P9-AZW-429

SIDNEY POITIER

Sidney

ARAM GOUDSOUZIAN

Poitier MAN, ACTOR, ICON

The University of North Carolina Press *Chapel Hill & London*

© 2004

The University of North Carolina Press

All rights reserved

Manufactured in the United States of America

Set in Sabon and Castellar types

by Keystone Typesetting, Inc.

The paper in this book meets the guidelines for

permanence and durability of the Committee on

Production Guidelines for Book Longevity of the Council

on Library Resources.

Library of Congress Cataloging-in-Publication Data

Goudsouzian, Aram.

Sidney Poitier : man, actor, icon / by Aram Goudsouzian.

p. cm.

Includes bibliographical references and index.

ISBN 0-8078-2843-2 (alk. paper)

1. Poitier, Sidney. 2. Actors — United States — Biography.

3. African American actors — United States — Biography.

I. Title.

PN2287.P57G68 2004

791.43'028'092 — dc22   2003019372

08   07   06   05   04   5   4   3   2   1

In memory of Andy Colligan

Along with the fight to desegregate the schools, we must
desegregate the entire cultural statement of America; we must
desegregate the minds of the American people. If we merely succeed in
desegregating the school buildings, we may very well find that we have
won the battle and lost the war. Integration begins the day after the
minds of the American people are desegregated.

JOHN OLIVER KILLENS
The Black Man's Burden (1965)

Entertainment is not, as we often think, a full-scale flight from
our problems, not a means of forgetting them completely, but rather
a rearrangement of our problems into shapes which tame them, which
disperse them to the margins of our attention.

MICHAEL WOOD
America in the Movies (1975)

We're all imperfect, and life is simply a perpetual, unending
struggle against those imperfections.

SIDNEY POITIER
The Measure of a Man (2000)

CONTENTS

A section of photographs follows p. 296.

ACKNOWLEDGMENTS

This book began when I was a student in the Department of History at Purdue University, under the direction of Randy Roberts. He taught me his approach to writing history, and his guidance shaped every stage of this project. I could not have asked for a more supportive, perceptive mentor.

Other historians at Purdue also helped mold me and this book. Elliott Gorn expanded my notion of biography, and he prodded me to consider some difficult ideas. Vernon Williams deepened my understanding of the African American experience. John Larson challenged me to both think more creatively and write more clearly.

More teachers and colleagues, both at Purdue and at other institutions, read chapters and seminar papers. They posed important questions and gave excellent suggestions. My thanks go to Anita Ashendel, Robert Bellinger, Jody Bresnahan, Susan Curtis, Chris Elzey, Kenneth Greenberg, Scott Hoffman, Art Leighton, Caleb Mason, Richard Moss, Michelle Wick Patterson, Caitlin Roper, Judith Smith, Yesuk Son, Steve Stofferahn, David Welky, and Chris Wells. My further thanks go to Debbie Butler for a canny research tip.

Ed Guerrero read the entire manuscript, and he provided invaluable suggestions and expert reassurance. My sister-in-law Lara Goudsouzian and her mother Seta Kousharian also asked vital questions after reading complete drafts. In addition, I gave talks on Sidney Poitier at a Department of History colloquium at Colby College, the Cambridge Adult Education Center, and the Armenian Library and Museum.

I owe particular thanks to my editor, Sian Hunter. She embraced the project, educated me about the publication process, and immeasurably improved the manuscript. Thanks also to David Hines, Eric Schramm, Paula Wald, and the other admirable professionals at the University of North Carolina Press.

Sidney Poitier, too, aided this endeavor. During sporadic telephone conversations, he answered my questions with grace and honesty. He also challenged me intellectually. I appreciate his cooperation and interest, and I hope that he respects my effort.

The Purdue Research Foundation funded me with a generous two-year grant. I thank the foundation, former History Department chair Gordon

Mork, and a succession of directors of graduate studies: Nancy Gabin, Charles Cutter, and Michael Morrison. My appreciation extends to past and present members of the History Department administrative staff: Barbara Corbin, Delayne Graham, Peggy Quirk, Jennifer Redden, Jan Whitehead, and others.

My research began during a final year in residence at Purdue University, aided by the Humanities, Social Science, and Education Library and the superlative Interlibrary Loan Department. For the next three years, I relied on Widener Library at Harvard University, which graciously granted me special borrowing privileges. Further thanks go to the staffs of the Margaret Herrick Library of the Academy of Motion Picture Arts and Sciences; the Special Collections Department at the University of California–Los Angeles; the Motion Picture and Television Library at the University of Southern California; the Wisconsin State Historical Society; the Black Films Collection and the Eli Lilly Library at Indiana University; the Schomburg Center for Research in Black Culture, The New York Public Library, Astor, Lenox and Tilden Foundations; the Celeste Bartos Film Study Center at the Museum of Modern Art; the New York Library of the Performing Arts; the Harvard Theater Collection; the National Archives at College Park; and the Motion Picture and Television Reading Room at the Library of Congress in Washington, D.C.

On research trips, I depended upon the hospitality of family and friends. In California, I stayed with Hagop and Araxie Boyamian, and their sons Michael, Samuel, and Daniel. Charlie Foley, and then Caleb Mason and Coleen McNamara, housed me in Washington, D.C. In New York, I stayed at various times with Jonathan Pappas, Chris Capozzola, and Josh Radoff. Randy and Marjorie Roberts put me up during return visits to Indiana. I extend thanks to all of them.

My deepest thanks are for my family: my father, Dr. Nishan Goudsouzian; my mother, Mary Goudsouzian; and my brothers, Steve and Haig. My further thanks go to my extended family of Goudsouzians, Boyamians, Derians, and Youssoufians.

Finally, I cannot thank all my friends in Boston individually, because I will not be able to stop. So many people have made my time here so fulfilling. They all know how grateful I am. Many also share with me one sadness, the loss of a great friend in Andy Colligan. This book is dedicated to his memory.

SIDNEY POITIER

INTRODUCTION

If Sidney Poitier had an acting trademark, it was the cool boil. In the movies, when injustice drove him to the brink, he became a pot of outrage on the verge of bubbling over. His eyes would blaze. His mahogany skin would tighten. His words would gush out in spasms of angry eloquence, carefully measured by grim, simmering pauses.

But the powder keg never exploded. It *could not* explode. For over a decade, from the late 1950s to the late 1960s, Poitier was Hollywood's lone icon of racial enlightenment; no other black actor consistently won leading roles in major motion pictures. His on-screen actions thus bore a unique political symbolism. The cool boil struck a delicate balance, revealing racial frustration, but tacitly assuring a predominantly white audience that blacks would eschew violence and preserve social order.

On 22 August 1967, life imitated art. During a televised press conference in Atlanta, reporters peppered Poitier with questions about urban riots and black radicals. Race riots had ravaged Newark and Detroit during a summer that had also seen race-related civil disorders in a spate of other cities. For five minutes, Poitier answered the questions. Then came the reined-in rage. "It seems to me that at this moment, this day, you could ask me about many positive things that are happening in this country," he lectured. Instead, the reporters fixated on a narrow segment of the black population. The movie star admonished their tendency "to pay court to sensationalism, to pay court to negativism."

Poitier further objected that the media had crowned him a spokesman for all black America. With controlled fury, he refused to be defined only by his skin color. "There are many aspects of my personality that you can explore very constructively," he seethed. "But you sit here and ask me such one-dimensional questions about a very tiny area of our lives. You ask me questions that fall continually within the Negroness of my life." He demanded recognition of his humanity: "I am artist, man, American, contemporary. I am an awful lot of things, so I wish you would pay me the respect due." His soliloquy won applause from the abashed reporters, who then confined their questions to the actor's career.[1]

Yet Poitier recognized his symbolic power, and he accepted political responsibility. One week before, also in Atlanta, he had delivered the keynote address at the tenth annual convention of the Southern Christian Leadership Conference (SCLC), the civil rights organization led by Reverend Martin Luther King Jr. The struggle for black equality had by then reached a crossroads. A decade of nonviolent demonstrations had won basic constitutional rights for black southerners, but had achieved little for the northern ghettos that burst into violence that summer. Moreover, a new generation of leaders now challenged King's core message of nonviolence and integration. That month H. Rap Brown, president of the Student Nonviolent Coordinating Committee (SNCC), had told 300 young blacks in Maryland to fight white racism with eye-for-an-eye violence. "Don't love him to death," he implored. "Shoot him to death." His rhetoric ignited a riot. In this volatile atmosphere, SCLC needed to maintain relevance. The Atlanta summit's theme was "Where Do We Go from Here?"[2]

Before 2,000 delegates at the opening banquet, King introduced his "soul brother." Then Poitier orated—celebrating the huge majority of peaceful blacks, condemning the "turmoil and chaos" that ruled politics, praising King as "a new man in an old world." When Poitier declared his continued devotion to civil rights, many delegates wept. Like King, who promoted economic boycotts as alternatives to riots, Poitier maintained faith in peaceful protest and interracial brotherhood.[3]

The civil rights movement had shaped the contours of Poitier's career. Nonviolent demonstrations for black equality had forged a culture in which his image resonated, and his movies had engendered racial goodwill. So Poitier shouldered political burdens unusual to movie stars. But then, as the press conference had indicated, he was an unusual movie star. Poitier said it best: *I am artist, man, American, contemporary.*

❖

Artist. Poitier was an actor of prodigious talent. Stanley Kramer once called him "the only actor I've ever worked with who has the range of Marlon Brando—from pathos to great power." Poitier infused grace and dignity into his characters, and he exuded a warm charisma. More, he possessed that indefinable quality of the movie star—an aura, a presence that dominated the screen. That Hollywood chose Poitier as its single black star was no whim; it was due, in large part, to his exceptional magnetism.[4]

Man. He was a fascinating man, at that, with a literally rags-to-riches story. Among family in the Bahamas and alone in New York City, Poitier grew up poor. Poverty shaped him, hovered near him long after his ascent to riches. This daydreaming dishwasher lived the great American myth of the self-made man, stumbling into a vocation and then applying himself with diligence. With fame came the burden of representing an entire race. It gnawed at him, even as he shone with urbane polish. He never stopped sizing himself by his parents. Through two wives, six daughters, and one tempestuous affair, he learned and taught his father's lessons about "the measure of a man."[5]

American. In an era when blacks demonstrated for rights guaranteed by the United States Constitution, Poitier was popular culture's foremost symbol of racial democracy. Before his 1950 film debut, images of blacks in film consisted of the stereotypes that justified racial segregation: oversexed bucks, absurd pickaninnies, beefy mammies, grinning song-and-dance men, and slothful comic servants. Poitier's image contradicted this burden. By the late 1950s, he was the Martin Luther King of the movies, an emblem of middle-class values, Christian sacrifice, and racial integration. Like college students staging sit-ins at lunch counters, like marchers weathering blasts from fire hoses, like civil rights leaders employing patriotic rhetoric, Poitier generated sympathy for black equality. In 1964, the year that King won the Nobel Prize and Congress passed the Civil Rights Act, Poitier won an Academy Award for *Lilies of the Field*, cementing his position as the film industry's token response to the civil rights movement.[6]

Contemporary. This final self-characterization might have drawn objections, because by 1967 many radicals, college students, and film critics were condemning Poitier's recurring role as a noble hero in a white world. Like other Hollywood stars, Poitier established an enduring image. Unlike other stars, his image changed meaning with the shifts in racial politics. He had always faced unique obstacles. Racial taboos precluded him from romantic roles. His pattern of sacrifice for his white co-star rankled many blacks. And his characters often seemed stripped of any black identity, instead promoting an exaggerated colorblindness. Yet his roles challenged convention enough that until the mid-1960s, few Poitier films played in the Deep South. So Poitier confronted difficult choices. As the single black film star, he had to balance mass appeal and political viability, an equilibrium difficult to maintain by the time of his anguished press conference.[7]

Poitier stewed that day because the public could not separate the image from the man, and the man from his race. Yet his stardom had depended on the blurred line between entertainment and reality, on the public's willingness to understand race relations through the prism of the movies. After all, everyone accepted that a movie star could deliver the keynote address for a political organization such as SCLC.[8]

Poitier, moreover, was at the top of his game. In August 1967 Poitier lived in a sumptuous Upper West Side penthouse, owned an Oscar, enjoyed the adoration of millions, and had two films — *In the Heat of the Night* and *To Sir, with Love* — climbing atop the box-office charts. A third film, *Guess Who's Coming to Dinner*, would buttress his brief reign as America's top movie star. That year Poitier soothed a liberal political center that seemed to be crumbling in the face of urban riots and black militancy. But with popular success came the disenchantment of critics and radicals. In the same month that *Variety* dubbed him "The Useful Negro," a *New York Times* column called him a "showcase nigger." Poitier could not escape the paradox of his "Negroness."[9]

❖

"How does it feel to be a problem?" asked W. E. B. Du Bois at the beginning of the twentieth century. That question articulated the frustration smoldering within Poitier at the press conference. Du Bois wrote of "double-consciousness," the African American's warring ideals of black identity and national assimilation. Poitier complicated the problem — as a man, as a public spokesman, and as a screen image that he could not entirely control. He endured teenage years of isolation and adult years in a withering public eye. He had to maintain progressive depictions of blacks while appealing to interracial audiences. He weathered the insults of racists and radicals, Cold War conservatives and Black Power militants. And he wrestled with his own demons, his own quest for manhood. His struggle was rooted in his balance of identity between the Bahamas, the land that instilled him with his values, and the United States, the nation whose racial dilemma he represented on movie screens.[10]

How does it feel to be a problem? Few lived that question, in all its complexities, as Sidney Poitier did.

PART I
POVERTY AND PROGRESS

❖ ❖ ❖

CHAPTER I

PATCHES

(1927–1943)

Sidney Poitier would stand tall, six feet and two inches. He would have broad shoulders, long legs, and perfect posture — almost a regal bearing. He would exude grace in every movement, emotion in every expression, conviction in every word. If only one quality could define him, it would be this energy, this vigor — this *life*. But in Miami, Florida, on 20 February 1927, he was born small and sickly. A premature baby of seven months, he weighed less than three pounds, and he seemed closer to death than life.

Reginald Poitier accepted that fate. The gaunt farmer had come to Miami to sell tomatoes, not bear a son. The Miami Produce Exchange offered the best prices for his goods, which he harvested and packed on his native Cat Island in the Bahamas. He arrived expecting to unload his crates, haggle with some merchants, and return home. The newborn delayed matters. He had endured similar ordeals before — previous children had died in infancy, by stillbirth or disease. It was fairly common on isolated Cat Island. Reginald found an undertaker and purchased a tiny casket, no bigger than a shoebox.

His wife, Evelyn, resisted this surrender. She, too, remembered her own lost offspring. But she resented Reginald's stoic realism. She had been only thirteen when she married the twenty-eight-year-old Reginald. Seven children and a lifetime of farming later, this dark, thin woman had hardened. Shy and inarticulate, she could barely communicate her frustration. Desperate for some reassurance, she paid a visit to a soothsayer.[1]

Evelyn had never been to a fortune teller, but she was willing to suspend disbelief. She sat before a wizened old clairvoyant with gray, braided hair and a string of beads tumbling over a loose dress. Soggy tea leaves congealed in a cup, portending the infant's fate. The room was silent. Finally the soothsayer's face trembled and twitched. A raw rumbling emerged from deep in her throat. "Don't worry about your son," she began. "He will survive and he will not be a sickly child. He will grow up to be" — she paused, amending her prophecy — "he will travel to most of the corners of the earth. He will walk with kings. He will be rich and famous. Your name will be carried all over the world. You must not worry about that child."

Evelyn might not have believed such grandiose predictions — the child of a poor tomato farmer, walking with kings? — but she cherished the words. She paid fifty cents, marched home, and insisted that Reginald expunge any trace of lost hope, starting with the miniature casket. For the next three months Evelyn and Reginald Poitier remained in Miami, far from their other six children, nursing Sidney back to health.[2]

The ordeal was the first link in a chain of improbable events that proved the soothsayer correct. Sidney's premature arrival in Miami gave him automatic citizenship in the United States, a twist of fate that benefited him fifteen years later. Fortune smiled on him, sparing him where others fell. But Sidney Poitier also shaped his life through his singular personality: proud, stubborn, intelligent, restless, resourceful, virile, outwardly confident, and inwardly insecure. He would return to the United States to become a man, an actor, and an icon. But he was a child of the Bahamas.

❖

The Bahamas lies close to the American mainland, its northernmost isle only fifty miles from Florida. Hundreds of tiny islands and cays stretch to the southeast, creating a flimsy shield between the Atlantic Ocean and the Caribbean Sea. Since 1492, when Christopher Columbus weaved his way through Long Island, Rum Cay, and Crooked Island, the Bahamas has been a crossroads between the Old and New Worlds.

Its history combines intrigue with exploitation. By 1542, the conquering Spanish had deported over 20,000 native Lucayans to Hispaniola, enslaving them on *encomiendas* under Spanish overlords. The islands soon became a popular corridor for European explorers. Ponce de Leon passed through in search of the Fountain of Youth, a legend gleaned from the Lucayans. English colonists landed at Cat Island in 1585 on their way to the "Lost Colony" of Roanoke. By the late 1600s, the international quest for gold had infested Nassau. British colonial governor Nicholas Webb complained that the capital city had become "a receptacle for all rogues." By 1713, over a thousand pirates called Nassau their home, including Benjamin Hornigold, the "lady pirates" Mary Read and Anne Bonney, and Edward Teach — better known as Blackbeard.[3]

The islands remained under British control well into the twentieth century, but the fortunes of Bahamians were more intertwined with their American neighbors. Following the American Revolution, hordes of scorned British Loyalists sailed to the Bahamas. The accommodating colonial government attracted the wealthiest Loyalist planters with huge land grants. Over 80 percent of the Loyalists came from Georgia and the Carolinas; most brought slaves. Slavery had flourished in the Bahamas since at least 1671, when the first list of settlers noted 443 slaves. By 1787, slaves composed 75 percent of the islands' 12,000 people.[4]

The Caribbean slave system differed from that of the American South. Because of the black majority, Caribbean slaveholders never developed an elaborate paternalistic ideology. Unlike their northern neighbors, they did not expect their slaves to act like appreciative children. They ruled through coercion, often working a slave to death. So Caribbean slaves more frequently organized rebellions and planned escapes. The Poitier ancestors, in fact, probably arrived in the Bahamas as fugitive slaves. "Poitier" is a French name, and there are no white Poitiers from the Bahamas. One of Sidney's uncles claimed that the family forebears hailed from Haiti—an accepted assertion, since that was the nearest French colony. Runaway slaves from Haiti established maroon communities throughout the Bahamas, including Cat Island.[5]

To the chagrin of colonial slaveholders, British reformers passed an 1833 Emancipation Act. But the end of slavery did not mean black prosperity. Black Bahamians now endured a more subtle, indirect form of exploitation. The white-dominated government established property qualifications to limit the black vote. The black majority won few land grants or educational opportunities, and the Bahamas never developed a stable class of black farmers. Without black autonomy and political power, the islands' economy stagnated.[6]

The malaise continued, mostly unabated, until 1919, when the United States government adopted the eighteenth amendment, banning the sale and manufacture of liquor. Nassau reclaimed its pirate roots and began bootlegging alcohol. "Adventurers, businessmen, soldiers, including a renegade officer or so, sailors, loafers, and at least one minister, they sought to make their fortunes by keeping America wet," wrote one observer in 1921. Bay Street, the city's main strip, "was no longer a sun drenched idle avenue where traffic in sponges and sisal progressed torpidly. It was filled with slit-eyed, hunch-shouldered strangers, with a bluster of Manhattan in their voices and a wary truculence of manners." William McCoy sold such quality whiskey that it earned a lasting nickname: the Real McCoy.[7]

The fortunes of bootlegging rarely trickled down to the black majority — especially not to poor Out Island farmers such as the Poitiers. Most blacks outside Nassau were subsistence farmers. Sometimes enterprising Out Islanders prospered from booms in demand for cotton, pineapples, sisal, or sponges, but the markets for these goods inevitably collapsed. Reginald's trips to Miami continued a long trend: Out Island farming families struggling within the web of the American market economy, operating in near isolation.[8]

On a map, Cat Island looks like a thin wisp. Fifty miles long but only ten miles wide, the island is divided by a long ridge that runs its entire length and affords spectacular views of the azure Atlantic, sandy beaches, and rocky cliffs, dotted by colorful explosions of poinsettias, casuarinas, bougainvillea, sea-grapes, and sapodillas. The Poitiers lived in the scattered community surrounding Arthur's Town, a village on the island's northern tip. It contained only a simple church, an all-age school, a lockup, and a wooden courthouse. Farming on Cat Island was a dicey proposition. The soil was fertile but thin. There were few rivers or streams. Wells drilled too deep produced brackish or salt water. Hurricanes, droughts, and disease posed constant threats.[9]

Yet Reginald grew fat and delicious tomatoes, thanks to superior resources, backbreaking labor, family cooperation, and ingenuity. Unlike most Cat Islanders, the Poitiers owned a horse, donkey, and cart. Reginald frequented a cave that held the key to his juicy tomato harvest: bat guano. He loaded the cargo and returned to his farm, where he created a rich base by mixing the topsoil with his precious bat feces.[10]

A large, strong family was not a luxury on Cat Island — it was an economic necessity. Cyril, the firstborn, was fifteen years older than Sidney. Following Cyril was Ruby, Verdon (nicknamed "Teddy"), Reginald, Carl, Cedric, and Sidney. From age six, they worked in the fields. The hardest labor came from October to March, when they lopped down bushes and prepared new fields. Farming, however, was a year-round undertaking. Besides growing tomatoes, the family kept an acre for subsistence farming. They grew string beans, sweet potatoes, navy beans, yams, okra, onions, peppers, and corn.[11]

After working in the fields all morning, Evelyn would come home to prepare their large mid-day meal. In a cast-iron pot, she simmered hog lard with onions, tomatoes, green beans, and okra, and then added grits, water, seasoning, and perhaps some fish or chicken to create their dietary staple. They ate by hand or by a spoon improvised out of a sea-grape leaf.

On rare occasions they had mutton or goat, and they ate rice on Sundays — a luxury, since it was imported from England.[12]

But despite such symbols of opulence as a donkey, horse, and sporadic rice dinner, the Poitier family lived daily with poverty. "We were poor, man!" exclaimed Sidney years later. "*I mean, we were bus-ted!*" The entire family lived in a three-room stone hut with a thatched roof and an outhouse in back. Reginald built the home himself. As the family patriarch, he instilled the discipline that ensured survival. The children not only worked in the fields, but also fetched water, shucked corn, shelled beans, fed chickens, washed clothes, ground grits, and slopped hogs. Evelyn reinforced that ethic by insisting upon proper manners: if Sidney sassed her, she slapped him across the mouth. He learned to respect his elders and himself.[13]

Poverty was no excuse. Evelyn tore empty flour sacks into two-yard strips, bleached them in a big pot, and made shirts for the boys. "She used to say that it was all right to wear patches as long as you were clean," remembered Sidney. "Well I want you to know that I wore me some patches!"[14]

Cat Island operated on an informal combination of barter and cash economies. Most farmed but others fished, built boats, kept shops, or dug wells. For these services, one offered goats, pigs, chickens, or labor in lieu of cash. The small population, good weather, and lack of taxes made this system possible. Cat Island culture also incorporated both African and European customs. African folk traditions included beliefs in ghosts and witches, "obeah-men" who charmed fields and bewitched enemies, and occasional desperate turns such as Evelyn's visit to the soothsayer. The Anglican church service in Arthur's Town allowed the Poitiers to connect with the rest of Cat Island. Occasional Saturday dances, holidays, or weddings also provided welcome breaks from farming.[15]

Adults scratched out sustenance, but for young children, Cat Island was a gigantic playground. After chores, Sidney often roamed the island unsupervised, wandering down narrow flower-lined paths, building mud huts, collecting turtle eggs, swimming in the Atlantic, and climbing sapodilla trees to shake down the plump, gray-brown fruit and eat until his stomach ached. He caught fish, added peppers and limes, and stewed it in a can over a fire on the beach. His imagination drifted out to sea, to the world beyond Cat Island. "I'd stand on the piers," he recalled, "and watch the ships until they disappeared and then I'd just stare at that line and dream. I was a real dreamer. I'd conjure up the kind of worlds that were on the other side and what I'd do in them. So *many* hours I stared at that line. . . ."[16]

From his earliest years, Sidney loved to act. He rustled up old clothes — even his mother's dresses — and wandered into the backyard, where he created characters and acted out scenarios. "When he was missing from the family group," remembered his brother Reginald, "we were sure to find him, off somewhere by himself, rigged up in different clothes and costumes." He had space and time to indulge his creativity, and he grew both confident and introspective — ideal qualities for a future actor.[17]

His unfettered existence centered around the ocean. Before he could walk, he could swim. When he was ten months old, Evelyn threw him into the ocean. Reginald fished him out. His mother tossed him back. This training occurred for days, until Sidney paddled about comfortably. He later joined his brothers on fishing expeditions. Constructing rafts out of bound coconut trunks, fishing lines out of thread waxed with tree sap, and hooks out of bent pins, the brothers floated out to sea. Holding the thread between their thumb and forefingers, they awaited the tug of Caribbean shad, turbot, grunts, and goggle-eyes.[18]

Sidney never wore shoes. "They were *tor-ture*," he winced, remembering the pinching. Shoes half a centimeter too large belonged to an older brother or sister. His parents forced him to don footwear, however, during their weekly visit to church. After squirming through the service, he would bolt out the front door, take off his shoes, tie them together, and sling them over his shoulder for the walk home.[19]

By age nine, Sidney grew curious about the fairer sex. He and his best friend, Fritz Campbell, cast a spell by placing two dead frogs in matchboxes. If one week later the frog bones formed a "V," they would wrap two strands of hair — one of theirs, and one from the object of their affection — around the bones. Whether because of the spell or his own charms, Sidney attracted a girl named Lurlene to an abandoned home, where they clumsily fondled each other. Smitten, he soon wrote her a love note: a brown paper sack with the words "I love you" scratched in pencil. Lurlene's parents found the note and gave it to the Poitiers. Sidney returned home one day to find his parents and siblings laughing on the front porch. "I can't tell you how *embarrassed I was*," he recalled.[20]

Despite such humiliations, Sidney would remember Cat Island as an idyll. He later yearned for the simplicity of his parents' life, especially the isolation from a consumer culture of automobiles, clothes, television, and movies. His amusements, by contrast, consisted of "the sound of the sea and the smell of the wind and your mama's voice and the voice of your dad and the craziness of your brothers and sisters—and that's it." Cat Island represented stability: a family, a community, a common struggle for survival. Forged by discipline, he trusted those around him.[21]

Yet his own personality contradicted this stability. His independence and restlessness as an adult stemmed from his childhood. When he escaped cramped quarters to explore the warm outdoors, he learned skills that later served him as an actor. Swimming and running and climbing, he negotiated tight spaces and vast expanses, shaping his athletic limber grace. And in his constant daydreams, he slipped into and out of characters. "I was free in body and spirit," he later said.[22]

Cat Island offered another freedom: a society free of racial hierarchy. The only two whites in Arthur's Town were a doctor and a shopkeeper. Most of the island's authority figures—the schoolteacher, the constable, the Anglican priest, and the island commissioner—were black or mixed-race. On Cat Island, skin color had little relationship to power. Unlike his American contemporaries, Sidney did not grow up mired in discrimination, forced to negotiate racial codes, or resigned to limited opportunities based on his skin color. "I was fortunate," he later said. "The overwhelming majority of the people were black. There was not a white community representing a larger community. As such, I did not have trouble with self-definition at an early age."[23]

But his fond memories should not obscure the serious problems of life on the Out Islands. The British colonial administration neglected its outposts. Cat Island's parliamentary representatives lived in Nassau and maintained their offices through election-year displays of beneficence. Politically unorganized Out Islanders traded their votes for gifts of rice and rum. Without state support, their overwhelming poverty continued: no farming loans, no electricity, no modern medicine. Women married too young, trying to achieve a semblance of stability in the family-based subsistence economy. Underfunded schools ensured that Sidney learned enough to write "I love you" on a paper sack, but little else. For adults, Cat Island was no idyll.[24]

The Great Depression exacerbated this distress. From the fringe of the American economy, Out Islanders saw their opportunities shrink and their poverty deepen. In 1936 Florida restricted tomato importation from the Bahamas, eliminating Reginald's main market. Bahamian governor Sir Bede Clifford had already proposed a bill in 1934 for a produce exchange in Nassau, but the legislature dawdled on the bill for two years, and the exchange never proved effective. In 1938 Reginald was fifty-one years old. Hollow-faced, white-haired, rheumatic, and arthritic, he decided that his family could no longer survive on Cat Island. They moved to Nassau.[25]

❖

"It is a long way from Nassau to some of the Out Islands," reported *National Geographic* in 1936. "But everywhere there is good order and respect for authority. To these scattered British subjects, Nassau . . . is a world center of beauty, wealth, and culture." It is true that blacks launched few challenges to the political order in the 1930s, and it is true that Nassau held a cosmopolitan allure. But underneath this facade of affluence lay an exploited black majority, reaping few benefits from a modern economy. The Poitiers joined their ranks.[26]

Eleven-year-old Sidney and his mother sailed for Nassau first. On a sailboat manned by three men, they left Cat Island at eleven o'clock one morning and arrived in Nassau twenty-four hours later. "I didn't sleep at all that night," Sidney remembered. "We stayed in the boat's hold and it was full of huge rocks for ballast, and it smelled awful of sponge and sisal." Seasick and lightheaded, he sealed his mouth and measured his breathing. The nausea yielded to excitement when he spotted Nassau on the horizon. Sidney thought he saw scurrying beetles. As the boat coasted into the harbor, he realized that they were automobiles.[27]

Nassau was a newer playground with better toys. He saw electricity at work for the first time. He wandered shops, enthralled by the elaborate clothes, the cameras, and the washing machines. "I didn't say a word that whole day, I was so amazed," he recalled. His mother bought him an ice cream cone. "It looked to me like a scoop of mashed potatoes. I bit into it and my mouth froze. I *panicked*!!"[28]

After staying with friends for a few days, Evelyn found a three-room place on Ross Corner, in a densely packed district called Over the Hill. The neighborhood was full of transplanted Cat Islanders. Thousands of blacks had migrated to Nassau in the 1930s, pushed off the Out Islands by poverty and pulled into Nassau by service industry jobs. But few migrants escaped destitution. A small black middle class of policemen, businessmen, school principals and lawyers did not offset a large black underclass. Young Sidney understood this reality on a most basic level: "There were haves and have-nots, and we definitely had very little."[29]

Race played a significant, if ambiguous, role in Nassau life. In Nassau about 15 percent of the population was white, and another 15 percent mixed-race. Marriages, sexual liaisons, and friendships across race lines occurred more frequently than in the United States. But whites dominated the colonial government and controlled the avenues to wealth. The mixed-race class had more access to education and white-collar positions; their outlook, dress, and social aspirations followed the white model. The dark-skinned majority looked for jobs in construction, food service, domestic work, and other forms of low-paying wage labor. Race thus established the boundaries of a colonial class system.[30]

Sidney learned these lessons firsthand. Upon moving to Nassau, he befriended a white boy named Carl. After a few weeks of loose cama-raderie, they discussed race. Carl smugly informed Sidney that blacks would never have the same opportunities as whites. "I waited for the punchline," remembered Sidney. "None came. He was dead serious!" Sidney launched insults at Carl; he had not considered that skin color might limit his progress. Three years later Sidney fell in love with a fair-skinned girl named Dorothy. Dorothy's mother was white, her father black. Her half-brother, the child of Dorothy's mother and a white father, was none other than Carl.[31]

Sidney's romance with Dorothy flourished, but Carl's predictions proved accurate. During the Great Depression, the Bahamian govern-ment further stifled the black underclass. The bootlegging industry had collapsed after the repeal of Prohibition in 1933. Instead of public aid, the Bahamian government championed the tourism industry: creating more frequent steamship service, building transportation facilities, taking over hotels from failing private companies, and sponsoring international ten-nis and golf tournaments. "Well gentlemen, it amounts to this," explained Governor Clifford to his Executive Council. "If we can't take the liquor to the Americans, we must bring the Americans to the liquor."[32]

Tourism transformed Nassau. It became "the social centre of the South," according to a 1935 observer, where "the society set of Palm Beach and other Florida resorts mingled with the fashionable colony here in a gay whirl of parties." Wealthy Americans, attracted by the gorgeous weather and the sheen of British class, propped up the Bahamian econ-omy. The American media praised this tourist delight (although the *New York Times Magazine* had one complaint: "The splendid Bahamas, other home of many Americans of wealth and social eminence, center for sport-ing fishermen, Utopia for yachtsmen, paradise of leisure, is equipped with entirely too many black children who go around strumming ukeleles and singing: 'Mama don't want no peas, no beans, no cocoanut oil' ").[33]

The city's wealth concentrated at the top, aggravating the racial divide. Even before the tourism boom, a 1927 public health report had chron-icled the squalid conditions of Nassau's black slums: festering garbage, filthy wells, and threats of tuberculosis, venereal disease, and typhoid fever. A world apart from the wealthy, white-dominated ridge that encircled the city, the slums further degenerated in the 1930s. Such conditions sparked sporadic protests from the black majority. When 300 men turned out for a small construction job at the Prince George Hotel in 1935, a near-riot broke out. Two years later, protesters burned down the racially segregated Nassau and Montagu Theaters. Nassau, feared a colonial official in 1940, was "becoming a gathering ground for a parasitic element and possibly a centre of dissatisfaction and slum existence with disproportionate incidence of petty crime."[34]

Poitier, looking back, agreed. "That place Nassau was not good for raising tomatoes or children." Bahamian culture was profoundly patriarchal, assigning prerogatives to male heads of household. Men, including Reginald, could earn reputations as both family men and philanderers. On Cat Island, Reginald fed his family and built their home. In Nassau, he struggled within the wage labor, cash-oriented economy. Pained by severe arthritis, he could only watch as Evelyn "beat rock." Sidney and his brothers carried home large rocks, up to twenty or thirty pounds. In their backyard under a tree, Evelyn crushed rocks into pebbles and sold them to builders for cement. She earned about twenty cents a day.[35]

Reginald worked in a bicycle repair shop for three years. He then reverted to agriculture, claiming "squatter's rights" on government land outside the city. Without his bat guano, however, the land proved infertile and unprofitable, and Reginald often spent his days in a straight-backed rocking chair, stiff from a lifetime of labor and jaded by the new economic order.[36]

Evelyn kept Reginald from the precipice of despair. She cushioned him from problems with the local grocer, who refused to establish credit without sufficient cash. She could not rely on community bonds; as Sidney lamented, "her new neighbors did not exchange corn for beans, yams for peas, or papayas for sugar apples." But Evelyn took jobs washing and ironing, and she stretched out the family's meager earnings. Sometimes she borrowed money from their daughters, unbeknownst to her husband.[37]

Sidney, unlike his father, could ignore their economic impotence. He remembered his early life in Nassau as "a remarkable experience cram-jammed with excitement." He made friends with the neighborhood boys, who congregated at the busy intersection of Ross Corner "to plan or improvise the scenarios of mischief that would send them off gleefully to tie tin cans to dog tails, 'accidentally' break windows with slingshots, and otherwise reduce the established order of the community." Yorick Rolle, a frail, high-strung, but entirely warmhearted boy, became his best friend.

But family bonds remained important. Soon after Sidney's arrival, an older bully named William approached Ross Corner and fixed a glare on the newcomer. Eager to lord his authority, William spewed insults. Sidney responded in kind, and William delivered an open-hand slap. Some observers related the incident to Sidney's sister Teddy — a meaty, big-boned woman. She gave the bully a vicious smack, buckling his knees. Several slaps, punches, and kicks to his rear end later, Teddy had established the Poitier reputation.[38]

Teddy's defense illustrated the family code from Cat Island. But that code had a harsh flip side, rooted in patriarchy. After four months living with her unstable and violent boyfriend, "Blood," Teddy moved back home. Reginald set one condition: to protect her, she could not visit Blood without first informing the family. When she violated the pledge, Reginald punished her for undermining his authority: he beat his adult daughter with a thorny tamarind switch. Teddy returned to Blood, and Reginald reminded her that she was leaving his protection. A few months later, Blood came home drunk. With a cow cock — literally a cured, smoked, and salted cow's penis, including the extension through the spine — he beat her. The word came back to Reginald. But under the patriarchal code of Bahamian society, neither he nor his sons could reciprocate Blood's cruelty.[39]

In Nassau, violence and crime constantly bruised the Poitier family. Cedric, Sidney's older brother by two years, spent time in jail for theft. Upon his release, he and his friend "Rooster" hatched an extortion scheme. In a letter, they demanded a ransom from a successful shop owner. They added: "P.S. Do not be in touch with the police or you will regret it." On the night of the proposed drop, Cedric and Rooster lay by the side of a road, cloaked in the underbrush. A package flew out of a car — their ransom! When they emerged, a gaggle of policemen pounced upon them. Cedric spent six more months in jail.[40]

Sidney, as the youngest child, was most vulnerable to the forces suppressing Nassau's black underclass. For the first time, he regularly attended school. It was a disaster. Sidney lacked both basic literacy skills and the self-discipline to improve; after a lifetime of wandering Cat Island, he could barely sit still. After eighteen months he learned, in his own words, "to read a little, write a little, and sing 'Rule Brittania.'" His sexual education progressed marginally better. At the age of thirteen, he visited a prostitute and lost his virginity. "It was really very nice. Absolutely neat," he looked back. "But the old broad gave me the biggest dose of clap I have ever seen." Stricken by gonorrhea, he underwent a series of painful sulfur treatments.[41]

Academically floundering and socially restless, he quit school to work. A Swedish industrialist named Axel Wenner-Gren had come to Nassau in the late 1930s as a tax refugee. On Hog Island, off the Nassau coast, he built a huge estate, named "Shangri-La" after the Himalayan utopia of James Hilton's novel *Lost Horizon*. In 1940, Wenner-Gren contracted workers to build a forty-foot-wide, twenty-five-foot-deep, two-mile-long canal connecting his mansion to his marina. Sidney started as a waterboy and became a digger. Swinging a pick and shoveling ditches helped Sidney develop muscles to complement his six-foot frame. But his employment proved fleeting when Wenner-Gren decamped for Mexico. The United States and Great Britain had declared him persona non grata for his business connections to Nazi Germany and his "quasi-fascist" ideas. Wenner-Gren built the canal, according to Nassau gossip, so that Shangri-La could house German U-Boats.[42]

Wenner-Gren was one of many rich refugees in the Bahamas during World War II — the new governor and his wife, the former King Edward and Wallis Simpson, had accepted their post to escape the taint of their controversial marriage. Yet the war did not directly affect the majority of Bahamians, including Sidney, until the United States entered the conflict. In early 1942, the American government contracted the Pleasantville Corporation to expand the military capacity of the Nassau airport, Oakes Field. The company advertised for 2,400 Bahamians at two dollars a day — the standard rate for black American labor, but four times the average for Nassau blacks.[43]

Sidney joined the legions who worked at Oakes Field. Fearful of social anarchy, the colonial government contradicted the original advertisement and pegged wages for unskilled labor at approximately half the original rate. The injustice enraged the workers; again, the color line reinforced the class divide. White American truck drivers earned six times more than black Bahamians for the same work. White Bahamian foremen supervised the gangs of black manual laborers such as Sidney.

In late May 1942, informal labor leaders began clamoring for higher wages and pay on rainy days. On 31 May, a small group went on strike and overturned a car. The next morning more than 2,000 workers, many brandishing sticks and machetes, gathered in Over the Hill and descended upon Bay Street. They raided a parked Coca-Cola truck and hurled the glass bottles through windows. They targeted white-owned businesses.

As colonial authorities declared martial law and read the Riot Act, the mob gutted a shop owned by the Speaker of the Assembly. But at the shoe store of labor organizer Percy Christie, they left not even a scratch.[44]

Sidney may have abstained from these violent labor politics, but he understood the precarious world of the Bahamian underclass. His frustrations manifested in a surface posture of brusque defiance. He learned to handle a deck of cards and to bluff his way through bad hands. Petty theft became his favorite weapon: a tool of survival, and an underhanded objection to his circumstances. "For instance," he described, "I would walk into a hardware store, saunter upstairs as if I knew exactly where I was going, stroll around, pick up a pair of skates, walk back downstairs and out the store." He stole everything from comic books to food. Some nights, he swam to a milk boat, climbed on deck, dumped empty bottles into the water, retrieved them, and traded them in for money. Masking an internal insecurity, he portrayed an image of assurance amidst danger.[45]

A cool demeanor, however, could not shield him forever. When he was fourteen, he and his friends stole corn from a farmer. Each took off with a filled gunny sack, and though they never could have eaten all their booty, they ran to a nearby field and started feasting. The police easily cracked the case; they followed the light of the guilty party's bonfire. All the boys suffered a reprimand and ten-shilling fine, but only Sidney spent the night in jail, because Reginald could not raise bail money. The next day the terror Sidney felt at his imprisonment melted into shame. He remembered how much his actions hurt his father: "There were tears in his eyes. I could tell he was hurt real bad. But he didn't say a word. He didn't even look at me."[46]

Just two months later Sidney came home drunk on rum. Reginald snapped. With withered fists, he tried to beat his tall and muscular son. Sidney begged him to stop. But Reginald would not, or could not, stop. For Reginald, Sidney's life encapsulated the devastating pressures of Nassau: a land where family ties unraveled, where a white minority dominated a black majority, where a man could not be a man. Reginald collapsed into his rocking chair, worn out by the exertion and worn down by Nassau.[47]

❖

Soon after Sidney's arrival in Nassau, his friends took him to a movie theater. Sidney withheld some compromising information: he had no idea what a movie was. "We went to this building," he recalled, "and I don't want to let on to them that I don't know where I am or what's going on. . . . I have to give the impression that I'm cool with all of this, whatever it is." The affected nonchalance disintegrated, however, when the lights dimmed: "There's this white wall, and suddenly on this white wall there's writing. And there's action! And then there are cows, tons of cows!"[48]

It was a Western, the first of many for Sidney. He soon idolized the young, well-mannered, straight-shooting, white-hatted heroes: Bob Steele, Tom Mix, Gene Autry, Roy Rogers, and a score of others. Perhaps the most popular film genre of the 1930s, Westerns were formulaic, low-budget affairs. The solitary hero always saved the day and kissed the girl, and the corrupt villain or plotting rancher always got his comeuppance. The films reinforced the myth of the American frontier, portraying a world distinct from the entanglements of modern society, a world where virtue was rewarded and justice was served. The message appealed to Sidney, whose own life seemed to contradict these values.[49]

Sidney thought of his heroes as real people. After that first movie, he sprinted out the theater's back door, "fully expecting to see them strut out through the stage door, followed by their horses and their cows and the bad guys and the good girls." He later told Teddy that he wanted to go to Hollywood, because he wanted to be a cowboy. He assumed that Hollywood was where cowboys lived. Film, in his mind, documented some version of the truth. "I was never so fascinated in my whole life," he remembered. "Nothing in life had been that . . . *impactful* on my imagination."[50]

This blurred line between fantasy and reality spoke to the power of film. More than a mere escape, Hollywood articulated a vision of American culture. Westerns, gangster pictures, screwball comedies, and musicals all emphasized narratives and individual heroes. The movies mollified social anxieties — sexuality, urban life, the Great Depression — in entertaining packages. By exhibiting charisma, resolve, and grace, the screen stars vicariously fulfilled their audiences' dreams. Sidney's cherished Westerns especially expressed a masculine version of heroism. The solitary figures wasted no words, endured pain, and forswore dependence of any sort, whether technology, religion, or women.[51]

Sidney's steady diet of Westerns fed a need for mythic role models. In dilapidated, segregated theaters, he absorbed the Hollywood version of the hero: solitary, masculine, and white. But this last characteristic left a void. Since arriving in Nassau, he saw himself more as black — in other words, he linked his personal identity to his race. And in the movies, he later explained, "I very rarely saw a Negro man when I was looking for myself." The only blacks in Westerns were idiotic sidekicks designed to elicit unthinking chuckles from white American audiences.[52]

Such images of blacks had infected American film since its birth. Early short films such as *The Wooing and Wedding of a Coon* (1905), *For Massa's Sake* (1911), and *The Dark Romance of a Tobacco Coon* (1911) portrayed dimwitted blacks who kowtowed to whites. Black simpletons were the objects of derision in the shorts series *Sambo* and *Rastus*, both produced around 1910.[53]

D. W. Griffith's 1915 *Birth of a Nation* best articulated the scope of white prejudice. An epic tale of Civil War and Reconstruction based on the Thomas Dixon novel *The Clansman*, the film insisted that radical Republicans had entrusted too much power to African Americans. The mulatto lieutenant governor of South Carolina betrays his white benefactor by winning the irresponsible black vote (while salaciously eyeing his mentor's doe-eyed daughter). As black politicians gnaw on chicken and sneak pulls of whiskey, black occupation troops bully well-meaning whites on the streets and at the ballot box. Yet aristocratic virtue survives in the hands of whites; a young southern belle plunges off a cliff rather than risk rape by a black man. The heroes of the climactic scene are the hooded protectors of southern nobility: the Ku Klux Klan.[54]

Birth of a Nation was phenomenally popular — not only because it was Hollywood's first feature-length film and full of cinematic innovations, but also because it played on prevalent white racism. It included almost every stereotype of black people. W. E. B. Du Bois complained that *Birth of a Nation* depicted the African American "as an ignorant fool, a vicious rapist, a venal and unscrupulous politician, or a faithful but doddering idiot." Its inaccurate portrayal of Reconstruction, he added, was "a gross perversion of a period of our history about which the people have been lied to for a generation."[55]

A protest campaign by the National Association for the Advancement of Colored People (NAACP) suppressed exhibitions in some cities, but the film garnered a huge following because it doubly resonated with American culture: it reinforced the myths of black inferiority and Reconstruction tyranny that perpetuated racial discrimination, and it portrayed them through a new and powerful visual medium. "It's like writing history with lightning!" marveled President Woodrow Wilson. "My only regret is that it is all so terribly true."[56]

The NAACP protest after *The Birth of a Nation* influenced the film industry by eliminating future portrayals of animalistic, sex-craving black brutes. But the myth of black sexuality endured. Whites enjoyed a privileged status as long as interracial sexual relations remained taboo. Hollywood could either castigate the image, as in *Birth of a Nation*, or sublimate it, as in every film featuring blacks for the next half-century.

In the 1920s and 1930s, blacks could only play comic and asexual stereotypes: bug-eyed pickaninnies such as the black children of *Our Gang*, loyal mammies played by Louise Beavers or Hattie McDaniel, grinning song-and-dance sidekicks such as Bill "Bojangles" Robinson. Black stereotypes pervaded mass culture; *Amos 'n' Andy*, the most popular radio program of the decade, featured two white men imitating black dialect. The Motion Picture Production Code of 1930 decreed that "MIS-CEGENATION (sex relationship between the white and black races) is forbidden." During Poitier's entire childhood, through the early 1940s, the only blacks on screen were those who "knew their place": serving whites, singing and dancing for whites, making whites laugh, or some combination of the three.[57]

The avatar of black inanity was Lincoln Perry, known to the world as Stepin Fetchit. Between 1929 and 1935, Fetchit appeared in twenty-six films. He played servants, slaves, and foolish country bumpkins, and he exaggerated every aspect of his performance: oversized clothes, bright white teeth, black dialect, and an achingly slow walk. "Nothing fancy," marveled a Hollywood fan magazine. "Nothing educated or emancipated. He typifies his race. All the traits and talents that legend gives to colored people are embodied in him. He has their joyous, child-like charm, their gaudy tastes, their superstitions." But his slothful image allowed for some sly subversions, too. Fetchit's characters hoodwinked whites to escape work, avoid punishment, or win money. Off-screen, he laughed loudest: he owned six houses, employed sixteen servants, wore $2,000 cashmere suits imported from India, and paraded through town in a champagne-pink Cadillac with his name on the side, emblazoned in neon lights.[58]

As Fetchit illustrated, by the 1930s films did not just duplicate the pernicious black images of *Birth of a Nation*. The next epic of the Civil War and Reconstruction era to inspire a fanatical following, David Selznick's 1939 *Gone with the Wind*, romanticized the Old South and presented an idealistic picture of slavery. But it also emphasized the dependency of whites on some black characters. Hattie McDaniel's Mammy chides Scarlett O'Hara for not grieving her husband's death, accompanies Scarlett to Atlanta despite her own legal freedom, and protects Scarlett by fashioning a magnificent green dress out of Tara's drapes. The performance earned McDaniel an Oscar for Best Supporting Actress, the first Academy Award ever accorded an African American.[59]

Yet McDaniel, like all her contemporary black actors, operated within a limited range of stereotypes — a restriction with profound consequences for race relations. The stereotypes suggested that blacks lacked individual personalities, that they could only be jesters, mammies, and servants. And if racial identity was fixed — if blacks "naturally" acted in certain ways — then one might justify their exclusion from legal rights. So blacks on screen remained subservient, desexualized, and asinine. To wit, *Gone with the Wind* also features helpless black idiots such as Butterfly McQueen's Prissy. After assuring Scarlett that she can deliver a baby, Prissy contradicts herself, screeching: "Lordy, Miss Scarlett, I don't know nothin' 'bout birthin' babies!"[60]

The issue of racial stereotype on film would one day dominate Sidney Poitier's career. But as a teenage Bahamian, he loved movies for the excitement, the heroes, and the world beyond Nassau. "Films taught me about other people," he reflected. "How to dial a telephone, geography, names of places, things I never knew before." He also launched a self-directed course in acting. Working on Wenner-Gren's canal or at Oakes Field, he earned enough to afford frequent movie screenings. He often returned home and acted out the film, scene by scene. He delighted in commanding the attention of family and friends even more than he enjoyed watching the film.[61]

Sidney later realized that the movies also taught brutality: "how to shoot, how to steal, how to kill Indians." He blamed Cedric and Rooster's failed ransom scheme on the fantastic movie plots that Cedric devoured. But he could not blame Hollywood for the forces in Nassau that placed so many poor black men in prison. Only a thin line separated Sidney from the same fate.[62]

❖

It was a rare occasion when Yorick Rolle and Sidney Poitier were apart. But one afternoon in Sidney's fourteenth year, fate divided the best friends for a few hours, sending them down opposite life paths. Sidney, for some reason now forgotten, failed to meet Yorick as planned. Yorick occupied himself with a joyride on a stolen bicycle. The police caught and sent him to the Boys Industrial School, a euphemism for the reformatory established in 1928 as a response to Nassau's rising juvenile delinquency. A judge sentenced Yorick to four years. "Yes, four years for stealing a bicycle," recalled Poitier years later, after Yorick had died from odd jobs and cheap rum. "Let's say the severity was one of the unfortunate aspects of minority rule."[63]

A few months later Sidney took a walk across the island to visit his incarcerated friend. Yorick presented the old neighborhood attitude —

defiant, self-assured, "cucumber-cool." In reality, his body had shriveled, and his oversized ocean-blue uniform and shaved head made him look forlorn. Sidney remembered his father's words upon hearing Yorick's sentence: "There but for the grace of God goes my son."[64]

Reginald could not stomach the same fate for Sidney, who at least had the advantage of American citizenship. The United States offered a glimpse of hope. Cedric had once tried to sneak into Miami via cargo freighter, only to be caught, deported, and jailed a third time. Cyril, the oldest brother, had had better luck. When the rest of the family moved to Nassau, he illegally immigrated to Miami and obtained citizenship by marrying an American. From the perspective of Nassau, Miami seemed like the Promised Land. Cyril sometimes shipped home boxes of clothes and shoes, and his letters described elegant cars and tall buildings. Cyril agreed to receive Sidney. He sent home ten dollars. The family spent seven of them on a passport, pants, a shirt, shoes, and a sweater for Sidney.[65]

Sidney left in January 1943. The day of his departure, Evelyn stayed home. Tears welled in her eyes as she fastened the buttons on his shirt. Gently, she touched his face. Without a word she guided him out the door, and Sidney and his father walked to the pier, exchanging few words. Reginald took him down Bay Street — not the most direct route, but the heart of the city. Sidney soaked it in, stopping to chat and bid friends farewell. As they approached the battered old passenger liner, Reginald stuffed the remaining three dollars into his son's hands. "Take care of yourself, son," he said. An ambivalent Sidney — troubled to leave his friends, family, and girlfriend but excited for the opportunities of Miami — boarded the ship.[66]

Unlike Yorick, unlike Cedric, and unlike the vast majority of young, poor black men, Sidney had escaped Nassau's colonial order. By strokes of fate, he had acquired American citizenship and sidestepped the Bahamian cycle of delinquency. But Miami was no paradise — not for any person with black skin, and certainly not for a cocksure, carefree, stubborn, functionally illiterate fifteen-year-old boy with a West Indian accent.

CHAPTER 2

GREAT MIGRATIONS
(1943–1945)

❖

Sidney retched himself to sleep that night. The ship's hole stank of sickly sweet motor oil, and his stomach churned with nausea. Finally morning arrived and he climbed above deck into sunshine and fresh air. As the ship coasted into Miami's harbor, he marveled at handsome buildings towering over steamships and sailboats. He recognized Cyril at the dock. Passing through customs and riding to his new home, he grew excited. Miami bore hope, the promise of education and opportunity and thrills.[1]

Had Sidney actually foreseen the next few months, he might have retreated into the ship's hole and retched his way back to Nassau. In Miami he felt isolated and unable to connect with Cyril's six children. Cyril's wife, Alberta, resented his presence. Sidney had hoped to return to school, but she demanded that he earn his keep. He began walking the city, ostensibly to find work but really to acquaint himself with Miami. Everything seemed new: American accents, taller buildings and longer streets, different sounds and tastes and smells. The white multitudes particularly struck Sidney. For the first time in his life, he was part of a racial minority.

Alberta chafed at Sidney's meandering, half-hearted job search. She was a nurse's aide, and Cyril was an airport porter with two extra part-time jobs. They barely made ends meet. After one week she insisted that Cyril use a contact at a department store to help find Sidney a job. Soon after, he was hired to deliver packages for the store's pharmacy. Traveling by bicycle, Sidney learned more of the city. During a delivery in Miami Beach, he learned a more harrowing lesson.[2]

Sidney pedaled through the wealthy white neighborhood, impressed by the mansions and their ornate grounds. He hopped off his bicycle at the appointed house and sauntered up the walk, package in hand. An older white woman answered the door. "What do you want?" she snapped. Confused, he showed her the parcel. "Get around to the back door!" she screamed. Sidney, unaware that southern protocol demanded that blacks enter white homes through the service entrance, simply asked why. The woman erupted, then slammed the door in his face. He shrugged, set the package by the door, and got back on his bicycle.[3]

Two nights later he accompanied a cousin to the movies. Returning home, they noticed that the house seemed dark. "Get in the house!" someone hissed. Alberta yanked them to the floor. All the children were awake, silent, and scared. Alberta informed them that the white woman from the delivery incident had called the department store. Sidney's white boss had provided his address. The Ku Klux Klan then paraded through their Liberty City neighborhood in white robes and hoods, ready to avenge the insult of a black teenager using the front door of a white woman's home.[4]

The lesson was a harbinger of the inevitable clash between the entrenched racial codes of Jim Crow and the stubborn independence of Sidney Poitier. Poitier had followed a long pattern of Bahamian migration to Miami, but he could not abide the Deep South.

❖

Miami, the *Nassau Tribune* proclaimed in 1911, was "to the Bahamians seeking a livelihood, what Mecca is to the religious Moslem world." Ten to twelve thousand people — about one-fifth of the Bahamian population — migrated to Miami between 1900 and 1920. Many returned home, but others stayed in south Florida. By 1920, Bahamian laborers, farmers, domestic servants, cooks, waiters, bellmen, hackmen, draymen, carpenters, painters, masons, launderers, and porters constituted over half of Miami blacks and over 15 percent of the entire city population. "In a very short time," complained one white planter from the Bahamas, "our lovely islands will soon be depopulated, gone to swell the millions on the great American continent."[5]

Despite a slackening of the influx by the mid-1920s, black Bahamians had few alternatives to emigration. In both Nassau and the Out Islands, they had limited access to education, social services, and political power. Families also encouraged emigration to improve their circumstances. "You always sent back money," explained Poitier, describing the unwritten rules for emigrants. "By long tradition in the Bahamas, that's simply *what you did* when you went to America."[6]

But the Bahamas paid a steep price for this cash infusion. The exodus of workers accelerated the decline of the agricultural economy. Subsistence money from abroad discouraged investment in the Bahamian infrastructure. And as male heads of household separated from their wives and children, patriarchal Bahamian families often crumbled.[7]

Nor, as Poitier's delivery episode illustrated, did Bahamians easily adjust to American racial patterns. "How unlike the land where I was born," recalled one Bahamian emigrant in the mid-1930s. "There colored men were addressed as gentlemen; here, as 'niggers.'" Race may have governed economic opportunity, but the Bahamian racial system did not sanction whites to call blacks "nigger" or "boy," to impose curfews on blacks, to refuse blacks at public facilities, or to require that blacks use service entrances. Like other Bahamians in Miami, Poitier grew up in a black majority and rejected this code. "I went to America with much of myself already congealed," he later explained. "Pride and entitlement I carried with me. I brought it from Cat Island."[8]

This sense of entitlement sometimes translated into acts of monumental cheek. For his next job, Poitier resolved to park cars, despite no driving experience whatsoever. At a downtown parking lot, he studied drivers' negotiations of the pedals and gears. Confident that he could adapt, he got a job at another garage, smoothly lying about his experience and driver's license. He accidentally put a car in reverse and began stripping the gears. The lot manager fired him, so he walked to another garage. This time he worked the gears, only to ram into another car. Another furious manager exiled him. He kept repeating this process, leaving a trail of dented fenders and shattered headlights in his wake. The next day, afraid of his reputation among the local parking fraternity, Poitier tried a different section of the city. He considered it a great triumph that he was not fired until the end of the day.[9]

Besides displaying Poitier's self-assurance, the fiasco revealed the economic limitations imposed upon a fifteen-year-old with minimal education and a thick patois. Discouraged by his prospects, he drifted back into delinquency. He tried to leave Miami by joining the Navy, which was recruiting blacks for menial service positions. At the main Miami police station, which granted the necessary pass to access birth certificates at the Bureau of Vital Statistics, a sergeant called him "nigger" and demanded that he remove his cap. By southern custom, blacks deferred to the instructions of white police officers. Poitier bucked custom. "Are you crazy?" he remembered asking. The sergeant was incredulous, and every officer in the station turned to watch as Poitier launched into a rant. Remarkably, the sergeant laughed. "But it sure was a peculiar laugh," Poitier qualified. "It was like saying he could just as well shoot me as laugh at me." The teenager's comically egregious violation of racial etiquette suggested more ignorance than ill will, so the sergeant gave him the pass. Poitier got his birth certificate and went to the naval recruiting center, only to be told that he was too young to enlist.[10]

More than a humorous exchange, Poitier's puffed-up pride represented a defense against Jim Crow. He may have been uneducated, but he was a young, intelligent outsider. "I couldn't understand it," he said. "Every sign, 'White' and 'Colored,' every rebuff, was like saying to me, 'You're not a human being.' "[11]

The Jim Crow system of World War II–era Florida, like that throughout the American South, was grounded in fear of black sexuality. In a 1944 survey, southern whites ranked miscegenation as their chief racial bugaboo. Whites manifested this sexual anxiety by treating blacks like children, demanding the doffing of their caps, calling them "boy" or "Auntie," or sending them to the back door for deliveries. But these social patterns also justified white monopolies on wealth and political power — as if only whites possessed work ethics, reasonable intellects, and moral principles.[12]

Southerners codified these views and practices, rooted in slavery, almost immediately following emancipation. In 1866, Florida enacted a series of Black Codes restricting blacks from sitting on juries, allowing fines or imprisonment for "leading an idle, profligate, or immoral life," and instituting a death penalty for inciting an insurrection or attempting to rape a white woman. State statutes in 1897 and 1901 disfranchised blacks, excluding them from the Democratic Party and charging a poll tax to cast a futile vote for the Republicans.[13]

In Miami, by 1920, only one in fifteen registered voters was black. Legalized segregation reinforced these political barriers. City ordinances prohibited black artisans and tradesmen from working in white neighborhoods. Blacks were barred from public parks and beaches, most labor unions, and the University of Miami. Like African Americans throughout the Deep South, Miami blacks sat in the backs of buses, had to step aside on crowded sidewalks in deference to whites, and could not try on clothes at department stores.[14]

Miami also had the highest degree of residential segregation of any major city in America. During his brief time there, Sidney lived in the city's two largest black neighborhoods. The Liberty Square Housing Project, home to Cyril's family, was a New Deal initiative with clean and modern facilities. Yet by 1942 many white neighbors had already sold their homes, and thrift stores and junk dealers surrounded the project.[15]

After the Klan paraded through Liberty Square, Cyril took Sidney to stay with his elderly Uncle Joe and Aunt Eva. They lived in Colored Town, a 105-block collection of ramshackle shotgun shacks, pockmarked streets, and piles of stinking trash. Throughout the first half of the twentieth century, as Miami had expanded and the black population had multiplied, white prejudice maintained Colored Town's boundaries. In 1920, social workers found 100 families living on one block. Few homes had electricity or indoor plumbing. The police force had only two officers, and the public school was tiny and underfunded. Insufficient public sanitation sometimes caused outbreaks of yellow fever.[16]

Yet Colored Town had its charms. "The Harlem of the South" survived because blacks developed their own resources within their own ghetto. The main strip, Avenue G, boasted a black-owned business district of groceries, general merchandise, pharmacies, funeral parlors, clubhouses, and ice cream parlors. There was a Chinatown, a prostitution district called Railroad Front, a Gambler's Lane, and a Good Bread Alley, where the aroma from a bakery wafted through the neighborhood. On Saturday nights, men in zoot suits and women in silks paraded through the city, laughing and flirting amidst the smells of sweet potato pies, hot fish sandwiches, and "sho-nuf" Georgia-style barbecue ribs. When downtown clubs closed, interracial cadres of performers headed for late night jam sessions at the Rockland Palace and Harlem Square. Bessie Smith, Cab Calloway, Count Basie, and Billie Holiday all played Miami, and they always visited Colored Town.[17]

Sidney stayed with Uncle Joe and Aunt Eva after the Klan incident. He still relied on Cyril for guidance and financial help, but Cyril had to provide for his own family. Unfortunately, although Uncle Joe and Aunt Eva were kind and docile, they could not replace the companionship of the Bahamas. Sidney also failed to replace his girlfriend, Dorothy; unsatisfied with short-term trysts, he was a hopeless and miserable romantic.[18]

He washed cars, cleaned rooms in a motor hotel, lugged crates around a warehouse, and grew depressed. He even tried a sales job with the Fuller Brush Company. He made only one sale: to Alberta. Most blacks could not afford the brushes and most whites refused to buy them from a black man, especially one with an accent. He got frustrated. "He'd get all worked up about the plight of the Negro here and the lack of opportunities," remembered Cyril. "I knew it couldn't last. I knew he had to take off."[19]

❖

The incident at the police station convinced Sidney to leave, and another episode involving the police soon after confirmed his decision. The afternoon before his departure, he stopped at a Colored Town cleaners to pick up a jacket and two pairs of pants. Unfortunately, the clothes were at a processing plant across town. Unwilling to lose a single day, Poitier took a bus there. By the time he returned to the station, the buses had stopped running. It was nearly dark, and he was stranded in a white neighborhood. He hitchhiked home. By this time, well-versed in southern folkways, he stuck his thumb out only at cars with black passengers. Finally a dark sedan stopped. Poitier had miscalculated. Inside the car were five white policemen.[20]

"What are you doing?" asked the driver. "I'm trying to hitch a ride back to Colored Town," he replied. A long, long pause followed. The cops looked him up and down, silently. They directed him to an alley and rolled alongside him, boxing him in. The officer in the passenger seat gestured to Poitier to approach the car and lean in. Then he put his gun on Poitier's forehead and made slow circles with the nozzle, talking to the others but looking squarely into Poitier's eyes. "What should we do with this boy?" they pondered. "Should we shoot him?"[21]

Poitier explained his story. For ten seconds, no one spoke. Finally the driver said that he could walk home. But if he turned around, they would shoot him. For thirty-five blocks, Poitier trekked home, looking stiffly straight ahead. For thirty-five blocks, the police car crawled beside him, the officers cracking jokes about their victim's humiliation. And for thirty-five blocks, as he alternately trembled with fear and stewed in anger, Poitier learned another lesson about black life in the South: Jim Crow was not just a dehumanizing institution, but a force backed by the deadly authority of the state.[22]

It may have been a new lesson for Poitier, but most Miami blacks had learned it repeatedly through decades of intimidation. In 1928, for instance, a white officer shot a black teenager for stealing eggs from a railroad car. The officer reportedly ran up to him shouting, "What did you run for? Did you think I wouldn't get you?" That same year a Dade County grand jury uncovered the use of a crude electric chair to elicit confessions from black suspects rounded up on unfounded charges of vagrancy, disorderly conduct, and vice. The police sometimes applied live electric wires to men's and women's exposed genitalia.[23]

The police also turned a blind eye to the Ku Klux Klan, which in 1921 had announced their presence in Miami with a downtown parade. During municipal elections in 1939, the Negro Citizens Service League conducted a voter registration campaign. The night before the election, the Klan sent a seventy-five-car motorcade into Colored Town. Hangman's nooses hung from car windows. "Niggers stay away from the polls," warned a Klan leaflet. Every block for twenty-five blocks, they burned a cross. Black effigies hung from lampposts, their chests bearing a chilling epitaph: "THIS NIGGER VOTED."[24]

Miami's black community actually defied this intimidation by turning out for the 1939 elections. But by early 1943, when Poitier's failed delivery prompted the Liberty City witch-hunt, Klan activity had intensified rather than abated. Race remained the primary division in Miami society. More than ever, Poitier craved escape. Lacking funds, he drew inspiration from the movies: he would ride the rails like a hobo. Put into action, however, reality trumped romance. On his first attempt he got stuck in Tampa. No northbound trains passed through for a few hours, so he returned to Miami.[25]

Poitier refused to quit, though. "I had just imagined that if you got in a boxcar, it would go all the way north," he remembered. On his second try, he reached a white, middle-class town north of Tampa, where he warily approached houses asking for odd jobs. One woman fed him and refused his offer of work. The kindness sustained him, and he later claimed that she illustrated the essentially good nature of people, even in the racist South.

For two days he mowed lawns, cleaned garages, and washed cars. At night he slept in the woods. By the third evening, he craved shelter. Apprehensive of getting arrested for vagrancy, he went to the police station and asked if he could sleep in jail. Once again, Poitier had mystified a white police officer. The policeman on duty had never encountered such a preposterous scheme, let alone from a black teenager. He let Sidney sleep in the lockup, but he insisted on telephoning one of his kin. The next morning a peeved Cyril took Sidney back to Miami.[26]

Sidney's third attempt showed a tad more forethought. At Cyril's suggestion he worked in the kitchen at a rural resort north of Atlanta. The lodge, perched atop a mountain plateau and sheltered by pines, offered spectacular vistas, fellow black workers, and steady wages. But for twelve hours a day, he washed dishes, scrubbed floors, peeled potatoes, and performed odds and ends. "My ass was dragging at the end of the day," he recalled. Nor did his labor earn a shred of autonomy. The resort operated like a paternalistic plantation: the workers could only draw a dollar or two from their weekly salary, and they received afternoons off only at the arbitrary dispensation of their "benevolent" boss.[27]

After six weeks Poitier had accumulated thirty-nine dollars and aggravated his itch to escape the South. He tendered his resignation and reached the central bus station in Atlanta. The next bus went to Chatta-nooga — not far enough, in Poitier's mind. The second went to Birming-ham — certainly not. But the third bus was to New York City — home of Harlem. And Harlem, as James Weldon Johnson once wrote, "is the rec-ognized Negro capital. Indeed, it is the Mecca for the sightseer, the pleasure-seeker, the curious, the adventurous, the enterprising, the am-bitious, and the talented of the entire Negro world." Harlem had enticed Sidney since childhood. He paid $11.35 in bus fare. It was the spring of 1943, and a sixteen-year-old solitary immigrant with minimal education, stubborn pride, and a little luck was on his way to New York City.[28]

❖

In fits and starts, without plans or prospects, Poitier participated in the most significant demographic shift of twentieth-century America: the Great Migration. Black Americans had begun moving from the rural South to the urban North during World War I, when northern cities needed new labor to replace soldiers and supply the war effort. The north-ward flow doubled during the prosperous 1920s, persisted through the Great Depression, and multiplied during World War II, when the number of black workers in war industries tripled. As the boll weevil, the mecha-nized cotton picker, poverty, and Jim Crow pushed blacks out of the South, economic opportunities pulled them into New York, Chicago, and Detroit. Singing "Farewell, We're Good and Gone" and riding trains chalked with "Bound for the Promised Land," the migrants embarked on an exodus that transformed the nation's political and cultural landscape. If geography was destiny, than black Americans altered theirs by heading north. They transformed race into a national issue.[29]

Harlem, on the northern tip of Manhattan, most embodied the frustra-tions, joys, and contradictions of black America. Harlem was a black world unto itself, but owned by white landlords. Harlem was a black haven from Jim Crow, but segregation defined its boundaries. And Har-lem was the historical quintessence of black culture, but within a system of white patronage.

A neighborhood of tree-lined streets and spacious homes at the turn of the century, Harlem absorbed an influx of blacks between 1910 and 1935. Its population multiplied by 600 percent. As realtors shepherded migrants there, landlords charged exorbitant rents for deteriorating apartments in cramped confines. Thousands lived in dank basements and squalid tene-ments. Segregation persisted, too, even within Harlem; a black woman could not try on clothes in large department stores on 125th Street, and the Loew's Theatre on 116th Street restricted blacks to the balcony. Employment prospects were similarly bleak. Sociologist E. Franklin Frazier described the two New York City hiring policies: "Those that employ Negroes in menial positions and those that employ no Negroes at all."[30]

Yet Harlem enchanted even white Americans. In the 1920s, the Harlem Renaissance tied black artistic life to white patronage. Heralding the arrival of the "New Negro," Alain Locke argued that blacks could achieve racial pride through the arts. White philanthropists, romanticizing the culture as bohemian, funded black intellectuals such as Langston Hughes, Countee Cullen, Jean Toomer, and Zora Neale Hurston. At the same time, liberal whites such as Van Wyck Brooks, Eugene O'Neill, and Du-Bose Heyward used black life for artistic inspiration.[31]

In popular culture, too, Harlem enticed crowds with an exoticized image of black America, a release from buttoned-down everyday existence. The Savoy, the epicenter of swing music since the late 1920s, had two bandstands, haughty café au lait hostesses, and an interracial clientele primed to see Duke Ellington, Benny Goodman, Louis Armstrong, and Ella Fitzgerald. "Rendezvous of famous and infamous cosmopolities, of privileged and titled and nondescript bohemians, celebrated in smart unconventional publications, the Savoy is the vast depot of dancing for the commonality of Negroes," marveled Claude McKay. But acid tinged his admiration. The Savoy, like so many Harlem institutions, was owned by whites.[32]

So why Harlem? Why did it attract migrants, stoke racial pride, or stir lingering memories of its charms? To the extent that Harlem flourished, it did so because it housed black cultural institutions, allowed for black leaders, and preserved black traditions without direct white control. Its allures were many: churches that doubled as social centers, serving hot meals and attracting Harlemites in their Sunday finest; grand funeral processions and fraternal parades along Lenox Avenue, complete with brass bands and dignitaries in full regalia; bridge parties, where the black middle class hobnobbed among their own; rent parties, where fifteen cents paid for chitterlings, pigs feet, all-night dancing, and access to corn liquor or a potential mate; the Apollo Theatre, where jazz, blues, and boogie-woogie entertained the masses; and Sunday afternoon "strolling," processions of men sporting such finery as silk toppers, homburgs, velvet-collared Chesterfields, monocles, and white gloves while accompanying women in wide-brimmed hats, suede shoes, and white satin frocks. This was the Harlem of legend, the Harlem that bore so much promise for Poitier.[33]

Harlem also housed the vast majority of West Indian immigrants. About 125,000 Harlemites — a quarter of the neighborhood's population — hailed from Jamaica, Barbados, Trinidad, and other Caribbean islands. West Indians did more than add yams, pawpaws, and ginger roots to the neighborhood's groceries; they were a powerful economic and political force. Insular, educated, and ambitious, they aggressively competed with white-owned grocery stores, tailor shops, and real estate offices. Many of Harlem's leading politicians and businessmen came from the West Indies. Called "monkey chasers" and "Black Jews" by resentful African Americans, West Indians accumulated reputations as clannish and hot-tempered Anglophiles. American blacks often complained that they exploited the black community and raised trouble with their insistent rejections of black servility.[34]

Poitier was both inside and outside this West Indian milieu. As his Miami stint illustrated, he loudly protested treatment based on skin color. He also possessed a powerful ambition associated with West Indian culture. Poitier later reflected on the distinctions between American and West Indian parenting. He argued that African American parents warned their children, "You're gonna have to be twice as good as the white folks in order to get half as much." His parental lectures, by contrast, consisted of another message: "Get that education. Get out there and work. Get out there and hustle. Take whatever opportunities there are, and use them as stepping-stones."[35]

But cultural differences did not entirely explain the prominence of West Indians. West Indians succeeded more frequently than African Americans because most arrived with schooling, some financial capital, and a network of contacts. Poitier lacked all these tools. He was uneducated, poor, and alone.[36]

With no one to greet or guide him, Poitier added to his string of misadventures. He stepped off his bus at 8th Avenue and 50th Street and noticed that someone had stolen the money in his suitcase. He had only the three dollars in his pocket. He first spoke to a pimp (declining the offer) and then asked a black man how to reach Harlem. Directed to the subway, he nervously clambered below ground. Rushing commuters, nickel slots for turnstiles, the A and C and D Trains — the subway mystified him. "How can trains run under the ground?" he asked himself. Finally his AA Train arrived and his mood changed. "I'm on a TRAIN UNDER THE GROUND," he thought, and "it's FANTASTIC!!!"[37]

He alighted at the 116th Street station and ascended to Harlem. Malcolm Little — soon called "Detroit Red" and later "Malcolm X" — had arrived there a year earlier. He had described Harlem as a "technicolor bazaar" of black soldiers and sailors, the cool Small's Paradise and the hot Savoy, hustlers peddling jewelry and pimps selling whores. Poitier's reaction was more muted. He walked to a nondescript hotel and asked for a room. It cost three dollars, the exact sum in his pocket. Poitier assumed that was the price for a month, or perhaps a week. But the hotel cost three dollars a night. A bit shaken, he returned downtown.[38]

He went to Broadway and 42nd Street. He drank in the buildings, the people, the lights that exploded in color with the onset of twilight. He gawked at a cigarette billboard that blew smoke all over Broadway. He gorged on hot dogs and chocolate malteds. He walked into pinball parlors, adult bookstores, and haberdasheries. He marveled at the movie theaters. It was a sensory feast.[39]

Although he did not notice it then, Broadway in 1943 also reflected subtle shifts in black entertainment. A number of all-black musicals — including *Carmen Jones*, *Razzle Dazzle*, and a revival of *Porgy and Bess* — debuted on Broadway that fall. Hollywood mirrored this fascination with black entertainers. The all-black movie musicals *Cabin in the Sky* and *Stormy Weather* both opened during Poitier's first few months in New York City. *Cabin in the Sky* starred Eddie "Rochester" Anderson, Ethel Waters, and Lena Horne. *Stormy Weather*, an entertainment cavalcade based on the career of Bill Robinson, featured Horne, Fats Waller, Cab Calloway, and "Mr. Bojangles" himself. Both movies had spectacular song-and-dance numbers. The musicals represented a slight improvement on the dim-witted servants and sacrificial mammies of Hollywood's past, even if they reinforced the perception that blacks were natural entertainers without brains or souls.[40]

On a more hopeful note, the later war years also included some roles for black character actors playing moral, intelligent men. Dooley Wilson's Sam may be a crooning, oversimplified sidekick to Humphrey Bogart's Rick Blaine in *Casablanca* (1942), but the two enjoy a legitimate interracial camaraderie unseen in previous American films. In the anti-lynching film *The Ox-Bow Incident* (1943), Leigh Whipper's Sparks preaches reason and compassion to an angry mob. In *Lifeboat* (1944), an Alfred Hitchcock film about Americans stranded by a German torpedo, Canada Lee's Joe earns respect by saving a drowning white woman and her child.[41]

The black images of stage and screen were Poitier's future; his present concern was that he had spent all his money on hot dogs and malteds. At 11:00 that night, he passed an advertisement for dishwashers at the Turf

Restaurant on 49th Street. He offered his services and immediately started. For $4.11 and two meals, Poitier worked through the night, stacking dirty dishes into gigantic washers in the restaurant's basement. The next morning, he dragged himself back to the bus station where he had stored his suitcase in a locker. He changed his clothes, washed his face, and looked for a place to catch a nap. Unwilling to waste his night's salary on a hotel room, he deposited a nickel into a bus station pay toilet. He put the seat down, propped his feet on the door, settled into an awkward crouch, and slept amidst the wafting aromas of urine and disinfectant.[42]

Since it was early summer, Poitier spent days wandering New York City. Splitting time between Harlem and Broadway, he fell in love with the energy and variety of New York City. One day he walked into the Brill Building, the center of the music industry on 51st and Broadway. He rode the elevator and caught a bird's-eye view of the city. After he learned that the building never closed, he sometimes slept on the Brill's rooftop, swathed in old newspapers.[43]

In time Poitier settled into stability. He saved money and rented a room on 127th Street for five dollars a week. The tiny space contained only a small cot, a rickety bureau, and a naked light bulb hanging off-center. The bathroom was down the hall. But compared to the pay toilet and the Brill Building rooftop, the accommodations were luxurious. He also found employment agencies specializing in placing restaurant staff. He worked as a dishwasher all over Manhattan: the Crossroads Cafe, Rudley's, the Savoy-Plaza, the Madison, the Taft, the Edison, the Waldorf-Astoria. At the Zanzibar, he poked his head out of the kitchen to watch Bill Robinson and his "soft syncopated dance."[44]

Poitier later listed job titles such as butcher's assistant, drugstore clerk, saladmaker, construction worker, porter, and longshoreman. Manual labor allowed him to experience the city, and he drifted from job to job with little care. "I had the freedom and the prerogative to walk off a job as a porter if I didn't like it or if it bored me to tears," he later explained. "I was a great daydreamer. I would wind up leaving the job and going and sitting near the water, or in Central Park, and just dream all day." He also took weekend jobs at resorts in the Catskills. On his own and with limited resources, he educated himself in the rhythms of the urban North.[45]

No incident taught him more than the Harlem Riot of 1943, a flashpoint of black frustration during World War II. If the United States was protecting democracy abroad, asked black leaders, then why did the country snub black rights at home? The Army segregated black and white units. The Navy allowed blacks only to serve as messmen. The Red Cross rejected blood donations from blacks. The federal government ignored southern blacks at the mercy of lynch law. War industries placed limits on black advancement. "We are disfranchised, jim-crowed, spat upon," noted one black man in 1942. "What more could Hitler do than that?"[46]

In New York, throughout the war years, the newspapers exaggerated a Harlem crime wave, and the police harassed blacks chatting on street corners. A $50 million apartment complex opened on the Lower East Side in 1943 and refused to accept blacks; its chief sponsor explained that "Negroes and whites don't mix." In April of that year, the police even shut down the Savoy, presumably to quell the practice of interracial dancing.[47]

On Sunday, 1 August, this smoldering discontent burst into flame. At 7:30 that evening at the Braddock Hotel, an unruly black woman named Marjorie Polite began arguing with a rookie white police officer named James Collins. A black soldier, Private Robert Bandy, heard Polite yell, "Protect me from this white man!" He intervened, knocking the white officer to the ground. Bandy fled and Collins shot him. Bandy suffered only a slight shoulder wound, but Harlemites immediately started spreading rumors: a black soldier had been shot in the back, a black soldier was crippled, a black soldier was dying. "They preferred the invention," explained James Baldwin, then a young observer, "because this invention expressed and corroborated their hates and fears so perfectly."[48]

White over black, trigger-happy cop over patriotic soldier, powerful over powerless—Harlem reached its boiling point. Blacks attacked the most visible symbols of this oppression. They smashed the windows of white-owned businesses along 125th Street. They tore white department store mannequins, limb by limb. Anger turned into anarchy. A black mob beat two British seamen leaving a 125th Street movie house. A glass bottle struck a 62-year-old woman. Crowds marched as far north as 135th Street, sparing only those storefronts with "COLORED STORE" or "NEGRO" hastily scrawled upon them. As sirens wailed and shadows stretched down the city streets, young black men broke street lamps and climbed rooftops to hurl bricks, bottles, and ashcans upon police in air raid helmets.[49]

Poitier was washing dishes downtown that night. He had heard about the riot, but nothing prepared him for the scene when he walked out of the subway station on 125th Street. "There was chaos everywhere," he remembered, "cops, guns, and people running and looting, with shots going off everywhere and debris and broken glass all over the street." During his walk up Lenox Avenue, he succumbed to mob psychology, scrambling through smashed windows and looking for something—

anything—to claim as his spoils. The riot offered Poitier an opportunity to lash out against an exploitative, discriminatory system. "I'm not essentially a looter," he tried to explain years later. But in the summer of 1943, he was poor, young, and angry at racial double standards—a typical looter.[50]

From inside a department store, Poitier heard gunshots. The police were close. Looters scattered. Poitier ran into a storeroom filled with large bags of flour and sugar. It had no exits. He heard screams. "They're not shooting in the air," he thought, terrified, "they're shooting at people." He threw himself onto a flour sack, waited for the door handle to turn, took a deep breath, and played dead. A flashlight shone in his face. He laid still until the door slammed shut. For now, at least, Poitier was safe.

After five minutes, he decided to escape. He launched himself through the smashed window and into the fracas of armored police, wailing sirens, and scurrying looters. Poitier scrambled up Lenox Avenue and turned onto 127th Street. Gunshots whizzed past him. Then a cool sensation penetrated his leg. Afraid to stop amidst the chaos, he kept running into his apartment. He had been shot, and blood soaked through his shoe.[51]

That night there was a 10:30 curfew. Black leaders Walter White and Roy Wilkins drove through the streets in a sound truck trying to dispel the rumor that a black soldier had died. Gunfire continued and fires burned through the night, as Poitier nursed his injury. The bullet had torn through his lower calf without lodging inside him. He limped for a few weeks, with his only medicine liberal applications of Vaseline. For the rest of his life he bore a scar.[52]

The scar on Harlem was deeper: 6 dead, 700 injured, 600 arrested, and 4,500 windows smashed. In the following weeks, New Yorkers dissected the riot. White newspapers lamented the destruction. Black newspapers rebuked the looters, but pointed at the riot's root causes. The Harlem Riot of 1943 had begun in the heart of the black community, and it targeted the main symbols of white authority: white-owned property and white police officers. Foreshadowing the riots of the 1960s, it sprung directly from the discontent of the inner city.[53]

Poitier nevertheless preferred the violence-marred summer to the approaching winter. The winds of November and snows of December disheartened the young Bahamian, who had seen snow only in the movies. He had no gloves, no hat, and no winter coat; he owned only light shirts, thin pants, and a summer jacket. In a sadly comical defense, he wore all his clothes at once. His dishwashing jobs dried up, and he rarely left his apartment. He ate less and could not pay his rent. In early winter his landlord evicted him. "I was lonely," he remembered. "So lonely."[54]

He slept on a bench in Penn Station and was arrested for vagrancy. He spent the night in a cold cell at a 32nd Street precinct, a single light bulb swaying above his cell. He neared his breaking point. The next morning, he wandered into a Catholic orphanage in Brooklyn. Although he was not Catholic, the nuns there provided him with a bed, food, and a toothbrush. He soon found more dishwashing work. Still cold, still alone, Poitier was surviving.[55]

❖

He decided to join the Army. Hunger and cold had scarred him; he wanted warm weather and three square meals. But he was only sixteen, and the minimum age for the Army was eighteen, so at the recruiting station he fibbed about his age. After basic training at Camp Upton on Long Island, he joined the 1267th Medical Detachment at the Veterans Administration Hospital in Northport, Long Island. The hospital tended to shell-shocked soldiers. Poitier's all-black company supported a white civilian staff. He learned how to perform physiotherapy, shock therapy, and basic health care.[56]

He hated the whole experience. His peers, older and native New Yorkers, taunted him. "I was oddball number one," he explained, "and the kickoff was my accent." He also witnessed staff abuse of patients. The medical professionals showed little appreciation of mental illness, and they sometimes beat the patients. Poitier also hated Army discipline. After an unfettered childhood and independent teenage years, he resented the emphasis on minor details and the blind acceptance of authority.[57]

He welcomed respites from the hospital, and he often joined his company on excursions to bars that catered exclusively to blacks. On one trip to Oyster Bay, the two black military policemen who supervised the company stopped at a roadhouse for beer and sandwiches, requesting their order takeout. The manager responded: "We don't serve niggers in here." The MP's departed to snickers and racial slurs.

When they told the company about the incident, the soldiers decided to order fifty beers and fifty sandwiches from the same roadhouse. Again came the answer: "We don't serve niggers in here." An MP punched the manager in the face, and Poitier's company destroyed the bar. They smashed bottles and tore pictures off the walls. When they left for Northport, the roadhouse resembled a war zone of jagged glass, splintered wood, and puddles of spilled liquor.[58]

The unit's captain restricted the entire company to base for the next three months as Army officials investigated the incident. But the men refused to divulge any information. Their response reflected black solidarity against second-class treatment. Poitier's company was quite typical; of the 500,000 blacks then in the Army, only about 79,000 were overseas. Most were mess attendants or performed grunt duties. Even more than the typical black citizen, blacks in the military understood the hypocrisy of fighting fascism abroad while tolerating discrimination at home.[59]

The war afforded the opportunity to demand equal participation in America's democratic tradition. Following the D-Day invasion in June 1944, for instance, black newspapers trumpeted the contributions of black soldiers and hoped that military success would end Jim Crow. And as Poitier's company evinced, blacks in the military tended not to accept such egregious displays of racism. Following their three-month restriction, the company returned to the roadhouse and ordered more sandwiches and beers. Their large group could not be seated and the order took twenty-five minutes, but the manager delivered the order in tidy little boxes. Poitier's unit won a tiny victory.[60]

But the rigidity of Army life still weighed on Poitier. He wanted to leave. The solution was simple: he only had to report his actual age — too young for the Army — and he would obtain his release. But Poitier misguidedly regarded such an admission as the tactic of a confused boy. He preferred a bolder, if more foolish, strategy: he would provoke a Section 8 discharge by faking insanity. He made an appointment with the head of the hospital. Poitier entered the office, closed the door, picked up a large wooden chair, and threw it across the desk. The administrator ducked, as Poitier had hoped. The chair crashed through a huge bay window and fell two stories. Poitier sauntered out the door, walked to the recreation building, and began shooting pool.[61]

He got sent to Mason General Hospital in Amityville, Long Island, for observation. But all the patients in his ward still had shoelaces and belts. Poitier knew that he would not get declared Section 8 for such mild insanity. So that first night, at dinner, he upped the ante. Huge dinner carts warmed by steam trays circulated food to the patients. He planted his feet and pushed one over. An unsavory hodgepodge of baked beans, chicken, steaming water, and chocolate pudding oozed across the ward. Ignoring the bewildered staff and patients, he maintained an unruffled pose.[62]

His plan finally bore fruit. He went to a ward where they took away his belt and shoes. He wore a gown and slippers and had to eat with his hands. The next day a psychiatrist questioned him. Poitier continued to portray a composed loner; when the doctor mentioned him pushing over the cart, he shrugged, "Yeah, it wasn't too bad, was it?" The cat-and-mouse continued. The psychiatrist played his trump card: he would arrange for shock treatments. Poitier knew all about shock treatment from his stint at the VA Hospital. He was suddenly on the defensive. In a calculated risk, he confessed that he had faked his own insanity.

The admission could have landed him in jail. But the psychiatrist questioned him further, and Poitier described his incompatibility with Army discipline, his own upbringing, and his tribulations in America. "I gave him everything," Poitier remembered. The psychiatrist respected the honesty. He arranged to see Poitier fifty minutes a day five days a week for the next five weeks, during which time Poitier elaborated upon his experiences and ordeals, his hopes and desires.

The sessions exposed the contradictions of Poitier's life. "In the discussions we'd been having," he remembered, "I kept repeating that I was as *good* as anybody." American race prejudice had pushed him into a bunker. The Klan march through Liberty City, the incident with the Miami police, the Harlem Riot, and the Oyster Bay donnybrook had all threatened his self-worth. Like many West Indians, Poitier struggled under the blanket of race that America threw over all people with black skin. Yet America also offered economic opportunity and democratic ideals. Some white people—the Florida woman, the Brooklyn nuns—had even harbored him. Now the psychiatrist urged him to remember the good nature of both whites and blacks. The sessions might not have purged Poitier's demons, but they sustained his faith in humanity.[63]

❖

Based on the psychiatrist's recommendations, Poitier avoided a court-martial. The Army sent him to Fort Dix in New Jersey for three weeks before releasing him on 11 December 1944. He had been in the Army for one year and eleven days.

Upon entering the Army, Poitier had specified that some of his pay be sent to his parents in the Bahamas. By a bureaucratic fluke, the Army had withheld the money but had not sent it home. So on top of his mustering-out pay, Poitier received this bonus allotment. He returned to New York City and rented a room on 146th Street with a Hispanic family. But he was still gloomy. Some awkward dates with a cute, plump, eighteen-year-old woman did little to lift his spirits. He still yearned for the warm romance of his Nassau days. Stilted conversations with this new girl did not quench his thirst for companionship.[64]

Financial pressures piled on top of these insecurities. His savings dissipated, even though he typically worked eight hours, returned to Harlem, and wandered the streets by himself. For all its charms, New York City seemed to have defeated Sidney Poitier. He wanted to leave America for Nassau, but he had no money. He refused to write home — not placing money in the envelope violated the West Indian code, but asking for money was an admission of total failure. So Poitier hatched a new plan, a ridiculous scheme carried out with beguiling earnestness.[65]

He wrote a letter. "Dear President Roosevelt," it began, "my name is Sidney Poitier and I am here in the United States in New York City. I am from the Bahamas." He expressed his desire to return home. He missed his mother, father, brothers, and sisters. He could not establish a toehold in the United States. Finally he asked to borrow $100 to return home. "I will send it back to you and I would certainly appreciate it very much. Your fellow American, Sidney Poitier." Every day he rushed down to his mailbox, expecting a $100 check from FDR, returning upstairs disappointed.[66]

Eventually he returned to manual labor, finding many of his jobs by perusing the want ads of the *New York Amsterdam News*, the black-owned newspaper based in Harlem. One day early in 1945 he was scanning over the typical jobs for chauffeurs, maids, factory workers, and dishwashers. A small ad on the opposite page caught his eye. He knew what it was like to be a dishwasher, or a janitor, or a porter. Here was something new. Out of part dissatisfaction with the drudgery of daily toil, part fanciful daydream of a better life, and part sheer restlessness, Poitier pursued the following ad: "Actors Wanted By Little Theatre Group; Apply in Person at the American Negro Theater."[67]

CHAPTER 3

STAGES

(1945–1949)

In appearance alone, Frederick O'Neal was intimidating. The generous cut of his suits accentuated his mountainous build, and his goatee punctuated a withering glare custom-tailored to pulverize the egos of cocksure eighteen-year-olds. To the black acting fraternity, O'Neal was doubly intimidating. Organizer of the Ira Aldridge Players in St. Louis, actor in the New Theatre School and the Rose McClendon Players in New York City, and co-founder of the American Negro Theatre, O'Neal stood atop the small world of black theater. His reputation extended downtown. In the spring of 1945, O'Neal won Broadway's Clarence Derwent Award for his performance in the play *Anna Lucasta*. That same spring, Poitier knocked on the door of the American Negro Theatre, then housed in the basement of the Harlem Branch of the New York Public Library on 135th Street and Lenox Avenue. To Poitier's misfortune, the man who answered was Frederick O'Neal.[1]

Poitier began his cool bluff, the one from Miami parking lots and Army recruiting offices. He pretended that he had been acting for years in Nassau and Miami. A skeptical O'Neal handed him a script. Poitier would read one part from the stage while O'Neal responded from the orchestra.[2]

Poitier had never set foot on a stage. He had never even heard the word "script." He had to deduce his expected lines while walking to the stage. He stared at the script. O'Neal looked impatient. Poitier read his first line—one word at a time, with plenty of pauses, and in his gelatinous singsong accent. O'Neal's first line never came. He commanded Poitier off the stage. "You can hardly talk," said O'Neal, as Poitier remembered. "You've got an accent, and that accent—you can't be an actor with an accent like that. And you can hardly read. You can't be an actor and not be able to read." O'Neal met Poitier at the stairs, snatched his script, grabbed his arm, almost pushed him out the door, and offered a parting shot: "Just go on and get out of here and get yourself a job as a dishwasher or something."[3]

The words seared through Poitier. "How the hell does he know I'm a dishwasher?" he wondered as he walked down 135th Street. "Is there a sign on me somewhere?" He knew that he lacked education, and he had endured teasing about his accent in the Army. But by 1945 he was excruciatingly sensitive about his position in America. Since landing in Miami, he had suffered from deep isolation, endured assaults based on skin color, and languished in dead-end jobs. Had O'Neal politely dismissed him, Poitier might have chalked up his acting tryout as yet another American foible. But that chance remark about dishwashing, he remembered, "was an immediate crystallization of all my insecurities and fears. My own feelings had been, 'I ain't worth much,' and they were confirmed." Unwilling to embrace that self-definition, he challenged himself. By the time he reached 7th Avenue, he had resolved to become an actor.[4]

For the next six months Poitier embarked upon a remarkable program of self-education. He returned to dishwashing and scraped together fourteen dollars to purchase a radio. After work, he brought raisin bread and soda into his apartment, listened to the radio, and repeated what he heard: news reports, commercials, soap operas, panel discussions, anything. He mimicked the clean diction of radio announcers like Norman Brokenshire, host of the *U.S. Steel Hour*. Poitier would imitate them, expunging the Bahamas from his voice. "How do you do, Ladies and Gentlemen? How do you do?" His landlord, listening through the door, thought he was crazy.[5]

He read magazines and newspapers at every chance. He had no real friends and little extra income, so reading filled his spare time. He also enlisted the assistance of a genial waiter at his regular dishwashing job. Late at night, as the waiters ate, Poitier read the *New York Journal-American* out loud. The elderly, bespectacled Jewish waiter supervised his coltish pupil, correcting his mistakes and expanding his vocabulary. Poitier then took the newspaper home and read the articles again, patterning his voice after the radio announcers.[6]

Poitier may have vowed to learn acting out of spite for Frederick O'Neal, but the decision shaped his course to manhood. Acting gave him a goal—a career rather than a job. Acting gave him an identity—a creative outlet and a sense of self-worth. Acting gave him human contact—true friends and exciting romances. And acting gave him an education—not only in his craft, but in racial politics. Sidney Poitier entered the theater in 1945 as an impulsive and illiterate teenager. He left for Hollywood in 1949 as a seasoned young actor, a man textured in American politics and culture, a member of a small black avant-garde, and a first-hand witness to the ironies of racial integration.

❖

When Poitier first walked into the 135th Street Library basement, he entered a theater in the midst of transformation, one whose success had planted the seeds of its dissolution. By 1945 the American Negro Theatre teetered on a fulcrum, balanced between Broadway and Harlem. The same dilemma had plagued black entertainment for years.

Downtown loomed fame and wealth — at a price. Popular black enter-tainers historically pandered to outside perceptions of their culture. For instance, the turn-of-the-century comedians Bert Williams and George Walker, though comic geniuses, acted like impudent dandies and hapless dimwits. Extravaganzas of smiling, shuffling singers and dancers sim-ilarly reinforced notions of innate black entertainers. White audiences rejected serious black drama. In 1917, Ridgely Torrence introduced three one-act plays with all-black casts on Broadway. White critics focused on recognizable stock figures, including a Mammy type named "Granny Maumee," instead of the plays' challenging implications about race rela-tions. Despite good reviews for Torrence's plays, black drama disap-peared from the Great White Way.[7]

Uptown, by contrast, endured the promise of independent theater free of white prejudice. But any such theater had to overcome significant bar-riers. Few blacks possessed training as dramatic actors, playwrights, di-rectors, or theater technicians. Due both to cultural apathy and financial limitations, Harlem had never fully supported a self-sustaining theater. A few independent companies had briefly overcome these hurdles: the Lafa-yette Players survived until the early 1930s, W. E. B. Du Bois organized the Krigwa Players in 1926, and the Harlem Suitcase Theater, the Rose McClendon Players, and the Negro Playwrights Company all came and went in the late 1930s.[8]

The American Negro Theatre (ANT) grew out of a conversation be-tween two veterans of the black theater. In 1940, O'Neal and Abram Hill, a drama director and former member of the Negro Playwrights Com-pany, discussed forming a theater company structured as a cooperative, teaching organization. The two men gathered eight like-minded actors and playwrights. When they passed a hat at the end of the meeting, they collected six cents.[9]

From these inauspicious beginnings ANT blossomed into the foremost black independent theater of the 1940s. Hill and O'Neal overcame a shoestring budget with cooperative ingenuity. They rehearsed in a rent-free funeral parlor before moving to the 135th Street Library. They scraped together funds through advance sales, subscription house parties, New Year's Eve bashes, program advertisements, fines on members who missed rehearsals, and pleas to Harlem celebrities (Bojangles Robinson gave ANT its largest contribution: five dollars). They rummaged through old trunks for props. They divided half of each show's profits among the members and placed the other half in the ANT treasury. They even contributed some income earned from outside acting work. This communal spirit was central to the company's purpose. "ANT is not a star-making organization," O'Neal liked to proclaim. "You may play a leading role in one production and be an attendant in the rest room during the following production."[10]

Unlike theater groups organized in the leftist cultural ferment of the late 1930s, ANT shunned overt political themes. Hill had left the Negro Playwrights Company because he believed that theater should aspire to artistic eminence over political consequence. ANT addressed universal themes through black characters, and it transcended Broadway's depictions of black butlers, maids, singers, and dancers. "Among the foremost aims," Hill later said, "was to destroy the black stereotypes." The Playreading Committee even established formal guidelines to promote positive black images. They blamed stereotyped caricatures for more than two-thirds of ANT's rejected scripts. The result, as one critic admired, was that "Negroes in this theatre are shown to be what they are: human beings with foibles and troubles that beset the rest of mankind, yet with mankind's greatness, goodness, and creativity."[11]

The June 1944 premiere of *Anna Lucasta*—one year before Poitier's initial audition—heightened ANT's reputation as a quality company addressing colorblind themes. Hill had adapted the play from Philip Yordan's script about a Polish-American family, called *Anna Lukaska*. On opening night, two hundred spectators crammed into folding wooden seats in the 135th Street Library basement on a sweltering night (one white critic called it "jungle heat"). *Anna Lucasta* revolves around a reformed prostitute who returns home, falls in love, and negotiates between her past and present. Featuring memorable characterizations of Anna's treacherous family and saucy companions, *Anna Lucasta* transformed a sweaty, uncomfortable crowd into enthusiastic patrons.[12]

The next day, the critics applauded the "serious story of average human beings (all highly individualized) who happen to have pigmented skins." Most praised Hilda Simms in the title role and Frederick O'Neal as her conniving brother Frank. One columnist warned Hill that unless he kept "a very sharp eye on his players, Broadway producers would pick them off one by one."[13]

Instead, a Broadway producer took the whole show. John Wildberg bought the rights to *Anna Lucasta* and staged it in August at the Mansfield Theatre. The Broadway debut prompted the same lusty laughs and thunderous applause. Again, scores of critics praised the robust performances and emotional impact. White critics again hailed the play's universal appeal. "It's a story that could be told with white characters as well as Negro," wrote Arthur Pollack of the *Brooklyn Daily-Eagle*. For Broadway, that was groundbreaking. *Anna Lucasta* was a hit. It ran for 957 performances, finally closing on 30 November 1946.[14]

But the play's crossover success raised questions about the future of black entertainment. Anna committed suicide in the original, but for the Broadway version, Yordan substituted a happy, love-conquers-all ending. Scenes once played for drama now garnered laughs. Scenes of straight humor now played as farce. And the Broadway Anna was no longer a complicated prostitute caught between two lives; she was one-dimensional and vulgar. Nora Holt of the *New York Amsterdam News* considered the new version tawdry. There were no shuffling butlers or pancake-flipping mammies, but the Broadway version did emphasize the seedy, bohemian side of black life. Holt added that "the exploitation of Negro talent does not go unobserved."[15]

Broadway royalties fortified the ANT treasury. Producers traveled uptown, searching for black talent. The *New York Times* printed a history of ANT by W. E. B. Du Bois. *Anna Lucasta* enhanced ANT's standing in the New York theater world, and it created opportunities for black actors. But it also caused complications.[16]

❖

Six months after beginning his self-improvement program, Poitier had another ANT audition, at the company's new location on the second floor of the Henry Lincoln Johnson Lodge on West 126th Street. The New York Public Library had evicted ANT from the tiny basement of its 135th Street branch, which became a fire hazard as more and more patrons flocked there looking for the next *Anna Lucasta*. The lodge provided double the seating capacity and a larger stage, but it tripled ANT's production costs. Now they had to pay rent; with utilities they owed over three hundred dollars a month. Nor was the facility ideal. Upstairs was the lodge's barroom. Downstairs was a dance hall that sent swing rhythms pulsating through the theater.[17]

Poitier's second audition was an open call for the ANT School of Drama, an apprenticeship program for theater production. Poitier saw seventy-five other hopefuls rehearsing their lines. He felt like a rank amateur. He wore a brown zoot suit — wide-shouldered, long-waisted, pegged-pants — with brown shirt, brown tie, brown socks, and brown shoes. The fashion usually suggested a stylish subcultural gesture, but the other auditioners were wearing casual clothes. Even more conspicuous was Poitier's material. The other students read scenes from actual plays. Poitier brought an excerpt from *True Confessions* magazine. Even worse, he chose a love story — told from a woman's point of view. "There I stood waiting for my Jim," he read, "my one and only Jim."[18]

The spectators' jaws dropped. Osceola Archer, the head of the School of Drama, mercifully interrupted him. She suggested that he perform an improvisation of a soldier caught in the jungle. Poitier placed his hands in the shape of a machine gun and spun around. Snarling "You dirty rats!" in his finest James Cagney imitation, he started shooting at imagined enemies. He pretended to be shot in the stomach. He would have crumpled to the ground, except that it might have soiled his suit. So he ended his improvisation holding himself up by his arm, half off the ground, staying clean in his imaginary jungle.[19]

Poitier thought the audition was a disaster, but he was accepted into the apprenticeship program for a trial period of three months. He later learned that he had been accepted because there were so few male actors. He did not care. He quit dishwashing and began a steady job packing clothes and pushing a hand truck around the Garment District. The new job paid less and offered no meals, but it freed his evenings for the School of Drama. For four hours, five nights a week, Poitier rotated through classes in acting, body movement, voice and speech, stagecraft, radio, choral singing, and playwriting.[20]

Monumentally insecure and painfully shy, Poitier struggled. "I was sensitive about my accent in those days," he remembered. "While people in the workshop were not as cruel as people in the street, they still snickered when I spoke." Many classmates were college graduates with theater experience; Poitier believed that he was the worst student in the company. But he possessed the tools of an actor. He had spent so much time by himself — exploring Cat Island, negotiating through Florida, struggling in New York City — that he had developed unique abilities for observation and reflection. That introspection fed his understanding of characters. He was so withdrawn, however, that few contemporaries from these early days even remembered him. Poitier must have exaggerated his acting inadequacy, because after three months he was neither dreadful nor impressive. When his trial period ended, he had to leave ANT.[21]

He pleaded for another chance. The nine months spent learning to read, enunciate, and act constituted Poitier's first real investment in his own future, and his fires of ambition had been kindled. But the School of Drama's faculty believed that he had not improved enough. Dejected, he mulled his options for a week. Then he struck upon an idea. He proposed to Abram Hill that he assume janitorial duties in exchange for another semester. Impressed with Poitier's initiative, Hill let him stay on.[22]

Poitier overloaded his schedule, spending days in the garment district, evenings at ANT, and late nights sweeping and scrubbing and emptying trash cans. He embraced the challenge, exuding energy. "He was like a jack-in-the-box," marveled Earle Hyman, who first met Poitier at an ANT Saturday night social. "I remember thinking, 'Oh God, why doesn't he sit down? He's everywhere.'" On stage, Poitier displayed this same electricity. The extra semester helped him channel his natural energy into his performances. Hill judged the young Poitier as raw but expressive. Archer remembered him as a restless, troubled soul, continually unsatisfied with himself.[23]

Poitier's ANT education transcended acting. Harlem offered firsthand exposure to black America's political thinkers and cultural movements. As he read newspapers and entered discussions, he developed an intellectual foundation for understanding his own experience. He formulated distinctions between Democrats and Republicans, socialists and communists, assimilationists and nationalists. His intelligent and educated friends at ANT became his informal tutors. One politically passionate woman named Louise angrily railed against "rhetorical bullshit" and the shortcomings of "bourgeoisie Negroes," and Poitier sought out her company.[24]

His first performance came in the spring of 1946. The School of Drama occasionally put on productions to showcase its pupils, and Archer was casting for Frank Gabrielson's *Days of Our Youth*, a two-act play addressing the anxieties and aspirations of college life. Poitier believed that he deserved the part of Liebman. To his disquiet, Archer recruited outside ANT. For the part of Liebman, she brought in a friend named Harry Belafonte.[25]

Like Poitier, Belafonte was tall, handsome, and peacock-proud. Unlike Poitier, he had light skin. Poitier believed that Archer chose the newcomer out of middle-class bias, since many white-collar blacks differentiated themselves from the black masses by their fair complexions. Belafonte's parents both descended from mixed-race families. In their integrated New York City neighborhood, Harry and his brother often passed as white.[26]

Belafonte and Poitier shared deep insecurity, though it sprang from different sources. Both used surface assurance as self-defense. Belafonte was born only two weeks after Poitier, and he spent four childhood years in Jamaica. During the exact period that Poitier was in the Army, Belafonte was in the Navy. And they shared a new fascination with the theater. The first play Belafonte ever saw was ANT's 1945 production of *Home Is the Hunter*. Acting — assuming different personalities, receiving adulation — allowed both to cope with their anxieties.[27]

They would become best friends and achieve celebrity. But at their first meeting, that future seemed improbable. More obvious was the pride and sensitivity that marked their frequent feuds. For *Days of Our Youth*, Poitier became Belafonte's understudy. Searching for props and costumes under the ANT stage, Belafonte opened with a jab: "You know, I've heard about you from somewhere. Were you ever in jail?" That put Poitier on the defensive. Belafonte had struck a nerve (Poitier was sensitive about spending the night in jail two years earlier) and he sustained the needling. Poitier landed his own blow: "No, I've never been to jail, but I will probably go to jail because I'm very hot-tempered and I will cut, stab, or hit somebody in a minute. I can't control myself." The back-and-forth continued, each feeling out the other, eventually settling into a wary mutual respect.[28]

Belafonte later missed a private rehearsal arranged by Archer for James Light, the original Broadway director of *Days of Our Youth*. Although an understudy, Poitier had mastered the part of Liebman. After the rehearsal, Light invited him to his office the following Monday. To Poitier's surprise, Light offered a small part in his upcoming all-black production of the Greek play *Lysistrata*. Poitier stammered out an acceptance. He returned to ANT as the first member of his class to make it to Broadway. His classmates slapped him on the back. "Hey, that's nice," Belafonte graciously added.[29]

Poitier's star was rising. Before joining the cast of *Lysistrata*, he earned his first role in an official ANT production, the Moss Hart and George S. Kaufman classic *You Can't Take It with You*. Although it was not a major ANT production, the role signaled that his apprenticeship was over.

Poitier played Boris Kolenkhov, a dance instructor, Czarist sympathizer, and dinner guest of the quirky Vanderhof family. It is a minor but meaty role, for which Poitier was an unfortunate choice. He struggled to portray the flamboyant character, especially failing to speak with a Russian accent. Yet because Kolenkhov takes pokes at Communist Russia, Poitier's performance brought him some attention. The *Daily Worker* complained that Poitier "got in a few vicious digs at the Soviet Union that 'a people's theater,' certainly a Negro people's theater, should avoid." Unlike other left-wing theater groups, ANT had no ties to the Communist Party. Their reputation relied on portraying blacks as universal characters, presenting a soft version of integration palatable to the mainstream left wing.[30]

The Broadway production of an all-black *Lysistrata* reflected a broader cultural trend in line with ANT philosophy. Originally written by Aristophanes, the comedy celebrates a scheme by Athenian women to end war with Sparta by withholding sex from the warriors. Gilbert Seldes translated the play into prose, and it became a Broadway hit in 1930. Light's all-black revival, with its ribald humor and gentle moralism, seemed designed to capitalize on the popularity of *Anna Lucasta*.[31]

Lysistrata joined the other race-oriented dramas flooding Broadway in the two years since *Anna Lucasta*, including *St. Louis Woman*, *Jeb*, *Memphis Bound*, *Strange Fruit*, and *Deep Are the Roots*. More blacks found roles in traditional musicals as well. In 1940 three plays had used black actors for important roles; in 1946 twenty-eight shows had racial themes. Black stars such as the Nicholas Brothers and Pearl Bailey especially benefited, receiving salaries far above Actors Equity minimums.[32]

Yet limitations remained for blacks on Broadway. Few shows spoke to the realities of black life. White playwrights penned the integrated dramas of racial hardship in the South. In the cases of *Anna Lucasta* and *Lysistrata*, white producers adapted all-black casts to works originally intended for white actors. A cloud of racial exploitation hovered over Broadway. As one African American columnist complained, blacks were "enjoying a relatively small taste of the accruing financial gravy, while Caucasian producers, playwrights and directors wax fat on 'the root of all evils.'"[33]

The taste of "gravy" and the Broadway atmosphere more than satisfied Poitier, however. He was earning about seventy-five dollars a week, and he cherished the four weeks rehearsing on a Broadway stage with professionals such as Etta Moten, Fredi Washington, Leigh Whipper, and Rex Ingram. He played Polydorus, a simple-hearted messenger who fawns over Fredi Washington's Kalonika. As rehearsals continued, his confidence grew. He had only nine short lines in the middle of the second act, but he was now a professional actor. He reveled in the thought.[34]

Poitier's aplomb crumbled on opening night, when he developed a first-class case of stage fright. Minutes before showtime, he peeked through the curtain and saw a sea of white faces. By the time the curtain rose, he could barely move. As the play wore on, his nerves further jangled. No one was laughing at this alleged comedy. *Lysistrata* was a disaster even before Poitier stumbled onto the stage, and he could not remember his lines. He looked at the audience instead of the actors. He gave the wrong line. A confused Washington fed him the correct line. Poitier blurted another mistake. Humiliated, he abandoned the stage in the middle of the garbled scene. He heard the audience laughing. This surprised him, but he assumed that they were laughing at him. He left before the end of the play, convinced that his brief theater career was over.[35]

Poitier would relate the aftermath in dramatic fashion. He remembered rushing to the newsstand the next morning to find reviews of *Lysistrata*. He claimed that the critics universally panned the play, but that some believed there was one "saving grace": "an unknown young actor who came out in the first act and absolutely devastated the audience with his acute comedic approach to the part of Polydorus." "According to them," he remembered thinking, "I was a hit. Overnight I was a hit!" He believed that he had fascinated the critics and that the *New York Daily News* had asked, in effect, "Who is this guy?"[36]

Poitier's recollection was skewed. He did suffer from stage fright; one critic complained about "actors darting about doing unaccountable things without rhyme or reason." The critics did pan *Lysistrata*; Light artlessly mixed burlesque with deadpan dignity and a misbegotten dance number. And Poitier did win chuckles; his stuttering anxiety actually fit the character of Polydorus. But the record does not support his account. The *Sun* noted that "Sidney Poitier has a few comical utterances as the sex-starved Polydorus" and the *World-Telegram* added that "Sidney Poitier gets laughs as the bachelor brave with a yen for Kalonika," but that was it. The *Daily News*, like the *Herald Tribune*, *Post*, *Journal American*, *PM*, and *Times*, did not even mention Poitier.[37]

For Poitier, years later, to deliberately misstate the critics' reception of his first Broadway performance would not only be out of character but unnecessary. His version of events did not serve his ego — the praise was undeserved, after all. The memory instead speaks to his persistent demons of insecurity. He always exaggerated his failings as a young actor, but no one else corroborates his mediocrity. He had groped for identity and security since landing in Miami. He craved affirmation so much that some cheers and a few critical asides made him feel like an overnight hit.

Lysistrata ran for only three more performances. Poitier recited his lines in order and elicited no laughter. Luckily, John Wildberg came to opening night. Wildberg had become quite rich since buying the rights to *Anna Lucasta*; the night of *Lysistrata*'s debut, *Anna Lucasta* had its 900th performance at the Mansfield Theatre. Another Wildberg production of the play ran for over a year at Chicago's Civic Theater, and the producer had just sent a traveling company through Connecticut, Massachusetts, and Pennsylvania. Wildberg asked Poitier to join the *Anna Lucasta* tour as an understudy, learning various roles and filling in when necessary. Poitier embraced the chance. He would earn eighty dollars a week, gain acting experience, and travel the country.[38]

He joined a cast of professionals with miles of tour experience. *Anna Lucasta* veteran Ruby Dee remembered her first glimpse of the shy rookie: slim, dark, neatly dressed in a navy coat and black pants, withdrawn, and preoccupied. He offered a pleasant glance but no smile, and then he returned his gaze to the bus window. "Sidney was about the quietest guy you ever saw," confirmed Dee's husband, Ossie Davis. "He tended to disappear into the background."[39]

As time wore on, however, Poitier became comfortable with his troupe. Cut off from their lives at home, the actors grew close. Bus rides allowed for long, sometimes passionate discussions. They traveled from Philadelphia to Detroit, Chicago to Minneapolis, Denver to San Francisco, linking them to black communities around the country. Some of the actors wrote plays; others planned to direct. They all shared optimistic visions for black artists. Poitier basked in the tour's intellectual energy.[40]

His understudy role extended beyond the theatrical. Maxwell Glanville, Duke Williams, and Roy Glenn tutored him in the world of romance and conquest. Since arriving in America, Poitier's love life had sputtered. His one girlfriend from his early ANT days came from a middle-class family, and she resented his financial limitations. After she dumped him, he moped for weeks. Glanville, Williams, and Glenn aimed to reconfigure Poitier's passive, overromanticized reverence of women. The tall, handsome, and ultraconfident trio were proficient at luring women into bed with aggressive savoir-faire, corny lines, and simple compliments. Later they bragged of their sexual wizardry. Like the cowboy heroes of Poitier's youth, they were masculine, confident, and emotionally detached.

Poitier was a slow learner. He sometimes botched his friends' efforts by interrupting flirtatious conversations. But he progressed. In Philadelphia, he dated a pretty southern nurse. In Baltimore, he enjoyed a one-night stand with a stylish woman he met at a poker game. In Boston, he pursued the daughter of an Army colonel. Here he ignored his tutors and fell in love. The brief, passionate relationship ended when the tour moved on, much to Poitier's torment. As with his earlier girlfriend, her family never approved of an uneducated actor dating their proper, middle-class daughter.[41]

By Pittsburgh, he had recovered from his heartbreak enough to attract a new mate named Y. A. Janey, a sophisticated, independent, and married actress then playing the title role in *Anna Lucasta*. Through Ohio and across Indiana, their affair flourished in spite of her marriage. By St. Louis, Poitier was sneaking out of his men-only (and black-only) hotel and picking up Janey at the women's hotel for late-night trysts. One weekend, jazz great Dizzy Gillespie and his band checked into the men's hotel. After their own performance, the *Anna Lucasta* cast attended Gillespie's show.

The men joined forces late that night in Gillespie's suite for a raunchy exchange of marijuana and funny stories. When Poitier tried to excuse himself, his friends teased him about Janey. Poitier insisted that he was going to sleep; he would even sleep in Gillespie's bed, he claimed. He then entered the bedroom and promptly jumped out the second-story window. Upon his return with Janey, he found a motley mixture of giggling, drug-addled entertainers in the hallway outside his room, offering such mock pleasantries as "My, my, my, I hope you had a wonderful evening" and "I think it's so nice of her to see him to his door."[42]

Poitier and Janey dated for a few more months, until she transferred into another tour of *Anna Lucasta* (by 1947 Wildberg had established multiple companies traveling the country). Poitier continued to appear in minor roles as Lester or Rudolph. During breaks in the touring schedule, he also performed in ANT productions. In August 1947 he took a small part in an all-black version of *John and Mary*, a comedy then playing Broadway with an all-white cast. The ANT version played one night only at the Music Box, the play's regular venue.[43]

The next month *Anna Lucasta* began a three-week engagement at New York's National Theater. Poitier played Lester, a sidekick to the rough sailor who lures Anna back to her seedy past. Lester is shy, wistful, handsome, and trying to shed his innocence — rather like Poitier himself. The role suited him and he performed well. The entire cast, for that matter, earned critical commendations.[44]

POVERTY & PROGRESS

Reviewers continued to hail the play's universality. "It is not necessarily the story of a Negro family," wrote one. "It is the story of the human family, and goes beyond any particular creed, color, or race." But *Anna Lucasta*'s return highlighted an old dilemma about black theater. Adapted from the story of a Polish family, twisted from Hill's adaptation into a lurid and bohemian farce, this "universal" play owed little to the black experience.[45]

❖

Black theater faced another, more concrete barrier: money. ANT gained only a crumb of the *Anna Lucasta* pie. Abram Hill originally sold the play's rights to John Wildberg under standard contracts that gave ANT 5 percent of the original production's net and 2 percent of any subsidiary productions. Hill filed the contracts with the Dramatists Guild just as the play won acclaim. Then the Dramatists Guild lost the contracts. Smelling profit, Wildberg refused to honor the original deal.[46]

After Hill threatened Wildberg with a court injunction, they agreed upon a new deal that gave ANT only 2 percent of the Broadway net. Hill compromised ANT for his own benefit; he received a flat fee of $25,000 for his adaptation. During a Broadway run that lasted over two years, *Anna Lucasta* brought in $20,000 a month. Despite developing the play, ANT received none of the revenue from the play's one-year run in Chicago, the multiple companies touring the nation in the late 1940s, or the 1949 film based on the play. Rubbing salt in the wound, the film version used a white cast. Philip Yordan produced it and took sole writing credit.[47]

Ironically, the success of *Anna Lucasta* had jeopardized ANT. Soon after Poitier joined, *Variety* reported the general feeling that ANT "has lost its original perspective and has turned into a feeder for Broadway, becoming an experimental showplace for new scripts." Another problem was the dearth of black writers. After *Anna Lucasta*, all ANT productions featured white playwrights. Even as its actors won acclaim, ANT faltered in its original mission to provide creative, experimental theater rooted in Harlem.[48]

The ghost of *Anna Lucasta* haunted ANT. Later productions inevitably inspired comparison to the original crossover success, and they all failed to measure up. *Home Is the Hunter* was "repugnant claptrap." *Walk Hard* received a "thumbs down" from all six major New York critics. *Garden of Time* was "a bit pretentious" and "pretty slow." *Henri Christophe* was "slow and fumbling . . . melodramatic and stagey." *The*

Peacemakers was full of "all kinds of breathless and ridiculous antics far beyond the limits of either respectable farce or fantasy," and *Tin Top Valley* was "a limp, generalized performance." Meanwhile, ANT's costs escalated. It started paying rent upon moving to the Henry Lincoln Johnson Lodge in 1945. Its Rockefeller Foundation grant expired in 1947. When ANT invested five thousand dollars in the stock market, it lost all but seven hundred. By the late 1940s, it relied almost solely on box office revenues. With every failure to produce a hit, frustration mounted.[49]

These pressures divided ANT members into two camps: an older group trying to salvage the company's original mission, and a younger group (including Poitier) looking for careers on Broadway. Tensions flared in early 1946 when Hill established an "iron rule" restricting ANT members to ANT productions. After banishing Gertrude Jeanette for expressing interest in a play at a 92nd Street theater, Hill gained a reputation as an autocrat. Some young actors left the company and others complained of the administration's "Gestapo set up."[50]

Older members blamed the new generation for the organization's instability. ANT staked its reputation on trained, well-rounded professionals. They fussed when Robert Earl Jones deserted the cast of *Walk Hard* for a Broadway show two days before opening night. Students in the School of Drama exacerbated the situation by telling casting directors that they were members of ANT rather than mere apprentices. "We are baffled at a solution to keep the kids from being exploited by Broadway," related ANT veteran Claude Sloan. "The damn fools are suckers for making $60 a week." But by the 1946–47 Broadway season, when *Lysistrata* joined the flood of Broadway shows using black actors, they had trouble convincing young members such as Poitier to turn down theater work and continue training.[51]

In 1947 and 1948, years that Poitier mostly spent on tour, ANT dissolved into bickering aimlessness. School of Drama students irked the ANT administration by ignoring fees and accruing debts. Abram Hill resigned in February 1948, worn by criticism of his ironhanded leadership. Yet even Hill's resignation could not quell the infighting. That November one member reported to Frederick O'Neal (then in London with a company of *Anna Lucasta*) that ANT was "in a state of revolution." Rather than solve the financial and artistic problems of ANT, they feuded. As older members left, upstarts spoke their minds at membership meetings, and one raged into a "near battle."[52]

Poitier returned from the *Anna Lucasta* tour soon after this fractious affair. In February 1949, he appeared in the ANT production of Kenneth

White's one-act *Freight*. The organization hoped that the play, presented in conjunction with *Riders to the Sea* at the Harlem Children's Center on 134th Street, would herald a rebirth for the ANT. *Freight* takes place in a boxcar filled with nine young black men on the run. As the train rolls, a white man named Jake hops on board. He speaks first with Poitier's character, Lottie, a scared young man sitting in a shadow. When Lottie steps into the light, Jake explodes with rage. He then realizes the number of black men in the boxcar. He brandishes a knife, spews insults ("God-damn stinkin' nigger-sister"), and reflects upon lynching as a cure for boredom. Midway through the play, the tables turn. The black men un-arm Jake. They humiliate him, forcing him to crawl on his hands and knees while a one-legged man rides him. They consider lynching him but deem him too pathetic. At the end, Jake protests, "You can even take mah *life*! But Ah'm white! White! White!"[53]

Freight's interesting premise and juicy roles prompted good reviews. The script needed editing, the lighting needed improvement, and the actors needed experience with the acoustics of the space, but ANT deserved plaudits. The *New York Times* suggested that "after floundering around for the last two seasons, the American Negro Theatre has taken a new lease on life." Unfortunately, the opposite proved true. *Riders to the Sea* and *Freight* were ANT's last major productions. Financial burdens and internal disorganization plagued the theater to its end.[54]

ANT had begun at the dawn of the 1940s and disintegrated as the decade closed. In between it had functioned amidst the tensions surrounding black entertainment: artistic integrity versus commercial success, racial pride versus mainstream appeal, organizational unity versus individual opportunity. ANT developed black actors, playwrights, stage managers, and set designers — all under black supervision. And for almost ten years, it presented dramas with nonstereotypical characters to integrated audiences. But that same universal appeal spelled the end of independent black theater. The popularity of blacks on Broadway in the years after World War II encouraged Poitier's generation to abandon ANT's original goals and accept lucrative roles on the Great White Way.

But as ANT dissolved, the number of jobs for black actors waned. In the era's conservative political climate, racial dramas such as *Freight* acquired a faintly subversive odor, while risqué melodramas such as *Anna Lucasta* seemed out of vogue. Harlem, too, lost its chic allure. As the Great Migration continued after the war, the black middle class moved to the suburbs, draining the neighborhood of its economic base and creative energy. Emblems of the black upper crust such as Count Basie, Billie

Holiday, and Ella Fitzgerald moved to St. Albans in Queens. Dizzy Gillespie and Thelonius Monk took their cutting-edge jazz to downtown clubs. "The heyday of Negro entertainment is gone," mourned the *New York Age* in August 1949. "Nobody comes to Harlem anymore. Nobody seems to care."[55]

So Poitier scraped by in 1949. Unwilling to return to dishwashing, he tried to create his own opportunities. He and Ossie Davis tried to bring theater to Africa, spending an entire night in futile negotiations with a Nigerian diplomat. Poitier then convinced Harry Belafonte to co-develop a nightclub comedy routine. Every day for one week, they rehearsed on the roof of Belafonte's 156th Street apartment. As neither man was a natural comedian, their skits inevitably failed. They spent the week frazzling each other's nerves. Then they tried to become entrepreneurs. They arranged to harvest a type of Caribbean conch so that they could extract the proteins and calories for a bodybuilding drink. Confronted with complicated federal food regulations and a lack of capital, they abandoned that idea, too.[56]

But Poitier and Belafonte developed a close friendship. They saw their own magnetism and insecurity in each other, and they shared a similar economic plight. Both went on unemployment insurance, splitting checks as they received them. They also shared theater tickets, one seeing the first act and returning with the stub and a plot summary for the other. This way, they kept their finger on the pulse of the theater world, even if they could not find work.[57]

Poitier staved off poverty through morsels of acting work. He had first appeared on film as an extra in the 1947 all-black *Sepia Cinderella*. In the spring of 1949 a Harlem talent agency sent him to Fort Jay on Long Island for an Army Signal Corps documentary called *From Whence Cometh My Help*. The film warned young recruits about the danger of venereal disease and examined religious life in the armed services. Poitier vaguely remembered playing a minister. He clearly remembered his pay rate, though: for three days work he received a hundred dollars.[58]

In spite of his financial woes, Poitier had joined a young circle of black actors, musicians, and writers — a cultural avant-garde, engaged in politics and a bohemian lifestyle. Poitier frequented the Sage Restaurant, a Greenwich Village coffee shop run by Belafonte and two friends, reveling in the after-hours folk music and poker games. He loitered around the Astor Drug Store, a favorite haunt of out-of-work actors. He swung by Birdland, the legendary jazz club where he befriended the young musician Quincy Jones. He joined the singer Leon Bibb at fundraising meetings for a failed literary journal called the *Harlem Quarterly*. He chased skirts with Julian Mayfield and William Marshall. And he befriended Alice Childress, an actress and playwright from ANT who encouraged him to learn black history. She introduced him to Paul Robeson, the black theater legend on the verge of complete mainstream vilification for his Communist ties.[59]

Poitier had joined Harlem's premier theater organization, appeared on Broadway, traveled the country, made lasting friendships, jumped out of Dizzy Gillespie's window, and learned a few lessons about himself—not bad for a shy, poorly educated kid whom Frederick O'Neal once shouted off a stage.

❖

For all these strides, Poitier's toehold in the theater world was tenuous. He did not even have an agent. In late 1949, he tried to audition for the Theatre Guild production of *Lost in the Stars*, a musical about South Africa based on the Alan Paton novel *Cry, the Beloved Country*. Poitier wanted to play Absalom, an important role that required no singing or dancing (he had no faculty for either). But without an agent, he could not even enter the playhouse.

In the alley outside the theater he noticed a young, elegant white man in a gray suit accompanying a group of black actors. Between pulls on his cigarette, the agent introduced himself as Bill Nichols. Luckily, Nichols had seen him in both *Freight* and *Lysistrata*. He agreed to represent Poitier for the day, and they entered the theater. In twenty minutes, Poitier learned the part. As his audition neared, his mouth dried. But he had progressed. He channeled his nervous energy into the part, and at the end of his reading, a voice from the theater's shadows suggested the possibility of another audition.[60]

His second audition, a few days later, improved upon the first, and he was pleased when they called him back a third time to read opposite a woman. Again he performed well. But he received no job offer. To his frustration, they called him back for a fourth audition. Poitier now realized that director Rouben Mamoulian needed male actors to read against women auditioners. But he agreed to a fifth audition, and at that point Mamoulian offered Poitier the role of Absalom. He accepted his first lead role on Broadway.[61]

Poitier was gleeful at the thought of steady work on Broadway. He floated into the Jules Ziegler Agency and informed Nichols. On his way home he told Julian Mayfield, who had also wanted the part. Mayfield graciously congratulated Poitier. Then Poitier saw Thompson Brown, yet another struggling black actor. Brown informed him that Twentieth Century-Fox was doing screen tests for a movie with black actors called *No Way Out*. Poitier and Brown investigated it the next day.

Tiptoeing along an ethical boundary, Poitier auditioned for the film one day after accepting a star role in a play. He convinced himself that he was merely establishing contacts. The chances of a part were slim, anyway; casting director William Gordon had screened over a hundred actors from Hollywood, San Francisco, Chicago, Cleveland, and New York City. The lead role in *No Way Out* was a twenty-seven-year-old doctor. On his application, Poitier added three years to his age. Along with scores of others, Poitier filmed a short screen test that Gordon sent to Hollywood.

Director Joseph Mankiewicz narrowed the field to six applicants. Thompson Brown did not survive the cut; Poitier did. Poitier's screen test also impressed Twentieth Century-Fox studio head Darryl Zanuck, then in Europe. Poitier returned to the Fox studios and filmed a longer screen test. The actor shot three takes of the same scene, each time receiving different, detailed, and incisive instructions from Mankiewicz. With the camera still rolling, the director sat down next to Poitier and interviewed him. He then offered Poitier the lead role in *No Way Out*.[62]

Poitier did not accept. He already had a part in *Lost in the Stars*. Mankiewicz, nonplused, suggested that he consult his agent before making a final decision. "Little did I know it at the time," Poitier later reflected, "but now I'm dealing with Hollywood, and what Hollywood wants — Hollywood gets." Poitier had not signed a contract with the Theatre Guild, and Fox had exponentially more resources at its disposal. On Broadway, he would earn seventy-five dollars a week. Mankiewicz offered ten times that amount.

Jules Ziegler, the head of Nichols's talent agency, told the Theatre Guild about Poitier's Hollywood offer. He claimed that Poitier wanted the Broadway part, but he needed a firmer financial commitment. Ziegler knew that the Theatre Guild would see this as a negotiating ploy, and he knew that the Theatre Guild would call his supposed bluff, which it did. Poitier then signed a contract with Twentieth Century-Fox. The Theatre Guild could not cry foul, because it had passed on the opportunity to retain Poitier. At the end of the Machiavellian maneuver, Ziegler had protected his reputation, allowed Julian Mayfield to play Absalom in *Lost in the Stars*, and sent Poitier on the Twentieth Century Limited, a luxury train rolling out of New York, through Appalachia, across the Great Plains, and over the Rockies. Sidney Poitier was going to Hollywood.[63]

PART II
RACE MAN

❖ ❖ ❖

CHAPTER 4

MESSAGE MOVIES

(1949–1952)

❖

"I been doing awful," moaned Stepin Fetchit. In February 1945, he turned to John Ford, director of four Fetchit movies and then a lieutenant commander in the Navy. Calling his situation a "Home Front emergency," Fetchit begged for a shred of screen time. He stroked the ego of the notoriously paternalistic Ford by delighting in "the lavish news that I was the recipient of a phone call from a Commander in the United States Navy and a Lieutenant Commander Star of Screen and Democracy." The flattery worked. The next year Ford pitched a revival of Fetchit's career to Twentieth Century-Fox studio head Darryl Zanuck. "I think we would have a great character to introduce to the Public again as bellboy, porter, night clerk, waiter, bootblack, bartender and chambermaid," wrote Ford.

Zanuck demurred. "No one has laughed longer or louder at Stepin Fetchit than I have," he wrote, "but to put him on the screen at this time would I am afraid raise terrible objections from the colored people." Since 1942, Walter White, the executive secretary of the NAACP, had been lobbying for more positive screen images of blacks. Zanuck remembered that White had singled out Fetchit "as an example of the humiliation of the colored race. Stepin Fetchit always portrays the lazy, stupid half-wit, and this is the thing that the colored people are furious about." Traditional portrayals of black jesters had acquired a political taint.[1]

Around this same time, in August 1945, Branch Rickey summoned Jackie Robinson into his office. The president of the Brooklyn Dodgers greeted the dark-skinned second baseman: "You got a girl?" Robinson did. Rickey proposed to make Robinson the first black player in organized baseball since the late nineteenth century. He had researched Robinson's background, including his UCLA education and military service. He had one final test: could Robinson withstand the fury of white detractors? For over two hours baseball's "Mahatma" scrutinized Robinson. He mimicked a rude white hotel clerk. He imitated an angry baserunner.

"How do you like that, nigger boy?" he taunted. And he expected Robinson to absorb it all.

"Mr. Rickey," asked Robinson, "are you looking for a Negro who is afraid to fight back?" "Robinson," Rickey erupted, "I'm looking for a ballplayer with guts enough not to fight back!" Rickey singled out a passage from Giovanni Papini's *Life of Christ*: "But whosoever shall smite thee on thy right cheek, turn to him the other also." Robinson accepted the challenge. He joined the Brooklyn club in 1947, and he answered the catcalls with stoic restraint. Robinson ultimately earned a Most Valuable Player award, a World Series title, and a place in the Hall of Fame. Robinson ushered baseball into an age of integration.[2]

Fetchit's fall and Robinson's rise illuminate the cultural forces that shaped Poitier's emergence in Hollywood. Resistance to Fetchit's image helped launch a "message movie" cycle that included *No Way Out*. Poitier's character in that film resembled Robinson, the era's preeminent black culture hero — an educated, talented, middle-class family man who practices Christian nonviolence. The new black icon expressed the feasibility of racial integration, even as it demonstrated its limits.

❖

"We seem to be well launched now on a cycle of pictures occupied with the Negro problem," wrote Arthur Knight in February 1950. Four major films with racial themes — *Home of the Brave*, *Lost Boundaries*, *Pinky*, and *Intruder in the Dust* — had appeared the previous year. *No Way Out* would arrive that summer. "There never has been anything quite like them before," he marveled. These "problem pictures" had both realistic characters and entertaining scripts. "But best of all," he argued, "these pictures prove how groundless was the fear so many of us shared that the Un-American Trials would drive all progressive thinking off the screen. Just the contrary seems to be the case."[3]

The House Un-American Activities Committee (HUAC) had started investigating Communism in the film industry in October 1947. Other government committees had probed the topic before, but in the new Cold War climate, the hearings included the cooperation of panicky studio executives and streams of "friendly witnesses," including such leading men as Gary Cooper and Ronald Reagan. In turn, a group of radical screenwriters known as the "Hollywood Ten" were blacklisted. Anti-Communist anxiety crept through Hollywood. Studio heads dreaded bad publicity, and accusations of radicalism constituted the worst kind of press.[4]

The rise of the message movie, then, seems incongruous. Why did a cycle of progressive films arise in such a conservative atmosphere? The answer lies in a larger paradox of Cold War culture. The HUAC investigations, like the 1948 trial of Alger Hiss, provoked hysteria over Communist infiltration into American institutions. Mountains of clandestine FBI files reflected the government's willingness to curtail individual freedom. Civil rights organizations made little progress in these years — the specter of Communism hung over basic liberal reforms.

Yet any justification for American leadership — both within and outside the nation's borders — hinged upon a celebration of democratic ideals. During World War II, many blacks had sacrificed for those ideals. So racial progress did occur in some public arenas: Jackie Robinson integrated the national pastime, and President Truman desegregated the armed forces in 1948. These milestones, like the message movies, reinforced rather than threatened established notions of democracy.[5]

This racial ambivalence coincided with a Hollywood crisis far deeper than the HUAC hearings. The middle class migrated to the suburbs, away from downtown movie palaces. The "baby boom" kept young families home at night. The 1948 Supreme Court decision in *United States vs. Paramount* forced Hollywood's five largest studios to sell their theater chains. Without direct control of exhibition, the major studios' monopoly power eroded. Competition with smaller studios and independent producers intensified. By the mid-1950s, as television rose to prominence, movie attendance had declined by 50 percent.[6]

Some studios tried attracting audiences by exploring new themes, including prejudice. In 1947, RKO's *Crossfire* and Twentieth Century-Fox's *Gentleman's Agreement* examined anti-Semitism. Meanwhile, black organizations pressured Hollywood to present new black images. The NAACP picketed Disney's 1946 *Song of the South*, and *Ebony* called James Baskett's character an "Uncle Tom–Aunt Jemima caricature complete with . . . the toothy smile, battered hat, grey beard, and a profusion of 'dis' and 'dat' talk." The old stock figures drifted off the screen, but black actors suffered from a dearth of roles.[7]

A turning point arrived in 1949, hailed by *Variety* as "the year of the Negro problem pic." *Home of the Brave* centered on a black soldier who needs help from whites. *Lost Boundaries* regarded a pale-skinned black doctor and his family "passing" as whites in a New Hampshire village. *Intruder in the Dust* examined one black man's rejection of southern racial mores. And Twentieth Century-Fox's *Pinky* — another treatment of racial passing — boasted the institutional resources of a major studio, a first for a progressive race film. Darryl Zanuck even replaced John Ford with Elia Kazan after Ford insisted on using the old racial stereotypes. The film proved the year's biggest box office draw for Twentieth Century-Fox.[8]

Thanks to these integrationist themes, optimists predicted a new era for black actors. But some black critics sounded ambiguous notes. Although they lauded these rejections of old stereotypes, they criticized the emphasis on passing, with its implicit message that blacks desire to be white. The use of white actors Mel Ferrer (in *Lost Boundaries*) and Jeanne Crain (in *Pinky*) for these roles added insult. Worst of all, wrote Ralph Ellison, was that "these films are not *about* Negroes at all; they are about what whites think and feel about Negroes." Message movies alleviated guilt for white audiences without assigning blame for racial injustice.[9]

No Way Out was the last film in the message movie cycle, and it stimulated high expectations. After a multi-studio bidding war, Darryl Zanuck bought the story rights in January 1949 for Twentieth Century-Fox, the same studio that had produced *Gentleman's Agreement* and *Pinky*. He paid writer Lesser Samuels $75,000. Samuels had coined the story after his son in-law, a doctor, related the indignities faced by his black colleagues. The writer realized that black professionals endured daily, humiliating discrimination. In this irony he saw dramatic potential. "To my mind," Samuels explained, "their plight is more acute than that of the uneducated Negro who never has tasted, in imagination at least, the fruits of real freedom. . . . They live in an economic and social no-man's land from which, at the moment, there seems no way out."[10]

But Samuels's original treatment revolved around a white doctor who gains appreciation for his black intern, all the while wooing the female lead. Zanuck insisted on reshaping the characters, lending *No Way Out* a progressive distinction. The black doctor, he instructed, "does not want to crash the white man's world. He does not seek admittance to white man's society. All he asks for is civility, not condescension, in the work he has chosen. . . . He has an inner dignity of his own." He wanted a non-threatening yet appealing black hero. Zanuck also advocated scrapping the romance and installing scenes that showed "how real Negroes in a metropolitan city live."[11]

Through early 1949, Zanuck and his writers shoved the black doctor into the dramatic center. In an early draft by Philip Yordan (who received no official writing credit), a fanatical white racist buries the black doctor alive. Zanuck, citing his cardinal rule to "never kill the leading man unless something is gained by it," demanded that the black man survive. Also in the original, the white doctor saves the killer's life. By the final draft, the black man performs this act of Christian compassion.[12]

Yet Zanuck also forged some necessary compromises. He already ceded that the frank depiction of white villainy and black heroism "will lose about 3,000 accounts in the South who will not play the picture under any circumstances." Then the Production Code Administration (PCA), the industry organization that screened controversial subject matter, advocated eliminating a race riot scene. Zanuck agreed, urging that they rewrite the scene as a barroom brawl or street fight. "In other words," he summarized, "we should be careful that we do not deliberately invite disaster. It is fine for us to be courageous, but we must also be sensible, and not too courageous with other peoples' money."[13]

Poitier arrived in Los Angeles in late October 1949, just as the studio put its final touches on the script. He had brimmed with excitement on the scenic cross-country train ride, and on the way to his Hollywood hotel, he drank in California's deep blue skies and casual atmosphere. Only upon arrival did Poitier grasp his incongruity in this swanky, all-white neighborhood. Los Angeles had not been immune to the Great Migration. Real estate brokers had segregated blacks in the city's valley, isolated from the prosperous areas and major industries — including Hollywood's film studios. Poitier compared his first stint in Hollywood to "being a visitor in a foreign culture, on the alert and at the ready twenty-four hours a day."[14]

The Twentieth Century-Fox lot bore the same stamp of de facto segregation. Except for staff members such as kitchen workers and janitors, the studio employed no blacks. The plight plagued the entire industry. Hollywood payrolls included not a single black grip, painter, carpenter, electrician, cameraman, editor, writer, director, publicist, hairdresser, guard, or receptionist. The actors also operated under double standards; Poitier was the lead actor, but he had fourth billing and received the same salary as supporting cast members.[15]

Poitier researched his role by observing emergency room interns at a Los Angeles hospital. He also befriended the film's villain, Richard Widmark, who displayed an incredible physical commitment to acting; he had lost twenty pounds in his previous role, gained back ten pounds shooting scenes when confined to a hospital stretcher, and lost the weight again during the rest of filming.[16]

The transition from stage to screen pleased Poitier. Live audiences still made him nervous, but not movie sets. The adjustment was tougher for Ossie Davis, a theater veteran. His first scene showed a family eating breakfast. Through three takes, as the other cast members spit their food into buckets, Davis cleaned his plate. Then the director called for close-ups. Davis went pale. They shot the scene again and again, with Davis choking down food, trying to show the same gustatory delight.[17]

The studio faced new challenges, too. The hairdressers had no idea how to fix black women's hair. Ruby Dee suggested a black hairdresser. Yet in wardrobe, Dee still felt uncomfortable; the white technicians barely contained their displeasure over serving her. For one scene at night in a graveyard, they dressed Poitier in a dark suit. "You could only distinguish his white cuffs and collar," recalled cameraman Milton Krasner. "He was literally as black as coal." They revised the script and refilmed the scene indoors.[18]

The studio also encountered a new generation of black actors less willing to accept the paternalistic patterns of early Hollywood. Director Joseph Mankiewicz once canceled filming for the race riot scene when black extras protested unequal pay by destroying dressing rooms and stuffing towels down toilets. They returned to the set only after the Screen Extras Guild negotiated a settlement.[19]

Yet Mankiewicz treated the main cast members warmly, producing fine performances from Poitier and Widmark. Drawing from the emergent school of Method acting, Mankiewicz insisted that their personal experiences inform their acting interpretations. "He kept asking me to feel what *Sidney*, not the character, would feel under the circumstances," recalled Poitier. The technique worked for Poitier, but it wore on Widmark, a politically liberal, genuinely kind man quite unlike his dastardly screen image. "The cameras would start rolling and I'd start cursing and swearing at Poitier," Widmark related. "Then I'd see his eyes flash and I knew something more than acting was going on between us." This energy caused "a nauseous bubble" inside Widmark, but it drove the dramatic conflict in *No Way Out*.[20]

The film begins when Ray Biddle (Widmark) enters a county hospital's prison ward staffed by intern Luther Brooks (Poitier). A policeman had shot both Biddle and his brother Johnny during an attempted robbery. Biddle objects to treatment from Brooks, a situation exacerbated by his brother's death under the black doctor's care. Biddle refuses to allow the autopsy that might clear Brooks. The villain threatens reprisal from his friends in the all-white, lower-class neighborhood Beaver Canal. "Wait till they found out how he got killed, and by *what*," he sneers. "Yeah, I'd sure hate to be living in Niggertown these days."

Despite Brooks's efforts, a black mob launches a preemptive raid. (To ward off criticism, Mankiewicz built up to the race riot and then cut away to the gory aftermath.) Now Brooks is desperate to clear his name. He forces an autopsy by confessing to the murder of Johnny Biddle. The autopsy proves his original diagnosis correct, but the results only infuriate Ray Biddle. With the help of a third brother, he escapes from the prison ward and tricks Brooks into a final showdown. Delirious with rage, Biddle calls Brooks "little black Sambo" and shouts "Nigger! Nigger! Nigger!" In the end, Brooks sidesteps death and the police capture Biddle.

No Way Out portrayed racial hatred more explicitly than any previous Hollywood film. Per Zanuck's orders, it mixes an examination of racial prejudice with fast-paced, entertaining action. The film's most important legacy, however, is its depiction of Dr. Luther Brooks. Brooks is socially polished, professionally accomplished, and politically acceptable to both blacks and white liberals. Poitier's protagonist reversed the stereotypes that plagued blacks for nearly a half-century.

First, unlike the villains of *Birth of a Nation*, Brooks presents no sexual threat. He displays no lust for white women. His demeanor is restrained and genteel. He loves his prim wife, but his mannerisms never suggest the slightest animal urge.

Second, unlike Bill Robinson, Brooks does not sing or dance. Poitier debunked the myth that all blacks possess innate musical talent. In fact, he later learned that he was tone deaf. If a scene in his 1967 film *To Sir, with Love* is any indication, he was a worse dancer.

Third, unlike Stepin Fetchit, Brooks has a white-collar job and middle-class values. He is a dramatic, not comic, character. The doctor has a supportive family and neat apartment. He dresses in dark suits. He has perfect manners. Poitier's unique diction—a West Indian singsong overlaid by his self-trained, precise radio voice—suggests neither the rhythms of the South nor the comic "dis and dat" of Fetchit.

Finally, unlike the stars of the "passing" films, Brooks implies no threat to established racial boundaries. Like Jackie Robinson or the singer Nat King Cole, Poitier had dark skin and typically black features. He could never pass as white. Dr. Luther Brooks is a black man competing for equal footing in a white world, a formidable development for the film industry. But Poitier's image in *No Way Out* presents no menace to the racial status quo, whether sexual, social, or political.[21]

An old Hollywood bromide states that the first five minutes of a film establishes the central conflict. The first five minutes of *No Way Out* did more: it established the icon that guides Poitier's career. Brooks must negotiate through a spectrum of racial attitudes. White doctors congratulate him for passing the state medical boards. The chief resident Dr. Wharton (Stephen McNally) offers a platitude of colorblind liberalism: "My interest in you, Brooks, is no greater than in any good doctor on my service." Brooks shrugs off the racial bitterness of the elevator operator Lefty (whose Dickensian name suggests a dangerous political orientation). But he also faces a symbol of prejudice in Ray Biddle, who spits on the floor and sneers: "Clean that up, where's your mop?"

Brooks survives in this integrated world, but only because he performs better than his white colleagues. He never brags about his accomplishments, but his wife reveals his work ethic and skill. As he falls asleep in her arms, she reflects: "You've worked so hard, harder than anybody to get where you are. The shoes you've shined, dishes you've washed, garbage you dumped, the food you couldn't buy because you needed books. . . . You told me 'A' was your passing mark. Not for the others, just for you. You got 'em. All A's. No wonder you're tired." Brooks's humility borders on the implausible. Despite his impeccable record and an offer to join an established black practice, he wants another year of training as a junior resident. "I think I need a little more time than the others," he says.

Brooks also commits a tremendous sacrifice. Even after an elderly white woman spits in his face, he risks imprisonment by confessing to murder and forcing an autopsy. Yet he still downplays white bigotry. "There are Negroes who are pathological white-haters," he says. "If one of them thought I'd murdered his brother, I'd be afraid too." He risks jail time not to gain personally, but to extinguish burning racial hatred.

Brooks is not a coward, a weakling, or an Uncle Tom. Poitier expresses an appealing dignity and barely controlled anger. His body language suggests the unacceptability of racial injustice. But by the end of *No Way Out*, Brooks has gone to exceptional lengths to maintain racial harmony. He pleads that by attacking Beaver Canal, the black community will sink to the depths of violent whites. Lefty, whose cheek bears a scar and whose sister is wheelchair-bound from the last white attack, responds: "Ain't that asking a lot, for us to be better than them when we get killed just trying to prove we're just as good?" Brooks holds steadfast.

In the final scene, his sacrifice stretches further. Both Brooks and Biddle are wounded, but the doctor tends to the villain. He refuses to let Biddle die. "Because I've got to live, too," he explains. "I can't kill a man just because he hates me." As police sirens wail, Biddle bawls with self-pity. Brooks offers a final salve: "Don't cry, white boy. You're gonna live."

❖

A middle-class emblem of excellence, a paragon of virtue, a bridge of racial understanding—Poitier's character suggested new dimensions in American popular culture's treatment of blacks. This development stemmed from the trends of the post–World War II era. By the late 1940s, as the black middle class expanded, the armed services integrated, and Jackie Robinson joined the Dodgers, more white Americans could identify with blacks—if not personally, then at least culturally. Since the major studios employed no black producers, directors, or writers, Hollywood's white liberals shaped the new black characters. Poitier thus represented an idealized black man. His character challenged racial conservatives accustomed to thinking of blacks as shiftless or sex-crazed. It comforted most whites, however, that blacks could be reasonable, intelligent, and nonviolent.[22]

Poitier's image also satisfied the black middle class. The "black bourgeoisie" occupied a curious middle ground in American culture. They identified themselves apart from the black masses, but they also bore a self-imposed responsibility as image-makers. As social symbols, they eschewed laziness, clowning, or hankerings for chitterlings or white women. Thus, as sociologist Nathan Hare later wrote, the black middle class believed "that all Negroes have to do to break down discrimination is to impress the white community with proper public manners and the sincerity of the Negroes' quest for integration."[23]

Was there a more apt public representative of this concern than Dr. Luther Brooks? The character dovetailed with Walter White's efforts. The NAACP, itself dominated by the middle class, was America's most influential black organization in the late 1940s and early 1950s. So even if Poitier's icon posed few challenges to racial problems, the most powerful segment of black America beamed its approval.

No Way Out won an official commendation from the New York foreign language press film critics for its "advancement of improved race relations in the United States." It also generated good reviews. "Its message flows straight out of the action, and as a piece of entertainment it is tense, explosive melodrama," noted *Time*. Poitier's debut prompted similar praise; the *New York Herald-Tribune* found him "particularly good as the doctor who has to hurdle both his color and the exacting demands of his profession. His Dr. Brooks has stinging conviction." Numerous publications, from *Newsweek* to the *New Yorker*, echoed that appraisal.[24]

The black press also lauded the film, mirroring the sentiments of such leaders as White and Dr. Ralph Bunche. With more than a little hyperbole, Frederick O'Neal predicted that the film "should provide the greatest step forward in the fight against racial prejudice since the Civil War." But among the predictable platitudes, Lillian Scott of the *Chicago Defender* raised some subtle objections: "It is, of course, a great relief to see Hollywood portraying Negroes as highly intelligent, trained people for a change. But why do these superior qualities always come packaged in an overly receptive humorless individual?"[25]

Other critics mused on Hollywood's tendency to portray personal rather than political conflicts, and its implications for American racial attitudes. *New Republic*'s Harold Clurman noted that bigotry rarely assumes the form of Widmark's psychopathic, irrational villain. Hollis Alpert of *Saturday Review* concurred: "My experience tells me that there are fairly normal, reasonably well-adjusted housewives who will not live on the same street as a Negro, who won't share a housing project with Negro families. I'm aware, too, of any number of intelligent, reasonably 'liberal' organizations, business and cultural alike, which will not hire Negroes. I wondered how much this sort of action or non action is allied to the kind of disorder the film portrays."[26]

Walter White protested Alpert's review, pointing to instances of overt racial villainy. Despite his valid points, however, the picture oversimplified racism by representing prejudice only through Widmark's scoundrel. It suggested that racism was the province of psychopaths, thus exonerating most viewers of personal guilt.[27]

No Way Out induced further contradictory impulses in its white audiences, according to social scientists Martha Wolfenstein and Nathan Leites. In *Commentary*, they argued that visual cues undercut the film's good intentions. For instance, the dialogue informs the viewer of Luther Brooks's sterling qualifications. But Poitier's mannerisms and facial expressions suggest self-doubt. And unlike the typical Hollywood hero, he relies on others to fight his battles. He survives his ordeal thanks to Dr. Wharton and the deceased's ex-wife, Edie Johnson (Linda Darnell). Even his climactic sacrifice—a passive rather than active deed—occurs off screen. Brooks's manner, restraint, and sacrifice may indicate his redemptive appeal, but they also insinuate that even this excellent doctor remains the white man's burden.[28]

Despite the fine reviews, *No Way Out* was a box-office disappointment. It was the last in the message movie cycle, and by 1950 moviegoers had tired of these socially conscious pictures. The race riot scene and epithets also frightened exhibitors, especially in the South. *Intruder in the Dust, Pinky,* and *Home of the Brave* had played in Atlanta, but no Georgia theaters showed *No Way Out.* Maryland, Ohio, and Pennsylvania review boards demanded cuts. The Massachusetts Department of Public Safety banned Sunday exhibitions.[29]

These local boards did not object to Luther Brooks. In a film with a race riot and an unrepentant villain, Poitier offers a glimmer of hope. The cut scenes instead included the most venomous of Biddle's insults and the black preparation for the race riot. These same scenes impelled the National Legion of Decency, a conservative review board, to give the film a "thumbs down." The film's detractors also included a black organization, the Negro Newspaper Publishers Association, that feared Biddle's flurries of epithets would "build up a vocabulary of undesirable expressions" among the racist element. From across the political spectrum, these groups feared that the film would exacerbate racial unrest.[30]

The controversy over *No Way Out* reached its apogee in Chicago, where the police censor board banned the film. The city's South Side had recently experienced racial violence over zoning laws, and police captain Harry Fullmer argued that the picture's "blunt" presentation would fan the flames. "The film would not cause trouble between normal whites and Negroes," Fullmer stated, "but there is always the chance it would stir up trouble among the more abnormal factions." The NAACP protested the ban. The film appeared in Chicago theaters only after a racially integrated committee cut over three minutes from the film.[31]

Sympathetic audiences did appreciate the cinematic glimpse into modern race relations. Colonel Jason Joy, Twentieth Century-Fox's director of public relations, reported that 99 percent of the letters sent to the studio hailed the film. But the other 1 percent provided a chilling reminder of virulent racial hatred. Joy saved a letter from a Minnesota man named Roger Foss. "All the propaganda in the world couldn't change me," Foss wrote, "and surely your (probable) government sponsored movie won't do anything but make me hate niggers and nigger lovers more." He continued: "America has always been 'the strongest' segregated. Now with this form of degeneration going on, anything may happen. . . . Go to New York City if you want to see what comes of mixing white with black. See all the white women and black niggers walking the streets; go to the school and college dances and see the mixed dancing. What always follows dancing, Mr. Zanuck? That's right, interdating."

This sentiment helped ensure the end of the message movie cycle. With southern theaters rejecting and northern markets wavering, Hollywood studios shied away from race-themed pictures. The example of Mr. Foss spoke volumes. "They say a lot of you producers are queer?????" he speculated. As if his points needed clarification, he signed off: "Damn you nigger lover!!!"[32]

❖

Poitier's movie debut triggered a new round of anxieties. During his ANT days, he feared that audiences would dismiss his talent and crush his fragile sense of self. Films layered heavy political burdens upon his insecurities, and he struggled under that weight. When the picture premiered, a group of friends accompanied him. "He was in quite a turmoil," remembered Alice Childress. His companions kept reassuring him that the film reflected well on him and all blacks.[33]

Yet Poitier also displayed a burgeoning self-assurance and political consciousness. At lunch with *New York Post* film critic Archer Winsten, Poitier ordered an orange flip. Winsten admired his polite admonition to the waiter: "Friend, this is not a flip. This is an orangeade." After providing instructions to add eggs and milk, Poitier spoke of his uncertain future: "Since Hollywood has broken the ice, I'm hopeful they will do what I've always wanted, integrate Negroes into the American scene, not as Negroes, but as persons."[34]

Poitier had a chance for another role in a film adaptation of Alan Paton's *Cry, the Beloved Country*—the same novel, ironically, that had inspired the musical that Poitier spurned to play Luther Brooks. When filming wrapped up in December 1949, Mankiewicz suggested that Poitier visit director Zoltan Korda back in New York City. Poitier craved the exposure of film work, so as soon as he arrived in New York, he opened a savings account, deposited his paycheck, and went straight to Korda's offices in the Empire State Building. As he entered, Korda was leaving. Dressed in a fedora and cape, with a sharp nose and striking forehead, inhaling snuff, and shouting instructions in broken English ("You think I know fuck nothing about pictures!" he once scolded. "I tell you I know fuck all!"), he made quite an impression. Korda arranged for a meeting with Poitier the following morning at the airport, before he was to fly to London. But the next day, Poitier overslept and missed the meeting.[35]

Poitier rued the missed job opportunity less than he brooded over his relationship with his family. He had not written home since leaving Miami. The inaction stemmed from insecurity, since Bahamian migrants always sent money home. "If you had nothing to put in the envelope," Poitier asked, "what do you say? What is your excuse?" He could not abide his mother opening an envelope, finding no money, and realizing his precarious existence in America. So he cut himself off, burying his torment underneath ambition. But $3,000 in the bank brought that guilt bubbling back to the surface. To atone, he paid a surprise visit. On Christmas Eve 1949, he flew to Nassau.[36]

In the airport, on the cab ride home, and back in Over the Hill, he recognized faces from his childhood. But no one recognized him: he was taller, heavier, more mature. He paused outside the wooden, two-room house, by a window propped open with a stick. For a few minutes, he listened to his parents' Saturday night dinner table conversation. He walked inside through the back door and soaked in the aura. His parents turned to him. Both bore the faintest hints of smiles, but neither recognized him. Then his mother screamed — a loud, joyful scream. "My Sidney, my Sidney, my Sidney," she shrieked. His parents embraced him, feeling his face and patting his shoulder and hugging him, confirming that their lost son was still alive.[37]

They listened to his unlikely tale. Sidney pulled out publicity photographs of him and Richard Widmark. The trip, in a way, represented Sidney's final transition into adulthood. They exchanged stories late into the night. At one point Evelyn almost raged at his familial neglect, but she caught herself. Her baby had grown up. On Christmas Day, he reunited with his siblings and promised never to lose touch again. He gave his parents most of the money from *No Way Out*. He also realized that he was now an American. Accustomed to running water, indoor bathrooms, and electricity, he stayed at a hotel instead of his boyhood home.[38]

Poitier might have drifted from his past, but his new career influenced Bahamian politics. The government's censorship board banned *No Way Out*, as it had *Lost Boundaries* and *Pinky*. These decisions irked even the mixed-race middle class, a social strata that traditionally accepted their intermediary status for its relative benefits over the black majority. But by the early 1950s, instances of overt discrimination — including bans on message movies — stimulated some cautious reformism.

After the *No Way Out* ban, A. F. Adderley, the only mixed-race member of the censorship board, resigned in protest. A group of middle-class nonwhites then organized the Citizens' Committee, which demanded an end to the film ban, published a newspaper called the *Citizen's Torch*, and drew up a constitution. Their liberal agenda of racial unity became an organized counterpoint to the white colonial order. Three years later the

Progressive Liberal Party (PLP) formed along these ideological lines. Led by the light-skinned middle class, it called for wider political representation and more government social programs. It was the first political party in the Bahamas.[39]

Middle-class, mixed-race control of PLP proved short-lived. In 1955 a populist black caucus assumed control of the party, and the Bahamas moved toward black control and political independence. But the Citizens' Committee reforms represented an important transition in Bahamian politics. Among other small victories, they forced the censorship board to rescind the ban on No Way Out. A Nassau exhibitor invited the Poitier family. Evelyn had never attended a movie. Like Sidney years earlier, Evelyn had trouble distinguishing reality from the screen. When Widmark hit her son with the butt of his gun, Evelyn jumped up and shouted, "Hit him back, Sidney! Hit him back!" Her family explained it to her, but for the rest of her life, Evelyn Poitier never liked Richard Widmark.[40]

Meanwhile, six weeks after Poitier flubbed his opportunity for Cry, the Beloved Country, Korda granted a reprieve. Poitier flew to London for a screen test, barely believing his good fortune. He sat in first class with sleeping accommodations. Upon arrival, he checked into a hotel and read the script; he would audition the next morning for the part of a young South African priest. Wanting to pick up "an authentic African accent," Poitier wandered London. While touring the sights, he conversed with a Kenyan and imitated his speech patterns. If the accent had scant connection to a Johannesburg priest, neither he nor Korda cared. The next day Korda offered him the role of Reverend Msimangu. He would leave for South Africa in early summer.[41]

That spring, he joined the cast of Longitude 49, a drama written and directed by the leftist playwright Herb Tank. It ran at the Czechoslovak House on the Upper East Side. The play is set on a tanker in postwar Iran. The ship's black first mate gets murdered, and the plot explores the controversies between black and white crew members. Longitude 49 garnered critical praise for the vitality of the cast, including Poitier, and Tank won plaudits for his "true characterizations, salty dialogue, and right-as-rain detail." The play earned more engagements, but it never made the transition to Broadway; as Variety predicted, " 'Too much message' hurts its professional chances."[42]

Before he left for South Africa, Poitier also began dating Dolores Weekes, a smooth-skinned, lightly freckled, curly-haired woman of demure charm. From the beginning, he was smitten. Like most women he dated, Dolores came from a middle-class family. Her West Indian parents logged long hours at their Harlem coffee shop so they could educate their children. Dolores waited tables at the luncheonette and studied social psychiatry at Hunter College. She offered Poitier a stability and structure long absent in his own life. They quickly fell in love. He asked her to marry him, and she accepted.[43]

The familiar obstacles then appeared. Dolores's parents dissuaded their daughter from marrying Poitier. They feared that a marriage to an uneducated actor with no steady paycheck threatened her long-term security. Poitier was doubly depressed: he lost the woman that he loved, and the estrangement exposed his latent anxieties. No less than his clashes with the Miami police or his initial ANT rebuff, the rejection assaulted his sense of personal worth. He sank into self-pity, eating little and roaming the city streets. Frank Silvera, his fellow cast member on *Longitude 49*, advised him to "remember all the pain of your experience, because someday you're going to use it all."[44]

That counsel influenced Poitier enough for him to quote it decades later. At the time, though, he only wanted Dolores. He managed to rekindle the romance before he left for South Africa, but the relationship died while he was away. Over the telephone, in about three minutes, Dolores called off the engagement. She explained that practical considerations outweighed romance. His malaise reached new depths, exacerbated by life in apartheid South Africa.[45]

❖

The story of how a Bahamian living in America worked in South Africa for a British company began, appropriately enough, in turn-of-the-century Hungary. As children, Alexander Korda used to read to his little brother Zoltan from Henry Morton Stanley's *In Darkest Africa*, relating tales of brave white men exploring savage lands. As adults in England, Alexander founded London Films and Zoltan became an accomplished director. Their enchantment with Africa never disappeared. With brother Vincent often designing the sets, the Kordas set films in Africa such as *Sanders of the River* (1935), *The Drum* (1938), and *The Jungle Book* (1942). But each film prompted animated squabbles. Alexander held a romantic, patriotic vision of Britain's responsibility on the Dark Continent. Zoltan loved African culture and wanted to portray the natives' humanity. As the producer with the financial backing, Alexander usually won. Their "Empire pictures" treat most Africans as backward savages.[46]

In the late 1940s, Alexander retreated from the day-to-day operations of London Films, freeing Zoltan to convey his own vision in *Cry, the*

Beloved Country, a white liberal's perspective on South Africa. Alan Paton published the novel in early 1948. Despite little advance publicity, it soon became a surprise bestseller. The lyric language and compassionate message touched readers worldwide, and Maxwell Anderson soon adapted it for *Lost in the Stars*. By February 1950, Korda and Paton were collaborating on a screenplay. John Howard Lawson — one of the Hollywood Ten — also contributed, but Paton disapproved of his radical interpretation. Lawson received no writing credit, moved to Mexico, and never worked in Hollywood again.[47]

Filming commenced in the small village of Ixopo, near Durban. Korda and Paton brought a liberal spirit to the production, inviting the local chief to the set and giving blankets, clothes, and food to villagers. They even rebuilt Ixopo's dilapidated church. But the racial divide dominated their existence. The Minister of the Interior delayed the entrance of the American blacks into South Africa. As *Variety* reported in August 1950, "Certain conditions have been laid down, chiefly that the men are brought to South Africa for the sole purpose of appearing in the film, and that they will take no part in politics during their stay." Poitier later learned that he had arrived in South Africa under the care of Zoltan Korda — as a legally indentured servant.[48]

He entered a country built on a foundation of racial oppression. Since discovering diamonds and gold in the late nineteenth century, both Britons and Boers had appropriated tribal land and exploited black labor. Franchise restrictions and color bars ensured white dominance. Black miners toiled under deplorable conditions, government policies transformed black sharecroppers into wage laborers, native reserves grew overcrowded and destitute, and black families disintegrated as fathers searched for work. These were the conditions that Alan Paton mourned in *Cry, the Beloved Country*.[49]

In the years between Paton's novel and Poitier's arrival, the status of black South Africans further deteriorated. The National Party rose to power in 1948 on a platform of Afrikaner nationalism. Under the new system of apartheid, whites had absolute political control. Legislation abolished black political organizations, banned sexual contact across racial lines, completely segregated public facilities, and forced all South Africans to legally register their race. For black South Africans, apartheid meant virtually no autonomy. For Poitier, it meant entering the country as the legal property of the director.[50]

Poitier's journey to Johannesburg began in New York, passed through London and Rome, and included stops in the Sudan and Kenya. He coveted a long night of sleep in a hotel room. To his dismay, a London Films representative drove him to an isolated country house. There he met fellow black actors Edric Connor, Charles McRae, and Canada Lee. Lee became Poitier's informal mentor. A former violin player, jockey, and boxer, Lee had played Bigger Thomas in the stage version of *Native Son*, performed as Banquo in an all-black *Macbeth*, donned whiteface for *Duchess of Malfi*, and appeared in the Alfred Hitchcock film *Lifeboat*. It was Lee who informed Poitier that they were indentured servants, legally forbidden from living in downtown Johannesburg or buying alcohol.[51]

Neither man could change their circumstances, but each carved some dignity out of the oppression. Poitier complained about their isolation, so London Films appeased them by stocking their house with food, beer, and whiskey. The company also provided a cook and a houseboy (the latter insisted on calling them "Massa"). Most evenings Poitier, McRae, and Connor talked, drank, and played cards. Only Lee — a notorious ladies' man — escaped the boredom, and in the riskiest possible manner, by romancing a liberal, upper-class white woman.[52]

White South Africans sometimes invited them to dinner parties in elegant Johannesburg suburbs. Poitier believed that these liberals, although sympathetic to blacks, thirsted for reassurance of racial peace. "They'd treat us like some kind of strange animal," he told the *New York Times*. "And inevitably they wanted to know: How did we feel about the African situation, and what had the natives told us. Everyone there is living in fear."[53]

Poitier also described the ramshackle conditions of the Johannesburg slums: "Their houses consisted of nothing more than corrugated boxes, bits of burlap sacks and sections of watertanks turned upside-down to provide roofs. Those shacks had no electricity, no sewers, no sanitary facilities of any kind. Often there was no water. It was pitiful." The experience honed Poitier's political consciousness. He and Lee met black activists who pleaded with them to convey the South African plight to Americans. Lee soon spoke on the subject at an NAACP fundraiser at Madison Square Garden.[54]

On location, the production's biggest hurdle was finding black actors. Although 2,000 locals auditioned, few had any training or experience. Korda's cast included a kitchen maid, a librarian, and a "dancer-poetess." Lionel Ngakane had been fired from the Johannesburg Zulu newspaper *Zonk* after failing to deliver a story. Korda hired him to play Absalom.[55]

The temperamental director was less kind to Canada Lee. Poitier marveled at Lee's charm, but Korda often berated the leading man. Alan

Paton hypothesized that Lee was punch drunk from his boxing years. More likely, he was weakened by the kidney disease that soon killed him. In any case, Paton noted, "life had knocked the fight out of the ex-boxer, and he received Zoltan's criticisms with pained smiles." He added that Korda never dared insult Poitier that same way.[56]

Location shooting ended in November 1950, but Korda did not release the film for over a year. First Lee underwent surgery to reduce his blood pressure, postponing interior shooting. Then, five minutes into the first screening at London Films headquarters, Alexander Korda flipped on the lights. "When does your film start?" he boomed, glaring at Zoltan. "When does your film start?" Zoltan aspired to portray the tragic, lyric sensibility of the novel. Alexander demanded a faster pace and more action.[57]

Zoltan tightened the film, but it retains a leisurely, poignant air as it explores the intertwined lives of the black Reverend Kumalo (Canada Lee) and the white landowner James Jarvis (Charles Carson). Kumalo must retrieve his sister from Johannesburg. The city scares the country priest. When he steps off the train, a con man steals his bus fare. He needs the guidance of Reverend Msimangu (Poitier), who empathetically explains that his sister is now a prostitute. Kumalo now understands the depravity of the Johannesburg shantytowns.

The two priests arrange to send Kumalo's sister home, but they cannot save Kumalo's son Absalom (Lionel Ngakane). During a house robbery, Absalom has killed Arthur Jarvis, a prominent white reformer who built native housing. Coincidentally, he is the son of James Jarvis, the major landowner in Reverend Kumalo's village of Ixopo.

James Jarvis is not a liberal, at least not at first. When he sees a picture of his son with black leaders, he says, "I understand about the houses, but why does he have to shake hands?" But after the murder, he reads his son's personal papers, and he starts to sympathize with poor blacks. At the funeral, it is James Jarvis who is shaking hands with black men. He even befriends Kumalo, the father of his son's killer. Jarvis sends milk to Kumalo's impoverished parishioners and pledges to build a new church. Kumalo similarly mends his spirit through Jarvis. At film's end, Jarvis asks Kumalo to keep his post in Ixopo: "How could you go? For what did my son die if you went away?"

The film's plea for interracial humanity is aptly represented by Poitier's Reverend Msimangu. The young priest is a tower of compassion and strength; Kumalo leans on him for both practical guidance and spiritual faith. Msimangu lives with both white and black priests. An ideological rift divides him from Kumalo's brother John (Edric Connor), a radical political speaker. John Kumalo dismisses the church, which ignores fundamental issues such as racial laws and low wages. "There is a new thing growing here, stronger than a church or chief," he proclaims.

But John Kumalo — the film's only overt political voice — is also its only villain. John Kumalo's son avoids incarceration, even though he helped rob Arthur Jarvis. Only Absalom is sentenced to death. "It was justice," John proclaims. "Justice?" responds Msimangu. "Is that what I heard you say? . . . Keep your words in your mouth. And when you open it again, in your great meetings, with your great bull voice, spare us your talk of truth and justice." Reverend Msimangu, like Luther Brooks, values understanding over violence. And *Cry, the Beloved Country*, like *No Way Out*, privileges Poitier's humanity over concrete political change.

Cry, the Beloved Country premiered in late 1951 in Durban, where the South African board of censors cut scenes featuring the liberal (though hardly inflammatory) political writings of Arthur Jarvis. The film then had a gala debut in Johannesburg attended by Prime Minister D. F. Malan and his wife. Mrs. Malan was shocked by the documentary-style footage of the Johannesburg slums. "Do you really think Johannesburg looks like that?" she asked Paton. The writer reflected that she was "not so much shocked by such places as by the fact that people write about them, especially in books that are read all over the world." She thought that Paton betrayed South Africa — "fouling one's own nest," in the idiom of the time.[58]

Cry, the Beloved Country nevertheless earned good returns in South Africa. The film, like the novel, contained no threat to the political order; it did not even mention Afrikaners, let alone Afrikaner nationalism or apartheid. Many white South Africans could appreciate its simple, heartwarming message without seeming unpatriotic.[59]

But the film fared poorly in the United States. "A little slow, grim, and even-toned," complained *Variety*. Trade reviewers suggested that it play art houses — an automatic deterrent to mass appeal. An ill-conceived marketing scheme by United Artists further crippled its prospects. The distributor changed the title to *African Fury* in late April 1952, weakening its association with the bestselling novel, and then reverted to the original name two months later.[60]

The title switches enraged Zoltan Korda, who expected bigger American audiences. But he had himself to blame. By adhering to the plot and feel of the novel, Korda eschewed standard Hollywood plot structures. He illustrated important plot points — Arthur Jarvis's activism, James Jarvis's change of heart, the conflicts between radicals and liberals —

through dialogue rather than action. Without stars or sex appeal, he could expect little more.[61]

Most critics did like *Cry, the Beloved Country*. *Time* and *Newsweek* praised the shots of impoverished shantytowns, bustling mines, and rolling green hills. The *New Yorker* and *New Republic* hailed its celebration of the "Golden Rule." Bosley Crowther of the *New York Times* called for more American filmmakers to address racial issues by understanding "that all distractions that make for social cruelty and human anguish are but reflections of the want for brotherly love." In this spirit, the film won the 1952 David O. Selznick Golden Laurel Award for its contribution to international understanding and good will. The next year, a grass roots campaign by two women in Richmond, Virginia, led to a successful week-long exhibition, with all proceeds to charity. If nothing else, *Cry, the Beloved Country* appealed for compassion.[62]

It further avoided the stereotypes that plagued most film treatments of Africa. Over forty Tarzan movies and scores of other pictures had painted the Dark Continent as an exotic playground for white conquerors. *Cry, the Beloved Country* challenged popular assumptions of black Africans as loyal servants or savage beasts. It questions the social effects of colonialism, and it portrays Canada Lee's Kumalo and Poitier's Msimangu as characters with both frailties and strengths. Both actors received excellent reviews.[63]

But *Cry, the Beloved Country* offered no solutions for the complicated tangle of greed and racism in apartheid South Africa. The *Pittsburgh Courier* noted that the film "makes no obvious statement as to which side is right or wrong." The black newspaper intimated that South Africa deserved a more realistic political analysis. By presenting a love-thy-neighbor message, the film performed no political function greater than alleviating white liberal guilt.[64]

❖

From South Africa, Poitier wrote letters home describing the horrors of apartheid. The experience had forged a deeper understanding of race prejudice, a lesson learned through firsthand experience. Once, while with Lee and Ngakane, he saw a white motorcyclist weaving through traffic. He collided with a van of black people. The white man was unhurt, but the crowd beat the innocent van passengers, including a pregnant woman. The police approved the mob rule by hauling away the battered blacks.[65]

Another time, at the Johannesburg studio, a young Afrikaner yelled at

RACE MAN

Poitier for using the white bathroom (the black one had no toilet paper). Poitier lodged a complaint with a studio executive, who reprimanded the white man in front of the black actor. But Poitier had violated a pillar of South African race relations. The white man later approached Poitier and casually asked when he planned to leave the country. Poitier answered, but the exchange troubled him. He and Lee arranged an armed escort for the ride to the airport. Poitier even carried a pistol, just in case.

It was almost necessary. For twenty miles a blue sedan followed them at high speed. Poitier's car cut through an open field and crashed through a fence to reach another highway. The blue sedan followed, right to the gates of the airport before finally turning away. "Sixteen weeks in that country," Poitier reflected, "but it was at that moment that the full impact of South African politics hit me."[66]

His flight back to London included an overnight stay in Lisbon, Portugal. When he reached his hotel room, he collapsed on his face. A bellman had to revive him. Whether from the fall or from stress, large welts covered his face and upper body. His failed relationship with Dolores, his burden as a black image maker, his uncertain future, and his harrowing experiences in South Africa had overwhelmed him. He would return to America searching for stability. He found it in his personal life. As an actor, he lost any shred of it.[67]

CHAPTER 5

BLACK LISTS
(1951–1954)

If Jackie Robinson's integration of major league baseball in 1947 foreshadowed Poitier's emergence in *No Way Out*, then Robinson's testimony before the House Un-American Activities Committee (HUAC) in July 1949 portended Poitier's subsequent dilemma.

At issue was a statement by Paul Robeson, the black star of song and stage. The large, handsome, All-American football player and Columbia Law School graduate had achieved celebrity for his deep bass singing voice and considerable acting skill. The star of the 1943 Broadway production of *Othello* had also acted in films, including *The Emperor Jones* (1933) and *Sanders of the River* (1935), but he abandoned that medium for its stereotypical portrayals of blacks. By the late 1940s Robeson's popularity was waning. Inspired by radical socialism after a 1934 visit to the Soviet Union, he became an outspoken critic of the United States, just as Americans grew paranoid about Communism. Robeson's concert dates dwindled, and angry picket lines greeted his performances.[1]

In April 1949, world press agencies reported Robeson's declaration that black Americans would not fight against the Soviet Union. "It is unthinkable," he told a Paris conference, "that American Negroes would go to war on behalf of those who have oppressed us for generations against a country which in one generation has raised our people to the full dignity of mankind."[2]

A public uproar ensued, culminating with the HUAC hearings. A string of prominent black leaders reassured white Americans of black patriotism, crowned by the star witness, Jackie Robinson. Whatever Robinson's misgivings about the committee's tactics, he was a World War II veteran and anti-Communist. He indicted Jim Crow and avoided criticizing Robeson, but he believed that blacks would "do their best to help their country stay out of war; if unsuccessful, they'd do their best to help their country win the war — against Russia or any other enemy that threatened us."[3]

Citations from civic groups, bags of fan mail, and media praise followed Robinson's testimony. Press accounts emphasized his critique of Robeson and ignored his denunciation of prejudice. Black reaction was more ambiguous. The *New York Age* reported that Harlemites "split sharply on the issue of whether the popular ballplayer should have gone before the committee. . . . Opinion was both congratulatory and condemnatory." As for Robeson, his career sunk to new depths. The next month, at a benefit concert in Peekskill, New York, a white mob protested his appearance by setting up roadblocks, burning crosses, attacking concert patrons, and torching the stage. Thirteen people were injured, and Robeson did not sing.[4]

Throughout the ordeal, few noted the absurdity of either Robeson or Robinson speaking on behalf of all black America. Robinson testified to that effect, but the nature of black celebrity outweighed his logic. For whites who knew about blacks only what they read in newspapers or saw on movie screens, Robeson's remarks constituted an actual threat, and Robinson's statement a genuine balm. Poitier would later assume this same mantle as spokesman for an entire race.

More immediately, the affair illustrated the line that Poitier tiptoed in the early 1950s. Like Robinson's testimony, Poitier's films offered reassurances of the black man's role in American democracy. But Poitier's political sympathies drifted closer to Robeson's, snaring him in a prickly tangle of politics and entertainment that stretched from Washington to Hollywood, and from Hollywood to Harlem.

❖

Poitier returned from South Africa in a shambles. He wandered Harlem's streets, hoping to cross paths with Dolores. He tried filling his emotional void by buying a new Buick, dating various women, and dallying once again in Harlem's nightlife. He still missed Dolores. Then a friend introduced him to a dancer and model named Juanita Hardy. "Just when my big-time bachelor pose was ready to shrivel and collapse in the heat of the torch I was carrying," he recalled. "Just when I wasn't able to deal with the loneliness anymore; just when I knew I *had* to have a steady girl in a steady relationship before I got any further on into the years where being alone was too tough, to say nothing of being unnatural; just when, for a fleeting moment briefer than the swiftness of the mind, all things were equal — I met my wife."[5]

Juanita had been on the beauty pages of *Sepia* and *Ebony*. But handsome young actors met many pretty women. On top of her looks, Juanita offered an anchor of domesticity. She was born in Alabama and raised in a large Catholic family. Although she had studied at Columbia University, she aspired to raise children. Her father was a successful dress designer. Her mother had taught her to cook and keep house. For the patriarchal Poitier, Juanita represented a stability absent since he left the Bahamas.[6]

It was a curious courtship. The second time they met, in January 1951, she was at a nightclub with a date. Poitier marched up to their table and announced, "I'll never marry a girl like you!" Juanita was dumbfounded. He later explained that he thought she was unstable, because she was so attractive and always had a different date. But a week later, he asked her out. After one month, he introduced her as "my future wife." His formal proposal came later, during a car ride. "Is this for keeps?" Juanita asked. "Yes," he solemnly replied. "This is for keeps." They married in a small ceremony in April 1951.[7]

Dots Johnson (Lefty from *No Way Out*) was Poitier's best man. He drove the newlyweds to their new home in Astoria, Queens. The converted attic space had ceilings so low that Sidney continually bumped his head. He had drained his bank account and sold his car to pay for the wedding and some furniture, so after a three-day "honeymoon" in the new apartment, Poitier returned to dishwashing. For three weeks he worked at a West Side hotel, loading hot dishes into huge, steamy machines. He grew frustrated. After touring the country with *Anna Lucasta*, appearing in two major films, and winning a bride, Poitier was working the same job as his first night in New York City. At that moment, eight years of training and sacrifice seemed to have reaped scant rewards.[8]

"I've been knocking my head against the wall ever since coming to New York," he complained to the *New York Times* that month. "I suppose I'll just have to keep doing it." Jobs for black actors remained scarce. Broadway's brief fascination with black performers in the late 1940s faded. Of the 692 cast positions available in the upcoming theater season, only 13 would be played by blacks. Three were supporting roles, and the other 10 were bit parts. As for Hollywood, Poitier grumbled that it "still doesn't want to portray us as anything but butlers, chauffeurs, gardeners or maids." His two roles remained minor exceptions to the film industry's rule. "As an actor, if I have the ability, all I ask is the opportunity," he said. "When it's denied me because of my color I can't help feeling resentful."[9]

The blame for Poitier's straits lay both in his black skin and the Red Scare. Hollywood and HUAC had declared a cursory truce after the 1947 investigation. But by 1950, after the Alger Hiss trial, the "fall" of China, the Soviet atomic test, the arrest of Klaus Fuchs, the onset of the Korean War, and the rise of Joe McCarthy, the truce disintegrated. Communism, many feared, included a Soviet propaganda campaign carried out by American agents. No facet of popular culture provoked more hysteria than the film industry. A congressional report labeled Hollywood "a reservoir for financing Communist objectives, without which the Communist Party and its fronts in the United States would have had difficulty operating." In March 1951, HUAC returned to Hollywood.[10]

HUAC subpoenaed over a hundred witnesses, and it expected them to both disavow Communist ties and expose others. "We hope those who have changed their views will cooperate to the fullest extent," said John Wayne. "By that I mean name NAMES and PLACES." The Motion Picture Industry Council, a group that included Ronald Reagan, took out full-page advertisements defending sympathetic HUAC witnesses. Gossip columnist Hedda Hopper resolved to "make public every scrap of evidence we can find" about Communist infiltration of Hollywood. The Screen Actors Guild established voluntary loyalty oaths. Unwilling to sacrifice their careers, fifty-eight actors, directors, and screenwriters named names. Those who refused were blacklisted.[11]

Poitier was far removed from these hearings. But the HUAC investigation merely undergirded the film industry's new anti-Communist practices. More pervasive and far more slippery than the actual blacklist, a "graylist" of liberals and socialists circulated through Hollywood studios. Both the American Legion and American Business Consultants compiled rosters of suspected Communists through HUAC reports, back issues of the *Daily Worker*, and letterheads of old Popular Front organizations. They submitted these lists to studio executives, who then relayed the charges to the agents of accused radicals. Actors often had no idea that they were on these lists. But when they found out, the burden of proof fell on them.[12]

Most black actors escaped any formal blacklist: they had no jobs to lose. "They're crying about being blacklisted," ran one dark joke. "Don't these people know we've been blacklisted our whole lives?" Yet many black celebrities aroused suspicion. *Red Channels*, an exposé of Communism in the entertainment industry, specified the leftist affiliations of Lena Horne, Langston Hughes, Hazel Scott, and Fredi Washington. Anti-Communists gained little from forcing them to name names; few blacks joined the Communist Party or possessed political influence. To get work, however, black performers often had to pledge loyalty. Before appearing on the *Ed Sullivan Show*, Horne promised American Business Consultants that she would avoid any "subversive" group. Hughes testified before HUAC that his work affirmed American democracy.[13]

Canada Lee refused to kowtow before Cold War conservatives, and he endured a harsher fate. During the 1949 trial of Department of Justice employee Judith Coplon, a file named him and actor Frederic March as "outstanding fellow travelers." Over forty television shows subsequently banned Lee. He called a press conference to distinguish his outspokenness on civil rights from Communist agitation. But in the early 1950s, his unapologetic stance scared away television and film executives. Even as *Cry, the Beloved Country* played to critical acclaim, he found no work. It devastated him. Once ebullient, he grew defeated, a penniless man resigned to shining shoes on a Broadway street corner. In May 1952, Lee died of uremic poisoning. The mourners at the funeral, including Poitier, believed that he died of a broken heart.[14]

Still, Canada Lee was a sideshow. Paul Robeson was the big black prize in the anti-Communist crusade. Once Robeson had been America's most respected black entertainer. Now he personified disloyalty. He never joined the Communist Party, but his praise for the Soviet Union and his leftist associations alienated him from the mainstream. In 1950 NBC banned him from their network. That same year he criticized American involvement in Korea, and the State Department rescinded his passport.[15]

HUAC demanded that other African Americans follow Jackie Robinson and denounce Robeson. A black entertainer's stance on the controversial giant became an anti-Communist litmus test. For instance, folk singer Joshua White condemned Robeson in September 1950 to avoid the blacklist. HUAC relished these denunciations, as they represented a reassuring consensus on American democracy.[16]

As the general public vilified Robeson, however, Poitier's cadre regarded him as a martyr and a mentor. Like Harry Belafonte, Ossie Davis, Ruby Dee, and others, Poitier admired Robeson's fearless political conscience. He and Belafonte often accompanied Robeson on long walks through Harlem or joined him at a Fifth Avenue bar off 125th Street, where they gobbled up Robeson's revolutionary rhetoric and pitched him ideas.[17]

"He was concerned about Harry and myself," Poitier later recalled. "He used to tell us not to be too radical because he never wanted us to lose our credibility." Even as he grew estranged from the mainstream, Robeson foresaw that black entertainers could nurture sympathy for racial integration. He wanted his protégés to work within the establishment.

Poitier and Belafonte mostly heeded the advice by avoiding formal ties to Robeson, even as they maintained affection for him. Robeson later visited Poitier's home and played with his children. Through their apprenticeship under the radical icon, these young artists learned important lessons about balancing politics and popularity.[18]

Robeson was not Poitier's only connection to the political left. In the early 1950s, Poitier traveled in America's most radical social circles. The HUAC investigations had driven many actors, directors, writers, and producers out of Hollywood and into New York City. Harlem, in particular, became a bastion of left-wing activity. In 1951 the Communist Party moved its national headquarters to 125th Street, where it cultivated the support of Harlem's arts community. Poitier remembered meeting white people "strikingly different from the majority of whites I had encountered before. They were friendly and sympathetic on the racial question, when most other people were decidedly not."[19]

Poitier attended dinners, cocktail parties, and meetings funded by left-wing political groups. He joined a radical *cause célèbre* by signing a petition to oust May Quinn, a local teacher infamous for racist remarks. He watched Davis and Dee perform in the A. S. Prevue, a satirical revue of HUAC and the Cold War; the play raised money for the Committee for the Arts, Sciences and Professions (ASP), a group that the anti-Communist newsletter *Counterattack* called "Moscow's top culture destroying agency in the U.S." He became friends with radicals such as Lester Cole, the play's co-author and a member of the Hollywood Ten.[20]

Poitier's associates moved in this same radical milieu, and accusations against them appeared in *Counterattack*. Paul Robeson was "used by the CP to attract people to dozens of Communist fronts and causes"; Leon Bibb marched at May Day parades and sang at meetings for various party front organizations; Alice Childress wrote "Communist propaganda plays" and was among the "younger leading lights in the CP cultural world"; Ossie Davis and Ruby Dee joined appeals to secure clemency for the Rosenbergs; Harry Belafonte sang at the Village Vanguard, a "Greenwich Village spot known for the rosy hue of entertainers." It was all legal activity, but *Counterattack* implied that these black men and women were unpatriotic.[21]

Partly due to his limited career, and partly due to luck, Poitier eluded the pages of *Counterattack* in the early 1950s. But the anti-Communist watchdog kept close tabs on him. In 1957 the newsletter charged that Poitier had spent "considerable time sponsoring, entertaining at, and otherwise supporting Communist front causes." Though he had no direct connection to radical politics, he had lent his talents to "subversive" activities. *Counterattack* listed his 1950 appearance in *Longitude 49* (playwright Herb Tank pleaded the Fifth Amendment before HUAC when asked about Communist ties). In 1951, Poitier helped sponsor the Citizens Memorial Committee for the Martinsville Seven and spoke at a Negro History Week celebration staged by the Teachers Union. In 1952, he appeared at "Harlem's Big Star Night," a benefit presented by the radical newspaper *Freedom*. He also signed a tribute to Robeson. And throughout 1951 and 1952, Poitier performed for the Committee for the Negro in the Arts (CNA), a cultural group sponsored by the Communist Party.[22]

CNA included white Communists, other whites on the far left, and black actors, writers, journalists, and social critics. Established in 1947 to eradicate stereotypes and fight for black employment in the arts, the organization grew with the anti-Communist purges in the entertainment industry. Membership in CNA did not mean membership in the Communist Party, but the group did obtain funds from the party and produce plays that served the party's political ends. Poitier — like Belafonte, Alice Childress, Maxwell Glanville, and others — relied on the organization for morsels of theater work. After ANT collapsed in the late 1940s, only CNA sponsored black theater in New York City.[23]

The connection of young black actors to Communist front organizations such as CNA and ASP deepened the wedge within the black theater community. The generational conflict that began when young actors abandoned ANT for Broadway now adopted a political dimension. The Negro Actors Guild advocated working within established channels to obtain black roles. President Leigh Whipper tried to convince the Young Turks that their leftist affiliations jeopardized all black actors. Poitier recalled that once, outside a Harlem tobacco shop, Whipper lectured him on his unsavory associates. Poitier listened, keeping his opinion to himself as the older actor fulminated. Whipper had even tucked a gun into his pants, and he threatened to shoot Poitier and his friends if they kept giving black entertainers a bad name.[24]

Poitier, as was his wont, let the incident blow over. He realized Whipper was venting, and he continued to perform under CNA auspices. During the Christmas season in 1950, he and Hilda Haynes headlined benefits at Sydenham and Harlem Hospitals. A few months later, at the Club Baron on Lenox Avenue, he starred in *Just a Little Simple*, a musical revue based on Langston Hughes's *Simple Speaks His Mind*. Poitier replaced Kenneth Manigault as Simple, a humorous and thoughtful master of ceremonies. The revue had an informal, entertaining air. "Even Mr.

Poitier entered into the spirit of the thing and played a couple of comedy pantomimic bits," noted the *New York Post*. He continued to perform in later CNA productions.[25]

But Poitier's acting, even combined with Juanita's modeling and dancing gigs, did not make ends meet. He worked for several months on a construction site, but they saved only enough for two weeks of unemployment. Poitier tried to keep acting. Every morning he circulated through casting offices, politely and persistently inquiring about work opportunities. For three weeks he faltered. In the face of constant rejection and an angry landlord, only Juanita's unflagging optimism buoyed him. He was looking for more construction work when, in the summer of 1951, he won a part in the Sidney Kingsley drama *Detective Story*, with $150 for two weeks of rehearsal and $150 for one week of performances. The play was at Harlem's legendary Apollo Theatre.[26]

The production failed. Poitier had the lead role of Detective McLeod. Despite his "carefully planned" and "well-spoken" performance, he lacked the requisite maturity for the role of the grizzled, inflexible officer. "Poitier is an intelligent actor but his facial expressions belie his problems, and his voice diminishes impact," opined *Variety*. "The goatee which he sports, apparently to add years to his youthful countenance, makes him look like a be-bop musician rather than a gumshoe."[27]

The Apollo followed *Detective Story* with another well-known drama, Somerset Maugham's *Rain*. Reviewers panned this play, too, and Harlemites avoided both productions. The theater canceled plans to stage two additional dramas; Apollo owner Frank Schiffman complained that blacks did not care for drama. At that accusation, theater veterans took exception. "The owner of the Apollo had insulted the Negro people by bringing to this community two inferior pieces with little meaning to our lives," stated the Council on the Harlem Theatre. "Ridiculous prices were charged, and when we exercised the buyer's right (of withholding patronage) we were accused of lacking taste." In the end, the Apollo productions only served the short-term interests of black actors — most notably Poitier's.[28]

Detective Story allowed Poitier to continue seeking work as an actor. It also opened the door on another opportunity. After rehearsals at the Apollo, he sometimes dropped by the Hotel Theresa, a Harlem landmark. There he befriended John Newton, the manager of the hotel's lounge, who convinced Poitier to open a barbecue restaurant with him. They subsequently rented a dilapidated storefront on 127th Street and Seventh Avenue and decided to name the restaurant "Ribs in the Ruff."[29]

Neither had capital, but Newton displayed exceptional pluck. A jukebox company gave them a $500 deposit, which they invested in building materials. They also salvaged lumber from an East Bronx dump for paneling and a counter, transforming their rundown space into a tiny restaurant. While Poitier worked on the renovations, Juanita provided the family with their only real income, sewing labels into clothes for thirty-five dollars a week. "We were putting that restaurant together with spit, with pure spit," he remembered. By late 1951, however, their resources were dwindling. Another opportunity saved them: a movie called *Red Ball Express*.[30]

❖

Poitier was lucky to find a role. After HUAC, cinematic examinations of racial issues bore an odor of anti-American propaganda. *No Way Out*, for instance, constituted evidence of Communist conspiracy for such rabid conservatives as Myron C. Fagan, head of the Cinema Education Guild. In his lecture "Hollywood Reds Still At It!" he charged that *Gentleman's Agreement*, *Pinky*, and *No Way Out* "effectively advance Red ideology." At the same time, African Americans rejected stereotypes: brief comebacks by Stepin Fetchit and Butterfly McQueen failed, and a television version of *Amos 'n' Andy* aroused protests by the NAACP and black media. Thus, just as grinning butlers, shiftless servants, and bossy mammies were fading away from the screen, message movies became politically unacceptable. By the early 1950s, film roles for black actors dried to virtually nothing.[31]

Universal-International originally considered casting James Edwards for *Red Ball Express*, but he refused to testify before HUAC in February 1950. The studio cast Poitier instead. Even though Poitier was in *No Way Out* and had been associated with radicals, he never assumed Edwards's position of public defiance. Heeding Robeson's advice, he was more performer than reformer. Nor did his nascent screen image form a political threat. His first two roles suggested deference to well-meaning whites.[32]

Poitier also acted with skill and presence, and his nibbles of film work had whetted his appetite. During filming in November 1951, he savored his opportunity. "I realized how much I had missed acting in the movies," he remembered. "I was hooked deeper than I had allowed myself to admit." He also appreciated the contract. He invested a large chunk of his $3,000 paycheck in the restaurant; with the remainder he moved his family to West 123rd Street, on the southern edge of Harlem.[33]

Red Ball Express celebrates the truck companies that supplied the

Allied Forces in Europe during World War II. Following the D-Day invasion in June 1944, the Allies attacked with armored tank divisions while stretching their supply lines thin. A chain of trucks battled long hours, muddy roads, and German resistance to supply these aggressive forces. Black soldiers comprised about 70 percent of this "Red Ball Express," fighting both the Germans and the racism of their fellow soldiers. The truckers rank among the most significant African American contributors to the Allied victory.[34]

Hollywood, however, nearly omitted the African Americans. In the spring of 1951, the *California Eagle* reported that the script for *Red Ball Express* focused on Italian rather than black soldiers. The *New York Times* picked up on the story, charging that such a film would be "irresponsible" and "slur Negro G.I.s." A studio spokesman, on his heels, insisted that nothing was decided. "We certainly don't intend to do anything to offend Negroes," he added. The studio then scrapped its original treatment.[35]

Universal-International may have incorporated blacks only after media cajolement, but the theme of democratic cooperation in *Red Ball Express* fit a common Hollywood pattern. War pictures typically portrayed an ethnic diversity of troops uniting under a common cause. By the early 1950s, including black soldiers seemed plausible. In the summer of 1951, during the Korean War, the troops fighting in integrated units increased from 9 percent to 30 percent. Thus, although the prevailing Hollywood mood frowned upon left-leaning message movies such as *No Way Out*, a studio could still salute interracial camaraderie in the name of patriotism.[36]

Given these limitations, *Red Ball Express* is no penetrating examination of race relations. The main dramatic conflict revolves around two white men, Sergeant Ernest Kallek (Alex Nicol) and Lieutenant Chick Campbell (Jeff Chandler). In a ridiculous premise, Kallek blames Campbell for his brother's death in a pre-war trucking accident, even as Campbell leads the truckers with daring. Predictably, Campbell earns Kallek's respect by saving him as they thunder through a burning city. There is also a light romantic subplot between a white private and a French girl.

Three blacks in supporting roles offer an oversimplified, historically suspect characterization of race relations in the Red Ball Express. Private Taffy Smith (Bubber Johnson) is a jovial jazz drummer whose warm spirit endears him to both blacks and whites. Private Dave McCord (Robert Davis) is similarly ingratiating; he dies while leading the unit past a minefield. Only Poitier's Corporal Andrew Robertson expresses any racial resentment. He tries to start a conversation with Campbell, who is sto-ically preoccupied. Robertson assumes he is prejudiced, muttering, "Sure lieutenant. I get it." Later, at a relief station, Robertson asks a Red Cross volunteer to hand him a doughnut. A soldier sneers, "Black boy, you give orders to nobody. You take them." Robertson replies, "Well I'm not tak-ing any from you!" and slugs him across the face. The two men brawl.

Poitier's punch could have been a milestone in American film: a violent act by a sympathetic black man, an expression of one man's essential dignity. But the script's melodramatic formula glosses over the punch's implication. After the fight, Robertson asks for a transfer. He believes that Lieutenant Campbell is racist: "He outranks us the way we've been out-ranked our whole lives." By the end, however, Robertson admires Camp-bell and embraces his unit's interracial camaraderie. He even aids his former rival during another punchout. Later, he symbolically places one arm around a black man and the other around a white man.

Reviewers divided on *Red Ball Express*, particularly on its treatment of race. "A completely stereotyped and shoddy film," complained the *New York Times*, adding that the film's "lip service to better race relations" was done "in a patronizing and superficial fashion." But others praised the integrationist spirit. "It is refreshing," wrote the *New York Herald Tribune*, "to see Hollywood at least show this enterprise in highlighting a problem which has been more or less taboo." In the age of the blacklist, merely addressing racial issues was considered significant.[37]

Black critics conceded that point. The *Chicago Defender* noted that certain scenes "give a wonderful picture of an integrated outfit." *Ebony* promoted the film in a three-page layout. Yet these publications perceived the film's compromises. *Ebony* reported on the segregated conditions during filming in Fort Eustis, Virginia. "I had to go to Jim Crow Virginia and work on a picture about an Army unit organized on democratic principles," complained one actor. The *Defender* protested that the final version had "three Negroes with speaking parts and something like 50 whites with speaking parts."[38]

Southerners took an opposite tack, naturally. The *Atlanta Journal* maintained that the filmmakers "have become so involved in proving that white and Negro troops just love to work and play together, that they've missed the drama of their theme. The thing boils down to a mediocre war melodrama, heavily larded with love-thy-brother angles."[39]

Reviewers at least agreed on Poitier's acting skills. Corporal Robertson cannot smile or dance away injustice, but his sullen facade flakes off, exposing a warm and amiable disposition. "Sidney Poitier adroitly commands sympathetic understanding as the colored soldier," wrote the *Hollywood Reporter*. "A sensitive performance," added *Motion Picture Daily*. Bruised by prejudice, he still embraces the colorblind spirit of the unit. Poitier's character again reassured white audiences of the black man's patriotism and human decency.[40]

But black Hollywood still faced a dearth of roles. Some sought jobs by pleading patriotism. In June 1952, sixteen black members of the Screen Actors Guild, including Louise Beavers and Hattie McDaniel, signed a statement condemning the Communist front organization ASP. "The ASP does not speak for the Negro people," the statement read. "There are a few Negroes who are communists. But they are very few. We urge all Negroes not to be deceived by communist double-talk." The age-old dilemma for black entertainers — whether to work inside or outside the dominant white medium — was now cast in the shadow of the blacklist.[41]

❖

Red Ball Express was a blip of employment, not the end of Poitier's dry spell. He kept making the rounds of casting agents. His efforts bore no fruit for almost a year, until November 1952, when he landed his first television role. He appeared on NBC's *Philco Television Playhouse*, a popular program featuring a different live drama every week. He played an anxious, earnest police officer in the episode *Parole Chief*, based on a David Dressler book. Like many episodes in the genre, neither the film nor the script has survived. Years later, even Poitier forgot about this job.[42]

Yet the role was notable, simply because so few blacks appeared on television during its so-called "Golden Age." Only programs with black caricatures — *Amos 'n' Andy*, *Beulah* — consistently featured African Americans. Live dramas typically shied away from black actors because of anti-Communist pressures, although *Philco* producer Fred Coe defied the blacklist. His use of leftist actors and writers earned *Philco* repeated admonishments in *Counterattack*.[43]

Poitier welcomed the pay for one week's work, especially since he and Juanita had their first child, Beverly. The baby stimulated more worries in her perpetually anxious father. He always remembered a lesson that his father once taught him: "The measure of a man is how well he provides his children." Poitier unceasingly measured his own worth, fretted about his success, and questioned his ability to provide for his family. Beverly's care taxed his financial and emotional resources. Nor could he articulate his anxiety to Juanita, who embraced motherhood. Poitier loved his wife but realized a gulf between them: "She was never able to understand my turmoil, why I was so frightened all the time."[44]

Poitier's tension explained his ownership of Ribs in the Ruff. "Acting can't feed my family," he said. "With restaurants they can eat." The barbecue joint did provide a small, steady income. It held only sixteen seated customers, but Poitier and Newton established a takeout business, made deliveries, and stayed open late at night, serving the spillover from the Apollo Theatre. Louis Armstrong, Nipsey Russell, and Baron Wilson all marched into Poitier's restaurant for 4 A.M. snacks. Despite these endorsements, Ribs in the Ruff struggled. "The surroundings were congenial," explained one friend, "but the barbecue tasted like a spicy glue."[45]

Poitier shared his professional plight with Archie Moore; the famous boxer dated Juanita's sister Joan. Moore had been the leading contender for the light heavyweight crown for over three years. Unable to secure fights with white champions, Moore plotted with Poitier to get rich. "The phonograph would be blaring," remembered Joan, "and Archie and Sidney would sit there planning business ventures by the hour. In no time at all they'll find a piece of land, put up a building, and start collecting rents. It never went further than the room." Finally Moore received his chance against Joey Maxim in late 1952. Poitier had more butterflies than the boxer. Moore won the title, four days after his thirty-sixth birthday. He earned only $800.[46]

While Moore fought two rematches against Maxim, Poitier remained a restaurateur. Yet he still defined himself as an actor. Three nights a week he took classes at Paul Mann's Actor's Workshop, on the third floor of a dusty former factory near Times Square. The studio's appearance was deceiving; professionals regarded the Actor's Workshop as highly as the famous Actor's Studio. Both schools taught the Method, a style first advocated by Constantin Stanislavsky of the Moscow Art Theatre. When Stanislavsky first came to America in the 1920s, good acting meant memorizing lines and projecting voices. Stanislavsky propounded a novel theory, that one must act "from the inside out"; in other words, the actor must immerse himself in his character's speech, mannerisms, background, and social circumstances. Moreover, he must connect his own experiences to his role. He must probe his past for events and emotions that lend insight into his character.[47]

Paul Mann, the heavy-set, bearded founder of the Actor's Workshop, helped pioneer the Method in America. He had trained with Elia Kazan, Lee Strasberg, and Harold Clurman. While his fellow Method advocates lent expertise to the Actor's Studio, Mann taught his own classes. He opened the Actor's Workshop in 1953, limiting his classes to twelve actors and removing students who displayed little promise. He also created a welcoming atmosphere across racial lines. A black man, Lloyd Richards, was chief assistant director, and Mann founded scholarships for black students in memory of theater greats Ira Aldridge and Rose McClendon. His students included Poitier, Ruby Dee, and Ossie Davis.[48]

Poitier improved at his craft. After the Actor's Workshop, he became a more nuanced actor. But the Method may have intensified his personal anxieties. The public exposure of inner feelings — "turning trauma into drama" — stirred his insecurities. His association with Mann also deepened his ties to the radical left. *Counterattack* chided Mann about his sympathy for Communist Poland, his friendship with Sean O'Casey of the *London Daily Worker*, and his connections to Communist actor J. Edward Bromberg. Poitier honed his acting, but he had few opportunities to apply it.[49]

For almost a year and a half, Poitier did not work in film. A break finally arrived during the summer of 1953. A minor producer named Alfred Palca signed Poitier for *Go, Man, Go!*, a film about the Harlem Globetrotters. Palca had already made a short film about the basketball team in 1951, titled *The Harlem Globetrotters*. Unsatisfied with that effort, Palca wrote another script and vowed to make it independently. He hired cinematographer James Wong Howe to direct, and they shot the film in New York City in only twenty days. Howe was so nervous about his directorial debut that he broke out in hives, but he overcame a meager budget with ingenuity. For scenes in the team car, Palca could not afford standard process shots or a mobile camera car. Instead Howe strapped the touring car to a trailer chassis. Unfortunately, the trailer's engine drowned out the dialogue. So they drove up hills, cut the engine, and rolled tape. For that reason, throughout the film, the Globetrotters always ride downhill.[50]

Go, Man, Go! did not escape anti-Communist hysteria. Palca was leaving his Upper East Side apartment one morning when two FBI agents intercepted him. While working as a television and comic writer, Palca had joined organizations and signed petitions sponsored by the Communist Party. He claimed never to have joined the party. Insisting upon his guilt, the agents offered a nugget of evidence: he hired Sidney Poitier. ("The one guy couldn't even pronounce his name," Palca later recalled. "He said, 'Sidney Popeeyay.' ")[51]

The FBI agents continued to stop by Palca's apartment, always urging him to name names. Palca refused. By September 1953, he had talked to

United Artists, Twentieth Century-Fox, RKO, and Paramount about distributing the film. But no studio would sign a contract attached to Palca. One executive even offered to arrange a trip to Washington so Palca could clear his name. He still would not testify. Finally Palca used a front, a common practice among the blacklisted. When he signed with United Artists, he gave his producing credit to Anton W. Leader, his assistant and brother-in-law. The writing credit went to his cousin Arnold Becker, a Connecticut pediatrician.[52]

Like its contemporary films on black sports, *The Jackie Robinson Story* (1953) and *The Joe Louis Story* (1953), *Go, Man, Go!* tells a story of achievement through cheerful pluck. It traces the Globetrotters from their modest beginnings through their barnstorming exploits in the 1930s to their rise atop the basketball world in 1940.

Unlike the other films, however, the hero of *Go, Man, Go!* is a white man, the entrepreneur Abe Saperstein (Dane Clark). Saperstein arranges winner-take-all pickup games in barns and dry swimming pools, and he orchestrates clever schemes to elude color barriers restricting the Globetrotters from major arenas. The story mixes truth with myth. It implausibly explains the origins of the trademark Globetrotter "clowning" as an opportunity for one player to perform while the others rest, thus soothing aches from their grueling schedule. At the climax, the players revert to "straight" basketball to convince an arena owner to book black teams. At the "World Professional Championship Tournament," they stage a come-from-behind triumph.

Palca paints an interracial rags-to-riches story in the Horatio Alger mold, ignoring the troubling implications of the Globetrotters' clowning — an unsurprising decision, since the team's appeal rested on comedy. The Globetrotters were the most famous sports team in the world, and almost every reviewer praised the entertaining antics of Sweetwater Clifton, Goose Tatum, and Marques Haynes. *Time*, for instance, admired a scene in which Haynes dribbles through all five opponents as his teammates relax. Haynes then passes to Tatum, who glances up from his comic book to flip the ball through the hoop.[53]

But these "Clown Princes of Basketball" reinforced the stereotype embodied by Stepin Fetchit. Their vaudevillian performances — passing to "Sweet Georgia Brown," sleeping on the court, eschewing rules for laughs — suggested that they were natural entertainers, not legitimate athletes suited to the discipline of professional sports. The actual Abe Saperstein, moreover, had a grittier sensibility than the Dane Clark version. Although adamant that his team generated racial goodwill, he gave "his boys" three important rules: never contradict white men, never drive a Cadillac, and never get caught with white women. Even southern whites would watch "happy darkies," Saperstein knew, but they would lynch an "uppity nigger."[54]

To preserve the integrationist folk tale, Palca needed a black character of intelligence and decency, a loyal ally to the white hero—a Jackie Robinson to Saperstein's Branch Rickey. That character is Inman Jackson, played by Poitier. Jackson is a veteran Trotter, team leader, and liaison to the benevolent boss. He becomes an assistant coach. He wears a tie in the office, is good with figures, and has a prim wife played by Ruby Dee. He embodies middle-class stability. Saperstein's mother urges her son to follow Jackson's model and "find a nice girl." When Saperstein does get married, Jackson is there, wearing a yarmulke. Poitier gives the film liberal credentials it might otherwise have lacked. It also enhanced his image as a clean-cut, well-spoken black man in an integrated setting.[55]

Go, Man, Go! premiered in January 1954 to minimal expectations and decent reviews. *Newsweek* called it "an ingratiating little film." Critics also appreciated the minimal "soapboxing of minority theme." Although the film hints that discrimination keeps the Globetrotters out of organized leagues, it never directly references race. This muted suggestion of racial barriers relieved liberal audiences without pinpointing America's social ills.[56]

In most of the country, the picture earned fair returns. In the fall of 1953, a promotional campaign followed the team's national tour, and in winter 1954 the team and the film "trotted the globe" from the Philippines to Singapore, Sydney, Hong Kong, and beyond. Yet the film's modest success did not compel most theaters in the Deep South to show *Go, Man, Go!* Although it soft-shoes on race relations and delights in black clowns, it also portrays interracial friendship and black achievement. Poitier's character, in particular, violated the racial order. Theater owners remained intransigent even while the film industry suffered and *Variety* reminded them of the substantial African American market. In New Orleans in late March 1954, whites organized protests outside the theater. The exhibitor pulled *Go, Man, Go!* before its scheduled run.[57]

This dismal environment for black entertainment vexed Poitier, even more so by April 1954 with the arrival of his second daughter, Pamela. Parenting did not come naturally to Poitier. When he was a child, his own father was already an old man. Now, as a young father, he himself struggled to reconcile his childhood on Cat Island—the hard work in the fields, the physical reprisals for transgressions of the family code—with his own circumstances. Worse, he was not providing for his family as he would have liked. For most of 1954, he ran Ribs in the Ruff and searched for work.[58]

His situation remained precarious even as, by the mid-1950s, the boundaries of the blacklist grew fuzzier. Poitier found work in *Red Ball Express* and *Go, Man, Go!* without threats from the FBI or the American Legion. Yet these jobs were rare. They usually came from small, independent producers such as Alfred Palca. Major studios often demanded some demonstration of anti-Communism. For instance, Harry Belafonte had to cleanse himself of a socialist taint before starring in the 1954 film *Carmen Jones*. He told *Counterattack* that he hated Communism, and he denied his presence at certain radical functions. He further claimed that he thought CNA was a cultural organization unattached to the Communist party—a dubious assertion.[59]

Belafonte's star kept rising, but not without triggering suspicion. Once, after appearing on *The Ed Sullivan Show*, he and Poitier went to a Harlem bar. A man with radical ties attacked Belafonte with a knife. As Belafonte recalled, "He thought, how could I have possibly gotten on the Ed Sullivan Show unless I finked?" Luckily, Poitier intervened and saved his friend. Both learned lessons about the costs of widespread acceptance.[60]

Poitier, meanwhile, urged equal opportunity in the entertainment industry. At Actor's Equity meetings, he demanded greater attention to the plight of black actors. Actor's Equity did stave off the blacklist that plagued film, radio, and television, but the well of black roles on Broadway still ran dry. At meetings for the American Federation of Television and Radio Artists, Poitier hammered at the same theme. During one session, the presiding officer advised Poitier to be patient. "Goddamn it, I *can't* wait," he responded. "I have to make it now, while I've got my hair and my teeth." Five years after his first trip to Hollywood, he remained a marginal figure, an actor whose black skin and Red politics fettered his success. His career hung by threads.[61]

❖

Unbeknownst to Poitier, his fortunes had already started turning. One morning in April 1954, Metro-Goldwyn-Mayer (MGM) producer Pandro Berman read a synopsis of the forthcoming Evan Hunter novel *The Blackboard Jungle*. He immediately requested galley proofs. He got a copy that afternoon, took it home, and began reading. He read all night. The graphic story of delinquents in an urban high school intrigued him. A film version would attract a huge youth market and tap into adults' anxiety about juvenile delinquency. The novel's upcoming serialization in *Ladies Home Journal* would further build an audience. As the clock struck midnight, Berman called MGM head Dore Schary and urged, "Let's buy it!"[62]

The studio purchased the rights to *The Blackboard Jungle*, but that hardly ensured a film. MGM had traditionally been the "Tiffany of Studios," known for glamorous Greta Garbo vehicles and all-American Andy Hardy movies, and run by paternalistic overlord Louis B. Mayer. Even after Mayer's forced retirement and Schary's ascension in 1951, the studio still relied on its conservative instincts. It passed on box office smashes *From Here to Eternity* (for fear of offending the Army) and *The Caine Mutiny* (for fear of offending the Navy).[63]

Berman and Schary rejected this trend and hired Richard Brooks, a writer and director with an affinity for sensationalistic material. Then Berman scheduled a lunch meeting in New York to assure MGM president Nicholas Schenck that a film about angry teenagers did not constitute Communist propaganda. Berman pleaded with passion. "I was mad for that one," he recalled. "There was my biggest fight of my life." He and Schary told Schenck that they could make the film for $1.2 million and gross near $10 million. With dollar figures dancing through his head, Schenck gave the green light.[64]

Still, the Production Code Administration objected to the "over-all tone of viciousness and brutality" and demanded softer language in fifteen different spots. It also insisted that Brooks pare down scenes of a beating and a rape. MPAA president Eric Johnston warned that the film would portray the country in a bad light. As a result, the film includes some clumsy Cold War compromises: a scrolling preamble celebrates "a school system that is a tribute to our communities and to our faith in American youth" and insists that the film highlights juvenile delinquency for "social awareness." The filmmakers also inserted a scene at another American high school where the teachers maintain order, the students are intelligent and obedient, and everyone sings the "Star Spangled Banner" at assembly. The scene has no basis in the novel.[65]

Those earnest white students from the tacked-on scene contrast with the polyethnic rowdies of the "blackboard jungle." Berman and Brooks searched coast-to-coast for alienated teenagers. To mirror the novel's gritty texture, they sought inexperienced actors with rough edges. In Hollywood, Brooks and Berman attracted 200 auditioners with a call for "boys interested in coming to MGM to play football." In New York, they interviewed 248 boys, gave 49 of them screen tests, and hired 7. Steve McQueen and John Cassavetes, among others, lost out to these novices.[66]

Among the few cast members with acting experience was Poitier. Casting directors throughout the city knew him as polite and eager. In the spring of 1954, an MGM representative informed Poitier of a role for a black teenager. The twenty-seven-year-old father of two assumed that he was too old and suggested some younger actors. A month later the same casting director called and requested that Poitier audition. They sent a screen test to Berman and Brooks, and the MGM team quickly cast Poitier. Only after they signed the contract did Brooks realize Poitier's age — not that it mattered. He thought that the baby-faced Poitier (who had fudged his age in the opposite direction for No Way Out) was perfect.[67]

In November 1954, Poitier flew to Hollywood. The week before filming, he met Brooks, did his wardrobe fitting, and learned the script. During this week a studio representative told him to stop by Pandro Berman's office. When he arrived, a secretary informed him that his appointment was actually with the legal department. She directed him through a maze of hallways until he reached the office of a studio lawyer, who accused him of associations with known radicals such as Paul Robeson and Canada Lee. The lawyer demanded that he sign a loyalty oath.[68]

Poitier said that he needed time to decide. Then, after they shook hands, Poitier never returned to the legal department. He knew that airing his actual political sympathies would cost him his job. Signing the loyalty oath, on the other hand, would betray his fealty to two mentors. So he avoided the matter. On the first day of filming he spoke with Brooks. The rumpled, iconoclastic director knew about Poitier's political record. He advised: "Fuck 'em." In practical terms, that meant ignoring rather than defying blacklist paranoia. They simply disregarded the lawyer's implied threat that Poitier could not work without signing the oath. They finished without incident, and by Christmas Poitier was back in New York City.[69]

The clamor over Blackboard Jungle, however, was just beginning.

CHAPTER 6

THREATS
(1955–1957)

Holding court in a dingy trade school bathroom, he presides over a band of incorrigibles. A cigarette dangles from his mouth. A white T-shirt, its sleeves rolled up to expose his sinewy muscles, offsets his smooth mahogany skin. He moves with an almost feline grace, and he exudes a self-assured calm. Only his eyes reveal an inner fire. He is Gregory Miller, Poitier's character in *Blackboard Jungle*. In his first scene, he dominates the screen. Like "Rock Around the Clock," the Bill Haley beat that rolls with the film's credits, he embodies a generation of Americans less bound by behavioral, sexual, or racial convention. He is, in a word, cool.

When an authority figure confronts him, Miller rebels. The teacher Richard Dadier (Glenn Ford) finds the boys smoking. Most scatter, but Miller just drops his cigarette slowly, nonchalantly, with an exaggerated parting of his fingertips. The teacher orders him to leave. "Can't a guy wash his hands, Chief?" he says. Dadier threatens to take him to the principal. "You holdin' all the cards, Chief," he shrugs. When Dadier commands Miller to stop calling him "Chief," the student smirks. "Sure, Chief. That's what I been doin' the whole time. Okay for us to drift now, Chief?"

Gregory Miller possesses none of the polished virtue of Dr. Luther Brooks, none of the earnest humility of Reverend Msimangu, none even of the integrationist credentials of Corporal Andrew Robertson or Inman Jackson. Nor does he recreate previous black stereotypes. He resembles the emergent hero of 1950s American youth culture: silky, sullen, sexually charged.

Marlon Brando created the icon in stage and screen versions of *A Streetcar Named Desire*. His rippled muscles, tight pants, animal rage, and emotional inarticulateness gave masculinity a sensuous, almost feminine edge. He recreated the image in *On the Waterfront* and *The Wild One*, and his popularity spawned a generation of kindred Method actors, from Paul Newman to Montgomery Clift to James Dean. In an age when social critics bemoaned the Babbittry of American life, this new culture hero threatened middle-class propriety.[1]

Poitier's character was the black version of this culture hero, lending him an extra element of subversion—a hint of a new racial order within the teenage rebellion. One year earlier, the Supreme Court had ruled in *Brown vs. Board of Education* that racially segregated schools were "inherently unequal." That ruling, though slowly implemented in the South, prefaced a new era in American race relations. Meanwhile, the Great Migration continued. Poorer, less educated blacks arrived in northern cities just as the demand for unskilled labor slackened. The middle class flocked to the suburbs. The rising black numbers, along with persistent white neglect, overwhelmed public housing and schools.[2]

In both the South and the North, then, white America confronted race in a new context. And as the *Brown* decision illuminated, youths constituted the frontier of racial change. Was the cool menace of Gregory Miller a harbinger of future black defiance?

That threat was too powerful, and it strayed too far from Hollywood mores. In those first frames, Poitier's character neither reinforced conservative stereotypes nor resembled the virtuous characters of his earlier films. If *Blackboard Jungle* were to please the masses, the danger posed by Miller had to dissolve. The picture thus recreates the pattern from Poitier's earlier films: Miller helps the white hero, proves himself decent, avoids trampling on racial sensibilities, and illustrates the success of American democracy.

The transformation of Miller from cultural threat to loyal citizen upheld Cold War democratic principles. But Poitier had tapped into a physical, sexual energy that personified the nation's rifts. *Blackboard Jungle* provoked the anxieties of parents, teachers, and politicians; it fueled national and international controversies, and it catapulted Poitier's career.

❖

The United States, by the mid-1950s, had surpassed the expectations of the previous decade. The nation led the free world, enjoyed unparalleled prosperity, and boasted abundant suburbs of nuclear families, picket fences, and new cars. Yet despite this affluence—because of it?—Americans seemed nagged by anxiety. Joe McCarthy and HUAC were only the most obvious examples of cultural paranoia. Senator Estes Kefauver led congressional investigations into organized crime in 1950 and 1951. A 1951 cheating scandal at the United States Military Academy disillusioned even ardent patriots. Water fluoridation, comic books, point shaving in college basketball, and the conduct of Korean War POWs all prompted ordinary Americans to fear conspiracies and corrupted morals.[3]

Between 1954 and 1956, a new fear captured the spotlight: juvenile delinquency. Radio and television specials, books, newsreels, magazine articles, newspaper editorials, and civic and church groups bemoaned the antisocial tendencies of America's teenagers. Many blamed the mass media; alienated young heroes populated *Blackboard Jungle*, *The Wild One*, *Rebel Without a Cause*, about sixty B-grade films, teen-oriented television programs, and comic books. The fear did not represent actual increases in juvenile crime so much as the transformations of the postwar era. Middle-class adults worried that decaying cities, a generation unweathered by the Great Depression, and burgeoning consumerism had created a layer of Americans without moral decency.[4]

As the paranoia over wayward teenagers intensified, Metro-Goldwyn-Mayer (MGM) advanced the release date of *Blackboard Jungle* to March 1955. The studio's publicity agents compiled evidence of a juvenile crime wave, touting newspaper headlines of violent crimes perpetrated by youths. They excerpted editorials that analyzed the hysteria over hoodlumism. They quoted J. Edgar Hoover and President Eisenhower. *Blackboard Jungle*, they suggested, merely portrayed actual conditions.[5]

The publicity targeted parents and educators, but the film's natural audience was teenagers. In the 1950s, young people had unprecedented amounts of spending money. They demanded products that reflected their sensibilities: tight clothes and slicked hair, hip slang and brooding cool, fast cars and fast music. Rock and roll bore the stamp of legitimacy. Still in its fledgling state, the music melted boundaries between pop, country and western, and rhythm and blues. Its pounding rhythms and suggestive lyrics challenged sexual and racial barriers. On their transistor radios and in their cars, white teenagers heard Chuck Berry, Little Richard, and Fats Domino, and they joined blacks at concerts ("Salt and pepper all mixed together," as Domino described). Rock and roll's growing popularity reflected teenagers' consumer power.[6]

Writer and director Richard Brooks captured this sensibility with *Blackboard Jungle*. On the set, he repeatedly played "Rock Around the Clock" between takes. He also featured the song in the opening credits, letting it play for over a minute, through two verses and a guitar solo, before cutting to the opening scene of first-year teacher Dadier approaching North Manual High School. The music reflects the school, a motley collection of Irish, Italian, black, Hispanic, and Asian boys from the economic margin. Brooks creates a leering, disconcerting aura by suggesting sexual confusion: boys swing each other around to "Rock Around the Clock," and one boy wolf-whistles at Dadier.[7]

The students exhibit defiance, with Miller and Artie West (Vic Morrow) the ringleaders. After one day, Dadier has dodged a baseball thrown at his head, quieted a rowdy chant of "Daddio" mocking his name, and thwarted the attempted rape of an attractive teacher. A few days later, a gang ambushes Dadier and his colleague Joshua Edwards (Richard Kiley) in a dark alley.

Dadier forges on. He tries to ally with Miller, whose intelligence surpasses his peers. Miller instead supplies disruptive comments. "How'd you like to bring your mother to school?" threatens Dadier. "How'd you like to bring yours?" cracks back Miller. Dadier's status only deteriorates during a lecture on tolerance: a student reports that he used racial slurs, and the principal mistakenly admonishes the teacher. Then Edwards quits after the students destroy his collection of swing records — a telling musical parallel to the unruly younger generation, which prefers rock and roll. "You're in my classroom now," sneers Artie West at Dadier, "and boy, what I could teach you."

Dadier suspects Miller of wrongdoing, but it is Miller who saves Dadier. He leads a group of black students in rehearsal for the Christmas pageant that Dadier directs. He inspires an interesting discussion during Dadier's first classroom triumph. He also explains his intentions to drop out of school and become a mechanic, because race limits his opportunities and makes formal education irrelevant.

Miller again saves Dadier after Artie West pulls a knife in class. As teacher and pupil dance through a final showdown, Miller stops West's sidekick from sneaking up behind the teacher. Dadier disarms West, the class restrains the villain's sidekick, and Miller approves Dadier's decision to turn in the miscreants. In the final scene, Dadier and Miller walk out the school's front door, Miller's white T-shirt replaced by an overcoat, and they both agree to return the next year. They have bridged the classroom gulf.

By the final frame, Gregory Miller resembles previous Poitier characters, displaying loyalty to a white mentor and emblematizing a polyracial American democracy. He is the moral counterweight to Artie West. By choosing education over crime, he has presumably embarked down a virtuous path toward middle-class stability. The scent of danger, the element of the picaresque from Poitier's early scenes, melts into a spirit of interracial, intergenerational cooperation. Miller's race and cool style exemplified the threat of juvenile delinquency. His actions defused that same threat.

The critics recognized Poitier's excellent performance. As one wrote, "Much of the suspense of the production comes from Poitier's subtle and sound characterization. He is thoroughly anti-social, but not yet criminal. Just wavering on the brink." Trade journals, New York newspapers, and national magazines all praised his acting talents. They also anticipated a box office hit. The graphic violence, the vivid characters, the facile ending to a complicated social issue, the pounding soundtrack — all promoted a visceral emotional reaction. "Even those who are repelled by it will go to see it," predicted the *Hollywood Reporter*.[8]

The forecast proved true. At a preview in Encino, California, 260 of the 273 viewers liked *Blackboard Jungle*. By early April the film had broken house records throughout the country. Even theater owners who despised the film (an Elk Rapids, Michigan, exhibitor complained that "pictures like this spread the disease of the big city") showed it to great gain. By September, *Blackboard Jungle* had grossed four million dollars. As one trade weekly stated, "Any 'showman' foolish enough to reject it unquestionably deserves the dunce's cap."[9]

Teenagers, drawn to the hip styles, slang, and music, led the rush through the turnstiles. *Blackboard Jungle* reflected Hollywood's new awareness of this youth market, an audience that received additional attention with the rise of the drive-in theater. If any film could distract teenagers from groping each other, it was *Blackboard Jungle*. At the beginning and end of the film, youths jumped out of their cars and danced to "Rock Around the Clock."[10]

Haley's song became the top-selling record of 1955. The song, like the movie, frightened adults. A Boston exhibitor refused to turn on the sound to *Blackboard Jungle* until the second reel; he feared an accident as young patrons poured into the aisles to dance. Even at august Princeton University, the music threatened social order. One warm spring day, students pointed their hi-fi sets outside dormitory windows and blared "Rock Around the Clock." A crowd of 1,000 students paraded down a main thoroughfare, blocked traffic, turned on a fire hydrant, and set off an alarm. Although no injuries or damage occurred, the faculty committee suspended four students.[11]

Shocking violence, young villains, black insolence, interracial homosociality, and rock and roll: anxious middle-class Americans wondered if *Blackboard Jungle* portrayed the truth. "Are there any schools where pupils are so completely arrogant and out-of-hand, so collectively devoted to disorder, as are the hoodlums in this film?" asked the *New York Times*. Teachers and administrators responded, some maintaining that the film highlighted a social ill, others arguing that it presented a "telescopic distortion" of urban school conditions.[12]

Blackboard Jungle prompted similar hand-wringing throughout the mass media. On television's *Claire Mann Show*, the host discussed the film for five consecutive days with twenty different mothers. Radio programs devoted similar attention. Some assumed that *Blackboard Jungle* authentically portrayed urban high schools. The *New York Daily News* praised "the honest, slam-bang lowdown on the junior punks and electric chair candidates who have been permitted to make shambles of some U.S. high and vocational schools." Other publications condemned the notion that Ford's "superman turned pedagogue" could reverse the social and economic forces that drive teenagers to delinquency.[13]

Mostly, Americans craved reassurance that the hoodlums of *Blackboard Jungle* would not infect their own lives. Art Buchwald wrote a humorous column about packing a gun before speaking to high school students ("We waited for one of them to call us 'Daddio.' If they did we would shoot them with our .45."), only to find them curious, intelligent, and polite. *Life* promoted the film but claimed it exaggerated the truth. The magazine featured a photo spread of studious youth that supposedly represented most American teenagers.[14]

Underlying this anxiety lay lingering fears of Communism. "Is it any wonder that the communist countries keep winning over millions of people?" asked one shocked viewer of *Blackboard Jungle*. "They advertise and exaggerate their virtues; we advertise and exaggerate our faults." A critic worried what would happen if the film "ever fell into Communist hands." William H. Mooring of *Catholic Tidings* argued that if movie producers exposed *Blackboard Jungle* and its ilk to foreign audiences, whose propaganda networks banned criticism of their own countries, then the American government should restrict the export of films that portrayed social problems.[15]

Domestically, censorship of *Blackboard Jungle* had already begun, led by the Memphis film board and its eighty-eight-year-old chairman, Lloyd Binford. "When the picture first started I thought we were going to have to pass a picture showing Negro and white students together," Binford said. But the board ultimately banned the movie because Artie West and his sidekick never reform. "It's the vilest picture I've seen in 26 years as a censor," proclaimed Binford. The mayor, however, rescinded the ban and classified the film "for adults only," prompting outrage from conservatives and relief from embarrassed liberals. Binford must have smiled when, a month later, a gang of teenage girls burned a cattle barn at a Memphis fairgrounds. Although no fires are set in the film, the ringleader claimed that she hatched the plan after watching *Blackboard Jungle*.[16]

Atlanta censor Christine Smith Gilliam also banned the "immoral, obscene, licentious" film. MGM parent company Loew's legally challenged the ban, and a federal court lifted it; in his decision, Judge Boyd Sloan raised doubts about the constitutionality of censorship. Gilliam seethed that only "college students, radio and newspaper people and librarians" agitated for free speech against the will of the majority.[17]

The hubbub over *Blackboard Jungle* spread beyond conservative southern film censors. Police in Schenectady blamed it for inspiring a teenage gang to rumble with their Albany counterparts. A censor board in Milwaukee held a contentious four-hour meeting before cutting four scenes. The Board of Selectmen in Winthrop, Massachusetts, removed the film from the local theater in response to demands from parents and clergy. The school board in Minneapolis resolved that MGM "failed in its responsibility to the American public." A Parent-Teacher organization in Farmville, Virginia, claimed that *Blackboard Jungle* inspired "new ideas of unbridled misconduct, rebellion against authority and unconcealed immorality."[18]

Organizations acting in the name of public virtue added their wrath. The Legion of Decency gave *Blackboard Jungle* the unfavorable "B" rating, based on "morally objectionable elements" that "negate any constructive conclusion." The Institute for Public Opinion, the National Congress of Parents and Teachers, the Girl Scouts of America, the American Association of University Women, and the Daughters of the American Revolution all denounced the film. The National Education Association resolved that the picture glorified scofflaws and perpetuated stereotypes about trade schools.[19]

Blackboard Jungle had exposed a national anxiety over youth culture. Estes Kefauver tapped into this vein — and mined political gold. The Tennessee senator had earned his reputation in 1951 leading televised hearings on organized crime. In 1954, he assumed chairmanship of the Subcommittee to Investigate Juvenile Delinquency. Drumming up publicity for a presidential run, he thundered against teenage crime as "a symptom of the weakness in our whole moral and social fabric." He led hearings on the role of the mass media, including the comic book and television industries. In July 1955, the Kefauver Committee came to Hollywood.[20]

Although one of many films investigated by the committee, *Black-*

board Jungle assumed a centrality in the proceedings. The senators spot-lighted it during the hearings, concluding that "many of the type of delinquents portrayed in this picture will derive satisfaction, support, and sanction from having society sit up and take notice of them." Producer Dore Schary defended *Blackboard Jungle* and other youth films for their basis in reality. The committee never established a direct link between popular culture and youth violence, but they did provoke popular fears and keep Kefauver's name in the headlines.[21]

But even the Senate hearings paled in comparison to the dispute sparked by the American ambassador to Italy, Clare Boothe Luce. In late August 1955, Luce demanded that the upcoming Venice Film Festival withdraw *Blackboard Jungle* because it was "too violent" and "derogatory" to America. She threatened to skip the festival and create "the greatest scandal in motion picture history." The festival substituted *Interrupted Melody*, an innocuous biopic of opera singer Marjorie Lawrence. Within days, Loew's International filed a protest with the State Department condemning "such unwarranted personal censorship at the hands of our diplomatic representatives."[22]

As the State Department investigated the objection, the media spotlighted Luce's action. *Variety* revisited the debate over whether Hollywood should distribute films abroad that showed America's "seamy side." Readers of the *New York Times*, meanwhile, divided on a Bosley Crowther column critical of Luce. Some applauded the film as a confirmation of American democracy, but the producer Arthur Hornblow argued that Luce performed a valuable service. "The smell of anti-Americanism and communism in Italy is no joke," he warned. Another reader reminded just how much *Blackboard Jungle* threatened many Americans: "It is a shame that it has not been banned in every city in our country."[23]

The State Department cleared Luce of accusations of censorship, concluding that she merely stated a preference to avoid *Blackboard Jungle*. Loew's countered that Luce's intimidation of Film Festival officials constituted a form of censorship. Whether censorship or not, it paid well. The spring's controversies, the summer's Kefauver hearings, and the autumn's Luce affair generated continuous publicity for *Blackboard Jungle*, and it won enormous profits.[24]

Blackboard Jungle became an international phenomenon. Capitalizing on the Venice fuss, MGM sent it to the Cannes Film Festival. The Edinburgh Film Festival gave it a "Diploma of Merit." A Chilean magazine named it best film of the year. Both the German and Finnish governments offered tax incentives to exhibit the picture. In Sweden, Belgium, Australia, Hong Kong, and Singapore, the film earned top returns.[25]

Yet *Blackboard Jungle* also stirred international fears that American popular culture could steer their own youths astray. Egypt and Uruguay admitted the film only after lengthy appeals by Loew's. Israel banned minors from the film, and India banned the picture outright. After MGM refused to allow Japanese censors to cut the film, Japan's national association of exhibitors called the refusal "a holdover of the occupation system" and threatened to ban all American films. The two sides compromised by restricting minors from the picture.[26]

By May 1957, *Blackboard Jungle* had grossed over eight million dollars, an exceptional return for a low-budget production. Millions of moviegoers had seen Poitier's turn as Gregory Miller. Poitier achieved this notoriety just as the blacklist began waning, as *Brown vs. Board of Education* focused attention on racial integration, and as the old comic stereotypes continued to fade away. The door for black dramatic actors had opened a crack, and *Blackboard Jungle* positioned Poitier to slip through it.

❖

Blackboard Jungle did not, however, gain Poitier an instant fortune. For all the film's national and international success, the actor earned only $3,000. With some of that money, he moved his family into a two-bedroom apartment on 146th Street and Riverside Drive. Ribs in the Ruff was earning a modest profit, so Poitier and John Newton invested the remaining capital in an additional three restaurants. Two failed immediately, but a third, The Encore, in Queens, cleared expenses and even paid out a small weekly draw.[27]

Poitier earned additional income with his first spoken-word album, called *Poetry of the Negro*, produced by his friend Philip Rose. Rose ran the rhythm and blues label Glory Records, and he cultivated friendships with struggling black artists on the cultural left in the early 1950s. He and his wife, Doris Belack, often socialized with the Poitiers. For the album, Poitier read poetry by Paul Laurence Dunbar, James Weldon Johnson, Countee Cullen, Langston Hughes, Gwendolyn Brooks, M. Carl Holman, and Armand Lanusse. Lorraine Hansberry, a young critic and playwright, wrote the liner notes. As expected, the album won kind reviews but sold few copies.[28]

Before the release of *Blackboard Jungle*, Poitier's career remained in doubt. MGM signed Vic Morrow to a long-term contract but rejected Poitier. In the newly decentralized Hollywood of the 1950s, studios could not afford exclusive rights on many actors, and Poitier may have been something of a political risk, since he had refused to sign the loyalty oath. For a while, he suffered from ulcers. He attributed the condition to his gnawing insecurities: "a worry bug about my future, my family's future, the future of my race."[29]

But MGM's decision to sign only Morrow benefited Poitier. Had the studio made an offer, he reflected, "the temptation would have been to accept. That's guaranteed salary, you know?" In the MGM stable, he might have acquiesced to routine supporting roles or languished without work. As an independent actor, he could accept projects that furthered his objectives and presented positive images of blacks. Moreover, after the Paramount decision, the studios were losing power to independent producers, directors, and agents, who could deliver talent and negotiate their own deals.[30]

So Poitier needed a good agent, and he found one in Martin Baum — or rather, Baum found him. Casting for a film called *Phenix City Story*, the agent requested that Poitier audition to play a janitor who witnesses a brutal crime at an Alabama casino. Organized criminals intimidate and threaten the janitor into silence. After Poitier read the script, he turned it down, even though the role paid $5,000. "There was nothing derogatory in it," he later explained. "I just didn't feel I should be playing parts like that."[31]

Poitier believed that the janitor lacked a certain dignity, and the movie illuminated nothing about the human condition. Over three decades later he advised Denzel Washington, then a struggling young actor: "Son, your first three or four films will dictate how you are viewed your entire career. Choose wisely, follow your gut and wait it out if you can." Poitier spoke from the experience of his initial lean years and subsequent success. His rejection of *Phenix City Story*, despite two young children and an anemic bank account, illustrated that he envisioned a future as an actor of social significance. He was actively participating in the construction of his image.[32]

Baum failed to understand Poitier's decision at the time, but a few months later — after the release of *Blackboard Jungle* — Baum called him into his Fifth Avenue office. He admired Poitier's values and wanted to represent him. Poitier accepted, and they began a lifelong, mutually profitable partnership.[33]

That journey began modestly, with Poitier's second television credit. In

June 1955 he acted in *The Fascinating Stranger*, an episode of live drama for ABC's *Pond's Theater*. An adaptation of a 1923 Booth Tarkington story, *The Fascinating Stranger* starred Larry Gates as the charming rogue Alfred Tuttle. Poitier played Clifford Hill, a genial man who sells a valuable ring for a pittance. Poitier also appeared on Merv Griffin's Sunday morning religious series *Look Up and Live*.[34]

Then Batjac, a production company run by John Wayne, secured Poitier for William Wellman's adaptation of the James Street novel *Goodbye, My Lady*. Lauren Bacall had recommended him after watching *Blackboard Jungle*. In a reverse of tradition, Wellman scheduled studio filming before going on location. That plan allowed more time to train the Basenji dog featured in the film.[35]

Location shooting in Georgia was grueling. Crew and cast of *Goodbye, My Lady* trudged through swamps and peanut fields, roasting under the August sun. A prop man had to kill a six-foot-long rattlesnake just as it neared the actors. Out of these surroundings Wellman crafted a simple, charming story of a boy and his dog. An orphan named Skeeter (Brandon DeWilde) lives with his Uncle Jesse (Walter Brennan) in a rural Mississippi cabin. Skeeter finds an African Basenji, a rare hunting dog that sheds tears but does not bark. He bonds with the dog, which has remarkable hunting instincts. As the dog, named Lady, becomes a local legend, the town storekeeper discovers an advertisement for a lost Basenji in a hunting magazine. He tells Uncle Jesse, who with folksy wisdom lets Skeeter decide the proper course. Despite his love for the dog, Skeeter returns Lady to its rightful owner.[36]

Goodbye, My Lady could have descended into mawkishness. To Wellman's credit, that never happens. On the strength of its family appeal and evocative message, the Daughters of the American Revolution deemed it the best children's picture of 1956. But trade newspapers realized its commercial limitations. For every reason that *Blackboard Jungle* thrived, *Goodbye, My Lady* failed: no villains, no violence, no edgy allure, no problems with censor boards. Most major publications did not even review it. Wellman called it "a financial fiasco."[37]

At least Poitier's scorecard of virtuous, integrationist characters earned another tally. He plays Gates, a chicken farmer and friend of Skeeter. In three brief scenes, Gates paints the black southern farmer in dramatically different shades than those of the typical Hollywood treatment. He speaks with authority, but he is sensitive to the boy's predicament. Before anybody else, he understands the Basenji's value and Skeeter's dilemma. He knows about the advertisement but does not tell Skeeter. "I never saw anybody aching so hard," he empathizes. Uncle Jesse and Skeeter even need Gates's help to send a telegram. Poitier's farmer possesses more intelligence and dignity than anyone else in the film.[38]

Goodbye, My Lady allowed Poitier to resolve debts accumulated by his overextended restaurants. Cleared of immediate financial burdens, he and Newton discussed their future. While Newton had been pouring his energies into the business, Poitier envisioned a full-time acting career. Newton therefore proposed that they split up. The suggestion surprised Poitier, but he accepted the proposal, perhaps too quickly: Newton would take The Encore in Queens and Poitier Ribs in the Ruff in Harlem.[39]

Alone at the helm, Poitier floundered. He lacked Newton's managerial expertise and cut his staff to a single waitress. One Tuesday, while the waitress had her day off, Poitier cooked the chicken and ribs, made the cole slaw, washed the dishes, scrubbed the counters, and opened the restaurant in mid-afternoon. By 9:00, he had sold one sandwich and one order of ribs. He shut off the gas and electricity, took the $1.50 in the cash register, and hung up his apron. He gave his supplies to a neighboring restaurant. Ribs in the Ruff was no more.[40]

❖

Poitier could accept the demise of his safety net, because his acting career was blooming. After watching *Blackboard Jungle*, writer Robert Alan Aurthur started designing a television play around Poitier. Aurthur based it on an actual black stevedore that he once knew. In August 1955, he pitched his story outline to executives at NBC's *Philco Television Playhouse*.[41]

Producer Gordon Duff liked the idea but foresaw problems casting Poitier. No television drama had ever featured a black protagonist — networks, advertising agencies, and corporate sponsors feared alienating southern viewers with race-themed dramas. (In 1954, for instance, CBS's *Westinghouse Studio One* series bought *Thunder on Sycamore Street*, a play about a black family moving into a white neighborhood. The studio substituted an ex-convict for the black family.) Duff suggested that Aurthur write the script without specifying a black character. After NBC approved the project, they could cast Poitier.[42]

Aurthur titled the script *A Man Is Ten Feet Tall*, always keeping Poitier in mind. For the first time, the actor negotiated from a position of strength — even if he still lacked the material trappings of stardom. Before negotiations with producer David Susskind, Poitier picked up Baum in his car. Like many agents, Baum cultivated an image of wealth and confidence. He wore tailored suits with fine leather shoes and silk ties. So he recoiled when Poitier pulled up in a battered Packard. After a few blocks the jalopy broke down. Actor and agent pushed it to the curb and walked to Susskind's office. Baum then secured Poitier a $1,000 salary, the top rate for an actor on *Philco Television Playhouse*. "If only Susskind could have seen us ten minutes earlier," Baum laughed.[43]

A Man Is Ten Feet Tall aired on 2 October 1955, at the tail end of television's "Golden Age," when live drama showcased the talents of writers and actors. In the early 1950s, television networks could not afford to purchase and adapt popular novels; they instead bought original scripts from such writers as Paddy Chayefsky, Horton Foote, and Rod Serling. These writers turned the limitations of live drama to their advantage: they wrote scripts with tight narratives, indoor settings, and psychological rather than physical conflicts.[44]

By the 1955–56 season, the three networks produced sixteen live anthology series. As viewers tuned in, corporations exerted pressure upon their programs. Philco executives constantly jousted with producer Fred Coe over scripts and casts. An anti-Communist watchdog group, Aware, Inc., stoked this anxiety. "If you watch television," testified leader Vincent Hartnett before HUAC in 1956, "there is scene after scene in which the police shoot the wrong teenager, or the court convicts the wrong person or the honest official abroad is suspected of supporting the Communists. We're being brainwashed."[45]

Television's blacklist was even more haphazard than Hollywood's. CBS directors requested approval for actors by calling a company telephone extension. An anonymous voice answered yes or no. "You never knew why or how," recalled director John Frankenheimer, "and you'd try to get at the bottom of it, and you couldn't." Some actors could work at NBC but not CBS, and vice versa. Perhaps because Poitier had already appeared in a major film, Philco executives approved Poitier for *A Man Is Ten Feet Tall*.[46]

The NBC legal department proved more problematic. The studio lawyers asked Poitier why he signed various civil rights and fair housing petitions; then they grilled him on his friendships with Paul Robeson and Canada Lee. They demanded that he sign a loyalty oath. They also made Poitier discuss his indenture to Zoltan Korda in South Africa. Humiliated and resentful, Poitier left the room sobbing and refused to do the show. Aurthur kept telephoning until Poitier accepted the call, and then he spent an hour cajoling his star. Eventually he negotiated a compromise that precluded Poitier from signing the oath. The actor ducked yet another threat.[47]

Rehearsals, at NBC studios in Rockefeller Plaza, lasted ten days. They began with actors Poitier, Don Murray, Martin Balsam, and Hilda Simms reading the script around a table. Aurthur attended these dry runs. When director Robert Mulligan found the dialogue deficient, Aurthur modified the script. Then the actors rehearsed in earnest, with Mulligan fine-tuning the sequence of camera angles and set changes. As the live performance approached, the cast grew tense. Technical failure or an acting blunder could doom the program—a particular fear for Poitier, who still suffered from stage fright. In fact, during one live televised scene, Poitier forgot a line. He panicked for a few seconds. Luckily, the silence resembled a dramatic pause, not an embarrassing blooper.[48]

A Man Is Ten Feet Tall opens with Murray's Axel North, a tortured man with no self-confidence and a mysterious past. He telephones his girlfriend but does not talk. He works as a stevedore under the gruff, corrupt Charlie Malik (Balsam), but he befriends another supervisor, Poitier's Tommy Tyler. Tyler is unfailingly ebullient. "You gotta laugh!" he says. "You gotta laugh at it or stomp on it!" He buys Axel a slice of pie, gives him his old baling hook, and arranges for Axel to work in his group, agitating an old conflict with Malik. He urges Axel to realize his own worth: "Look, there are the men, and then there are the lower forms, you know? A guy's gotta make a choice. You go with the men and you're ten feet tall. You go with the lower forms and you're down in the slime."

Tyler invites Axel into his blissful home, where he teases his pretty wife (Simms), bangs on bongo drums, and dances to jazz. He reveals his dreams of becoming a musician, doctor, or lawyer. When Axel confesses that he is AWOL from the Army, Tyler insists that they are still friends. When Malik challenges Axel, Tyler sacrifices for his friend. "It's me he wants," Tyler insists. A long fight with baling hooks ends with Malik killing Tyler. A police investigation reveals nothing: the dockworkers, including Axel, adhere to a code of silence. But after self-reflection, Axel adopts Tyler's faith in humanity. He tells his girlfriend that he loves her, and he beats up Malik before turning him into the police. "You're crazy, you'll go to jail," screams Malik. No, says Axel. "You can't hurt a man who's ten feet tall."[49]

The liberal message and graphic style surprised television audiences. Mulligan remembered so many laudatory calls that the NBC switchboard shut down. That night in Harlem, a crowd congratulated Poitier as he walked down the street. Poitier called Aurthur from a drugstore telephone booth. "I'm talking to the guy who wrote it," he announced to the crowd. "Tell him what you think." A roar came through the telephone line. In November the program captured Sylvania's annual award for best dramatic show on television. Poitier was particularly good, and he won Sylvania's prize for best male acting performance. The drama also won the Brotherhood Award of the National Conference of Christians and Jews.[50]

But racial conservatives found it jarring: a major television program had featured a black actor in a lead role, supervising a white friend and challenging a white villain. Many viewers also thought that the café-au-lait Simms was white. Some of the telephone calls flooding the NBC switchboard protested the casting decision, and the studio received over 200 letters in that vein. Southern editorialists condemned the writer, cast, and Philco. "Programs such as this," cautioned one Mississippi newspaper, "are part of the brain-washing scheme to prepare southern minds to accept the monster of integration and intermarriage."[51]

❖

Two weeks after the drama aired, MGM announced plans to finance and distribute films for a company headed by Aurthur, David Susskind, and Alfred Levy. The first project was *A Man Is Ten Feet Tall*. After the success of the teleplay and film *Marty*, writers, directors, and producers were migrating from New York to Hollywood. The talent exodus helped the film industry, but it enfeebled television. Programs such as *Philco Playhouse* lost their best assets. With the innovation of videotape in 1956, live television drama became unnecessary. The last *Philco Playhouse* aired in February 1956, and the demise of similar programs soon followed. Television's "Golden Age" was over.[52]

As Aurthur adapted the script, Susskind replaced most of the cast, signing John Cassavetes to play Axel North, Jack Warden to play Charlie Malik, and Ruby Dee to play Tyler's wife. Only Poitier reprised his role, signing in December 1955 for $15,000. For the first time in his life, he received billing as a co-star. Although the fee was Poitier's largest, it was small by Hollywood standards. The racial theme ensured a limited market in the South, so MGM budgeted only $500,000. Susskind shot on location in New York with low-priced talent. All the actors, with the exception of Poitier, worked primarily in television.[53]

Susskind's director also came cheap. He hired Martin Ritt for only $10,000. In the early 1950s the television actor and director had "helped Communist-controlled unions put on propaganda shows," according to

Counterattack. Blacklisted, Ritt earned a living by acting in bit parts, teaching at the Actors Studio, and betting on horses. He flew to Hollywood to meet with MGM president Spyros Skouras, who urged him to clear his name before HUAC. The director refused. "Suddenly," Ritt recalled, "for no reason that I could discern, he said, 'Okay, you're a good boy. You come to Hollywood and make pictures for Twentieth Century-Fox.'" Perhaps Skouras could not decline the bargain price. In any case, the incident reflected the diminishing power of the Hollywood blacklist.[54]

With cast and director secured, Susskind arranged to begin filming in late March. Location shooting in Central Park, on St. Nicholas Terrace, and all through Harlem posed hurdles that required patience, ingenuity, and a sense of humor. Susskind had trouble procuring a railyard with locations for both interior and exterior scenes; he convinced a railroad executive to allow filming at his yard while the man's wife was in labor. On location, turret trucks and tractor trailers sometimes rolled into shots unannounced. Other times, the squeals of freight trains drowned out dialogue. When an April snowstorm threatened to delay exterior shooting, Susskind paid early-morning passersby to shovel the railyard.[55]

The lightest moment involved a real-life hot dog vendor, hired to play himself on screen. The vendor haggled with the film crew before signing the necessary waiver forms. They began filming the scene, which called for a character to complain about his hot dog. With cameras rolling, the vendor howled in protest. The crew mollified him with ten dollars.[56]

The most exciting moment came during the baling hook fight. The New York Central had refused to allow the fight in their Manhattan yard, so Susskind arranged an alternate location in Queens. Just before filming, with a doctor on standby in case of an errant swipe, the actual railyard workers climbed onto the cage that surrounded the actors. Poitier and Warden thrust and parried through their choreography, and when the long scene ended, the laborers gasped. An awed hush followed, at least until Ritt called for another take.[57]

In adapting the drama, Susskind claimed that they "tore up the TV script and began again," and Aurthur insisted that he spent three and a half months writing a new script. But the film version—retitled *Edge of the City* at the last moment—maintained the basic plot, characters, and dialogue of the original. The modifications mostly fleshed out Axel North: his father blames him for his brother's death, and he has since cowered before authority figures. Additionally, Axel makes silent calls to his mother, not his girlfriend. That change increased his psychological peculiarity, and it allowed for a Hollywood-style romance with a sweet schoolteacher played by Kathleen Maguire. *Edge of the City* thus adhered to the televised play, but added a dab of Hollywood polish.[58]

Aurthur also expanded on the rivalry between Tyler and Malik. Malik takes a percentage of Axel's salary until Tyler adopts Axel into his group, and he resents black supervisors on the dock. He prompts their baling hook duel with the goad, "Tyler, you're the blackest ape I ever saw." But Tyler does not change. The charm, wisdom, and goodness of Poitier's character remain intact.

MGM executives, presumably uneasy with the racial theme, delayed the film's release. But a New York City screening earned raves — almost every viewer included "terrific" or "excellent" in his or her appraisal. An early review from *Variety* hailed the "courageous, thought-provoking and exciting film." Representatives from the NAACP, Urban League, American Jewish Committee, and Interfaith Council later lauded the message of racial brotherhood.[59]

When the film arrived in early 1957, critics marveled at its presentation of the friendship between Tommy Tyler and Axel North. Hollywood historically portrayed interracial friendships only when whites occupied positions of authority. *Edge of the City* was different. "Surprisingly enough in a Hollywood movie," remarked *Time*, "the Negro is not only the white man's boss, but becomes his best friend, and is at all times his superior, possessing greater intelligence, courage, understanding, warmth, and general adaptability." Neither man acknowledges race as a barrier to friendship. *Variety* called the film, without exaggeration, "a milestone in the history of screen in its presentation of an American Negro."[60]

Poitier's magnificent performance helped make the interracial relationship plausible. Critics rained praise upon him. "Sidney Poitier, the Negro of the piece, does a magnificent job." "Sidney Poitier, as his Negro friend, turns in the most distinguished of his many first-rate characterizations." "With this performance Poitier matures into an actor of stature." "Here is an actor who deserves major leading roles." His reputation soared.[61]

Cassavetes earned plaudits, too. His scarred, inarticulate hero resembled Marlon Brando in *On the Waterfront*, another film examining corruption on the docks. Cassavetes further suggests an ambiguous sexual identity. Axel calls his mother without saying a word, allows his eye contact with Charlie Malik to linger, avoids conversations with attractive women, and establishes an unusually close relationship with Tommy Tyler. (These innuendoes unnerved the Production Code Administration. Although it approved the script, it urged "extremely careful handling to avoid planting the suspicion that he may be a homosexual.")[62]

By contrast, Poitier never implies any threat. He speaks in "bop" slang, walks with a chipper strut, and delights in jokes and dancing. But his body language and marital status do not suggest the sensuousness of Axel North or his own Gregory Miller. Tommy Tyler exudes optimism. "Man, don't you know that you gotta have faith?" he asks Axel. He carries this faith to the end, fighting Malik only to protect Axel's life. Even after capturing his rival's baling hook, Tyler pleads for peace. But Malik stabs Tyler in the back. Axel rushes in and cradles his dying friend, rubbing his face against Tyler's head and whimpering, "It was my fight all along." The white man learns from the black man's death, achieving manhood and self-esteem and love. The black man reaches the height of Christian sacrifice.[63]

❖

Christian sacrifice was the order of the day. Between December 1955 and December 1956 — soon after *A Man Is Ten Feet Tall*, a month before *Edge of the City* — the black citizens of Montgomery, Alabama, staged a bus boycott protesting segregated seating. The city's black leaders understood the power of symbol. In April 1955, the police had arrested an unwed pregnant teenager for refusing to vacate her seat to a white woman. In October, after a similar violation, the police arrested a child living in a dilapidated shack with her alcoholic father. Neither case resulted in a boycott. The protest began after the arrest of Rosa Parks — a soft-spoken woman with rimless spectacles, an NAACP secretary and part-time seamstress, an emblem of middle-class dignity.[64]

Even more than Parks, however, Montgomery's public face was Reverend Martin Luther King Jr. The twenty-six-year-old preacher led the boycott only because he had avoided the rivalries that plagued the city's older ministers. After one night, however, King had displayed his oratorical powers. As he raised the multitudes to a fever pitch, he fused American democracy and Christian righteousness: "If we are wrong — the Supreme Court of this nation is wrong. If we are wrong — then God Almighty is wrong! If we are wrong — Jesus of Nazareth was merely a utopian dreamer and never came down to earth! If we are wrong — justice is a lie."

For 381 days Montgomery's blacks walked and organized carpools, enduring frequent stops and harassment from unsympathetic policemen. Angry whites bombed the homes of black leaders, including King. Police arrested King for driving thirty miles per hour, five over the speed limit. Ten thousand whites lauded segregation at a Montgomery Coliseum rally organized by White Citizens Councils. King still preached passive resistance: "We must meet hate with love."[65]

By February 1956, newspapers worldwide featured the boycott on their front pages. Reporters described white violence and black sacrifice. King was a hero — "Alabama's Modern Moses," according to *Jet*. After the Supreme Court upheld an Alabama state court decision against segregation on buses, King's stature rose even further. A long, sympathetic profile appeared in *Time*. Clare Booth Luce, scourge of Italian communists and *Blackboard Jungle*, wrote to King that "no man has ever waged the battle for equality under our law in a more lawful and *Christian* way than you have."[66]

The Montgomery boycott unleashed a tide of attention to racial equality, and *Edge of the City* rode the crest of this wave. Robert Alan Aurthur recognized that he exaggerated his characters, but he defended it based on Montgomery: "In these times, when excesses of the most distasteful kind are being repeated on our front pages each day, a little idealization on the other side might be excusable." Tommy Tyler was the ultimate victim-hero, an icon of moral purity fighting a white supremacist, a vehicle designed to elicit white sympathy.[67]

With *Edge of the City*, black critics drew connections between entertainment and politics. "Dixieland won't like it," warned Evelyn Cunningham of the *Pittsburgh Courier*. "There's so much integration in this picture, it almost scares you." Hollywood films had profound implications: "The picture makes you realize more forcefully than ever before how conditioned we all have become to Negroes staying in their place."[68]

As Martin Luther King gained a national profile through the Montgomery bus boycott, Sidney Poitier solidified his public image in *Edge of the City*. The *Chicago Defender* predicted a special Oscar for the black actor, celebrating that "just as Hollywood has grown up and ceased limiting Negro actors to burlesque and strictly menial roles, so Negro fans themselves are not barred from winning because of race or color." Poitier had become a standard-bearer for black participation in the American democratic tradition, and the actor endorsed his character's vigor, charm, and benevolence as universal human virtues that "made his color invisible."[69]

Poitier, like Jackie Robinson, had become an archetype of racial integration. John D. Silvera, chairman of the Coordinating Council for Negro Performers, lobbied for more black roles in 1956 on the basis of Poitier's success: "He has proven in the field of movies and the occasional TV roles given him that he can compete with the white actors." MGM wedded Tommy Tyler to Sidney Poitier. One article in the promotional literature for *Edge of the City* noted the "uplift philosophy" of the black protagonist; another article detailed Poitier's rise from poverty in a story headlined "Optimistic Uplift Outlook Has Paid Off for Ex-Busboy Sidney Poitier." The actor's image matched the values of the era's progressive racial politics: faith, hard work, nonviolence, sacrifice.[70]

Dorothy Masters of the *New York Daily News* carried this connection between actor and character to even greater heights. During her original review of *Edge of the City*, she named Poitier an early favorite for best actor of the year. She considered his "innate perceptivity" the foundation of his success. One week later, after interviewing Poitier, she claimed to fully understand his power: "Sidney had only to be himself." Like Tommy Tyler, Poitier possessed compelling warmth — he was "a philosopher who has arrived at an excellent adjustment to the world."[71]

She also wrote that "Sidney would, if he elected to change careers, make a fine minister of the gospel." This final observation spoke potently to how the doctrine and demeanor of Martin Luther King had shaped the contours of the actor's image. After *Blackboard Jungle* and *Edge of the City*, Poitier had become one of Hollywood's few established representatives for black Americans. Professionally and personally, that position opened new possibilities, new responsibilities, and new tensions.[72]

CHAPTER 7

NOBLE SAVAGES
(1956–1957)

"Negro Actors Get Pix Breaks," announced *Variety* in May 1956. No longer confined to playing maids, porters, singers, or dancers, black actors now had small but important parts in a few pictures. But progress was slow. Although black urbanites thirsted for more roles like Poitier's turn in *Blackboard Jungle*, the major studios still had to consider the substantial southern market. "In the question of Negro casting," the trade journal summarized, "Hollywood is somewhat caught between the devil and the deep blue sea."[1]

At the time, Poitier was shooting *Edge of the City*, a picture that illustrated this dilemma. The film confronted racial discrimination, and it featured a compelling black character. Yet it found few bookings or willing theatergoers in the South. Without its low budget and independent production team, *Edge of the City* never would have been made.[2]

Poitier's next role promised a better opportunity for large-scale success. He reunited with MGM producer Pandro Berman and writer/director Richard Brooks for *Something of Value*, a film based on Robert Ruark's novel about the recent Mau Mau rebellion in Kenya. The studio poured enormous resources into the project, paying a record $300,000 for the film rights in January 1955, three months before the book's publication date. It borrowed Rock Hudson from Universal for $400,000 and paid the actor $200,000. It claimed to have spent $250,000 fact-checking Ruark's novel. Then in September 1955, Brooks and Berman scouted locations in East Africa. MGM seemed determined to create an entertaining, big-budget picture that portrayed racial conflict in an African nation.[3]

Ruark's book, meanwhile, became a bestseller. The Scripps-Howard columnist reshaped his Kenyan experiences into a novel about two friends—one white, one black—and how political circumstances divide them. Echoing Alan Paton, Ruark lamented that whites destroyed black tribal life and failed to replace it with "something of value." But the book's appeal lay more in its lurid depictions of Africa: grotesque female circumcisions, blood-soaked massacres, and brotherhood oaths involving animal penises, sodomy, and the consumption of human brains. The *New Yorker* snickered that the novel had "the lean and hungry look of imitation Hemingway," and Ruark himself seemed a pastiche of the legendary writer. Hefty, hearty, and more than a little pompous, Ruark bragged that between movie rights and book sales, he made over three million dollars from *Something of Value*.[4]

MGM banked on similar success. Following the formula of *Blackboard Jungle*, Brooks adapted a popular novel based on current events. Both projects depicted violence frankly. Both included roles for popular leading men such as Glenn Ford and Rock Hudson. And both cast Sidney Poitier as a young black man torn between two codes of behavior. Just as Poitier's race lent a key subtext to the anxiety provoked by *Blackboard Jungle*, his Mau Mau rebel implied a threat of black rebellion in America. Again, that danger was defused.

❖

When Poitier arrived in Kenya, he saw mostly black faces. Nevertheless, it was a white man's country. When settling Kenya in the late nineteenth century, the British envisioned a fertile land of European farmers and subservient African peasants. Whites seized land and political control. Wage labor and tax codes weakened traditional systems of land ownership and local rule, creating a huge, rootless black underclass from Nairobi to the countryside.[5]

World War II stimulated change. Returning black veterans demanded jobs and political reforms, and protest organizations sprung in both cities and rural areas. Some developed elaborate oaths. By 1950, rebel protests included murder, arson, and the maiming of animals. By 1952, the government had declared a state of emergency, imprisoned leader Jomo Kenyatta, and summoned the British army. By 1955, the so-called Mau Mau rebellion had been suppressed.[6]

Press reports, government statements, and missionary accounts shaped a popular image of Mau Maus as bloodthirsty savages captivated by primitive voodoo rituals. Few examined the legitimate nationalist sentiment behind their actions, and fewer understood that most black Kenyans desired the same reforms as the rebels. Ruark's novel—the best-known account of the Mau Mau—enshrined the myth that blacks either stayed loyal or betrayed paternalistic whites. It never questioned the English right to "civilize" blacks. And it graphically described Mau Mau savagery, dominating the public's perceptions of Kenya.[7]

MGM marketed the film on these myths. "The Most Dangerous Big-Game in Africa . . . Man!" advertised the posters. The studio suggested that theaters emphasize "the fantastic Mau Mau ceremony and frightful oath of murder, which revived the incredible Witchcraft, Voodooism and Rituals of Darkest Africa." But Brooks had to reduce the book's brutality. In the novel, the white and black protagonists (Peter and Kimani, respectively) sleep with prostitutes and guzzle booze. Peter eventually strangles Kimani to death. Brooks made them more sympathetic, brightened Peter's romance, and cleaned up explicit scenes. He also eliminated lines that openly disparaged blacks as savages. Most important, he changed the ending so that Peter and Kimani try to bridge the racial divide.[8]

Cast and crew departed for Nairobi in July 1956. "There isn't one thing here that won't kill you," Brooks announced. Besides scorpions and malaria, he had logistical problems. The hotel refused to admit Poitier, and Brooks would not cave in by housing the black actor in a separate bungalow. His resolve surprised the hotel manager, who asked how much Poitier earned. When the director said $30,000, the man's jaw dropped. Poitier could stay. According to Brooks, the hotel decided that "anyone who makes thirty thousand dollars for three months work is not black."[9]

Brooks, Hudson, and Poitier were three very different men. Brooks was an ex-Marine who wore garish flowered shirts, smoked a pipe, and had a gruff manner—he was the man, after all, who once advised Poitier to "fuck 'em." Hudson, by contrast, carried himself with the smooth arrogance of the quintessential movie star. In Hollywood, he never carried money, put change in parking meters, or made reservations at a restaurant. He also possessed an insatiable sexual appetite, especially for men.[10]

Poitier possessed the grace missing in Brooks and the humility absent in Hudson. "With his dancing eyes and million dollar smile, Sidney was wonderful company," remembered Hudson's wife, Phyllis. "Whenever the conversation dragged, he would liven it up with a bright remark." But Kenya tested his good cheer. Restaurants turned away the black cast members, forcing them to improvise with picnic lunches.[11]

During penny-ante poker games with Brooks and Hudson, Poitier often discussed race relations. He had become an authority on that and many other subjects. After years of deprivation from his semi-literacy, he now read voraciously. At home, he regularly read the New York Times from cover to cover, and he devoured books on religion and history. His self-education fostered confidence. Thanks to his West Indian upbringing, he had never deferred to whites in social situations. Now, armed with reserves of intellectual firepower, he became an eloquent spokesman for his beliefs.[12]

In Kenya, however, Poitier operated under some Western misconceptions. Years of Tarzan movies had convinced him that poisonous snakes lurked in every corner. Before he slept, he checked under his bed. He locked the door and shut the windows. He tried to sleep in the exact center of the mattress. His terror multiplied when the production went to Nanyuki, a town near Mount Kenya, home to black mamba snakes. One scene called for him to run through the woods, his feet in sandals, as a camera truck filmed from an adjacent road. Visions of angry mambas filled his head. Out of professional pride, Poitier promised to sprint the path for a single take. Afterward, Brooks was unsure about the shot. Citing his promise, Poitier refused to run again.[13]

The shooting schedule set a grueling pace, and the actors often returned to the hotel exhausted, their hair tinged with red dust. Sometimes conditions were hazardous. A pair of hunters accompanied the crew to fend off rhinoceroses and lions. One morning on the set, a script girl found a baboon in her safari wagon. Hunter had to scare off the animal with a shovel. The girl escaped with scratches, minor bruises, and frayed nerves.[14]

They also met Mau Maus. Through the anthropologist Louis Leakey, Brooks arranged an excursion into the backcountry. Arriving in rebel territory, they spilled out of a Land Rover. The guide advised them to stand still, or they might get shot. The Mau Maus emerged. As the guide communicated in Kikuyu, the parties eyed each other warily. The rebels had predicted their arrival from the smell of soap, and they recognized Poitier as an American by the way he walked and spoke. In time the two groups discussed Kenyan and American race relations. Brooks remembers a stimulating discussion. Hudson recalls nothing of the sort. "I never saw such hatred in the eyes," he later said. "Black, piercing eyes. They could look right through you and sever you in two."[15]

In mid-August the production returned to California, a fire-eating "witch doctor" in tow as a consultant. Poitier left Africa wiser, more textured in the nuances of race and world politics. While exploring Nairobi, he had realized his ambiguous position. "I walk down the street and the Africans know I'm not one of them," Poitier told Brooks. "I feel like a stranger here." He also decried the effects of colonialism. "I didn't like Kenya at all," he said. "I found Africa in need of a great many things—

opportunity is only one of them. They are in need of opportunity for education, better opportunity to learn trades, better opportunity to learn what the rest of the world is like." For a black child of a British colony, the injustice stung.[16]

The film, like the book, offers no solution for colonialism. It only suggests that the white man has ignored his burden. Peter McKenzie (Hudson) and Kimani (Poitier) are lifelong friends torn apart by race. "You can't treat an African like a brother and expect to have a good servant," warns Peter's brother-in-law Jeff (Robert Beatty). When Kimani acts insolently, Jeff hits him. Cultural differences create broader rifts. When Kimani's father approves the killing of a child born feet first, in accordance with Kikuyu custom, he is arrested.

Kimani now grasps his futility. "Is that to be my life?" he asks. "Head man for a white boss? 'Yes, Bwana. No, Bwana. Yes, Bwana.' This land can serve me, too. I want my own land." He joins a band of guerrillas. Though horrified by their tactics, he cannot escape the oath that makes him a Mau Mau. His humane instincts torture him while they raid the McKenzie farm. As the others kill Jeff and his children, Kimani's conscience prevents him from murdering Peter's sister.

Peter joins the hunt against the Mau Mau. Still, he yearns for peace. As others urge reprisals, Peter distinguishes Mau Mau from loyal blacks. He also laments the pressures on Kimani: "He started out as a good kid with a fine father, but they civilized the outside of him and forgot all about the inside." The old friends negotiate a truce. But a militant white farmer sabotages their rendezvous and kills Kimani's wife. His trust shattered, Kimani runs. As Peter chases after him, trying to salvage their friendship, Kimani falls into an elephant pit and dies. Peter raises Kimani's child as his own, hopeful that the next generation can avoid their mistakes.

Many sniffed at the sentimental climax. "The come-to-Jesus ending is just plain bad," proclaimed Ruark. A critic called it "a sad piece of hokum." But a hardened Rock Hudson strangling an unsympathetic Sidney Poitier would never have played in Peoria. Despite the African setting, audiences drew connections to American racial politics, and only racial reconciliation satisfied the white liberal vision for race relations. The film's two main publicity stills reinforced these politics. In one, Hudson carries Poitier on his back. In the other, the two men grapple. The first suggested that black Africans were the white man's burden. The second implied that ignoring that responsibility threatened white society, too.[17]

Something of Value depicted Africa on a grand scale, with star actors, grand vistas, timely themes, and grisly violence. *Variety* predicted boxoffice success. Even those affronted by racial brotherhood could relish "the blazing guns and scenes of natives cowering before the blows of the white man, smouldering with hate, but taking it all the same." The reviewer added that southerners "may find some apt parallels in this film."[18]

That a race-themed film might attract audiences across the political spectrum seemed a contradiction. This paradox centered around Poitier. *Variety* suggested that he gave "a glimpse of the new Africa — young, easily misled through appeal to bitter resentments, and yet conscious of new responsibilities." Others noted how aptly Poitier conveyed the frustrations that drove men into the Mau Mau: he dignified a revolutionary anti-colonialist stance. Yet Kimani also reassured audiences by fretting about Mau Mau tactics: "When he agrees to surrender without a final fight, it is like an act of expiation, a triumph of reason over emotion." That whites betray him, that his politics are dismissed, and that he perishes escaped reviewers. Kimani dies so that others may learn. The film thus discourages black action while encouraging white compassion.[19]

Even this compromised message threatened the mores of racial conservatives. As *Something of Value* opened to excellent returns in New York City, most southern exhibitors rejected it. They objected to scenes of black-on-white violence and a white woman receiving a blood transfusion from a black man. Southern attitudes crippled its commercial potential, and the film never achieved the success of *Blackboard Jungle*. It did, however, lend its principals a political cache. Brooks trumpeted: "Any film which reflects the world as it is today, historically and from the viewpoint of humanity, cannot do any harm because in the long run, people who see the film will be moved to a greater understanding of each other."[20]

Poitier's status kept escalating — among African Americans, in the national media, and worldwide. The *New York Amsterdam News* considered Kimani his best role, and *Ebony* praised his "Academy-Award-type acting." Although he was not nominated, *Something of Value* won the National Brotherhood Award from the National Conference of Christians and Jews. Ironically, it was an American entry at the Venice Film Festival, sight of the *Blackboard Jungle* contretemps, and won the St. George Statuette for its humane message.[21]

Publicity for the film also clued in the American public to Poitier's intelligence, work ethic, and humility. The actor realized his position as a black image-maker. He presented himself as a diligent, middle-class American, one who saw racial solutions within the democratic tradition. During a *Newsweek* interview, Poitier described the links between professional ambition and social conscience: "I've reached the point in my career where I can eat, sleep, and pay the rent. No, what I want now is the kind of role that makes me feel worth-while. I will work anywhere — movies, theater, TV — provided the material has texture, quality, something good to say about life."[22]

He walked a fine line between movie star and racial emblem. "I have no politics," he said, "but I am a Negro. For this reason, I try to do and say nothing that might be a step backward. I believe in integration, though I'd rather call it equality of opportunity." He sounded charming and humble, a black man living the American dream. He described a journey from self-doubt to peace. "I found I could learn to accept what I had to accept and to try to change what I wanted to change," he said. "Now? I dig my work, I love my family, I booze with my friends, I go to church, I play a lot of golf. What else is there? I mean, *what else*?"[23]

❖

On one level, Poitier spoke the truth. By the time he expressed this utter contentment, he had filmed two more pictures. A third daughter, Sherri, arrived in July 1956. With most of his paycheck from *Something of Value*, he and Juanita placed a down payment on a two-family home in Mount Vernon, New York, near their friends Ossie Davis and Ruby Dee. Mount Vernon was an integrated middle-class community just north of New York City. Poitier wanted his children in a "multiracial cultural milieu," not an "antiseptic" white suburbia.[24]

They embraced their new neighborhood. On weekends, the Poitier residence turned into an open house, with children playing and watching television, and parents cooking and gossiping. A woman named Jean Walker helped with childrearing, cooking, and cleaning. The girls dubbed Davis "Uncle Ossie" and Dee "Aunt Ruby." Poitier relied on their companionship. "I treasure the times when he would come barefoot to our house," Dee later recalled, "and the three of us might wind up in the kitchen, joking, laughing, and discussing some issue of the day."[25]

But as Poitier's professional fortunes soared, his marriage disintegrated. His evidence of internal peace — time with friends, golf — also suggested domestic trouble. Juanita serenely stayed outside the orbit of black protest. Sidney, by contrast, was enmeshed in the intellectual ferment of the black artistic community. He often escaped to Harlem, where he laughed and debated with old friends from his theater days. Other days he indulged his mounting obsession with golf, leaving early in the morning and not returning until dusk.[26]

They also clashed over their children. Juanita doted on the girls. Sidney's entire experience suggested that success followed self-discipline. He demanded that his children avoid mindless entertainment, and he insisted upon the privilege due a father. "I'm a patriarchal kind of man," he once said. "I happen to believe that the man should be the head of a household, make the decisions, and have the respect of his family." But his frequent trips to Harlem, golf courses, and movie sets diminished his authority. Also, Jean Walker and Juanita's parents shared the mother's permissive approach. The father fought a losing battle.[27]

Poitier was also tall, young, handsome, famous, and a frequent traveler. Willing women were constant temptations. While filming *Something of Value* in California, he met David Susskind and two women for dinner. They decided to have a nightcap at the home of one of the women. On their way there, Poitier, already loosened by a bottle of wine, drove through a yellow light and hit an empty bus. Poitier and his date were thrown out of the car, and the others remained amidst the mangled metal. Miraculously, no one was hurt, and the drivers absolved each other of blame. Whether his wife learned of the accident, or of other dates that did not end with a car wreck, Poitier does not discuss. But Dee noted that Juanita had gained weight, and that perhaps Sidney had judged "the book by its cover" in letting his marriage deteriorate.[28]

Temptation followed him back to Africa for his next picture, a Lloyd Young film called *Mark of the Hawk*. Funded by the Board of Foreign Missions of the Presbyterian Church and the Methodist Church of America, the project promoted the work of Christian missionaries. Poitier judged its political value more important than the meager pay, so he took the role. In late 1956, after complications obtaining a work visa, he packed his bags for Nigeria. The British colony resembled Kenya in economic structure. Every morning in Enugu, thousands of poor blacks descended from the outlying mountains into the commercial district to work for middle-class blacks and upper-class whites.[29]

At the government-run hotel, Poitier met his co-star: the beguiling, leggy, mercurial Eartha Kitt. The diva of song and dance, though needed only for interior shots in London, had insisted upon the trip to Africa. She sometimes explored Enugu by bicycle, dressed in a bikini. A sexual tension infused her relationship with Poitier. Each claims that the other suggested a walk into the hills. Poitier remembers a sociological excursion, being "swept upward by the crowd of homeward-bound workers" and following them into villages of corrugated tin buildings, mud huts, and communal kitchens. Kitt tells a different story: "It was calm and romantic, the moon was full. Only the sound of crickets could be heard. The night was soft and gentle and right for romance." She qualified, however, that it was "the wrong timing and the wrong man, a married man." They witnessed a large dance before returning to the hotel.[30]

While the others filmed, Kitt returned to the hills, where she met the Ebos, a tribe that worshiped bats. She returned to find the cast sitting in the restaurant, with Poitier "giving his grandiose speeches as usual, eulogizing on the fabulous use of the English language." Kitt interrupted and solemnly presented writer/producer Lloyd Young with a Christmas gift. It was a gigantic bat. He screamed and sprinted away. Poitier leapt through an open shutter window. The humorless Young never returned, but everyone else laughed and called for stronger drinks.[31]

Young departed early the next morning for London, and the cast followed him there for interior shooting in January 1957. They strained to present every point of view on African colonialism while trumpeting Christian missionaries. At the center of this drama stands Obam (Sidney Poitier), a new member of the Legislative Council of an unnamed African colony. (Blacks fight for the rights of "African" people, and they speak the "African" language.) Obam, like Kimani from *Something of Value*, is caught between political cultures. Terrorist radicals want his support, and many whites fear him. Yet he joins the political establishment at an elegant reception. There, a councilman argues that schooling Africans plants the seeds of rebellion. A missionary laments social injustice for blacks. The governor just wants order without martial law.[32]

At the next day's council meeting, Obam demands basic rights: a broader franchise, democratic elections, and an abolishment of the curfew. Rebuffed, he takes his case to the workers. "They have taken your wealth and what have they given you in return?" he orates. "Do you have more land? Those of you who once plowed your fields now work the land of the white planter. For what? For a white man's salary?" His rhetoric frames a radical solution of self-government.

But the Reverend Amugu (Juano Hernandez) and the American missionary Bruce Craig (John McIntyre) convince Obam to forswear violent upheaval. During a bloody white ambush of a black raid, Craig dies in the crossfire. A court investigates Obam's culpability in the raid. Though cleared of wrongdoing, he stands before the court. "I, too, am guilty," he announces. "I am guilty because I had already yielded to hatred." He advocates racial brotherhood. "God grant that I will work with them towards our country's freedom, and love, and understanding. . . . For I am no longer alone." The ending suggests that Christian love can resolve the ills of colonialism.

"Unfortunately," as one reviewer stated, "there is far too much talk — at the expense of dramatic continuity." While praising its sincerity, critics agreed that the film bogged down in solemn lectures. The one commercial concession failed. Kitt, who played Obam's wife, Renee, sang the torchy "This Man Is Mine," a scene that *Cue* deemed "completely, and comically, out of place."[33]

Despite her minor role, Kitt received first billing. At the time she was more popular than Poitier, and her song generated royalties for the Board of Foreign Missions. For the first time since *No Way Out*, however, Poitier played the clear-cut lead role. Trade newspapers applauded him. Clad in African garb and demanding social justice, he commanded the screen. In keeping with his image, he opposes violence and advocates interracial cooperation.[34]

In September 1957, Harlem's Apollo Theatre held a sneak preview. An overwhelming majority praised the film. "This picture makes me glad to be a Negro," wrote one man. Others drew parallels to the emergent struggle for black equality in America. Clebert Ford of the *New York Amsterdam News* cheered that *Mark of the Hawk* presented African problems from a black point of view. But he questioned Hollywood's use of Poitier as the sole actor "to bear the social stigma of the Negro." He also bemoaned the recurrent Poitier pattern: "Humiliated in 'No Way Out,' pitifully sacrificed in both 'Edge of the City' and 'Something of Value,' one seriously wonders whether Mr. Poitier will ever be given an opportunity to show his talents in more wholesome surroundings." On the verge of stardom, Poitier had been typecast.[35]

Mark of the Hawk failed at the box office, no surprise considering its lackluster plot and shoddy production values. Universal-International did not release it in the United States until March 1958. A unique promotional campaign did, however, reach at least one important citizen. Protestant ministers advertised the film from the pulpit. At the National Presbyterian Church in Washington, D.C., the pastor recommended it to a congregation that included President Dwight and Mamie Eisenhower, Secretary of State John Foster Dulles, and Secretary of the Army Wilbur Brucker. The president had already seen it at a special White House screening.[36]

Poitier's public profile expanded. In his syndicated column, Bob Considine marveled at the great American success story of a "Bahamian version of a Dead End kid" made good. A Broadway producer tried to cast Poitier opposite Kitt in the musical "Shinbone Alley." Another producer pursued him for a show tentatively titled "Jamaica" or "Pigeon Island." "Mr. Poitier is said to have the necessary qualifications for the assignment," reported the *New York Times*. "He is a baritone and is able to sing the required Calypso numbers."[37]

Poitier could no more sing calypso than flap his arms and fly. The mistaken assumptions about the tone-deaf actor revealed both the pervasiveness of black stereotypes and Poitier's peculiar position. No black actor had ever become famous solely for his dramatic talents; the media took for granted that any black performer could sing. And at the time, the nation was in the throes of a calypso craze. By early 1957, calypso dominated the Billboard charts. Its popularity inspired calypso dances, fashions, and B movies. Leading the way, with a bestselling album featuring "Day O" and "Jamaica Farewell," was Harry Belafonte.[38]

In 1957 Belafonte sold more records than Elvis Presley and Frank Sinatra. He adapted calypso and ethnic folk music into popular songs. His popularity, however, rested on his sex appeal. His stage show emphasized his seductive charisma. Lit in warm hues of lavender, cornflower, and pink, he wore tailored "bullfighter" shirts with plunging necklines. Looping metal rings met at the belt of his form-fitting silk pants. His delivery conveyed an animal urgency. When he hit the stage, crooning a sultry ballad, women of all ages and races swooned.[39]

Belafonte shared Poitier's anxieties. "Success was traumatic for me," Belafonte reflected. "Here I was, a Negro, being accepted by people of all denominations, in all walks of life, by millions as a performer and an artist. Yet in my personal life, I was nowhere, not ready for it." He tore himself up with self-analysis. He called friends in the middle of the night, complaining of loneliness. He alienated others with long-winded monologues on culture and politics. On occasion, he developed a psychosomatic case of laryngitis. He blamed his guilt over his success; his first wife, Marguerite, believed that he used it to avoid difficult decisions. Like Poitier, Belafonte had married at a young age. When he achieved fame, he drifted from Marguerite. His decision to divorce her and wed white dancer Julie Robinson in January 1957 kindled controversy in the black community.[40]

He also appeared in movies, starting with *Bright Road* (1953) and *Carmen Jones* (1955). In the summer of 1957, *Island in the Sun* appeared in theaters. The film explores interracial romance on a Caribbean island. "A sickening, repulsive, indecent spectacle," spat South Carolina senator

John Hart. Ku Klux Klan protests or exhibitor bans occurred in Memphis, New Orleans, Charlotte, Atlanta, and the Bahamas. The furor raged even though Belafonte and Joan Fontaine never kiss. Belafonte's sex appeal still threatened southern mores. But the popular stage performer toured the world, spoke about race relations, and appeared on the cover of *Time*.[41]

Belafonte's popularity explains something of white expectations of black male performers in the late 1950s. In his 1957 essay "The White Negro," Norman Mailer argued that "the source of Hip is the Negro." He explained that the black man, living on society's margin, indulged in the "enormous present" of "Saturday night kicks, relinquishing the pleasures of the mind for the more obligatory pleasures of the body, and in his music he gave voice to the character and quality of his existence, to his rage and the infinite variations of joy, lust, languor, growl, cramp, pinch, scream and despair of his orgasm." The white "hipster," he continued, emulated the primal urges of the urban black man. For all its gross oversimplification, Mailer's essay illuminated the cultural power that many whites assigned to blacks.[42]

Belafonte's appeal rested in this white perception of black sexuality, although his skin color and facial features smoothed that edge. His friend Bill Attaway explained that Belafonte was a "bridge Negro — one who serves to connect white and Negro." He was a black man who conformed to white standards of beauty. His music, too, bridged a cultural divide. When he quickened pulses with lively rhythms and seductive gestures, he allowed whites to appreciate black culture and sexuality, and he only nudged at their racial boundaries. Whites could deflect their racial guilt by savoring his charisma.[43]

Unlike Belafonte, Poitier had dark skin and more African features. Nor was he swinging his hips to fawning white audiences. On screen he had no opportunity for romance. His characters either had unassuming wives or displayed no interest in women. The sensuous energy he displayed in *Blackboard Jungle* — an energy he had no occasion to act upon — remained an exception to the rule.

But his recent film roles had conveyed elements of black exoticism, conforming to the same white expectations that drove Belafonte's success. His costumes, accent, and revolutionary rhetoric in *Something of Value* and *Mark of the Hawk* stirred viewers without directly facing America's own racial ills; the Third World was a safer forum for appreciating blacks on screen.

In this recurrent role as exotic white ally, Poitier updated the American literary tradition of the Noble Savage. Like Queequeg in *Moby Dick* or Jim in *The Adventures of Huckleberry Finn*, he exhibited an alternative to the dominant white culture, even as he served white interests. Poitier now embodied this compromised vision of the black man's place in American society. His body language and diction infused dignity into his characters, even as his basic goodness reassured viewers of racial peace. So in February 1957, when director Raoul Walsh needed a young actor to play an educated, angry, but ultimately loyal slave, he naturally turned to Poitier.[44]

❖

Robert Penn Warren, acclaimed author of *All the King's Men*, dipped deep into the past to write *Band of Angels*. He had researched a true, pre–Civil War story about two daughters of a Kentucky gentleman. After their father's death, the girls learned that their mother was black, their father was in debt, and they were chattel. In New Orleans, the new slaves disappeared from the public record. From this tale Warren fashioned an epic novel of slavery, the Civil War, Reconstruction, and westward expansion. As the mixed-blood female narrator searches for freedom, she obsesses over identity. "Oh, who am I?" she cries. Her virtuous husband, her owner and lover, and an educated slave all grapple with similar problems of self-definition.[45]

The novel garnered mixed reviews, but Warner Brothers bought the film rights for $200,000. In *Band of Angels*, the studio could recreate the Hollywood stereotype of the tragic mulatto—a woman caught between two worlds, endeared by her white identity and exoticized by her black blood. Fredi Washington in *Imitation of Life* (1934), Jeanne Crain in *Pinky* (1949), and Dorothy Dandridge in *Carmen Jones* (1955) all played some version of this ill-fated temptress.[46]

Yet *Band of Angels* might have presented opportunities for more progressive depictions of African Americans. Hollywood films from *Birth of a Nation* to *Gone With the Wind* had portrayed slaves as dim-witted, indolent, and inherently loyal. Poitier's character, Rau-Ru, is not this type of slave. He resents his owner, Hamish Bond, who benevolently reared and schooled him. Rau-Ru decries racial double standards, joins the Union Army, and orchestrates Bond's death. This character could have eased the burden of Hollywood's past.[47]

That possibility evaporated the moment Warner Brothers signed Clark Gable. Gable *was* Hollywood's past, a living symbol of the Golden Age. Under contract to MGM for twenty-three years, he had worked in top-shelf productions with an assortment of stars in a variety of genres. Now he was pallid and overweight, worn down by a lifetime of drinking, smoking, and womanizing. Haunted by the ghost of his beloved third wife, Carole Lombard, he let a fourth marriage end after one year. He trembled with palsy. After a string of mediocre films, he wanted to retire.[48]

But Gable still possessed an almost mythic status. In an age of anxiety, he exuded self-assurance. "I was in awe of him," recalled Poitier. "He was incredibly disciplined, the ultimate professional." Gable rehearsed his scenes exactly as he played them, and he rarely flubbed a line. When MGM re-released *Gone With the Wind* in the mid-1950s, it catapulted him back to superstardom. He was burned into the American consciousness—especially below the Mason-Dixon Line—as the cocksure rogue Rhett Butler.[49]

When Gable arrived in Baton Rouge in January 1957 to film *Band of Angels*, he was received like royalty. Socialites begged for his presence at country club dinners, cocktail parties, and gala balls. His fifth wife, Kay, dined with the wife of Louisiana governor Earl Long. Adoring fans ringed Gable's hotel, deluged the switchboard, wrote mountains of fan mail, and popped flash bulbs at every opportunity, including his exits from trailer toilets.[50]

The black actors enjoyed no such adulation. Upon arrival, they found Jim Crow in place. At a restaurant in the New Orleans airport, three black cast members ate behind an improvised screen. Warner Brothers tried to approach the problem with sensitivity; they arranged for the "colored" Chamber of Commerce to confer with black actors prior to arrival. At great expense, the studio complied with state segregation statutes: housing black cast members separately at Southern University, transporting them in separate cars, arranging meals at separate facilities, and providing separate portable toilets.[51]

Since his scenes were all interiors, Poitier avoided Louisiana. The weekend before he reported for duty in California, he appeared in a dramatic musical about the bus boycott called "Montgomery Walk." Ossie Davis had written the play, and the cast included Ruby Dee and Frederick O'Neal. Pete Seeger sang. "Montgomery Walk" earned Poitier neither money nor notoriety; it was part of a Negro History Week celebration held at Local 1199 Retail Drug Employees Union, AFL-CIO. Moreover, Nelson Frank of the *New York World-Telegram* had accused union leader Leon Davis of Communist ties, an allegation with potentially damaging implications for an actor entering the mainstream. Poitier nevertheless lent his services.[52]

Filming for *Band of Angels* wrapped up by the end of March, and it premiered in July. The movie adhered to the novel at first, but abandoned it by the end. It opens in 1853 at a Kentucky plantation, where young Amantha Starr (Yvonne DeCarlo) plays with house slaves and adores her benevolent father. Years later, after boarding school in Ohio, she returns for her father's funeral, after which she learns that her mother was black, her father died in debt, and she is a slave. She endures a New Orleans slave auction, where a lecherous man prepares to inspect her. Hamish Bond (Gable) intervenes, buying her and protecting her honor.

Amantha seethes at her slave status, but Bond coolly smiles and houses her in elegant quarters, eventually taking her to his rural plantation. In time, of course, she falls in love with him. He offers her freedom; she stays with him instead. But when Bond reveals that he was once a cruel slave trader, a horrified Amantha leaves for New Orleans, now occupied by the Union army.

Here the film departs from the book. As the Civil War draws to a close, Amantha leaves a kind Union captain (Efrem Zimbalist) to avoid revealing her tainted ancestry. She still wants Bond, despite his past. By then, Union armies are chasing Bond, a fugitive Confederate hero. Rau-Ru (Poitier) captures him first. Once Bond's top slave, the educated black man is now a Union lieutenant. He resents Bond's paternalism and swears revenge. But after Bond relates how he saved him from murderous African slave catchers, Rau-Ru has a change of heart. He orchestrates Bond's escape, and he guides Amantha to Bond. The two lovers escape the closing Union army on a tiny boat, rowing out to meet a sailboat of freedom.

That final scene punctuates the film's conservative reformulation of *Band of Angels*. In the novel, Amantha marries the Union officer, slaves hang Bond, and Rau-Ru remains embittered. In the film, Rau-Ru forgives his master and enables his romantic reunion. Two slaveowners—Amantha's father and Hamish Bond—paternalistically reign over their loyal minions. Only Rau-Ru articulates the injustice of the slave system, and his final actions accommodate the white hero.

The white hero, moreover, has been reconstructed to garner adoration. Hamish Bond is Rhett Butler redux, puffed to preposterous proportions. In his presence, men cower, women swoon, slaves sing and dance. When he beds Amantha, thunder rumbles and lightning crackles. Rau-Ru even absolves his sinful past. The secondary male characters reinforce the mentality of the Lost Cause. The effeminate, cruel Charles de Marigny (Patric Knowles) is rewarded with disloyal slaves. Union troops disrespect southern women and exploit blacks. The abolitionist Seth Parton (Rex Reagan) betrays his own self-righteous proclamations by lusting for Amantha. Only Hamish Bond is benevolent, manly, and superlatively suave.

In its elevation of Gable, *Band of Angels* subordinates his co-stars. The film's publicity implied that blackness scarred both Rau-Ru and Amantha. "You're the same color I am!" taunted Rau-Ru in one advertisement. "He bought her . . . she was his," read a promotional poster swimming in sexual imagery. It pictured DeCarlo grasping at Gable, his cane held up at crotch-height. Poitier was turned the other way, but he gazed upon the lurid embrace. That erotic subtext insinuated that both the mulatto woman and the black man need the affirmation of the white patriarch.[53]

The film further diminishes Poitier in its ostensible portrayal of miscegenation. Rau-Ru chides Amantha for sleeping with a white man, but as Henry Popkin noted in *Commentary*, visual cues weaken that message. DeCarlo is so white that audiences do not viscerally react to the interracial romance. Poitier is so dark, by contrast, that only he carries the burden of "real" black people. When he facilitates the romance of the stars, he directly contradicts his earlier position. Also, in the novel, Rau-Ru lusts after Amantha — "but not in the film, for that would be *real* miscegenation, which is quite a different thing from the union of two high-powered gods of the market place as Clark Gable and Yvonne DeCarlo."[54]

That same ironic tone infused most reviews of *Band of Angels*, and with good reason. The picture offered wilted acting, absurd dialogue, corny melodrama, uninspired direction, an intrusive score, and crude stereotypes. Gable, in particular, looked bored and tired. Many drew the inevitable comparisons to *Gone With the Wind*, and none thought that it measured up. *Newsweek*: "Here is a movie so bad it must be seen to be disbelieved." *New Yorker*: "A spate of romantic hokum." *Los Angeles Mirror-News*: "Just when Hollywood seems to be making a little progress, a movie like 'Band of Angels' comes along."[55]

For all the film's compromises, Warner Brothers had distribution problems. The National Legion of Decency gave the picture an unfavorable Class B rating for its "suggestive costuming and situations." Censorship boards in Chicago and Richmond demanded cuts of lewd dialogue, especially exchanges that suggested black sexuality. Because of the miscegenation theme, Chicago also restricted minors from the film. Notoriously conservative boards in Memphis and Atlanta approved the picture through gritted teeth. A Memphis censor explained that "we didn't like the picture, but we couldn't put our finger on any legal reason for banning it."[56]

Warner Brothers tried to anticipate southern objections, especially over a scene where Poitier slaps DeCarlo. A studio executive sent a transcript to their Atlanta office that established Amantha's drop of black blood. The accompanying note emphasized that "it is a negro striking a negress, and not a negro striking a white woman." With that plot twist, censors could sigh with relief. The mythical virtue of southern white women stayed unsullied.[57]

The black press followed these censorship issues, and it recognized the political value of films that challenged the racial status quo. It further delighted in movies that ruffled white racial sensibilities. Before the film's release, the *Pittsburgh Courier* anticipated a "most daring trip into the realm of interracial romance." Two weeks later, it reported on the tittering speculation about light-skinned black women at the premiere.[58]

Ultimately, however, *Band of Angels* insults black people. Besides Rau-Ru, the slaves worship Bond. Some are morons. There are also ill-advised musical bits, including an embarrassing, clearly dubbed sea chanty by Poitier. Perhaps the most objectionable scene occurs when Gable and DeCarlo arrive at his plantation via steamboat. The black writer John Oliver Killens saw the film with a friend, and he vividly remembered that moment: "When the boat neared the shore, all of his happy faithful slaves were gathered there singing a song of welcome to old massa. White people in the theater were weeping, some slyly, some unashamedly, at the touching scene, when suddenly my friend and I erupted with laughter, because we thought that surely, in the time of Montgomery and Little Rock, this must have been put into the film for comic relief."[59]

❖

Killens had reason to be discouraged with the black image on film, and not just because of *Band of Angels*. In 1957 a Hollywood studio asked Harry Belafonte to star in *The Emperor Jones*, a remake of the Eugene O'Neill play and 1933 film. Belafonte expressed reluctance about the crap-shooting, razor-toting stereotypes. He asked Killens for help. Killens outlined a revamped script: Brutus Jones was no longer a porter but a slave, and he killed a white whipping boss instead of a black gambler. Killens then fashioned an epic of Haitian history featuring Toussaint l'Ouverture and Napoleon.[60]

Poitier was in town during the writer's visit, and he joined them one night in Belafonte's hotel suite. They discussed the plight of blacks in Hollywood, and they anticipated black control over the creative process. "I will never make a movie that will reflect against the dignity of the Negro people," proclaimed Poitier. The next day, the studio rejected

Killens's idea. Belafonte declined the part. The studio searched for another actor. "As sophisticated as we three deemed ourselves," recalled Killens, "we naively thought we could set jaded Hollywood on their uppers."[61]

A new era *had* begun — but not with the seismic shift anticipated by the three artists. No black actor accepted the stereotyped role of Brutus Jones, and the film was never remade. That year *Variety* (which one year earlier had argued that race films were "between the devil and the deep blue sea") noted more pictures with black actors. Urban blacks and international audiences were counterbalancing the lost revenue in the South.[62]

That autumn, the NAACP visited Hollywood. In meetings with the major associations and guilds, it lobbied for more employment in all facets of film production. In the fifteen years since its last visit, black membership in the Screen Actors Guild had dropped from approximately 500 to 125. Blacks also remained outside both creative and technical processes: no writers, no directors, no producers, no camera men, no scenic designers, no press agents, no make-up artists.[63]

Market forces and political trends suggested that Poitier would keep finding vehicles. As the NAACP visit revealed, however, his screen image was in white hands. He could reject unfavorable scripts and stamp his own interpretation on roles, but whites wrote, directed, and produced his films. Well-intentioned liberals such as Martin Baum, David Susskind, and Pandro Berman sought and developed roles for him, but they had white, middle-class sensibilities. Poitier could simmer with outrage, but he could not strike against the institutions of racism. He could express virtue and intelligence, but he had to sacrifice for Rock Hudson or Clark Gable. He could represent black Americans, but he could not find scripts from any black perspective.[64]

Considering Hollywood's past treatment of blacks, however, his noble image carried weight. "Young Sidney Poitier deserves a pat on the back," wrote the *Pittsburgh Courier* in February 1957, "not only for his brilliant screen and television portrayals but for practically creating a new era for budding Negro thespians." The newspaper quoted his condemnation of stereotypical butler and maid parts. "The 'Uncle Tom' is an opportunist," said Poitier, "and when I can get across a true picture of him to the point when Negroes who see the picture can say, 'I could never be an Uncle Tom,' then I feel that I have communicated and they have gotten the message."[65]

By contrast, when Stepin Fetchit praised southerners and blamed his unemployment on "some fellows supposed to be liberal out of New York

City," black critic George Pitts pounced on him. "These are modern times," Pitts wrote, "and your old head scratchin' role is outdated, offensive, not only to your race, but to mankind in general."[66]

Poitier embodied the new politics of image. Especially in the North, whites only learned about blacks from newspapers, magazines, television, and movies. Incidents such as the Montgomery bus boycott spurred sporadic media coverage of political leaders. The public related more often to athletes and entertainers. As long as neither the Republican nor Democratic Parties actively courted black votes, these spokesmen had to focus public attention on racial equality. For instance, at the Prayer Pilgrimage to Washington on 17 May 1957, 30,000 neatly dressed blacks heard speeches not only from political leaders Martin Luther King, A. Philip Randolph, and Adam Clayton Powell, but also entertainers Sammy Davis Jr., Ruby Dee, Harry Belafonte, and Sidney Poitier.[67]

Poitier and Belafonte, in particular, donned the crown once worn by Joe Louis, Paul Robeson, and Jackie Robinson: race man. More than heroes, they symbolized black equality. Their success reflected upon the entire race. To be sure, this position caused complications. For one, it marginalized black women, since only males had this duty. For another, it placed political burdens on men outside politics. "A white entertainer can say anything," explained Belafonte. "No one assumes that he is talking for anybody but himself. But as soon as a Negro celebrity says anything, his words are immediately seized as a statement — not for himself but his people."[68]

But Poitier and Belafonte nevertheless held astonishing power over public sympathies. In September 1957, as Arkansas governor Orval Faubus ordered the National Guard to prevent nine black children from entering Little Rock High School, *New York Post* columnist Barry Gray interviewed Sidney and Juanita Poitier. The couple admired the black children's courage, condemned the white mob outside the school, and demanded that President Eisenhower intervene (as he eventually did, after considerable vacillation). Their comments were reasonable and informed.[69]

Gray did not merely solicit their opinions, however. "Sidney is my friend," he wrote. "He is a Negro, and one of the finest men I've ever met." Gray saw the Little Rock crisis — indeed, the entire racial struggle — through Poitier. He did this despite the actor's Bahamian upbringing and sporadic stints in the South. "It is of Sidney I think of when I read of Governor Faubus in Arkansas, for it was the Faubuses of our time who willed to Sidney, as a child, the park bench and alley as a bed — or, on good nights, the pool table in the small hours when the night's snooker action was over." The writer dramatized Poitier's past with little regard for accuracy or applicability to Little Rock. "It was the Faubuses who denied Sidney the opportunity for equal education, and forced him to grab learning on the run, in short-order joints as a pearl diver, as a boot-black and delivery boy." Faubus personified racism, and Poitier the black Everyman. The nuances of race relations, like the details of the actor's life, were distilled into a basic struggle between good and evil. "What great riches Faubus denies this land when he refuses to give the Sidneys of the future a chance to walk into the better schools of the whites." In Poitier, Gray discovered the tragedy of the past, the resolve of the present, and the hope of the future.[70]

For an established actor brimming with self-confidence, it was quite a burden. For Poitier, with his confused domestic life, perpetual insecurities, and tenuous grasp on security, it was even heavier. His image had political consequences for an entire race. And as he soon learned, it was very important who controlled that image.

PART III
BLACK MAN'S BURDEN

❖ ❖ ❖

CHAPTER 8

DECISIONS

(1957–1959)

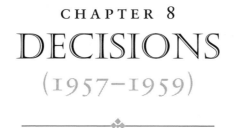

Late 1957 was Poitier's calm before the storm: soft breezes, sandy beaches, and magnificent views. He had signed a generous contract to appear in *Virgin Island*, a picture produced by the British company Countryman Films. He lived in a small hotel on Guana Island, an eleven-acre stretch of paradise near St. Thomas. The cast included friends John Cassavetes, Ruby Dee, and Julian Mayfield. He had a fun, light role as a zesty West Indian. Pressures were few, telephones nonexistent. And each morning, as a motorboat ferried the cast to location, the amply endowed British actress Virginia Maskell removed her top and soaked in the warm Caribbean sun.[1]

The film itself is part travelogue, part fiction from a lowbrow women's magazine. Lush scenery and good humor compensate for the simplistic plot. Poitier plays Marcus, a jovial fisherman who helps newlyweds Evan (Cassavetes) and Tina (Maskell) build a house on a secluded island. The trio endure legal interference from the island commissioner (Colin Gordon) and a visit from Tina's crusty mother (Isabel Dean). Tina gets pregnant and her baby almost arrives prematurely; they sail that night for the hospital. Alas, there is no wind, so Evan swims for help. Marcus fixes his outboard motor and rescues them. At the end, Marcus agrees to marry his girlfriend, Ruth (Dee), and share the island with the white couple.[2]

"A standout performance is given by Sidney Poitier as a gentle, comic islander," wrote *Variety*. The role let him reclaim the singsong speech rhythms and carefree spirit of his youth. He also followed the pattern of his earlier films: Marcus shares the robust good nature of Tommy Tyler in *Edge of the City* and the exotic appeal of his African characters, and he befriends well-intentioned whites, whose interests he serves out of innate warmth.[3]

Poitier cherished his time in St. Thomas. He told columnist Whitney Bolton that he wished to build a house there. He explained that, in contrast to other black colonies (and, one might add, to the sunny picture of white colonialism of *Virgin Island*), "it is native to the core." He preached nonviolent, liberal resolutions to global racial problems: "Sooner or later the African continent will come into the sun of freedom, and unless the West and the whites give it room and a chance, it can be a violent time." St. Thomas was a peaceful alternative; Poitier appreciated the island's black governor and population. "I have a feeling there such as no other place gives me. I am with my own and we work in a common, self-respecting destiny."[4]

As a career vehicle, *Virgin Island* was of less consequence. Despite predictions of nationwide exhibition, it crawled into American theaters in March 1960 as the second feature behind *Sink the Bismarck!* Yet Poitier's Caribbean stint proved important. On location in November, he heard from agent Martin Baum that Samuel Goldwyn had offered him the lead in the Gershwin folk opera *Porgy and Bess*. He would receive first billing and a $75,000 paycheck, two personal milestones. But he rejected the part. *Porgy and Bess* presented blacks as dice-rolling, gin-swilling, razor-toting stereotypes. Poitier played characters of dignity, not emasculated beggars.[5]

A week later, however, Poitier picked up a three-day-old *New York Times* and read that Goldwyn had announced his participation in *Porgy and Bess*. Against his wishes, and against the black political tide, Poitier was roped into a controversy that revealed his limited control over his own image. It was a time of difficult decisions, and a firsthand lesson in Hollywood power. He flew to New York. The calm ended, and the storm began.[6]

❖

Back in March 1947, Samuel Goldwyn had been on top of the world. At the podium of the Shrine Auditorium, surrounded by the Hollywood establishment in elegant evening wear, the producer was holding his second Academy Award of the ceremony. The first time, he accepted the Oscar for his picture of returning war veterans called *The Best Years of Our Lives*. Now, as he grasped the Irving Thalberg Award for "the most consistently high quality of production" that year, he choked back tears. By night's end, *The Best Years of Our Lives* would win seven Oscars. Goldwyn counted his Thalberg Award and an honorary Oscar for Harold Russell in his tally, so that his picture bested *Gone With the Wind*'s record of eight Academy Awards.[7]

That was typical salesmanship for the man born Schmuel Gelbfisz in

Warsaw, Poland, an immigrant glove salesman who changed his name to Samuel Goldfish and helped start the movie business. He co-produced the first feature-length picture filmed in Hollywood, the 1914 Cecil B. De-Mille western *The Squaw Man*. Like the other great movie moguls, he was an Eastern European Jew creating a national popular culture of glamorous, idealized stars. Unlike the others, he thrived without heading a studio.[8]

Ousted in power struggles from the studios that became Paramount and MGM, the man now known as Samuel Goldwyn became Holly-wood's first great independent producer. He developed Ronald Colman and Vilma Banky, Gary Cooper and David Niven, Danny Kaye and Eddie Cantor. Impeccably tailored in old-fashioned suits, proud to a fault, he chafed at his reputation for high-pitched, heavily accented "Goldwyn-isms" ("Include me out"; "A verbal agreement isn't worth the paper it's written on"; "Anyone seeing a psychiatrist should have his head exam-ined"). He survived with an extraordinary business sense, a persistent de-mand for the finest quality talent, and a salesman's gift for manipulation.[9]

By 1957, Goldwyn was the last of the movie moguls. The studio system had disintegrated. His old rivals were dead, dying, or retiring. Box-office receipts had dropped, and Universal and RKO had been sold to television companies. The films had changed, too. A 1956 overhaul of the Produc-tion Code removed bans on many old screen taboos, including mis-cegenation. Some opted for low-budget psychological dramas such as *Marty* or *On the Waterfront*. Others experimented with technological innovations unavailable on the small screen: large-scale biblical epics and musicals, Cinemascope, Cinerama, 3-D, even Smell-O-Vision.[10]

Goldwyn, well into his seventies, demanded bigger and better. He pro-duced lavish films with gigantic promotional campaigns, always looking for the next *The Best Years of Our Lives*. "My father got compulsive about producing each picture as though it were his last," remembered his son Samuel Jr. "*That* was the one he would go out on, the one he'd be remembered for."[11]

Goldwyn believed that *Porgy and Bess* would be his ultimate achieve-ment, the fulfillment of a longstanding dream to bring Gershwin to the screen. Over three decades earlier, in Charleston, South Carolina, a cot-ton checker named DuBose Heyward toiled on the docks with Low Coun-try blacks. Inspired by the story of a crippled beggar, he wrote the 1925 novel *Porgy*.[12]

In 1927 Heyward and his wife Dorothy adapted the book to stage. Their successful Broadway play trafficked in negative stereotypes of African Americans: Porgy begs for pennies by day and rolls dice by night; Bess succumbs to temptations both narcotic and sexual; Crown abuses liquor and women; Sportin' Life is a cocaine-sniffing ne'er-do-well. The denizens of Catfish Row sing away hardships, kowtow to whites, and superstitiously panic when buzzards fly overhead. The drama itself addresses Bess's decision between Porgy's moral kindness and Crown's seductive power. In the end, neither wins: Porgy kills Crown and avoids imprisonment, but Sportin' Life seduces Bess with "Happy Dust" and the lure of New York City. With eternal faith, Porgy hitches up his goat cart and searches for Bess.[13]

Heyward then collaborated with George and Ira Gershwin on a 1935 opera. That version garnered mixed reviews and mediocre gate receipts, but no one denied the genius of George Gershwin's music: "Summertime," "I Got Plenty O' Nuttin'," "Bess, You Is My Woman Now," "It Ain't Necessarily So." When Cheryl Crawford replaced the recitatives with spoken dialogue for a 1942 reinterpretation, it flourished. *Porgy and Bess* embarked upon a three-year nationwide tour and won status as a "classic."[14]

Producers Blevins Davis and Robert Breen staged another revival in 1952, traveling to American cities and European capitals before a triumphant Broadway landing in 1953. Then came a comprehensive national tour, and then another international tour under the auspices of the State Department. *Porgy and Bess* toured Europe, the Middle East, and Latin America. Soviet Premier Nikita Khrushchev broke protocol and attended the second Moscow show; he could not wait for the final performance.[15]

The black press was ambivalent. Although the production showcased black talent, it sold a government-endorsed image of black vice and sensuality. The *New York Amsterdam News* called it "a degrading play which the Negro needs like he needs a hole in his head." Trade newspapers had no such reservations. Davis and Breen, *Variety* suggested, were cultural ambassadors. "They have better than a portfolio; they have 'Porgy and Bess.' "[16]

As early as 1935, Hollywood wanted *Porgy and Bess*. Over ninety producers sought the film rights. Goldwyn finally won the property in May 1957 and began searching for the finest talent. Writers Langston Hughes, Sidney Kingsley, Clifford Odets, and the team of Jerome Lawrence and Robert E. Lee all declined before Goldwyn settled on Richard Nash. Directors Elia Kazan, Frank Capra, and King Vidor also passed. Goldwyn hired Rouben Mamoulian, director of the original stage version.[17]

Goldwyn next sought a top-notch cast. He wanted Harry Belafonte for Porgy, but the singer rebuffed him. "He says he'll never play any role which demands that he spend all his time on his knees," reported the *Pittsburgh Courier*. Belafonte also lobbied Dorothy Dandridge to reject playing Bess. The response bewildered Goldwyn, who blamed "an underground movement by radicals." His press releases to black and Jewish newspaper syndicates trumpeted the picture as a triumph over racial prejudice. In the 1930s, that might have been true. By 1957, black image politics dictated a resistance to *Porgy and Bess*. Still, Goldwyn forged on. He donated $1,000 to the NAACP and pledged profits to charity. *Porgy and Bess* would be a monument to his resolve.[18]

Goldwyn's biggest coup was landing Poitier, whom he signed with equal parts luck and pluck. Martin Baum had a West Coast associate named Lillian Small. When Goldwyn inquired after Poitier, Small promised the actor's services without consulting him. On 4 November, a Goldwyn spokesman announced that Poitier would play Porgy. When Poitier flew back to New York, he consulted with Belafonte, Ossie Davis, Ivan Dixon, and Loften Mitchell. Then he met with Mamoulian and Nash and asked if they planned significant changes from the stage version. They said no. He declined the part again.[19]

Poitier called Goldwyn and explained his decision. Before returning to St. Thomas, he told the *New York Amsterdam News* that he bore a responsibility to play roles "constructive to my life as a Negro." In *Porgy and Bess*, "there is simply one too many crap game." The newspaper applauded him: the front-page headline read "Poitier Puts $75,000 Tag on Race Pride." The article linked him to a "new and young militant group of Negro actors" demanding more dignified roles.[20]

The folk hero treatment ended there, as Goldwyn's publicity machine spun the negotiations to make Poitier look arrogant. On 10 November, Goldwyn announced that the actor had demanded script approval before leaving the film. Rumors swirled. Barry Gray reported that Belafonte "put the 'Uncle Tom' bee in Poitier's noggin." The *Daily Defender* wondered if success had spoiled Poitier. At Goldwyn's behest, *New York Post* columnist Leonard Lyons wrote that Poitier's friends were lobbying him to play Porgy. Lyons even quoted Ralph Bunche, who believed that *Porgy and Bess* was "a classic, and ought to be preserved on film."[21]

When Poitier returned from St. Thomas in late November, Baum urged him to meet with Goldwyn. "I smelled a trap," Poitier remembered, but he wanted to avoid ruffling the ego of a powerful Hollywood producer. Actor and agent flew to Los Angeles. Poitier fumed at Lillian Small, especially after she mistakenly drove them to the house of Columbia head Harry Cohn. After Mrs. Cohn gave directions to the Goldwyn estate, they finally met Goldwyn and Mamoulian. Baum acted as moderator, briefly recounting the situation. Goldwyn and Poitier then exchanged long compliments, each drowning the other in a sea of honey.[22]

Two versions exist of what next transpired: the media version, and the Hollywood back-room version. The initial report cast Poitier as Goldwyn's pupil in racial politics. Supposedly, after Poitier expressed his reservations, Goldwyn launched into a passionate soliloquy, extolling *Porgy and Bess*. Then Mamoulian explained the "poetry and emotional richness" within Porgy. After two hours, with "chills running up and down his spine," Poitier leapt to his feet and proclaimed: "I will come to you completely pure, virginal and unprejudiced!" The actor claimed to have previously understood *Porgy and Bess* from an album cover synopsis. After their meeting, he embraced Goldwyn's racial sensitivity, and he agreed to play Porgy.[23]

Poitier tells a different story. Goldwyn did recount the folk opera's glorious history, even calling *Porgy and Bess* "one of the greatest things that has ever happened to the black race." But Poitier considered that opinion "outrageous bullshit." Also, after Goldwyn finished, the mogul merely urged that Poitier delay his final decision. With a sly smile, Goldwyn bade farewell.[24]

While still in Los Angeles, Poitier met Stanley Kramer. Like Goldwyn, Kramer was an independent producer, and he was Jewish. The similarities ended there. Kramer was sturdily built, boyishly handsome, and unfailingly direct. A product of Hell's Kitchen, New York University, and the Army Signal Corps, he wore his liberal politics on his sleeve. Part of the postwar generation rising from the ashes of the studio system, Kramer had made some innovative, socially conscious films: *Home of the Brave* (1949), *The Men* (1950), *High Noon* (1952), *The Wild One* (1954). Kramer had just signed a six-picture distribution deal with United Artists. His survival in the movie industry challenged the common Hollywood adage that "if you want to send a message, call Western Union"—an adage attributed to Samuel Goldwyn.[25]

Kramer handed Poitier a script for *The Long Road*, a story of two escaped prisoners—one black, one white—linked by handcuffs. He later changed the title to *The Defiant Ones*. Poitier loved it. The taut, action-packed drama challenged racial prejudice. His character had passion and depth. The film would propel his career. Kramer offered Poitier a lead role, with a caveat: Poitier needed a release from Goldwyn. Although

Poitier had signed nothing, Small had promised his services. Kramer feared a lawsuit, which would cripple the production.[26]

Now Goldwyn's glossy charm melted away. He held the actor to Small's promise. Poitier had two choices: accept both parts, or accept neither. "Suddenly," he recalled, "decisions of a very political nature were on my doorstep." *The Defiant Ones* would open doors, and rejecting Goldwyn might damage his reputation within Hollywood. In early December 1957, out of some combination of ambition and racial responsibility, he signed a $75,000 contract for *Porgy and Bess* and a $15,000 contract for *The Defiant Ones*. Goldwyn staged a press conference, parading Poitier before reporters. The actor endorsed Goldwyn's whitewashed account. His reservations, he claimed, had been "washed away in the warm and wonderful explanation of the plans." Poitier looked indecisive, naive, and supplicant to the paternalistic producer.[27]

With Poitier on board, resistance from other quarters fizzled. Dorothy Dandridge signed one week later, followed by Pearl Bailey and Brock Peters. Goldwyn wanted Cab Calloway as Sportin' Life, but he signed Sammy Davis Jr., whom he had once dismissed as "that monkey." The popular nightclub performer had campaigned for the role. Itching to escape Las Vegas for Hollywood, he wanted to star opposite Elvis Presley in *The Defiant Ones*, but Presley's manager Colonel Tom Parker squelched the idea. Davis then enlisted Frank Sinatra, Jack Benny, and George Burns to lobby Goldwyn on his behalf. Goldwyn appeared backstage at the Moulin Rouge. "Mr. Davis, you are Sportin' Life," he announced. "The part is yours. Now will you get all these guys off my back?"[28]

Poitier was less enthusiastic than Davis. He returned to New York in December, his image compromised. The *Amsterdam News*, Langston Hughes recalled, "never informed Harlemites as to just what happened, so they were left wondering if Goldwyn's price went up, or Poitier's pride went down." Friends and associates expressed disappointment. When Poitier explained his decision to Belafonte, he listened, but he never accepted the rationale. Worse, a doubt niggled at Poitier: had Goldwyn, Small, and Baum conspired to put Poitier in *Porgy and Bess*? They all knew about Kramer's property, and they all anticipated his decision. "In other words," he recalled, "I think I was manipulated. As smart as I thought I was, that time the white folks were smarter."[29]

❖

Kramer had Poitier first. Because of Poitier's *Porgy and Bess* commitments, he had to release the actor by early April 1958. He scrambled for a white actor to play the other fugitive. He sought Kirk Douglas, Gregory Peck, Frank Sinatra, Burt Lancaster, Anthony Quinn, and many others. He really wanted Marlon Brando, then at his peak. Kramer salivated at the thought of Brando and Poitier together: "You wouldn't need a script. Just turn on the cameras and let things happen." Brando embraced the script's integrationist politics but rebuffed Kramer. Kramer later claimed that Brando was stuck in Tahiti shooting *Mutiny on the Bounty*. In fact, Brando did not go to Tahiti until 1960. He turned it down because he disliked Kramer's direction in *The Wild One*.[30]

Kramer cast Tony Curtis, a decision that amused the industry establishment. Stuck playing fluff parts in comedies, Curtis yearned for respect as a legitimate actor. With characteristic manic energy, he later joked that Kramer hired him only because Brando wanted to play the black part, and Kirk Douglas wanted to play both parts. Actually, he overcame Kramer's doubts during their interview, when he passionately discussed his craft. After winning the job, he even forsook his pretty-boy image by donning a misshapen plastic nose.[31]

On set, Poitier flexed the muscles that came with a lead role. In the first week, he twice pulled Kramer aside and questioned whether Curtis could play the role. Later, Poitier assured Kramer that Curtis was doing well, bolstering the director's confidence. Kramer held Poitier in high esteem, higher than he ever held Curtis. Yet Curtis asked to share top billing with Poitier, even though their contracts specified that only Curtis's name appear above the title. With that generous gesture, Poitier officially became a star.[32]

They filmed *The Defiant Ones* in just one month, in March 1958. Kramer closed the set to avoid distractions or controversies over the film's racial theme. He shot 80 percent on exterior locations throughout southern California, often in arduous conditions. Poitier and Curtis rarely used stunt doubles. Bound by a twenty-nine-inch chain, they sloshed out of a sloppy clay pit, brawled down the side of a hill, and crossed a swollen river. During the river crossing, they wore skintight diving suits under their prison uniforms to endure the thirty-eight-degree water, and they struggled from rock to rock until midstream, where the current pushed them into rapids. Luckily, stunt men downriver saved them, and the scene became a memorable one.[33]

The Defiant Ones was a benchmark for all three men: stardom for Poitier, legitimacy for Curtis, profit and pride for Kramer. It also struck a blow against the blacklist. By the late 1950s, blacklisted writers, directors, and actors often worked under assumed names. For instance,

"Hollywood Ten" member Ring Lardner Jr. had co-written *Virgin Island* under the pen name Philip Rush (prompting an indignant letter to the *London Times* from a British historian actually named Philip Rush). For *The Defiant Ones*, Kramer hired screenwriter Nedrick Young.[34]

Young had acted on Broadway and in B movies before HUAC subpoenaed him in 1953. He refused to testify and was blacklisted. After stretches behind a bar and on a Chevrolet assembly line, he hatched *The Defiant Ones*. With Harold Jacob Smith, he drafted revisions over three years. Young wrote under a pseudonym. When Kramer bought the script, he not only gave the writers a cut of the profits, but also cast them as prison truck drivers in the opening scene. In a sly cinematic joke, Kramer superimposed the credits on the drivers. Under Young appeared his pen name, "Nathan E. Douglas."[35]

As Smith and Young drive, Noah Cullen (Poitier) howls the folk song "Long Gone." John "Joker" Jackson (Curtis) snaps: "You heard what the man said, nigger, now shut up." Cullen leaps up: "You call me nigger again, Joker, and I'm gonna kill you!" They establish their mutual hatred just before the truck gets sideswiped. The handcuffed pair escape, sprinting for miles. When Cullen demands to head north, Jackson protests that they are not married. "You married to me all right, Joker," Cullen says, holding up the chain, "and here's the ring."

They cross an angry river and dive into a clay pit, cooperating in spite of their differences. At night, they learn about each other. Joker chafes at his old dead-end service jobs; he wants money, power, to be "Charlie Potatoes." Cullen hates Jackson's racial slurs; he wants respect and equality. They discuss their family problems. Yet race still divides them. After residents of a small company town capture them, a lynching is imminent. "You can't go lynching me," Jackson protests. "I'm a white man."

They escape, but when they stop, Cullen rages at Jackson. "You're not even a man," he growls, "you're a monkey on a stick." He resents that Jackson used his race to plead for mercy, and they wrestle. They finally remove their chain at an isolated farm, where they meet a lonely woman (Cara Williams). Jackson, though weak from infection, romances her. She and Jackson agree to escape by car. Cullen again steams that Jackson has abandoned him. Only later does Jackson learn that she has sent Cullen into a deadly swamp. He forsakes the woman to find Cullen, taking a bullet in the shoulder as he leaves. By the time the pair reunite, Jackson is weak.

They reach railroad tracks just as a train pulls away. Cullen leaps on and holds out his arm, but Jackson cannot reach. Jackson tumbles down the hill, and Cullen leaps off. The film ends as the bloodhounds bark and the sheriff approaches. The black man tends to the white one, cradling him and howling "Long Gone."

The intimate physical contact in that final scene culminates a barrage of images with homoerotic undertones. After they cross the river, the men lie in exhaustion on each other. As they sleep, Cullen's head rests on Jackson's chest. Cullen holds Jackson's hand while tending to his infection. In one ironic turn, Cullen smears mud onto Jackson's face to avoid detection in the moonlight. Even after they remove the physical chain, a psychological chain links them. When they separate, they resemble a romantic couple: Cullen is angry, and Jackson guilty. Both enjoy their reunion, even as they trudge through a swamp. Their friendship, not their failed escape, is the film's climax.[36]

The Defiant Ones first appeared at the Berlin Film Festival, in June 1958. European critics loved it. Kramer had given the film a spare, direct feel. He eliminated all dissolves and fadeouts in favor of straight cuts, and he eschewed background music to highlight Poitier's dissonant song and a deputy's transistor radio. His direction complemented the tight script and lightning performances. The praise was so strong that Kramer hastened its American premiere.[37]

Poitier received the Silver Bear Award as the festival's best actor. "His human warmth and modesty, combined with dignity and honesty, gave an unusual demonstration of tolerance and kindheartedness which is indispensable between people of good will." A month later, Eleanor Roosevelt presented Poitier with the trophy at her New York home.[38]

The black press celebrated Poitier's achievement as "a giant step toward fulfillment of his ambition — top rating as an untyped star of stars, period." His eminence, along with the film's liberal message, woke United Artists to the financial potential of the African American market. The distributor concocted promotions that targeted the black community. It urged exhibitors to contact local preachers and suggest sermons about the film. It also suggested tying Poitier's award to the good works of local black organizations. In New York City, *Amsterdam News* editor Jimmy Hicks and *Post* reporter Ted Poston won a "Defiant Ones Award." In Chicago, Ghanaian prime minister Kwame Nkrumah accepted the same honor.[39]

The mainstream promotional material, conversely, emphasized sex. Posters pictured Poitier and Curtis snarling at each other, bound by a chain, bare muscles flexed to the point of caricature. An inset recalled the poster from *Band of Angels*: Curtis and Williams are locked in embrace, with Poitier looking on. The accompanying text reads, "He watched them — and listened for the dogs!" Actually, in the film, Poitier's character sleeps at the kitchen table during the romance. But the advertisement underscores Kramer's quasi-erotic treatment of their interracial connection. At film's end, Cullen and Jackson bond only after casting off the woman. Poitier again competes with a white woman for the white man's favor.[40]

Before the August premiere in Chicago, representatives of the city's civic, fraternal, and union groups attended special screenings. Kramer appeared on eight television and fifteen radio programs, and he judged a black beauty contest for "Miss World Premiere." One week later, Poitier appeared on ten television and twenty-one radio programs, and he led the annual "Bud Billiken Day" parade on the city's South Side. The effort paid off, as *The Defiant Ones* broke records at the Roosevelt Theatre and earned good reviews.[41]

The Defiant Ones opened in New York City in late September, and in other major cities the following week. Some lauded the lofty social aim. "Here is a visible symbol of a basic social idea," waxed Bosley Crowther of the *New York Times*. "To wit, that categories of human beings are fettered by powerful restraints, which men would do better to work together, rather than separately, to throw off." Trade newspapers applauded the fast-paced action, downplaying the racial message: "Kramer takes no sides, avoids any direct preachment." "At no time is the film a 'preachment' or a castigation." "It never goes from rousing to rabble-rousing."[42]

Poitier became Hollywood's first black actor to achieve stardom solely for his dramatic talents. He did not sing, dance, or joke. *Newsweek* called him "the country's finest Negro actor." Black publications trumpeted him for an Academy Award nomination, and one speculated that *The Defiant Ones* might be "the greatest motion picture to come out of Hollywood in many years."[43]

It captured a host of accolades. In 1958, the New York Film Critics awarded it Best Picture, Best Director, and Best Screenplay. The Film Critics' Circle of the Foreign Language Press, the British Film Academy, and the Newspaper Guild of New York gave it awards. Film festivals in Venice, Mexico City, San Francisco, and Sydney bid for its exhibition. In early 1959, it won nine Academy Award nominations: Best Picture, Best Director, Best Original Screenplay, Best Cinematography, Best Film Editing, Best Supporting Actor, Best Supporting Actress, and two for Best Actor — one for Tony Curtis, and one for Sidney Poitier.[44]

Black Hollywood reached a milestone. Hattie McDaniel had won Best

Supporting Actress for *Gone with the Wind* (1939), and James Baskette had received a posthumous special Oscar for *Song of the South* (1946), but Poitier's nomination was the first accorded a leading black actor. Unlike the others, Poitier fulfilled no traditional black stereotypes. Unfortunately, the nomination of Curtis cost each actor a chance at victory. Those favoring *The Defiant Ones* split their votes. David Niven won for *Separate Tables*, as expected.[45]

Nedrick Young and Harold Jacob Smith did win Best Original Screenplay, signaling another important shift in Hollywood politics. Before the nominations, Young had announced that he co-wrote *The Defiant Ones* under a pseudonym. The Academy, realizing the superiority of the script, rescinded its 1957 edict banning blacklisted talent from the Oscars. After the ban's repeal, "Hollywood Ten" member Dalton Trumbo admitted that he wrote *The Brave One*—winner of Best Original Screenplay two years earlier—under a pseudonym. The next year, Kramer hired Young and Smith to write *Inherit the Wind*, and Otto Preminger tapped Trumbo to adapt *Exodus*. The blacklist further dissolved.[46]

After the Oscars, *The Defiant Ones* kept winning awards for fostering humanitarian bonds. It even became a direct weapon against racial segregation. Under the sponsorship of a Methodist Church board, the Protestant Film Council arranged an integrated exhibition in Louisville. The World Council of Churches then began a campaign for similarly integrated shows in church halls and meetings throughout the South.[47]

Yet as *The Defiant Ones* basked in critical acclaim, earned large profits, and enlightened audiences, few saw the film in the Deep South. Southern theater owners still refused pictures that touched on racial issues; they feared negative publicity or boycotts. In Montgomery, Alabama, theater manager A. B. Covey canceled a one-week run of *The Defiant Ones* after receiving a telegram from the White Citizens Council that branded the picture pro-integration, anti-South, and Communist-inspired. "I just didn't want any trouble," said Covey. "And you can never tell about those things." Council president Bruce Wyatt elaborated: "We just don't like it. We think it's a dangerous film."[48]

The "danger" stemmed from Poitier's characterization of Noah Cullen. "His presence, sprung with inner tensions, radiant with force, amplifies the character even beyond what the authors have written," wrote Stanley Kauffman. Cullen rages at a life of "Yassuh, boss." He references a lynching with chilling gravity. He aches with the memory of debt-ridden farm life. And he seethes with frustration at his wife's timid acceptance of racial codes: "From my wife, 'be nice.' They throw me in solitary confinement, and she say 'be nice.' Man short-whip me when I turn in my crop, and she say 'be nice or you're gonna get in trouble.' She teach my kid that same damn thing. I never could get that woman to understand how I was feeling inside. All of a sudden there was nothing left to say." Poitier displays remarkable range: snapping with fury, simmering with resentment, smiling with understanding, caring with love. He does not idealize Noah Cullen; with astonishing sensitivity, he breathes three-dimensional life into him.[49]

Still, no matter how powerful Poitier's performance, *The Defiant Ones* exhibited the perspective of white liberals. Kramer and the screenwriters saw triumph in the convicts' friendship, but they compressed racial problems into a personal relationship. The resolution ignored Cullen's second-class citizenship. When Cullen jumped off the train, it replicated Poitier's pattern. As in *No Way Out*, as in *Edge of the City*, as in *Band of Angels*, racial understanding occurs only after the black man's sacrifice.[50]

James Baldwin saw *The Defiant Ones* twice: first on Broadway, then in Harlem. The first time, at the end, the white audience sighed and clapped, moved by Cullen's noble gesture. Baldwin scoffed. "He jumps off the train," the writer explained, "in order to reassure white people, to make them know that they are not hated; that, though they have made human errors, they have done nothing for which to be hated." As Montgomery and Little Rock exposed white racism at its most objectionable, liberal whites craved the racial message inherent in Cullen's sacrifice.

Then Baldwin went uptown. Again, Cullen jumped off the train and stayed with his white friend. Only this time, a black audience roared, pleaded, and howled: "*Get back on the train, you fool!*"[51]

❖

Poitier recognized the compromises of black sacrifice. Liberal white film-makers presented him as a figure of great humanity, a symbol of prejudice. "So they make a statement," he said. "And the statement finally is, 'You should be nice to your colored friends. They too are human beings.' Well, this is messy, you know."[52]

Before the civil rights demonstrations of the 1960s, the message did have weight: if people sympathized with his virtuous characters, they could sympathize with others enduring racial injustice. But reducing race problems to human relationships — and constantly sacrificing Sidney Poitier — ignored the wider dimensions of prejudice.

Poitier thus attempted to disassociate *The Defiant Ones* from larger race issues. "It doesn't try to tell the South anything," he told Mike Wallace. "It just says here is one guy, a Negro, who says this guy, a white man, is all right. It's kept on a strictly personal basis and doesn't try to answer the world's race problem." Perhaps to sidestep black criticism, perhaps to avoid an outsized responsibility, he often touted this message.[53]

Publicity for the picture also addressed Poitier's personal life, a treatment befitting his new stardom. In interview after interview, he crafted a persona with broad appeal: a middle-class family man, a tolerant soul, a loyal patriot. A brief profile in *Look* included sketches of his family life. The *New York Amsterdam News* described him as a doting father with a weakness for beans and rice. He told Hedda Hopper about Juanita's domestic virtues. He also soft-pedaled on racial discrimination, arguing that he moved "in a world where primarily a man functions on merit." When Hopper sank into condescension ("I've never known any of your people who couldn't sing"), Poitier responded with grace. When she asked about *Brown vs. Board of Education*, he painted in Cold War hues: "Let's not give the other fellow an edge so he can say — you sell a hypocritical kind of democracy."[54]

Poitier's rising profile built anticipation for *Porgy and Bess*, slated to begin shooting in July 1958. Samuel Goldwyn fidgeted while Richard Nash finished the script. One night Goldwyn called at 3:00 A.M. Nash groggily asked if he realized the late hour. Goldwyn shouted to his wife, "Frances, Mr. Nash wants to know the time."[55]

By April they submitted a draft to the Production Code Administration. The PCA worried about the impropriety of Bess living in Porgy's home. Goldwyn and Mamoulian assuaged that since "Porgy is a cripple . . . there would be no suggestion whatever of a sex relation between them." With Porgy's neuterdom established, Goldwyn's anticipation grew. He announced that they would film in Todd-AO, a colorful wide-screen process with six-channel stereophonic sound. Goldwyn insisted that it was worth the $1.5 million price tag.[56]

Poitier worked with Robert McFerrin, the voice of Porgy, to hone his lip-synchronization of the lyrics. In late June he met with Goldwyn and underwent wardrobe fittings. Then, in the wee hours of 2 July, a fire burned down Sound Stage Eight at Samuel Goldwyn Studios, site of the elaborate Catfish Row set. Goldwyn estimated the damage at $2 million. By that afternoon, some were suggesting that black protesters had burned down the stage. (Witnesses reported a series of explosions precipitating the fire.) Although Goldwyn and NAACP representatives denied the possibility of arson, they never determined the fire's cause.[57]

Goldwyn pressed on. At an emergency meeting that afternoon, he resolved to build a better set, and he passed out a new production schedule that set a new start date of 27 August. At this meeting, Poitier met Diahann Carroll. The light-skinned, high-cheekboned nightclub singer had a minor part. She was slender, with alluring eyes and a slightly prim reserve. She had fashioned some fabric into an elegant headdress. Poitier was intrigued.[58]

Carroll was overwhelmed. When Poitier had entered the room, he had introduced himself to each cast member. "His presence was so mesmerizing, his whole bearing so unashamedly sexual, that I was overtaken by the moment," Carroll confessed. She already admired him for his talent and reputation. As Poitier made his rounds, she crossed and recrossed her legs. She was moved, stirred by his grace. He sensed her nervousness. He greeted her, bellowed a deep laugh, pulled her in for the slightest second, and flirted: "Nice to see you. We must talk." Their "talk" came later, after they returned from their unexpected month off.[59]

During the hiatus, he and Juanita vacationed in Acapulco, Mexico, with Martin Baum and his wife, Bernice. Retired baseball pioneer Jackie Robinson and his wife Rachel joined them. One day Poitier and Baum waded into the ocean. The undertow pulled them away from shore. For minutes, they fought the tide, clawed at the sand, and screamed for help. But their wives chatted far away, and the lifeguard had his nose in a magazine. With their muscles near submission, a wave swept them near shore, and the lifeguard pulled them to safety. Twenty minutes later Baum was snapping off wisecracks. But Poitier took stock. "We love; we work; we raise our families," he later wrote, remembering that day's lesson. "And love and work and family are the legacy we leave behind when our little moment in the sun is gone."[60]

Love, work, family — it sounded simple. As he returned to Hollywood, however, maintaining a firm grasp on those basic categories was anything but simple.

❖

The set of *Porgy and Bess* was bedlam, a cauldron of conflicts and accusations. Goldwyn resented the press attention accorded Mamoulian. The director, a monumental ego in his own right, suspected that Goldwyn was growing senile. Mamoulian also criticized the airing of films on television, which irked his boss, who wanted to sell his properties to the networks. Goldwyn ordered Mamoulian to fire his press agent. He insisted on identification as "sole creator" of the film, and he demanded that Mamoulian work without pay during the layoff. They feuded.[61]

In late July, Frances Goldwyn sent a peace offering, inviting the Mamoulians over for dinner. They enjoyed a fine evening. The next morning, Mamoulian learned that Goldwyn had already fired him. Goldwyn's press release explained that "he and I could not see eye to eye on various matters." Mamoulian thundered back that the producer's "bland statement hides a story of deceit and calumny."[62]

Goldwyn replaced him with Otto Preminger. Again, filming was delayed. Mamoulian took his production manager, cameraman, and assistant director with him, and Preminger demanded script revisions, set changes, and three more weeks of rehearsal. That pushed the start date to 16 September. Then the Screen Directors Guild interrogated the producer about his abrupt dismissal of Mamoulian. Goldwyn remained atypically serene and refused to expound upon his original statement. On 3 August, the guild announced a boycott against Goldwyn. Preminger defied the edict.[63]

A few days later, race politics entered the cauldron. Leigh Whipper—president of the Negro Actors Guild and stage veteran of *Porgy and Bess*—withdrew from the production, claiming that Preminger "has no respect for my people." He argued that only Mamoulian could stage the production with dignity, and he alluded to a mysterious, ten-year-old incident that allegedly illustrated Preminger's prejudice.[64]

Whipper's charges actually helped Goldwyn. The media noted that Mamoulian's press agent staged the press conference; Whipper seemed a pawn of the ousted director. He also seemed a blowhard for exaggerating his minor role as the "Crabman." Pearl Bailey, Sammy Davis Jr., Brock Peters, and NAACP spokesman Loren Miller issued statements supporting Preminger and Goldwyn. Poitier—who remembered Whipper waving a gun at him in the early 1950s—termed the accusations "ridiculous."[65]

But the conflict burned on, stoked by black voices. In a two-page advertisement in the *Los Angeles Tribune*, Almena Lomax of the Council for Improvement of Negro Theatre Arts criticized Goldwyn's paternalistic command of *Porgy and Bess*. "The air is heavy with sycophancy," she wrote. Decrying the producer's smug dismissals of suggestions to hire a black writer, she noted that Goldwyn's only full-time black employees hauled trash. She also criticized "a Negro leadership which prostitutes itself for a handful of blacks." She singled out Poitier, who "had his brains washed by Goldwyn a long time ago." At a press conference, Poitier "put on his beamish black boy act. He did everything except scratch his 'haid.'" For the first time, Poitier received public criticism as an Uncle Tom.[66]

Poitier was no toady of the white establishment, but he did lend some contrived overstatements. From Chicago, he expressed optimism that *Porgy and Bess* would rank as an all-time great film musical. On a brief trip home, he rubber-stamped Goldwyn's version of their negotiations. He later proclaimed that "other roles may come and go, but I expect the role of Porgy to stay with me for a lifetime." He admired the character's faith and resolve: "Ten years from now, somebody will call out 'Porgy' and I'll stand up and salute and say, 'Yes, sir.'" More than a fulfillment of responsibility, this was outrageous hyperbole. To rationalize his participation, he had deluded himself into believing that Porgy deserved his complete reverence.[67]

Meanwhile, Goldwyn won his battle with Mamoulian. The Directors Guild rejected Mamoulian's claim that he deserved partial screen credit. But Goldwyn and Mamoulian had a love affair compared to Goldwyn and Preminger. A man of massive frame, shiny bald head, and glowering blue eyes, Preminger had directed and produced another all-black musical, *Carmen Jones*. He was staunchly independent and notoriously stubborn. When he agreed to direct *Porgy and Bess*, clashes with his meddling boss seemed inevitable.[68]

They were. Crew members congregated under Preminger's open window to hear their screaming matches. Once Goldwyn complained that Preminger was not shooting with two cameras, one for 70 mm film and another for 35 mm film. He did not understand that the 70 mm print could be reduced if necessary. According to Preminger, Goldwyn was "the laugh of the lot." They also bickered over the music. Preminger wanted jazzy arrangements treated as extensions of scenes, not distinct musical numbers. Goldwyn, faithful to Gershwin, insisted upon an operatic style.[69]

On the first day of rehearsal, Preminger battled anew—this time with the cast, led by Poitier. The original script contained servile, stereotyped dialogue that jangled with Poitier's polished middle-class image. Although the script lacked the exaggerated rhythms of Heyward's play, Richard Nash had revised such words as "crying," "singing," and "looking," to "cryin'," "singin'," and "lookin'." The tension was palpable. "It wasn't like a sound stage," recalled an observer. "It was like a guerrilla war."[70]

Poitier started in dialect. Then he changed to standard English. Then, noted a witness, "Sidney got positively Shakespearean." The cast followed his lead. Poitier got off his knees and walked over to Preminger: "All right, Otto, should we talk it over?" The director authorized the elimination of dialect. Pearl Bailey enforced the provision forthwith, ranting at an actor who kept saying, "Ain't I done told you?"[71]

Preminger's accommodation of the actors' demands revealed a degree of racial sensitivity. The Austrian Jew had fled Hitler and hated bigotry, and he charmed many cast members with his hearty laugh. He befriended Sammy Davis Jr. "All he ever wanted to talk about was broads," remembered Davis. The song-and-dance man's dressing room was an unofficial clubhouse of music, liquor, and women. Davis delighted Preminger by arranging dates with a half-dozen women for the two of them.[72]

Preminger was not a racist, but he was a tyrant. After a week of location filming in Stockton, California, the cast returned to the Catfish Row soundstage. The first day back, he crushed the will of Dorothy Dandridge. She had both stunning beauty and tragic insecurity; she hungered for Hollywood fame, and she had tasted some glory with *Carmen Jones*. At that time she had also carried on a relationship with Preminger, who had played her vulnerabilities like a concert pianist. So when Preminger replaced Mamoulian, Dandridge crumbled. The manipulation began afresh. He demanded that she cry during a song. She refused, and they argued. Preminger repeated the scene all afternoon, spewing invective with each take. Dandridge's emotional rope frayed. At last, on the sixth take, her chest heaved with exhaustion, and tears streamed down her face. Preminger rolled tape. He had his scene, at his ex-lover's expense.[73]

Dandridge's anxieties reignited the racial tension. She was aloof, and her relationships with white men rankled many blacks. Once she pleaded with Preminger to recast Brock Peters, who played Crown. She cried for fifteen minutes. "When he puts his hands on me I can't bear it," she said. "And—and—he's so black!" Preminger thickened the strain by telling Peters about her plea. Later, he directed Dandridge to caress Poitier's head. She hesitated, and he erupted. Perhaps she was avoiding the racist folk legend of rubbing a black man's head for luck, but after the incident, cast and crew murmured about her aversion to the respected actors.[74]

Poitier tried avoiding controversy. Although opposites in style and temperament, he and Sammy Davis Jr. became good friends. Davis recalled Poitier's anxiety—he "was all inside himself, bottling up most of his emotions." After hours on his knees, Poitier had to skip rope to restore circulation. He practiced lip-synchronization. He took pride in preparation. So when Preminger tried to intimidate him, Poitier stood firm. While filming "Bess, You Is My Woman Now," Preminger sat on a highly perched camera crane. He bellowed that Poitier transmit more emotion. The set froze. Poitier warily accepted some borderline insults. Filming resumed. Again, Preminger yelled, "Cut!"[75]

As Poitier recalled, Preminger disparaged him: "You don't even know how to play a warm scene with the woman you love." When Poitier explained his interpretation, the director interrupted. He ranted on: "What am I dealing with here—children?" As Preminger raged, Poitier slipped off his shin shoes. Preminger screamed. Poitier rose. Preminger kept screaming. Poitier left the set, drove home, and lay on his bed until Preminger called and apologized. Poitier returned the next day, and Preminger never yelled at him again.[76]

Diahann Carroll watched the altercation from a safe distance. It confirmed her earlier impression of Poitier: "I had never seen . . . any black man deal with the white world with his kind of self-assurance and strength." She was attracted to him despite herself, twisting her already-confused self-image. Carroll possessed light-skinned "exotic" beauty, but she behaved by the circumspect guidelines of her middle-class upbringing. When she married the white casting director Monte Kay, problems surfaced. Kay married her to escape bourgeois convention; she craved that very stability. Kay was private and withdrawn; she needed constant affirmation.[77]

Both Poitier and Carroll were staying at the legendary Chateau Marmont on Sunset Boulevard. They saw each other constantly. Carroll sensed danger. "I was a traditional wife," she explained. "Casual sex was out of the question for me." Poitier nevertheless invited her to dinner, explaining that since both were safely married, they could use companionship. She vacillated, then agreed. Warmed by the potent drink concoctions and glowing tiki torches of a Polynesian restaurant, they talked and laughed, sharing stories. That night, Poitier said goodbye at her apartment door.[78]

In the coming weeks, there were more dinners, more long conversations, more laughs and subtle glances. They studied lines in his apartment. She tagged along on horseback rides and trips to the driving range. Poitier adored her independence and fire; she once hurled a hairbrush at him in anger. Carroll admired his self-respect, and she marveled at his improbable history and appetite for knowledge. "He thought about everything," she observed, recalling the stacks of books that littered his apartment. "He was the most political human being I had ever met."

They did not sleep together, however. Carroll knew that attractive women pursued Poitier, and she assumed that some succeeded. But this was different: "A casual extramarital affair was one thing to Sidney. A serious love affair that threatened the stability of his family and home was quite another." If the situation worried Poitier, it terrified Carroll. One night a group of friends left her apartment, and only Poitier stayed. She entered the bathroom and ran water until he departed. Another time her husband visited. Poitier knocked on the door while she was packing. She hid in the closet. After that weekend — an awkward disaster that left Kay hurt, Carroll confused, and Poitier jealous — they ignored each other all week.

The next Saturday, Carroll received a message from Poitier. He was at a local piano bar. She walked in and they stared into each other's eyes. "Let's go," he said. They walked up the hill, away from the Sunset Strip. Pulling each other close, strolling above the city lights, they acknowledged their mutual love. Their future, they knew, held some important personal decisions.[79]

Midway through December, filming of *Porgy and Bess* finally wrapped up. By then, along with the legal spats and political jousts, Dandridge had bruised her ribs, Davis had twisted an ankle, Joel Fluellen had crashed off cobblestones, and Porgy's goat had run amok chewing scenery. Goldwyn had closed the set and banned smoking to avoid another fire. He estimated the cost at $7 million. He bragged about the Todd-AO process, the elaborate orchestra, and the painstaking details in set and costuming design. "But I'll tell you one thing," he pronounced. "I will not disguise 'Porgy and Bess.' The ads will state plainly that it is an opera." He planned to accompany his picture around the world. The last of the movie moguls anticipated a masterwork, a magnificent coda on his career to the tune of Gershwin.[80]

Poitier and Carroll took a red-eye back to New York City, their future uncertain. They held hands the entire flight. Although exhausted, Poitier kept the light on. "I want to look at you," he said. When they landed, some friends greeted them, and Carroll squirmed beneath their suspicious glares. They waited for luggage, an awkward silence between them. When the suitcases arrived, they parted like strangers.[81]

❖

Porgy and Bess premiered to massive fanfare at New York's Warner Theatre in June 1959. The celebrities on hand included Sammy Davis Jr., Dorothy Heyward, Marlene Dietrich, Edward R. Murrow, and Henry Cabot Lodge. Goldwyn was the toast of the town. At a Waldorf-Astoria tribute, he won both a Bronze Medallion from New York City mayor Robert Wagner and a special award from the George Gershwin Memorial Foundation. Brokers sold reserved seats for the premiere at $3.75 each. Scalpers found willing buyers at double the face value.[82]

Goldwyn carried off the folk opera with lavish production values, charming the bulk of trade reviewers into such lauds as "timeless," "a triumph of the cinematic art," "a rousing musical success," and "one of the monumental milestones in the theatre's long history of entertainment." New York critics, entranced by the premiere's gala atmosphere, lavished similar praise. Bosley Crowther of the *New York Times* wrote not one, not two, but three articles in praise of *Porgy and Bess*.[83]

Yet others found the film curiously plastic. The elaborate costumes and set looked cartoonish, conveying nothing of Catfish Row's squalor. The stereophonic sound boomed the dubbed voices of classically trained professionals, distancing the audience from the actors. The Todd-AO screen, moreover, transmitted an artificial theatricality. Preminger filmed almost entirely in wide-angle boom shots, holding the same shot for minutes, especially during songs. He rarely cut from one angle to another, and he used no closeups. The faithful stage translation failed on film, a medium that demands visual variety. One critic wrote that *Porgy and Bess* "is not so much a motion picture as a photographed opera."[84]

Goldwyn's plan to travel the world, releasing his film to international hosannas, never fully materialized. Although the picture played 2,700 domestic dates, garnered good grosses in major cities, and had long runs throughout Europe, it only earned back half its cost. Ponderous two-and-a-half-hour folk operas rarely translated into box-office bounty. To Goldwyn's additional displeasure, Broadway producer Robert Breen sued him in April 1959 over the financial terms of their original agreement. Four years later, Goldwyn won the lawsuit, an anticlimactic epilogue to his eightieth and final film.[85]

By then, race politics had once again besieged *Porgy and Bess*. In January 1960, fifteen members of a black youth group ordered tickets at the segregated Brown Theatre in Louisville. Ushers turned them away at the door. The NAACP picketed the theater, and a Unitarian church organized an interracial bus trip to Indianapolis to see *Porgy and Bess*. A similar picket followed in Chapel Hill, North Carolina.[86]

These small youth- and church-oriented protests now characterized the battle over segregated public facilities. That *Porgy and Bess* might become a locus for political action horrified Goldwyn; he pulled the picture from theaters throughout the South, ensuring himself a financial loss. The *Atlanta Journal* chided Goldwyn's "excessive timidity or excellent press agentry." The situation was awash in irony: Atlanta's notorious censorship board approved the film, but Goldwyn withheld it.[87]

Contradiction also marked the film's contribution to the quest for positive black images. By its very nature, *Porgy and Bess* cataloged black stereotypes: animalistic brutes, oily hucksters, dice-rolling indolents, God-fearing mammies, cream-colored harlots, and a cripple burdened by folk superstitions and masochistic faith. The musical form further suggested that blacks were innate, happy-go-lucky entertainers. But the film showed little penury or poverty. "Sidney Poitier's Porgy is not the dirty, ragtag beggar of the Heyward script," described *Time*, "but a well-scrubbed young romantic hero who is never seen taking a penny from anybody." Clean characters with precise diction softened complaints of insensitivity. But with Catfish Row sanitized, Porgy and Bess seem distant, unconnected to any time or place, incongruous and implausible.[88]

The black press mostly cheered *Porgy and Bess*—they had to, given the array of black talent. The *Chicago Defender* even championed Goldwyn: "We cannot hide our heads in the sand and say that these conditions never happened, or that they are still not happening." The *New York Amsterdam News* only suggested that Goldwyn next produce an epic biography of a black hero such as Ira Aldridge, Frederick Douglass, or Booker T. Washington. The NAACP took no official stance.[89]

But black intellectuals chafed at the step backward. In a debate with Otto Preminger on a Chicago radio station, playwright Lorraine Hansberry criticized the American literary tradition that portrayed blacks as exotics and Uncle Toms. African Americans, she believed, "cannot afford the luxuries of mistakes of other peoples." James Baldwin echoed this critique in *Commentary*. He called *Porgy and Bess* "grandiose, foolish, and heavy with the stale perfume of self-congratulation." He condemned the "white man's vision of Negro life," detached from black culture, designed to assuage white guilt.[90]

Baldwin added that Poitier was miscast: "The very qualities which lend him his distinction—his intelligence, virility, and grace—operate against him here." The man who stewed with righteous passion in *Blackboard Jungle* and *The Defiant Ones* looked tragically out of place. There were political consequences. African Americans relied on public expressions of racial dignity, and their most prominent leading man was on his knees singing, "I got plenty o' nuttin', and nuttin's plenty fo' me."[91]

Poitier had compromised his image to achieve stardom, and he never fully rationalized his decision. Eight years later, it still gnawed at him. "I toyed with the idea of being steadfast," he said, remembering the dilemma, "but I weakened and ultimately did it. I didn't enjoy doing it, and I have not yet completely forgiven myself."[92]

CHAPTER 9

BURDENS
(1959–1961)

When Poitier returned home from California, his wife was making breakfast. There and then, in the kitchen, before the children awoke, he told her that he loved Diahann Carroll. Juanita was shocked. Her world was crumbling. Her father had recently died, and now her husband loved another woman. She blamed Carroll. Sidney insisted that he deserved the blame, and she sobbed. As the children stirred, Juanita reined in her tears, and they postponed their discussion until that night.[1]

They resolved nothing that morning, nothing that night, and very little in the days ahead. Poitier was torn. He loved Carroll, and he agonized at the gulf between him and Juanita. "Why couldn't she develop a meaningful interest in my work so I could have someone with whom I could intelligently discuss all my never-ending problems?" he reflected, with a touch of self-indulgence. Yet guilt gnawed at him. He remembered his own father's lesson that "the measure of a man is how well he provides his children." Poitier equated parental responsibility with manhood, and he feared that he was forsaking his family.[2]

He carried this luggage into his next job, the lead role of Walter Lee Younger in the Lorraine Hansberry play *A Raisin in the Sun*. As he returned to the stage, his turmoil molded his interpretation. He identified with Walter Lee, who struggled with economic barriers, self-respect, and his father's legacy. Actor and character both sought to fulfill themselves through their larger duties. That quest left Poitier torn between his family and Carroll. It influenced his public image as his celebrity soared. And it drove the conflict that shaped a Broadway phenomenon.

❖

Lorraine Hansberry was an odd mixture of bourgeois and radical. Her father, a wealthy Chicago executive, sent her to segregated public schools. When she was eight, they moved to an all-white neighborhood, and her father challenged Chicago's restrictive housing covenants in the 1943 Supreme Court case *Hansberry vs. Lee*. She moved to New York City in 1950, where she ran in the same avant-garde circles as Poitier. While writing essays and reviews for leftist journals, she honed a worldview that combined liberal individualism with a critique of capitalism.[3]

She struggled to forge these sensibilities into her own work. For years, she could not finish a play. Her inspiration came in 1956, after witnessing yet another play mired in black stereotype. "I suddenly became disgusted with a whole body of material about Negroes," she recalled. "Cardboard characters. Cute dialect bits. Or hip-swinging musicals from exotic sources." From her third-floor Greenwich Village walk-up, the twenty-six-year-old woman wrote *A Raisin in the Sun*.[4]

The entire play takes place in the cramped South Side apartment of the Younger family. It opens as the family awaits a $10,000 check from the life insurance policy of the patriarch, Big Walter. His son, Walter Lee ("a lean, intense young man in his middle thirties, inclined to quick nervous movements and erratic speech habits — and always in his voice there is a quality of indictment"), chafes at his chauffeur job, and he wants to invest in a liquor store. Walter Lee's wife, Ruth, is tired, old beyond her years. His sister, Beneatha, sparkles with ambition. Mama Younger bears her husband's torch; she resists besmirching Big Walter's legacy in a liquor store.[5]

But Walter Lee *needs* the opportunity, because he equates money with manhood, and he suffocates under his burdens: his child sleeps on a living-room couch, his wife lacks life's finer things, his job offers no upward mobility, and his mother controls the household. He complains that no one understands him: "Man say to his woman: I got me a dream. His woman say: Eat your eggs. Man say: I got to take hold of this here world, baby! And a woman will say: Eat your eggs and go to work. Man say, I got to change my life, I'm choking to death, baby! And his woman say — Your eggs is getting cold!"

So Walter Lee anguishes when his mother places a $3,500 down payment on a house in all-white Clybourne Park. He abandons his job and drinks for three days. Mama Younger, realizing that she has crushed her son's dream, gives him the remaining $6,500. He must save $3,000 for Beneatha's education, but he can invest the rest. Walter Lee now tackles life with buoyancy.

One week later, Mr. Lindner from the Clybourne Park "welcoming committee" arrives. The white man wants to keep blacks out of his neighborhood, so he proposes to buy the house at a profit to the Youngers.

Insulted, Walter Lee dismisses him. But then comes bad news: his partner in the liquor store has absconded with the entire investment. Worse, Walter Lee gave him the entire $6,500. He prepares to accept Lindner's offer.

Mama pleads that he reconsider, but Walter Lee has approached the brink. He drops to his knees, "groveling and grinning and wringing his hands in profoundly anguished imitation of the slow-witted movie stereotype." Only after Mama Younger summons his son Travis does Walter Lee upright himself. With newfound resilience, he sends Lindner away. The family finishes packing and leaves for Clybourne Park. "He finally came into his manhood today, didn't he?" Mama asks. "Kind of like a rainbow after the rain."

A Raisin in the Sun explored themes atypical of American drama: the search for black manhood, the generation gap in black expectations, the meaning of wealth in the black community. It promoted liberal uplift, yet contained radical indictments of ghetto life. Hansberry presented these issues within an authentic milieu, humanizing her characters. Each possessed individual faults, charms, idiosyncrasies, and speech patterns. Walter Lee is neither grinning entertainer nor paragon of virtue: he is a bundle of complexities. Mama Younger, Beneatha, and Ruth transcend stereotypes of mammies, jezebels, or prim housewives. The racist Lindner is calm, mannered, almost rational.[6]

A typical Broadway producer would not have staged a black drama without singing or dancing. But Philip Rose was no typical Broadway producer. Actually, before *A Raisin in the Sun*, he was not a producer at all—he was a record executive, a friend of Hansberry, and an idealistic liberal. As Hansberry wrote the play, Rose learned the theater business and drew up an option agreement. Yet to get to Broadway, he needed a marketable commodity. He had one: his good friend Sidney Poitier. Rose convinced him to star in the play.[7]

Poitier's prestige proved crucial. Producers such as David Susskind and Roger Stevens now returned Rose's telephone calls, though they backed off funding the risky proposition. An accountant named David Cogan had originally offered $500; now he raised $30,000. At Poitier's behest, Rose hired director Lloyd Richards, the former chief assistant at Paul Mann's Actor's Workshop. Claudia McNeil signed to play Mama Younger, and Ruby Dee would play Ruth.[8]

Poitier helped Rose and Richards interview other cast members. From Poitier's Chateau Marmont bungalow, during the filming of *Porgy and Bess*, they interviewed Carroll for the part of Beneatha. Carroll thirsted for the role, but she detected a chill from Poitier. "He couldn't bring himself to acknowledge that my work really mattered to me," she believed, blaming his patriarchal upbringing. Unnerved by this perceived lack of support, she gave a wooden reading. They cast Diana Sands instead.[9]

After returning home, Poitier began rehearsals at the New Amsterdam roof garden theater in Times Square. He also contemplated his future with Carroll. They often met at a seedy 42nd Street moviehouse. The two models of elegance would intertwine hands and lock eyes. But instead of bathing in soft violins and fine wine, they sat in rickety chairs under cover of darkness, the only sound another humdrum picture, the only scent crushed popcorn. Unsatisfied with these rendezvous, they agreed to leave their spouses and move into separate apartments, so that they could be together whenever they wanted.[10]

Only Carroll moved out. At the last moment, Poitier lost his nerve, citing the guilt of leaving his children. Carroll subsequently returned to her husband. Poitier seethed, because he wanted the privacy of her apartment, and he accused her of abandoning their relationship. She retorted that only *she* had moved out. Carroll then became pregnant by her husband, and she and Poitier drifted apart. Without sufficient consideration for either woman, Poitier wanted both the stability of Juanita and the romance of Carroll. Now his grasp slipped from his family and his mistress.[11]

A Raisin in the Sun was similarly unsettled. Rose scheduled an opening in New Haven, Connecticut, and a two-week run in Philadelphia, but he still had no Broadway theater booking. Meanwhile, Richards and Hansberry pared the play down, cutting scenes of a neighbor gossiping about the bombing of a black house in a white neighborhood, Travis reporting that he chased a rat, and Beneatha coming home with a "natural" haircut. The cuts served a dramatic purpose, but by omitting scenes exploring segregation, poverty, and Afrocentrism, Hansberry and Richards dulled the play's political impact.[12]

Two weeks into rehearsals, Hansberry grew distressed with the actors. She griped that Sands played Beneatha with too much humor and not enough intellect. She worried that Ruby Dee gave Ruth too much force. But mostly, she complained about Poitier. As it stood, Claudia McNeil's Mama Younger dominated the play. Hansberry thought that Walter Lee needed more strength and anger.[13]

Poitier agreed. It is Walter Lee, after all, who rages at life's inequities, arrives at the edge of the abyss, and achieves manhood by repudiating materialistic fantasies. It is Walter Lee who must simultaneously portend black disenchantment and endear himself to the audience. And it is Walter Lee who lives the Langston Hughes words that lend the play its title: "What happens to a dream deferred? / Does it dry up / Like a raisin in the sun?" When Mama Younger dominates the play, it stifles the dramatic impact. It also reinforces stereotypes of the bossy black matriarch and emasculated black male.[14]

Hansberry later admitted to the play's "enormous dramatic fault" of no clear-cut main character. Fearing that the audience would latch onto Mama Younger, she and Rose had resisted casting the popular Ethel Waters. She also tried revisions that strengthened Walter Lee, but her efforts proved futile. Perhaps out of creative frustration, she blamed Poitier. After their final rehearsal, Hansberry praised McNeil and offered constructive criticism for Dee and Sands. For Poitier she wrote only: "It was just one of those things."[15]

But while Hansberry expected Poitier to strengthen his performance, Poitier expected Hansberry to flesh out his character. Instead of exchanging opinions, their relationship slid into cold silences and grumbled innuendoes.[16]

Despite the infighting, the play succeeded. When *A Raisin in the Sun* debuted at the Shubert Theatre in New Haven on 21 January 1959, the *Hartford Times* asked: "Where has Miss Hansberry been?" Hansberry thought that she wrote a straight drama, and Richards had prepared it that way. But during the four-night stint, the audience laughed. The characters had a comic warmth that balanced their dramatic trials. Poitier gained personal satisfaction, too. Live audiences no longer prompted crippling episodes of stage fright for him.[17]

His on-stage confidence heightened his off-stage dissatisfaction. When they arrived in Philadelphia, Martin Baum scheduled an emergency meeting with Rose. With *The Defiant Ones* in theaters and *Porgy and Bess* forthcoming, movie studios were inquiring about Poitier's availability. Baum told Rose that his client would gladly leave the play. The producer tried to assuage the agent, because the play received great reviews and played to a full house at the Walnut Theatre. Rose had a hot property.[18]

James Baldwin was at the Walnut, and he was awestruck. "I had never in my life seen so many black people in the theater," he wrote. "Never before, in the entire history of the American theater, had so much of the truth of black people's lives been seen on stage." That racial honesty was unusual enough that FBI agents maintained a file on Hansberry. They reported with relief that whites mostly "appreciated the drama and the quality of the acting. . . . Relatively few people appeared to dwell on the propaganda messages." *A Raisin in the Sun* appealed to whites while resonating with African Americans.[19]

The critical and commercial success landed a Broadway booking at the Barrymore Theatre. But *Look Homeward, Angel* still had one month left on its run there, so Rose accepted a four-week offer from the Blackstone Theater in Chicago. His decision panicked Hansberry. Chicago was home to a cabal of notoriously persnickety theater critics, led by Claudia Cassidy of the *Chicago Tribune*. But Cassidy celebrated the "remarkable play, acted to the Blackstone hilt on its warm heart, its proud backbone, and its quicksilver funnybone." Word of mouth sparked a triumphant run. McNeil and Poitier both received fine reviews and copious cheers.[20]

Still, Poitier was dissatisfied: Mama Younger was garnering the warmest responses. He stopped speaking with McNeil, squabbled with Richards, and alienated himself from most of the cast. Poitier believed that Hansberry had sabotaged his character. But Hansberry wanted a stronger Walter Lee, too. Unfortunately, she never conveyed that opinion to Lloyd Richards. The director saw no reason to reconstruct the play just weeks before the Broadway debut.[21]

Poitier worried that his concerns smacked of ego gone awry. "Could I be that far out of touch?" he remembered thinking. "I wasn't exactly a Rock of Gibraltar at that time." He also thought that Richards discounted his position because he was leaving after six months to fulfill film commitments, while McNeil's contract covered the entire run. But in his mind, he bore a duty to reclaim the play's integrity.[22]

His objections stemmed from the bonds between actor and character. Based on his Method training, Poitier identified with Walter Lee. He had once approached the brink himself: sleeping in pay toilets, throwing chairs through doctors' windows. Now, with his own family's future in doubt, Poitier interpreted his character's resurrection as a triumph of fatherhood. He thought of his own family's patriarch. "My father was with me every moment as I performed *A Raisin in the Sun*," he later reflected. His vehemence in clashes with the writer, producer, director, and co-star all derived from this deep-seated emotional understanding of his character.[23]

Midway through their Chicago run, Poitier and Ruby Dee discussed the conflict over drinks. At that point the play was "frozen"; no new lines would be added. They decided that Poitier would play *against* McNeil, injecting more anger into Walter Lee and challenging Mama Younger's dominance. Hansberry might have wanted this change, but she neither articulated her plea nor revised her play. It was Poitier who pushed Walter

Lee into the dramatic center. Now he plunged to such emotional depths that the audience identified with his despair. When he saved his family, it surged with passion. Poitier's strategy had paid off. The audience's dramatic reactions testified to Poitier's will, stature, artistic judgment, and ego. Before reaching Broadway, he had won the battle for the play's soul.[24]

❖

Poitier returned to Broadway for the first time since September 1947, when he played Lester in the *Anna Lucasta* road show. Little had changed. Broadway theaters had staged only three works by black writers: *Take a Giant Step* by Louis Peterson (1953), *Mrs. Patterson* by Charles Sebree (1954), and *Simply Heavenly* by Langston Hughes (1957). None had a substantial run. Black performers still worked predominantly in musicals.[25]

Poitier knew firsthand about this scarcity of dramatic roles. Two years earlier, Shelley Winters met Poitier at Sardi's Restaurant, and they discussed her new play *The Saturday Night Kid*. No one had been cast yet to play opposite her as the genial, educated photographer. Poitier wanted the role. But director George Keathley believed that a black actor would distort the play's meaning, and he cast Alex Nicol instead.[26]

A Raisin in the Sun did not just feature a black actor: the writer, director, and all but one actor were black. One critic called it "a small hunk of history." But as opening night approached, that hunk seemed to be crumbling. On 10 March 1959, they gave a preview performance before some theater veterans. An air of panic hovered over the polite applause; the racial drama had no successful precedent. Between the second and third acts, the press agent suggested closing for two weeks. Rose had neither the inclination nor the money to postpone. The next night, he took his seat next to Hansberry, and they watched their history-making enterprise.[27]

"It was an electric night," Poitier remembered. "The most electric night I spent in the theater." Poitier, McNeil, Dee, and Sands were in top form, and the audience alternated between flowing tears and peals of laughter. Even jaded veteran photographers cried. When the play finished, the crowd roared and stomped. The actors came out for curtain calls. The critics, who usually rushed out to write their reviews, stood and clapped. Then the cries turned to "author, author." Ruby Dee pounded on Poitier's arm. "Go get her, you son of a bitch," she stage whispered. Poitier gracefully bounded to Hansberry. He escorted her on stage, inspiring the loudest roar yet.[28]

The next day's reviews saluted the integrity of Hansberry's vision and the fluidity of Richards's direction. The actors earned excellent reviews. McNeil offered humor and humanity, avoiding stock characterization. And Poitier, as Walter Kerr noted, was "superb." He conveyed an astounding range of emotions. "There is nothing more moving in 'A Raisin in the Sun,'" wrote Kerr, "than the spectacle of Sidney Poitier biting his lip, clutching the back of a chair, and turning himself into a man." Others shared this admiration for his silent eloquence.[29]

The plaudits continued after opening night. They played to standing-room-only crowds for months, and each time they inspired emotional reactions. Hansberry received buckets of fan mail, and her "elfin, slim-hipped, tousle-headed" good looks made her a media darling. The *New Yorker* featured her in the "Talk of the Town" section. In her syndicated "My Day" column, Eleanor Roosevelt hoped that the play would "sink into the conscience of America." The black press reveled in the theatrical triumph. Martin Luther King Jr. lauded Mama Younger during a sermon on Mother's Day.[30]

Poitier's gut-wrenching portrayal of Walter Lee kept audiences on an emotional swing. Lerone Burnett of *Ebony* described Poitier's late arrival before a Sunday matinee. He rushed into his pajamas costume just five minutes before curtain. Then he sullenly flipped through some letters. With the call for "Places," he leaped up and performed calisthenics until he sprinted on stage. After three acts and three curtain calls, he had undergone a transformation. He had lived Walter Lee's catharsis, and he wept in exhausted embrace with Lloyd Richards.[31]

Six days a week for six months, he sustained this same ordeal. He dropped nine pounds off his lean frame, and he ate spoonfuls of honey to calm a scratchy throat. Worse, the play's interpretation still generated conflict. Poitier and Hansberry resented the credit accorded each other, while McNeil grumbled about slights true and imagined. Off stage, she backed down from conflicts with the star. But on stage, Poitier recalled, she "wasn't giving me what I needed. She knew what my big moments were, and she knew when to hold back and take the air out."[32]

Despite the discord, *A Raisin in the Sun* kept packing the Barrymore. In April it won the prestigious Drama Critics Circle Award. Hansberry was the first African American to gain the honor, edging out Eugene O'Neill, Archibald MacLeish, and Tennessee Williams. Her victory sparked some suggestions of tokenism. Tom Driver of *New Republic* contended that the play owed its success to sentimental racial consciences.[33]

He overstated the case, but he had a point: the play tugged white heartstrings beyond expectations. A *Village Voice* critic admitted to difficulty distinguishing the actors from their characters. "Young Miss Lorraine Hansberry," he eulogized, "has done nothing less than to pick her people up and shove them dramatically — as *people*, not as A People — into the middle of the twentieth century." In print and in Broadway chatter, praise for the play followed that opinion: *A Raisin in the Sun* presented issues and concerns that transcended black life and applied to all human beings, regardless of race.[34]

At first Hansberry encouraged these proclamations of universality. She told the *New York Times* that "this wasn't a 'Negro play.' It was a play about honest-to-God, believable, many-sided people who happened to be Negroes." More than one critic expressed relief that the play had "no axe to grind." "She argues no causes," wrote Brooks Atkinson, encapsulating a popular sentiment. "Note that she resolves the situation not in terms of social justice but in terms of the pride of a family that has ethical standards."[35]

That white audiences acknowledged the universal dimensions of black characters spoke to Hansberry's genius: she had crafted endearing characters, avoiding both stereotype and propaganda. Like Jackie Robinson's baseball career, Ralph Bunche's Nobel Prize, or Poitier's finest films, *A Raisin in the Sun* opened white eyes to the plausibility of integration. In 1959, that was a powerful weapon.[36]

This widespread reading, however, diluted Hansberry's leftist critique of American society. She had intended that the ending sound an ambiguous note: Clybourne Park is hostile territory, and the Youngers' house payments will force tremendous sacrifices. Moreover, Walter Lee's debasement suggests the corrosive effects of materialism. Critics and audiences ignored these themes. For them, Walter Lee's rejection of Lindner was no awakening to the upcoming black struggle. It was an unmitigated triumph, an inclusion in the democratic tradition.[37]

When Poitier thrust Walter Lee into the play's center, he shaped this popular understanding (and misunderstanding) of *A Raisin in the Sun*. Walter Lee became more than a weak-willed symbol of black anger. Now he was a hero who saved his family from tragedy. Alas, this obscured the racial problems in store. Poitier's artistic judgment — combined with his acting ability and instinctive likability — both fueled theatergoers' cathartic journeys and blunted the play's politics.

A Raisin in the Sun brewed mixed legacies. As a 1961 film, 1974 musical, mass-market paperback, and regular selection in anthologies, it reached broader audiences than the typical Broadway play. Inspired by its success, black playwrights pursued their own visions. Yet many black intellectuals later dismissed the play as an appeal to white liberal guilt, an anachronistic saga of bourgeois aspiration, a token that soothed whites. Most blamed Lorraine Hansberry. At the time, few understood the play's radical aspects, and fewer still the dilution of that ideology at the hands of Sidney Poitier.[38]

❖

"Poitier's Stock Has Gone up Up UP," cheered an April 1959 headline. A serendipitous confluence of accomplishments had placed Poitier in the public eye: the upcoming release of *Porgy and Bess* prompted considerable hype, *A Raisin in the Sun* was the "must-see" play on Broadway, and Poitier won an Oscar nomination for *The Defiant Ones*.[39]

This deluge of success unleashed a flood of publicity on Poitier: sundry features in New York newspapers, continued commemoration in black newspapers, long cover profiles in *Life* and *Ebony*, a four-part series by black journalist A. S. "Doc" Young in the *Los Angeles Mirror-News*, and an enormous five-part series in the *New York Post*. Poitier keenly understood the importance of this attention. As his fame mounted, he meticulously selected his political affiliations. He no longer aligned himself with radical causes, as he had in his early career. He also refused to hire a press agent. Instead, he carefully chose his promotions. "The statements one puts in print aren't just for the moment," he once said. "They stay with you forever, so you must take complete responsibility for them."[40]

He bore a double burden: furthering his career, and furthering the status of African Americans. At this point, those two goals went hand-in-hand. If Poitier could humanize his public image, he could effect the transition to full-fledged movie star, with all its trappings of money, fame, and status. He could also display that black people shared the aspirations of other Americans — a significant feat when many blacks still lacked basic civil rights.

In his 1961 classic *The Image*, Daniel Boorstin wrote that American culture blurred the lines between hero and celebrity, hard news and puff features, actual events and media creations. "The American citizen thus lives in a world where fantasy is more real than reality, where the image has more dignity than the original." More than ever, Americans understood their world through popular culture. The celebrity thus had profound power. The public connected with their stars, both admiring their glamorous distance and identifying with their personal stories. Poitier did not revel in fame; after years of isolation, he was on one level quite shy. But he exploited his celebrity for professional and political ends.[41]

He emphasized his traditional nuclear family, despite the actual unsettled state of his marriage. *Life* pictured Sidney reading on his living room floor, with Juanita sitting nearby. *Ebony* described him as "a devoted family man" with no valet or secretary, whose wife good-naturedly complained that he should dress "like a young actor, instead of a West Indian farmer." The *New York Post* delighted that daughters Beverly and Sherri shared the patriotic birth date of the fourth of July. Doc Young admired that the Poitiers lived in a comfortable middle-class home, not a mansion with a swimming pool.[42]

That domestic bliss consummated a tale of uplift, pulled from a Horatio Alger fable and adapted to a West Indian immigrant. As Poitier himself described, he was a "Do-It-Yourself Man," an independent entity with an intense work ethic. He constantly searched for suitable scripts, and he studied movies with perspicacity. An admirer summarized his life's lesson: "Through perseverance and taking the bull by the horns . . . our hero becomes a self-respecting citizen and a credit to his country."[43]

Poitier embodied the black image for the dawning Age of Integration. Though a Bahamian immigrant, he represented Black America. His persona shared the joys and concerns of ordinary middle-class Americans. Thanks to his diligence and talent, he deserved inclusion in his chosen field. Yet he deflected resentment with humility, often exaggerating his inadequacies. He also evaded any overt political label. "I am not a crusader consciously," he said. "I am a guy who is aware that I am a Negro and have certain responsibilities as such." Only a bigot could attack Poitier's stated goal to "spread just a little love, just a little understanding." Only a fool could dismiss his by-the-bootstraps fulfillment of the American Dream.[44]

Now many Americans learned the complete, extraordinary Poitier story: the humble origins of Cat Island, the delinquency of Nassau, the jolt of Jim Crow Florida, the poverty of Harlem, the initial ejection from ANT, the birth of a career with *No Way Out*, the failed Ribs in the Ruff, and the breakthrough in *Blackboard Jungle*. Oft-repeated anecdotes — his self-education, his panicky debut in *Lysistrata*, his rejection of *Phenix City Story* — elicited admiration for his resolve.

The media also painted his traits and idiosyncrasies. Poitier could be irritable, and he sometimes seemed anguished. More often, he was a fount of amiability, a gregarious fellow with deep reserves of charisma. As the public perceived his mercurial temperament, it could picture him off screen: the absentminded gnaw on sport shirts while sunk in gloom, the dancing eyes during impassioned late-night conversations, the graceful stride into Sardi's as heads swiveled. His eager-to-please charm caused complications — incapable of turning people down, he might make three dinner plans for one night and arrive at the last appointment six hours late.[45]

A competitive fire guided his leisure hours. He hated losing at golf, liked picking horses at the racetrack, and loved cards. He also possessed a strong self-discipline. Although he ate with abandon, Poitier drank and smoked in moderation. He preferred health shakes with asparagus and spinach juice. He performed calisthenics, favored walking over driving, and took frequent naps. He avoided the telephone. He rarely watched television but constantly read books. He played bongo drums.[46]

Poitier enjoyed flaunting his intelligence, but he avoided pedanticism. He spoke in a curious amalgam of black slang and polysyllabic elocution, eloquently pontificating before injecting a familiarity. "Too many dramatists look only for the shock value in racial conflict," he once said. "They look for the kicks rather than the statement of import. Dig?" His favorite topics included race relations, jazz music, and Eastern religions. "I dig all of those Oriental religions and philosophies," he told *Newsweek*. "Like the Upanishads, and Taoism. Confucius and all that stuff. Man! I really dig all that jazz!"[47]

Every article was sympathetic, an organic function of Poitier's charm and good nature. At times, however, the media confused the man and the image. *Life* praised Poitier's "unspoiled natural virtue" and "innate wholesomeness," suggesting that he suited his familiar role as "good man and good companion." Dorothy Masters, who in 1957 had proposed that Poitier become a minister, now wrote "with his tremendous empathy, acute sensitivity and inner fire, he ought to approach the Pearly Gates as an evangelist." A year later, she rehashed the theme a third time, marveling that he "has the attributes of an evangelist — spontaneity, compassion, warmth, courage, and integrity." She continued to blend the man with his sacrificial screen hero.[48]

But other profiles included thoughtful analyses of Poitier's consequence. A few mentioned his good looks — a significant reference, considering the taboos on black sexuality. The *New York Post* noted that he neither danced nor sang, and his handsome face conformed "with none of the Caucasian standards of beauty." Indeed, Poitier had black features: dark skin, pronounced lips, tight curly hair. He also possessed a certain virility, though not a growling, Brando-esque vigor. Thanks to his prim housewife, gaggle of daughters, clean diction, and impeccable manners, he was a "safe" sort of sexy, the type that white women could admire without feeling threatened. Philip Rose recalled Poitier's mounting celebrity: "I began to see these white ladies coming over to the restaurant and asking for an autograph for their daughters. *For their daughters!*"[49]

The *Post* also interviewed Martin Baum, who had recently asked a producer what would happen if Poitier declined an offer. "We'll get a white actor," was the answer. Compelled by this solitary status, Poitier planned for the future. "I'm hot now," he told the *New York Herald Tribune*, "but suppose I get cold next year. What do I do? Open a haberdashery?"[50]

Poitier did not savor his isolated perch. He mentored some young black actors, including nineteen-year-old Billy Dee Williams, who trained with Poitier for about a month. "The moments I had with Sidney were good moments," recalled Williams, "because he gave me the feeling, as a minority, that there was an opportunity for me, that there was a place for me in America to make certain kinds of achievements." Poitier also urged studios to create opportunities for blacks in all phases of film production. For his own professional stability, he sought roles that avoided racial issues, met with executives about diversifying his career, and predicted that he would soon direct.[51]

In January 1959, Poitier appeared on David Susskind's live television program *Open End* with Harry Belafonte, Shelley Winters, and Tony Franciosa. The opinion show ended when they exhausted their subject—hence the program's name. (Some referred to it by the unfortunate title *David Susskind's Open End*.) Usually Susskind baited his panel into confrontation, but the liberal host let the two black celebrities expound unfettered. "This was Poitier's and Belafonte's show," reported *Variety*. Poitier noted the industry's limitations: "My dream is to be able to function as an artist first. As things are now, I rarely can play the part of a human being caught in conflict. There is great narrowness in our work." The stars further orated on American democracy and African nationalism. Most *Open End* programs ran less than two and a half hours. That night, they finished at 1:45 A.M., after three hours and twenty five minutes. And as black critic Jesse Walker admired, both Poitier and Belafonte "pulled no punches."[52]

The black community revered Poitier. The Harlem YMCA gave Poitier a special award for inspiring black participation in the arts. The *Chicago Defender* saw him as a vehicle of racial progress. The *Ebony* cover feature prompted effusive letters to the editor. Fans delighted in his acting ability, his happy family, his work ethic, and his avoidance of hair straighteners. One wrote: "I personally think articles of this nature, which so richly demonstrate the ambition and the capability of the Negro race, should be more frequently publicized. I am sure this kind of literature in the hands of the public would constitute a substantially better view of race relations. Sid, we're proud of you." Like Joe Louis or Jackie Robinson, he was a "hard moral man," a black symbol in a white world, a folk hero who expressed new racial possibilities with dignity and decency.[53]

African Americans held the same esteem for Harry Belafonte. The singer continued to perform around the world, even as he presided over a small entertainment empire. He established two music companies, and his films were big moneymakers. In 1957 he founded Harbel Productions. Some speculated that Belafonte would propel black film beyond Poitier's pattern of loyal aid to the white hero. His public statements bolstered this perception; where Poitier smoothed sensibilities with social grace, Belafonte ruffled them with defiant pronouncements. "Nobody dictates to me," he growled to *Redbook*.[54]

But after two 1959 films, the promise of Belafonte faded. In *The World, the Flesh, and the Devil*, Belafonte, a white woman, and a white man are the only survivors of a nuclear holocaust. After some sexual tension, the film ends inconclusively with all three hand-in-hand. That compromise capped what Belafonte called "one of the worst experiences of my life." *Odds Against Tomorrow*, produced by Harbel, featured Belafonte as a musician-turned-robber whose criminal partners include a southern bigot. Harbel never made another picture. Belafonte's wooden hero, sulking in film noir gloom, seemed to scare off future investors. He disappeared from films for over a decade.[55]

Poitier was the only black actor working consistently in Hollywood. After 198 performances as Walter Lee Younger, Poitier left *A Raisin in the Sun* on 29 August 1959. Ossie Davis replaced him. Poitier returned to the movies, hoping that his next picture might escape the "narrowness" of his early career. But nothing changed. On screen, he remained a symbol of black integrity first, and a human being second.[56]

❖

All the Young Men was a war drama written, produced, and directed by Hall Bartlett. Like his mentor Stanley Kramer, he possessed a strong social conscience. He designed a script for Poitier, and he signed the actor to a huge contract, for $100,000 and a cut of the profits. The film is set during the Korean War, the first American military action with integrated units. Poitier's protagonist is a proud sergeant who earns the respect of white troops. But Bartlett aspired to more than a prestige picture. He wanted to make money.[57]

At the turn of the decade, that endeavor remained difficult for a racial drama. Ninety percent of American families owned televisions, and studios fought for smaller slices of financial pie. Only Columbia would finance the picture, and it insisted that Bartlett build up a part for a white co-star, even if the modifications warped the story's structure. He still had trouble finding a white star to play opposite Poitier. Civil rights remained a cause for blacks and isolated liberals; many actors hedged at playing second fiddle to Poitier and limiting one's appeal in the South. Finally Bartlett procured Alan Ladd.[58]

Bartlett's supporting cast appealed to specific segments of the moviegoing public. Comedian Mort Sahl, *Variety*'s "king of the eggheads and college students," made his motion picture debut. Handsome boxing champion Ingemar Johansson attracted sports fans and women. Teen idols James Darren and Glenn Corbett satisfied the bobbysoxer contingent.[59]

This potpourri of actors, jokers, boxers, and crooners assembled in Hollywood in early October. By mid-month they descended upon Glacier National Park in northwestern Montana. The bone-chilling location, near Canada and 6,000 feet above sea level, marked Bartlett's attempt to replicate the American invasion into mountainous North Korea. Clad in parkas and heavy boots, they moved from one arctic locale to another, ending up in Timberline, Oregon.[60]

The attention to detail did not include ethnic accuracy. Bartlett cast his wife, Ana St. Clair, as a Korean woman, Mario Alcalde as an American Indian, and Blackfoot Indians as North Korean soldiers. Other than the Swede Johansson and the Blackfoots, they all hated the cold. During one scene, as the unit ran across an icy expanse, Sahl actually fainted.[61]

Poitier, miserable, kept his distance from the other actors. The artistic conflicts and emotional reactions of *A Raisin in the Sun* had been replaced by a business-as-usual melodrama, and no self-respecting Cat Islander enjoyed the cold. Moreover, he was the only black person on the set. Later, when shooting interiors, an electrical grip yelled a racial slur across a sound stage. Poitier checked his temper, forcing himself to turn the other cheek.[62]

Exacerbating the torment, his personal life stalled. He still loved Diahann Carroll, and he telephoned her constantly. But he was mired in a muddy no man's land, because he refused to leave his family. Carroll loved Poitier, too, but she resisted subordinating her career and family to him. When she gave birth, they drifted apart again. Tearing emotionally, enduring the cold, Poitier survived his tour of duty as a screen soldier.[63]

He nevertheless dominated the picture. His emotive style overshadowed the restrained Ladd. The old star of *Shane* was by then severely depressed. Overwhelmed by a domineering wife, he starved himself and drank heavily. He vomited blood every morning, and he quietly acceded to the picture's artistic direction.[64]

Even in better states of mind, however, neither Poitier nor Ladd could have saved a script of war film banalities and stale racial melodrama. Poitier's Sergeant Towler takes command of nine white Marines after an ambush kills their lieutenant, and the unit worries. The veteran ex-sergeant Kincaid (Ladd) refuses to endorse the black leader. Towler nonetheless gives orders with confidence, saves lives by setting off mines, and stands up to a southerner who complains that where he comes from, blacks do the menial labor. "We are not where you come from!" Towler replies.

Predictabilities abound, including a dying soldier who misses his girl, a Navajo scout who sacrifices himself, Sahl's city-slicker riffs on conventional morality, Johansson's immigrant paeans to American democracy, Darren's doe-eyed rendition of the title song, and the racist's attempted rape of a Korean woman, only to be thwarted by Towler. The black sergeant leads the capture of a crucial bypass and then orchestrates its defense against repeated invasions. An American battalion then rescues them. Towler thus enables a victory and earns respect. He even gives a blood transfusion to Kincaid — perhaps the most ham-fisted symbol of racial brotherhood in Hollywood history.

The critics groaned. "The lessons to be gained," wrote *Newsweek*, "are that racial tolerance and courage are good, war is hell, and any movie soldier who talks about home is almost sure to be dead inside of 50 frames." The plot and characters conformed to musty war movie clichés. Some critics also noticed what black reviewers had long suggested: that Poitier is "so discriminated against because of his color that he will probably never be allowed to play a character that is not strong, sensitive and noble." His character has no background, no weaknesses, no personality — he is a bland black Superman.[65]

But the something-for-everyone casting in *All the Young Men* roped in customers, including black audiences. Columbia Pictures created two separate advertising campaigns: one for whites, one for blacks. Part-time black publicists targeted black newspapers, radio stations, and political organizations. The poster for black theaters touted Poitier's rejection of white authority as the central theme. It pictured Poitier gripping Ladd by the collar. "Spit out what's on your filthy little mind," it read, assigning Poitier a line that does not exist in the film, "and then take your orders from me!"[66]

To Columbia's surprise, the black campaign also appealed to white audiences. *All the Young Men* earned high grosses at downtown movie theaters throughout the North and West, and exhibitors pointed to the unique marketing strategy of a black man defying a southern white. Racial justice was turning profits![67]

This remarkable development reflected a new era in American race relations. On the first day of February 1960, four black college freshmen walked into a Woolworth's Department Store in Greensboro, North Carolina, and ordered coffee at the lunch counter. This small act defied Jim Crow, and the waitress refused them. But neither the manager nor the police forced them to leave. The next day, twenty more students joined them. Two days later came white students from a local women's college. In one week, protests spread to Hampton, Virginia, and Rock Hill, South Carolina. In another week, they widened to Chattanooga and Nashville. By year's end, some 70,000 people had participated in sit-ins, pickets, marches, and rallies. They protested segregation at lunch counters, parks, swimming pools, restaurants, buses, beaches, and movie theaters.[68]

The protesters shared a basic style. They created white allies by appealing to America's core democratic values, seeking basic rights guaranteed by the Constitution. They also relied on public figures, especially Martin Luther King Jr., for symbolism and media accessibility. Finally, they were sympathetic and nonthreatening, neatly groomed and polite. Framing their quest in the Christian tradition, they practiced nonviolence and avoided radical rhetoric. They were college students, after all — the future of the black bourgeoisie. Their peaceful demonstrations, alliances with white liberals, and middle-class ideology molded the civil rights movement.

Sharing these values, in both his personal politics and screen image, was Sidney Poitier. He wanted more scripts like *The Defiant Ones* — scripts that conveyed man's capacity for kindness, scripts that he called "pro-human." He wanted to play realistic characters with worthwhile messages. There was no better vehicle for these goals than a film version of *A Raisin in the Sun*.[69]

❖

"Nobody's going to turn this thing into a minstrel show," proclaimed Lorraine Hansberry in March 1959, as her play piqued the interests of movie producers. "If this blocks a sale, then it just won't be sold." After the Broadway premiere, United Artists, MGM, Paramount, Twentieth Century-Fox, Walter Mirisch, Hall Bartlett, and Harry Belafonte all considered purchasing the screen rights. The author hesitated; even theater producers had wanted it "just a little sexier," and she feared that Hollywood's "glossy little paws" would compromise her message. After friends convinced her that *A Raisin in the Sun* should reach a broader audience, Hansberry changed her mind. Still, she insisted on writing the screenplay herself.[70]

David Susskind bought the rights at the end of March. Per Hansberry's demands, he co-produced with Philip Rose. Susskind was sometimes pedantic and often obnoxious; Oscar Levant called him "salami dipped in chicken fat." Yet he and Rose realized huge risks in bringing *A Raisin in the Sun* to the screen, since the racial theme sacrificed the southern market. Susskind downplayed its political dimensions in favor of the human relationships. "It's a warm, frequently amusing and profoundly moving story of Negro life in which, *for once*, the race issue is not paramount," he wrote, adding that after *The Defiant Ones* and *Porgy and Bess*, "Sidney Poitier should be an important box office element."[71]

Poitier had star power — a film version without him would have crashed before takeoff. So he drove a hard bargain. In April 1960, his representative broke off negotiations with Susskind. Poitier then signed a favorable deal, and most of the play's cast joined the film. But Lloyd Richards did not make the cut. Columbia vice-president Sam Briskin had investigated Richards's work at CBS Television; the director communicated well with actors but needed help in the booth. Refusing to hire a technical novice, Briskin signed Daniel Petrie instead. The barrier between black directors and major studios stayed intact.[72]

Meanwhile, Hansberry installed scenes outside the Youngers' apartment. Besides breaking the visual monotony of a single set, the additions made the family's context more specific to the black working class. One new scene showed Mama Younger paying exorbitant prices at a South Side supermarket, and another portrayed her white employer's patronizing disbelief when she quits her job. Walter Lee faced similar condescension when a paternalistic liquor store owner discouraged him from starting his own business. In another scene, Walter Lee watched a radical soap-box orator.[73]

Columbia eliminated these additions. Studio executives warned that "the introduction of further race issue elements may lessen the sympathy of the audience, give an effect of propagandistic writing, and so weaken the story." Then, when Briskin provided line-by-line suggestions on the screenplay, he eviscerated dialogue with black slang (calling money "bread"), references to African American culture (Travis needing money for books about black history), direct allusions to racism (Walter Lee sneering at "them cool, quiet-looking restaurants where them white boys are sitting back"), and points about African politics (Beneatha describing "the Great Sore of colonialism"). Rather than sharpen the comment on the African American experience, Columbia whitewashed the Youngers.[74]

Poitier returned from a European family vacation in July 1960 to begin location shooting in Chicago. The cast encountered racism in more places than the script. The University of Chicago would not let Susskind use the school's name. Some whites cooperated for street scenes until the cast arrived, and then disappeared or carried on grudgingly. The actors showed little surprise. "We live every day, so we're not shocked to find actual circumstances coinciding with the script," Poitier told the *New York Amsterdam News*.[75]

One pregnant white woman — a Poitier fan — consented to filming near her home. When the production returned three weeks later, she was shaking with fear. She had received death threats. Even so, she courageously allowed them to proceed. Forty years later, Petrie remembered the ride home: "We drove a bit in silence. Then Sidney started to swear and he became so angry, and I mean angry. He was disillusioned and heartsick that this woman had to suffer that unconscionable terror." Only when away from the media did Poitier unleash his bitterness at American racism.[76]

In black neighborhoods, filming adopted a more convivial atmosphere. Black spectators flooded the South Side for glimpses of Poitier. The cries of peanut hawkers, ice cream men, and souvenir salesmen silenced only when the cameras rolled. Just one resident objected. "You're ruining my business!" he screamed at Poitier. The actor, always in the edifying mood, explained the benefits of location shooting for the local economy. "You don't understand, man!" the man interjected. "*I'm a bookie!*"[77]

When they moved to Los Angeles in August, the cast again found their lives and scripts in unpleasant harmony. Poitier offered to rent a house for $1,500 a month, but no one would rent a respectable home to a black family. Instead he took three rooms at the Chateau Marmont. A number of hotels turned away the other actors. Just before moving into cheap motels or black neighborhoods far from the studio, they found rooms at the Montecito Hotel. Poitier blamed their troubles on racial bias. His comments underscored that even movie stars faced discrimination.[78]

They spent two months in Los Angeles filming *A Raisin in the Sun*. On stage, the actors had ridden an emotional roller coaster every night. Now they had to summon dramatic depths for isolated scenes, without any give-and-take from an audience. They also adjusted to the "cool" medium of film by underplaying their sweeping gestures. Still, Poitier relished bringing his character to the screen. "The entire thing was an experience rather than a performance," he reflected, especially appreciating that he could repeat scenes to his satisfaction.[79]

Petrie designed a tiny set to convey the confinement of the Younger apartment. On the first day, Poitier, immersed in the Method, started vaulting around over furniture and crossing the set's boundaries. Then he harnessed his energy under control. "He can turn on a dime," marveled Petrie. "He can bend a finger and make it look like an explosion. Every limb moves and talks." If the film has one distinction, it is Poitier's anguished grace amidst his imaginary, suffocating walls.[80]

"This is by far the most ambitious opportunity yet presented this black actor," wrote *Films and Filming*, "and he grabs it greedily, playing to a full character pitch, often beyond it, in a galvanic, almost electric performance." Poitier is exquisitely expressive: pacing with anger, imitating an African warrior, shimmying to jazz, dropping to his knees in torment, standing upright with reclaimed manhood. When the picture opened in late March 1961, critics rained acclaim upon him. He owns the film. For all of Claudia McNeil's durable grace, Ruby Dee's emotional subtlety, and Diana Sands's bubbly hope, they look like stationary props next to Poitier.[81]

In other roles, Poitier could only add warmth and dignity to one-dimensional social symbols. Walter Lee Younger, by contrast, had complexity. He avoided the servant/comic/singer/dancer burden, and he eluded the traditional Poitier icon of loyal ally to the white hero. Moreover, the female characters stepped outside the boxes in which Hollywood placed black women. *A Raisin in the Sun* shattered stereotypes again, and on a larger scale.

The *New York Amsterdam News* trumpeted the picture as "even better than the award-winning play," published a letter calling it "the best all-Negro motion picture ever made," and quoted Poitier explaining his pride "in aiding understanding between human beings." Bosley Crowther of the *New York Times* spent a Sunday column condemning southern censorship and praising Poitier's films, culminating with *A Raisin in the Sun*.[82]

But most screen critics, like their theater counterparts, praised the "universality" of *A Raisin in the Sun*. Walter Lee's struggle, admired one, "is not peculiarly a Negro's but a man's struggle." Another waxed that "their problems, trials, hopes, and aspirations, despite any superficial differences, are those of mankind." A third marveled at the "simple and purely American story" of hard work and progress. They ignored the threat of white racism, and they embraced the affirmation of democracy.[83]

A Raisin in the Sun had a bigger problem. Although its antithesis in plot and politics, it shared a predicament with *Porgy and Bess*: it looked like a photographed stage production. Petrie sometimes held the same shot for minutes, awkwardly pulling the camera in and out. His few unconventional shots looked contrived. And except for three scenes, the entire film takes place on one set. "The result," concluded *Newsweek*, "is excellent to listen to, but not much to look at."[84]

The lack of action, combined with southern reluctance, ensured that *A Raisin in the Sun* would not shatter any box-office records. Columbia promoted it as a prestige picture, and it captured a few minor awards. In May 1961, Poitier traveled to the Cannes Film Festival, where he built goodwill by holding forth for the media, losing huge sums on the roulette table, and sending studio executives' wives atitter. *A Raisin in the Sun* failed to capture any of the festival's regular prizes, though. International audiences complained that without any visual emphasis on ghetto conditions, they could not understand the Youngers' desperation to leave. The picture did win a new award for "outstanding humanitarian values" honoring the late Gary Cooper. When Poitier accepted the prize, the crowd roared.[85]

For all the warmth that the picture engendered, it received no Oscar nominations. Insiders considered it a deliberate snub of Susskind—a vociferous critic of Hollywood. Without the Academy's prestige, *A Raisin in the Sun* proved neither a box-office winner nor loser, its low cost roughly offset by modest gate receipts.[86]

But the film's legacy lay beyond dollars and cents. Even though Columbia resisted Hansberry's changes, even though southern audiences never saw it, and even though critics insisted upon universalizing the Youngers, a Hollywood studio had addressed racial integration. As the *Christian Science Monitor* noted, a new era had dawned: "Whether he occupies a delegate's chair at the United Nations or protests segregation from a lunch counter stool in the South, the young Negro in today's world belongs to a historic forward movement." In the quest for full citizenship, the newspaper added, *A Raisin in the Sun* "writes a significant chapter."[87]

❖

For Poitier, too, *A Raisin in the Sun* defined a critical era. On stage and screen, he had articulated a genuine black voice to mainstream audiences. He had polished a reputation once tarnished by *Porgy and Bess*. His fame, will, and sheer ego had forced his character into the center of *A Raisin in the Sun*, shaping a popular understanding that placed the Youngers within the tradition of American upward mobility. And his life and his role had intertwined, as both Sidney Poitier and Walter Lee Younger grappled with issues of manhood and family responsibility.

"There were so many firsts, so many unique experiences," Poitier later reflected. "Much of it was too fast, and too much." The insecure Bahamian teenager had become American popular culture's foremost expression of racial possibilities, and it burdened him. "I was under great stress and pressure," he added. "I had on my shoulders the dreams of people I didn't even know. I was being asked to represent necessary fantasies for people who desperately needed fantasy representation." He sometimes felt unequipped to handle the responsibility. He could not even order his personal life.[88]

That ordeal would continue. Every day after filming *A Raisin in the Sun* in Los Angeles, Poitier returned to the Chateau Marmont to prepare for his upcoming role in *Paris Blues* by learning to play tenor saxophone. He practiced and practiced, but he was tone deaf. The cacophony of his futile efforts bounced through the elegant quarters, and Juanita heard it all. Every bleat, every wail, every flub of the fingers signaled the confusion that lay ahead. Because in *Paris Blues*, Poitier's co-stars included Paul Newman, Joanne Woodward, Louis Armstrong — and Diahann Carroll.[89]

CHAPTER 10

BLUES

(1960–1962)

As Diahann Carroll arrived in Paris in early October 1960, she resolved to choose restraint over passion, logic over emotion, and responsibility over romance. She had given birth to an infant daughter and tried to repair her marriage. She had studied with the legendary Lee Strasberg of the Actors' Studio, broadening her career and bolstering her self-confidence. She had a dramatic, romantic lead in *Paris Blues*, a rarity for a black woman. Despite her continued feelings for Poitier, she steeled herself. "Perhaps," she thought, "we could just do the work and leave each other alone."[1]

Carroll deliberately checked into a different hotel than Poitier. Their impending reunion made her stomach churn. But when she saw Poitier, her butterflies flew in formation. At a script reading, they exchanged lines across a table with Paul Newman and Joanne Woodward. Afterward, Poitier escorted Carroll outside, and they discussed their past. Neither wanted to hurt their loved ones, and they agreed to end their relationship.

But this was Paris, where romance wafted along the cobblestone streets, in the open-air markets, on the quays of the Seine, and in the shadow of Notre Dame. "It was becoming difficult to separate our lives and our roles," Carroll remembered. They played new lovers, and their scenes called for long walks and romantic talks. Neither admitted it, but they were still in love.[2]

Newman and Woodward might have recognized the situation. Newman had divorced his first wife to marry Woodward in 1958, and the couple had collaborated on three films before coming to Paris, where they stayed in a quaint Montmartre apartment, acting by day, exploring jazz clubs and bistros by night. They had a comfortable relationship. But Newman and Woodward shared affluent backgrounds, established Hollywood careers, and enough individual security to allow each other space. They were friends first and lovers second, quite unlike their confused co-stars.[3]

After a few weeks, Poitier and Carroll met for a drink. Poitier played it cool, adopting an ostensibly rational approach to an emotional dilemma. He contended that they could not end their relationship unless they first slept together. Carroll recognized his argument for what it was: "total bullshit." But the sexual frustration was too much. The next afternoon, Carroll took a long milk bath and donned a simple black dress. She arrived at Poitier's room, and amidst the elegance, they sat together, taking their time, establishing their natural chemistry. At the right moment, Poitier reached to her.

Carroll coiled up. She realized that she could not have sex without some future implication. She felt "like trash, like absolute trash," and she refused to continue. They had the same poisonous conversation: Carroll wanted commitment, Poitier refused to leave his family. Two years after *Porgy and Bess*, they were back where they started.[4]

❖

The only thing more muddled than their romantic future was the script of *Paris Blues*. Based on Harold Flender's second-rate novel, it revolves around an expatriate black musician torn between an American woman and the racial fluidity of Paris. Indeed, Paris had attracted black entertainers and intellectuals since the 1920s. By the 1950s, the City of Lights harbored a black literary circle that included Richard Wright, James Baldwin, and Chester Himes. Jazz great Sidney Bechet called Paris home. Gordon Heath, star of *Deep Are the Roots* on Broadway, moved to Paris in 1949. Instead of competing for roles with Poitier or James Edwards, Heath sang folk music at his nightclub on Rue L'Abbaye.[5]

A still photographer named Sam Shaw, enchanted by the scenery and mood of the Left Bank, wanted to film Flender's novel. Once Shaw secured Poitier, Newman and Woodward signed on. Under Pennebaker Productions, a company nominally run by Marlon Brando's father, the budget escalated from its original, modest total of $400,000 toward $2,000,000.[6]

The producers worried about the financial prospects of a film featuring black romance. An ancillary plotline in the book involves Benny, a Jewish pianist. Three screenwriters later, that minor character was Ram Bowen (Newman), a white trombonist of indeterminate ethnicity. For his love interest, they turned a sixtyish spinster into the attractive American tourist played by Woodward. The main story became Bowen's choice between love and music. The black saxophonist Eddie Cook (Poitier) was now Bowen's sidekick, and his racial dilemma the secondary plot. *Paris Blues*, too, would conform to the established pattern of race relations in Poitier films.

Alas, the script verged on incoherence. The producers summoned a "script doctor," screenwriter Walter Bernstein. Apparently his main contributions were to curse like a sailor and frequent the Paris bars. They finally patched together an eighty-five-page script that plugged the plot's most gaping holes. Putting a smiling face on the ordeal, director Martin Ritt told *Newsweek* that "rather than clutter it up with a lot of talking and dramatic close-ins, we thought we'd achieve the effort much better by letting the actors go through their motions and let the action speak for itself." To compensate for the deficient script, he installed long musical numbers and repeated sequences of strolling couples.[7]

The production did boast Paris scenery, a handsome cast, and vintage jazz. Rather than wait for sunlight in Paris in November, Ritt captured the city's gray autumn mood, providing a fine visual counterpart to the Duke Ellington score. The film also featured such Ellington classics as "Take the A Train" and "Mood Indigo." For the jazz club scenes, Newman conquered the trombone, but Poitier's hours of practice never resulted in saxophonic mastery. While shooting Poitier, Ritt had to quickly pan in and out.[8]

At a late date, Louis Armstrong joined the cast. In the novel, the character "Wild Man Moore" is rather disagreeable. The producers turned him into a jovial jazz legend, a fictional version of Armstrong himself. Satchmo possessed astounding popularity in Europe. Parisian artists, poets, actors, and intellectuals adored him. French authorities even feared a popular riot during filming at the Gare St. Lazare. The picture's most memorable scene stars Armstrong: his orchestra enters a cozy jazz club and engages Newman's band in a good-natured "cutting contest." Seventy-five young Parisians with tight pants and turtleneck sweaters played witnesses to the musical duel. Later the crew realized that some extras were men dressed as women. "Good looking women," added Ritt.[9]

The presence of Ellington and Armstrong engaged a musical debate. In a publicity interview, Ellington bemoaned "the modernists, who come on with this so-called *cool* jazz." He referred to the cutting-edge bebop of Miles Davis, Thelonius Monk, and John Coltrane. Based in Greenwich Village, featuring smaller combinations and abstract compositions, they suggested a certain black defiance, a refusal to pander to white expectations. Davis, for instance, matched restrained music with an imperious demeanor — a revolt against Armstrong's grinning exuberance.[10]

As the avant-garde lauded bebop, traditionalists retreated to Europe.

"Here they dig *Satchmo's* style," said Ellington. *Paris Blues*, by romanticizing two expatriates who play Ellington standards and revere Armstrong, sides with the traditionalists. That stance had political ramifications. Jazz was a significant black contribution to the American arts, and the traditionalists symbolized American racial brotherhood to the world. By saluting them, *Paris Blues* promotes a less threatening form of African American music.[11]

The film, however, devalues *all* jazz. Ram Bowen composes a piece called "Paris Blues." (Ellington actually wrote it, and he often championed his work as art.) The arbiter of its value is not Wild Man Moore but the French composer Rene Barnard, who dismisses the piece and urges Bowen to formally study harmony, theory, and counterpoint. In the end, Bowen forsakes his love for the American woman Lillian (Woodward) to follow the composer's advice. His decision implies that jazz cannot rival the European tradition as serious music.[12]

The film's other plotline deals more explicitly with race. Eddie Cook (Poitier) falls for an American schoolteacher named Connie (Carroll), but he likes Paris. He explains: "Sit down for lunch somewhere without getting clubbed for it, and you'll look across the ocean and say: Who needs it? Who needs it?" Connie appeals to his race pride: "Things are much better than they were five years ago, and they're still going to be better next year. And not because Negroes go to Paris." In the end, Eddie chooses Connie. Unlike Ram Bowen, who chooses art over love, Eddie Cook must answer his racial responsibilities. His decision suggests that he can obtain his due civil rights in the United States.[13]

Paris Blues thus subscribes to the optimistic liberalism that infused other Poitier films: Eddie bears a moral responsibility to uplift his race. But the film also marked a milestone. Racial taboos had precluded him from romantic roles. In *Paris Blues*, however, he displayed flirtatious charm. Eddie escorts Connie through moonlit streets and jokes that "if I had a teacher like you when I went to school, boyyyyyyyy, I might have learned something!" As the romance develops, his sexuality remains overt. In the film's penultimate shot, as Connie's train pulls away, Eddie leaps to the window, and they kiss.

The romance is palatable to mass audiences because both characters are black, attractive, and genteel. Moreover, their relationship seems tame within the sexual freedom of Paris. The opening scene shows interracial and same-sex couples, and Ram Bowen first flirts with Connie. Then the film pulls back to safety: Lillian pursues Ram, and the white and black couples pair off. Ram and Lillian appear half-naked in bed. Eddie and Connie remain fully clothed throughout.[14]

The publicity walked the same line between taboo-breaking titillation and racial rigidity. Advertisements dangled miscegenation before potential customers. "Two American girls in Paris," one read. "They give the love they'd never give at home." Yet visual cues smoothed over the implication. In all the posters, Newman and Woodward embrace. In some, Woodward is wearing only lingerie. Poitier always plays the saxophone, alone.[15]

Paris Blues combined stars, scenery, jazz, and sexual innuendo. "All it lacks," *Time* qualified, "is something to pull these parts into a sensible whole." Many critics echoed this appraisal, and some yearned for more progressive fare. Newman's conflict glossed over Poitier's more interesting racial dilemma. The black critic Albert Johnson chided the superficial presentation, characterizing Poitier and Carroll as "likable puppets quite unlike any Negroes one might meet in Europe or America. They are, ultimately, only figments of a white person's literary fancy, and once past the initial hint of misceginative romance, the film loses its nerve."[16]

At the time, none of the principals acknowledged that early scripts featured interracial couplings. But three years later, in a private conversation, Poitier said that he believed United Artists "chickened out on us." The "guts" of the film, in his opinion, was the two interracial romances. "Cold feet maneuvered to have it twisted around—lining up the colored guy with the colored girl. It took the spark out of it."[17]

Filming *Paris Blues* could have been a stimulating experience. Poitier worked with great actors, dined in fine restaurants, and slept in luxury hotels, but he wallowed in self-pity. He could not choose between his marriage and his mistress, and he could not reconcile his disciplined code with his celebrity lifestyle. That agony manifested itself in bursts of emotion, sometimes with a dangerous edge. At one cast party, he and Carroll argued. "Oh, if you would just get out of my life!" said Poitier. According to Carroll, he grabbed her face, pulled her toward him, and then pushed her away. He always bottled up his anger in public. But in private, passion sometimes overwhelmed his self-discipline.[18]

During the holidays, his family came to Paris. Juanita refused to abandon their marriage, explaining that a divorce would not only forsake their responsibilities, but also absolve Sidney of his deserved guilt. Her sound morality removed any convenient solution to his ethical torment.[19]

The night before Christmas Eve, Poitier wandered the city. In a restaurant window he saw Diahann Carroll, eating dinner with a friend. She, too, was escaping from a visiting family. When Poitier entered the restaurant, Carroll's friend excused herself. Poitier and Carroll talked that evening, and the next night, and the next. In secret, under cover of darkness, during long walks, they convinced each other of their romance's inevitability. Poitier had planned to keep his family in Paris until filming finished; now he sent them home. He and Carroll planned a vacation in Sweden before arranging their respective divorces. They finally made their agonizing decision.

Or so it seemed. Poitier then received a wire from John F. Kennedy's inauguration committee, inviting him to attend the upcoming gala. He canceled the trip to Sweden. Carroll assumed that he had an alternate plan for their future, but there was none. Poitier used his perceived political duty to deflect his personal crisis. He flew to Washington, she flew to New York, and nothing between them changed.[20]

❖

John F. Kennedy represented the ultimate marriage between national politics and celebrity culture. The new president was right out of Central Casting: handsome, breezily charming, elegant wife on his arm. His telegenic appeal swung votes during his famous debates with Richard Nixon. And Kennedy's camp understood the cache of famous names and faces. Poitier joined an election committee called "Hollywood for Kennedy," whose chairmen included Andy Williams and Gene Kelly. Harry Belafonte and Henry Fonda did television spots, and Frank Sinatra led the "Rat Pack" in campaign performances.[21]

Sinatra also produced the inauguration gala that lured Poitier away from Carroll. The celebration at the National Guard Armory in January 1961 raised $1.5 million dollars for the Democratic campaign fund. It starred Belafonte, Jimmy Durante, Nat King Cole, Leonard Bernstein, and many others. Poitier performed a skit with Anthony Quinn, Bette Davis, Fredric March, and Sir Laurence Olivier. The integrated cast reflected the new administration's appreciation for racial symbols: African Americans attended various inaugural balls, and Kennedy even danced with black women. Yet the colorblind spirit had limits. Notably absent was Rat Packer Sammy Davis Jr., who had already postponed his marriage to Swedish actress May Britt at the behest of the Kennedy campaign. Three days before the inauguration, the new administration asked Davis to avoid parading an interracial couple on a national stage. Davis was crushed.[22]

Celebrities also contributed to the civil rights movement. Poitier and

Belafonte chaired the cultural division of the Committee to Defend Martin Luther King and the Struggle for Freedom in the South, a Harlem-based fundraising association. The organization gained notoriety with a March 1960 advertisement in the *New York Times* entitled "Heed Their Rising Voices," which applauded the courage of protesters, celebrated Dr. King, and condemned "Southern violators of the Constitution." A host of famous names signed it, and contributions flowed in. It sparked a bizarre lawsuit by Alabama officials, who claimed libel against the *New York Times* and four black ministers in Montgomery. During the dragged-out case, the newspaper's lawyers defended the committee's reputation for "truthfulness and trustworthiness," citing such endorsers as Eleanor Roosevelt, Marlon Brando, and Poitier.[23]

In May 1960, Poitier and Belafonte led the committee's commemoration of the sixth anniversary of *Brown vs. Board of Education*. After an interfaith ceremony at the Statue of Liberty, they arrived at a rally in the Garment District. Fifteen thousand people cheered as the performers took the podium. Poitier was present, he said, because he had three children in school, "and I wish for them the freedom that was not forthcoming when I was a child." That night Poitier, Belafonte, and Shelley Winters headlined a "theatrical spectacular" at the 369th Armory in Harlem. Belafonte, Mahalia Jackson, and Diahann Carroll sang, and Poitier performed in a skit written by Lorraine Hansberry. Attendees paid an entrance fee and threw $10,000 into passing hats. Two other shows that month—one at the Apollo, the other at the Village Gate—also raised money for civil rights.[24]

In January 1961, one week after Kennedy's inauguration, Poitier joined a "Tribute to Martin Luther King" at Carnegie Hall. He introduced Mahalia Jackson, who sang the national anthem. The Count Basie Orchestra played, Tony Bennett sang, Nipsey Russell joked, Belafonte introduced Reverend King, and the Rat Pack revived their famous "Summit Meeting" routine. The show raised $35,000 for the Southern Christian Leadership Conference.[25]

Poitier committed not only his celebrity stature, but also his money. In 1960, for instance, he sent emergency funds to King to fight a trumped-up tax evasion case in Alabama. Poitier's politicization reflected a new era in Hollywood-Washington relations. In the heyday of the studio system, actors encountered subtle pressure against political activity. In the conservative 1950s, the House Un-American Committee and gossip columnists checked the careers of overt liberals. But by the early 1960s, movie stars could—and did—endorse political causes such as black equality.[26]

Yet black inequality characterized Hollywood itself. In November 1961, the NAACP charged the film industry with employment discrimination and inaccurate portrayals of black life. Los Angeles chapter president Edward Warren threatened boycotts, pickets, and possible legal action unless studios took remedial steps. "Any time they have a crap game they show plenty of Negroes," he said. "But when do you see a Negro doctor or lawyer except on some Amos and Andy show?" The Writers Guild, Directors Guild, and Motion Picture Producers Association pledged support for the NAACP goals. As civil rights demonstrations thrust race into the public eye, the black image in popular culture also won attention. The NAACP even established a permanent Hollywood–Beverly Hills chapter in 1962.[27]

In this context, Poitier became a touchstone for black progress. *The Progressive* ran a five-part series on "The New Negro on Screen" that revolved around him. In February 1961, the *New York Amsterdam News* announced that two one-act plays were each searching for "a Negro actor of Sidney Poitier's type." On the same page, another article promoted Trinidadian actor Errol John as "another Poitier." Poitier's mannered, intelligent image was in vogue, the model for future black stars.[28]

Poitier thus searched for important vehicles in the vein of *The Defiant Ones* or *A Raisin in the Sun*. He wished, he told the *New York Times*, to appear in "the first honest, three-dimensional drama on integration in the schools." At his best, Poitier compelled casual filmgoers to consider the changing racial landscape. His screen persona elicited sympathy from white, middle-class voters. At the same time, he remained legitimate to African Americans. Black theater columnist Jesse Walker believed that "Poitier is still the same engaging fellow who barely 10 years ago was half-owner of a Seventh Avenue barbecue spot and making many of the deliveries. Simply a nice guy."[29]

He had graduated from up-and-coming star to established authority on race and acting. In an interview with drama critic Lewis Funke, Poitier reflected on his background, artistic interests, and the Method. When asked to advise black actors embittered by the lack of opportunities, he said, "Go and prepare yourself to be an artist, and if you become an artist — if you are on your way to realizing your potential as an artist — and some bastards superimpose restrictions on your effort, get as bitter as you want — you follow?"[30]

Poitier's tone betrayed frustration with his own career. Stardom had created many opportunities, but few materialized. In 1959, he planned to play a western gunfighter opposite Harry Belafonte. First called *The Ex-*

odusters and then *The Last Notch*, the script examined black migration to the West following the Civil War. Two years later, they canceled the project. In 1960, he agreed to co-star with Spencer Tracy in *The Devil at Four O'Clock*. Then his deal collapsed and Frank Sinatra replaced him. He also considered the film *Call Me by My Rightful Name*, and rumors connected his name to *The Interns*, *The Gallery*, and *Synanon*.[31]

The most persistent reports concerned *Othello*. Every great black dramatic actor from Ira Aldridge to Paul Robeson to Canada Lee had played Shakespeare's tragic Moor, and Poitier felt beholden to follow that tradition. But he also had misgivings. Othello, though proud and commanding, gets tricked by his lieutenant Iago into strangling his wife Desdemona. Poitier feared that the play harmed the quest for positive black images. Othello is manipulated by a white man, which might displease black audiences, and murders a white woman, which might offend white sensibilities. So he dismissed his earlier interest. "It's a bad part," he said in September 1960. "I see now that the character is a little wanting."[32]

Yet the following spring, he considered *The Iron Men*, a modernization of *Othello* directed by John Cassavetes and set in World War II Italy. Cassavetes envisioned Poitier as head of the 99th Pursuit Squadron, a unit of black pilots. In August, Poitier confirmed that he would soon begin filming in Italy. Then he dropped out. According to Lester Cole, the "Hollywood Ten" exile who co-wrote the script, Poitier's friends warned him that a modernization would amplify the controversial racial impact. It seemed an undue risk. Without him, first United Artists and then Paramount abandoned production. *The Iron Men* was never made.[33]

Poitier similarly waffled on his ambitions to direct. In September 1960 he told *Newsweek*, "I'd like to direct the same way a guy would like to try many things. But now, man, I just don't want his problems! I see them now, man!" Six months later, the *New York Times* reported that he planned to direct *Uhuru!*, a musical documentary about African freedom struggles. That project never panned out. In August 1961, he related his aspiration to produce low-budget films examining "certain myths of modern living," especially the pervasiveness of corruption. He and Belafonte also shook hands on a deal that required each star to appear in films produced by the other's company. They publicly announced their partnership, but the deal never came together.[34]

Poitier did option the screen rights to the Paule Marshall novel *Brown Girl, Brownstones*. The story of Barbadian immigrants in Brooklyn examined a young female protagonist, her unwavering mother, and her tragic father caught between cultures. Poitier identified with the story, but he never made the film. Although once staged on television, the film proved difficult to finance. The characters spoke in dialect, coped with personal rather than physical struggles, and were all black—hardly the stuff of box-office gold. Manilo Productions, the company that Poitier formed to purchase the rights, disappeared.[35]

Poitier also considered returning to Broadway. Playwrights William Branch, Loften Mitchell, William Herman, and John Oliver Killens all wanted Poitier for their projects. Poitier certainly wished to replicate the satisfaction of A Raisin in the Sun. When asked in 1961 about his future on stage, he said, "You can very well expect me next season." In June 1962, he contemplated playing a Brazilian psychiatrist in Roger O. Hirson's Journey to the Day. He ultimately declined the part, however.[36]

Another intriguing possibility was James Baldwin's Blues for Mister Charlie. The two men had been friends since January 1959, when Baldwin saw A Raisin in the Sun. From Puerto Rico in the summer of 1962, Baldwin sent Poitier a draft and publicly hoped that Poitier would accept the lead role in his new play. Loosely based on the 1955 murder of Emmett Till, it examines the roots and aftereffects of a black man's death at the hands of an angry white storekeeper. The murder victim, a former drug addict who returns to his southern hometown, interested Poitier; the character was proud, defiant, intelligent, sexual, contemptuous of racial mores, and resentful of his accommodationist father. In November, Baldwin proclaimed that Poitier would star opposite Rip Torn in an Actors Studio production. But Poitier decided against it. He never again appeared in a major stage production.[37]

Poitier's disappearance from Broadway reflected a broader trend. In the early 1960s, jobs for black actors declined. While the stage actors' union held panels on racial discrimination, the Congress of Racial Equality (CORE) and the Committee for the Employment of the Negro Performer (CENP) held mass meetings and picketed two plays without black actors. The next month, at a rally at Judson Memorial Church in Greenwich Village, Poitier was the featured speaker.[38]

Of course, Poitier operated under different circumstances than most black actors. CORE and CENP protested that Broadway producers did not incorporate blacks into racially nonspecific roles. But unlike other blacks, Poitier's exclusion from the stage was by choice. He considered most Broadway fare asinine and valueless. "I hate the theater," he said, while in a particularly prickly mood. "You know that? I feel like yelling, 'Come on, man, this is 1961. You're not starving. You don't have to write this stuff. Show us your guts.'" He resolved to direct, to produce, even to write his own play. He bounced with frustrated energy: "I'm going to live swinging, and I'm going to die swinging. The pessimism bit isn't my scene. I know there are 100-megaton bombs. I can't sit here waiting for them to drop."[39]

Poitier's main reason for choosing Hollywood over Broadway, however, was money. Complaints aside, he recognized theater's artistic potential. As he told James Earl Jones, then a young off-Broadway actor, "If you're not hungry and you don't have kids to feed, don't rush to Hollywood, because they will only ask of you what you are, and not that you grow." But he supported a wife, his parents, assorted family members, and especially his children. (A fourth daughter, Gina, was born in May 1961.) He wanted to act in both plays and films, solving the dilemma between "integrity and the icebox." In the end, though, he stayed off the stage.[40]

His decisions were rooted in his past — in his parents' struggle to stay afloat, in his father's lessons about providing for his children, and in his own early poverty. "When you are poor," reflected Poitier, "the question of food, the question of lodging, becomes so immediate that you are constantly at the precipice, in terms of how you're going to deal with it." Even after achieving material comfort, he sometimes put his arm around his plate, protecting his food. When he ate at expensive restaurants, he considered all the groceries that he could have bought with the same money. He even demanded contracts that spread out payments over twenty-five years.[41]

But Poitier was also an inveterate gambler, a foible humorously immortalized by Art Buchwald during the 1961 Cannes Film Festival. Buchwald claimed that both lost so much money playing roulette that they applied handcuffs to each other. In an arch reference to *The Defiant Ones*, Buchwald wrote that "in spite of the antagonism we held for each other the gambling casino had made us brothers." Some time later Sammy Davis Jr. invited him to Las Vegas and reserved a room for only nine dollars a night. Poitier arrived at the hotel, gave his bags to the bellboy, walked into the casino, and promptly lost $1,000. "I don't seem to have much sense about handling money," he sighed to the *New York Daily News*.[42]

Poitier often gambled at Philip Rose's legendary Thursday night poker game. As others smoked cigars and guzzled whiskey, Poitier — nicknamed "Big Daddy" — ate hard-boiled eggs and drank milk. He needed his wits about him. "A player could easily drop fifty thousand a year in that game," an anonymous regular told William Hoffman. "Sidney was a consistent loser. One time he visited my office and gave a detailed analysis of what he was doing wrong and how he was going to change. But he never practiced what he preached. He stayed in too many hands."[43]

Gambling attracted Poitier for a number of reasons. He enjoyed the camaraderie, the escape from feminine entanglements. He loved competition and reveled in the cool bluff. Most of all, gambling filled a cavern carved by poverty. In other situations, he fretted about finances, arranged long-term investments, and placed himself on a budget. Gambling, though, provided the visceral thrill of winning and losing large sums. When he won, he experienced the sudden rush of tangible wealth, an alien phenomenon in his early life. When he lost, he still knew that he could survive frittering away money, bolstering his ego. These emotions explained his irrational faith in mediocre poker hands. No longer wandering New York City, no longer sleeping in pay toilets, he still had not escaped his past.

❖

After filming *Paris Blues*, Poitier moved his family to Pleasantville, New York, a village in northern Westchester County. The twelve-room Tudor estate sat on seven acres of land and lay amidst similarly grand estates, populated by affluent whites. Poitier did not embrace the move, since it isolated his children in upper-class comfort. He also cherished golf and social outings with New York City friends. But Juanita demanded the change. It satisfied her vision of upward mobility, and it distanced her husband from the city's temptations. In the wake of the Paris debacle, he could not refuse.[44]

Poitier and Diahann Carroll continued to alternate between devotion and frustration. Both remember a meeting with Monte Kay, Carroll's husband, but each pins responsibility on the other. According to Poitier, Carroll insisted that he meet Kay at a hotel cocktail lounge. Kay calmly questioned him before requesting a private discussion with his wife. According to Carroll, Poitier demanded to confer with Kay. At an intimate restaurant, he announced his love for Carroll. She fled the restaurant, overcome by Poitier's insensitivity. As the contradictory stories reveal, mutual insecurities still plagued their relationship.[45]

The stories do share a conclusion: Kay obtained a divorce and moved out. Poitier and Carroll now dated openly — and even, after three years, consummated their relationship. At dinner in a dark, private booth of an opulent restaurant, Poitier uncharacteristically ordered a cocktail before dinner and wine with the meal. They relaxed. "There was nothing forced, nothing unnatural—we had a wonderful dinner," Carroll recalled. "And then we went back to my apartment, and we made love. Finally."[46]

Poitier kept spending time with Carroll in Manhattan. At night, though, he always returned to Pleasantville. He hemmed and hawed about divorcing Juanita, citing his complicated family situation. Juanita's friends and family implored him to stay with his wife, and in 1961, Juanita invited Sidney's mother to Pleasantville. "Not the least among her many reasons for coming," Poitier remembered, "was to talk some sense into her son—who, she had been told, was neglecting his children something awful and ignoring his marriage vows." The visit exacerbated Sidney's guilt. His family seemed to be crumbling. That year, his brother Cedric died of carbon monoxide poisoning after falling asleep in his car. Then, after Evelyn's visit, Reginald neared death.[47]

Sidney made an emergency visit to Nassau, arriving to find a vigil of family and friends. After some solemn hugs, he saw his father, more gaunt than ever. Reginald squeezed his youngest son's hand. Sidney rambled, put up an optimistic veneer, assured his father that they would travel America together. Reginald knew better. Weeks earlier, he had dictated a two-page will. Then he stopped eating. When Evelyn brought him meals on the porch, where he sat in his wheelchair, he fed the neighborhood dogs. After seventy-seven years, he was at peace. He starved himself to death.[48]

Reginald died in December 1961. Friends from throughout the Out Islands paid respects. Sidney and his brothers carried the coffin through Over the Hill, with Evelyn trailing. None of the pallbearers cried. Even on this occasion, the West Indian code of masculinity prevailed. Back in America, that code tortured Sidney. Neither his wife nor his mistress lived by his patriarchal whims. He was confused. He wanted personal fulfillment, a loving family, financial stability, artistic accomplishment, and political respect. Above all, he wanted internal peace. When he juggled these needs, he tortured himself.[49]

Poitier's depression compelled him to call Harry Belafonte, who was then performing in Miami Beach. Poitier visited, and they sat with Belafonte's wife, Julie, to discuss his problems. Belafonte confessed the pressures of his own career, political responsibility, and high-visibility interracial marriage. "He understood the aloneness," Poitier recalled, "because he was walking the same road." The couple suggested that Poitier visit Julie's therapist, a Columbia University psychologist with a private practice. Although hesitant about revealing weakness to a woman, Poitier scheduled an appointment.[50]

Poitier respected Dr. Viola Bernard from the moment he entered her Fifth Avenue office. He slouched into a chair and closed his eyes. He discussed his childhood, and then he moved to a couch and addressed his own shortcomings. Poitier had always been introspective, but now he was articulating his anxieties. His sporadic appointments turned into regular visits, four to five times a week. He achieved some self-awareness. "Maybe I'm worrying too much about the needs of my position," he said in June 1962. "I wish I'd discover the real needs of just me. Then I could do more justice to my position. Man, that's why I got me an analyst."[51]

For his next film, ironically, Poitier moved to the other side of the psychiatrist's office. In October 1961, he signed onto *Pressure Point*, based on a chapter from Robert Lindner's book of actual case studies, *The Fifty Minute Hour*. Lindner was a Jewish doctor assigned to cure a fascist lunatic. It had aired in January 1960 as a one-hour television drama entitled "Destiny's Tot." Then Stanley Kramer bought the property and assigned Hubert Cornfield to adapt the script and direct. In Cornfield's early drafts, Lindner's character remained Jewish. After revisions, however, the doctor was black.[52]

The bold casting move illustrated Kramer's penchant for liberal social commentary, a reputation polished by such films as *On the Beach*, *Inherit the Wind*, and *Judgment at Nuremberg*. He said that the switch reflected the reality of the black middle class: "There should be no reason why any number of properties could not be changed to reflect the improving position of the Negro in our society." Poitier echoed his producer; he hoped that his role might stimulate black youths to become psychiatrists.[53]

Kramer continued his unconventional casting by hiring teen idol Bobby Darin to play the racist patient. He had never seen Darin act, but he thought that the singer's notorious temper suited the part. During filming in late 1961, Poitier developed a fondness for his temperamental co-star, tutoring him on acting's finer points. He later explained to the media that Darin was big-hearted, hard-working, and given to angry fits out of insecurity. In many ways, *Pressure Point* marked a new stage for Poitier. He had top billing, a huge salary ($87,500 up front, $87,500 deferred, and 12.5 percent of profits), and an established reputation as a thoughtful man of experience, both on and off screen.[54]

The bulk of *Pressure Point* is set in a prison in 1942. Darin, a member of the German-American Bund, is in jail for sedition. He cannot sleep and visits the prison psychiatrist. Upon entering the office, however, Darin cackles disbelievingly. "Whoever heard of a Negro doctor anyway?" he says. "Don't you people have enough troubles?" A composed Poitier draws out Darin's laundry list of psychological afflictions: an abusive father, a spineless mother, a subordinate imaginary playmate, a failed romance with a Jewish woman, and acceptance among hate mongers.

Cornfield shot Darin's past in surrealist flashback sequences, set to shrill background music. They are lurid. In one scene, a miniature Darin crawls out of a sink drain. In another, members of Darin's gang play tic-tac-toe all over the walls, floors, and tables of a bar, and then draw tic-tac-toe lines in lipstick on a woman's bare body. Other flashbacks have blank backgrounds, absurdist sequences, or quick cuts from past to present. Their effect is wearying: the ninety-minute film seems much longer.[55]

Poitier's character is simply a social symbol, a vehicle for a liberal viewpoint. He has no background, no home, no family, no psychological issues of his own — not even a name. His chief responsibility is to weather Darin's racist goading. That white audiences of 1962 accepted Poitier as a psychiatrist represented progress. But it is Darin who addresses bigotry. "What can you do?" he asks Poitier.

> Can you walk on a bus or a streetcar or a train with a little dignity, like a free human being, like a free man? You wanna go see a movie, can you walk into just any theater? Some flapjacks cookin' in a window — can you say, "Hey, I'll have some of those flapjacks!"
>
> You're a Negro with some brains, you could use a little education. Can you go to the school where you get it best? Maybe you see a house you like and you've even got the money to buy it. Can you live there? Huh? You live in the ghetto. North, South, East, or West, you live where they let you live. In Harlem, USA!
>
> Now maybe you're good at some job. Can you go to work where you can make something out of it? Can you do any of those things, doctor? And how about your kids? Are your kids gonna do any of those things?
>
> They got you so hypnotized you're singing "My Country Tis of Thee" while they walk all over you!

It is a comment on the limits of Hollywood liberalism that the most scathing indictment of American racism in the film — in the entire body of Sidney Poitier films — comes from the mouth of a crazed, despicable Nazi sympathizer.[56]

The black critic Albert Johnson described two reactions to Darin's diatribe: as whites murmured acknowledgment, blacks cheered this recognition of racist double standards. But Poitier only sits stone-faced. After this scene, the psychiatrist board grants Darin parole over Poitier's objection. The disillusioned doctor prepares to resign. Darin delivers a final taunting: "Who would they believe? . . . The big black boy who's supposed to be running this place, or the white Christian American?" Finally, Poitier explodes. "You vicious slimy rat!" he yells. "This is my country! This is where I've done what I've done!" He lauds American democracy and predicts Darin's demise. Now, Johnson noted, the white audience roared with patriotic pride. The black audience quietly contemplated the black man's ambiguous position in America.[57]

Late changes to the script underscored the relevance to contemporary race relations. In March 1962, they filmed two additional scenes set in the present. One opens the picture. Poitier, graying at the temples, now supervises a mental institute. A psychiatrist played by Peter Falk begs to be removed from a case involving a white-hating black teenager. Poitier admits that he considered assigning a black doctor. "I didn't for just one reason: I have more confidence in you than in either one of them. They're good — they're just not as good as you are. And I do understand." Then the film flashes back to 1942. It returns to 1962 at the very end, when Poitier reveals that Darin was hanged for beating a stranger to death. Poitier also discloses that he did not resign, implying that he achieved success by working within the system. In a color-reversed emulation of Poitier, Falk forges on.[58]

While equating the past experience of the black doctor with the present crisis of the white doctor, the film also likens white fascists of the 1930s to black extremists of the early 1960s. Many Americans knew something of black radicals, especially the Nation of Islam. Known to most as the "Black Muslims," they had been "exposed" by Mike Wallace in a 1959 television special called "The Hate That Hate Produced." Scores of magazines then ran features on the organization and their charismatic spokesman Malcolm X.[59]

Poitier himself had met Malcolm X in 1962, at the Mount Vernon home of Ossie Davis and Ruby Dee. They learned something about the Nation of Islam. The philosophy of Islamic discipline, eye-for-an-eye justice, and black separatism empowered masses of young, poor, urban African Americans. The media ignored such aspects, instead focusing on the Nation of Islam's condemnation of "white devils." Most middle-class whites could sympathize only with blacks who espoused Christian sacrifice, nonviolence, and integration. Just as Martin Luther King exemplified these ideals in politics, Poitier personified them on screen.[60]

Pressure Point opened in September 1962 and faltered at the box office. The dialogue-heavy script and unconventional flashbacks limited its appeal, and it played few southern markets. Attempts to market the picture on its prestige failed. As for Poitier, the critics paid lip service to his acting abilities, even though Darin's villain overshadowed him. Poitier did expand his repertoire, playing his first middle-class professional since *No Way Out*. But *Pressure Point*, like other Poitier movies, reduced racism to a personal (and in this case psychological) issue. The *New Republic* called the film "half cheap liberal sermon and half opportunism" and bemoaned Poitier's static, predictable character. "He is here only marking time until he gets parts worthy of his powers."[61]

❖

In early 1962, Poitier rented a one-bedroom apartment on West 57th Street. He left Pleasantville and committed to Carroll. Now his separation from Juanita was irrevocable.[62]

The guilt gnawed at him. "My mother and father had done so much better," he remembered. "My brothers Reginald and Cedric had done so much better. And then came Sidney, who simply wasn't measuring up. In fact, I was *giving* up." He tried to compensate by becoming a more active parent. He met his children after school, ate dinner with them in Pleasantville, hosted them for weekends, and telephoned when he was away. Of course, the girls resented the separation, and they justifiably blamed their father. Sometimes there were long, awkward, guilty silences. Beverly, a young teenager by then, took it hardest. For a time, she stopped speaking with him. Poitier tried periodic peace offerings, but he had already crossed his personal rubicon.[63]

During this same time, Poitier assumed more political roles. In May 1962 he received an invitation for a White House state dinner honoring Felix Houphouet-Boigny, president of the Ivory Coast. Since the burst of African independence in the late 1950s and early 1960s, the State Department had worried that international disapproval of American racism might wound their Cold War efforts. But Poitier was the perfect symbol of American racial enlightenment. The actor bought an elegant, tailed tuxedo for the occasion. Afterward, he displayed the formal wear in a glass case.[64]

Five months later, Poitier testified before New York congressman Adam Clayton Powell's Labor Committee about racial discrimination in entertainment. His statement equated the civil rights struggle with the plight of black actors, and it castigated Hollywood for failing to honestly explore African American life or race relations. He blamed the lack of black employment. "I'm probably the only Negro actor who makes a living in the motion picture industry," he said. "Except for the coffee boy, I am the only Negro on the set." He mourned his own tokenism: "It is no great joy to me to be used as a symbol, an example of how they don't really discriminate."[65]

Poitier could have added that in 1962, only *Pressure Point* featured a black star. Harry Belafonte still had drawing power, but he was very selective. He declined the lead in a film of the William Barrett novella *The Lilies of the Field*. He called the story of a black veteran and Eastern European nuns "highly meaningless" and "nonthreatening to the culture." The main character offered nothing: "He didn't kiss anybody, he didn't touch anybody, he had no culture, he had no history, he had nothing." Belafonte could afford to be discriminating, thanks to his popularity as a singer. But he also believed that films should provoke people, not comfort them.[66]

Poitier, by contrast, jumped at the chance to play the lead character, Homer. "If anyone plays this part I'll go shoot him dead," he said after reading the script. "This part is for me!" He liked characters of basic goodness and universal humanity, and he liked the story's interracial friendship. But the major studios rejected *The Lilies of the Field*. Finally, Fred Earl, the agent who first believed in the project, found a taker in Ralph Nelson, an independent producer and director with a tarnished reputation after his dud *Requiem for a Heavyweight*.[67]

Nelson searched for funding with little success; the plot had neither sex nor violence, and the protagonist was black. One producer suggested casting Steve McQueen as the veteran and injecting a romance with a young, attractive nun who has not taken her final vows, à la *The Sound of Music*. Nelson finally convinced United Artists to finance a scant $250,000. Poitier's going rate was over half the total budget. Nelson proposed a drastic pay cut. When he heard the offer, Poitier slid off the sofa. "You're kidding," he said. But Nelson convinced him to work for $50,000 and 10 percent of the gross.[68]

United Artists was still skeptical. The distributor doubted that Poitier could carry a picture without a white co-star, and it wanted a big name to play the mother superior. Instead Nelson hired Lilia Skala, a Viennese stage actress before the Nazi invasion. Nelson knew her from previous television and theater jobs, but the last that he heard, she was working at a Long Island City factory. She and the cast's four other professional actors earned the union scale of $350 a week.[69]

They filmed in November 1962 at an abandoned farmhouse outside Tucson, Arizona. Nelson cut every conceivable cost. He shot interiors inside actual buildings, not on sound stages. He hired his secretary and construction workers as extras. He cast himself as a contractor, and he changed his character's name to Harold Ashton to match the construction equipment. He gave the actual Harold Ashton a copy of the book; Ashton liked it so much that he donated the use of his equipment.[70]

Poitier was a dynamo. He lifted huge beams and ran up ladders with 100-pound rolls of tarpaper on his shoulders. Other actors might have insisted on light props. "Heck, when you believe in a picture like this you do anything to help get it made," he said. "I *had* to lift the timber . . . on this project we got no money to spare for falsies." He stayed optimistic even after a near-disaster, when he fell through a rickety roof. He saved himself by grabbing an exposed joist. But neither a dollar nor a minute was wasted. They filmed *Lilies of the Field* in just two weeks — under budget and ahead of schedule.[71]

It seemed innocuous, this low-budget, black-and-white picture about a handyman and immigrant nuns. But Nelson saw something bigger. Headlines of the last two years had described the violent southern responses to peaceful black campaigns, including the interstate Freedom Rides on public transportation, the failed protest campaign in Albany, Georgia, and James Meredith's attempt to integrate the University of Mississippi. Nelson's film avoided such overt racial politics. In the original script, some scenes directly addressed racism. In one, a southern policeman called Homer "boy" and kicked him out of town. Another line referred to Jim Crow. During filming, Nelson eliminated them.[72]

Instead, Poitier would foster racial understanding by forging warm, human connections. One crew member — a southerner without particular compassion for blacks — sat down to the daily rushes, then remarked: "I liked that Homer." At that moment, Nelson said, "I knew we had won the battle."[73]

CHAPTER 11

LONG JOURNEYS
(1963–1964)

In April 1963, Poitier went to Yugoslavia to film *The Long Ships*, a historical epic based on a Swedish novel. Neither Poitier nor co-star Richard Widmark were particularly enthused by the project. The action-adventure clash had a terrible script, and it lacked the political cache of Poitier's better films. Poitier took the role while his career seemed stuck in a rut. In Belgrade, the mood was glum, the locals seemed hostile, and the weather was freezing. "I have been spending hours on the set dreaming about tropical climates and little shacks on pink beaches," Poitier told the *Los Angeles Times*.[1]

He won a two-week reprieve in late May. He flew to Glen Canyon National Forest in Utah to play Simon of Cyrene in *The Greatest Story Ever Told*. Producer-director George Stevens, legendary for his perfectionist gusto, had been planning a motion picture version of the Fulton Oursler biblical epic since 1959. He vowed to avoid another biblical "spectacular," but by 1960, he had announced a $10 million budget, hired Pulitzer Prize–winner Carl Sandburg, and already secured Poitier and John Wayne for cameos.[2]

More than $2 million deep, Twentieth Century-Fox shelved production in September 1961. Stevens forged on, independently producing it with a United Artists release. By the end of filming, he created 117 speaking parts, hired 30 Oscar winners, built 47 major sets, and imported a bevy of animals, including four white donkeys. Equipment complications, housing shortages, and bitter cold created more delays, but by the end of Poitier's stint in early June, expectations ran high that *The Greatest Story Ever Told* would live up to its name.[3]

Meanwhile, as Poitier journeyed from Yugoslavia to Utah and back to Yugoslavia, America's moral conscience awakened. That spring Martin Luther King and the Southern Christian Leadership Conference (SCLC) led nonviolent mass demonstrations against segregated businesses and public facilities in Birmingham, Alabama. Jailed from Good Friday to Resurrection Sunday, King wrote his famous open letter from a Birmingham Jail, painting the protesters as upholders of America's founding principles. On the evening news, Americans watched Birmingham policemen blast high-pressure fire hoses at demonstrators, swing nightsticks into crowds, and set attack dogs upon teenagers and young children. These images of black sacrifice helped forge a critical mass of white middle-class support for racial integration.[4]

In a televised address on 11 June, President Kennedy called civil rights "a moral issue" that was "as old as the Scriptures" and "as clear as the American Constitution." Hours later, a white extremist killed the Mississippi civil rights leader Medgar Evers, and demonstrations resumed throughout the South. Now Kennedy moved beyond hollow gestures. Appealing to delegates black and white, northern and southern, Republican and Democrat, he pledged a comprehensive civil rights bill.[5]

The blooming liberal consensus coincided with a renewed campaign to end discrimination in Hollywood. At the end of June, the NAACP threatened pickets and economic boycotts against studios that stereotyped black characters. The grievance had been aired before, but never had the NAACP devoted it such attention. Producers had to move beyond glib promises and token jobs. "Reality," wrote the *New York Times*, "has forced Hollywood to realize that it is part of the United States and must deal with the same issues as the rest of the nation." Studios now incorporated blacks into crowd and street scenes. The NAACP pushed for more middle-class black characters and threatened legal action against discriminatory craft unions. Motion pictures, many hoped, might soon reflect the growing sympathy for black equality.[6]

In this atmosphere, Poitier's political importance magnified. He symbolized the liberal notion that extending basic rights to black Americans reflected the virtue of the American system. In July 1963, he and Stanley Kramer showed *The Defiant Ones* at the Moscow Film Festival. Poitier trumpeted the movie as an example of American freedom. "Such a picture could only be made in a free country, unafraid of self-criticism," said Poitier. After the film, the 8,000 spectators at Moscow's Sports Palace applauded for minutes and wiped tears from their eyes. They also streamed toward Poitier, who was standing in the corner of the auditorium. The Russians carried the actor on their shoulders, celebrating Hollywood's beacon of racial democracy.[7]

One month later, Poitier participated in the quintessential demonstration of faith in a colorblind society: the March on Washington. Harry

Belafonte and attorney Clarence Jones organized an interracial celebrity delegation. The movie stars had been galvanized by a recent visit from Martin Luther King. At Burt Lancaster's home, King had told them a story about how his children could not enter a white-only amusement park. Tears welled in the stars' eyes. King raised $75,000.[8]

As the march approached, the actors debated strategy. Marlon Brando wanted to chain himself to the Lincoln Memorial; Charlton Heston demanded order. They all agreed on their mission: in Heston's words, "to get as much ink and TV time as possible." The *New York Times* interpreted their participation as a watershed — a flash of political conscience, a chance to "lift the ceilings of fear" from the blacklist era, and a harbinger of more challenging material on screen.[9]

From New York came Poitier, Diahann Carroll, Paul Newman, Joanne Woodward, Tony Curtis, and Jackie Robinson. Brando and James Garner helped organize a Hollywood delegation. James Baldwin, Josephine Baker, and Burt Lancaster arrived from Paris. Sammy Davis Jr. flew in from Toronto. Although their relative numbers were small, their presence was important. Even sympathetic whites feared black violence: Washington banned liquor sales, area hospitals girded for the worst, and President Kennedy kept thousands of troops on alert. But the public trusted celebrities. FBI Director J. Edgar Hoover actually thought that the stars were Communist dupes. In a futile effort on the morning of the march, his agents called the actors' hotel rooms and suggested that they stay indoors.[10]

But on 28 August, Poitier walked with Martin Luther King and 200,000 others to the Lincoln Memorial. They sang freedom songs, marched peacefully, and smiled through the eighty degree heat. White students, intellectuals, union workers, and nuns mingled with blacks from every class and region. Bob Dylan, Mahalia Jackson, Josh White, Joan Baez, Odetta, and Peter, Paul and Mary sang. Ossie Davis was master of ceremonies. A cavalcade of black leaders — John Lewis of the Student Nonviolent Coordinating Committee (SNCC), Floyd McKissick of the Congress of Racial Equality (CORE), Whitney Young of the Urban League, Roy Wilkins of the NAACP — delivered speeches, along with Rabbi Joachim Prinz of the American Jewish Council and Walter Reuther of the United Auto Workers. As the shadows grew long, King delivered his "I Have a Dream" speech, finishing with the stirring hope that all Americans could cheer: "Free at last! Free at last! Thank God almighty, we are free at last!"[11]

Behind the dais, under the statue at the Lincoln Memorial, Poitier,

Belafonte, Baldwin, Heston, and Brando gave interviews. The five celebrities appeared together on television. Later some luminaries met at Belafonte's hotel suite. Still swept by emotion, Belafonte instructed Sammy Davis Jr. to call Robert Kennedy and request an audience with the president. The attorney general rebuffed them, pointing out the difficulty of even getting King and Wilkins to the White House. "He was right, of course," Davis later remembered. "We'd served our purpose by getting our pictures in the papers." Poitier instead took seven friends to a French restaurant in Georgetown.[12]

The March on Washington represented a pinnacle of cooperation among the civil rights organizations and their white liberal allies. All agreed upon the necessity of legislation that guaranteed blacks constitutional rights, and all endorsed the mood of interracial fellowship. The impassioned orators, noble marchers, and respected celebrities had opened eyes to the justice of racial integration. Laws were not passed, facilities were not integrated, voters were not registered. But hearts and minds had been won. At his best, Poitier had achieved that same impact. When he portrayed a compelling humanity — as in *The Defiant Ones* or *A Raisin in the Sun* — he advanced racial goodwill. Now, in the wake of Birmingham and the March on Washington, movie theaters showcased the perfect vehicle for Poitier's talent: *Lilies of the Field*.[13]

❖

Poitier plays a good man. He is Homer Smith, a veteran who lives simply, takes odd jobs, and travels the country in his used Cadillac. He values his independence, takes pride in his work, and carries a small Bible among his few belongings. When he pulls off a dusty Arizona road to find five dour nuns staring at him, he smiles warmly: "Car's thirsty. Can I please have some water?"

Mother Maria (Lilia Skala) looks heavenward. Her small flock of nuns, who had escaped Communist Eastern Europe, needs the help of a healthy, strong man. Homer tries to decline her offer of work, but his conscience prevails. He cannot resist helping them. That day, he fixes their roof. That night, he stays for dinner. After dinner, he gives them English lessons!

Mother Maria pays him nothing, feeds him little, and calls him "Schmidt." She refuses to thank him, and she commands him to build a chapel. He brays at first. Soon, however, building a chapel becomes Homer's odyssey. Adobe brick by adobe brick, the structure rises. He finances the project with a part-time construction job, and he teaches them more English, drives them to church, buys them groceries, and spoils them with lollipops. His goodness attracts donations and volunteers. But Homer squirms. "I was going to build it myself," he says. "I wanted to really build something, you know? Well, maybe if I had had an education, I would have been an architect or even an engineer, see? You know, throw the Golden Gate Bridge across San Francisco Bay and even maybe build a rocket ship to Venus or something." The speech is touching. Homer's frustrations are endearing, universal, and only subtly informed by his skin color.

Race is underplayed throughout *Lilies of the Field* — most references to black culture are employed for laughs. For instance, the nuns mimic Homer to learn English. "I stand up," he says. "I stand up," they say. "I stands up, y'all!" he laughs. "I stands up, y'all!" say the oblivious nuns through heavy accents.[14]

The only real allusion to racism comes from Homer's employer Harold Ashton (Ralph Nelson), who calls him "boy." Homer exhibits no outrage, instead using charm and pluck. His strategy wins. At first Ashton assumes that the black man is "shiftless and irresponsible." By the end, he offers Homer a foreman job and calls him "Mr. Smith."

Homer's altruism borders on saintliness. Mother Maria labels his arrival a "miracle." His strength and faith make the chapel a reality. Three times, Homer leads the nuns through the gospel song "Amen." He even places the cross atop the chapel. "This part is mine," he says. "This part is mine." From the worshipful camera angle below the steeple, the white cross frames his face. *Lilies of the Field* ends as Homer drives away to "Amen," concluding a cinematic prayer for love and tolerance.

In less capable hands, Homer Smith might have seemed ridiculous, a wholly pliant stooge to the white characters. But Poitier invests him with self-respect and charisma. The picture's best moments rest on his visual, nonverbal accents: his contemplation under the stars, his camaraderie with the nuns and Hispanic workers, his amused pique while absorbing Mother Maria's commands. These touches flesh out the character; as Albert Johnson wrote, Homer "can be thoroughly appreciated both by Negro spectators (because they will recognize the humor in his intonations, the smile *behind* the smile and the truth of Homer's reactions), and by non-Negro spectators (because Homer is not presented as a 'problem,' but as an ordinary human being)."[15]

Because Poitier's character is likable rather than annoyingly pious, *Lilies of the Field* avoids oversentimental slushiness. Still, it was a box-office risk. The black-and-white film lacked sex and violence, and it had no white stars. Poitier told *Variety* that the film "will determine my bankability." Nelson planned a gradual release, starting in Europe and moving to New York City art houses to build word-of-mouth support.[16]

In late June 1963, Nelson entered *Lilies of the Field* in the Berlin Film Festival. Critics raved; "Sidney Poitier: A Gift from Heaven," read one headline. Poitier captured another Silver Bear for best actor; he was the first to collar the prize twice. The picture itself won honors from both Catholic and Protestant film boards, and columnist Hedda Hopper gave an early endorsement. By the official premiere in Berlin on 15 July, some optimism seemed justified. Trade newspapers labeled the movie "thoroughly charming" and "good, clean honest fun." The State Department, recognizing the contrast between the sunny humanitarianism of *Lilies of the Field* and the negative publicity generated by southern resistance to black civil rights, endorsed the picture. Poitier promoted the film in London, Paris, Rome, and Copenhagen.[17]

Nelson's marketing strategy coaxed out more advance praise. *Scholastic* awarded *Lilies of the Field* the Bell Ringer Award for outstanding motion picture, *Parents* gave it the Family Medal, and *Seventeen* selected it as September's Picture of the Month. The National Screen Council gave it a Blue Ribbon Award. Nelson built the black audience by linking the picture to civil rights. A special September screening at Loew's Victoria Theatre on West 125th Street in Harlem benefited the NAACP, CORE, SCLC, and SNCC.[18]

When *Lilies of the Field* arrived at New York's Murray Hill Theatre on 1 October, critics predicted a sleeper hit. "It really doesn't matter a hoot in hell that Sidney Poitier is a Negro," marveled the *New York Morning-Telegraph*. "He is simply just a man." The actor again transcended old comic stereotypes, but now his subtle inflections of humanity inspired declarations of colorblind tolerance. "It is the dignity of man that Poitier epitomizes," wrote Judith Crist. "Unless a better actor comes along, he has got my vote for the Oscar," added Hedda Hopper.[19]

Poitier hated publicity tours, but he agreed to one for *Lilies of the Field*, because it fulfilled his political objectives, and because he gained a percentage of the gross. "It's such a warm, human movie," he said. "I want it to be successful all over the country." In early October he attended a special screening at Catholic University in Denver with 600 nuns. Predictably, the sisters applauded. Unpredictably, they flooded toward him. "They don't usually ask for autographs!" exclaimed Poitier. The commendations kept flowing in. The National Catholic Theatre Conference, the National Audience Board, and the Federation of Motion Picture

Councils added their plaudits. By April 1964, *Lilies of the Field* had earned $2.5 million, and Poitier had made $250,000.[20]

Only the naive ignored the connection to the contemporary climate of race relations. By avoiding a "militant" racial stance, *Lilies of the Field* allowed a broad cross-section of American society to appreciate Poitier without assaulting racial sensibilities. Yet as Bosley Crowther noted, Poitier's skin color lent depth to the character. "There is this need for affirmation, this heat of racial pride that puts an aura around him," he wrote. "It is idealistic and sentimental, but it is warm."[21]

Some were not convinced. Indeed, Homer Smith exhibits the same limitations as other Poitier characters, exaggerated to the nth degree. Not only is he without family or community, but he wanders the country in complete solitude. Not only does he lack outlets for sex or romance, but his female friends are elderly nuns. Not only does he sacrifice for whites, but his actions are explicitly cased in religious imagery. *Newsweek* complained that the screen "overflows with enough brotherhood, piety, and honest labor to make even the kindliest spectator retch." *Film Quarterly* sniggered that Poitier could have been more obsequious only if the nuns had "seduced him to their Romish ways."[22]

Ten years later Sharon Scott, a former critic for a black newspaper, remembered attending *Lilies of the Field*. She had eagerly anticipated the widely praised film. "But as the story unfolded," she recalled, "I found the character Poitier portrayed as solicitous, and self-sacrificing, without the dimensions characteristic of any normal male human being." She was not alone. Most appreciated Homer Smith, but some young black men yelled "chump" and "fool." Poitier's paradox thickened. *Lilies of the Field* won him more popularity, but only after submitting to the compromises structured by mainstream racial attitudes. It foreshadowed the dilemmas to come.[23]

❖

Poitier persisted as a spokesman for the black plight in Hollywood, displaying an awareness of his peculiar status to both white and black reporters. "I remain, regrettably, a token symbol of the possibilities open to Negroes in motion pictures," he told the *Los Angeles Times*. "I thought there would have been more progress in the arts by this time," he brooded to the *Chicago Defender*.[24]

With *Variety*, Poitier discussed the social impact of motion pictures. "Films are the most effective communications medium in the world today," he said. In a gentle plug for *Lilies of the Field*, he added that movies are foremost entertainment. The social message should be subtle, he argued, "like the fragrance of a good perfume." He also addressed the racist structure of the film industry, courting white liberal allies by proclaiming that desegregating Hollywood would "have to be a moral act."[25]

Some white celebrities embraced that responsibility, such as Marlon Brando, who became a valuable spokesman for civil rights. In February 1964 Brando announced that he, Laurence Olivier, Vanessa Redgrave, and nine others would henceforth insist upon contracts that barred their films from segregated theaters. Unfortunately the threat had little impact, since most white actors refrained from such risky stands. As SCLC counsel Clarence Jones reflected, "It was probably easier for James Garner and Burt Lancaster and Charlton Heston to get involved in the March on Washington than to deal with the institutional racism in the industry." Staging boycotts to integrate Hollywood studios or southern theaters entailed a financial sacrifice that most white stars declined to make.[26]

Poitier thus advocated that black entertainers create their own opportunities, often referencing his own ambitions. "I'm not going to sit around waiting for a white producer to find a play to fit me," he said. "I'll find it myself. D'you understand?" Despite his rhetoric, he found no suitable properties to direct or produce. He did, however, complete his own play, titled *600 to 1*. By July 1962, he was tinkering with the final act. In May 1964, he showed a draft to Philip Rose. The play, which examined black and Puerto Rican dropouts in New York City, was never produced. Presumably Rose found it wanting.[27]

The failure of *600 to 1* marked a temporary end to Poitier's career-broadening aspirations. Already, he was reappraising his situation. In January, his mother had died. "When I looked into her face for the last time," he reflected, "I took stock." He turned thirty-seven in February. His ambition drove him into "untenable positions" and "perpetual dissatisfactions." He decided to simplify, to concentrate on acting. "That writing-directing-producing jazz, that's past," he announced. "A man should only do what is within his innate capabilities, not dissipate himself in efforts whose sole goal is to gratify ego." For the moment, anyway, his decision engendered some serenity.[28]

Poitier spent much of the winter of 1964 entertaining offers from his regular perch at the Russian Tea Room. For some time he reconsidered *Othello*. David Merrick and Tony Richardson were staging a traditional production, and the prestige of the Shakespearean tragedy once again pulled Poitier. He ultimately declined, however, due to film obligations. That winter he also collected some honors. At Carnegie Hall in early

February, New York City mayor Robert Wagner presented him, Duke Ellington, and three others with a bronze plaque recognizing black contributions in the performing arts. Then in late February came an even greater honor: for his performance in *Lilies of the Field*, an Academy Award nomination for Best Actor.[29]

The accolade was not unexpected; in October 1963 the *Pittsburgh Courier* reported that 75 percent of Academy voters had already reserved a nomination for Poitier. But the actor wavered on whether to attend the award ceremony. He agreed only after cajoling from Martin Baum and Diahann Carroll. Eventually, he remembered, "I realized that there was a great deal riding on my chances, that a victory on Monday night would mean an enormous amount to a great number of people, and it would be unfair of me to take the edge off it for them by not appearing." He removed his tuxedo from its glass case.[30]

Poitier arrived in Los Angeles a few days before the ceremony. With every good luck wish, he felt a pang of anxiety. His fellow nominees were Paul Newman for *Hud*, Rex Harrison for *Cleopatra*, Richard Harris for *This Sporting Life*, and Albert Finney for *Tom Jones*. With typical public modesty, Poitier considered Finney the favorite. With typical private pride, he measured his performance against the others. He believed that if he won, his victory would not be "a charity case." As 13 April approached, Hollywood buzzed that a black actor might win a major Academy Award.[31]

Media critics later bemoaned that the Oscars had lost some allure, that too many stars stayed home, that the show seemed stale. But as Poitier rolled down palm-fringed avenues toward the Santa Monica Auditorium and alighted from his limousine to the roars of fans and the popping bulbs of paparazzi, the atmosphere felt electric. Poitier stepped out alone, followed by Martin Baum and his wife Bernice. (Carroll had accompanied him to Los Angeles, but they avoided appearing in public together.) Hollywood's Great Black Hope looked suitably glamorous in his tailed tuxedo.[32]

Poitier calmed his nerves enough to announce the winner for film editing, Harold F. Kress for *How the West Was Won*. Later, the nation's racial demonstrations lent the program its lightest moment. When Sammy Davis Jr. presented an award, he was handed the wrong envelope. "Wait till the NAACP hears about this!" he shouted. Meanwhile, Poitier's stomach churned. He fidgeted in his chair. He drummed his fingers. Sweat rolled down his forehead. His mind ping-ponged between composing a speech if he won and maintaining composure if he lost. Finally Anne

Bancroft—dressed in a white gown with spaghetti-thin straps, her hair fetchingly piled atop her head—announced the Oscar for Best Actor. As she recited the nominees, the screen behind her flashed their pictures. "The hush was *deafening*," Poitier recalled. His mouth dried. Upon opening the envelope, Bancroft smiled demurely, then gleamed. "The winner is Sidney Poitier."[33]

He literally jumped from his seat. "I won, I won, I won!" he beamed to the Baums. A deep, affectionate cheer washed over him. Screenwriter James Poe reached out—partly to congratulate him, partly to steady him. Poitier bounded to the stage in graceful, exuberant strides. With one hand at his side, he climbed the stairs and met Bancroft, who seemed equally elated. "Annie, I won," he said. They exchanged a tender hug. ("In fictional TV such a touchingly sincere and realistic scene would have been written out lest Southern sensibilities be disturbed," observed one perceptive critic. In fact, the newsreel account edited out the embrace.) She handed him the Oscar, and he steeled himself. He realized his symbolic importance, and he wanted to convey an appropriate dignity. He opened with a felicitous phrase concocted during the ceremony: "It is a long journey to this moment. . . ."[34]

He wanted to thank his friends and associates, but the moment overwhelmed him. "I am naturally indebted to countless numbers of people," he said, before breaking into an exhilarated grin. He was fighting back tears by digging his fingernails into his palms. "For all of them, all I can say is a very special thank you." He floated backstage, where Sammy Davis Jr. jumped into his arms. Bancroft escorted him to the press room. She dabbed tears from her eyes as Poitier spoke: "When it came to the moment and Annie opened the envelope, I thought I'd faint! I thought I'd fall down! I almost did!" A reporter then asked if his race made the moment more special. Suddenly Poitier sobered. "You're gonna have to let me mull that one for a while," he said, contemplating each word. "It's a very interesting question, and I would prefer not to answer it in my present anxiety. I'd rather be much more collected to deal with such a delicate question."[35]

Poitier may have dodged the question, but numerous critics and fans welded his award to the film industry's belated racial conscience. Poitier had delivered more subtlety in *The Defiant Ones*, more depth in *A Raisin in the Sun*. But *Lilies of the Field* captured the spirit of the times. As Bosley Crowther wrote, "The fact that a plurality of the Hollywood elite wished Mr. Poitier to win is strong evidence of a warm and liberal feeling." The audience's tremendous roar acknowledged not only Poitier's performance, but also the toppling of a racial barrier.[36]

To many, the Oscar was more than recognition of Poitier: it was a demonstration of interracial goodwill, an analogue to the March on Washington, even a symbolic absolution of Hollywood's complicity in racial prejudice. A *Washington Post* editorial celebrated the actor, adding that "the selection of Mr. Poitier, a Negro, had special significance in a year when civil rights has become a subject of such intense concern to the people and in Congress." A New Jersey man assigned redemptive power to Poitier: "God grant that this great artist's words will penetrate the minds and very souls of the instigators and perpetrators of racial hatred and violence so that we may live, as we were intended, in Peace on Earth."[37]

Blacks took particular pride. One letter to the *Chicago Defender* called the Oscar a victory for the NAACP, Urban League, CORE, SCLC, and SNCC. The NAACP suggested a ticker-tape parade through New York City. Hazel Garland wrote that when Poitier won, "millions of black, brown and beige viewers ached to reach through their sets just to shake his hand." Izzy Rowe waxed patriotic: "I have never been prouder of Sidney Poitier and the industry he represents so well. . . . From audience to stage the 36th annual Academy Awards looked like something out of the dream of the founding fathers of this nation who inscribed on the tablets of immortality the Godly words, 'And we hold these truths to be self-evident. That all men are created equal.' " She added that the Academy "put a glowing spotlight on democracy" for the world to witness.[38]

Yet some reserved judgment on the award's implications. The Negro Press Bureau extolled Poitier but interpreted the Oscar as an "easy out" for craft unions that excluded blacks. Poitier himself took a middle ground. On one hand he appreciated the symbolism: "This cannot be politically and sociologically exploited in anything but a healthy status." On the other hand he doubted that the award would wipe away discrimination like a "magic wand."[39]

In the aftermath of the Oscar, Poitier endured relentless questions about its political consequences. It soon frustrated him. One week after the Academy Awards, he received the Handel Medallion, New York City's premier cultural honor. After the City Hall ceremony, two reporters probed him about his political views and affiliations. Poitier boiled. "Ever since I won the Oscar the only questions the press seems to be interested in are what my feelings and actions are about civil rights movements," he said. "I don't object to being asked about it, but it's the incessant harping that annoys me." An Academy Award did not make him a political expert, he argued. Furthermore, the questions diminished his individual accomplishment: "Why don't you ask me human questions? Why is it everything you ask refers to the Negroness of my life and not to my acting?" Previous winners simply basked in Oscar's glory; Poitier wanted that same privilege, even if his peculiar position made that impossible.[40]

In early May, Poitier returned to Nassau. As he stepped off the airplane at Windsor Field, thousands waved flags and danced to calypso, including a tune created for the occasion, "Sidney's Comin' Back Home." Poitier led a two-hour motorcade for ten miles, and thousands more lined the streets, standing atop cars and roofs, hanging from trees, and displaying banners: OUR HERO SIDNEY; WELCOME HOME SIDNEY; YOUR GLORY IS OURS. A heavy rain soaked through his navy wool suit. Someone offered an umbrella, and Poitier refused. "*They* don't have any umbrellas," he said. A woman then barged into his car with a huge beach umbrella. He kissed her, and the crowd stomped their feet in delight. The motorcade culminated with a ride down Bay Street to a dais in the Public Square, before the statue of Queen Victoria. As the procession passed, he shook hands and recognized faces from his childhood.[41]

In the Bahamas, as in the United States, Poitier struck a political balance. That January, his native land had adopted a new constitution that assigned less power to the British colonial governor. But the white-dominated United Bahamian Party controlled the House of Assembly, which elected the premier. The black majority, represented by the Progressive Liberal Party, remained a political minority. Although Poitier supported the PLP, his four-night stay included a posh reception at the Government House, where Governor W. H. Sweeting, the colonial elite, and their wives honored him with polite questions and dignified toasts. White-jacketed black waiters circulated and a police band serenaded with music from *Porgy and Bess*.[42]

Later that night, Poitier reconnected with his roots. He left for The Cat and Fiddle, a club in Over the Hill with chicken-wire roofing. The calypso stopped and limbo dancers straightened as Poitier addressed the crowd. "Today's reception was the most moving event of my life," he said. "It rained but I was bathed in love." His fans bellowed, and Poitier reveled in their company, hailing old friends and following them to the Banana Club, where he flirted with swooning young women.[43]

The testimonials continued throughout the weekend. He was showered with gifts and lauded in speeches. "I have cried a little," he said on his final night, during a gala at the Sheraton-British Colonial Hotel. "I am now charged by this evening and this effort to go out in life and live up to this tribute." The trip had been a particular occasion for reflection. His parents missed his triumph—his mother by just months. Seemingly arbitrary episodes had separated him from the Bahamian masses—he visited the graves of three childhood friends killed by lifetimes spent drinking filthy, one-shilling-a-bottle rum. And guilt still plagued him—Juanita had accompanied the children to Nassau only to keep up appearances, to preserve his image on the land where Reginald Poitier had once taught him about "the measure of a man."[44]

Whatever his strains, his wallet fattened. Taking a percentage of the gross from *Lilies of the Field* proved among Poitier's most fortuitous decisions. After the Academy Awards, theaters snatched up all 300 prints for the next five weeks. Even southern exhibitors, who had first resisted a picture featuring interracial chumminess, began booking *Lilies of the Field*. It performed well throughout the South, a once-unthinkable scenario for a Poitier film. In August 1964, United Artists predicted that the picture would triple its estimated take thanks to Poitier's award.[45]

The Oscar also ensured Poitier long-term security, as studios now began seeking Sidney Poitier vehicles. "Doors have been opened to me that I never expected," he said the following year. "I no longer have to search for a role. Perhaps even more important, I now can say 'no' to mediocre parts." With increased career options came greater control over his own image—a critical development, as the politics behind the black screen image grew complicated.[46]

❖

Unfortunately, Poitier's first picture after the Academy Awards was *The Long Ships*, the saga of Vikings and Moors filmed in Yugoslavia during the spring of 1963. The preposterous story revolves around the competition between Norse adventurer Rolfe (Richard Widmark) and Moorish sheik Aly Mansuh (Poitier) over "The Mother of Voices," an enormous golden bell of legend. Actually, the plot is an irrelevant backdrop to a succession of hammy adventure-film conventions: duels and battles, storms and shipwrecks, tortures and escapes, drunken brawls and lusty bacchanals. Director Jack Cardiff, better known as a cinematographer, sacrificed any pretense of narrative for these lushly photographed, elaborately staged, eminently ridiculous scenes. When the picture premiered in June 1964, Judith Crist called it "one of the best awful spectacular adventure movies around."[47]

Because he played a black villain opposite a white hero, Poitier advertised his role as a breakthrough. Yet his performance is forgettable, even embarrassing. He looks foolish in a long-haired wig and flowing robes.

His accent constantly changes. He tries to appear both ruthless and solemn, and he fails. In another context, Aly Mansuh might have been a milestone: a black man extols Islam and denounces Christianity, two rarities on the American screen. But Poitier's villain hisses threats and savors torture all too seriously, an incongruous interpretation next to Widmark's swashbuckling, tongue-in-cheek hero.[48]

The Long Ships also upheld tradition by desexualizing Poitier. Aly Mansuh should be a character with sexual energy. He presides over an interracial harem, and an early publicity still shows him kissing a white woman. But in the film's final cut, he has taken a bizarre oath of celibacy. He swears to spurn women "until Allah's divine guidance brings me to the treasures of Islam." Even the entreaties of his favorite wife Aminah (Rosanna Schiaffino) fall flat. Later he calls the Viking princess Gerda (Bebe Loncar) to his quarters, but any passion between them ended up on the cutting-room floor.

The Production Code Administration ordered editing of sexually suggestive scenes, which not only contributed to the plot's inconsistencies, but also reinforced these racial taboos. Some southern exhibitors demanded to completely eliminate Aly Mansuh's minimal contact with Aminah and Gerda, but Columbia executives refused to further mangle the narrative. Still, *The Long Ships* was a colossal misstep. Four years later, Poitier called it "a constant reminder that I must never let my head get too big."[49]

Poitier spent minimal effort promoting *The Long Ships*, instead lending his fame to civil rights. In May 1964, he appeared with Harry Belafonte, Sammy Davis Jr., Richard Burton, Elizabeth Taylor, and others before 12,000 spectators at Madison Square Garden to celebrate the tenth anniversary of *Brown vs. Board of Education*. The NAACP broadcast the event in forty-six closed-circuit theaters, including sixteen in the Deep South. The event's timing coincided with the civil rights bill then before Congress. Poitier's Oscar had made him a sounding board for debate over federal desegregation of public facilities. The same month, following a glowing profile of Poitier by Hedda Hopper, some fans responded to the syndicated gossip columnist with pledges for racial understanding. One, however, issued a challenge: "Put Mr. Poitier right on the issue by telling him that this horrendous bill will do for him just what it will do to all of us — take *all* our rights away."[50]

In early June, Poitier traveled to Washington, D.C., for a firsthand look at the Senate filibuster delaying passage of the bill. He publicly railed against one senator's stall tactics: "He was bored; the men around him were bored. I was fascinated by the air of apathy." He also promoted the bill, calling it "a healthy, positive step forward." On 10 June, the Senate ended a 534-hour filibuster, ensuring future passage of the Civil Rights Act. That day Poitier attended a ceremony on the South Lawn of the White House, along with Leonard Bernstein, Harper Lee, Katherine Anne Porter, and other liberal artists. Munching on hamburgers under red-striped tents, they congratulated President Lyndon Johnson on the legislative triumph.[51]

Just three days later, Poitier found himself in very different circumstances: an informal summit of black leaders and intellectuals, at his own Pleasantville estate. Here, devoid of his lone symbolic status, Poitier was a sideshow. He arrived late because of professional commitments. Juanita, not he, was the host. After their separation, she had become an active civil rights fundraiser. With Ruby Dee, she hatched the idea and invited the major participants. From a Florida jail, Martin Luther King sent Clarence Jones. A. Philip Randolph, Dorothy Height, Whitney Young, Ossie Davis, and John Oliver Killens came. Most notably, Malcolm X was there. By this time Malcolm X had separated from the Nation of Islam and returned from his hajj to Mecca. In Pleasantville he reached out, ready to rescind his blanket comments about white "blue-eyed devils" and participate in the civil rights struggle. They bandied about ideas, including drafting a Declaration of Human Rights for Black Americans and creating a small, behind-the-scenes organization for the next stage in the movement.[52]

The presence of Malcolm X was important. Although he lacked a political base, only Malcolm X had addressed how racism had destroyed the black self-image, leading to dangerous compromises such as reliance on white patronage and black sacrifice. His ideas pointed to a future when a progressive black culture, more than any legislation, might shape American race relations.

The next week, in stream with this ideological current, a group of black artists debated three white liberals in a Town Hall forum called "The Black Revolution and the White Backlash." Davis, Dee, Killens, James Baldwin, Lorraine Hansberry, Paule Marshall, and playwright Leroi Jones confronted author Charles Silberman, columnist James Wechsler, and producer David Susskind. The black intellectuals foresaw an era that depended more on black unity than white sponsorship, and they intimated that nonviolence had served its purpose. Their comments outraged many white liberals, who felt betrayed by this lack of gratitude. "For generations it has been assumed that what Negroes wanted more desperately than anything else was simply to be absorbed into 'this house,' " wrote Hansberry, summarizing the brouhaha. "Perhaps it seems an affront to some that the most thoughtful elements of the Negro people would like to see this house rebuilt."[53]

By then Poitier was in Germany, heading the American delegation to the Berlin Film Festival. He had already undergone a briefing at the State Department. While Baldwin was saying that "there is much in that American pie that isn't worth eating," Poitier was playing the urbane black ambassador of American democracy, protecting the broad liberal consensus that governed the March on Washington, the Civil Rights Act, and his Academy Award.[54]

In Berlin he watched all the films, attended a myriad of cocktail parties and dinners, and discussed his career, black stereotypes, civil rights, and Hollywood's social responsibility. His public pronouncements continued to place blacks within the American democratic tradition, an ideology with added resonance in the shadow of the Berlin Wall. During an exhibition of the American documentary *John F. Kennedy in Berlin*, the Oscar winner received the evening's biggest ovation.[55]

Poitier's rhetoric balanced between progressive politics and public appeal. He recognized his position as a spokesman and fundraiser, which suited his philosophical, nonconfrontational nature. He thus typically refrained from overt activism. His connection to the civil rights movement mostly came through Harry Belafonte, whose palatial West End Avenue apartment had become an informal common ground for black activists. Belafonte had graduated from racial spokesman to the civil rights inner circle. He had established himself as a liaison between disparate black organizations and the Washington establishment: a close friend and adviser to King, the original bankroller of SNCC, a trusted link to Robert F. Kennedy. Because he communicated with everyone from preachers to radicals to attorney generals, Belafonte helped forge a political consensus. The movement relied on his fame, energy, and deep pockets.[56]

Ironically, despite his influential work, Belafonte resented that Poitier was America's single black movie star. Poitier worked within the system. His dark-skinned, sexually restrained, moral icon drew a clear line between blacks and whites, but insisted that blacks were good American citizens. Belafonte's light-skinned matinee idol challenged sexual boundaries, and he was out of Hollywood fashion. Nor did he have Poitier's dramatic gifts. But Belafonte also rejected pictures such as *Lilies of the Field*, insisting upon his own terms. So only Poitier became a star. Belafonte also knew that Poitier would not blindly follow his political orders. More than Poitier, he counted on Marlon Brando to build civil rights support in Hollywood.[57]

Yet sometimes, Belafonte needed his old friend and rival. One Thursday in early August, he telephoned Poitier. He was flying to Greenwood, Mississippi, to present $70,000 in donations to civil rights volunteers, and he wanted Poitier to join him. Poitier hesitated. For a black man in the summer of 1964, Mississippi was the most dangerous place in America. It was "Freedom Summer," when an interracial army of volunteers registered and educated black voters, only to suffer arrests, beatings, bombings, and assassination attempts. Just days before, three civil rights workers had been discovered in an earthen dam, brutally murdered. Belafonte explained that the celebrities' presence would boost the volunteers' morale. Plus, he added, "they might think twice about killing *two* big niggers." The explanation was less than satisfying, but out of political responsibility — and maybe some brotherly rivalry — Poitier accepted the challenge.[58]

Around 10:00 the next night, the two celebrities emerged from a rickety charter plane onto an airstrip outside Greenwood. A lone outdoor light, hung above a latch gate and obscured by night bugs, barely cut through the dark. By the small shed that served as a passenger terminal, James Forman and five other SNCC workers awaited. Their two cars had been stripped of chrome and paint finish, sanded down to avoid white ambushes. As they left the airstrip, a bank of headlights flashed on in the distance. Belafonte indicated relief at the extra protection. No, said Forman; "That's the Klan." Poitier and Belafonte sat silently as they weaved down pitch-black country roads. A truck with a two-by-four strapped to the front bumper approached from behind, trying to ram them. The other SNCC car maneuvered between their car and the Klan truck until they reached an Elks Hall in Greenwood's black district.[59]

They sprinted in. "Freedom! Freedom!" cried Forman, leading the two stars through the crowd. The young volunteers and local blacks gasped. Even Greenwood's schoolteachers, who had cautiously avoided Dr. King's recent visit, came to see the two matinee idols. They forgot about the Klansmen stationed outside the door. They cheered through Bob Moses's introduction, boomed out Freedom Songs, danced with the stars, and feasted on chicken and spareribs. One volunteer observed that the evening seemed to change their guests, stripping them of their confident composures, answering their needs for spiritual depth. "I am 37 years old. I have been a lonely man all my life," Poitier told them. "I have been lonely because I have not found love, but this room is *overflowing* with it."[60]

Before they left, Belafonte sang "Day-O," and even the Klansmen outside belted out the chorus. Then the stars retreated to private quarters with all-night sentry protection. Some volunteers grumbled at the special treatment; Poitier and Belafonte missed the complaints, but they hardly enjoyed a sound sleep. Peeking through blinds, they thought that they saw intruders lurking by a chicken coop. At 4:00 A.M., a car stopped in front of their house for ten minutes — only later did they learn that their guards kept the vehicle in their cross-hairs the entire time. The two old friends talked throughout the night, except when one heard a twig snap. Belafonte told ghost stories. Poitier did calisthenics.[61]

The next day, they were back in their opulent Manhattan high-rises, safe from battering rams and assassins. The experience had solidified Poitier's commitment to SNCC, and that month he helped finance the Mississippi Freedom Democratic Party's important trip to the Democratic National Convention in Atlantic City.[62]

But if Poitier had accomplished political good, he had also revealed his inner tumult. His confession of loneliness to the Greenwood crowd indicated that his relationship with Diahann Carroll had again bottomed out. Carroll had begun sessions with her own therapist. Both, separately, were sifting out the sources of their mutual attraction and passionate quarrels. Carroll delved into her background in the black bourgeoisie, caught between the white middle class and the black masses. Poitier dissected his own past, probing the anxieties that once drove him to crash cars in parking lots and toss chairs through windows. Both started to realize that their looks, elegance, and celebrity fluffed each other's external confidence, at the expense of addressing their emotional shortcomings.[63]

Furthermore, neither Sidney nor Juanita Poitier wanted a messy divorce. Juanita told reporters that although they had separated, her husband was a devoted father. The actor's business manager Arthur Fine dismissed all the divorce and Diahann Carroll rumors as "a lot of hokum." Indeed, by the time Carroll toured the tent circuit with *No Strings* that summer, they had halted their affair. Then, in early fall, Poitier flew to Los Angeles to film *Synanon*, a story of a narcotics rehabilitation center. He never appeared in the picture, but he did learn that *No Strings* was also in Los Angeles, and Carroll was staying at the Chateau Marmont.[64]

As Carroll recalled, her telephone rang at 6:00 one morning. "You bitch! You whore! You tramp!" shouted Poitier. Carroll had been dating her show's company manager. Poitier saw him on the street, provoking his jealousy. He demanded that Carroll come to his suite. Passion again outweighed prudence. She arrived, they embraced, and her heart melted.

Their exciting, enraging push-and-pull started anew, and in fifteen minutes they journeyed from declarations of love to impassioned clashes. "I won't have you running around with other men," he protested. "You belong to me!"[65]

Carroll weathered this sexist proclamation, because she still wanted a long-term commitment. This time Poitier agreed. That morning, they drove to a downtown jewelry store, and while she waited outside, he bought a diamond engagement ring. She bid farewell to her erstwhile beau, and he informed Juanita that a lawyer would serve divorce papers. Two days later, they drove to Tijuana. Poitier obtained a Mexican divorce. They ate dinner, drank margaritas, and returned to Los Angeles that evening.[66]

After fourteen years and four children, the Poitier marriage was over. In early October Poitier went to Tokyo to promote *Lilies of the Field* and watch the Olympics. "If Sidney jets," asked the *Hollywood Reporter*, hinting at his life's next chapter, "can Diahann Carroll be far behind?"[67]

❖

In Tokyo, Poitier touted *Lilies of the Field* as the most popular film ever among black audiences. "It has been preached about from the pulpits," he reported, adding that ministers implored their congregations to consider the picture "an exercise in Christianity." He also prickled at the constant questions about his own racial significance. "What I have to say is too often printed under the heading of race," he told *Variety*. "I have lived for 37 years and I'm offended when a reporter suggests by the nature of his questions that I've been pre-occupied for 37 years with race. I have not." He wanted recognition of not only his acting, but also his unique humanity.[68]

The future looked bright. He had shaken off the personal indecision of the last five years, ending his marriage and proposing to Carroll. He saw his children at every opportunity. He bathed in constant job offers. "Studios are actually on the lookout for stories for Poitier, who is not only a fine actor but a fine gentleman," wrote Louella Parsons. He even recorded another spoken-word album, a philosophical reading entitled *Poitier Meets Plato*. And after journeys to Yugoslavia, Utah, Moscow, Washington, Berlin, Los Angeles, Mississippi, Mexico, and Tokyo, Poitier had become a critical symbol of the black man in America.[69]

But his promotion in the Hollywood ranks made Poitier a lightning rod for black grievances. In November 1964 *Variety* reported the complaints of Bill Gunn, a black actor and writer stuck with minor parts and piles of excuses from casting directors. "When a good part for a Negro actor does come along, they always offer it to Sidney Poitier," he said. "If he turns it down, they rewrite it for a white actor." The gripe was nothing new, and it did not condemn Poitier himself. But after the civil rights triumphs and Poitier's Oscar, Hollywood's discrimination against blacks not named Sidney Poitier won a spotlight. Poitier's films had to both push boundaries and find a consensus between blacks and white liberals. That political minefield required ever more delicate steps.[70]

PART IV
ALONE IN THE PENTHOUSE

❖ ❖ ❖

CHAPTER 12

CROSSROADS

(1965–1966)

After six years of hype, almost two years after Poitier filmed his cameo, *The Greatest Story Ever Told* premiered in February 1965. Despite the $20 million cost, including an expensive new single-lens Cinerama technique, producer-director George Stevens demanded a subdued advertising campaign based on the picture's prestige. He won endorsements from major political figures; Lyndon Johnson, Harry Truman, Hubert Humphrey, Earl Warren, and Dean Rusk attended various exhibitions. Martin Luther King went to a special Los Angeles screening to raise money for the SCLC.[1]

For years Stevens had insisted on avoiding the elaborate staging and sexual innuendo of Cecil B. DeMille–style biblical epics. At that he succeeded: *The Greatest Story Ever Told* is a reverent, restrained take on the Gospels. Jesus Christ, played by Max von Sydow, is solemn and godly. The Utah landscape is striking, and a prayerful mood suffuses the picture from birth to rebirth. That interpretation induced some into lavish praise: "a memorable film," "a classic, timeless picture," even "the most majestic production the screen will ever have in the time and scope of current dimensions." On the strength of these reviews, support from religious and film organizations, and a series of cameos—including John Wayne, Shelley Winters, and Charlton Heston—the picture did well at the box office.[2]

But many critics trashed the film, and justifiably so. The *New Yorker* labeled it "a disaster . . . neatened and prettified and simultaneously blown up and diminished to the point where, if the subject matter weren't sacred in origin, we would be responding to the picture in the most charitable way possible by laughing at it from start to finish." The action is minimal, the dialogue stilted, the cameos excessive, the mood self-importantly sanctimonious. Worst of all, the film is long—"3 hours and 41 minutes of impeccable boredom," not counting the ten-minute intermission. Stevens mercifully cut twenty-eight minutes before it reached most theaters.[3]

Poitier's cameo raised some eyebrows. Simon of Cyrene helps Jesus carry his cross up Cavalry. He then watches the crucifixion with dreamy reverence, never uttering a word. Bosley Crowther labeled the casting choice "a last-minute symbolization of racial brotherhood," and other critics intimated similar opinions. Stevens did champion racial equality, and he hired a black assistant director, Wendell Franklin. But he was innocent of exploiting recent headlines. He had hired Poitier in 1960, before the ferment of Birmingham and the March on Washington.[4]

Furthermore, casting a black man as Simon of Cyrene had a legitimate foundation in the Gospels. Matthew, Mark, and Luke all describe an outsider from North Africa. Black Christians assigned great significance to this dark-skinned figure; his bearing of the cross signifies a larger inclusion of blacks in the Christian tradition. Poitier's role thus had allegorical significance: civil rights leaders framed the black struggle in terms of Christian sacrifice, and here was its screen personification. The black man does not just enlighten whites through his goodness; he actually, literally facilitates mankind's salvation.[5]

Now, however, the civil rights movement approached a crossroads. The spirit of nonviolent sacrifice still resonated: Martin Luther King won the Nobel Peace Prize in December 1964, and news footage of Alabama state troopers assaulting a peaceful march from Selma in March 1965 helped win support for national voting rights legislation. But cracks in the liberal consensus widened. Malcolm X was assassinated in February 1965, eroding the optimism of the Pleasantville summit. In Alabama, members of SNCC chafed at SCLC's conservative tactics. And that August, just five days after President Johnson signed the Voting Rights Act, the Los Angeles ghetto of Watts erupted in a riot. Urban blacks still endured frequent harassment, informal segregation, and economic stultification. Now they lashed out.[6]

Appeals to conscience could not solve the ghetto's ills. That summer, as King explored a potential protest in Chicago, he realized that this new phase lacked the clear moral imperative of the early 1960s. Urban problems needed an overhaul of the economic order, which threatened the interracial consensus. Middle-class moderates might have sympathized with black poverty, but not with black violence or socialism.[7]

Poitier approached his own crossroads. His image was tied to nonviolence and integration, but those values were coming into question. He had always presented a progressive black image and still appealed to a mass audience. By 1965, that was a very tricky balancing act.

❖

Before he overdosed on heroin in 1966, Lenny Bruce liked to spoof *The Defiant Ones*. He named his Poitier character "Randy." His white friend described an "Equality Heaven" run by Darryl Zanuck and Stanley Kramer. "Thass why they make them pictures," he said. "Cause they *believe* in equality, Randy, and up theah, it's gonna happen, cause they caused it, an, an, an then you gonna be livin' in Zanuck's house with all yo colored friends, and next dore Kramer on his property in Malibu, you be helpin' dem people, Randy—polishin' dem cars." For Bruce, Poitier movies presented a deficient vision of race relations, one where white liberals relegated blacks to loyal allies, where "To Play the Star Spangled Banner It Takes Both the White Keys and the Darkeys."[8]

Black pundits took shots at Poitier, too. In his 1966 book *White Papers for White Americans*, Calvin Hernton titled a chapter "And You, Too, Sidney Poitier!" Hernton objected to Hollywood's "systematic attempt to castrate Sidney Poitier." The taboo of black sexuality ran deep in the white psyche. "Insofar as Poitier in the movies must be a symbolic representation of America's concept of the Negro in general," Poitier's neuterdom reflected "the outright denial of manhood with reference to all black Americans."[9]

Without more black actors, writers, directors, and technicians, progress seemed unlikely. The NAACP's threats of mass demonstrations and boycotts had integrated most studios and craft unions, but only at token levels. In the spring of 1965, the NAACP renewed their demands. Still, integration proceeded at a snail's pace, and black intellectuals fumed. "We black writers and performing artists are ready to pool our creative strength to make our statements to our country," wrote John Oliver Killens in 1965. "Where are the big-talking liberals?"[10]

Ironically, Hollywood had become somewhat of a liberal enclave, at least in comparison to the conservative 1950s. In August 1965, Poitier cohosted a SNCC fundraiser with Belafonte, Elizabeth Taylor, Richard Burton, and Burt Lancaster at a Beverly Hills discotheque. Poitier delivered a short but passionate speech, arguing that the Watts riot was "only a symptom of the underlying social diseases eating away at the fabric of society." After SNCC director James Forman spoke, Poitier contributed $5,000, and celebrities from Marlon Brando to James Garner announced pledges for the civil rights organization most drifting toward radicalism.[11]

But as movie stars examined America's racial divide, movie screens ignored it. In the previous few years, some low-budget films had depicted proud, subtly defiant black protagonists: *The Cool World* (1963), *One Potato, Two Potato* (1964), *Nothing but a Man* (1964). Yet in 1965, the year of Selma and Watts, Hollywood produced no such honest delineations of black life.[12]

Nor did any blacks join Poitier in the ranks of stardom, a stagnation that displeased him. "Now I can't believe that I, Sidney Poitier, am the only man of talent for films from among twenty million Negro people," he said. "It's simply that Hollywood will not give people of my race a chance."[13]

Poitier wanted his creative juices stirred. To that end he planned a solo tour on the university circuit, envisioning a performance based on "the male-female relationship in which the world empties itself." He also resuscitated his ambition to create his own films. "I want to deal with questions of the human personality that are recognized by every individual—questions of loneliness, fear, love, violence." He sought to film in Africa, so that he could avoid commercial temptations.[14]

But Poitier never acted upon these notions. Nor did he exploit opportunities to render a more authentic black experience on screen. When James Baldwin approached him and Brando about a film of *Blues for Mister Charlie*, both actors expressed interest. Baldwin, however, never obtained the necessary funding. Then, producer Robert Young offered Poitier the lead role in *Nothing but a Man*. The low-budget film's script had a defiant hero who challenges his white employers, perhaps disturbing mainstream audiences. So Poitier spurned arguably the most complex, interesting black movie role of the 1960s.[15]

Instead he occupied a niche based on his integrationist prestige. "We don't have race films," wrote *Variety*, explaining the Hollywood psychology, "we have Sidney Poitier films." By March 1965 Poitier ranked among the industry's busiest actors. His four upcoming pictures carried a "soft-sell pitch" on race relations, emphasizing entertainment and deemphasizing race. Poitier favored this method; he told Ralph Nelson that *Lilies of the Field* "made a more important social statement than the March on Washington." So he selected roles in that tradition—roles that cemented his virtuous image, downplayed race, and appealed to white audiences.[16]

"I'm the only Negro actor earning a living in movies, the only one," he justified to the *New York Times*: "It's a hell of a responsibility." He believed that if he reversed derogatory images of silly maids and bug-eyed servants, then Americans would expect more black actors. "Why is Sidney Poitier the only one?" they would ask. Then, he hoped, his opportunities would transcend race, and he could play not just *Othello* but *King Lear*.[17]

Harry Belafonte was more cynical. He believed that when Poitier became "anointed," he severed his radical ties and embellished his virtuous image. "He handpicked each one of those pictures," Belafonte later said, "to continue to exercise that beauty and make sure that he never, ever disturbed the white psyche in anything he did. Not once."[18]

❖

In Mark Rascovich's novel *The Bedford Incident*, the character Ben Munceford is "a rawboned southerner" with a "round red face," a weak-kneed womanizer, a freelance journalist of average ability. James Poe rewrote the character for Poitier. Poe obviously changed Munceford's background. He also removed his tinge of mediocrity; like other Poitier characters, Munceford would be principled, intelligent, and upstanding. But Poe did not inject a racial story line. In a Hollywood milestone, *The Bedford Incident* never references Poitier's race.[19]

Poitier orally committed to the project in the winter of 1964. Admirably, he adhered to those contract terms after he won the Oscar. Producer-director James B. Harris raised his salary anyway. (In typical Poitier fashion, he wanted only half the $400,000 salary up front. He received the other half in payments spread out from 1973 to 1978.) For the last ten weeks of 1964, they filmed at Shepperton Studios in England.[20]

The Bedford Incident, in line with a recent trend, critiqued the paranoid militarism of the Cold War. The construction of the Berlin Wall and the Cuban Missile Crisis had widened a rupture in the nation's cultural politics. Although many Americans still endorsed vigilant anti-Communism, some 1964 Hollywood films had exposed a strain of dissent: *Dr. Strangelove* painted the Cold War as self-perpetuating lunacy, and *Fail-Safe* illustrated a tragic sequence toward nuclear Armageddon.[21]

The Bedford Incident mirrors the grim, quasi-documentary style of *Fail-Safe* more than the farcical nihilism of *Dr. Strangelove*. Richard Widmark's Eric Finlander captains the *Bedford*, an American destroyer tracking a Russian submarine in the Denmark Strait. He keeps his crew on edge, berating incompetents and running constant drills. Poitier's journalist dodges the captain's intimidating rebuffs, and he goads the captain into baring his militarism. "I'm proud to be an old-fashioned patriot!" Finlander explodes. "And I'd destroy any enemy if it meant saving my country. Now what's wrong with that?"

But Finlander is a monomaniacal Captain Ahab, and the Russian submarine his white whale. He ignores warnings from Munceford, his medical officer Chester Potter (Martin Balsam), and his adviser Commandant Schrepke (Eric Portman), a former Nazi U-Boat captain. As the *Bedford* stalks the submarine through iceberg-pocked waters, Finlander pushes his crew beyond the brink, and he interprets NATO orders to suit his aggressive whims. His sonarman has a nervous breakdown.

After twenty-four hours of pursuit, Finlander steers his ship directly over the surfacing submarine, provoking a desperate response from the Russian captain. "You're not chasing whales now, Finlander, you're pushing him too far!" warns Munceford. Commandant Schrepke echoes him. The captain assures them that the *Bedford* will not fire first. "But if he fires one, I'll fire one." A frazzled officer hears only the last words, "Fire One," and launches a missile. The Russians reciprocate, and the picture ends in mutual nuclear annihilation.

When *The Bedford Incident* opened in November 1965, Columbia astutely marketed it as an action picture rather than a bleak jeremiad. No advertising, however, could obscure its clichés. Critics likened Finlander to those other obsessed captains, Ahab and Queeg. Others tabbed the picture a hackneyed offspring of the 1964 classics: Arthur Knight called it *The Fail-Safe of the Sea*, and Hollis Alpert *Captain Strangefail*. Unfortunately *The Bedford Incident* lacked not only the satire of *Dr. Strangelove*, but also the drama of *Fail-Safe*. After beginning with brisk Cold War tension, the film bogs down before its unsatisfying conclusion.[22]

Poitier's performance is unremarkable. The actor's fans might have expected a lightning clash between Widmark's fanaticism and Poitier's humanity. Instead, Widmark dominates. Poitier displays some hints of charming insouciance, but soon he merely joins the cavalcade of voices preaching reason to Finlander. He suffered in the diminished role. Neither the part nor the performance befit an Oscar winner.[23]

The Bedford Incident was significant for Poitier only because the film never referred to his race. Columbia promoted this Hollywood landmark by hiring the black advertising firm D. Parke Gibson and Associates, which released editorials to black newspapers hailing the integrationist achievement: "Poitier's breakthrough represents one of the best assignments we as a race have received thus far, and again proves that if given the opportunity, we can produce in any field."[24]

Most white critics, conversely, followed the picture's logic and ignored race. Perhaps after seeing white violence in Selma and black violence in Watts, they appreciated the chance to watch Poitier without confronting the nation's most divisive issue. Yet *The Bedford Incident* asked audiences to accept that a black reporter, in 1965, could step onto an all-white Navy destroyer, and that no one would mention his race. Among the few critics to question this leap of faith was Arthur Knight: "Everyone on shipboard seemed miraculously, unbelievably color-blind."[25]

That gloss of Hollywood fantasy also coated *The Slender Thread*, which premiered one month later. Screenwriter Stirling Siliphant had adapted a *Life* article called "Decision to Die," progressively calling the script *Call Me Back!*, *Down Will Come the Sky*, *Soft Talk Me Home!*, and finally *The Slender Thread*. Sydney Pollack directed his first motion picture, and Anne Bancroft signed to star as a suicidal woman. Playing a young Crisis Center volunteer — a character absent in the original article and not specific to any race — was Poitier.[26]

"We felt a Negro explaining the meaningfulness of life would add a dramatic dimension to the picture," admitted producer Stephen Alexander. Casting Poitier ensured a racial subtext — the racial difference would be visually apparent, even if the script neglected the theme.[27]

The Slender Thread was filmed entirely on location in Seattle, starting in June 1965. Once, during a scene of an attempted suicide at the Golden Gardens beach, crew members had to rescue Bancroft from actually drowning. Poitier encountered no such excitement; his counselor was anchored to a telephone. Pollack rigged a live wire on set, so that when Poitier performed before the cameras, Bancroft could respond from her dressing room.[28]

On screen, Poitier's Alan Newell exhibits a comfortable, middle-class, graduate-student chic: books on his arm, pencil behind his ear, elbow patches on his corduroy coat. When he arrives at the clinic, his boss Dr. Coburn (Telly Savalas) calls him "Mr. Newell." He hopes to study for his next exam. After Coburn leaves, however, he receives a call from Inga Dyson (Bancroft). She has taken barbiturates and refuses to reveal her whereabouts.

Pollack employs European-style flashbacks to explain Inga's suicidal devolution. She has let her marriage deteriorate and tried to drown herself. These dreamy sequences contrast to the documentary-style footage of Alan Newell, the Seattle police, and telephone operators trying to save Inga. The juxtaposition illustrates the irony of thriving technological communication and degenerating human connections.[29]

Yet this structure hampered the picture. The Crisis Center scenes rely on dialogue, while the flashbacks move languorously. Some shots seem pretentious, especially in contrast to the predictable main narrative. The contrast betrayed the television roots of Alexander and Pollack. A plot centered on one telephone conversation lacked the action to drive a full-length motion picture.[30]

Throughout the picture, Newell tries to convince Inga of her life's value. He coaxes out a personal connection. When she descends into self-pity, he discards conventional wisdom and berates her, even yelling, "Go ahead, baby, go ahead and die!" But he balances these outbursts with sentimentality: "I love you, Inga! You're gonna stay right here in this lovely, lovely, lovely land of the living!"

Unfortunately, Poitier overplays these attitude swings. His despair appears forced, and his optimism Pollyannish. The physically expressive actor suffered when chained to a telephone. He bounds around with nowhere to go, and he gesticulates far too wildly — "like a windmill trying to dodge Sancho Panza," according to *Newsweek*. "Poitier," added *Time*, "behaves precisely like an Oscar-winning actor who has to work up an hour or more of excitement with a hot line as his only prop."[31]

Even though the audience cannot ignore it, Newell never reveals his race to Inga. Only once does he imply his racial experience, when Inga suggests that he use her as a "lesson." He erupts: "I am up to my ears in lessons. I've been taught — long before I picked up this phone tonight, I've been taught. So lessons I don't need, understand? Good people I do. You've watched the walls close in on you, me too. You've been ignored or studied out of the corners of people's eyes, me too. You've been suffered, intolerated, me too, okay? Times are bad, things stink, the world's a cinder in your eye, but what is the alternative? Now I ask you, Inga, what in God's name is the alternative?" One reviewer celebrated the obvious message: "If a young Negro, with his special frustrations and embarrassments, can value life so highly, it seems churlish, to say the least, for someone with fewer problems to give up."[32]

In theory, another actor, either black or white, could have played Alan Newell. But that is hard to imagine. As it stands, the picture suggests racial prejudice while ignoring racial conflict, which could only occur by casting Poitier. White audiences swallowed the colorblind perspective thanks to Poitier's image; before stepping foot in the theater, they knew that Poitier was a virtuous man in a white world. But his blackness lent legitimacy to otherwise trite lines. Without Poitier, *The Slender Thread* would have been unworthy of the screen—a comment on Hollywood, race relations, and Poitier's career that rings both sanguine and sad.[33]

❖

The Bedford Incident and *The Slender Thread* both aspired to colorblindness. *A Patch of Blue*, the third Poitier film of late 1965, had no such ambition: it featured an interracial romance. It nevertheless conformed to Poitier's pattern. His character is a model of middle-class respectability, a conscience and savior to whites. Moreover, the film suggests the expediency of ignoring racial distinctions. His white love interest is not just colorblind—she is actually blind.

From the start, *A Patch of Blue* was a Sidney Poitier vehicle. In June 1964, MGM producer Pandro Berman sent him the Elizabeth Kata novel *Be Ready with Bells and Drums*. On the way to the Berlin Film Festival, the actor read the story of a black man who befriends a poor blind white girl. At the end, she is surprised to learn his race, but she has overcome her prejudice, and they fall in love. Poitier expressed interest. When he met with studio executives that August, he appreciated the couple's relationship: "I think that's the kernel and the seed and it's from there you can build an extraordinarily touching, warm, humorous, tender, human story." But he also voiced objections. "It leans very heavily on the nature of race," he said, "and it ought not to." He thought that the picture should emphasize romance, not prejudice.[34]

Berman agreed that the film could not include the book's surprise ending. With the help of his wife, Kathryn, they reshaped the female hero to bear no racial prejudice. The studio and the actor shared a basic philosophy, as Berman summarized: "We want something we can be proud of and that will do the world some good from a racial point of view. We want to make a picture that is anti-prejudice and yet has as few message words in it as is possible to make."[35]

MGM needed Poitier. British director and screenwriter Guy Green had optioned the film rights, but no one had yet invested significant money. *A Patch of Blue* was economically feasible only with America's single black movie star. Berman had two other scripts with white lead actors. He could interchange Jack Lemmon, James Garner, George Peppard, or some other white star in those roles. "But if I don't have Sidney Poitier," Berman said, "I don't want to make this picture."[36]

The next month, Poitier agreed in principle to a $120,000 salary. In October, MGM bought the rights to the novel. In November, Poitier signed his contract (at the insistence of MGM's New York office, which wanted to cut costs, Poitier instead took an $80,000 advance and 10 percent of the gross). By the end of the year, MGM signed Shelley Winters. Story editor Russ Thacher marveled at the project's speed. "Never underestimate the power of a star, Thacher," responded Berman, "in this case Sidney Poitier."[37]

Even before filming began on 15 March, Poitier conferred with MGM executives to shape the picture's racial strategy. He urged that they render a range of white attitudes, not just racism. He also suggested revisions for scenes portraying disagreements between his character and his militant brother. Thanks in part to Poitier's input, only the blind girl's mother vents crude prejudice, and his own character never voices a racial philosophy. By the time shooting completed on 1 May, five days early and $65,000 under budget, Poitier had sculpted a film's politics to a degree unprecedented in his fifteen-year career.[38]

His character, Gordon Ralfe, suited both his political agenda and acting talents. A journalist, he speaks with good grammar, appreciates classical music, and wears cardigan sweaters. At a park, he meets the young blind woman Selina D'Arcey (Elizabeth Hartman). He learns about Selina's mother Rose-Ann (Winters), a slatternly maid and part-time whore. When Selina was five, Rose-Ann threw acid at her father, but she missed her target and blinded her daughter. Gordon buys sunglasses to cover her scars.

Over the next few days, Gordon treats her to lunch, helps her string beads, and teaches her such daily tasks as crossing the street, buying groceries, riding the elevator, and dialing the telephone. His guidance contrasts with her wretched home life. Her grandfather "Ole Pa" (Wallace Ford) is a pitiful drunk. Selina has never attended school, let alone learned braille. Rose-Ann berates and beats her daughter at a hint of insolence. Selina has even been raped by a "client" of Rose-Ann's.

As Gordon enlightens her, Selina falls in love. But Gordon refrains from revealing his race. When his brother Mark (Ivan Dixon) questions him about the social consequences of his relationship, Gordon deflects the interrogation, simply contending that Selina needs his help.

In another scene (suggested by Poitier himself) Mark is more vehement. He urges Gordon to cast aside Selina. "You plan on educating a white girl?" he asks. "Man, that's not your job! Let Whitey educate his own women." Gordon spurns the bait: "Look, on race and politics we don't agree, so let's drop this." The scene illustrates Hollywood's baby steps on America's preeminent issue. Mark espouses black identity politics new to the movie screen. But Poitier's hero sidesteps the debate. He prefers racial integration based on goodwill, and he avoids any overt political message that might discomfort whites.[39]

Poitier's virtuous image is complicated—and ultimately strengthened—by sex. Gordon falls for Selina, too. When she breaks a dish, he kisses her forehead. She pulls them together, and for a few seconds, they kiss on the lips. Here was another milestone, Hollywood's first interracial kiss. But the situation is fraught with ambiguity. After the spurt of passion, Gordon pulls back. Although Selina desires him, he refrains from exploiting her tragic past. This action refined Poitier's neuterdom. Unlike in past pictures, where his isolated position or marital status precluded romance, his character has sexual opportunities in *A Patch of Blue*. Now he must personally reinforce racial taboos by exhibiting Victorian restraint.[40]

After checking his passion, Gordon saves Selina. With her equally repugnant friend Sadie (Elisabeth Fraser), Rose-Ann plans a new brothel, perhaps with Selina as a prostitute. But in the park, Gordon escorts Selina away, leaving Rose-Ann to spew racist threats amidst unsympathetic onlookers. That night Gordon arranges for Selina to attend a boarding school for the blind. Selina wants to marry, but Gordon suggests that they wait a year to sort out their feelings. Their future remains undetermined, their sexuality unexpressed. Race trumps romance.

The ending revealed the continued limits on Poitier's control over his image. Although he bore enough influence to shape the script's racial philosophy, he lost the battle to develop the loving relationship in line with conventional Hollywood narratives. Two years later, he complained about his screen sexuality: "Either there were no women, or there was a woman but she was blind, or the relationship was of a nature that satisfied the taboos. I was at my wits end when I finished *A Patch of Blue*."[41]

Given the shifting context of black politics, Poitier's Good Samaritan frustrated some intellectual critics. "This caricature of the Negro as a Madison Avenue sort of Christian saint, selfless and well groomed, is becoming a movie cliché nearly as tiresome and, at bottom, nearly as patronizing as the cretinous figure that Stepin Fetchit used to play," wrote Brendan Gill. Gordon Ralfe is an abstract symbol of black goodness with no background, no complexity, no motivation for befriending little white girls in parks. "Would it not have been more interesting to write the Negro as a character of some difficulty, a character whose motives have at least the ordinary ambivalence?" asked Joan Didion. Poitier had become his own one-man stereotype.[42]

The picture itself inspired similar denunciations. Gordon is so virtuous, Selina so sweet, and Rose-Ann so vulgar that they lack credibility. The plot is implausible, and the resolution a maudlin tearjerker. Critics called *A Patch of Blue* "a compound of specious contrivance," "tepid tokenism," "bad art and ineffective propaganda," and "literally sickening in its sentimentality." One accused Guy Green of "trying to coax the last treacly tear out of scenes that, in dialogue and setting, are already so much softly bubbling penuche." Another claimed that "no other film has ever managed to simultaneously insult the Negroes and the blind." Still others drew parallels to the ultimate racial melodrama, *Uncle Tom's Cabin.*[43]

But for every acerbic review, another lauded the picture's sensitivity. Green, praised *Time*, prevented a collapse "from pathos to bathos." Others maintained that the actors overcame the picture's potential for mawkishness. Poitier radiated goodness, Hartman lent subtlety, and Winters was over-the-top evil. Thus, despite the ham-handed symbolism, the actors forged sympathy for the interracial relationship.[44]

That warm sentiment aroused grass-roots support for *A Patch of Blue*. "I cannot remember," wrote Berman to Green, "when I have had so many phone calls and letters from old folks and children and everyone in between who felt impelled to state their emotional reactions. It is very gratifying and very unusual." A young teacher hoped that it would speed racial integration. A Pennsylvania woman related her sister's shock ("Things like that just don't happen around here"), but she embraced the message: "It shows that Negroes are people just like we are, and that they have feelings too."[45]

Out of this goodwill emerged a box-office triumph. Positive word-of-mouth built audiences throughout the country. In March 1966 *Variety* reported that in nearly every exhibition, the tallies from the second and third weeks topped those from the first week. *A Patch of Blue* was Poitier's most successful picture to date, grossing over $6.5 million dollars. Because MGM had insisted that Poitier receive less up front and a percentage of the gross, Poitier earned over six times more.[46]

By spring 1966, a number of awards had fortified the picture's reputation. The Hollywood Unity Awards Committee gave an award for "outstanding contributions to the betterment of human relations," and the Hollywood Foreign Press Association nominated it for Best Picture, Best Director, Best Actor (Poitier), and Best Actress (Hartman). Hartman and Winters then won Academy Award nominations, and Winters took home the Oscar for Best Supporting Actress.[47]

The most extraordinary reaction came from the Deep South, where *A Patch of Blue* earned excellent grosses. No one had anticipated such solid returns in every major southern market, including Atlanta, Savannah,

Knoxville, Tulsa, Charlotte, Miami, Houston—even Birmingham. The only parallel to its Atlanta premiere, wrote one awed studio executive, was the recent re-release of *Gone With the Wind*, and Vivien Leigh and Olivia de Havilland had attended that gala affair. Even more surprising, *A Patch of Blue* played in many small southern towns.[48]

Alas, southern audiences were not privy to eight seconds of film, the eight seconds where Poitier and Hartman kiss. As one confused Texas woman described, "One minute she's about to kiss him, and the next thing you see are the two embracing." It might have been a milestone for southerners to witness the emotional connection between a black man and white woman, but the edit curbed the picture's romance even beyond the farfetched circumstances. Below the Mason-Dixon line, then, Poitier's virtuous sexual restraint was even more exaggerated.[49]

Even with Poitier's nobility, Hartman's blindness, and MGM's cuts, *A Patch of Blue* inflamed some southerners. In March 1966, in Jacksonville, Florida, protesters planted a seven-foot wooden cross covered in burlap, soaked in kerosene, and dotted with live shotgun shells. When the cross ignited, an exploding shell damaged an adjacent police car. In May, six Ku Klux Klansmen picketed a downtown Memphis exhibition. "We are here to get the people of Memphis and the Mid-South not to see this movie because it is ungodly," one said, as the others brandished a sign proclaiming "Bourbon and Water, Not White and Black." They also objected to "the nigger's name above the white woman's on the marquee." In August, authorities discovered a homemade bomb with five sticks of dynamite planted in a Concord, North Carolina, theater. Luckily, the bomb malfunctioned.[50]

The range of reactions to *A Patch of Blue*, from critical barbs to liberal praise to racist outrage, illustrated Poitier's evolving position in the American racial consciousness. *A Patch of Blue* opened days before *The Slender Thread* in December 1965, and only one month after *The Bedford Incident*. Poitier was a marquee name. But as the liberal consensus on black politics began to fracture, so had the consensus on Poitier. That audiences flocked to *A Patch of Blue* signaled that many Americans still craved sentimental racial goodwill. That some critics resorted to snide hyperbole portended the demise of Poitier's image. That Klan members picketed his picture revealed just how long the journey remained.[51]

❖

That December, Poitier won attention for another reason: he had signed to play Bumpo Kahbooboo, crown prince of Jolliginki, opposite Rex

Harrison in *Doctor Dolittle*. It seemed a curious decision to accept a supporting position in a droll musical. In fact, Poitier never played the part. Behind his initial pact and subsequent exclusion lay a tale of Hollywood ego, excess, and lunacy.[52]

Harrison had abruptly rejected Sammy Davis Jr., insisting upon Poitier as Bumpo Kahbooboo. Director Richard Fleischer and producer Arthur Jacobs panicked, since they had already signed Davis. But they bent to Harrison's whims. For Poitier, they laid it on thick. After insisting that he was their only choice, they acted out the score. Poitier sat stone-faced, thoughtful, chin in hand. After the elaborate spiel, he accepted.[53]

That night Fleischer and Jacobs attended Davis's Broadway smash *Golden Boy*. They planned to break the bad news after the show, a chore made more difficult as Davis played directly to them, ad-libbing, "I'm putting on my Rex Harrison hat" and affecting a ridiculous British accent. It got worse. After the show, as they sat with Davis in his dressing room, someone knocked on the door. It was Poitier.

Fleischer and Jacobs envisioned egg on their faces. Luckily, Poitier handled the situation better than he ever played a poker hand. He only confirmed his golf date with Davis. Fleischer and Jacobs fired Davis, and Davis explained the confusion to Poitier the next morning. But as Poitier orally agreed to a $250,000 contract, the production of *Doctor Dolittle* bloated. They built up Poitier's part to justify his salary. Then Harrison quit, so they bought out Christopher Plummer's Broadway contract to replace him. They reconsidered, however, and rehired Harrison.[54]

To cut costs, Twentieth Century-Fox insisted that they buy out Poitier, Harrison's fancies be damned. Then Jacobs received a telegram from Martin Baum that insisted upon the immediate resolution of some minor points in Poitier's contract. Not believing his good fortune, Jacobs rejected the demands, and Poitier left the cast. *Doctor Dolittle* appeared in 1967, a high-budget flop even without Poitier's golden opportunity to win money for nothing.[55]

More satisfying was Poitier's return to television in a spectacular, one-hour, all-black salute to Harlem called *The Strollin' Twenties*. Harry Belafonte conceived the program after reading Langston Hughes's novel *The Big Sea*. He co-wrote the script with Hughes and procured a cavalcade of black talent including Poitier, Duke Ellington, Sammy Davis Jr., Diahann Carroll, and Nipsey Russell. Belafonte had created the first television show ever written, produced, and performed by blacks.[56]

Television had played a contradictory role in the black quest for equality. On one hand, television news and documentaries were indispensable tools; visual images of peaceful black marchers and brutal white police-men had built support for civil rights legislation. On the other hand, television lacked even a token black star. After southern sponsors balked, Nat King Cole's variety show in the late 1950s was canceled. A deal for a series of Belafonte-hosted variety shows fell through. For the first half of the 1960s, no programs featured blacks in important roles.[57]

Since *A Man Is Ten Feet Tall* in 1955, Poitier had not appeared in a television drama. He often spoke about television's untapped potential for black performers. But the financial imperative to appease southern viewers meant that studios hesitated to air even innocuous fables such as *The Jackie Robinson Story* and Poitier's own *Go, Man, Go!* ABC refused to broadcast *The Defiant Ones* during the 1962–63 season because of its thirty southern affiliates.[58]

By the time *The Strollin' Twenties* aired in February 1966, there had been some progress. Sammy Davis Jr.'s variety show on NBC had pre-miered one month earlier to mixed reviews. Of more significance was Bill Cosby's role opposite Robert Culp in *I Spy*. The comedian had won mass acceptance by excising racial material from his act, instead spinning hi-larious routines on children, athletics, and the Bible. His intelligence agent in *I Spy*—a Rhodes scholar who speaks seven languages—was television's analogue to Poitier's film icon. Culp got the women, but Cosby was smart, funny, and comfortable around his white partner. He "could just as well be a white man," wrote one critic. Except for four in the Deep South, all NBC affiliates carried the successful program.[59]

The Strollin' Twenties, by celebrating "that dusky sash across Manhat-tan," forsook the colorblind approach. Poitier played "The Stroller," the narrator of Hughes's poetry: "Harlem is a tear held back into a smile; Harlem is a sunrise you know has got to come up after a while." He introduced America to Harlem culture: strolling, rent parties, The Savoy. Peppered by spirited musical numbers, the show also depicted Harlem's poverty. *The Strollin' Twenties* resonated among black viewers. One mar-veled: "This is the first time Negroes have let the white man see how he once lived."[60]

Alas, for Poitier, the show included some personal agony, since one co-star was Diahann Carroll. By then, the couple had almost cemented their bond, only for it to crumble apart in mutual misunderstandings and hot-blooded brawls.

After Poitier obtained a Mexican divorce in late 1964, gossip colum-nists predicted his impending nuptials to Carroll. By the next spring, Poitier and Carroll were a public item, attending such galas as a Writer's

Guild ball and the Academy Awards. Yet the stars played down the rumors. Carroll only spoke of her growing maturity regarding relationships. Poitier skated past inquisitions about his personal life; he told one reporter that besides his children, "the people who mean the most to me are — well, a lady I've known for seven years."[61]

Their relationship fascinated the media. While Poitier was filming *A Patch of Blue* and Carroll was singing at a Los Angeles nightclub, press hounds followed them to Sunset Strip bistros and the ultra-hip club "Whiskey A Go Go." The speculation was a milestone in itself: never had a black couple attracted such attention.[62]

They remained publicly evasive until Juanita sanctioned the divorce. Under New York State law, a divorce needed both parties' consent, and Juanita refused to sign the papers. To protect their daughters, she had even threatened to sue various newspapers for printing rumors of their divorce. Finally, in July 1965, Juanita disclosed her marriage's imminent end. At that point, Poitier and Carroll released a brief press statement announcing their plans to wed in the fall, when Poitier's divorce was complete and Carroll had returned from an Australian tour.[63]

Soon the couple signed a long-term lease on a nine-room apartment on Riverside Drive, and Carroll oversaw its redecoration to match her opulent standards. As carpenters, painters, plasterers, electricians, and upholsterers passed through, Carroll hired a caregiver for her young daughter, Suzanne. They installed bunk beds for visits from Poitier's girls.[64]

Juanita coped by expanding her interests. She co-produced two one-act plays by Douglas Turner Ward for the 1965–66 season at the St. Mark's Playhouse. According to John Oliver Killens, both *Happy Ending* and *Day of Absence* "magnificently spoofed the ways of white folk." The plays mirrored an emerging trend in black theater: creative control lay in black hands, and the plays strove more for cultural authenticity than mainstream acceptability.[65]

In September Poitier left for Kanab, Utah, to film *Duel at Diablo* — another picture where, in Poitier's words, "I play a guy, not a Negro." The divorce was still not complete, and he and Carroll had not set a wedding date. His distance from New York triggered new complications — and, per tradition, Poitier and Carroll colored their accounts in clashing hues.[66]

Poitier contended that they had reached an agreement: for six months, Suzanne would live with Carroll's parents in Yonkers. He did not want to jump straight from one domestic situation to another. But then Carroll announced that "the deal was off." After consulting her therapist, she had realized her misgivings about living apart from Suzanne. Poitier boiled. He had satisfied all her requests: moving from Pleasantville, divorcing Juanita, signing the apartment lease. Now Carroll was rejecting his sole request.[67]

Carroll denied the charge. "Sidney must have panicked," she explained. She claimed that he telephoned her to say that Juanita was having second thoughts about the divorce. Then, after she had rented out her old apartment, Poitier called again. He told her not to ship Suzanne's belongings to Riverside Drive. According to Carroll, they had agreed that Suzanne would stay with her parents for six weeks, "but there was never any question about her living with us. She was always part of our plans." Only then did she consult her therapist.[68]

They had built a relationship not on solid foundations of trust and commitment, but on flimsy floorboards of passion and insecurity and arguments. For this fight, Poitier recalled, "I could smell my own blood in the caverns of my sinuses." When Carroll told him about her therapist's recommendations, he hissed, "To hell with you and your doctor." That night, he changed the locks on the new apartment. Carroll emptied her bank account and borrowed the rest to take over the lease. They shelved their marriage plans. It was the beginning of their end.[69]

❖

By night Poitier's personal life shattered, but by day he realized a childhood dream. He had once idolized Bob Steele, Tom Mix, William S. Hart, and the other white-hatted heroes of Westerns. Now he played a cowboy in *Duel at Diablo*.

The black cowboy was a historical reality. *The Negro Cowboys*, a popular 1965 book by two UCLA professors, documented the preponderance of blacks in the West: cattle drivers and cattle thieves, "Buffalo Soldiers" and pro-Indian renegades. The historians argued that novels and movies had erased black cowboys from popular memory. Now, studios considered new takes on Westerns. In May 1965, at their Guild headquarters, seventy-five screenwriters listened to a presentation about black cowboys. "I have no doubt that what you say is true," responded one writer, "but how much can we expect the public to take? Will they believe it?"[70]

Poitier's integrationist image greased the skids for a black cowboy on screen. *Duel at Diablo*, like *The Bedford Incident* and *The Slender Thread*, would not mention race, a strategy that producer-director Ralph

Nelson might not have risked with a lesser-known black actor. There would be no racial tension among the cowboys. "None of that crap," said Poitier. "That's old hat."[71]

Poitier later admitted that he disliked the script. But he wanted audiences — especially black children — to see a black Western hero. In Marvin H. Albert's novel *Apache Rising*, the character Toller is a white gambler from the Deep South. Although likable and intelligent, he dies midway through the story. When Albert and Michael Grilikhes adapted it to screen (originally under the title *29 to Duell*), they made Toller a black ex-Army sergeant, a natural leader, as skilled with a gun as a pack of cards.[72]

Poitier's co-star, James Garner, was a more familiar cowboy. In fact, the star of the television hit *Maverick* feared that he was typecast. After leaving the show in 1960, he swore off spurs and a big hat. But Garner aspired to produce, and he knew that a western picture starring him was a bankable asset. He negotiated a stake in *Duel at Diablo* through his company, Cherokee Productions.[73]

Producers Ralph Nelson and Fred Engel planned to begin filming in the spring of 1965 in Durango, Colorado, on a set already constructed for *The Sons of Katie Elder*. Lamentably, locals ransacked the facility, so they rescheduled for Utah in September 1965. Striving for authenticity, they borrowed 500 silver dollars from a local bank, hired fifty Navajos as extras, and procured 200 horses trained by the black rodeo star Roy Quirk, who pulled extra duty as Poitier's stunt double. Once when Poitier was riding, however, his horse reared back onto him. He endured some painful bruises, but he kept acting and frequenting Las Vegas casinos on the weekends.[74]

Filming ended in December, and *Duel at Diablo* premiered in May 1966. The story takes place in the American Southwest during the 1870s or 1880s, when roaming Apache bands violently resisted white encroachment. A green unit of United States Cavalry, accompanied by scout Jess Remsberg (Garner) and bronco buster Toller (Poitier), travel to Fort Concho. Upon encountering Apaches, they stage a military chess match. When the Indians lay siege in Diablo Canyon, Remsberg rides for reinforcements, and the film climaxes with a cavalry rescue.[75]

A subplot concerns the ambiguous moral choices faced by Remsberg, a stubble-faced cowboy obsessed with avenging the murder of his Comanche wife. Three times Remsberg saves Ellen Grange (Bibi Andersson), a beautiful blonde once forced to bear the child of an Indian warrior. She is scorned both by Indians and whites, including her husband Willard (Dennis Weaver). In an improbable twist, Remsberg learns that Willard raped and killed his wife to avenge Ellen's abduction. Remsberg returns to Diablo Canyon intent on torturing him, but the Apaches have already slow-roasted Willard to death's door. Remsberg's humanity outweighs his malice, and he lets Grange kill himself.

By presenting these difficult choices and confused identities, *Duel at Diablo* revised the frontier myth of traditional Westerns. Remsberg can follow no virtuous path to justice, because it is unclear what constitutes virtue or justice. The graphic battle scenes do not glorify white heroism, and Remsberg's love for his Comanche wife complicates any easy racial dichotomy. Remsberg's sympathy for his enemy reinforces the ambiguity. "The Apaches have been holed up on that hellhole reservation at San Carlos — tricked, lied to, murdered," he says. When Ellen wonders if the warriors will remain on their reservation, he spits, "Why should they?"[76]

Still, *Duel at Diablo* is hardly pro-Indian. When the Apaches are not launching bloodthirsty raids, they remain faceless, stoic, tragic Noble Savages. If the picture condemns prejudice, it condemns prejudice against blacks. Critics again applauded the colorblind casting of Poitier; one revived a paternalistic chestnut by calling him "a credit to his people." Nelson crowed about Poitier's symbolism: "Even if the whites succeed in eliminating the redskins, there will still be the Negro problem." That analysis smacked of not only liberal self-congratulation, but also inaccuracy. By disregarding Poitier's race, the picture ignores "the Negro problem." Instead it bands blacks and whites together opposite a common Indian enemy.[77]

At first, Poitier's Toller cuts a ridiculous figure. He wears an ostentatious pearl gray hat, matching glossy vest with cigars in the breast pocket, bright white shirt, and big black boots. With a cigar jutting from his mouth, he utters absurd gambling analogies in a gravelly voice.

But underneath the dandified veneer lives a true cowboy. Toller breaks wild mustangs, lends military advice, takes an arrow in the arm, and directs the defense of the Apache siege. The troops obey his orders without question. Poitier also brought his character a subtle defiance, posturing opposite white officers and snapping off wisecracks. When a lieutenant orders him, he smiles bemusedly: "You're the cockle-doodle-doo around here." After assuming leadership, he is no longer silly but stalwart, a film figure of some significance. "In these transitional days," wrote one critic, "a Negro smart aleck who winds up saving Whitey from himself *and* from the Apaches may still draw gasps from audiences who are not quite so liberated from the Stepin Fetchit stereotype as they may have imagined."[78]

Poitier again rankled some racial extremists. In Glendale, California, three self-proclaimed "American Nazis" picketed *Duel at Diablo*. According to one report, the unemployed teenagers "flaunted placards crudely objecting to the idea of a Negro, Academy Award winner Poitier, portraying a cowboy." Their gripes gained no support. Theatergoers heckled the racists, not Poitier.[79]

But Poitier still operated within familiar boundaries. He has no romance, no complexity, no real identity. His social symbol plays second fiddle to James Garner's morally tortured and sexually charged protagonist. Moreover, it is inconceivable that an entire cavalry unit, just decades removed from the Civil War, would blindly accept a black man's authority. Hollywood's sole comment on the black experience was Poitier, and his films were ignoring the black experience, even as the political winds drifted away from his integrationist icon.

❖

In June 1966, a white man shot James Meredith on Highway 51 in Mississippi. Meredith had been marching from Memphis to Jackson as a public demonstration of defiance against white intimidation tactics of black voters. He survived, and so did his march. The major civil rights organizations agreed to continue his trek.[80]

They agreed on little else. SNCC, now led by Stokely Carmichael, and CORE, now headed by Floyd McKissick, foresaw a political future independent of white liberals. They believed that inner cities needed black leadership, and they lost patience with nonviolence. Their radical ideology drove the Urban League and NAACP out of the march. That left Martin Luther King and SCLC to negotiate the divide, to preach nonviolence, to smooth over Carmichael's incendiary rhetoric ("White blood will flow!"). Yet the split widened. At a rally in Greenwood, Carmichael named the militant mood. "What we gonna start saying now is Black Power!" he proclaimed. "We . . . want . . . Black . . . Power!" he chanted. Headlines throughout the nation reported the response: "BLACK POWER! BLACK POWER! BLACK POWER!"[81]

Poitier was involved in the Meredith march, first through his family, and then directly. While recuperating, Meredith had granted interviews from the Poitier estate in Pleasantville. On 20 June, at 3 A.M., Juanita discovered a five-foot-high cross burning in the driveway. Then, on 25 June, Poitier joined over 8,000 marchers at Tougaloo College in Jackson. They held a rally before the final march to the State Capitol. Sammy Davis Jr., who avoided the Deep South, swallowed his fear and flew to Jackson. He remembered feeling safe around Belafonte and Poitier: "Harry and Sidney . . . were like two black knights."[82]

For more than just his elfin friend, Poitier remained an icon of black nobility and racial justice. In December 1965 he read the Human Rights Declaration before the United Nations General Assembly. In May 1966 the American Jewish Committee recognized his commitment to racial understanding. In December 1966 President Johnson appointed him, Marian Anderson, Charlton Heston, and Helen Hayes to the National Council on the Arts. He projected dignity, on screen and off. None of his insecurities — his finances, his family, his romantic life, his political and professional responsibilities — could diminish that magnetism.[83]

He also continued to team with Belafonte on political endeavors, from the local to the international. In February 1966 they entertained an East Harlem elementary school during Negro History Week. The next month they bailed out John Lewis, James Forman, and three other SNCC members who had been arrested for demonstrating against apartheid at the South African Consulate on Madison Avenue. Poitier fronted the cash and grimly answered questions. "South Africa is absolutely hell," he said, recalling the indignities while filming *Cry, the Beloved Country*.[84]

For all Poitier's political engagement, however, his professional isolation seemed more glaring than ever. In July the NAACP announced the establishment of a full-time Hollywood bureau. Their periodic visits had resulted in "less than token" progress. True, admitted NAACP labor secretary Herbert Hill, "grotesque caricatures" had disappeared, but movie and television screens still lacked "the full diversity of the Negro social experience." Even the Marine Corps base in *Gomer Pyle* and the southern town in *The Andy Griffith Show* lacked black characters. Only Bill Cosby starred on television, only Sidney Poitier in the movies.[85]

So Poitier had to keep weighing the political ramifications of every job offer. He considered a film of Irving Wallace's bestseller *The Man*, about a black congressman who assumes an unexpired term as President of the United States, but he wanted "changes in the characterization" to match his scrupulous hero image. He rejected Otto Preminger's *Hurry Sundown* for its inferior script.[86]

In June 1966, Poitier once again contemplated *Othello*, this time for a two-hour NBC special, with David Susskind as producer and George C. Scott as Iago. Poitier had entertained offers to play the tragic Moor since the late 1950s, on the widespread assumption that *Othello* was the pinnacle of any black actor's career. But after twelve weeks of creative hashing with Susskind, he backed out. Despite popular pressure, he could not embrace the role. He had built an image on characters of sound judgment and moral rectitude. No matter the interpretation, Iago tricks Othello into murdering his wife. Poitier could not, as he later told James Earl Jones, "give audiences a black man who is a dupe."[87]

One could argue whether Poitier's persona fulfilled integrationist ideals or betrayed black identity, but one could not dispute his popularity. Poitier placed seventh on a list of top box-office attractions for 1966. His world had changed. "I don't suffer from economic insecurity or a lack of self-importance any more," he said. "But along the way I have acquired other fears and uncertainties." The emergence of Black Power foreshadowed his icon's eventual demise. The media circus surrounding his professional and personal missteps stung him. He retreated from the public eye, granting fewer interviews. He could not satisfy everyone. No one man could.[88]

CHAPTER 13

USEFUL NEGROES

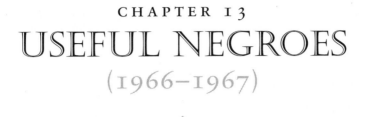

(1966–1967)

On a Caribbean sailing trip in 1967, Poitier's relationship with Diahann Carroll arrived at its ignominious end. After their ugly spat the previous year, they had begun dating other people. Even so, they stayed close. When Poitier invited her to sail, Carroll accepted, hoping to sort out their feelings in quiet conversations. But two friends of Poitier joined them. Tension infected the vacation: Carroll burned at these unexpected companions, and Poitier glared when she made small talk. After dinner onshore, they fought in earnest. When he got into their bed that night, she got out. "I suppose sex had become the final battleground between us," Carroll mused.[1]

The next morning, Poitier and Carroll boarded a dinghy to take them to the yacht. Poitier could not start the outboard motor. Some locals offered to help, teasing, "You're an *actor*, Sidney. You don't know anything about boats." They laughed, meaning no offense. Carroll chuckled too. Finally the motor started. Poitier boiled, glowered, stabbed at the air with his finger. He hissed at Carroll, "Don't you ever — ever, *ever*, as long as you live — laugh at me again."

For Carroll, it was over. "Sitting there in the dinghy," she looked back, "watching Sidney nurse his imagined humiliation, the veil dropped from my eyes and I saw him for the first time. I saw the incompleteness. I saw the insecurity. I saw the lack of humility and the need to be regarded as some sort of god." He *had* been a type of god. "Both in his life and his work he was able to touch people and make them care about him in a way I never thought I could." For years, her self-esteem had depended upon his affection. But he no longer filled her emotional voids. When together, they only tormented each other. In Nassau, Sidney Poitier and Diahann Carroll shook hands and bid farewell after nine years of passion, love, and anguish.[2]

Poitier returned to New York City. He now lived in a huge apartment atop a twenty-nine-floor building on the Upper East Side, a glass-encased urban palace with views of Central Park and the Hudson River. On a clear day he could see the Statue of Liberty. His housekeeper kept his thick, ivory, wall-to-wall carpet spotless. A plush red easy chair sat near a dark bar of Spanish inspiration. He dined by candlelight, on bone china, with full table settings of crystal and silver. The epitome of elegance, he was alone in the penthouse.[3]

❖

Over the years, some critics had suggested the limitations of Poitier's image. But not until 1967 did these grievances trigger debates over his iconography. In February, *Los Angeles Times* critic Bert Prelutsky fired the opening salvo. He called Poitier a "Negro in white face," a symbol with no relevance for Black America. "We have rid the screens of one stereotype only to replace it with another," he wrote. "Exit Stepin Fetchit, enter Sidney Poitier." He lamented the dearth of complex black characters. "It is Hollywood's hypocrisy that it can only envision a Fetchit or a Poitier, not a combination of the two — or a Negro who's both charming and evil, witty and corrupt, intelligent and criminal." According to Prelutsky, Poitier fulfilled the patronizing vision of white liberals unable to consider genuine black humanity.[4]

A fusillade of letters sallied back. One man wrote that Prelutsky "is in no ethnic position to pass judgment on what kind of hero Negroes should have." Another faulted him for characterizing blacks as incapable of pure integrity. But a black woman from Los Angeles cheered Prelutsky; she had wearied of Hollywood's "Lily White Negro, Poitier, who has (in the movies) no mother, no father, no sister, brothers or natural origin." His "clean cut Eunuch in the white world," she continued, "is not symbolic of us and we do not identify with him."[5]

Poitier stayed aloof from the debate. Instead, in early 1967, he supported the black majority of the Bahamas. By the mid-1960s, black opposition had weakened the white-controlled United Bahamian Party (UBP). Lynden Pindling, leader of the Progressive Liberal Party (PLP), adopted the techniques of moral suasion and political symbol that had spurred black revolution worldwide. Pindling and his populist associate Milo Butler sometimes visited Poitier's Manhattan penthouse for financial support.[6]

When the UBP called a general election for 10 January, Poitier campaigned for the PLP. Just as his celebrity lent appeal to the black struggle in America, it bolstered the possibility of black rule in the Bahamas. The PLP, like the American civil rights movement, employed political symbols of Christian virtue. The UBP had unwittingly chosen an election date with biblical significance — on "the tenth day of the first month," the Pharaoh had ordered the Israelites released from bondage. The PLP exploited that coincidence with three campaign songs: the theme from *Exodus*, the civil rights anthem "We Shall Overcome," and "Amen," Poitier's bouncy hymn from *Lilies of the Field*.[7]

Days before the election, the PLP fretted that its shipment of walkie-talkies had not arrived. Without communication among campaign coordinators, they could not move voters from outlying districts to the polls. Poitier entreated a resourceful friend. In New York, Harry Belafonte called a retailer at home on Saturday night, charmed him into opening his store on Sunday morning, bought six walkie-talkies, and wheedled the gadgets onto a commercial flight to Nassau. Poitier waited at the other end. The walkie-talkies arrived in time, and the PLP transportation plan succeeded.[8]

Despite lacking the political networks of the UBP, the PLP won an equal number of representatives in the House of Assembly. After two independent legislators broke the stalemate, the PLP controlled the Bahamian government. Pindling soon appointed a cabinet of progressive black leaders. One month later, 5,000 spectators cheered the new legislature. Poitier, Belafonte, Bill Cosby, and Miriam Makeba attended the celebratory reception at the Government House.[9]

In the United States, too, Poitier upheld political and professional commitments. In late January, he and Belafonte sponsored a benefit for SNCC at Small's Paradise in Harlem. In April, he attended the Academy Awards, presenting the Best Supporting Actress award to Sandy Dennis for *Who's Afraid of Virginia Woolf?* That same month, he reappeared on television for another all-black special produced by Belafonte, *A Time for Laughter: A Look at Negro Humor in America*.[10]

Humor had always been central to the African American experience — a subversion of the white power structure, a system of meaning for the black community. Historically, however, black comedy had poked into popular culture only through the haze of stereotypes. Stepin Fetchit's trickster hero, for instance, could fool whites only while fulfilling expectations of black idiocy. But the new generation of black comedians — Dick Gregory, Godfrey Cambridge, and Nipsey Russell — used humor to challenge racism. Cambridge used to sprint onstage and say, "I hope you noticed how I rushed up here. We do have to do that to change our image. No more shuffle after the revolution." The past decade's transformations allowed these comics to ridicule racial neuroses, killing Sambo with laughter.[11]

A Time for Laughter, an hour-long revue for *ABC Stage 67*, showcased the rich tradition of black humor. The show featured new stars Gregory and Cambridge, old vaudevillians Moms Mabley and Pigmeat Markham, up-and-comers Redd Foxx and Richard Pryor, and icons Belafonte and Poitier. "For the most part, America has seen only a caricature of our humor," narrated Poitier. The skits presented the genuine article, roasting such elements of the black experience as white exploitation of the minstrel show, the oily posturing of the poolroom hustler, and the pretensions of the black bourgeoisie.[12]

Although the show pulled respectable ratings, critics split over its value. The *New York Times* found the production haphazard and tasteless, even calling it "a minstrel show in the dress of the 1960s." The *Pittsburgh Courier*, however, suggested that whites missed the point: *A Time for Laughter* was hilarious, but "some of the humor went over the head of most whites. It was strictly 'dark' humor which only non-whites could understand."[13]

The gulf in perceptions indicated a larger rift: a nation "moving toward two societies, one black, one white, separate and unequal." That chilling conclusion came from the National Advisory Commission on Civil Disorders (the so-called Kerner Commission) after the race riots of 1967. That summer, almost 150 disturbances broke out, from Boston to Buffalo, New Haven to South Bend, Rochester to Toledo. In Newark, the arrest of a black cab driver triggered a bloody race war. Blacks looted stores and burned tenements, while the police and National Guard shot to kill. In Detroit, a mass arrest at a nightclub kindled six days of anarchy; nearly 4,000 fires destroyed 1,300 buildings.[14]

The summer's toll included at least 90 deaths, over 4,000 injuries, and almost 17,000 arrests. The destruction spawned from the conditions of the ghetto: police harassment, unemployment, tenement housing, and run-down educational and recreational facilities. "White society is deeply implicated in the ghetto," argued the Kerner Commission. "White institutions created it, white institutions maintain it, and white society condones it." So poor urban blacks lashed out.[15]

The entertainment world fretted over the riots; television stations had to assess their complicity in the carnage. "I think a lot of the riots have been stirred up by the great amount of time given on the news media to rioting and looting," opined Texas senator Ralph Yarborough, echoing a common complaint. Because of television's visual immediacy, footage of black rioters fomented anger on both sides of the racial divide. Images of black nonviolence had once awakened the nation's moral conscience. Now, images of black violence tore at the social fabric.[16]

The riots compounded a popular sense that America was unraveling. That summer, President Johnson sent 45,000 more troops to Vietnam, stoking a groundswell of disillusionment among moderates. Meanwhile, countercultural hippies and New Left radicals mocked the foundations of middle-class American life. Within black politics, young and charismatic advocates of Black Power such as Stokely Carmichael and H. Rap Brown captured the media's fancy. Both virile and violent, they delivered revolutionary rants that made great theater. Brown's outlandish pronouncements ("Violence is as American as cherry pie") attracted more interest than the older generation's staid appeals to man's better nature.[17]

These radicals challenged the conventional wisdom of the civil rights movement. The Black Power philosophy advocated that blacks reclaim their identity from white control. Political parties offered no solutions. Integration and nonviolence did not address issues of social justice and cultural integrity. Nor could token leaders substitute for black community-based control. Even popular culture heroes preserved the status quo, as Eldridge Cleaver wrote in *Soul on Ice*: "While inflating the images of Uncle Toms and celebrities from the apolitical world of sport and play, the mass media were able to channel and control the aspirations and goals of the black masses. The effect was to take the 'problem' out of a political and economic and philosophical context and place it on the misty level of 'goodwill,' 'charitable and harmonious race relations,' and 'good sportsmanlike conduct.'" Without mentioning Sidney Poitier, he condemned the effects of the actor's stardom.[18]

The black establishment lamented the reversal in the politics of image. "Who can say how many millions of white people have frozen up their public school policies, hardened their resistance to open housing, and planted still more booby traps to equal employment after they saw and heard Negroes cursing and threatening and acting anti-socially on TV screens?" wrote Roy Wilkins, executive director of the NAACP. He called upon those "far down on the totem pole" to project "a better image of Negroes."[19]

For white Americans, "black protest" now meant alienated, brick-throwing mobs. The Kerner Commission described the typical rioter as a young black male, a high school dropout, a lifelong resident of an inner city, underemployed or working a menial job, aggressively race-conscious, and distrustful of middle-class blacks, all whites, and the political system. That black image, however indicative of enduring racial barriers, shook faith in the possibility of colorblind democracy.[20]

Into this crisis stepped Sidney Poitier, his icon stripped clean of the ghetto's cultural baggage. The riots betrayed hope for equal citizenship and racial harmony; the Poitier hero still insisted upon that dream. More than ever, he played mature, cultured, nonviolent, and middle-class characters. He deemphasized race and sacrificed for whites. And he sparked a curious contradiction: as more people grew disenchanted with his icon, Poitier became America's favorite movie star.

❖

"Too soft, too sweet, too sentimental, and most of all too special" — these were the reasons, according to Poitier, that most Hollywood executives had passed on *To Sir, with Love*. E. R. Braithwaite's 1959 memoir about teaching in London's East End won the Anisfeld-Wolf Award for racial understanding and was published in seven languages. Though it interested producers, none made the movie. They worried that the English setting would not appeal to American audiences. Some, perhaps, also fretted about the book's romance between Braithwaite and a white teacher.[21]

After Columbia Pictures bought the rights, Martin Baum launched the project. The agent interested his client James Clavell, a screenwriter, director, producer, and author of two popular novels. Then Poitier signed on. Braithwaite's self-made success story resembled Poitier's own journey. Poitier admired his values of integrity and fellowship. In a time of turbulence, he thought that the warm story of a black teacher and his interracial classroom might make a worthwhile statement.[22]

Baum structured a contract for Poitier that paid no money up front and 10 percent of the gross. Clavell signed a similar deal for a percentage of the net. These "share-the-risk" contracts appeased Columbia, which assigned a measly $750,000 budget. Still, studio executives remained dubious of its commercial potential. One complained that the script lacked something, which he tried to denote by sweeping his hand in an arc. Clavell asked what he meant. "You know," said the executive, explaining with another inarticulate sweeping gesture. After an awkward pause, Clavell feigned a whiff of understanding. "I'll just put in a little more . . . ," he said, adding a silent arc of his own.[23]

That hurdle cleared, filming commenced in London in August 1966, with interiors at Pinewood Studios and location shots in the East End. Clavell cast the students from assorted British drama schools and repertory companies. Unlike young Hollywood actors, the youths arrived professionally trained and prepared. Yet they learned a great deal from Poitier. "When you act a scene with Sidney Poitier," said Judy Geeson, "he listens intently to every word you say. You can feel your words hit him. He makes the scene utterly real."[24]

Poitier enjoyed his young castmates, but the cosmopolitan star sniffed at London's offerings. "It doesn't swing like Las Vegas or Miami Beach or even New York," he told journalist Sally Marks, who provided a telling anecdote. She arrived on the set early one morning, only for Poitier to delay their appointment with affectionate promises of "a big, fat interview." Finally, at 2:15 P.M., they sat in a limousine. She asked whether he minded if she smoked. After gesturing to find matches, he seized her cigarettes and tore them to shreds. "See how much poison you inhale?" he lectured. "So don't sit here and interview me and smoke a cigarette — that's an AFFRONT to me!" But then he granted a long, friendly interview. At the end he reassured, "Don't worry, Kiddo, you ask the right kind of questions." The story captured Poitier's distinctive combination of ego, moralism, grace, and good nature.[25]

In the film, Poitier plays Mark Thackeray, a teacher sent to an experimental high school in the East End. An engineer by training, he flounders. His students slam doors, toss books, drop water bombs, play with lewd squeeze toys, saw a leg off his desk, and read at grade-school levels. Thackeray retains his composure until he finds a feminine napkin on a heating grate. Then he explodes. He evicts the boys and lectures the girls: "I am sick of your foul language, your crude behavior, and your sluttish manner! There are certain things a decent woman keeps private, and only a filthy slut would have done this!" He storms out.

The outburst prompts an epiphany. Thackeray reenters the classroom, scraps his books, and announces his new curriculum. Now he demands courtesy. They will call the girls "Miss," the boys by their surnames, and him "Sir" or "Mr. Thackeray" (not the mildly disrespectful "Guv'nor"). He also insists upon cleanliness. Finally, they will spend class time discussing "life, survival, love, death, sex, marriage, rebellion . . . anything you want."

Immediately, incredibly, the plan works. Pamela Dare (Geeson) demonstrates the proper way to enter a classroom. They discuss life skills, from marriage to cooking. They take a field trip to the Victoria and Albert Museum, cinematically portrayed by a musical photo montage. Denham (Christian Roberts), at first a skeptic of the new agenda, in time embraces

Thackeray's lessons. The plan works almost too well: Pamela develops a crush, which the teacher deftly evades. The path from surly to fresh-faced encounters few roadblocks.

Thackeray's race shapes this metamorphosis. Instead of overt references to racial prejudice, the jaded teacher Theo Weston (Geoffrey Bayldon) baits Thackeray with coded barbs, calling him a "black sheep" and suggesting that he use "voodoo." Denham also tries agitating Thackeray by inquiring about bare-breasted African women. But Thackeray stays cool, ignoring innuendoes and preaching tolerance. His strategy works. When he cuts his hand and a student blurts, "Blimey, red blood!" Pamela shames the offender into regret. Later, when the mother of a mixed-race student dies, the class resists delivering a wreath because they fear neighborhood gossip. Thackeray grimaces through this bigotry. After the class attends the funeral, however, he radiates pride.

By graduation, Thackeray has achieved complete success. Students inform him of their jobs, and colleagues praise his methods. He dances with Pamela (performing some sort of awkward chicken dance, in a presumably involuntary reinforcement of his distance from black stereotypes). The students present a gift and card. Thackeray is composing himself in his classroom when two cads enter. "Evening, Guv," says one. "I'm in your bleedin' class next term." Thackeray had planned on accepting an engineering job offer. But he rips it up, silently resolving to transform more hoodlums into industrious young adults.

Twelve years earlier in *Blackboard Jungle*, Poitier had embodied the threat of urban rebellion. Now *he* tamed the disaffected youth of the inner city. "The Sidney I saw in *Blackboard Jungle* was a lithe, restless, smart but unmotivated kid with contempt for authority," recalled the writer Nelson George. "This was someone I knew from the projects, someone I could be in a rebellious moment, precisely the kind of kid my mother had taken me to *To Sir, With Love* . . . to prevent me from becoming."[26]

Thackeray is dignity incarnate, a buttoned-down, bottled-up symbol of middle-class values. Like Poitier, Thackeray rose from poverty. When he recounts old jobs as a fry cook and janitor, one student objects: "But you talk posh and all!" He explains how he shed his native patois through personal training. "If you're prepared to work hard," he preaches, "you can do anything. You can get any job you want."

In line with this ethic, Thackeray is preoccupied with self-restraint. He eats oranges for lunch because "I'm a weak man. When I eat, do I love to eat!" He avoids wine, pastrami sandwiches, and cheesecake because they arouse his epicurean passions. Furthermore, he ignores the cracks of students and skeptics. Even during his sole classroom outburst (which he immediately regrets) his rage is not frenzied but repressed, quivering, icy.

Thackeray also espouses nonviolence, a theme unaddressed in the book. After a student threatens a cruel gym teacher, Thackeray lectures the class on peaceful resolutions. When Denham challenges him to a boxing match, Thackeray refrains from annihilating him. "Hitting you wouldn't have solved very much, would it?" asks Thackeray. Thackeray instead advocates a soft, cultural uprising. He cites the Beatles: "The fashions they set in hairstyles and dress are worldwide now. Every new fashion is a form of rebellion."

To Sir, with Love thus offered a recipe for the generation gap: mix old-fashioned civility with liberal uplift, and add a splash of Mod style. In Braithwaite's book, students dance the fox trot and waltz. In Clavell's movie, they spend lunch breaks grooving to rock n' roll. They wear smart jackets and mini-skirts, and they style their hair in the shaggy but neat Mod fashion. The movie even features the rock band The Mindbenders and the bubbly pop star Lulu. Her title track is heard at the beginning, middle, and end of the film.[27]

The picture may have occupied the cutting edge in youth style, but it was decidedly conservative in its portrait of interracial love. In Braithwaite's book, the teacher enjoys a mature relationship with a white colleague. In the script's first draft, Clavell maintained the relationship, even injecting some quips about sexual taboos. Thackeray flirts: "Didn't you know that all able-bodied, healthy, resident Negroes are celibate by inclination — or masters of the art of sublimation? We abhor the opposite sex!" In the second draft, Clavell purged that dialogue, but he preserved the mutual attraction, installing a conversation planning a future relationship.[28]

In the final draft and film, Thackeray squelches their romance. The teacher Gillian (Suzy Kendall) still welcomes a liaison. She moons at Thackeray, and she volunteers to help chaperone the museum field trip. After warning him about Pamela's crush, she adds, "Not that I blame her." Yet Thackeray remains a passionless monument to self-control. An older teacher urges him to pursue Gillian; "Oh, I thought you'd be wiser," he replies. Just as he harnesses gastronomic urges, he insists on restraint in all matters sexual.[29]

Like *A Patch of Blue*, then, *To Sir, with Love* opens doors to intimacy with white women, then shuts them through Poitier's Victorian inhibition. Unlike *A Patch of Blue*, however, there is no reason for Poitier's sexual reticence except to reinforce racial taboos. Of course, Thackeray must evade Pamela's flirtations out of professional responsibility — like the blind Selina, Pamela is young and fragile. But Gillian is mature, intelligent, beautiful, aware of the obstacles facing interracial couples, and beguiled by her handsome colleague. The glimmers of romance titillated, but never trampled upon racial sensibilities. Another Poitier film deflected white anxieties off an unimpeachable moral exemplar.[30]

To Sir, with Love arrived in theaters haphazardly. Some magazines published reviews in April 1967, but Columbia held no trade press screenings until just before its June release — "a manifestation of fear on the part of a distributor who either has a dud on his hands, or doesn't know what to do with a good film," according to *Variety*. Most likely, the strategy evinced some confusion over how to advertise a Britain-based picture featuring only one marquee name.[31]

Columbia followed a two-pronged marketing strategy. First, it targeted teenagers. Promotional posters included such phrases as "The story of the new-beat bold-tempo mods and minis and the teacher who had to make them cool it — and call him 'Sir'!" Second, Columbia emphasized the film's educational value and prestige. The initial screening at the American Film Festival, a convention put on by educators, won raves. That July, the picture earned a minute of solid applause at the Moscow Film Festival.[32]

The approach soon seemed unambitious. *To Sir, with Love*, despite its cotton-candy sweetness, possessed an undeniable charm. The teenagers had a quaint charisma, and Clavell's script flowed quickly. Poitier held it all together. "The actor towers over the film," wrote one critic. Poitier balances classroom homilies with self-deprecation, projects emotions with subtle gestures, and reinforces his lessons with his noble bearing. Most reviewers pooh-poohed the abrupt classroom transformation — "but Poitier, electric personality that he is, almost makes us believe that such miracles are possible."[33]

The picture's popularity derived in part from its racial understatement. "Racial differences do not enter into it, thank goodness," sighed one critic. Because there is neither interracial romance nor overt racism, the picture rarely confronts prejudice. The result, according to Bosley Crowther, is "a cozy, good-humored and unbelievable little tale of a teacher getting acquainted with his pupils, implying but never stating that it is nice for the races to live congenially together."[34]

Black publications cheered the message, and they lauded Poitier's variation on Mr. Chips ("Mr. Chocolate Chips," according to one). Mel Tapley of the *New York Amsterdam News* entreated the NAACP to establish a "Communications and Understanding" award honoring *To Sir, with Love*. Yet black critics also lamented Poitier's desexualization. "Had Thackeray been white," speculated *Ebony*, "the Thackeray-Gillian relationship would have been a love affair." Tapley, in the gentlest of admonitions, suggested a sequel where the friendship blossoms into romance.[35]

Some veteran critics hit harder. Andrew Sarris mocked the facile conversion of the class, contending that the students "come on less like stragglers in a slum school than like a well-drilled troupe from a British high school for the performing arts." Stephen Farber called *To Sir, with Love* "a foolish, offensively simple-minded movie." He argued that Poitier's superficial platitudes slapped a thin coat of gentility over the serious problems of economic class. The teenagers await menial jobs with sparkling cheer, and all it takes is some museum visits and "milky aphorisms."[36]

The *New Yorker* accused Columbia of exploiting race. "If the hero of this Pollyanna story were white, his pieties would have to be whistled off the screen and his pupils blamed for cringing." No white actor could mouth such moralistic clichés. But Poitier aroused liberal affection, layering racial sympathy underneath the classroom drama. His skin color "draws on resources of seriousness which the film does nothing to earn."[37]

Poitier's image shaped reactions to the film, and some critics drew their line in the sand. Farber called him "the suburban audience's dream of a well-adjusted Negro" with "no desires, no passions, no weaknesses." *To Sir, with Love* paraded "another of his sweet, saintly, sexless performances." Added Pauline Kael: "Poitier has been playing the ideal boy-next-door-who-happens-to-be-black for so long that he's always the same; he acts about as well in bad roles as in good ones. This self-inflicted stereotype of goodness is destroying a beautiful, graceful, and potentially brilliant actor. What can he do? He can't pass as a white man in order to play rats or cowards or sons of bitches, and if he plays Negro rats or cowards or sons of bitches he'll be attacked for doing Negroes harm. Yet if he goes on smiling much longer, the audience may begin laughing."[38]

Kael suggested that Poitier diversify his image, even at the risk of alienating his fan base. But that summer came another film in the Poitier mold, sparking more debate over the black icon: the murder mystery *In the Heat of the Night*.

❖

John Ball's novel *In the Heat of the Night* was a conventional crime caper with a timely twist: a racist white sheriff and a proud black detective team to solve a murder. In 1965, producer Walter Mirisch bought the rights and signed Poitier to a $200,000 contract. The *New York Times* celebrated the "first Negro detective hero," an advance on the comic foils of most police movies. But his services came with a qualification. The picture was set in Mississippi, and Poitier was unwilling to stomach segregation. "I am not going to work in a city where I can't move about, where I can't eat if I want to," he proclaimed.[39]

Director Norman Jewison chose the small town of Sparta in southern Illinois. Only some brief location shots would be done in Tennessee. One month before filming began in September 1966, while Poitier was vacationing in the Virgin Islands, Jewison telephoned the actor to request his approval for the locales.[40]

Over sixty cast and crew members swooped into Sparta. "It's like Randolph County Fair week, the Rotary Club's Halloween Mardi Gras and the annual Sparta-Chester football game rolled into one," marveled the local newspaper. The citizenry tasted both the tedium and excitement of filmmaking. Extras milled about for hours, bundled in hats and coats, removing their warm garb only before the cameras. "It beats cleaning house," explained one woman, citing the $1.50 daily salary, the free lunch, and the chance to rub elbows with the stars. Jewison delighted the locals by changing the town's name to Sparta in the film. Poitier's trademark grace made him a fan favorite on the set.[41]

From his hotel suite in nearby Belleville, Poitier performed publicity interviews, expounding on such topics as his withdrawal from *Othello* ("I was doing it for all the wrong reasons"), his taste in music ("from popular rhythm to the blues to rock and roll to Bach"), and his brown rice diet ("You wouldn't put cheap oil in a Cadillac"). He also participated in long arguments over the script. Mirisch, Jewison, co-star Rod Steiger, and screenwriter Stirling Siliphant all endorsed black equality, but they debated over effective presentations of southern race relations.[42]

The film's most famous scene occurs when a Southern aristocrat slaps Poitier's detective Virgil Tibbs, and Tibbs slaps back. In *No Way Out*, Poitier's doctor endures spit in his face without retaliation. Seventeen years later, his detective's reaction connotes a measure of progress, an insistence on black dignity. Poitier remembered reading a first draft where Tibbs absorbs the slap and turns the other cheek. He claimed to have insisted upon the revision.[43]

In fact, Tibbs's response is in the revised original script, a draft completed before filming began. After getting slapped, Tibbs returns fire, "slapping him back as hard—or possibly harder, the blow virtually rattling Endicott's head." For the film, they even underplayed the reaction: although Tibbs strikes the old man, the jolt is hardly "rattling."[44]

Poitier's account was less willful misrepresentation than time-addled defensiveness. He deserved pride in his accomplishments, of course, and the slap was a benchmark in black dignity. But the actual changes did not include such dramatic additions. Siliphant's adaptation mostly sharpened the personal conflict between Tibbs and the white sheriff, Bill Gillespie. In later drafts, Siliphant cut segments that displayed a general southern bigotry, such as one where a hotel lobby clerk instructs Tibbs to wait outside. He also changed the characters' origins, inflating their symbolism. In the first draft, Tibbs came from Arizona and Gillespie had newly arrived from Texas. In the film, Tibbs hails from Philadelphia and Gillespie is a Mississippi native. In sum, Siliphant boiled racial conflict down to the relationship between the two protagonists.[45]

Rod Steiger played Gillespie. Poitier had employed the Method for years, but working with Steiger, he realized, "I had been a-c-t-i-n-g! Pretending, indicating, giving the *appearance* of experiencing certain emotions, but never, ever, really getting down to where real life and fine art mirror each other." Free of the expectations heaped upon Poitier, and too much a quirky loner to embrace stardom, Steiger had managed to win Hollywood success without a consistent image. From *On the Waterfront* to *The Pawnbroker* to *Doctor Zhivago*, he submitted memorable performances shaped by his complete immersion in the role.[46]

While Poitier ate brown rice, Steiger ballooned to 243 pounds, keeping his belly hanging over his belt. Off the set — at dinner, at the movies, even shooting the breeze with Poitier — Steiger never broke character, measuring his voice in a southern cadence, patrolling the premises in an arrogant waddle, revealing insecurities underneath a cocksure veneer. His character constantly chewed gum, so Steiger constantly chewed gum. Columbia claimed that he finished 263 packages during filming.[47]

An improvised exchange between Steiger and Poitier is the picture's finest moment. Tibbs sits in Gillespie's ramshackle apartment, and the sheriff exposes his frailties. "I got no wife, I got no kids, I got a town that don't want me," he says, gulping a shot of bourbon. "I got an air conditioner that I got to oil myself, I got a desk with a busted leg, and on top of that I got . . . this place. Don't you think that would drive a man to take a few drinks?" He asks Tibbs, "Don't you get just a little lonely?" Tibbs replies, "No lonelier than you, man." The tender moment snaps. "Oh now, don't get smart, black boy!" barks Gillespie. "I don't need it. No pity, thank you." Their relationship stays ambiguous, their common humanity blocked by race.[48]

When the production moved to Dyersburg, Tennessee, they filmed

Poitier's favorite scene, as Gillespie and Tibbs drive past cotton fields manned by poor blacks. "None of that for you, eh Virgil?" says Gillespie. Tibbs says nothing. The camera follows his face as he watches the fields, silently responding to Gillespie's crack, suggesting his complex responsibilities as an educated, middle-class black man.[49]

But filming in Tennessee was a trial. One hotel refused to admit Poitier, so the entire production switched quarters. The populace objected to the race-related plot. Two state policemen patrolled the hotel during the day, but at night local thugs harassed them by honking car horns, lighting firecrackers, and barging through the hallways. According to Jewison, Poitier kept a gun under his pillow. The actor left the hotel only to work, and the production departed a day and a half early. They completed *In the Heat of the Night* in early December 1966, after three weeks at Producers Studio in Hollywood.[50]

Quincy Jones wrote and compiled the score, mixing soulful blues with twangy country. Ray Charles wails the title track, crying out the frustrations of black life, suiting Jewison's direction and Haskell Wexler's cinematography. In the film, Sparta steams with suffocating tension. Neon signs glow through haze. Police cars roll down streets in eerie silence. Shadows dominate, hiding and imprisoning characters. Light pokes through in isolated bands. The sounds and images are striking metaphors for the constraints of southern life.[51]

The murder mystery itself is almost irrelevant. Late one night, a police officer finds industrialist Philip Colbert dead on Main Street. Colbert had planned to build a factory that would boost Sparta's economy. A range of suspects are introduced and discarded. But the case never develops an engaging narrative, and the resolution seems contrived.

In the Heat of the Night succeeds, however, thanks to charged performances by Steiger and Poitier. Gillespie must solve the murder to save the factory. He suspects Virgil Tibbs, found alone in a train station. Arrested only because he is a black loner with money in his wallet, he offers Gillespie only staccato responses. "A colored can't earn that kind of money, boy," protests Gillespie. "That's more than I make in a month! Now where did you earn it?" Seethes Tibbs, "I'm a police officer." In fact, he is Philadelphia's top homicide expert, en route home after visiting his mother.

Racial tension drives the film. Tibbs's chief in Philadelphia orders him to help Gillespie's investigation. By admitting that he lacks expertise in murder cases, Gillespie sacrifices the southern racial code; he calls the black man "Officer" with only a dash of sarcasm. Tibbs further corrodes racial mores by imperiously commanding autopsy supplies, smugly correcting the diagnosed time of death, and confidently informing Mrs. Colbert (Lee Grant) of her husband's death. When he clears another suspect, Gillespie explodes. "Well you're pretty sure of yourself, ain't you Virgil?" he rants. "Virgil, that's a funny name for a nigger boy that comes from Philadelphia. What do they call you up there?" The detective bellows back, "They call me Mister Tibbs!"

Only Mrs. Colbert preserves their uneasy partnership. Impressed by Tibbs, she threatens to cancel the factory if he leaves the case. Gillespie must again beseech Tibbs for help. Tibbs suspects Eric Endicott, the local aristocrat. At Endicott's plantation, two patterns of race relations collide. Outside the mansion stands a lawn ornament of a grinning, big-lipped black jockey. When Tibbs tramples convention by questioning the paternalistic squire, Endicott muses about orchids: "Like the Nigra, they need care, and feeding, and cultivating." When Tibbs presses on, Endicott slaps him, and Tibbs slaps back.

Gillespie only gapes. As Endicott notes, another sheriff might have shot the black detective. But Gillespie stands pat, and then he saves Tibbs from a gang of rednecks. The two men establish a precarious bond. When Tibbs insists on arresting Endicott without sufficient evidence, Gillespie marvels, "You're just like the rest of us, ain't ya?" Tibbs realizes his own prejudices, and he clears another of Gillespie's suspects through logical analysis and keen psychology. He then finds clues in the pregnancy of Sparta's Lolita, a lusty exhibitionist named Dolores Purdy (Quentin Dean). Tibbs arrests the killer at the home of a local black abortionist.

They solve a murder, but not an immoral social structure. *In the Heat of the Night* never pretends to cure racism. In his shabby apartment, for instance, Gillespie bristles at Tibbs's empathy. Hope survives, however, in the final scene. Gillespie takes Tibbs to the train station, even carrying the black man's bag. As Tibbs boards, Gillespie says: "Virgil? You take care, y'hear?" They exchange knowing smiles.

When the picture opened in early August 1967, critics hailed "a modern classic of its genre," "a taut, tingling, cinematic gem," "a film that has the look and sound of actuality and the pounding pulse of truth." Jewison's direction, Wexler's cinematography, and Siliphant's script earned deserved praise. Poitier was excellent, and Steiger superlative. Together, contended *Time*, they "break brilliantly with black-white stereotype." Their tense alliance avoided sentimentality. "They do not suddenly become brothers under the skin, put down their old prejudices, or vow to be better men," wrote Richard Schickel, with admiration.[52]

In the Heat of the Night discards romantic notions of the Old South. Sparta is all desolate parking lots, garish neon signs, and blistering cotton fields. The white natives are sweaty, slovenly, and slurred-of-speech. "My God," says Mrs. Colbert. "What kind of people are you? What kind of place is this?" Northern witnesses of news footage of Birmingham and Selma had already been asking that question.[53]

By contrast, Tibbs breathes dignity. The black man represents law, order, and civility. The white supremacist publication *The Thunderbolt* moaned that the film was designed "to make the viewer ashamed of being white." It certainly privileges Poitier's cultured blackness over the rednecks' cartoonish buffoonery. It also debases southern white women, embodied by the whorish Dolores Purdy. Like *The Defiant Ones*, the drama revolves around the two men. It does not address the stickier economic problems evidenced by the urban riots. *In the Heat of the Night* thus displaces liberal anxiety about a seemingly intractable racial divide.[54]

Tibbs does show periodic disdain for his fellow man. He is sometimes vain, sometimes contemptuous. He relishes ruffling the feathers of local officials. He claims that Mr. Colbert was stabbed at an angle of exactly seventeen degrees. He knows his weekly salary down to the cent, and he enjoys rubbing it in Gillespie's face. Some critics cheered that Poitier had a testy edge. As Roger Ebert exclaimed, "What a relief to see Sidney Poitier angry!"[55]

But Virgil Tibbs is more social symbol than human being. Gillespie dictates their relationship: Gillespie arrests Tibbs; Gillespie asks for help from Tibbs; Gillespie insults Tibbs; Gillespie rescues Tibbs; Gillespie opens up to, then antagonizes Tibbs; Gillespie tells Tibbs to "take care." In yet another film, the white man learns from the integrity of Sidney Poitier. And despite flashes of ego and emotion, Virgil Tibbs is another of Poitier's shrines to isolated black excellence. He has no wife and children, no black community, no sexual interests. He is an incomplete superhero.[56]

In the midst of the summer riots, that persistent pattern provoked some jeers. The *New Yorker* scoffed at the "primitive rah-rah story" with "a spurious air of concern about the afflictions of the real America at the moment." Stories of elegant black men enlightening whites seemed trivial compared to ghetto violence. Some doubted that a southern sheriff would ever carry a black man's bag; one called the ending "a cynical sell-out." Others lamented the too-perfect Tibbs; his encyclopedic knowledge and cultured air seemed exaggerations of previous Poitier characters. Andrew Sarris criticized the entire premise, faulting "the bland assumption that any Negro, however noble and privileged, could find rapport with a white man who was capable of addressing (and undressing) him as 'boy.' "[57]

But many blacks applauded the sophisticated supersleuth. In Detroit, just days after the rioting, one black critic wrote that "what was happening in the audience was as electric as anything happening on the screen." When Tibbs embarrassed the whites, the black audience burst into cathartic cheers. Another reviewer screened the picture on Broadway. When Tibbs slapped Endicott, "the repressed wrath of the Black Man for his American bondage finally was portrayed on screen." The predominantly black audience roared. The moment seemed "invested with atonement for the shufflin' indignities and foolish 'singin' darkies' of a dreadful past."[58]

James Baldwin disagreed. He appreciated elements of *In the Heat of the Night*: the virile energy of Virgil Tibbs, the brief scenes of Mississippi blacks. But the film fulfilled white fantasies. It showed no awareness of the black perspective. It asked audiences to identify with Steiger's racist, a "descendant of *Birth of a Nation*." The final scene was an interracial, homosocial version of the "obligatory, fade-out kiss," absolving whites of guilt. "The effect of such a film," Baldwin concluded, "is to increase and not lessen white confusion and complacency, and black rage and despair."[59]

❖

Poitier had become a lightning rod for racial opinions among blacks and whites, critics and audiences, conservatives and liberals and radicals. But it was only because the nation was in the throes of a Sidney Poitier phenomenon.

To Sir, with Love arrived first, playing limited engagements in early July. As the picture set house records in New York and Boston, the industry scuttlebutt was that Columbia had a sleeper hit. In early August the film appeared nationwide. It quickly climbed to third in the national box-office survey.[60]

In the Heat of the Night won more immediate success. In early August it established several New York City house records. By the end of the month it was America's most popular movie. Meanwhile, *To Sir, with Love* set house records in Dallas, Pittsburgh, Baltimore, Philadelphia, and Detroit.[61]

The best lay ahead. *Variety* proclaimed September "Sidney Poitier Month." *In the Heat of the Night* stayed atop the box-office charts until

To Sir, with Love supplanted it. In November, *In the Heat of the Night* opened at eighty more venues, and *To Sir, with Love* won a rare "encore" engagement in New York showcase theaters. Both movies had profitable runs throughout the South. In December, United Artists re-released *Pressure Point* and *Duel at Diablo* in five New York movie houses. The New York Film Critics named *In the Heat of the Night* the best picture of the year, and Protestant, Catholic, and Jewish organizations all commended the movie. By the end of the year, *To Sir, with Love* had grossed $7.2 million dollars, the most ever for a Poitier film.[62]

Poitier's popularity was not limited to the big screen. Television producers barraged him with offers, and networks featured his vehicles. *Lilies of the Field* was the highest-rated motion picture telecast of the 1966–67 season. *The Defiant Ones, Porgy and Bess, A Raisin in the Sun*, and *The Bedford Incident* all appeared on prime time in 1967. The indisputably execrable *The Long Ships* was on CBS twice: once in April, once in July. *The Slender Thread* and *Pressure Point* played in early 1968. Even the music world felt reverberations. Lulu's mawkish "To Sir with Love" topped the singles charts in October 1967. The soundtrack remained a bestseller through early 1968.[63]

Columbia commissioned a Gallup poll to investigate the startling success of *To Sir, with Love*. The survey determined that Poitier topped a list of actors — including Julie Andrews, Burt Lancaster, Steve McQueen, Paul Newman, and Elizabeth Taylor — whose name alone would draw customers to otherwise unknown movies. Poitier ranked especially high among women; the *New York Times* called him "Hollywood's first Negro matinee idol."[64]

Poitier entered virgin territory for black actors. In late June, he integrated the famous forecourt of Grauman's Chinese Theatre. A crowd cheered as he knelt onto the red carpet, placed his hands and feet in wet cement, signed his name, and threw in a dime (the only thing in his pocket). "Now make a mudpie," cracked Bill Cosby. The honors continued two weeks later, when he took office as the first vice-chairman of the American Film Institute.[65]

The barriers kept falling that November, when Poitier became Hollywood's first major black producer. He formed E&R Productions, named after his deceased parents Evelyn and Reginald, and inked a three-year, nonexclusive contract with Columbia Pictures. Poitier would produce original properties distributed by Columbia. The pact reflected not only his expanding clout, but also his concern for long-term relevance. As long as Columbia approved the property, Poitier and Columbia would split profits equally, and Poitier would assert significant creative control.[66]

Poitier also continued to perform the functions of the black celebrity: raising funds with Harry Belafonte at a Harlem elementary school, appearing with Cosby at the National Association of Radio Announcers Convention, narrating a performance at Harlem's Town Hall called "The Langston Hughes Scrapbook." Also that summer, Juanita Poitier hosted a black-tie fundraiser in Pleasantville for the Urban League, but Sidney did not attend.[67]

Martin Luther King won his continuing support. In August Poitier delivered the keynote speech at the annual convention for the SCLC. That fall, he emceed fundraising rallies for King's program to launch civil disobedience campaigns in inner cities. King was trying to adapt his nonviolent philosophy to the problems of unemployment, inadequate housing, and poor education. In one speech he lauded Poitier as "one of the great performing artists of the world," a man "bearing great gifts."[68]

Poitier was experiencing an astounding burst in popularity, and many sought to explain it. In a Sunday column entitled "The Significance of Sidney," Bosley Crowther argued that Poitier's films gained noble objectives, because they urged racial compassion. Pointing to *In the Heat of the Night*, Crowther wrote that "it is most appropriate and gratifying to see Mr. Poitier coming out at this moment of crisis in racial affairs in a film which impressively presents him as a splendid exponent of his race, maturely able to stand up to the abuse and patronage of racist whites."[69]

Variety called him "The Useful Negro." Noting the simultaneous rise of ghetto riots and Poitier's superstardom, the trade journal recounted the many pictures where he aided white co-stars and promoted social harmony. It surmised that "Poitier on the screen is the only Negro which myriads of Americans feel they know and understand." If that analysis spoke to Poitier's ability to humanize characters, it also suggested the dismal state of American race relations. Whites could identify only with an image of flawless morality, not an actual black man.[70]

Poitier's icon actually gained salience with the summer riots. His films were soothing balms on the nation's racial wounds. The end of *In the Heat of the Night* was "at least a comforting sight for eyes sore from watching the television tube recently out of Newark and Detroit." All his films presented a black figure of culture and grace, a symbol far removed from urban violence. Poitier occupied a safe middle ground, embodying the promise of racial brotherhood without engaging the ghetto's messy tangle of race and class. He was a comforting fictional alternative to the very graphic, very tangible threats on the television news.[71]

Poitier received mountains of fan mail, much of it asking for more than autographs or photographs. He described "letters from real people with real problems," reaching out to him "because there is not enough love for them to give — or to take." Man and image, intertwined, represented the compassion absent in Detroit, Newark, or even Vietnam.[72]

Poitier was also a sex symbol, albeit a unique one. His appeal, as the Gallup poll indicated, was highest among women. Of course, he was tall, trim, and handsome. But he never played romantic leads, and he publicly avowed his preference for black women. Sexually too, then, Poitier occupied a middle ground. He had undeniable virility, which let white women fantasize about taboo-defying interracial sex. But his mannered style counteracted the stereotype of the black buck, a threat heightened by the ghetto riots.

Most blacks supported Poitier, since their single star presented an upstanding image. *Variety* reported that although African Americans constituted only 10 to 15 percent of the population, they represented nearly 30 percent of movie customers. Blacks, it admitted, "have been more loyal to pix than the film industry has been to them." Still, the path to box-office riches lay in middle-class appeal, a strategy based on established stars and light plots. Hard-hitting examinations of social issues alienated audiences, jeopardized international distribution, and threatened television syndication. So the only race films remained Sidney Poitier films.[73]

After the summer riots, the Poitier film boom, and the inflation of his noble image, a tide of critics bellowed. Exasperation with Hollywood's racial strategies had historically come embedded within movie reviews. Now, entire articles disparaged the Poitier icon. Andrew Sarris spent his *In the Heat of the Night* review mourning how race constricted the actor's gifts. Poitier possessed no ambiguity, no complexity. His moral excellence made him bland and predictable. "It is not Poitier's fault that he is used to disinfect the recent riots of any lingering racism," he wrote. "It is his destiny to be forbidden the individuality to say 'I' instead of 'we.' "[74]

Hollis Alpert compared him to Gary Cooper. The stars shared dignity, sensitivity, and masculinity. But unlike Cooper, Poitier never got the girl. Alpert bemoaned that each passing role reinforced his isolated symbolism. Others echoed this notion. Poitier's image, argued one critic, "is now so idealized that it doesn't seem more appreciably honest." Another warned that if Americans were to fathom the summer riots, then they needed to understand the black experience — a possibility unexpressed by Poitier, "Hollywood's Stepin Fetchit of the Sixties."[75]

Academics joined the fray, excoriating Poitier's icon as they meditated on Hollywood's historic portrayal of race relations. Thomas Cripps wrote in *Phylon* that in the 1960s, "Negro characters had changed into perfectly abstinent, courageous paragons of virtue as stifling and destructive of mature characterization as the old Rastus stereotype." In the Canadian journal *Take One*, Catherine Sugy called Poitier "Uncle Tom refurbished."[76]

In *The Crisis of the Negro Intellectual*, an influential tome castigating a range of black political and cultural strategies, Harold Cruse exhorted black intellectuals to employ cultural nationalism and portray a black perspective. That included action against the "film-producing conspiracy" that delivered Poitier as the single representative of black culture. Entertainers bristled at the same problem. "It seems Whitey can accept only one successful Negro in each field at a time," grumbled Brock Peters on the front page of *Variety*.[77]

The isolation frustrated Poitier, too. In public, however, he related this tension only in measured pronouncements. "Let's face it," he told one reporter. "The American film industry isn't even prepared to deal with white life on a realistic level. I'm not surprised that the same thing is true about Negro life." Instead, he trumpeted the message of human understanding: "I like to have people coming out of a theater feeling better than when they went in." Whether holding court at the Russian Tea Room, speaking to nuns and priests at Fordham University, or signing autographs with a smile, Poitier promoted these ideals.[78]

Behind his public actions lay private convictions. Drama coach Frank London marveled at Poitier's integrity and intelligence. "Sidney's like a sponge," he related. "He's a glutton for knowledge. He reads a lot. He has friends all over the world who send him books they think will interest him." Poitier enjoyed fame and wealth, but he also sought stability and meaning. So he deeply pondered each career decision, balancing pragmatism with principles. Once he made a decision, he stuck to it. When he lauded his pictures' politics, he did so with sincerity.[79]

Poitier understood the nation's wounds. He lent perceptive opinions on race in America, imploring the government to create jobs rather than devote resources to the Vietnam War. "People don't riot for fun," he told one reporter. "There's no fun in tearing up your community or going to prison. There's no fun in being shot at or beaten. People riot for reasons that are very real to them." He cited unemployment rates for young black males of over 35 percent. "They have reached the chronological age of manhood and have nothing to do but stand on street corners, without enough money to take a girl to a movie," he explained. "So what are they going to do? . . . Strike out, of course, if only to use up energy." Poitier had once rioted himself, after all. The scar on his leg was a reminder.[80]

But he staunchly defended his image. "I'm the only one," he said. "I'm the only Negro actor who works with any degree of regularity. I represent 10,000,000 people in this country, and millions more in Africa." He would continue playing steadfast heroes until more blacks became movie stars. If his roles were stereotypes, at least they were positive stereotypes. He consistently refused to apologize for his career.[81]

To Joan Barthel of the *New York Times*, Poitier betrayed a more vulnerable side. At his Upper West Side penthouse, through cocktails, filet mignon, and coffee, they discussed his life and career. Poitier shed his armor of formality. Weary of predictable questions from the publicity trail, he urged Barthel to explore his human side. "I don't want to get bored with you," he warned, while plopping ice into her highball glass. "I expect you to stimulate me. I want you to tap me."[82]

Barthel's feature appeared on a Sunday in early August, under the headline "He Doesn't Want to Be Sexless Sidney." They sat amidst the warm glow of candlelight, a peach-colored rose as their centerpiece, majestic views of the Hudson River and Central Park surrounding them. She noted the irony as Poitier recounted the brutality of Miami policemen and nights in New York pay toilets. His speech patterns betrayed that duality. Between grandiloquent pronouncements and references to Camus, he laughed, "You sure got me to runnin' my mouth tonight."

Usually, reporters did not ask about — and Poitier did not volunteer — observations on his screen sexuality. But to Barthel he expressed frustration. Creative control lay with white writers and white studio executives, who still thought it "avant-garde" to present intelligent, principled, white-collar blacks. That image had neutralized his humanity. "To think of the American Negro male in romantic social-sexual circumstances is difficult, you know? And the reasons why," he paused, then sighed, "are legion, and too many to go into." Even while resolving to eschew neutered roles, he exhibited trademark restraint on this thorniest of taboos.

Poitier still defended his career. He insisted that he chose to operate within the Hollywood system. His pictures may have sacrificed realism, but they contributed positive messages: "They are interesting, marvelous fables, and I like what they have to say. They warm the heart, and there's nothing wrong with that." He regretted only *Porgy and Bess* and *The*

Long Ships. Other roles failed to challenge him, and some movies flopped, but blacks derived pride from his pictures. He would keep playing virtuous, intelligent heroes.

"I guess I was born out of joint with the times," he mused, as the lights of Manhattan twinkled below. "I have not made my peace with the times — they are still out of kilter — but I have made peace with myself."[83]

❖

That peace shattered one month later, after another article in the *New York Times*. Clifford Mason, a black playwright, drama critic, and radio show host, maligned Poitier on the front page of the Sunday drama section. The headline read: "Why Does White America Love Sidney Poitier So?"[84]

Mason condemned the entire premise of Poitier's career, "that the Negro is best served by being a black version of the man in the gray flannel suit, taking on white problems and a white man's sense of the world." Alluding to Barthel's article, he argued that Poitier had a misguided conception of a positive black image. In *Porgy and Bess* "at least we have a man, a real man, fighting for his woman." Poitier's villain in *The Long Ships* was "nobody's eunuch or black mammy busting his gut for white folks as if their problems were all that's important in the world." He contended that Poitier should instead demonstrate shame for his integrationist pictures.

Lilies of the Field sapped him of racial identity. *Duel at Diablo* stripped him of dignity. *The Bedford Incident* assigned him to pander to whites. And *A Patch of Blue* "was probably the most ridiculous film Poitier ever made," because he had no apparent motivation for befriending Elizabeth Hartman, besides perhaps his presidency of the BSPCBWG, or "the Black Society for the Prevention of Cruelty to Blind White Girls."

To Sir, with Love, Mason went on, "had the all-time Hollywood reversal act. Instead of putting a love interest into a story that had none, they took it out." *In the Heat of the Night* "exhibited the same old Sidney Poitier syndrome: a good guy in a totally white world, with no wife, no sweetheart, no woman to love or kiss, helping the white man solve the white man's problem." Poitier always played "the antiseptic, one-dimensional hero" that allayed white racial neuroses and promoted stifling political gradualism. Poitier was a tool of the white establishment — in Mason's cruelest words, "a showcase nigger."[85]

Responses to Mason's assault revealed the depth of controversy over Poitier's image. The industry stance came from Jay Weston, co-producer of an upcoming Poitier film. Weston lamely defended his meal ticket: "Progress, even if it may appear to be slight, is being made and, certainly, this *is* better than no progress at all!"[86]

That attitude typified the moderation that many blacks could no longer stomach. One writer to the *New York Times* saluted Mason, comparing him to Malcolm X and Lorraine Hansberry for revealing white hypocrisy. He recognized Poitier's breakthroughs but argued that the actor had stagnated over a seventeen-year career. "Will it be another 17 years before he, or some new young black star, can be violent, make love to all the girls and be the true hero, like his white contemporaries?"

Another man questioned Mason's assumptions about the proper black image. Why, he asked, must blacks identify themselves strictly by their race, dismiss racial brotherhood as Uncle Tomism, or define manhood as an expression of violence? Poitier addressed social concerns in integrated settings, acted benevolently, and espoused peace—all admirable traits. A woman faulted Mason blaming the film industry's historical mistreatment of blacks on Poitier—the one man who worked within Hollywood to reverse those stereotypes.[87]

Poitier called Mason's article "the most devastating and unfair piece of journalism I had ever seen." In time he dismissed the playwright as an opportunistic hack, but the damage was done. He suffered a bruised ego, courtesy of his hometown newspaper. As his friend Robert Alan Aurthur said, "That article hurt him because of the truth in it."[88]

Poitier refrained from defending himself in print, having seen too many ugly, fruitless exchanges of correspondence. Even before the article, he knew that his iconography neared its end. "I used to sit and evaluate the decline," he once recalled. "The quality of the decline, the rapidity of the decline, and the nature of a decline of a career." He wanted to engineer that descent with dignity. Now Poitier despaired. "On that Sunday morning," he later wrote, "I was convinced that the brick-by-brick growth of my career was complete—it had peaked, and there was no place to go but down."[89]

Not quite yet. In the coming months every aspect of the Sidney Poitier phenomenon intensified. Again, a Poitier film soared atop the box-office charts. Again, Poitier extended his own idealized stereotype. And again, critics denounced his one-dimensional image. Illustrating both the enduring strengths and emerging weaknesses of racial liberalism, delivering the ultimate expression of the Poitier icon, was *Guess Who's Coming to Dinner.*

CHAPTER 14

LAST HURRAHS
(1967–1968)

They were Hollywood's perfect pair, relics from the Golden Age. Through twenty-five years and eight films, Spencer Tracy and Katharine Hepburn had refined a remarkable chemistry, one a yin to the other's yang. Tracy: the rumpled Irish pug, the snowy-haired Everyman, the iron-willed champion of the human spirit. Hepburn: the blue-blood scion of a Connecticut doctor and a liberal activist, the regal product of Bryn Mawr and Old Money, the pants-wearing, tennis-playing emblem of female independence. Tracy was the grumpy hero, Hepburn his sovereign alter ego. On screen, they rarely touched, let alone kissed. But through jokes and arguments and glances, they conveyed an appealing mutual respect. They were the Great American Couple.[1]

Off-screen, their partnership was less ideal. In 1941, while shooting *Woman of the Year*, they began a rocky affair. Tracy — filled with self-loathing, tormented by Catholic guilt, plagued by insomnia — treated her with cold silences and cruel outbursts. He drank hard and often. Hepburn weathered, even welcomed, the abuse. She had a romantic weakness for troubled souls, and she fussed over Tracy. In their early days together, Hepburn sometimes curled asleep outside his hotel door, while Tracy sat inside with a case of Irish whiskey, blind drunk and stark naked.[2]

Their romance endured through *State of the Union* and *Adam's Rib* and *Desk Set*, Tracy periodically chastening himself for betraying his marriage vows, Hepburn continually sacrificing her independence. She embraced her old age; he grumbled that he was the last of his tribe. By the late 1950s she was preserving his career, lobbying John Ford (Hepburn's former lover and Tracy's former mentor) for the lead in *The Last Hurrah*. She also nursed Tracy's myriad ills from a lifetime of drinking.[3]

Tracy had another cheerleader: Stanley Kramer, who produced and directed the Tracy films *Inherit the Wind* (1960), *Judgment at Nuremberg* (1961), and *It's a Mad Mad Mad Mad World* (1963). Like Poitier, Kramer had been drawing more scorn from sophisticates. Pauline Kael decried his self-righteous melodramas, which fit the "formula of using 'controversial' subjects in noncontroversial ways." *Inherit the Wind* condemned religious extremism, *Judgment at Nuremberg* exposed Nazi war atrocities — not exactly subjects of great debate.[4]

In 1966, screenwriter William Rose pitched Kramer *Guess Who's Coming to Dinner*, a story of a liberal couple whose daughter plans to marry a black man. Kramer wanted Tracy and Hepburn for the parents, and Poitier had to play the groom — there were no other black stars. While Rose worked on the script, Kramer set to convincing three stars and a major studio to make a movie about interracial marriage.[5]

Kramer had a contract with Columbia Pictures for an adaptation of the Civil War novel *Andersonville*. Columbia tanked what would have been a gloomy, expensive picture. Kramer could substitute another picture with a budget under $2.8 million dollars. He sold studio head Mike Frankovich on *Guess Who's Coming to Dinner*. Frankovich, in turn, told Columbia's New York executives that the bride was marrying a Jewish man. They could face any repercussions if they signed Poitier.[6]

Kramer met Poitier at the Russian Tea Room. They had long ago formed a mutual admiration society. Poitier respected Kramer's courage; Kramer appreciated Poitier's trust. So Kramer was frank. "Look," he said, "the revolution is only a backdrop with a thing like this." The picture would be something less than honest social drama, instead presenting a light plea for tolerance. Kramer fibbed, however, that Tracy and Hepburn were already on board. Would Poitier join? "Of course," the actor responded. "My God, it's beautiful."[7]

Yet the project's racial sensibilities sat well behind the cutting edge; Rose described a black maid character as a "tough but lukewarmhearted darkie." In an early treatment shown only to Kramer, Rose sketched the background of Poitier's character, John Prentice. Rose imagined that Prentice was the grandson of a slave whose owner was also named John Prentice. Prentice the slaveowner "liked his niggers, treated them well" and freed them before the Civil War. A racist neighbor then shot the white man for his racial enlightenment. Rose defined Poitier's character against black nationalism, especially Muhammad Ali, the boxing champion who converted to Islam and renounced his given name. "Cassius may be ashamed of someone named Clay," Rose wrote, "but Prentice isn't at all ashamed of Prentice. Nor does he really care who he might have been, or what he might have been called, somewhere in the Continent of Africa."[8]

Though Rose never intended this material for the script, it illustrated his vision of a black character that quelled white liberal neuroses. The modern John Prentice not only forsook black militancy — he revered his grandfather's owner! Prentice was so deferential that during two conferences at the Plaza Hotel, Poitier urged Rose and Kramer to give the character more backbone — or, in his words, "ballsiness." Satisfied with the revisions, Poitier signed in November for $250,000 and 9 percent of the profits.[9]

By then, Kramer had cast his other stars. Hepburn joined readily, but Tracy needed convincing. He was ill, grumpy, and reluctant to work. "But I get tired," he groaned. Kramer promised a light schedule, so that Tracy would be home by lunch. "Spence, are you going to sit there in your rocker and wait for oblivion?" asked Kramer. Tracy signed for less than Poitier, though he received top billing. Even so, Columbia refused to insure Tracy, since he had emphysema and was recuperating from prostate surgery. Kramer and Hepburn placed their salaries in escrow. If Tracy died, that money would pay his replacement.[10]

Mirroring the plot of *Guess Who's Coming to Dinner*, Tracy and Hepburn hosted a dinner party to appraise their co-star. The situation smacked of condescension: no one would have expected Paul Newman or Kirk Douglas to put themselves on display. The couple was no more racially enlightened than Rose. "I can't consider Sidney as a Negro," said Hepburn. "He's not black, he's not white, he's nothing at all as far as color is concerned." But Poitier recognized their good intentions, and he respected them both. So he jumped through their hoops.[11]

In fact, Poitier exhibited a nearly debasing awe. He feared becoming stagestruck around the screen giants. That was hardly a typical attitude for an Academy Award winner on the verge of superstardom. "Working with the two of you is a dream to me," he gushed on the first day of rehearsal. During scenes with black actors Roy Glenn and Beah Richards, he performed without flaw. But with Hepburn and Tracy, he bungled lines like a rank amateur. Once Kramer sent the couple home, leaving Poitier to play a scene opposite empty chairs.[12]

Between takes, Poitier fidgeted with a golf club, a recent nervous habit. He remained the same bundle of self-doubt. One day Hepburn turned to him. "Spencer can see right through you," she said. "You're very much alike. He knows how you are made." Poitier agreed. Tracy was a gruff teddy bear, and Poitier a smooth black stone, but both projected an outward strength that masked their insecurities.[13]

Hepburn drove the making of *Guess Who's Coming to Dinner*, which was also the screen debut of her real-life niece Katharine Houghton. Hepburn rehearsed at dawn with Tracy, worked all morning, sent Tracy home after lunch, and then rehearsed with Houghton in the late afternoon. She bounced around the set, frazzling Kramer with opinions on camera angles, costumes, and set design, insisting upon an intellectual justification for every mannerism and delivery.[14]

Tracy scoffed at such exercises. He had two acting rules: "Know your lines and don't bump into any furniture." But he struggled to maintain form. His long, climactic monologue took six days to film. He looked haggard, and he forgot dialogue cues. His frustration landed on Hepburn. During one rehearsal she knelt by his feet, and he objected. When she explained herself, he needled her. "Spencuuuh," he said, affecting a mock Yankee accent. "Christ, you talk like you've got a feather up your ass all the time!" She softly acceded to his commands, as she had for twenty-six years.[15]

In late May, during the production's final week, Tracy took Kramer aside. "If I die on the way home tonight," he said, "you can still release the picture with what you've got." A few days later Tracy filmed his last scene, a location shot at a drive-in restaurant. At the final call of "cut," Kramer rushed to embrace him, and the cast wept. The dying legend avoided the wrap party, instead cracking open a beer and telephoning friends, exulting "I made it! I made it!" Two weeks later, Tracy awoke at 3 A.M., made a cup of tea, and collapsed from a heart attack. The crash startled Hepburn. She discovered him in the hallway, dead.[16]

Anticipation for *Guess Who's Coming to Dinner* ran high. In tribute to Tracy — and in promotion of her niece — the notoriously private Hepburn submitted to numerous media profiles. Roy Newquist turned interviews with the principals into a popular book called *A Special Kind of Magic*. Poitier's marketability inflated with *To Sir, with Love* and *In the Heat of the Night*. And in 1967, two events focused national attention on interracial love. In June, the Supreme Court ruled in *Loving vs. Virginia* that states could not prohibit marriages on racial grounds. In September, Margaret Rusk, daughter of Secretary of State Dean Rusk, married a young black man named Guy Gibson Smith.[17]

The picture was a monument to Tracy, a last hurrah for a Hollywood legend. He propelled the drama with curmudgeonly charm, in a performance warmed by his ninth and final pairing with Hepburn.

It was a last hurrah for Poitier, too — at least for his icon. *Guess Who's Coming to Dinner* arrived in December 1967, just as the box-office momentum from *To Sir, with Love* and *In the Heat of the Night* waned. It proved an astounding success, thanks largely to comic-book exaggerations of Poitier's trademark intelligence, gallantry, and sexual sterility.

❖

The premise of *Guess Who's Coming to Dinner* borders on the ludicrous. Matt Drayton (Tracy) and his wife, Christina (Hepburn), reign over San Francisco's liberal high society. He publishes a newspaper; she runs an art gallery. They sit on committees, take public stances for social justice, and keep a picture of Franklin D. Roosevelt in the study. Their daughter Joanna, or "Joey" (Houghton), arrives from Hawaii with a surprise: Dr. John Prentice (Poitier). They plan to marry, and they seek her parents' blessing before flying to Switzerland that night. Thrown into this frothy brew are a snooty socialite, a sassy black maid, a bubbly Monsignor, and Prentice's own parents. The Draytons must decide, in about eight hours, whether they can practice the colorblind tolerance that they preach.

But Prentice is no jive-talking hipster. His speech, dress, and manners are polished to a sparkle. He has taught at Yale Medical School and helped direct the World Health Organization. He earned fame developing health programs in Africa. He lost his wife and young son in a car accident eight years ago. And he is preposterously deferential to the Draytons. Unbeknownst to Joey, he informs her parents that if they disfavor the union, he will forfeit his fiancée. The Draytons will determine his romantic destiny.

Just as Prentice is the acme of black distinction, Joey is the embodiment of colorblindness. She never grasps that her parents might disapprove of an interracial marriage. Her sunny ignorance plants a recurrent sight gag: everyone learns about their romance on screen. Kramer employs a light touch, preserving particular sympathy for the flustered parents.

Although an original screenplay, the story resembles a farcical stage comedy. Ninety percent of the film occurs in the Drayton home. Characters rotate from room to room, scrambling scenes of earnest conversation, improbable surprises, and humorous banter. The supporting characters are symbols, designed to elicit reactions from the protagonists. Further suggesting a plastic absurdity, Kramer shot in 1940s-style Technicolor. The skies glow a bright blue, the sunsets burn a disturbing orange. Nothing about *Guess Who's Coming to Dinner* implies subtlety — it paints characters, settings, and issues in broad, colorful strokes.

The only complete articulation of racial prejudice comes from a black woman: Tilly (Isabel Sanford), the Draytons' loyal maid. "I don't want to see a member of my own race getting above himself," she objects. "You're one of those smooth-talking, smart-ass niggers just out for all you can get, with your Black Power and all that other troublemaking nonsense. . . . You bring any trouble in here and you're going to find out just what Black Power really means!" Tilly's equation of the middle-class, integrationist Prentice with the militant philosophy of Black Power reveals a pathetic illiteracy in black politics. Her viewpoint bears no credibility in 1967 America, and her comic relief scars the picture. The mammy stereotype lets audiences indulge in outdated paternalism. "Civil rights is one thing," she rails, "but this here's another." That statement, at least, rings true.[18]

Poitier's continued desexualization compounded the picture's alienation from any black perspective. Although in the throes of young love, Prentice and Joey kiss only once, in a taxi. Kramer compromised even that brief smooch, filming from the cab driver's perspective, through the rear-view window. (Kramer had shot racier versions of the kissing scene; Poitier told one radio interviewer during filming that "if the scene is still in the movie when it's released, I suggest that your listeners hurry down to the theater and see this scene, and just . . . take some aspirins with them.") Kramer's chosen shot shrinks the kissing couple to a tiny portion of screen space, and it distances the audience from their embrace.[19]

In another scene, Prentice admires Tilly's attractive black helper Dorothy (Barbara Randolph). This contrived episode further defuses the threat of black masculinity, by implying that Prentice bases his attraction to Joey on genuine love, not the myth that black men yearn for white women.[20]

Prentice refuses to sleep with Joey, despite her willingness. Ostensibly, he protects Joey in case her parents reject their marriage. Actually, he exacerbates his own neuterdom. Later, Tilly sees him bare-chested, and Prentice drapes his shirt between them. The glimpse of his naked chest puts his masculinity on display, only for Prentice to consciously, awkwardly enforce his own sterility. The sociologist Stanford Lyman ranked this scene as "one of the most subtly debasing scenes to blacks" in Hollywood history.[21]

Poitier's primary task is to convey restraint. He barely touches his fiancée, absorbs snide remarks with pursed lips, and tiptoes around the Drayton home with self-conscious manners. Again, Poitier plays less man than social symbol, and this time his archetype bloats beyond plausibility.

Prentice's only outburst comes against his own father, played by Roy Glenn. Mr. Prentice worries that by marrying a white woman, his son will fritter away his accomplishments. Dr. Prentice snaps back: "If I try to explain it to you for the rest of your life you will never understand. You are thirty years older than I am. You and your whole lousy generation believe that the way it was for you is the way it's got to be. And not until your whole generation has lain down and died will the whole weight of you be off our backs. You understand, you've got to get off my back!"

"You think of yourself as a colored man," he adds. "I think of myself as a man." This scene has only a shred more viability than Tilly's scoldings. It purports that Dr. Prentice stands at the vanguard of a new colorblind philosophy. In fact, Black Power criticized this very stance. Instead of asserting his blackness, Poitier again cast it aside.

Prentice's first convert is Christina Drayton. She insists that she and her husband cannot abandon their principles. When a snobbish employee at the art gallery mourns the family's predicament, Christina fires her, delivering a catty monologue. *Guess Who's Coming to Dinner* followed a pattern: like Gillian in *To Sir, with Love* and Mrs. Colbert in *In the Heat of the Night*, Christina first advocates racial acceptance. The films' "feminine" message of compassion resonated with the white women — on screen and in the audience — who especially appreciated Poitier's quasi-sexual appeal.

But if white women are the shock troops of colorblindness, white men are the judge and jury. Like Denham and Chief Gillespie, Matt Drayton ultimately validates Poitier's character. And Drayton, despite a lifetime of justice crusades, endures a moral dilemma. "We're being pressurized!" he moans to his wife. He thinks the couple fails to appreciate their future hurdles. His best friend calls him "a broken-down old phony liberal coming face-to-face with his prejudices." Drayton grows absurdly irascible: strewing socks and ties throughout his bedroom, backing into the car of a hip young black man, putting his razor in his scotch.

By that night's dinner party, Drayton decides the couple's fate. Mrs. Prentice (Beah Richards), who supports the marriage, grieves that Drayton has forgotten the power of young love. That triggers a flash of self-awareness. Drayton gathers everyone and delivers a long monologue, recapping the day's events: Joey surprised him, Prentice set unfair conditions, Tilly acted disruptively, Christina turned against him, and Mrs. Prentice accused him of neglecting romance. He objects to this last charge, insisting upon his endless love for Christina. She loves him back with moist eyes. Drayton then gives the couple his blessing, and he expresses confidence that Mr. Prentice will soon concur. The real romance in *Guess Who's Coming to Dinner* is that between Matt and Christina Drayton — or, perhaps, between Spencer Tracy and Katharine Hepburn.

The views of the black characters are irrelevant. After the speech, Mr.

Prentice looks sour, but Drayton just pats him on the back. His son, moreover, abides only the decision of the white patriarch. For all the discussions, arguments, and alliances, the only approval of consequence belongs to Matt Drayton.

And for all the superb acting, clever screenwriting, and lavish production values, *Guess Who's Coming to Dinner* captivated audiences because they had to answer Matt Drayton's question: would you allow your daughter to marry a black man? Interracial sex remained the prickliest taboo, a final frontier for racial liberals. The film boiled Drayton's predicament down to the single factor of skin color. No class or cultural issues clouded the scenario. Instead, the circumstances are so exaggerated that Drayton must allow the marriage. Dr. Prentice reverses black stereotypes through his professional accomplishments, mannered demeanor, and Victorian restraint. But these qualities are so bloated that Poitier's character enshrined his own one-man stereotype for the Age of Integration.

❖

Guess Who's Coming to Dinner opened in New York and Los Angeles in late December 1967 to staggering success. When national distribution began in February 1968, *Variety* asserted that the picture "looms as one of the industry's all-time biggest grossers." America's most popular movie through March, it earned excellent grosses into May. The well-made, entertaining, and heavily hyped picture boasted both the final pairing of Tracy and Hepburn and the star power of Poitier. Industry insiders tried to remember the last time an actor starred in three top films within a six-month period. Poitier's prominence, they surmised, killed the old notion that "message movies" could not win profits.[22]

The picture inspired piles of fan mail, much of it pondering America's racial troubles. Some cheered that the picture restored hope in integration. A Massachusetts woman wrote that the film sparked a long office discussion about interracial marriage. Others resolved to treat blacks fairly after seeing the picture. A white Air Force lieutenant recalled his college days, when he fell in love with a black woman but acted too slowly; *Guess Who's Coming to Dinner* revived pangs of regret. Other correspondents invited prejudiced friends to see the movie and gauged their reactions. One woman, who coaxed her date with the promise of a hilarious maid, wrote that "the effect was fabulous. He could only shake his head after. What can you say about such a TOTALLY absorbing experience?"[23]

The early critical reaction reiterated these sentiments. New York reviewers recognized the excellence of the writing, acting, and production, and they commended Kramer for tackling a controversial subject. Bosley Crowther of the *New York Times*, an enduring advocate of Poitier, devoted a review and a column to the film. *Variety* cheered the "landmark in tasteful introduction of sensitive material to the screen." In a later column titled "Films, Poitier, and Race Riots," the trade newspaper praised the casting of Poitier, even if his extraordinary qualifications made "Ralph Bunche look like a high-school dropout."[24]

But Poitier's "composite Schweitzer, Salk and Christ" induced another slew of bleating critics. "Sidney Poitier, the surgeon, cuts one more slice off his by-now stale performing loaf," wrote Stanley Kauffman. Arthur Knight suspected reverse racism in the distended Poitier icon. Others lamented Prentice's desexualization, and some questioned why a sophisticated thirty-seven-year-old doctor would fall for a naive twenty-three-year-old, except that she has white skin.[25]

Most conceded the picture's charms. Even jaded Brendan Gill of the *New Yorker* softened at Tracy's soliloquy, a speech informed by his life-long partnership with Hepburn. But critics lambasted Kramer's irrelevance. "Hollywood lives!" proclaimed Wilfred Sheid, tongue-in-cheek. The film showed "the old Hollywood knack for misstating a situation so grossly that the problem never arises." Robert Kotlowitz announced an unwillingness to watch the picture in Watts or Harlem. As riots plagued inner cities, as radicals proclaimed black revolution, *Guess Who's Coming to Dinner* presented cartoonish characters and silly scenarios. Judith Crist wrote:

> It would be easy to accept this film, as thousands of mindless movie-goers are doing, because it is designed to satisfy the smugs in its lip service to decency while it sloughs off our most pressing national problem in frighteningly insidious terms. In essence it says that it's perfectly fine for the slightly silly daughter of a millionaire to marry a Negro provided that (a) he's Sidney Poitier (b) he's the second smartest scientist in the whole wide world (c) his mother keeps her gloves on while drinking sherry with her prospective in-laws . . . and (d) the happy miscegenated couple gets the hell out of this country by midnight and spends the rest of their lives peddling medicine to the natives in Africa.

The story might have seemed more dramatic when Rose and Kramer first conceived it. "Now," *Newsweek* concluded, "it seems an absolute antique."[26]

College students registered further disgust. When Kramer embarked upon a nine-campus tour in early 1968, they scolded the director about

Guess Who's Coming to Dinner. "The primary objection," Kramer recalled, was "that the film was made in the first place." The young adults already accepted interracial love affairs. They objected that Poitier and Houghton never have sex, and they roasted the flawless black hero. But Kramer insisted that reviewers and students missed the point. *Guess Who's Coming to Dinner* was a deliberate fantasy. "The film is an adventure into the ludicrous — the characters so perfect that the only conceivable objection to this marriage could be ludicrously enough, the pigmentation of a man's skin." "That was the point of the film," he later added, "and it worked."[27]

Guess Who's Coming to Dinner also surfaced the political divisions among African Americans. The picture received heavy promotion in black publications, thanks to the controversial theme and sterling cast. Doc Young supported Kramer. Young wrote one detractor: "Your problem is that, like so many other Caucasians connected with the daily press and television, you are overly impressed by the loudmouths created by that media as 'Negro Leaders.' These people represent virtually no one but themselves." That white intellectuals assumed radicals spoke for the black majority frustrated Young, a member of the integrationist old guard.[28]

But even mainstream black publications indicted the film's compromises. Jesse Walker of the *New York Amsterdam News* wrote that "we wouldn't be human if we didn't carp a bit" about Poitier's ridiculous credentials and self-imposed neuterdom. In a long profile of Poitier, Charles Sanders of *Ebony* mourned the actor's desexualization. He claimed that publicity stills showing passionate kisses between Poitier and Houghton remained locked in the New York offices of Columbia Pictures, "marked with bold red Xs and the word HOLD."[29]

Other black criticisms ranged from thoughtful to theatrical. Psychiatrist Alvin Poussaint contended that Poitier's heroes placed undue burdens on black youths. Black children shared a joke about Poitier: "Is it a bird? Is it a plane? No! It's Superspade!" Lindsay Patterson argued that *Guess Who's Coming to Dinner* was "a perfect exercise in Hollywood's escapism, blithely disregarding the genuine and maybe altogether unendurable problems to be encountered in a mainland interracial marriage." Maxine Hall Elliston took the argument further: "Whites will love to see this Black nigger try to crawl his way into white society, and at the same time hate him for kissing a white girl. And non-thinking Blacks will wallow in the glory of their Black movie star." In sum, the film was "warmed over white shit."[30]

Bashing the Poitier icon became high fashion. The British magazine *Punch* satirized Poitier as a Nobel Prize–winning jungle hero in a piece called "You Sidney Poitier, Me Jane!" Then came an attack from, of all people, Stepin Fetchit. A recent television program had criticized his eye-rolling, slow-moving, dialect-speaking image. Anathema in Hollywood, now a hanger-on in Muhammad Ali's entourage, Fetchit assailed Poitier as an ineffective token. Fetchit had won fame by reinforcing the noxious stereotypes that once justified Jim Crow, but he argued that *Guess Who's Coming to Dinner* "served the purpose of white supremacy."[31]

Poitier's box-office aura did stretch into the South. Once associated with integrationist upheavals, now Poitier represented an alternative to radical violence. "He hasn't been one of those militants," said a southern theater owner. "Whites can identify with him." He added that if Stokely Carmichael appeared on his screen, whites would demolish the theater. Only one exhibitor, in New Orleans, edited out the kissing scene in *Guess Who's Coming to Dinner*. Billboards featured Poitier and Houghton arm-in-arm, and the picture grossed well throughout the region.[32]

White supremacists nevertheless attacked the picture as a Jewish conspiracy to undermine Christianity, a Communist plot to subvert Americanism, and a threat to racial order. The *Thunderbolt* lampooned Poitier's character: "Has any of our readers ever heard of a nigger with these qualifications?" Hate mail to Stanley Kramer feared the dismantling of racial taboos: "The puberty crowd will snicker through it, and come home with all kinds of new ideas for Mom and Pop about the interracial bit." "Certainly Poitier sees nothing wrong with holding a pretty white girl in his arms and making love to her. That is the ambition of all Negro men." "I felt like throwing up every time that *black* Poitier touched the little white girl." "We hate *Superspade* Poitier and now we despise Pig Houghton. She sucks niggers."[33]

These loathsome convictions inspired some protests at venues showing *Guess Who's Coming to Dinner*. In Lexington, North Carolina, twenty Ku Klux Klan members picketed a drive-in theater, carrying signs that read "Fight for Your Rights" and "Mom and Dad — It Could Happen to You." In Chicago, an undercover officer revealed a Klan scheme to set off tear gas bombs at a 3,900-seat movie palace. In Westwood, California, a vandal poured ammonia into a theater's ventilation system two days after a demonstration by the American Nazi Party. In Cleveland, delinquents planted stench bombs in three movie houses.[34]

Racial hatred existed side by side with popular support for the picture. In Hamilton, Ohio, ten picketing Klansmen sparked a counterprotest by young blacks, who launched rocks through windows. Police armed with riot gear had to quell the disturbance. Only twenty-six miles away in Cincinnati, integrated crowds set attendance records at the 3,000-seat Albee Theater.[35]

Guess Who's Coming to Dinner was a sounding board for American racial convictions. For intellectual critics, college students, and African Americans, Poitier's icon had outlived its purpose, even if racial conservatives found Poitier's interracial love repugnant. The loudest comment, however, was the incessant clicking of theater turnstiles. A large liberal contingent sought its message. Hollywood had polished and adorned a controversial issue, rendering it digestible, fulfilling Stanley Kramer's purpose: audiences accepted the marriage of a white woman and a black man, at least provided that the black man was Sidney Poitier.[36]

Few grasped Poitier's significance better than James Baldwin. Poitier's equivalent in the literary world, he understood the peculiar dilemmas of the black artist. Baldwin admired his friend's energy, grace, and capacity to both ignite and reassure. But he hated *Guess Who's Coming to Dinner*. It offered black people nothing; "they felt that Sidney was, in effect, being used against them." An "essential inertia and despair" marked any film where the black man curried favor only by possessing extraordinary qualities, surrendering his destiny to a white man, and relinquishing his sexuality.[37]

But Baldwin also forecast its implications: "*Guess Who's Coming to Dinner* may prove, in some bizarre way, to be a milestone." No picture could carry the saintly, sexless stereotype any further. "The next time," he wrote, "the kissing will have to start."[38]

❖

Baldwin profiled Poitier in *Look*, one of many articles contemplating Poitier's popularity after *Guess Who's Coming to Dinner*. Most were sympathetic. Fan magazines printed features titled "What's the Secret of Sidney Poitier's Zooming Appeal?," "Why Negroes Love Sidney Poitier — but Not Sammy Davis," and "Why White Women Dig Sidney Poitier." They lauded Poitier's combination of affability and dignity, which drew white fans and retained black respect. Also, Bill Cosby and football star/actor Jim Brown publicly appreciated Poitier's barrier-breaking career. In the *Washington Post*, Richard Coe mourned the unfair criticism of Poitier. A white man wrote to *Ebony*: "Please don't make it too hard for those of us who want to help, and who honestly will do our best to overcome our clumsiness. Poitier movies — while not yet the whole answer — are moving in the right direction."[39]

Poitier articulated his own philosophical justifications. "I try to make motion pictures about the dignity, nobility, the magnificence of human life," he said. He also insisted that *Guess Who's Coming to Dinner* was entertainment, not propaganda. "I have no way of determining how important it will be in a racial sense," he said. Instead he spoke generally about American culture. He argued that values of "pleasure and materialism" cultivated a "propensity for hate." He championed a culture that educated people "to understand, to tolerate, to love, to enjoy." The implication hung that his pictures performed this service.[40]

But now the crown of racial symbol weighed heavier. When New York City mayor John Lindsay asked him to join a walking tour through Harlem, Poitier declined. When Dorothy Manners mentioned a contentious television debate about race, Poitier only commented, "What I have to say I want to say through my pictures." He knew that his image disenchanted some people, but he also cited statistics showing the high percentage of blacks at his movies. He pointed the finger at Hollywood, decrying the imposition of undue responsibility: "I am not about to be all things to all people."[41]

So Poitier returned to Broadway, this time as a director. Robert Alan Aurthur, a friend since penning *A Man Is Ten Feet Tall*, had written the film script *Carry Me Back to Morningside Heights*. He wanted Poitier to star. But Poitier proposed that he adapt it on stage. Instead of acting, he wanted to direct. Aurthur consented. In January 1968, Poitier began rehearsals with his five-member cast at the John Golden Theater. An actor's director, he let each performer express their interpretation before softly adding his own changes. The job opened doors to self-discovery. Waving his nine-iron like a baton, bounding about the stage to check sightlines, instructing actors in such details as passing a plate, Poitier cherished the experience. "You control," he described, explaining the appeal. "You have absolute *control*." So often frustrated by Hollywood's conservatism, he appreciated the artistic freedom.[42]

He possessed rare power among blacks on Broadway. Black actors still found few opportunities on stage. Repertory companies consigned blacks to minor "buddy" roles, and drama schools restricted blacks from important roles in classics. Successful plays by James Baldwin and Ossie Davis were exceptions to the rule.[43]

Yet the theater also augured a trend in black culture. The Harlem Black

Arts Repertory Theater and School, co-founded by Leroi Jones in 1965, envisioned black theater as a revolutionary art form. Renouncing white custody and drawing heavily from African heritage, the school promoted black nationalism through art. Its stance included actual revolutionary measures; a 1966 police raid revealed a cache of weapons. *Carry Me Back to Morningside Heights* — with a white playwright and integrated cast — stood well outside this trend. Poitier and Aurthur patterned it on the warm formula of Poitier's films. They sought widespread acceptance.[44]

They failed, and prodigiously. Ostensibly a comedy, the play addressed white liberal guilt. Seymour Levin (David Steinberg), a Jewish civil rights activist, volunteers to become the slave of Willie Nurse (Louis Gossett), a black law student at Columbia. This premise disintegrates into stale gags based on reversed racial stereotypes: Seymour refers to steamed chad and potato knishes as "soul food"; Seymour borrows a pen and gets accused of stealing; Seymour kisses his girlfriend and is likened to a sexually overcharged animal. By the end, racial superiority corrupts the once-decent black folk. Willie exploits Seymour, and Willie's girlfriend (Cicely Tyson) sexually assaults the white slave. She cries "Rape!" when they are discovered.

Upon its February 27 debut, critics lambasted the insignificance. "It is that grand old platitude — tolerance — sprinkled with references to Negro militancy and white liberal guilt, but clear enough beneath the earnest disguise," wrote one reviewer. "Just plain old pre-crisis middle-browism, as simplistic as ever." Worse, the play lacked humor. The best jokes elicited quiet giggles, and the rest met with silence. The play closed after one preview and seven performances.[45]

Poitier did not elude the barbs. Aurthur's script needed stringent cuts and creative staging. Instead, Poitier's limp hand sustained overacting and poor timing. One critic called his direction "an embarrassment." Despite creative control, Poitier made no comment of consequence. *Carry Me Back to Morningside Heights* told yet another story from the white liberal perspective, and without any panache. Its failure pierced Poitier's ego and stoked fears of a career decline.[46]

One month later, Martin Luther King was assassinated. King had been in Memphis with striking sanitation workers, another stage in his evolving application of Gandhian principles to ghetto problems. Now that hope seemed dead. A new spate of urban riots erupted: over 130 disturbances, 46 deaths, 2,600 fires, 20,000 arrests. Floyd McKissick captured the militant spirit: "Dr. King was the last apostle of nonviolence, and with his death the philosophy of nonviolence died."[47]

Poitier flew to Memphis for a memorial march led by Ralph Abernathy and attended by Bill Cosby, Ossie Davis, Ruby Dee, and Walter Reuther. (The FBI tracked their participation, fearing that the presence of high-profile figures might stoke more violence.) Then Poitier went to Atlanta, where Harry Belafonte invited him to discussions on a memorial service for the slain leader. Belafonte advocated holding a rally at Atlanta Stadium. Poitier disagreed, arguing that it might deflect attention from King's funeral. Their voices rose. Poitier accused Belafonte of dominating the proceedings. Julie Belafonte entered the fray, attacking Poitier personally. Harry soon froze out of the argument, yielding to Poitier with icy disenchantment. Poitier and Belafonte, best friends and brotherly rivals, stopped speaking to each other.[48]

After the funeral, in Marlon Brando's hotel suite, the celebrity branch of the civil rights coalition gathered one last time: Poitier, Belafonte, Brando, Sammy Davis Jr., Eartha Kitt, Tony Franciosa, Peter Lawford, and others. That month celebrities remained public voices for the King legacy. Ossie Davis and Ruby Dee appeared on a televised tribute to King. Sammy Davis Jr. publicly urged a reaffirmation of nonviolence. Brando briefly quit acting to devote more energy to civil rights. And Poitier, Sammy Davis Jr., Diahann Carroll, and Louis Armstrong withdrew from the Academy Awards out of respect for Dr. King. They reconsidered only after the Academy postponed the initial ceremony.[49]

The assassination shook the entertainment world. Television networks highlighted urban violence, while downtown movie houses shut down for the weekend. Columbia recalled all prints of *Guess Who's Coming to Dinner* and edited out the scene of Joey Drayton asking Tilly to "guess who's coming to dinner." Tilly sasses back, "The Reverend Martin Luther King Jr.!"[50]

Poitier remained a symbol of King's philosophy. The Easter holiday adopted an extra significance for African Americans in 1968. The issue of the *Pittsburgh Courier* that reported the assassination also ran a biblical quotation describing Christ's crucifixion. Next to the passage was a still from *The Greatest Story Ever Told*, with Max Van Sydow carrying the cross up Calvary, aided by Sidney Poitier.[51]

Poitier received no Oscar nominations that year, thanks to his stereotype. "When Sidney returns to playing believable parts in pictures and forgets his role as Super-Negro," wrote Vernon Scott, "people will no longer find it necessary to ask why Poitier wasn't nominated." In the days between King's assassination and the Academy Awards, columnists mused further on Poitier. Charles Champlin maintained that his films had increased racial understanding, but King's death had compelled a reexamination of race in America, including Hollywood. Champlin captured Poitier's import: "He is a reminder of the progress made, among all the reminders of the distance we have to go." His symbolism comforted many Americans, but it bore little applicability for the nation's racial future.[52]

King's shadow hung over the Oscars. Emcee Bob Hope alternated between tasteless jokes about the postponement and crass remarks of Hollywood self-congratulation. (He compared Jesse Lasky and Samuel Goldwyn to King because "they, too, had a dream.") Academy president Gregory Peck was more eloquent, calling upon the industry "to continue making films which celebrate the dignity of man, whatever his race or color or creed." He asked viewers to contribute to the Martin Luther King Jr. Fund. Peck also noted that two nominations for Best Picture implored racial understanding: *In the Heat of the Night* and *Guess Who's Coming to Dinner*.[53]

Poitier's image adopted extra significance. When arriving at the Santa Monica Auditorium, then again when presenting the Best Actress award, the actor won thunderous applause. His films dominated the proceedings. *In the Heat of the Night* won Best Picture. Katharine Hepburn won Best Actress. Stirling Siliphant won Best Adapted Screenplay for *In the Heat of the Night*. William Rose won Best Original Screenplay for *Guess Who's Coming to Dinner*. And Rod Steiger won Best Actor. On stage, he thanked Poitier for deepening his understanding of racial prejudice. He ended, "We shall overcome."[54]

The Oscars boosted the fortunes of Poitier's films, especially *In the Heat of the Night*, which grossed over two million dollars in the week after the ceremony. The three pictures stayed popular through most of 1968. That summer Columbia reissued *A Raisin in the Sun*. Industry organs ranked Poitier the top draw of the year. Poitier recorded his third spoken-word album, another philosophical reading called *Journeys Inside the Mind*. A Miami producer even tabbed his brother Cyril to play a gas station attendant in a low-budget melodrama about motorcycle gangs. Cyril had no acting experience. At the time, he was running a nursery school.[55]

Internationally, Poitier gained enormous prestige. A Reuters poll deemed him a "world film favorite." His pictures played from Bangkok to Beirut, Caracas to Copenhagen, Tel Aviv to Tokyo, and they carried political implications. To American allies he represented faith in American democracy. In South Africa he subverted apartheid; a government board banned *To Sir, with Love* and *In the Heat of the Night*. In the Soviet

Union, a 1969 stage version gave *In the Heat of the Night* a telling twist: at the end, an offstage voice says to Tibbs, "Not that way, fellow; the colored car is at the rear of the train," suggesting that capitalism cannot overcome racism.[56]

Within American borders, Poitier represented a fleeting era of interracial optimism. In May, he came to Washington to support the Poor People's Campaign, an interracial protest led by Ralph Abernathy. Poitier organized a volunteer clean-up brigade of the Mall, where the protesters had constructed an impromptu city of plywood huts. In June, Poitier was one of 600 honorary guards keeping vigil over the grave of Robert F. Kennedy, the fallen presidential candidate who had most embodied the old idealism. That month Poitier also joined the National Committee of Inquiry, a panel of black leaders and celebrities that recommended presidential candidates. The organization incorporated a political spectrum, from Abernathy to Andrew Young to Stokely Carmichael. This stab at reviving a black consensus failed; Richard Nixon's victory buried the old liberal coalition.[57]

If an epoch had ended, at least Poitier emerged wealthy. Other actors received higher flat fees, but Poitier earned higher percentages of his pictures' earnings. His three 1967 films, combined with the upcoming *For Love of Ivy*, gained him close to ten million dollars. Poitier was also receiving paychecks from earlier contracts, which spread his fees over the long term. In January 1969 Martin Baum surmised that Poitier was the highest-paid actor in the world.[58]

To be sure, Poitier pursued riches. "That's what makes Sidney run," said a friend. "He just *has* to have all that money." He chose mass-market film projects, and he delighted in superstardom's trappings enough to stay at the Plaza Hotel when his housekeeper broke her toe, or to stop for a "sandwich" and order cold lobster. Yet he still struggled to reconcile his wealth with his values. To compensate, he enforced a rigorous self-discipline. He drank a glass of juice for lunch, ate only organic fruits and vegetables, maintained a daily routine of calisthenics, and ordered smokers to extinguish their cigarettes. He chose stimulating, diverse New York City over the Babylonian excess of Beverly Hills.[59]

Poitier still possessed enough hang-ups to carry around a MacGregor nine-iron, even into Sardi's or the Russian Tea Room. He called it his "insecurity rod." But years of therapy allowed him to challenge his neuroses. He related a recurring daydream, where jungle animals claw at each other. "And then," he went on, "there is one who is different. But it is a difference that is *earned*. There is one animal, walking about, making choices, not out of greed or lust, but exercising control." He envisioned himself as this higher order, a man whose isolation demanded difficult choices, but a man in control of his destiny.[60]

To this end, he invested time in Pleasantville, spent weekends with his daughters, and left a telephone number when he traveled. In July 1968, he took the girls on a European vacation, traveling to San Sebastian, Rome, Amsterdam, and Pamplona, where they watched the running of the bulls. Poitier had evolved as a father. "I used to behave like they were my property," he said. Now he softened a bit from the rigid codes of his own childhood. He also assumed some responsibility for the teenage daughter of his family's housekeeper.[61]

Yet his continued separation from Juanita strained his relationship with his daughters. He remained the disciplinarian, yet he never stayed in Pleasantville. The girls blamed him for the estrangement, but he avoided direct conversations about the fractured marriage. Sixteen-year-old Beverly alternated between retreats into books and open rebellion. Fourteen-year-old Pamela loved riding horses, and she often argued with her father over its detraction from her studies. Twelve-year-old Sherri struggled with undiagnosed dyslexia, and she compensated with humor. Only seven-year-old Gina was too young to understand much of the turmoil.[62]

Sidney did maintain a cordial alliance with Juanita, and he often praised her as an excellent mother. She still refused to sign the legal papers for an official divorce. A strong and traditional woman, she refused to sanction her husband's frailties. Sidney could live with the marriage, too. He avoided the financial penalty of divorce, and he had no plans to remarry. In one's mate, he averred, "we think there is perfection, *eternally*." Now he believed that was a myth.[63]

Instead Poitier tasted the fruits of bachelorhood, as befit a matinee idol. Fan magazines reported Poitier's intrigues with famous, attractive women such as Myrna Lee, Leslie Uggams, and Nancy Wilson. In early 1968, gossip hounds spotted him all over New York City with Haitian model Yolande Toussaint. He escorted television personality Joan Murray to the premiere of *Guess Who's Coming to Dinner* and actress Jean Seberg to the Cannes Film Festival. He spent time with actress Linda Cristal in both Hollywood and New York.[64]

Intermittent rumors had him staging reconciliations with either Juanita or Diahann Carroll, but in general, he sought neither housewives nor divas. He required control. "I like a woman who accepts her femininity, her womanhood — her *femaleness*," said Poitier. He deplored women who challenged his authority; summing up his dating philosophy, he proclaimed, "Ballsy Women Turn Me Off." This chauvinistic stance protected him from emotional exposure or messy entanglements. He eschewed commitment and guarded his privacy. After Cristal publicly discussed their dates, he stopped calling her.[65]

When confronted with an intelligent and accomplished woman, Poitier erected barriers of stiff formality. He briefly courted the attractive stage actress Ellen Holly. For every date, Poitier drove out to suburban Richmond Hill, ferried Holly to his Manhattan penthouse, hosted her for dinner, entertained her with the movies or the New York nightlife, and then returned her to Richmond Hill with chaste grace. A date with Poitier, Holly reflected, "was akin to being granted an audience with the Pope." He rang a tiny dinner bell when they finished each dinner course. The housekeeper attended to each detail "like an abbess conscripted to assure the preservation of his priestly virtue." Holly never penetrated his armor of decorum.[66]

Poitier was approaching dating as a duty. He attended premieres, sampled cosmopolitan hot spots, satisfied expectations of pretty women on his arm. But he had grown cynical, and he seemed more aloof. With his controversial ascent to superstardom, he retreated into a bunker of good form and self-discipline. That posture shaped his response to his career's descent.[67]

❖

Black radicalism and urban riots had opened a window of opportunity for Poitier. His cultured hero had becalmed anxiety, allowing audiences to disengage from entrenched racial problems, indulging myths built on black sacrifice. But the window slammed shut.

King's assassination again spotlighted the absence of blacks in entertainment. In the ensuing months, television networks rushed so many race-themed specials into production that *Newsweek* called it "The Summer of the Negro." CBS ran a seven-part series called *Of Black America*. Bill Cosby narrated an episode on black history, part of which examined cultural distortions of black identity. One visual sequence depicted baneful images of Stepin Fetchit and his ilk. "Today," Cosby added, "black actors are in a new stereotype. It's Sidney Poitier helping little old ladies across the street, whether they want to go or not."[68]

An emergent generation proclaimed the death of the Poitier icon. "Mr. Negro is gone, definitely," said Yaphet Kotto in June 1968. Blacks would now play realistic characters. Even when praising Poitier as "a trail blazer for Negro acceptance in films and television," Kotto sounded like he was eulogizing a relic.[69]

That summer black Hollywood brimmed with optimism. *Variety* had already boosted former football star Jim Brown as a leading man *"a la Poitier."* Now films in production employed black actors such as Calvin Lockhart, Al Freeman Jr., Geoffrey Holder, and James Earl Jones. Warner Brothers signed Gordon Parks to direct the film version of his autobiographical novel *The Learning Tree*, finally breaking the barrier between black directors and Hollywood studios.[70]

Studios also hired some black writers. John Oliver Killens co-wrote the script for *Slaves*, and Columbia signed James Baldwin to write a biopic of Malcolm X. Baldwin spent sixteen frustrating months in Hollywood butting heads with Columbia executives. Baldwin wanted to convey Malcolm X's indictments of American racism; Columbia urged him to tone down the radicalism. Baldwin wanted Billy Dee Williams in the lead; Columbia preferred James Earl Jones or Poitier.[71]

Poitier never commented on the Malcolm X movie, but he did find himself ensnared in another political tangle. William Styron's Pulitzer Prize–winning 1967 novel *The Confessions of Nat Turner* had infuriated black critics, who condemned the white author for interpreting the slave rebel as a sex-crazed madman. When Twentieth Century-Fox bought the rights in 1968, Ossie Davis spearheaded a protest against a screen version. Reporters sought Poitier's point of view. Again, the questions asked for more than artistic opinions — they expected him to speak for an entire race. Poitier downplayed the controversy, only maintaining that he avoided period films (he had also declined the slave comedy *The Skin Game*). Later that year, he remained vague on Nat Turner. "A political evaluation of the material is not necessarily the determining factor in my position on the book," he said. "I just don't like to play period pieces."[72]

"And I don't like that *particular* book," he added, finally, "nor am I *particularly* enamored of that *particular* character as he is constructed in the book." Even then, he bottled himself up, meticulously phrasing his qualifications. His public persona had smoothed ruffled feathers for so long that he stifled his genuine convictions. Poitier loved to be liked. So he continued to select and mold projects that lured broad segments of the American public, even if that meant sacrificing the progressive vanguard. He embraced the messages of *To Sir, with Love* and *Guess Who's Coming to Dinner*. He wanted to warm people, counteract gore and greed with smiles and laughter, unite in times of divisiveness. If, in the coming years, that sentiment seemed a quaint anachronism, then so did Sidney Poitier.[73]

Poitier in his first film role, as Dr. Luther Brooks in
No Way Out (1950). This character established the virtuous,
intelligent, mannered persona that lasted his entire career.
(Courtesy of the Academy of Motion Picture Arts and Sciences)

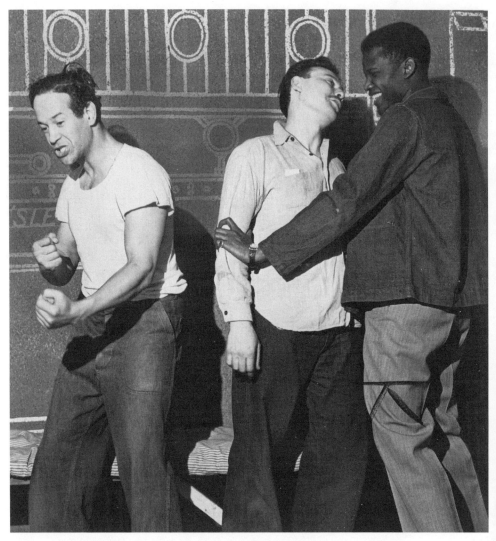

Frank Silvera, Herb Armstrong, and Poitier on stage in Longitude 49,
a play that had a brief Off-Broadway run in the spring of 1950.
(Photograph by Vivian Cherry; courtesy of the
Schomburg Center for Research in Black Culture)

Edric Connor, Canada Lee, and Poitier in Cry, the Beloved Country
*(1952). The three black men had to enter South Africa as the legally
indentured property of director Zoltan Korda. (United Artists;
courtesy of the Schomburg Center for Research in Black Culture)*

*"Parole Chief," a long-forgotten episode of the live television
series* Philco Television Playhouse *in November 1952.
(Courtesy of the Schomburg Center for Research in Black Culture)*

*Poitier strikes an angry pose for his
breakthrough hit* Blackboard Jungle *(1955).*
(Courtesy of the Schomburg Center for Research in Black Culture)

Poitier and Tony Curtis in The Defiant Ones *(1958), bound first by chains and later by friendship. (United Artists; courtesy of MGM and the Schomburg Center for Research in Black Culture)*

With the actor and his wife, Juanita, former First Lady Eleanor Roosevelt commemorates Poitier's 1958 Silver Bear Trophy, awarded to the Best Actor of the Berlin Film Festival. Poitier won for The Defiant Ones. *(Courtesy of the Schomburg Center for Research in Black Culture)*

Poitier on his knees before Brock Peters in Porgy and Bess *(1959). (Columbia Pictures; courtesy of the Schomburg Center for Research in Black Culture)*

*With Diana Sands, Ruby Dee, and Claudia McNeil
for the film version of* A Raisin in the Sun *(1961).
(Courtesy of Columbia Pictures and the
Schomburg Center for Research in Black Culture)*

Poitier teaching nuns English in Lilies of the Field *(1963),
the performance that won him the Academy Award.
(United Artists; courtesy of MGM and the
Schomburg Center for Research in Black Culture)*

Poitier in Lilies of the Field.
(Courtesy of the Academy of Motion Picture Arts and Sciences)

With Diahann Carroll at the 1965 Academy Awards,
during an "on-again" stage of their passionate nine-year relationship.
(Courtesy of the Schomburg Center for Research in Black Culture)

Twelve years after playing the cool teenager in Blackboard Jungle, *Poitier stepped to the other side of the classroom to play the cultured teacher in* To Sir, with Love *(1967). (Courtesy of Columbia Pictures and the Academy of Motion Picture Arts and Sciences)*

Poitier and Rod Steiger emitting disdain for each other in
In the Heat of the Night *(1967). (Courtesy of MGM and
the Academy of Motion Picture Arts and Sciences)*

Seeking Spencer Tracy's approval in Guess Who's Coming to Dinner *(1968). Katharine Houghton looks on. (Courtesy of Columbia Pictures and the Academy of Motion Picture Arts and Sciences)*

An interracial coalition of entertainers donated their talents to
King: A Filmed Record . . . Montgomery to Memphis, *a 1968*
documentary about the slain civil rights leader Martin Luther King Jr.
From left to right: Charlton Heston, producer Ely Landau, Leslie
Uggams, Walter Matthau, director Joseph L. Mankiewicz, Sammy Davis
Jr., Sidney Poitier, Ben Gazzara, James Earl Jones, Clarence Williams III,
Diahann Carroll, Anthony Quinn, and Burt Lancaster.
(Courtesy of the Schomburg Center for Research in Black Culture)

With Martin Landau in They Call Me Mister Tibbs *(1970). Here Poitier declares that he is "through playing God." (Columbia Pictures; courtesy of MGM and the Schomburg Center for Research in Black Culture)*

Bossing around best friend Harry Belafonte in
Buck and the Preacher *(1972). (Courtesy of Columbia Pictures
and the Schomburg Center for Research in Black Culture)*

*Behind the camera with Esther Anderson
during the filming of* A Warm December *(1973).
(National General Pictures; courtesy of the
Schomburg Center for Research in Black Culture)*

*Poitier and Joanna Shimkus in London's Heathrow Airport,
with their first child together, Anika, 1970s.
(Courtesy of the Associated Press/Wide World Photos and
the Schomburg Center for Research in Black Culture)*

PART V
THROUGH
PLAYING GOD

❖ ❖ ❖

CHAPTER 15

EXILES

(1967–1971)

❖

As much as popular culture distorted the black male, it performed a greater disservice to the black female. Skin color confined her to two basic roles: dark-skinned women played domestics, and light-skinned women played exotic sex symbols. Suffering the double prejudice of race and gender, black actresses such as Ruby Dee and Diana Sands either played housewives or stayed off screen. For years, there was no female equivalent to the Sidney Poitier icon.[1]

In 1968, NBC launched the sitcom *Julia*. Ironically, it starred Diahann Carroll. She played a nurse, war-hero widow, and single parent. The show exposed Carroll to the same criticisms faced by Poitier; "Watts it ain't," commented *Variety*. Like Poitier, Carroll staked no claim to ghetto authenticity. She admitted that whites comprised her target audience: "I'd like a couple million of them to watch and say, 'Hey, so that's what they do when they go home at night.'" Her nurse exhibited the same refined integrity as Poitier's teachers, detectives, and doctors.[2]

Poitier wanted to present a more genuine black woman, an imperative guided by fatherhood. On television, in the movies, and in magazines, his daughters saw only white standards of beauty — even when the celebrity was black, such as Diahann Carroll. He wanted his girls to develop positive self-images. He also wished to stretch Hollywood's tight boundaries on black intimacy. So he coined his own story, featuring himself as a romantic hero. After three weeks of isolation in his study, he emerged with a nineteen-page outline called *Ivy*. In the treatment, his wealthy playboy falls in love with a domestic.[3]

Martin Baum took it to three major studios. All declined, honestly explaining that an all-black romance fettered its appeal. In March 1967, Baum presented it to Palomar, the new film production wing of ABC Television, which gambled on it. They hired Robert Alan Aurthur to write the screenplay, now titled *For Love of Ivy*.[4]

Nearly 300 women auditioned for the title role. Few major pictures had ever offered black women such a developed part. The winner was Abbey Lincoln, who had last acted in *Nothing but a Man*. An accomplished jazz singer, wife to famed drummer Max Roach, and political activist, Lincoln transmitted pride. She also possessed demure beauty. Poitier paid her a high compliment: after an excellent take, he shouted out, "Man, she's so *colored*!"[5]

Starting in October 1967, they filmed in Nassau County and Manhattan, racing to beat the New York winter. The location shooting included a day in Greenwich Village, where a casting call for extras, posted throughout the Bohemian neighborhood, effected a cavalcade of scraggly beards, steel-rimmed glasses, peace beads, and headbands. One man arrived with a monkey on his shoulder. The extras earned twenty-seven dollars, some camera exposure, and an endorsement from Poitier. "Give them time, they may come up with something," he said. "As long as they hold on to love, they'll be all right."[6]

Poitier's recent success occasioned copious publicity, most of which trumpeted the picture's pioneering presentation of blacks. Poitier played a sophisticated hustler, a departure from his morally impeccable heroes. Lincoln's maid was not a stereotype but a complex protagonist. They had a genuine screen romance, the kind unavailable to Poitier throughout his career. "If *For Love of Ivy* delivers even a fraction of what it promises," anticipated one critic, "it may well be the most shatteringly revolutionary film to be done in this country in years."[7]

❖

When the picture arrived in July 1968, that assertion seemed laughable. Underneath the patina of contemporary significance lay an old-fashioned, ultra-conventional romantic comedy — "a descent into an ocean of matinee goo," according to Gordon Gow. Ivy Moore (Lincoln) works for the Austins, a wealthy Long Island family. After nine years, she wishes to move to New York City and attend secretarial school. But the Austin children — the shaggy Tim (Beau Bridges) and the cute Gena (Lauri Peters) — want her to stay. They figure that Ivy needs a beau, "a good-looking no-goodnik" who will charm but not marry her. That man is Jack Parks (Poitier), who runs a trucking operation by day. By night, he operates a roving casino from the back of an eighteen-wheeler. Tim threatens to expose the scam unless Jack takes out Ivy.[8]

Predictably, Ivy and Jack fall for each other, despite Jack's professed self-image as a "piranha." Ivy spends the night, and for the first time in

Poitier's career, he romances a woman into bed. But the next day Ivy learns that Tim blackmailed Jack to set up their date. Jack must woo Ivy back with a long, romantic speech. He divests himself of the gambling business and drives away with Ivy, presumably to live happily ever after.

"Bourgeois to the bootheels." "A completely frivolous American sex comedy." "One more bon bon from Nevernever Land." Critics likened *For Love of Ivy* to the formulaic Hollywood comedies of the 1940s, comparing Poitier to Cary Grant and Lincoln to Doris Day. They also realized that frivolity was the point: Hollywood had never allowed this type of black romance. Simultaneously slick and stale, the film addressed race only through light quips. The *New Yorker* mourned its irrelevance, but it also wished "that the film could be shown free on every broiling street in America, because its benignity is genuine, and it brings the comforting illusion that this long, hot summer of infamous dread doesn't really exist."[9]

For Love of Ivy had strong points. Lincoln combined dignity with vulnerability, and her smile lit up the screen. Bridges and Peters exuded fresh-faced charm. Quincy Jones wrote another fun and funky score, and Poitier displayed his usual competence. But Poitier was a much better actor than writer. He shares blame with Aurthur for hatching the ridiculous premise behind the romance.[10]

Writing, however, allowed Poitier to inject himself into his character. Jack Parks is a West Indian with subtle traces of his old accent. Like Poitier, his front of cool reserve melts into smiling charm. If his alleged roguishness is indigestible, he still has his moments: mocking the teenagers by pretending his aspirin pills are drugs, mocking himself when explaining why he speaks Japanese at a restaurant ("Maybe it's because I'm pretentious"). Poitier even wore his own natty clothes on screen.[11]

Like Cary Grant, he was a mannered dreamboat. *For Love of Ivy* elaborated upon his "safe sexy" appeal, a unique fashion among Hollywood stars by 1968. Vietnam and black radicalism were exposing political cleavages, and so was the film industry. On the left were the alienated antiheroes of *The Graduate*, *Bonnie and Clyde*, and *Cool Hand Luke*. On the right loomed traditional heroes promoting vigilante justice, such as John Wayne or Clint Eastwood. Only Poitier stood in the middle. For white actors, nonthreatening masculinity was obsolete. But because Hollywood had historically restricted black sexuality, Americans accepted Poitier's old-fashioned charm.[12]

By contrast, the white people in *For Love of Ivy* are clumsy and self-indulgent. The script takes sundry pokes at the racial obsessions of white liberals. For instance, Mrs. Austin (Nan Martin) offers to send Ivy on vacation, "any place you want to go. Uh, Africa?" Later, when Ivy first meets Jack, Gena tries to stimulate conversation by asking about Black Power. Jack is too debonair to talk politics; his cool pride reigns over the white silliness.

Unfortunately, Daniel Mann's direction sapped the pungency from the better one-liners. He rendered the actors excessively mannered, and the picture moves slower than the light script demands. *For Love of Ivy* already faced the economic hurdle of presenting a black love story. Thanks to Mann, the romantic comedy had little comedy. It never neared the commercial success of *To Sir, with Love, In the Heat of the Night,* or *Guess Who's Coming to Dinner.*

For Love of Ivy nonetheless stimulated attention, because it featured Poitier as a romantic lead. Its audience comprised all ages and races, but predominantly women. Many appreciated the much-anticipated expression of Poitier's sexuality, though others judged it a botched exercise. At least, as one black reviewer wrote, "there is pleasure drawn just because the pitting of two Negroes against each other is for something more enjoyable than violence."[13]

Even though the picture was deliberately innocuous, Poitier's presence invested it with political meaning. A *New York Times* article spoofed the film's vapidity in a mock letter from "Beulah," a southern black visitor. In the same newspaper, a white correspondent argued that Poitier lent a distinctive black voice, even associating him with Black Power. Surprisingly, Maxine Hall Elliston (who called *Guess Who's Coming to Dinner* "warmed-over white shit") liked *For Love of Ivy.* In a reversal of Hollywood convention, the white characters are the comic window dressing.[14]

Moderate blacks seemed most pleased with *For Love of Ivy. Ebony* devoted its cover to the black romance. Roy Wilkins cheered that Poitier "might undermine the heavy thinkers in the Black Revolution," because he showed that blacks possessed universal tastes and aspirations. A correspondent to *Newsweek* praised that it showed that "we (blacks) are not all superlovers chasing white women; that we do dig our black women; that we are not all good guys sweating the black revolution. We are the same as you, no better, no worse — maybe just a little more soulful."[15]

Even V. S. Naipaul weighed in on *For Love of Ivy.* A cynic of both colonialism and Third World culture, the esteemed author grasped the international influence of Poitier's image. In his novel *Guerrillas,* a depiction of a failed Caribbean revolution, the most bloodthirsty character is Bryant, a tormented henchman for a populist leader. Floundering in personal and political confusion, he attends a Poitier double feature. "The second film was *For Love of Ivy*," writes Naipaul. "It was Bryant's favorite; it made him cry but it also made him laugh a lot, and it was his favorite. Soon he had surrendered to it, seeing in the Poitier of that film a version of himself that no one — really no one, and that was the terrible part — would ever get to know: the man who had died within the body Bryant carried, shown in that film in all his truth, the man Bryant knew to be himself, without the edginess and the anger and the pretend ugliness, the laughing man, the tender joker." Bryant never unearths this identity outside the theater, but his fleeting pleasure revealed the finest element of *For Love of Ivy*: Poitier is neither brute nor ninny, neither Uncle Tom nor neuter. He is a Cary Grant that blacks could call their own.[16]

Alas, as Renata Adler wrote, Poitier was trying to achieve the impossible, trying "to grab the consensus around the middle and . . . lug it, like some great cow, to a vanguard outpost." Poitier attracted the grievances of both racial conservatives and radicals. If he was the only black star, then his films were inherently political. That explained his ascent to superstardom, and now it portended his demise.[17]

❖

Poitier was no Pollyanna. He understood Hollywood economics and American politics, and he knew that his image would lose its resonance. In November 1967, at his career's apex, he signed a $750,000 deal with Universal Pictures to make *The Lost Man*, a remake of the 1947 thriller of Irish rebellion, *Odd Man Out*. Reversing his icon, Poitier explained, he would play "a *revolutionary*."[18]

Robert Alan Aurthur, author of *Carry Me Back to Morningside Heights* and *For Love of Ivy*, wrote the script and directed. Poitier helped make script and casting decisions. He and producers Edward Muhl and Melville Tucker bandied about names for a leading lady — she needed to be white, young, pretty, and sophisticated. After pursuing Joan Hackett, they turned to Joanna Shimkus.[19]

A slim twenty-four-year-old with alluring green eyes, Shimkus bore an attractive combination of innocence and sensuality. Thanks to a strict mother and convent school, she had a conservative upbringing in Montreal. But she became a prosperous model in Paris, where she caught the eye of Jean-Luc Godard, which led to roles in various French films. Aurthur, Muhl, and Tucker all wanted the *Vogue* cover girl for *The Lost Man*. Only Poitier dissented. For some mysterious reason, he was not impressed. She flew to Hollywood over his objection.[20]

Poitier soon reversed course. Shimkus possessed genuine self-confidence. Content to alternate between modeling in Paris and visiting London (home of her boyfriend, producer John Heyman), she serenely refused a screen test. Her nonchalance captivated Aurthur, who convinced the producers to hire her. Poitier was also beguiled — romantically. Shimkus was stopping over in New York, so upon his arrival home, Poitier sent her flowers and took her to dinner. He suggested another meeting soon, since he had upcoming business in Paris.[21]

That was a white lie. Poitier had no intention of going to France until Shimkus called him ten days later. But when she cracked ajar the door to romance, he flew to Paris. His fondness for Shimkus intensified. She could be both elegant and shy, poised and self-deprecating, mature and fun. They went to the Louvre, ate dinner on the Left Bank, and danced in trendy discotheques. He even talked his way through her apartment door. Then Shimkus applied the brakes. Poitier's trinity of fame, looks, and charm typically overwhelmed women, but the self-possessed model bade Poitier a polite farewell, and they did not see each other again until filming *The Lost Man* in October 1968.[22]

In the meantime, Poitier attacked Hollywood's institutional exclusion of blacks. Although the integration of craft guilds had begun, few black technicians gained substantial professional experience. Poitier personally approached each department at Universal Studios and requested that they assign black personnel to *The Lost Man*. Thanks to him, nearly 50 percent of the crew was black, including electricians, production assistants, makeup artists, publicists, grips, and still photographers. Poitier also participated in a Brooks Foundation program that taught inner-city youths about film technology and entrepreneurship.[23]

They filmed in the Philadelphia ghetto, around 12th and Diamond Streets, and infused needed cash into dilapidated neighborhoods. They donated to local charities, and they patronized black-owned restaurants, bars, laundries, and taxicabs. One participant estimated that during two months of location shooting, they spent one million dollars there. Locals also received work as extras. For over seven months, picketers at nearby Girard College had been protesting the school's refusal to admit black students. Universal hired them to play striking workers.[24]

The integrated set did not escape racial tension. Two days into filming, black crew members organized a get-acquainted meeting, and some whites became needlessly suspicious. A groggy Poitier — he had been napping — had to relate the whites' concerns. The blacks then explained their harmless intentions. Later, a white crew member angered his black colleagues by making a salacious pass at a young African American woman. Another time, two white editors left a nightclub after receiving threats from black patrons.[25]

Racial anxiety also influenced the picture's final cut. Universal executives nixed a scene depicting a race riot; they assigned a second unit crew to shoot a less gory sequence. Despite such compromises, *The Lost Man* appeared a landmark for black Hollywood. Much of the credit belonged to Poitier. His efforts had fostered black pride on the set, and the production had improved ghetto conditions. A black assistant director named Tom Hurt had once resented the movie star. During filming, however, Poitier won his respect. "He does his thing — quietly and well," said Hurt. "I dig him."[26]

For all the indignation Poitier had provoked among intellectuals and militants, he remained a folk hero to most blacks, including those in the inner city. He always approached the public with grace. "Sidney doesn't just teach you how to be a film actor," said actor Paul Winfield. "He teaches you how to be a star." Even after long, sweaty days on location — they sometimes wore flea collars around their wrists — Poitier shook hands, signed autographs, and bantered with the fans behind the ropes.[27]

This concern for humanity extended beyond public relations. In 1969 he helped establish a new foundation called AHAB. The organization was designed to help the poor, lessen neighborhood tensions, and foster civil rights in black communities. Poitier was president, and the board included James Baldwin, Harry Belafonte, Bill Cosby, Stanley Kramer, and Marlon Brando. Poitier donated space at his E&R Productions office on West 57th Street. The foundation never became an influential force, but it was further indication that the old civil rights celebrities, led by Poitier, sought solutions for the problems of the inner city.[28]

As the launch date of *The Lost Man* approached, Poitier's pronouncements stoked hopes that his picture would relate the frustrations of urban African Americans. He discussed ghetto life for a March 1969 ABC television special called *Three in Search of Survival*. He also condemned shortsighted responses to urban violence, and he explained Black Power an an assertion of ethnic identity. Furthermore, he claimed to now gear his movies to a younger generation that already accepted racial integration. Poitier seemed more relaxed and candid. "There was for a long time the awesome responsibility of trying to be all things to all people," he said. "It's not as terrifying any more."[29]

So Poitier abandoned his integrationist, middle-class hero. His character, Jason Higgs, broods from underneath dark glasses. He dismisses appeasement of whites. "Nonviolence is one thing," he says. "Passive dying is another." A former civil rights activist, Higgs now leads a crime organization based in the ghetto. He orchestrates an elaborate heist of a factory, aided by a nonviolent labor leader (Al Freeman Jr.) who stages a diversionary picket line. He steals $200,000 from the factory vault. Then the robbery goes awry: a security guard and a gang member die in a shootout, and Higgs is on the lam with a briefcase full of cash.

Higgs needs help from Cathy Ellis (Shimkus), an upper-class liberal who teaches remedial reading to underprivileged black children. Before the heist, she had fawned over Higgs ("Do you enjoy being a tall dark secret?"), but he dismissed her advances. Now she shelters him. During the manhunt, their romance flourishes. At the end, he confesses his ardor, and they kiss. Alas, love cannot save them. A gunshot wound weakens Higgs to near-death, and police surround the fugitive couple. Ellis, rather than allow capture, induces gunfire. They die in each other's arms.

Trade critics reviewed *The Lost Man* in May 1969, and although they recognized that Poitier might not sustain the prosperity of recent years, they did predict a solid success. Poitier garnered his strongest praise from *Variety*, which applauded his "moving into the tumult of the times interpreting a Malcolm X-type leader."[30]

But *The Lost Man* exhibits no grounding in black politics. Aurthur adopted an Irish story, and he preserved the saintly Poitier archetype. The plot presumes an alliance between the militant Higgs and the nonviolent labor leader, a twist that discounts the deep rifts in black politics by the late 1960s. Also, Poitier's so-called *"revolutionary"* advocates no political upheaval. Nor does he address such bedrock issues as the limits of liberalism or the importance of black culture. Instead, he belongs to "The Organization," a mythical Robin Hood–type gang that steals from wealthy whites to help poor families of jailed activists. His robberies fund milk, education, and medicine for children. In sum, he is a liberal white fantasy of a black revolutionary.[31]

Poitier could not have it both ways: he could not portray an angry militant and a sympathetic hero in the same movie. His gifts were charm and dignity, and Aurthur took advantage of neither. While scolding gang members or strutting through the ghetto, he appears utterly fatuous. When *The Lost Man* appeared in theaters in the summer of 1969, it was a critical and commercial fiasco.[32]

The cinematic turkey inspired new meditations on Poitier's career. "Sidney Poitier is *the* black hero in America," wrote Jacob Brackman. "This country has gotten more of its notions of the quality of Black

Experience from Poitier than from anybody else." His pictures bore serious responsibilities, and *The Lost Man* failed to uphold them. Vincent Canby added that Poitier's racial symbolism sacrificed creative expression. His films demanded social interpretation, not artistic comment. He worked with political liberals, not virtuoso directors. "Sidney Poitier does not make movies, he makes milestones." Now Poitier's eager-to-please instincts clashed with the emergent black militancy. His star dimmed.[33]

The Lost Man alienated many blacks. Unlike Poitier's previous pictures, which promoted integration, this film obfuscated Black Power. Even if most African Americans did not advocate violent rebellion, they appreciated messages of black pride, independence, and beauty. *The Lost Man* ignored those messages, because it came from a white perspective. In the *New York Times*, black intellectual Larry Neal criticized Poitier for not working with black writers and directors. "Brother Sidney," he wrote, "there is no sense in being a million-dollar shoe shine boy."[34]

The rebukes smarted. Once considered a pennant of black dignity, now Poitier was labeled a lickspittle. Too proud to change his virtuous image, too concerned with appeasing everyone, too ambitious to sacrifice mainstream appeal, Poitier ended up with a halfhearted muddle of a movie and a reputation on the brink of obsolescence.

He faced another confusion: he had fallen for Shimkus. During filming, they had long dinners together, ostensibly to discuss the script. They connected emotionally: she appreciated his depth and passion, he savored her unadorned refinement. But her relationship with John Heyman complicated their affair. When Heyman visited the set of *The Lost Man*, Shimkus constantly burst out in unexplained sobs. Heyman still proceeded with plans to divorce his wife. He and Shimkus also arranged a wedding date for Valentine's Day 1969.[35]

But when the production moved to California, the feelings between Poitier and Shimkus deepened. They spent almost every evening together at his rented home in Hollywood. Poitier understood her turmoil, having once lived it himself. At his suggestion, they separated to sort out their feelings. It was a disaster. Shimkus brought Heyman to California, and Poitier invited a casual girlfriend to keep him company, but neither star could shake their affection for each other. Poitier and Shimkus again found themselves in each other's arms, confused by love and loyalty.[36]

When filming ended in December 1968, Poitier returned to New York intent on expunging her from his memory. "I am now totally free, owned by no man or women," he told one reporter. Fearing another jumble of broken marriages and bruised feelings, he adopted a cynical stance toward love. He pulled out his address book and embarked upon a sexual binge. (He later likened himself to "a drunken sailor or a bee in the botanical gardens.") Unfulfilled, he left New York for Nassau. Shimkus called from London on Christmas Day. Surprising them both, Poitier invited Shimkus to the Caribbean.[37]

They met in Puerto Rico, where they watched a Sammy Davis Jr. show, and took a helicopter to an uninhabited island, where they swam, snorkeled, and strolled down empty beaches. They then toured Barbados, Saint Vincent, Grenada, and Antigua. The experience was sublime. Flying home, staring out the window, holding her hand, he knew that his life had changed.[38]

There were ramifications to an interracial relationship. The coupling of black men and white women had always been a sensitive issue in the black community, and even more so in the burgeoning "black is beautiful" atmosphere. Poitier himself had declared his preference for black women. He once told Harry Belafonte that he could never marry a white woman.[39]

Poitier did date white women, however. A Hollywood fan magazine even speculated that his tastes were changing from black to white women. One white woman, Julie Andrews, stirred controversy in January 1969. Andrews sued two publishers for libel after they romantically linked her with Poitier. The offending magazines printed a retraction, but Andrews emerged the true loser. The squeaky-clean movie star looked like a bigot for objecting to a romantic union with a black man, and her litigiousness was deemed unladylike. "If I were Sidney Poitier, I'd sue Julie Andrews," sniffed the Los Angeles Times.[40]

Poitier stayed above that fray. In any case, his romantic life was focusing on Shimkus. "For the first time in my life," he recalled, "I was with a woman whose presence seemed to calm the turbulence in me rather than challenge it to battle." Shimkus was also young and gorgeous, with trappings befitting a Paris fashion model, such as a fur bedspread. She satisfied Poitier's need for stability, once answered by Juanita, and his attraction to glamour, once embodied by Diahann Carroll.[41]

In Poitier, Shimkus found an intelligent and complex man, a man grounded in his past but appreciative of life's finer things. He accorded her a respect that he chauvinistically denied other women. After their Caribbean excursion, she canceled her engagement to John Heyman. Poitier joined her for one week in the south of France, where she filmed The Guest. In April she accompanied him to California, where he presented an Academy Award. She watched the ceremony from Bill Cosby's home, and the relationship remained somewhat private. Shimkus publicly insisted that they were "just very good friends."[42]

Indeed, through early 1969, Poitier continued to date other women. A rumor linked him with Abbey Lincoln, his co-star from *For Love of Ivy*. Photographers also caught him kissing the actress Gail Fisher outside a movie premiere. After the Oscars, however, Poitier's commitment took root. He took Shimkus to the Bahamas, and that summer they traveled to North Africa for a month. Then Poitier followed her to London, where she filmed *The Virgin and the Gypsy*. Meeting Shimkus had delivered him harmony. His friends noticed the difference. "I haven't seen him this happy in years," said one. "Sidney is a warm, affectionate man, but he does *not* fall in love easily." Now he smiled more and brooded less. He stopped seeing his psychiatrist, and he better understood his needs.[43]

Those needs included some protection from long-term commitment. "Don't push us toward the altar," he warned reporters. He believed that if he belonged in a marriage, he would have stayed with Juanita. The Diahann Carroll ordeal disillusioned him. So he and Shimkus fashioned a modern partnership unfettered by wedding rings and legal formalities. "As far as long-term, forever-and-ever relationships are concerned, I am a bad risk. I'm good for one to nine years—that's my limit." He seemed comfortable with that assessment.[44]

But self-awareness did not mean peace. He worried about the future at the expense of the present. His shoulder always ached, and he popped pills to ease the pain. During his Bahamian vacation, he revisited Cat Island for the first time, and the ruins of his old house conjured up old conflicts. He dealt with resentment of his new relationship, especially from his own family. And he struggled to maintain his career as black Hollywood underwent a revolution.[45]

❖

"Can Black and White Artists Still Work Together?" asked a *New York Times* headline. By the turn of the decade, black celebrities from the Age of Integration were scuffling to stay relevant. Despite the popularity of *Julia*, Diahann Carroll agonized that her sitcom said nothing of consequence about African American life. "*Of course I'm a sellout,*" she told one magazine. "What else would I be? I've sold my talents for a job I'm not particularly crazy about." Like Poitier, Carroll was alienating many blacks, youths, and intellectuals. "I'm a black woman with a white image," she explained. Distraught and emaciated, she opted out of her contract in 1970, and *Julia* went off the air after two seasons.[46]

To avoid similar dilemmas, Poitier sought creative control over his future projects. In June 1969, he founded First Artists Production Company with Paul Newman and Barbra Streisand. They agreed to produce and star in three films each. For each picture, they would forgo an upfront fee in exchange for a $150,000 salary and 10 percent of the gross. Their distributor, National General Corporation, would finance two-thirds of the cost, and First Artists would bankroll the rest. The budget was only three million dollars per picture, but the actors possessed artistic control.[47]

First Artists was an important component of Poitier's strategy to preserve his career into the next decade. He had already formed E&R Productions for his deal with Columbia. Now he created Verdon Cedric Productions (named after his sister and brother) for his First Artists projects. Agents no longer barraged him with scripts, and Columbia had just canceled his vehicle *I Am Somebody*. But the production deals won him some future autonomy.[48]

Poitier needed that leverage, because Hollywood now sought vehicles that reflected a disenchantment with the Poitier icon. Roles for black actors tripled between 1966 and 1969, with many spots for athletic, brash, virile young men. Studios cast a number of professional football players, including Jim Brown, Fred Williamson, O. J. Simpson, Rosie Grier, and Deacon Jones. Brown and Williamson, in particular, represented the black anger and sexuality so long repressed in the Poitier image.[49]

The old guard of black celebrities fell into disfavor. Poitier realized the changing tide, and he detected animosity toward his isolated success. During the filming of *Cotton Comes to Harlem* in 1969, Poitier consciously avoided the set — even though Ossie Davis directed, even though old friends were in the cast, even though the Harlem location represented a landmark in black film production.[50]

Soon afterward, Anthony Quinn wanted to cast Poitier, Harry Belafonte, and Sammy Davis Jr. in his police drama *Across 110th Street*. He planned to shoot on location in Harlem. But community activists objected to the integrationist heroes. They wanted actors who flaunted ghetto culture and rejected white authority. Quinn needed community support, so he cast Yaphet Kotto, Paul Benjamin, and Antonio Fargas instead. Poitier, especially, had gone from Hollywood hero to exile.[51]

In 1970 Poitier moved to the Bahamas. He brought only Shimkus and his housekeeper. At the time, he justified moving to "the most successful black country in the world" as an expression of Bahamian pride. Indeed, since the 1967 victory of the Progressive Labor Party, the government had enacted moderate social reforms, and the Bahamas had enjoyed some economic prosperity. Poitier also expressed a fondness for Bahamian simplicity and an exasperation with American cities.[52]

But he actually moved for personal reasons. "I didn't particularly relish criticism of my work then as 'too white,'" he later explained. "In fact, I hated it. I got a lot of bad vibes from my actor friends, too." So he retreated to a lush fortress. He built a mansion, a six-bedroom palace of white stone and gold trim, with fountains cascading down three floors into a swimming pool, grand staircases descending to a living room with a formidable stone fireplace, and a mammoth modern kitchen of light oak and chrome. Sliding glass doors opened onto sundecks with views of Nassau's harbor.[53]

The man who once craved the stimulation of Manhattan now chose solitude in paradise. He read books and the Sunday *New York Times*, and he fished off a small boat. When Sammy Davis Jr. bought an adjoining property, Poitier fretted. He loved his friend, but he wanted to escape Davis's fast-paced world.[54]

While carpenters added final touches to his majestic sanctuary in late 1969, Poitier reprised his character from *In the Heat of the Night*. Borrowing a famous line from the original, the sequel was titled *They Call Me Mister Tibbs!* Publicity agents touted Virgil Tibbs as a "Black James Bond," a recurring hero in a series of pictures. The idea had some merit: if any Poitier character fit the task, it was his ice-cool supercop. Moreover, given Poitier's fleeting box-office stature, a sequel seemed a safe bet for commercial success.[55]

On the set, Poitier banished the press. Both in Los Angeles and San Francisco, he refused to even chat informally with reporters. Interviews with his co-stars had to occur at restaurants during lunch. His ground rules reflected the pain inflicted by controversies over his image. Instinctively gracious and gregarious, Poitier had become so sensitive to criticism that he retreated from the public eye.[56]

United Artists released the picture the following summer. It bore few similarities to *In the Heat of the Night*. Without explanation, Virgil Tibbs moved from Philadelphia to San Francisco, married and fathered two children, and spent twelve years in his department — all without aging. The sequel also expunged the tense racial drama of the original. *They Call Me Mister Tibbs!* is a traditional murder mystery, overlaid by references to urban discontent and middle-class black life.

Tibbs is still a sleuth par excellence, but with new dilemmas. His friend

Reverend Logan Sharpe (Martin Landau) leads a movement for community control over schools. Days before an important referendum, Tibbs must investigate Sharpe for the murder of a young prostitute. The detective again displays a panoply of skills. He interrogates suspects with cool aplomb, and he analyzes carpet lint and fingernails with expert assurance. He judo-chops attackers, and he sprints through city streets to subdue evildoers. He clears a range of suspects: a lascivious realtor (Ed Asner), a pathetic janitor (Juano Hernandez), and a pimp/slumlord/drug dealer (Anthony Zerbe).

The night before the vote, Tibbs deduces that Sharpe murdered the prostitute. The minister's arrest will inflame the city's class and racial tensions over community control, and Sharpe begs the detective to delay the arrest. Tibbs cannot. Exposing his dilemma—and alluding to the larger forces shaping Poitier's career—he responds, "I'm through playing God." The film ends tragically, as Sharpe throws himself before an on-rushing truck, avoiding negative publicity and preserving his political cause.[57]

Slices of Tibbs's home life are interspersed within the detective drama. Tibbs flirts with his wife (Barbara McNair) and teaches his daughter (Wanda Spell) to stand on her head. To his son (George Spell), he suggests opportunities for blacks in the age of affirmative action: "Do you know that any school you want, you can have it? The best there is. They're looking for you." He implores his underachieving tyke to watch less television and clean his room. Upon catching him smoking, Tibbs forces him to drink brandy and vomit. Yet Tibbs also realizes that his adamant discipline alienates his son. "You're not perfect, are you?" he asks the boy. "And I can't forgive you." The moment is poignant.

Unfortunately, his domestic life bears no relevance to the murder investigation. Nor does the script thread the city's political tensions into the main narrative. Even the action scenes are standard ingredients in a predictable recipe. *They Call Me Mister Tibbs!* resembles a television movie: each scene creates and resolves its own conflict, with no consideration of the larger story. The formula appealed to short attention spans, but it also guaranteed the picture's dramatic failure.[58]

Poitier seemed bored. Without an arrogant foil like the southern sheriff, his hero operates in a vacuum. Although some critics cheered that his race could now be ignored, the lack of resistance to Tibbs's prideful intelligence defuses the drama. And because the scenes of his home life float in isolation, Detective Tibbs remains a one-dimensional character, another sample of the timeworn Poitier image.[59]

"Is Sidney Poitier obsolete?" asked Vincent Canby. The *New York Times* critic had already lamented that Poitier sought political landmarks rather than good movies. Now, those "milestones" were "millstones," pictures that shackled his talents by perpetuating his iconography. "The terrible thing about being a point of view and a social symbol is that time, even before age, may suddenly overtake you," he wrote. The political imperative to convey black goodness had dissolved. If he kept playing one-dimensional characters in ordinary police dramas, Canby believed, Poitier denied African Americans their cultural identity.[60]

But Poitier's image still held some residual resonance. His character struck a balance: he expresses black pride without frightening whites, sympathizes with urban activists while following his principles, and confronts the issues of typical bourgeois existence. *They Call Me Mister Tibbs!* did not replicate the success of its predecessor, but the conventional hero presided over enough car chases, crime labs, and domestic quandaries to ensure a decent box-office return.

So the next year, Poitier resuscitated Virgil Tibbs for *The Organization*. During filming in the spring of 1971, producer Walter Mirisch hoped that a fourth Tibbs movie would follow. Poitier was less sanguine. Ennui was setting in. "It's the same guy," he said, "doing the same thing."[61]

Indeed it was. Tibbs retains his smooth cool in *The Organization*. For this installment, which Mirisch hustled into theaters that October, Tibbs investigates the murder of a furniture factory executive. A young, hip, interracial band secretly approach him. They have stolen a suitcase of heroin from the factory, which is a front for an international drug syndicate known as "The Organization." The outlaws sabotage corporate villains, but they deny the murder and offer to help Tibbs in exchange for immunity.

Tibbs now walks a fine ethical line: "You want me to play it cool with the department, where teamwork and discipline is everything. One slip and I've had it!" But he covertly allies with the vigilantes, even as he questions suspects through official channels. His superiors learn about his actions and suspend him. Still, Tibbs stays on the case. After a climactic shootout, Tibbs deduces that a night watchman's wife is the principal drug runner, and he compels her to identify the murderers from the crime syndicate. The film ends on an ambiguous note, when a sniper kills the murderers. Justice is served, but "The Organization" lives.

The idealistic anti-drug band, the mysterious "Organization," and the complicated plot twists stretch credibility. This picture, too, had the prosaic look and structure of a television movie. But it improves upon *They*

Call Me Mister Tibbs! The script has more unity, the domestic scenes are assigned some relevance, and the action sequences in San Francisco's bays, city squares, and subways are unquestionably entertaining. The picture also eliminates the first sequel's excursions into political commentary. *The Organization* is a standard action movie, comfortable in its own skin. Had Poitier continued playing Virgil Tibbs, this picture could have been a launching pad for future efforts.[62]

But *The Organization* was the final installment in the Virgil Tibbs series. Audiences soon embraced black film heroes far removed from the clean-cut, middle-class detective. Poitier had tired of Tibbs as well. Seeking a larger canvas, he became a movie producer.

❖

Between *They Call Me Mister Tibbs!* and *The Organization*, Poitier made *Brother John*, his first picture for E&R Productions. The project was personal. He hatched the idea, he recalled, after a quiet evening "fueling my imagination with collected fragments from my checkerboard life." His Columbia deal allowed him to put the vision on screen. As executive producer, he collaborated with screenwriter Ernest Kinoy in the spring of 1969. He and Joel Glickman planned location filming for northern California the following April.[63]

Poitier again integrated the crew. About one-third of the personnel was African American and Hispanic. A Ford Foundation grant funded an additional five interns. Some craft unions initially balked at the favoritism toward ethnic minorities, citing traditions of seniority, but no problems arose on the set. The multiracial crew harmoniously completed filming in eight weeks, exactly on schedule. The only roadblock before its March 1971 release was the title. Originally called *Kane*, the picture was renamed after objections from the copyright holders of *Citizen Kane*.[64]

Unfortunately, *Brother John* bore no other likeness to the classic, nor to any other well-made or entertaining movie. The picture is a disaster of Promethean proportions. Poitier plays John Kane, a stoic visitor to his Alabama hometown. His enigmatic presence disconcerts the town. The sheriff (Roman Bieri) suspects that he is an labor agitator. The district attorney (Bradford Dillman) hopes that he is a "foreign agent" whose capture might propel him to the governorship. The schoolteacher (Beverly Todd) falls in love with him.

Only Doc Thomas (Will Geer) fathoms the truth: John Kane is an angel of judgment, a man of infinite wisdom and power, a keeper of mysterious journals filled with blank pages, an owner of a passport stamped in London, Krakow, New Delhi, Havana, Saigon, Peking, Dar es Salaam, Nairobi, and elsewhere. This imperious hero speaks eight languages and dispatches rednecks with effortless karate chops. He remains impassive and tight-lipped. "I've seen death and starvation and cruelty," he says, and he believes that evil has vanquished good.

Director James Goldstone shot Poitier in reverential close-ups, bathing light behind the dark angel. His metaphysical aura makes the authorities' fears seem petty. They imprison him, suspecting that he may inflame the labor conflict at an industrial plant. In the end, Doc Thomas frees him, and Kane presumably continues traveling the earth to judge sinners.

The heavy-handed direction, clichéd cinematography, and preachy script earned well-deserved knocks. "What did they think they were making here?" asked Richard Schickel. After beginning with a realistic labor dispute, the picture ends with vague references to Armageddon. Worst of all was Poitier's stiff, humorless, pretentious performance. Critics seemed perplexed that following so much public dissatisfaction with his image, Poitier would play a Christ figure.[65]

"The apotheosis of Sidney Poitier is now complete," proclaimed Vincent Canby. For all its surface dabbling in issues of race, greed, and love, *Brother John* exerts meaningful effort only in painting Poitier as a supernatural superhero. Moreover, because Poitier put forth the concept, produced the movie, and considered the project a personal mission, he bore complete responsibility for this monument to bloated ego. "Time has run out," Canby wrote. "It's too late to believe that he's still a passive participant in his own, premature deification."[66]

Poitier's mystical angel seemed especially contrived next to the most popular black pictures of 1971: *Sweet Sweetback's Baadassssss Song* and *Shaft*. Melvin Van Peebles's Sweetback and Richard Roundtree's Shaft embodied Hollywood's new black icon, a conscious reversal of the Sidney Poitier stereotype. These outlaw heroes dressed in urban styles, spoke in black slang, and shunned white authority. Moreover, they exercised the tools denied Poitier: violence and sexuality. They lashed out against criminals who harmed black neighborhoods, and they casually discarded their female conquests, both black and white.[67]

Each picture grossed over eleven million dollars. Blacks composed the chief audience, filling the downtown movie palaces vacated by the white middle class. The fresh icons appealed specifically to urban African Americans. Gordon Parks, director of *Shaft*, explained his picture's success: "A new hero, black as coal, deadlier than Bogart and handsome as Gable, was doing the thing that everyone in the audience wanted to see done for so long. A black man was winning." The new leading men did not seek racial harmony. They acted out revenge fantasies.[68]

Lerone Bennett recognized the import for the Poitier icon: "We can never again see black people in films (noble, suffering, losing) in the same way." Particularly for young blacks — unweathered by Montgomery or Birmingham, resentful of ghetto poverty, eager for cultural expressions of black style — Sweetback and Shaft offered an emotional satisfaction that Poitier's doctors, teachers, policemen, and angels could never approach.[69]

Their success spawned a boom in black movies, starting with the next year's *Superfly*. Hollywood had been in crisis since the late 1960s, with five of every six pictures losing money. The so-called "blaxploitation" movies could stop some bleeding, since they had low budgets and built-in audiences. For the first time, studios designed pictures specifically for blacks. In September 1972 *Variety* reported plans for over fifty black films. Soon came *Blacula, Black Jack, Black Eye, Black Caesar, Black Jesus, Black Rodeo, Black Samson,* and *Black Belt Jones.* For Hollywood, black had become beautiful, or at least profitable.[70]

Poitier absorbed the blaxploitation craze from the Bahamas, enduring Saturday nights in Nassau theaters, listening to cheering audiences as Ron O'Neal, Jim Brown, or Fred Williamson struck another blow against Whitey. Poitier started attending drive-ins, where he could analyze the pictures in relative peace. He was cynical. Blacks still occupied few positions of institutional authority, and he predicted that the cycle would soon run its course. Bitterness laced his assessment. Bemoaning the current climate in both Hollywood and society at large, he protested that "to be accepted you have to be appropriately hostile and obviously militant and sufficiently anti-white."[71]

Personal torments exacerbated this professional pain. Poitier's relationship with his oldest daughter, Beverly, had been strained; the intelligent, bookish teenager resented that Poitier assumed parental prerogatives while abandoning his marriage. Her father was too rooted in his patriarchy to find a middle ground, and they grew estranged. In September 1970, at the age of eighteen, Beverly married a young Ghanian engineer. Poitier disapproved of marriage at such a young age, and he refused to attend the ceremony in Pleasantville. Even before the wedding and her subsequent move to Ghana, they stopped speaking to each other.[72]

The estrangement distressed Poitier, but it did not sour him on fatherhood. In early 1972 he had his first child with Shimkus — another daughter, named Anika. Poitier avoided any public announcement of the birth. When a reporter spotted Shimkus holding a newborn in a London airport, Poitier just smiled and joked and avoided personal details. Poitier and Shimkus mostly flew below the media's radar screen. Burned by the high-profile Diahann Carroll affair, resentful of recent criticism, and wary of public disapproval of his interracial relationship, Poitier retreated to his Bahamian cocoon.[73]

He did not disappear from American shores, however. Besides filming his own vehicles, Poitier narrated a 1970 documentary called *King: A Filmed Record . . . Montgomery to Memphis.* Along with Harry Belafonte, Ruby Dee, Paul Newman, Burt Lancaster, and Charlton Heston, Poitier read sermons and speeches by King, bridging gaps between newsreel footage. The project—there was both a 150-minute version and a longer cut for educational purposes—raised money for various civil rights organizations. Poitier also sat on a board that lobbied for a King memorial, and he was a trustee at the Martin Luther King Jr. Center for Social Change.[74]

In fact, for a man who lived abroad, Poitier remained exceptionally active in American public life. He joined the board of trustees at Virginia Union, a college of mostly black students; helped found the Black Academy of Arts and Letters, an organization that recognized contributions to black culture; sat on an American Civil Liberties Union advisory board; won another election as vice-chairman of the American Film Institute; and supported Reverend Jesse Jackson's Operation Breadbasket, a program designed to alleviate black poverty.[75]

Even at his nadir, Poitier never lost his position among black America's elite, a status evinced by his attendance at Muhammad Ali's comeback bout against Jerry Quarry. That night in October 1970, recalled Julian Bond, was a "coronation . . . the King regaining his throne." Banned from the ring since 1967 for refusing induction into the Army, Ali augured the emergence of the forthright, sexually charged black culture hero of the 1970s. But even the liberal old guard embraced the controversial boxer; almost all blacks resented his exile, which reflected the double standard imposed upon black public figures. Bill Cosby, Coretta Scott King, Jesse Jackson, Ralph Abernathy, the Supremes, and the Temptations were at the Atlanta arena.[76]

Minutes before the fight, Poitier entered Ali's dressing room. They embraced. Ali, unfazed by the imminent clash, admired Poitier's trim physique and elegant gray suit. "Hey, give me a rhyme to psych Quarry—when we're giving the referee instructions," said Ali. He held an imaginary microphone to the actor's face. "You met your match, chump," phrased Poitier softly and carefully. "Tonight you're falling in. . . ." Stuck, he cast out an arm, searching for a rhyme. "You're falling in *two*." Ali teased him to stick to acting, went out to beat Quarry, and soon began his second reign atop the heavyweight division. But their playful exchange had symbolized something deeper. Poitier was an elder, far removed from the black cultural frontier.[77]

As afros and dashikis replaced neat trims and three-piece suits at the forefront of black fashion, liberal high society indulged in what Tom Wolfe called "Radical Chic." Park Avenue socialites entertained Black Panthers at their cocktail parties, and limousine liberals contributed money to overthrow their own society. The Leonard Bernsteins, Otto Premingers, and Sidney Lumets of the world—the artistic liberals who once admired men like Poitier—now alleviated their racial guilt in such surreal displays. Gritty ghetto styles and African-inspired fashions were exotic and sexy, and Poitier was not.[78]

"Don't compare me with Sidney!" proclaimed Fred Williamson. "His movies don't make money anymore." Poitier's image had challenged convention in the 1950s, exemplified the liberal consensus in the early 1960s, and alleviated anxiety in the late 1960s. Suddenly, he seemed a relic. A full-page color cartoon in *Players* magazine illustrated this new and popular perception of Poitier. In the cartoon, a black executive from "Uhuru Films" advised a cocky young actor. "I have great faith in you, Otis," he said. "I think you could be the black Sidney Poitier."[79]

❖

Publicly confronting his detractors was never Poitier's style. In interviews, he mused on broad philosophical issues. Within his statements—decrying the "social cannibalism" of modern American life, indicting technology for deteriorating human relationships—lurked a deeper frustration that the media had sensationalized his plunge in popularity. He lamented that reporters never probed his complexities, never asked his opinions on classical music, Vietnam, the environment, or international economics. "The total man I am is almost never explored," he complained.[80]

When discussing his films' politics, Poitier stayed devoted to his principles. "I have no interest in putting 'whitey' down," he said. He would keep playing doctors, lawyers, and teachers while entertaining both blacks and whites. The new black heroes freed him to pursue that vision. "I used to think that my success as an actor was essential to the success of all other black actors who followed me, or maybe even all black people," he admitted to *Ebony*. "But I'm not going to be put in that bag anymore. That goes for the black actor, the black politician, that goes for anybody who thinks

I'm the carrier of his dreams. Screw him. Let him carry his own dreams." This declaration, intended for a black magazine, was as resentful as Poitier allowed himself in public.[81]

Only in a private interview with Ruby Dee did Poitier ever reveal his complete indignation. The session, recorded not for publication but for historical posterity, took place in January 1970. Alone with a good friend, Poitier let down his guard. He excoriated those who accused him of ignoring fellow blacks in the film industry, and he chafed at those who expected him to solve Hollywood's racial problems himself. "What kind of shit is this," he griped, "waiting for Sidney Poitier to lead the way out of the fucking wilderness?"

Instead, "let them review the twenty-two years of scuffling and trying and developing and learning and going without food in this goddamn town to learn this craft, sleeping on rooftops and parks in this city — trying to learn this business — trying to learn how to be an actor — trying to develop skills." If others shared his work ethic, he maintained, blacks could progress. Gone was the humble charm, the pensive air, the generosity toward the changes in black Hollywood. Instead there was bitter pride. "Listen," he said, "the self-improvement of Sidney Poitier should be a goddamn lesson to a lot of people today."[82]

Poitier had met with those advocating a "revolutionary film scene," but those people ignored the economic dynamics of the industry. No studio executives cared about radical black thought, and without Hollywood's financing and distribution, no black filmmaker could survive for the long term. So Poitier worked within the system: investing in independent black films, securing grants through the American Film Institute, and employing black writers, technicians, and administrators. Yet black critics Clifford Mason and Larry Neal targeted him. "These guys must be willing to accept the fact that it's an accomplishment to be successful in Charlie's world," he said.

He admitted that the critical bashing bruised him. He once believed that he could work with the rising generation, but no longer. "I have come to the point where I don't give a shit what they're talking about." Now he made films that satisfied him. He planned them with trusted associates, not political committees. And he would appeal to interracial audiences, because survival depended on profit. "Pay the goddamn $2.50 and go see it," he advised. "If they don't want to see it — don't go to the theater."

For all his indictment of black detractors, however, Poitier never forgot the larger problem: the "hostile community" of Hollywood. The film industry remained conservative. White society, moreover, was unwilling to accept three-dimensional black characters. "They are accustomed to seeing us within the framework of the have-nots who preceded us," he said. "We stir their indignation, we stir their sense of being put out, their sense of order." If black culture on the silver screen still discomfited whites, then the only solution was more blacks on both sides of the cameras. For that task, Black America needed Sidney Poitier. Because for all the diminishing appeal, for all the critical sniping, and for all the lame efforts from *The Lost Man* to *Brother John*, Poitier remained the most powerful black man in Hollywood.[83]

CHAPTER 16

SURVIVORS

(1972–1978)

When Poitier fell from Hollywood's heights, he responded with a retreat to the Bahamas and a string of mediocre movies. Now he climbed back. That journey began when blaxploitation still reigned, when his future was still uncertain, and when he and his best friend still refused to acknowledge each other's existence.

Since their spat before Martin Luther King's funeral in April 1968, Poitier and Harry Belafonte had completely avoided contact. Mutual friends had to avoid inviting them to the same functions. In time, their animosity drained away. "But we were two proud West Indians," explained Poitier, and "stubborn pride is a quality West Indians tend to husband beyond any reasonable usefulness." For over two years, neither offered the peace pipe.[1]

Then, late in 1970, Belafonte called Poitier. He opened with a joke, and they chatted, never acknowledging their squabble. Belafonte revealed his purpose: Drake Walker, an intern on his 1970 film *The Angel Levine*, had written a script about blacks in the Old West. Over a decade earlier, Belafonte and Poitier had planned a similar project, but in 1959 a black-themed picture was a rarity. Now Hollywood recognized the black audience. Moreover, Poitier had a production contract. Poitier agreed to make the picture, called *Buck and the Preacher*.[2]

The erstwhile rivals staged demonstrations of tact. Poitier insisted that Belafonte co-star and co-produce; Belafonte modestly declined equal billing. At a dinner meeting, they traded compliments, with Poitier raving about Belafonte's popularity. "Yeah, Sidney, I guess you're just applesauce," cracked Belafonte. They laughed at their own diplomacy and planned the picture. Under Poitier's existing contract, Columbia Pictures distributed the joint effort between E&R Productions and Belafonte Enterprises. The two executive producers hired Poitier's team from *Brother John*: Joel Glickman produced, and Ernest Kinoy fleshed out Walker's script. Joseph Sargent directed. To cut costs, they filmed in Durango, Mexico.[3]

Upon arrival in February 1971, problems besieged the production. When Glickman hired whole families from El Paso, Texas, as extras for a black wagon train, both the Screen Extras Guild in the United States and the Actors Guild in Mexico complained. The Mexican actors also protested low pay, despite receiving scale wages (a French company had recently paid them more). Later, Poitier and some reporters faced disaster when a bus barreled toward their car halfway into a wide curve. When the bus passed them — by inches — it was up on two wheels.[4]

The greatest upheaval occurred when Poitier replaced Sargent as director. Poitier and Belafonte had envisioned a certain style, one invested with respect for the black heroes of the American West. After three days viewing the rushes, they believed that Sargent lacked that vision. According to co-star Cameron Mitchell, "he was shooting the picture like a TV show," a treatment unbefitting a historical epic. Belafonte insisted that Poitier direct, contending that if Columbia had to send a replacement, the production would be delayed and possibly canceled. Poitier concurred. They fired Sargent. The deposed director handled the situation with grace, shrugging it off as a case of artistic differences.[5]

Belafonte was more forthright: "If the nature of the subject wasn't such that it was working and dealing as deeply with the black psyche, it might not matter." But the artistic differences had racial consequences, and Poitier and Belafonte refused another white interpretation of a black experience. Now, however, a first-time director faced a rapid shooting schedule, a cast with hundreds of extras, and a hodgepodge crew that spoke little English — in the middle of the Mexican desert.[6]

Poitier had long aspired to direct, and he had trained himself in lens sizes and camera angles. He had directed a few scenes of *They Call Me Mister Tibbs!*, but that brief exercise was scant preparation. Poitier primed his first scene, a long outdoor shot of him and Belafonte riding into a band of Indians; it involved many actors, a wide expanse, and an intricate choreography. After a few takes, Poitier's anxiety dissipated. The scene worked.[7]

Poitier and Belafonte still needed approval from Columbia. They told a studio executive that Poitier would keep on until a new director arrived. But no director wanted to replace Poitier halfway through a pet project, especially as rumors circulated through Hollywood that Poitier had engineered Sargent's dismissal. Instead, two studio representatives flew to Durango to supervise the production. "When that happened," said Belafonte, detecting some racist paternalism, "we started to know the real meaning of slavery." Columbia had two choices: let Poitier continue directing, or shut down the picture. Poitier had shot a week of film by then. The executives gave him the green light.[8]

Poitier enjoyed directing. He liked the control. Planning camera angles perched from a crane, pacing around with his East African walking stick, he reigned over the set. The cast and crew respected his guidance, and he delighted when a scene clicked. He also appreciated the company of friends. Julie Belafonte played an Indian woman, Ruby Dee played Poitier's wife, and Ossie Davis visited. "It felt a little like old times," recalled Dee. But in old times, the only other blacks were cafeteria workers and shoeshine boys. Now blacks controlled the production.[9]

The producers maintained their sibling-style jealousies. Belafonte reportedly chafed that Poitier left his birthday party while he sang with the mariachi band. Poitier allegedly fumed that Belafonte arrived late for the daily rushes. But after an article in *Look* detailed their animosities, the stars refuted the charges on television. Indeed, their fits of pique revealed nothing more than their historic rivalry and thin skins.[10]

Belafonte had long chafed as Poitier scooped up plum roles, even as he disagreed with Poitier's career choices. But now, Belafonte raged that everyone scrutinized Poitier's failures while ignoring those of white stars. "I refuse to be part of the parade of pain that is heaped upon him," said Belafonte. "An awful lot is expected of that man, and for no reason except that he is black." Of course, when Belafonte learned that he, and not Poitier, had made a list of celebrities with "studly appeal," he yelped, "Hot damn! Wait till I send him a copy. He can't even say it's racial discrimination!"[11]

They finished *Buck and the Preacher* in forty-five days, after working six-day work weeks through broiling Mexican days, cold desert nights, sticky red dust, a common cold epidemic, and dwindling morale. Poitier worked seventeen-hour days and barely slept. In April 1971, Poitier went straight to San Francisco to film *The Organization*. At night he edited *Buck and the Preacher*. Completing both pictures exhausted him. He sustained himself with a diet of milk and protein, a self-imposed ban on tobacco and alcohol, and a daily intake of thirty-six vitamins. With discipline, political conscience, and a dose of ambition, Poitier directed his first film.[12]

❖

Buck and the Preacher takes place on the heels of the Civil War, as freed slaves journey west to escape their former slaveowners. It chronicles an important chapter in the African American story: these "Exodusters" defined their own freedom by rejecting the South's enduring racial codes, enforced by white violence. The film opens with a scroll dedicating the picture to "those men, women, and children who lie in graves as unmarked as their place in history."[13]

But *Buck and the Preacher* is no in-depth social history. It recreates the familiar pattern of Hollywood heroes, except now the heroes are black. Poitier plays Buck, a noble guide for the wagon trains. He eludes bounty hunters, and he negotiates with Indians for safe passage. Belafonte plays the Preacher, a roguish minister with a six-shooter hidden in his Bible. He wavers between self-interest and social conscience. Predictably, Buck and the Preacher begin as rivals and end as allies.[14]

Deshay (Mitchell) leads an evil white posse that raids wagon trains and pursues Buck, the linchpin for the black migration. At first, the Preacher seems willing to report Buck's whereabouts for a $500 reward, but they soon become uneasy partners in shootouts, chases on horseback, and daring bank robberies. They kill most of the posse and steal back money for impoverished migrants.

The picture tweaks traditional Westerns not only by painting whites as outright villains, but also by presenting a black/Indian alliance. Indians aid the blacks' escape from the posse. Their chief adds his own pained account of white imperialism. Together, the black heroes and Indian guides save the wagon train from a final ambush. To many, Indians already embodied nobility; a recent intellectual fad romanticized the American Indian's tragic plight. *Buck and the Preacher* expanded upon that myth by linking minority cultures and portraying them as ethically superior to violent, exploitative white society.[15]

Most whites never before realized that blacks settled the West, allied with Indians, and admired their own cowboys. "I was watching western heroes with whom I could identify completely for the first time," wrote Maurice Peterson in *Essence*. "Judging from the howling cheers, thunderous applause, and even the tears that were in some eyes, I know that the rest of the Black audience felt as gratified as I did." The picture delivered a lesson in black history, and it forged black pride.[16]

Yet in terms of plot and character, *Buck and the Preacher* resembles bygone B-movies. "They ain't made Westerns like this for nigh onto thirty year," ridiculed Judith Crist. The characters lack complexity: Buck is extraordinarily virtuous, Deshay impossibly evil, the Indians stereotypically noble. The wagon train, the bank robbery, and the shoot-'em-ups fulfill Western clichés. Besides its racial reversal of heroes and villains, it is thoroughly conventional.[17]

The adherence to Hollywood formula included pairing two male stars as the lead characters — a strategy that, in an era of burgeoning feminism, earned Poitier and Belafonte some accusations of chauvinism. Ruby Dee does have one affecting scene where she pleads to leave for Canada. "It's like a poison soaked into the ground," she says. "They're gonna give us nothing. Not no forty acres, and no mule. And not freedom, neither." But this plot point never develops. Dee stays a background figure, a role unworthy of her prowess. The plot, as the title implies, centers on Buck and the Preacher.[18]

As Poitier's directorial debut, *Buck and the Preacher* was a mixed bag. The story provided excitement, the visuals of the landscape were impressive, and Belafonte won laughs. But Poitier employed an overabundance of close-ups, and he allowed his actors long, unnecessary pauses. The action sequences demanded tighter editing. Worst of all, Poitier the director restrained Poitier the actor. His stoic, upright hero is dull. Poitier later admitted that Sargent would have directed a more entertaining film. But he and Belafonte wanted "a certain substance, a certain nourishment, a certain component of self. We wanted black people to see the film and be proud of themselves, be proud of their history." Whatever its other limitations, *Buck and the Preacher* accomplished that goal.[19]

Alas, with the blaxploitation craze still at its apex, their picture failed to capture the fancy of the black masses. Although *Buck and the Preacher* was the best of the recent "soul westerns" — *The Legend of Nigger Charley, Soul Soldier, Cool Breeze* — it lacked the slick production values of Hollywood blockbusters. The film grossed about six million dollars, three times its production cost. After printing, advertising, and distribution expenses, it roughly broke even.[20]

Poitier and Belafonte did use *Buck and the Preacher* for political ends. They donated receipts from an April 1972 premiere in Newark to the New Jersey delegation of the National Black Political Convention, an event climaxed by Jesse Jackson's rousing call for black unity against white politics. Later, Poitier and Belafonte narrated William Greaves's documentary about the convention, called *Nationtime: Gary*. Despite the celebrities, however, television networks refused to air the film. The public accepted ghetto hustlers on their movie screens, but it remained unnerved by genuine black frustration with the American political system.[21]

Since neither *Brother John* nor *Buck and the Preacher* turned a profit,

Columbia did not renew Poitier's production contract. He could still, however, make pictures through the First Artists Corporation. He merged E&R Productions into Verdon Cedric Productions, and he hired Melville Tucker to produce his First Artists ventures. Tucker had produced *The Lost Man*, and despite Tucker's conservative politics, they had become good friends. In 1971 First Artists offered 25 percent of its shares to the public, creating enough capital for the stars to launch their initial projects. Poitier and Tucker bought Lawrence Roman's black love story, *A Warm December*.[22]

Poitier wavered at again donning the three hats of actor, director, and producer, but ambition trumped exhaustion. While Tucker handled the business end, Poitier searched for a female lead in New York, Los Angeles, Paris, and London. "I looked and looked and looked," he said. "And I looked and looked and looked and looked and looked and looked." He found a relative unknown: Esther Anderson, a tall, slim, gorgeous actress, born in Jamaica and trained in England.[23]

They filmed in London, where Poitier had bought a home. Through the summer of 1972, Poitier worked another arduous schedule, averaging eighty-hour weeks as he attended to company business, instructed the actors, learned his own role, consulted with the film editor, and supervised the costumes. He hired four designers to craft Anderson a sexy, elegant look. They shot all over London, from Trafalgar Square to Bond Street to Hyde Park to the British Museum. Poitier also refined his directing style; although extremely specific with instructions, he never shouted at his cast. Instead he arranged quiet, individual huddles. "I understand an actor's psyche," he explained. For the word "psyche," he might have substituted "ego."[24]

A Warm December, as Poitier himself described, is "an old-fashioned love story," with the twist of black protagonists. The story showcases two appealing personalities. Poitier's Matt Younger is a widower, a doctor devoted to serving the Washington, D.C., ghetto, a single father, a motocross racer, and a man of impeccable taste and copious charm. On holiday in London, he meets the stunning Catherine (Anderson), the niece of an ambassador from the fictional African country Torunda. Mystery surrounds her. Ominous men stalk her, and she periodically disappears. Younger is enchanted.[25]

In the first half, their romance blossoms. Sprinkled in are travelogue-style explorations of London's tourist attractions. In the second half, Catherine reveals that she has sickle cell anemia. Her "stalkers" are bodyguards from the Torundan embassy, and she "disappears" to receive shots. Younger proposes marriage, and although Catherine loves both him and his daughter, she cannot let them endure another death. She leaves him with a Swahili phrase — translated, it means "Goodbye, my husband, thank you for a warm December."

Upon release in April 1973, critics called the film "a black *Love Story*," alluding to the schlock-packed 1970 tearjerker. They meant no compliment. *A Warm December* was "a cornball soap opera," "a series of brilliantly edited 30-second cigarette commercials," and "some impossibly typical, transcendentally awful issue of *Reader's Digest*." Reviewers faulted the contrived plot, the overdone shots of London, and the one-dimensional characters. The discussions of black consciousness and sickle cell anemia seem out of place, part of a slick composite of stale conventions.[26]

A Warm December flopped. Poitier deserved the blame: he bought the script, guided the actors, starred in the story, and approved the final cut. But Poitier also won kudos, because he continued to achieve milestones. He contributed to public awareness of sickle-cell anemia, and he depicted an old-fashioned romance with black protagonists. Poitier and Anderson were genuine sex symbols. Both were graceful, charismatic, and virile, yet neither trafficked in the myths of exotic black carnality that endured in the blaxploitation films. True, *A Warm December* was a commercial and critical calamity, but as Judith Crist wrote, it presented black romantic heroes "who aren't pushing dope or pimping, who aren't out to kill whitey and who make us empathize and care. Isn't that what screen entertainment entails?"[27]

In 1973, the answer was unclear. Poitier had won some appreciation, if only for injecting blacks into old Hollywood formulas. But while Jim Brown and Ron O'Neal drew customers with violent action fantasies, Poitier reaped no profits. If his career were to survive, the trend had to run its course. It soon did.

❖

Blaxploitation begat a backlash. By the end of 1972, a high-profile debate arose over the merits of films starring virile, violent black heroes. "Black Movie Boom: Good or Bad?" ran a *New York Times* headline. "The New Films: Culture or Con Game?" asked *Ebony*. "Black Movies: Renaissance or Ripoff?" screamed the cover of *Newsweek*.[28]

Numerous black leaders criticized the genre. "If black movies do not contribute to building constructive, healthy images of black people and to fairly recording the black experience, we shall have lost our money and our souls," claimed Junius Griffin, president of Hollywood's branch of the NAACP. Roy Innis of CORE echoed that films glorifying pimps and drug dealers "are subtle ways of promoting Black genocide in the Black community." Both organizations lobbied studio executives and picketed theaters featuring derogatory black images.[29]

James Baldwin called the new movies "a desperate effort to fit black faces into a national fantasy." Alvin Poussaint bemoaned that "violent, criminal, sexy savages" had become role models for ghetto children. Amiri Baraka indicted the films' individualist, capitalist ethic. Huey Newton suspected a conspiracy against actual black revolution. Others faulted the movies for treating black women as mere sexual objects.[30]

Some used the attention to promote black capitalism within the film industry. The Black Artists Alliance, a network of creative and technical personnel, formed to protest inequality within the entertainment world. Jesse Jackson met with performers and executives about fostering black control over the financing, production, and distribution of films for black audiences, and he threatened protests unless studios hired more black personnel. Blacks now composed 40 percent of the American movie audience; Jackson argued that blacks should be reaping some rewards. He also joined the chorus condemning film treatments of blacks as savage, super-macho stereotypes.[31]

Black Hollywood responded, defending its new lifeblood. Gordon Parks dismissed the racist assumption that black audiences could not distinguish fact from fantasy. Curtis Mayfield, who composed the score for *Superfly*, argued that the pictures portrayed actual ghetto life. Fred Williamson wondered why only black violence stoked fear, when white gangsters and cowboys were equally bloodthirsty. And Jim Brown asserted that the trend created jobs for black directors, writers, and actors. Although Hollywood was no racial utopia, the black film boom had blasted down doors once open only for Sidney Poitier.[32]

Nevertheless, by January 1974, *Jet* was declaring the genre "a thing of the past." The pictures had poor production values, tired plots, and similar heroes. The criticism from prominent blacks tainted the argument that the boom represented progress. More important, Hollywood no longer needed these low-budget black-oriented pictures. As *The Godfather* (1972) and *The Exorcist* (1973) drew large black audiences, studios realized that they could capture the African American market while casting a wider net. The blaxploitation trend soon fizzled out.[33]

Thanks to his deals with Columbia and First Artists, Poitier had worked through the early 1970s. Without them, he surmised, "I might have found

THROUGH PLAYING GOD

myself twiddling my thumbs." His sporadic acting offers were for second-rate scripts. Though he now had directing and producing credits, he possessed little stature. During a two-hour meeting in the summer of 1972 with First Artists executives, he weathered pleas to abandon his next production, a comedy called *Uptown Saturday Night*. Poitier stood firm. The argument was moot, since the corporation was contractually obligated to fund him. But Poitier realized that if he submitted another dud, his reputation would lie in tatters.[34]

Despite a budget of only two million dollars, Poitier assembled an all-star package of black entertainers. On vacation in Nassau, Bill Cosby asked for the co-star role. Flip Wilson and Richard Pryor agreed over the telephone, script unseen. Harry Belafonte signed up. Each comedian could have made millions through live shows, but they accepted small salaries. "It's for Sidney," explained Belafonte. Movie roles helped them, too, since they exposed the stars to wide audiences. Celebrities in hand, Poitier promised to entertain all ages and races. He trumpeted a "healthier exploration of black life" distinct from the "pimps, prostitutes, and dope pushers who represent only a minuscule portion of the black community."[35]

Poitier assembled cast and crew at MGM studios in November 1973. Even more than his previous productions, the set illustrated Poitier's contribution to racial progress in Hollywood. The cast included the cavalcade of stars, a legion of black actors, and hundreds of black extras. More than one-fourth of the crew was black. The *New York Amsterdam News* estimated that over 1,300 blacks worked on some aspect of *Uptown Saturday Night*.[36]

Poitier presided over his kingdom, meeting with cinematographers, consulting with costume designers, rehearsing actors. He rarely rehearsed Bill Cosby, though; he just unleashed the man's comic energy. "Richard Pryor," Poitier recalled, "was another question altogether." The young, manic comedian — known for his profanity, ghetto-based humor, and brazen use of "nigger" — improvised hilarious scenes. After Poitier changed the camera angle, Pryor improvised different, even funnier scenes. Poitier managed this challenge, and they completed filming before Christmas.[37]

Uptown Saturday Night was light fare for the masses. The plot revolves around Steve Jackson (Poitier) and Wardell Franklin (Cosby), two working-class stiffs from Harlem who splurge one Saturday night at an upscale nightclub. Masked thieves rob the clientele, including Jackson and Franklin. The next day, Jackson learns that he won $50,000, but his lottery ticket is in his stolen wallet.

In their hunt for the ticket, Jackson and Franklin encounter a grandstanding preacher (Flip Wilson), a paranoid private eye/con artist (Pryor), a two-faced congressman (Roscoe Lee Browne), and a troika of gangsters: Little Seymour (Harold Nicholas), Silky Slim (Calvin Lockhart), and Geechie Dan Buford (Belafonte). The heroes trick Silky Slim and Geechie Dan into bringing a suitcase of stolen goods — including the wallet — to a church picnic. After some shootouts, car chases, and leaps off a bridge, they frame the criminals and recoup the winning lottery ticket.

Throughout these madcap hijinks, the film seems comfortable in its black milieu, as characters speak in dialect ("homeboy"; "chump"; "your ass is grass") and play the dozens ("You sooooooo ugly, 'til it's against the law in twenty states to marry you"). There are scenes with fried chicken and gospel music, smug integrationists and low-life gangsters. African American life informs much of the comedy. Before they enter the congressman's office, for instance, Browne changes into a dashiki and reverses his picture of President Nixon to a portrait of Malcolm X. Removed from the racial sensitivities of the civil rights era, *Uptown Saturday Night* let blacks laugh at themselves.[38]

The film also features broad, physical jokes without racial connotations. Cosby plays a mugging, smirking, wisecracking cab driver. Belafonte sends up Marlon Brando's Godfather: puffy-faced and scratchy-throated, he snorts nasal spray, eats raw eggs, and dresses as a woman during an escape. Many appreciated this old-fashioned comic sensibility. Everyone in the picture seems to be having fun.[39]

With one exception: Poitier. As a nervous straight man for Cosby, he saps away his own noble aura. "Poitier's idea of comic acting is to bulge his eyes out, as if doing a Manton Moreland impression," wrote Jay Cocks of *Time*. Although he always possessed a likable aura, Poitier never drew guffaws. He was not a natural comedian, and he appears tentative.[40]

Worse, his direction shows little comic timing. Poitier's sluggish pacing crippled the comedy. Poitier also maintained his propensity to overuse television-style close-ups. Finally, Richard Wesley's screenplay needed funnier gags. The actual jokes contributed less than the warm, loose energy supplied by the assemblage of black talent.[41]

Although a benign farce, *Uptown Saturday Night* got ensnared in racial politics. Following the premiere at the downtown Criterion Theatre in June 1974, buses took the celebrity-studded audience to a gala at Vincent's Place in Harlem. As guests filed in, a hostess handed each lady a red rose. The men received protest cards. "Jim Crow lives!" read the cards. "125th Street is still the back of the bus — moviewise that is." Bobby Schiffman, manager of the Apollo Theatre, objected that the picture would not play his uptown venue for weeks. A premiere and first-run showing at the Apollo would have injected money into Harlem.[42]

The next week, the "Harlem Salute Committee" picketed the Criterion, demanding that Poitier donate seed money for a black museum in Harlem. The ugly ploy soon faded from sight, but in early July, another brouhaha erupted. Cosby had recorded three promotional radio spots, including one that said: "Remember the good old days when you used to go to uptown to Harlem and have a good time — before it became very dangerous? Well, you can still go uptown without getting your head beat in, by going downtown to see *Uptown Saturday Night*. This way the people are all on the screen and won't jump off and clean your head out. . . ." Painting Harlem as a den of vice, even if tongue-in-cheek, inflamed tensions from the downtown premiere. The theater chain that owned the Apollo lodged complaints with CORE, the NAACP, the Urban League, and the Federal Communications Commission. Schiffman cited a larger conspiracy against first-run premieres in Harlem. Despite Cosby's public apology, he and Poitier faced accusations of complicity in Harlem's economic woes.[43]

But marketing *Uptown Saturday Night* to interracial audiences proved astute. White patrons filled theaters during first-week runs in New York, Chicago, and Detroit. Warner Brothers, which had replaced National General as distributor for First Artists, booked typically white venues such as Sioux City, Billings, and Salt Lake City. Among recent black films, only *Sounder* and *Lady Sings the Blues* had attracted large white audiences. *Uptown Saturday Night* — a harmless frolic of African American humor, and a breath of fresh air from blaxploitation — was the first "crossover" comedy of the 1970s. It grossed over ten million dollars, boosting Poitier's fortune and reputation.[44]

His acting might have regressed, and his directing needed improvement. But Sidney Poitier was back.

❖

It seemed especially cruel, then, that Poitier soon faced a final, all-out attack on his image and humanity. Amiri Baraka, founder of the Black Arts movement, wrote a play in 1969 entitled *Sidnee Poet Heroical*. He had difficulty getting it produced; it involved twenty-nine short scenes and combined drama, dance, music, and film. He also feared a lawsuit from Poitier. The Henry Street Settlement's New Federal Theater finally staged it in May 1975.[45]

Sidnee Poet Heroical caricatures Poitier. A young man named Sidnee arrives on American shores with confidence, "cause I'm big and black and fast and strong as Westindian African with manicure and sporty pants and all up in there." He meets a spoof on Belafonte named Lairee Elephont, who asks Sidnee if he would like to "grow up to be a famous nigger in the world and sleep with white women." Sidnee patterns himself after Lairee, "the world's greatest nigger."[46]

There are parodies of famous Poitier movies: Sidnee joins Tony Curtis at the hip, dances with adoring nuns, helps a blind girl who cries, "Nigger Helper, Nigger Helper, Big Sid, Help I'm blind I'm blind please come love me," and performs a sexy dance for Katharine Hepburn before passing a quiz from Spencer Tracy. Moreover, Sidnee internalizes the cultural implications of his image. "We are good and perfect helping them," he says. "Otherwise we barely exist."

In the second act, Sidnee pays for his celebrity. His skin turns white and a giant Oscar statue taunts him. When a director wants him to play White Pongo, an educated white ape, Sidnee rebels. But when he tries to make films about "real black life," reporters say that he is "preaching hatred." Sidnee searches out his abandoned black lover, and he becomes an apostle of black nationalism.[47]

Sidnee Poet Heroical has all the subtlety of a punch in the face. Baraka paints the black celebrities with broad strokes and ugly colors. *New York Times* theater critic Mel Gussow praised this "corrosive indictment of an American dream." But the punches are so below-the-belt that it seemed less a satire than a disparagement of Poitier. Baraka showed no appreciation for the complexity of the stars' positions. In 1969, when Baraka wrote the play, his points might have carried some weight. By 1975, after a generation of films rejecting the Poitier icon, *Sidnee Poet Heroical* was just mean.[48]

Even though the play had a short run at a small theater, it infuriated Poitier. *Sidnee Poet Heroical* not only maligned his films, but also portrayed him as a greedy simpleton. He remained sensitive to criticism that he forsook the black community. When Paul Winfield said in 1974 that Poitier "sold out by defining what's saleable," Poitier stopped talking to him. He had given Winfield his break by hiring him for two films, and he felt betrayed. "It never occurred to me that Sidney *could* be hurt by anything I said," mourned Winfield. "I'll always be sorry about that, because what I owe Sidney can't be measured."[49]

Meanwhile, Poitier searched for vehicles that satisfied his recurring interest in Africa. He explored opportunities for film distribution throughout Africa, and he considered making *Cabral*, a First Artists production filmed in Tanzania. Instead, he took a brief vacation from directing and producing for *The Wilby Conspiracy*, an old-fashioned movie with old friends. Martin Baum, his longtime agent who briefly ran ABC Films, had signed an independent production deal with United Artists. Baum hired Poitier and Michael Caine for the South African thriller. He also hired Ralph Nelson, Poitier's director from *Lilies of the Field* and *Duel at Diablo*.[50]

In March 1974 Poitier returned to the foothills of Mount Kenya, where eighteen years earlier he had made *Something of Value*. The nation had changed. In 1963 Kenya declared independence from Great Britain. Now Jomo Kenyatta was president, not an imprisoned political agitator. Poitier faced no racial segregation on this trip. He and Shimkus stayed in a huge bungalow at a luxury safari club. According to Caine, the locals viewed Poitier as "a god. Everywhere he went he was treated with awed respect." His reputation stretched even to remote rural areas without movie screens. Poitier cherished the adoration, and he further prized his invitation to a reception with Kenyatta—at least until the reception. When they shook hands, Kenyatta politely asked Poitier what he did for a living.[51]

Returning to Africa compelled Poitier to mull his life and career, his triumphs and compromises, his celebrity and obligations. During a break in filming, Caine saw Poitier at the end of a long runway, silhouetted by Mount Kenya, lost in contemplation. "Feeling your roots, Sidney?" asked Caine. Poitier smiled, paused, and said, "They don't go through Gucci shoes, Michael."[52]

Yet Poitier's African experiences informed his performance in *The Wilby Conspiracy*. He plays Shack Twala, the vice-chairman of South Africa's Black Congress. Shack is resentful of his second-class status, unbowed by confinement and torture, and possessed of a gallows sense of humor. Imprisoned for ten years on Robben Island, Shack wins freedom thanks to his lawyer Rina Nierkirk (Prunella Gee). Upon his release, however, constables arrest him for violating pass laws. When Nierkirk intercedes, they shove her. Then her boyfriend Jim Keogh (Caine) strikes the officers. Although indifferent to the apartheid state, Keogh must join Shack on the run.

The plot mimics *The Defiant Ones*: two fugitives, divided by race, united by common purpose. Shack needs Keogh, because the police will harass a lone black traveler. Keogh needs Shack, because Shack can arrange escape to Botswana. Major Horn (Nicol Williamson) from the Bureau of State Security stalks them. The fugitives drive from Cape Town to Johannesburg, pursuing not only freedom but also hidden diamonds. They withstand threats and double crosses, and they even elude the South African Air Force. In Botswana, Shack delivers the diamonds to Wilby, the outlaw chairman of the Black Congress. When Horn raids their rendezvous, Shack helps save Wilby. The once-apathetic Keogh kills Horn. "Now you understand," says Shack.

Upon the release of *The Wilby Conspiracy* in late summer 1975, Poitier, Caine, and Williamson won kudos. Poitier broke little new ground, but he projected dignity with a wry sensibility. For instance, Shack tells Keogh about his electroshock torture: "I gave them all the names they already had, and one they didn't." "Jesus," exclaims Keogh. "That's the one," replies Shack. Other moments created human connections between the heroes; most memorably, Keogh helps a handcuffed Shack urinate. But this snappy style undercut the drama. Like *The Defiant Ones*, the script reduces race relations to a personal interaction. "*The Wilby Conspiracy* plays like a 20 year old, well intentioned American film that tries to tell white people that black people are just as good as white people, as long as they look and act like Sidney Poitier," wrote Gene Siskel. "In 1975, that attitude, even in a political thriller, doesn't wash."[53]

The approach diluted any comment on apartheid, a point readily conceded by its creative team. Baum and Nelson avoided overt politics, instead emphasizing the message of common humanity. Screenwriters Rod Amateau and Harold Nebenzal insisted upon the unattainable: "an anti-apartheid point without politicizing it." They noted its parallels to Hollywood westerns, especially *Shane*: "The guy comes into town, does his job, and moves on." The audience identifies with Caine, not Poitier.[54]

This strategy deprived the black characters of political legitimacy. The strains of black resistance in South Africa, from Nelson Mandela's African National Congress to Steve Biko's Black Consciousness Movement, are melded into a vague, fictional "Black Congress." Only Williamson's Major Horn expresses any ideology. He defends apartheid, because whites built "every town, every factory, every farm, mine, and Christian church," and "no Zulu twenty years out of a tree" should usurp white control. Although Shack and Keogh defeat Horn, neither articulates an opposing viewpoint.[55]

South African exhibitors nevertheless banned the film. Movies about Africa rarely featured white villains, but Major Horn is utterly, undeniably evil. Moreover, Shack Twala never defers to white authorities or even Keogh. His Black Congress fights for revolution—a far cry from the passive acquiescence to the racial system in *Cry, the Beloved Country*.

Before widespread media attention to apartheid, and before the divestiture movement among American corporations, *The Wilby Conspiracy* addressed the repulsive nature of a racially segregated state.[56]

The picture also evinced the changes wrought by blaxploitation. Where once Hollywood sought to purge the screen of black sexuality, now the writers injected a superfluous romp between Poitier and Persis Khambatta, a former Miss India. The screen coupling sparked unfounded rumors of a real-life romance. By then, Poitier and Joanna Shimkus shared a child and a Nassau home.[57]

Also by then, the polite understanding between Sidney and Juanita Poitier had eroded. Sidney had paid alimony since their 1964 Mexican divorce, and for years the estranged pair avoided airing their dirty laundry. But in December 1972, Juanita claimed that he was violating their agreement; she termed his haphazard payments "humiliating." Juanita took legal action, asking the New York State Supreme Court to order an accounting of his net earnings. During this time, she moved from Pleasantville to a 580-acre property in Stuyvesant, New York, where she ran the Blue Heaven Farm, a rehabilitation center for children ages eight to eighteen. In a gesture perhaps as personal as it was political, she also co-chaired the New York State "Democrats for Nixon" campaign in 1972.[58]

As Poitier's estrangement from Juanita widened, his union with Shimkus tightened. In December 1973 they had their second child together. Despite an excited article in the *New York Amsterdam News* claiming that Poitier fathered his first son, named Sidney, he actually had his sixth daughter, named Sydney.[59]

The next year, they left Nassau. Poitier had grown disappointed with the Bahamas. After establishing independence in 1973, the nation suffered from the same dependence on tourism that existed under colonialism. Poitier also bemoaned the lack of Bahamian cultural life. Moving to Nassau had been a misguided stab at refuge from his problems. He called his exile "a fool's errand, a waste to all concerned." At Joanna's behest, they moved to Beverly Hills.[60]

Upon their return, gossip columnists tittered with speculation about the couple. In 1974 Poitier allowed that they had discussed marriage, but he offered little else. Unfounded rumors circulated: one claimed that Poitier would marry after she bore a son, another that Shimkus had cold feet. In reality, Shimkus, despite her cosmopolitan sophistication, was traditional to the core. Before meeting Poitier, she had professed admiration for marriage, and she never shook the notion. She confronted Poitier after a doctor's appointment, when the receptionist seemed confused that she and her children had different surnames. Luckily, he had overcome his long-term commitment issues. In July 1975, he secured a binding divorce from Juanita. On 23 January 1976, in his Beverly Hills mansion, surrounded by friends, with Harry Belafonte the best man and Julie Belafonte the matron of honor, Poitier slipped a wedding band over Shimkus's finger, and their life together received the sanction of the law.[61]

He was forty-nine years old. Behind him was a remarkable life and a fascinating career. He had an attractive, intelligent wife who understood his insecurities and peculiarities. His daughter Beverly now wanted peace, and together they repaired their relationship. The previous year, she bore his first grandchild. His next two daughters, Pamela and Sherri, sought acting careers with his uneasy blessing. Gina was in high school. And now he had two little girls, Anika and Sydney. He realized his luck, and he appreciated the contours of what he once called "a long journey." He was too smart, too restless, and too ambitious to let that journey end.[62]

❖

By mid-decade, Poitier was both a symbol of the past and an engine for the future. He achieved honors befitting his stature: hosting the 1976 NAACP Image Awards, gaining induction into the Black Filmmakers Hall of Fame at the Oakland Museum, getting named honorary knight commander of the Order of the British Empire for "his contribution to the performing arts through which he enhanced the image of the Bahamas." Broadway producer Philip Rose related that almost every black actor who passed through his office paid homage to Poitier, both for the images that he presented and the barriers that he shattered.[63]

Poitier looked forward, seeking new avenues to control and diversify his career. Throughout 1975, he negotiated to direct films through the Mirisch Corporation. Though the pact never materialized, he was anticipating the future. That same year Poitier made his third First Artists picture. Like *Uptown Saturday Night*, this comedy co-starred Bill Cosby and featured an all-star black cast. Poitier again directed and served as executive producer. Melville Tucker again produced; Richard Wesley again wrote the script. The title, appropriately, was *Let's Do It Again*.[64]

Principal photography began in Hollywood in March 1975, and location filming in Atlanta and New Orleans wrapped up by May. Throughout, cast and crew enjoyed a loose atmosphere. Poitier had obtained a larger budget, and he and Cosby relished each other's company. Poitier's brothers Cyril and Reginald had bit parts, and Beverly visited the set with her baby.[65]

The public no longer depended on Poitier to symbolize the entire race. *Let's Do It Again* had no message besides that all Americans could enjoy black people's humor. "This movie will not win an Academy Award. This movie will not be remembered in ten or fifteen years," said Jimmie Walker, the young comic making his motion picture debut. "It's a fun movie. And that's enough."[66]

Poitier and Cosby play Clyde Williams and Billy Foster, two officers in an Atlanta lodge called "The Sons and Daughters of Shaka." The lodge faces eviction, so they hatch a scheme. They travel to New Orleans and hypnotize a spaghetti-limbed coward named Bootney Farnsworth (Walker) into believing that he can knock out a boxing champion. They place huge wagers with the lodge's savings, and Farnsworth wins. But while saving their lodge, the heroes bilk rival gangsters Kansas City Mack (John Amos) and Biggie Smalls (Calvin Lockhart).

Six months later, they are back in New Orleans, caught between the two gangs. They concoct another ruse, this time hypnotizing both boxers. With the help of their wives (Lee Chamberlin and Denise Nicholas), they bet that both boxers, mesmerized into frenzies, will not last the first round. Their plan works. Williams and Foster then lure the criminals into a police station. Brandishing an envelope of evidence, they compel the gangsters to donate money to charity. The heroes win again.

When the film arrived in October 1975, the critics had ample grievances, among them a ridiculous story (hypnotized boxers, first-round double knockouts), tired plot devices (escapes out windows, leaps between buildings), and sloppy direction (poorly framed shots, repetition of plot points). None of them mattered. *Let's Do It Again* is both fun and funny, because the stars had free rein to flaunt their talents. Cosby is hilarious while bluffing his way through tight spots. Walker's goofy affability almost steals the picture. The movie shines with star power, including a score by Curtis Mayfield and cameos from George Foreman and Billy Eckstine. *Let's Do It Again* grossed over fifteen million dollars, an even greater success than *Uptown Saturday Night*.[67]

With this engaging farce, Poitier reigned over black Hollywood. He produced, directed, and starred in a triumphant response to blaxploitation. But he again shortchanged his own talent. In a *New Yorker* essay, Pauline Kael mourned his sacrifice. Poitier cannot shake his inherent reserve, dignity, or grace. He cannot play low comedy, even as the straight man. His stabs at humor mostly comprise silly facial expressions. In one scene, he actually gapes bug-eyed while munching on a chicken bone — a total contradiction of his historic image. "He can't even hold the screen," grieved Kael. "He loses the dynamism that made him a star. Sidney Poitier, who was able to bring new, angry dignity to black screen acting because of the angry dignity inside him, is violating his very essence as a gift to his people."[68]

Poitier suggested that his critics go to black theaters, where audiences were "falling down in the aisles, enjoying themselves freely without any fear of a put down." He would keep making films that satisfied black people. As the only black producer, and one of two black directors (along with Michael Schultz), he bore new responsibilities. A reporter asked if he was still trying to satisfy everyone, still "carrying the black man's burden." "But those were white guys' pictures," Poitier responded. "I was part of *their* statements for 20 years. Now these are mine and those of my constituency." So he produced, directed, and starred in a third film with Cosby, called *A Piece of the Action*.[69]

Although he had fulfilled his three-picture commitment, Poitier made the movie under First Artists. The company was troubled. It had added Steve McQueen and Dustin Hoffman as partners. Studios flooded the other stars with A-list scripts and upfront fees, so they devoted less energy to their risky, time-consuming First Artists ventures. Most First Artists pictures lost money. In 1975 the company hired Phil Feldman, and he diversified into film distribution, television and music production, and a sport shirt company. He also considered buying casinos. His strategy failed, and in 1978 Hoffman sued the company for contractual violations. By the end of the decade, First Artists made no movies—just sport shirts.[70]

Unlike his partners, Poitier received few and substandard offers, and he needed First Artists to satisfy his "constituency." He touted his newest installment as an improvement upon the first two comedies, since it would combine rollicking entertainment with a social message. Before filming began in March 1977, he worked with screenwriter Charles Blackwell. He hired another all-star cast, including James Earl Jones and Denise Nicholas. He also hired his brother Cyril and daughter Sherri. From studio filming in Los Angeles, to location work on Chicago's North Clark Street, through editing and scoring, Poitier crafted a personal vision in *A Piece of the Action*.[71]

This time, Poitier and Cosby are not average Joes but suave criminals. Poitier is Manny Durrell, a high-stakes con artist who scams the Chicago drug dealer Bruno (Titos Vandis). Cosby is Dave Anderson, a safecracker who jumps from twelve-story windows. One day, a deep bass over the telephone reveals evidence of their guilt. The distinctive voice presents an ultimatum: devote time and money to a black community center, or go to jail. Naturally, they "volunteer" for the center.

In an American ghetto twist on *To Sir, with Love*, Durrell tames rowdy teenagers in a job skills training program. Anderson works with employers to secure jobs. They also seek the identity behind the deep voice, and each has a personal subplot. Anderson romances the center's director Lila French (Nicholas), while Durrell endures a surprise visit from the devout family of his girlfriend Nikki (Tracy Reed). Durrell grudgingly admits that they will someday get married.

Finally they learn that retired detective Joshua Burke (Jones) framed them into volunteering for the community center, which was founded by his late wife. By then, Durrell has transformed the teenagers' attitudes, and Anderson has found them jobs. Alas, Bruno has kidnapped Nikki. In a final confrontation, Durrell shows Bruno evidence of the villain's underworld activities. Durrell thus earns Bruno's respect, ensures his own safety, and protects the South Side from a drug dealer. He returns to the community center in time for an ecstatic graduation ceremony. In another echo of *To Sir, with Love*, he and Anderson enlist for another stint.

Unlike the previous two Poitier/Cosby ventures, *A Piece of the Action* was less straight comedy than stew of comedy, action, and romance, seasoned with social conscience. When it arrived in October 1977, most critics looked past the absurd plot and smiled upon the warm-hearted amalgam of "corny and hip, cynical and sentimental, formulaic and funky." Cosby's wooing of Nicholas was amusing, the teenagers supplied innocent charm, and Curtis Mayfield submitted another sensational score. Poitier's direction showed more discipline. As an actor, freed of comic duties, Poitier played the combination con man and educator with panache. The movie was no blockbuster hit, but it earned fine profits.[72]

A Piece of the Action placed a capstone on an era in Poitier's life. In Manny Durrell, Poitier put his self-image on screen: an outsider who survives with pragmatism, a debonair character with a sense of social duty, an erstwhile bachelor who commits to one woman. Both Poitier and Durrell live in the penthouse, but each has lessons to teach the ghetto.[73]

One month after filming *A Piece of the Action*, Poitier spoke at a Los Angeles elementary school. He told the children that they bore a responsibility to improve the world. In the film, his character faces teenagers who never learned that code. "You wear your ignorance like a badge of honor and you call that being cool," he lectures. He teaches basic courtesy, because courtesy earns respect. He conveys the value of an earned dollar. The class learns humility, self-esteem, sacrifice, history. They understand the lessons of Reginald and Evelyn Poitier, the lessons that took Sidney from Cat Island to Nassau to Miami to Harlem to Hollywood, the lessons that forged a survivor. "You want to be a man? You want to be a woman?" he says. "Feed your family!"[74]

❖

As he turned fifty and started a new family, Poitier often reflected on his past, especially upon visits to New York. Now he stayed at Quo Vadis and ate calves' liver for breakfast. He pulled up to the Stage Deli in a white stretch limousine to eat a sandwich called "The Sidney Poitier." But New York also prompted memories of cold nights, empty stomachs, and washing dishes.[75]

He remembered his old heroes, especially Paul Robeson; he narrated a short, Oscar-winning 1979 film called *Paul Robeson: Tribute to an Artist*. He also contemplated a movie about the black leaders who had shaped his world. In a seminar at the American Film Institute, on the ABC television program *Like It Is*, with Louie Robinson of *Ebony*, he discussed the economics of filmmaking. But the subject always turned to his path from poverty to celebrity: hopping Florida freight trains, sleeping in Harlem pay toilets, stumbling through his American Negro Theater audition, panicking during his Broadway debut, traveling to Hollywood and South Africa and Mississippi.[76]

For years, Joanna had been urging him to put the stories to paper. He was spurred to action after a dinner party in 1977, when the writer Alex Haley turned to him and said, "You know, of course, you're going to have to write a book." Poitier's career shone light on Hollywood's treatment of race from the post–World War II era through the rise and fall of Black Power. Poitier also wanted others — especially his children — to separate the man from the movie star. "Even those close to me," he later said, "tend to relate to the image of me projected in my films." So he wrote an autobiography.[77]

Following *A Piece of the Action*, Poitier disappeared from the public eye for over a year. He first learned the form by cleaning out a bookstore's biography, autobiography, and bestseller sections. He then wrote a twenty-page proposal and secured a venerable publisher, Alfred A. Knopf. Too proud to use a ghostwriter, he penned the manuscript himself. It proved more difficult than anticipated. Although an avid reader, Poitier was accustomed to oration and physical expression. So he dictated into a tape recorder and molded the results onto paper, a technique that captured his unique mix of the formal and colloquial. He entitled the book *This Life*.[78]

In one revealing passage, he recalled himself as a nine-year-old boy, overhearing adults bragging about sexual conquests: "The unmistakable conclusion is that 'pleasure' is derived from this kind of involvement, and such deliciousness falling on tender ears creates anticipation. You say, 'Gee, I'd like some of that.' . . . You become so drunk with the fantasy image of yourself exploring the naked body of a young girl that your heart begins to pound in your head and your blood races as you think what it must be like to look at an exposed vagina. You ain't ever really seen one of them exposed—right there staring back at you." Cerebral yet colorful, stilted yet slangy, macho yet modest, his language revealed the contradictions of his personal path and complicated celebrity.[79]

No less than his films, *This Life* nudged racial preconceptions while presenting an attractive hero. Poitier professed his virility, but he also painted the young Sidney as a sweet, dogged pursuer of true love. He addressed his affair with Diahann Carroll, but the Sidney Poitier of *This Life* is a man torn between two women, not the manipulative egomaniac of Carroll's 1986 autobiography. He discussed his admiration for Paul Robeson and Canada Lee, but he downplayed just how radical most Americans considered his early professional circles. He also acknowledged the shortcomings of his screen image, but he concentrated on his personal experiences. Few pages addressed the difficult period when he drew such ferocious criticism.[80]

Nevertheless, *This Life* contains more honesty, introspection, and intelligence than the typical self-serving celebrity memoir. Knopf published it in 1980. On the strength of good reviews and the buying habits of adoring middle-aged women, the book sold well. It also marked a transition in Poitier's public image. His autobiography signaled that he belonged to history. He had left a legacy, and he could still shape it.[81]

CHAPTER 17

GHOSTS

(1978–2002)

❖

"Everybody wants Sidney Poitier (and why not?)," announced the *New York Post* in December 1978. That month Poitier signed a four-year deal with Columbia Pictures to write, direct, and/or act in movies and television programs. After his successful comedy trilogy, he owned a reputation for low-budget, high-grossing movies. Now Hollywood's trade newspapers relayed potential Verdon-Cedric projects: *China Blues*, an adventure film about three Americans in China in the 1920s; *Midtown Experience*, a suspense movie starring three women; *Timbuktu*, an NBC miniseries adaptation of Eartha Kitt's Broadway show; *The Cabral Story*, a revisitation of a scrapped project set in Africa; *Christmas Is Coming Uptown*, a film musical set in Harlem; and an installment in Peter Sellers's *Pink Panther* series.[1]

Poitier chose *Prison Rodeo*, a comedy starring Richard Pryor and Gene Wilder and later entitled *Stir Crazy*. For the first time, he directed without acting. Few scripts contained roles for middle-aged black leading men, and his talents did not suit character roles. Moreover, dividing between acting and directing impaired both responsibilities. Now he would concentrate on one task, and in a picture geared to the mainstream. "I can't allow myself to be circumscribed as simply a black director," Poitier said. "I have to reach beyond repeating myself and test my wherewithal against other American directors who function outside the special arena of black movies."[2]

In March 1980, they started filming in Tucson at Arizona State Prison. "It's bizarre," said Wilder. While shooting a comedy, they were "working shoulder-to-shoulder alongside rapists, killers, you name it." They all signed waivers indemnifying the prison in case of a riot or hostage situation. But the close quarters bred familiarity. Over 300 inmates signed on as extras. Between takes, Wilder played checkers and dominoes with them, and Pryor kept them laughing with impromptu routines.[3]

Poitier put this improvisational energy to use. "Don't stifle one impulse," he instructed. "You're two racehorses. I want to steer you, not tell you how to run." Pryor and Wilder already had chemistry from their 1976 film *Silver Streak*, so rather than provide detailed instructions, Poitier gave silent facial cues as the cameras rolled. On the first take of a courtroom scene, Pryor and Wilder burst into tears. The next time, they both had laughing fits. The third time, they picked a fight with the lawyer, throwing a glass of water at him. "Making this film," said Wilder, "was an exercise in controlled anarchy."[4]

They lost control in late April, when Pryor abandoned the set. The tortured comic had isolated himself, avoiding the luxury hotel where Poitier and Wilder stayed. He instead rented a small, secluded home to indulge his all-consuming drug habit. Even before his walkout, Pryor often arrived after noon, weak and irrational. He also snuck drugs to inmates. When he fled, production halted. The next day, Poitier filmed Wilder over the shoulder of a Pryor body double. As Poitier huddled with Columbia executives about how to complete the picture, Pryor returned from a four-day absence. They finished shooting in late May. Three weeks later, Pryor suffered near-fatal burns, after an explosion while freebasing cocaine.[5]

Stir Crazy premiered that December to universally bad reviews. Pryor and Wilder played unemployed New Yorkers driving through the Sun Belt. Unjustly framed for bank robbery, they escape during a prison rodeo. "It's a slovenly, loose-jointed movie, with anecdotes that lead nowhere and minor performances that don't come off," wrote one critic. Poitier drew blame for languid pacing, sloppy plot development, and misusing his stars' talents. Wilder's pie-eyed innocent dominates the film. Pryor mostly cringes and cowers — trying to be both street-smart and cowardly, fulfilling various black stereotypes, and finding few outlets for his rough-edged genius. Critics also faulted the lowest-common-denominator humor, especially Georg Standford Brown's effeminate homosexual.[6]

But the movie packed theaters through the Christmas season and beyond. It grossed over $13 million in its first week. A Times Square theater canceled two late shows during the premiere weekend, because customers were pushing against the theater's glass walls, posing a safety hazard. A huge crowd spilled onto the streets, disrupting traffic until police arrived. By May 1981 the film had grossed over $100 million. Its success even spawned a short-lived television series in 1985.[7]

Poitier had recaptured the winning formula from *Uptown Saturday Night* and *Let's Do It Again*, and on a larger scale. At its best, *Stir Crazy* offered a fun energy. By letting his stars improvise, Poitier elicited some hilarious moments: Wilder fruitlessly imitating Pryor's "We baaaaaad" strut, Wilder and Pryor feigning insanity. Theatergoers cared little about the hackneyed script and clumsy direction. *Stir Crazy* deflected national worries. In late 1980, at the tail end of the Carter administration, in the midst of an economic malaise, at the height of the Iran hostage crisis, the public appreciated the mindless entertainment. By farcically updating *The Defiant Ones*, the film further allayed racial anxieties. At the end, Gene Wilder gets the girl. Richard Pryor chauffeurs them into the sunset.

With its successful black director and interracial comedy team, *Stir Crazy* foreshadowed an era of growth for black Hollywood, even as it illustrated the resilience of barriers from Poitier's heyday.

❖

In 1982 the NAACP once again initiated its well-practiced dance with Hollywood. At "summit talks" with the Motion Picture Association of America, the NAACP promised boycotts unless studios improved their minority hiring practices. As in the past, the threat won incremental changes. But also, as in the past, few blacks occupied positions of authority.[8]

Poitier remained a rare black presence in Hollywood, and after *Stir Crazy* he possessed myriad options. He decided to avoid acting. "I haven't been stretched as an actor in over ten years," he said in 1981, citing *In the Heat of the Night* as his last challenging role. Few worthwhile offers passed his desk. So he spent time with his family, avoiding the Hollywood limelight of parties and premieres. He also resolved to focus on directing. It offered him artistic control, and it allowed him to work with people that he liked and trusted.[9]

Gene Wilder had a "romantic-comedy-thriller" property called *Traces*, and he brought in Poitier. Columbia assigned a $14 million budget to the project, eventually renamed *Hanky Panky*. Richard Widmark — Poitier's first friend in Hollywood — signed to play a mobster. *Saturday Night Live* alumna Gilda Radner also joined the cast. In the summer of 1981, during shooting in New York, Connecticut, Massachusetts, Arizona, and New Mexico, Radner split from husband G. E. Smith and began to date Wilder.[10]

Their chemistry never translated to the screen. Wilder plays an innocent architect caught between an international crime gang, the New York police, and government security forces. Radner, cast 180 degrees against type, plays a genteel ingenue. The alleged comedy involves the mystery of a secret computer tape. Without Pryor, Wilder flails about in a comic vacuum. Radner plays it straight. Poitier's direction muddles the mystery, and the jokes consist of burping, hitting people with purses, and men in drag. "An ungainly turkey," wrote one critic. "Dreck for boobies," wrote another.[11]

Hanky Panky exhibited all the bad qualities of Poitier-directed comedies — scrambled plots, drawn-out scenes, juvenile humor — with none of the genial charm of his successful pictures. When it appeared in June 1982, the public stayed away.

Poitier fared no better with *Fast Forward*, his stab at capitalizing on the national fascination with dance movies. Tone deaf and clumsy on the dance floor, he nonetheless claimed "an energy source, an instinct that tells me what is fascinating about motion." The story, based on Poitier's original idea, concerns "The Adventurous Eight," a teenage dance troupe from Ohio that wins a New York City talent search competition. After whittling three thousand applicants down to eight spots, Poitier filmed his dancers all over New York City and Los Angeles in late summer 1984. He billed it as "a picture as much about self-sufficiency as it is about dance."[12]

Released in February 1985, *Fast Forward* nettled critics with its simplistic plot, cornball dialogue, and dull dancing. Conceived as a classy amalgam of breakdancing and "youthsploitation" films, it instead smacked of a misguided movie-by-the-numbers: "four clones of the girl in *Flashdance* join forces with two clones of the guy in *Footloose* to create a jazzy ensemble of break dancers cloned from the gang in *Fame*." Another critic called it "a terpsichorean disaster that may finally sound the death knell for twinkle-toed teen movies." A third suggested: "Fast forward! Rewind! Eject!"[13]

"Sidney Poitier," added the *Boston Globe*, "should leap back to the other side of the camera before his well-deserved acting reputation is completely tarnished by his directorial career." Indeed, Poitier never directed a taut picture. When he gave free rein to established talents, his pictures absorbed their stars' charisma. But unlike good directors, he could not impose an overarching vision. Nor did he ever direct with a first-class script. Even his best efforts have a rambling, amateurish style.[14]

After *Fast Forward*, Poitier's Columbia contract expired. For over two years, he did not produce, direct, or act in a movie. (He did narrate *Bopha!*, a documentary of life in South African townships.) He played golf and tennis, and he sometimes went skiing, a sport that he learned at age fifty. His health remained an obsession. He waited three hours after eating to drink any liquids, insisting that the practice aided digestion. He became a vegetarian, except for the occasional piece of fish.[15]

Poitier traveled and read, and he started another book — "a contemporary novel that has flourishes of astronomy, a novel rooted in the cosmos," according to the author. His protagonist was a metallurgist. Poitier drafted over 300 pages. Despite his joking threat to independently publish it with his children's inheritance, the novel stayed out of the public record.[16]

He testified before Congress in September 1983, charging a "conspiracy" against studios that refused to allot projects to minority-owned firms, terming it "a rampant, inexcusable, unjustifiable, immoral discrimination." Later that year, Poitier's name again surfaced, this time against his will. A federal grand jury indicted two small Wall Street firms of concealing over $130 million in taxable income. Their high-profile clientele included producer Norman Lear, composer Henry Mancini, and Poitier, who unwittingly took over $650,000 in bogus deductions. Poitier did nothing wrong, but his reputation was dragged into the messy affair.[17]

For much of the mid-1980s, however, Poitier slowed down. After years of driving himself to break boundaries, achieve milestones, and represent a race, he enjoyed the hiatus, even achieving some long-desired serenity. His introspection no longer tortured him. Gone was the bubbling, frustrated anger of his years in the spotlight. "I like me," he said. "I like me because I set out to prove to myself that I was capable of moving a mountain." Even if the mountain moved only a little, he respected his own determination.[18]

He also accepted his frailties. He realized that his constant dissatisfactions — with his career, with his family, with himself — had ruined his first marriage. (Sadly, Juanita filed for bankruptcy in 1990. Her rehabilitation center sank more than $250,000 into debt.) He admitted to some male chauvinism. Though hardly a feminist, marrying Joanna and raising two daughters in the wake of Women's Liberation had alerted him to some patriarchal biases. Sidney and Joanna Poitier had achieved a Hollywood rarity, a stable marriage built on mutual understanding. He had become a happier, more secure man. "I don't think I am going to save the world," he said. "Life disabuses one of that slowly."[19]

That self-acceptance returned him to acting. Directing, while satisfying to the ego, cost time and energy. So in 1987 he just acted in *Little Nikita* and *Shoot to Kill*. In both he played an FBI agent, and in neither did he feel a racial responsibility. For a long time, he said, "I had to satisfy the action fans, the romantic fans, the intellectual fans. It was a terrific burden." But now there was Denzel Washington, Danny Glover, Morgan

Freeman, Louis Gossett Jr., and Eddie Murphy. "It's like the cavalry coming to relieve the troops!" he delighted.[20]

But Hollywood was no racial Zion. Blacks still wielded no power at major studios. Black actresses still found few worthwhile roles, and Latinos and Asians suffered from similar limitations on their screen humanity. The institutional and cultural limits on Poitier's career persisted.[21]

He first shot *Little Nikita*, starting in February 1987. The project had begun as a Jack Nicholson vehicle. But David Puttnam, the new head of Columbia Pictures, wanted Poitier. "It's merely fighting for who's *right* as against who's 'bankable,'" argued the idealistic English producer. Poitier liked the script, which concerned the relationship between his FBI agent and a teenager whose parents are Russian spies. Poitier, who turned sixty during location shooting in San Diego, now possessed the gravitas to play this father figure. He appreciated that the role hinged not on race, but on the human connection between the two characters.[22]

Soon after, Poitier made *Shoot to Kill*. He had agreed to the project, originally called *In the Hall of the Mountain King*, in early 1986, but it suffered long delays. Not until summer 1987 did they start location shooting in the Pacific Northwest. "This was the toughest film, physically, that I've ever done," he said upon completion. "I was in exquisitely good shape when I started and a wreck when I finished." At altitudes up to 8,000 feet, Poitier and Tom Berenger performed many of their own stunts, including rock-climbing up a narrow crevasse called "The Chimney." At sea level, the rigors continued. For one scene, as he pursued a killer onto a ferry, Poitier improvised by bounding over a car's hood. Director Roger Spottiswoode loved it so much, he made Poitier do it eight more times.[23]

Shoot to Kill arrived first, in February 1988. On its opening weekend, it grossed $5 million dollars, a healthy tally driven by the stars, action, and scenery. Audiences did not come for a complex or original story. In the film, FBI agent Warren Stantin (Poitier) and backcountry guide Jonathan Knox (Berenger) chase a killer through the mountains. The villain has kidnapped Knox's girlfriend, Sarah (Kirstie Alley). Before the climactic shootout in Vancouver, British Columbia, the two men overcome their predictable hostility and forge an even more predictable friendship. Poitier's fans had seen it before. One critic called it "an opportunistic pastiche" of *In the Heat of the Night*, *The Defiant Ones*, and *Lilies of the Field*.[24]

Poitier's role contained few new challenges: the humor rotates around his city-slicker foibles in the wilderness, and the drama involves the standard arrival of mutual respect between the two protagonists. There were also some logical breaches (a trail guide and American agent fighting crime in Canada) and corny exchanges ("Ain't no elevators out here, Mister"). But critics and audiences relished Poitier's comeback, his retread of familiar territory as an upstanding lawman who befriends a skeptical white man. Remarkably fit and handsome for a sixty-year-old man, he seemed to be enjoying his comeback.[25]

He gave a more nuanced performance in *Little Nikita*, which premiered one month later. This FBI agent, named Roy Parmenter, tracks two undercover Soviet agents to southern California, where they pose as a middle-class family. Parmenter must tell Jeff Grant (River Phoenix) that his parents are spies. Parmenter combines Poitier's typical rectitude with undertones of duplicity. He also woos a woman (Loretta Devine) with mischievous charm. Meanwhile, Jeff must balance his loyalties to family and country. The relationship between the authority figure and the confused teenager offers great dramatic potential.

But the story nosedives into spy thriller pap. Even before filming ended, Puttnam mourned that director Richard Benjamin and his screenwriters shortchanged the characters. "It became a mishmash," he said. The KGB agent Karpov (Richard Bradford) and rogue Russian "Scuba" (Richard Lynch) are one-dimensional, and the overdrawn plot spins out of control. Further damaging the picture's prospects, Puttnam got fired before its release, and Columbia launched a lukewarm distribution campaign. *Little Nikita* cost fifteen million dollars to produce, and it grossed less than two million.[26]

Neither *Shoot to Kill* nor *Little Nikita* inspired reflections on American race relations. After an eleven-year break from the screen, Poitier needed not worry about satisfying any constituency. But his comeback movies illustrated that Hollywood still designed pictures to ease racial anxieties. The 1980s had yielded a proliferation of black/white "buddy" pictures: *Stir Crazy*, the later *Rocky* pictures, the *Lethal Weapon* series, and Eddie Murphy's *48 Hours*, *Trading Places*, and *Beverly Hills Cop* series.[27]

The trend hearkened to Poitier's films. Some pictures replicated the interracial homoeroticism of Poitier's early films: at the end of *Die Hard*, *Lethal Weapon*, and *Lethal Weapon II*, an exhausted and wounded white hero collapses in the arms of his black friend, recalling *The Defiant Ones*. White and black cops, achieving friendship after overcoming initial apprehension, mirrored *In the Heat of the Night*.[28]

Poitier provided the model for the black heroes. He had first conveyed the charm that won white sympathy, and he had first shown the dignity that demanded white respect. He had also played by the system's rules: curbed sexuality, contained anger, tacit pledges of racial cooperation. Poitier's descendants followed that pattern — often deflecting issues of prejudice, usually assigning romances to white stars, always assuring audiences of racial peace. The new generation lived by Poitier's old rules.

❖

The ghost of Sidney Poitier hovered not just over Hollywood, but over all America. Race continued to mold American life in the 1980s. The expanding black middle class integrated social and economic arenas, but the poverty of the black lower class persisted. Racial anxieties mixed with fears of deteriorating inner cities, burgeoning drug problems, and "welfare queens." Now the civil rights generation seemed distant heroes, men and women of clear moral power. Martin Luther King was enshrined as a national hero. Poitier, too, represented the goodwill of a lost era. A generation of liberal whites revered his cool grace. The best illustration of his status came from a nineteen-year-old black man named David Hampton.[29]

Hampton arrived in New York City in 1983, after police twice arrested him for breaking into dormitory rooms at SUNY-Buffalo. He started milling about Columbia University, dropping the name of a campus gay-rights leader and convincing students to house him. Columbia authorities banned him from campus after accusations of stealing. Around this time, Hampton and a friend tried to enter the exclusive nightclub Studio 54, pretending to be children of celebrities. His white friend became the son of Gregory Peck. Hampton had three choices. He had light skin like Harry Belafonte, but Belafonte had a well-known son named David, and people might recognize Hampton as an impostor. Sammy Davis Jr. was too garish. "Poitier was the class act of the three," Hampton said. "And he was the only one to have won an Oscar." As the doorman graciously ushered in "David Poitier," Hampton reveled in the moment.[30]

A scam was born. Hampton walked into restaurants, claimed that he was meeting Sidney Poitier, enjoyed the gracious service, and ate for free when his "father" failed to show. He arrived at the homes of prominent New Yorkers, avowing that he had been mugged and needed a place to sleep. Once he showed up at Melanie Griffith's apartment, where Gary Sinise was staying. Sinise talked to him until 4:00 A.M., bought him breakfast, and gave him ten dollars.[31]

Hampton usually played his charade on wealthy parents of alumni of prestigious Phillips Andover Academy. Hampton always claimed to know their children, and he discussed growing up as Sidney Poitier's son. Charming and well spoken, he even helped cook dinner. After claiming that his father was arriving the next morning to cast a film version of the Broadway show *Dreamgirls*, he accepted money, room, board, and the admiration accorded a celebrity's son.[32]

He learned who to swindle from the address book of Robert Stammers, an Andover graduate and student at Connecticut College. Hampton had pulled the same fraud at the New London campus, claiming that he was the casting director for his father's film. "I don't know why everyone fell for him," recalled Stammers years later. "Maybe it was the strength of his persona. But when he identified himself as Sidney Poitier's son, no one could have suspected he could be anyone else."[33]

Had a white con artist claimed Marlon Brando or Paul Newman for his father, he would have aroused more suspicion. Hampton played on the racial neuroses of his white hosts. He was articulate, gracious, and intelligent. He assuaged their liberal guilt without attacking their status. Who else's son could he have been?

The string of hoaxes halted in October 1983. At the home of Osborn Elliott, dean of Columbia's School of Journalism, his wife, Inger, found Hampton in bed with another man. When the Elliotts contacted their children, they learned that they had been tricked. The police arrested Hampton after he called Elliott to apologize. (Hampton had earlier asked to borrow money so he could send flowers.) The judge spared him jail time if he paid back $4,500 to his various hosts. Alas, Hampton failed to make restitution, ignored the court order banning him from New York City, and rented limousines from his luxury hotel room — reserved under David Poitier. The police caught him, and Hampton spent twenty-one months in Dannemora State Prison.[34]

The curious saga might have ended then, except that the Elliotts visited playwright John Guare and announced, "Have we got a story for you!" Guare did some research, but the clippings about Hampton's arrest sat on his desk for six years. When he found them again in 1989, inspiration struck. He went to the Strand Bookstore, bought Poitier's *This Life*, and started the play *Six Degrees of Separation*.[35]

From this story of confidence schemes and celebrity worship, Guare fashioned a dark, tragicomic comment on the gulf between ideals and realities, a *Guess Who's Coming to Dinner* through a funhouse mirror. Every character disguises themselves, not just the con artist, here renamed Paul. The art dealers Flan and Ouisa Kittredge live in the aristocratic circles of the Upper East Side, but they need money and view art as a commodity. Under his surface confidence, their South African visitor Geoffrey fears black rule. The children condemn spiritual emptiness, but they are repugnantly spoiled. Only Ouisa, played by Stockard Channing, uses the encounter with Paul to search for genuine humanity. *Six Degrees of Separation* won extraordinary reviews, and it became New York City's high-culture phenomenon of 1990.[36]

The play prolonged Hampton's time in the spotlight of ignominy. In October 1990, he pretended to brandish a gun at a cab driver. At his trial, he gave the judge forged documents. In November 1991, he was charged with sexual assault and impersonating a police officer. He also appeared in court for threatening Guare's life. ("I would strongly advise that you give me some money or you can start counting your days," he said into Guare's answering machine.) Hampton later crashed a press party for *Six Degrees of Separation* at Tavern on the Green, and he sued Guare for $100 million. A judge threw out the case.[37]

Six Degrees of Separation, meanwhile, moved from stage to screen. Guare wrote the script for the 1993 film, directed by Fred Schepisi. The movie mostly adheres to the play. Stockard Channing reprised her turn as Ouisa Kittredge. But unlike the play, where Channing occupied the moral center, the film belongs to Donald Sutherland, who artfully conveys Flan Kittredge's surface goodness and moral ignorance. The picture also provided a breakthrough for Will Smith, then known for his rap music and television sitcom, *The Fresh Prince of Bel Air.* Smith first consulted Poitier, who had long refused comment on *Six Degrees of Separation.* "Mr. Poitier said it was well written," relayed Smith. "He said, 'And you're a handsome young man and I think you could be my son.'" With that light endorsement, Smith joined the ranks of black leading men indebted to Poitier.[38]

But throughout the media attention to Hampton's scam, Guare's play, and Schepisi's film, few studied the tight bonds between *Six Degrees of Separation* and Poitier's own life. In the play and film Paul says that Poitier has no real identity, only the experiences of his fictional characters. Just as Poitier blurred the line between image and reality for political ends, so does Paul for personal gain. Both Poitier's icon and Paul's hoax are masks that satisfy white expectations. Yet when Ouisa seeks to crack through society's artifice, she reads *This Life.* To grasp her own identity, she seeks Poitier's actual humanity. His legacy weaves through the story. The Poitier icon represents a larger compunction to smother problems by presenting an unruffled public front.[39]

By the late 1980s, that public function belonged more to Bill Cosby. The comedian was a one-man institution: star of the nation's top-rated television series, author of three bestselling books, standup comic earning $250,000 per night, and pitchman for Jello, Coca-Cola, Kodak, and E. F. Hutton. Yet many complained that Cosby reassured whites that barriers to black advancement had fallen. "He no longer qualifies as black enough to be an Uncle Tom," sneered one critic. On *The Cosby Show* he played a genial father, a dedicated husband, and a skilled obstetrician. The sitcom's humor revolved around slices of domestic life, bouncing Cosby's amiable hero off his lawyer wife and cheerful children. Poitier defended Cosby. As Poitier once did, Cosby let the average white American identify with a black man.[40]

Cosby struggled, however, to translate his appeal to the movies. His 1987 effort *Leonard, Part 6* bombed with both critics and audiences. In January 1989, script problems plagued his next venture, and it appeared that he had no screen project for his seven-month hiatus from *The Cosby Show*. Then his agent recalled an old script, called *Thursday*, once intended for Steve Martin. In February Cosby met with Universal executives and suggested Poitier for director. By late April, they began shooting the film, renamed *Ghost Dad*. Sixty-seven days later, filming completed. In six months, a forgotten script became the vehicle for America's brightest black star.[41]

While filming, Poitier and Cosby shared their old jokes. Now Poitier complained about low pay, as Cosby had done while shooting their 1970s comedies. Cosby seemed excited to play a less-than-perfect character, a man who must solve his family's problems from the afterlife. Denise Nicholas, Cosby's love interest in *Let's Do It Again* and *A Piece of the Action*, played his raunchy next-door neighbor. A softball game against the cast and crew from another predominantly black production, *Harlem Nights*, starring Eddie Murphy, Redd Foxx, and Richard Pryor, drew 1,200 spectators.[42]

But *Ghost Dad* flopped. The script had languished for good reason: a parent's death is a rickety foundation for a family-oriented comedy, and the jokes about Cosby's supernatural state grow tedious. The star mines smiles with his rubber-faced mugging, but goofy grins do not sustain feature-length films. Poitier cut the neighbor's seduction of Cosby to ensure a PG rating, even though the scene was quite innocuous. The public remained unable to think of its black stars in sexual terms, even if the black man was a ghost.[43]

The picture suffered under Poitier's direction. "Every scene appears either overedited, using a separate shot for every line of dialogue, or stilted, with uncomfortable configurations of cast members standing around gazing in the general direction of a special effect, with subsequent dialogue broken down into sluggish close-ups," wrote the *Hollywood Reporter* in June 1990. "If only it was a film *with* Sidney Poitier," mourned the *Los Angeles Times*.[44]

Poitier had planned on directing another feature for Columbia. The studio canceled a project called *Hard Knox* in January 1988, but under Poitier's deal, he received $1.5 million anyway. In November 1989 he attached his name to another Columbia project, entitled *Beat the Eagle*. Three weeks later, however, he renounced his interest, avowing that fatigue and family responsibilities precluded him from another time-consuming venture. Indeed, during filming Poitier skipped lunch and slept three hours a night. At his age, he took longer to recuperate. Rumors swirled, however, that Poitier actually declined *Beat the Eagle* out of loyalty to Creative Artists Agency, which had just endured a spat with high-profile screenwriter Joe Eszterhas. Whatever the reason, after *Ghost Dad*, Poitier never directed another movie.[45]

In June 1990 Poitier agreed to play Thurgood Marshall in the ABC television miniseries *Separate but Equal*, the story of the 1954 *Brown vs. Board of Education* decision. Marshall had argued the case on behalf of the plaintiff before the Supreme Court, years before President Johnson appointed him to the Court. The role was Poitier's first dramatic television appearance since *A Man Is Ten Feet Tall* in 1955. To prepare, he met the eighty-one-year-old Marshall, then at the end of his career. During a long lunch in Georgetown, Justice Marshall reminisced in his deep baritone. "He told me about the places he'd been and the battles he'd fought—tales of his car being surrounded on lonely roads by people with bad intentions," said Poitier. "It was a revelation for me, what his life was really like."[46]

George Stevens Jr., whose father directed Poitier in *The Greatest Story Ever Told*, wanted a star to play the defense attorney John W. Davis. He signed Burt Lancaster. The seventy-six-year-old legend had always had trouble memorizing lines. Now, for long courtroom speeches, he needed TelePrompters to surround the set. He looked thin and tired.[47]

Lancaster nevertheless represented Davis with grace, a difficult endeavor for a character that defends segregation. Richard Kiley, as Chief Justice Earl Warren, conveyed the personal principles behind the legal decision. In all, *Separate but Equal*, which aired over two nights in April 1991, recounted the *Brown* decision in emotional, human terms. "At the end I was in tears," wrote columnist Anthony Lewis. "That testifies to the power of the film—and the events it describes." Poitier earned high praise. He did not so much portray Thurgood Marshall as be Sidney Poitier, effusing resolve, pride, dignity, and warmth. His approach imbued *Separate but Equal* with moral power, an apt virtue for the subject and the medium.[48]

Separate but Equal also proved that Poitier could still spark political debate. The day before the miniseries aired, a *New York Times* op-ed piece condemned the casting of dark-skinned Poitier to play light-skinned Marshall. "Such lack of color consciousness is an insult to African Americans," wrote Richard Carter. "But it's par for the course in TV and movies." He likened it to casting a blonde actor to play a real-life figure with jet-black hair.[49]

The response recalled when everyone read racial significance into Poitier's movies. Many reflected upon the prejudices against blacks with darker skin. Some advocated colorblindness: "Abilities and qualifications, not skin color, count." Others countenanced black unity: "Our bond should be with all blacks, not divided into dark-skinned blacks versus light-skinned blacks." Hollywood still shaped perceptions of the African American experience, and Poitier still participated in the process.[50]

Yet he participated sporadically. Since his acting comeback, Poitier averaged about one project per year. Though freed of financial pressures, he was too restless to completely retire, and he returned to the big screen in 1992 with *Sneakers*. The comic thriller starred Robert Redford, Dan Aykroyd, Ben Kingsley, and River Phoenix. For the first time in decades, Poitier took a supporting role. "Sidney's an American icon," marveled writer/director Phil Alden Robinson. "To get him in an ensemble film was incredible." He was the cast's venerated old timer. In February 1992, on his sixty-eighth birthday, cast and crew sang "Happy Birthday." For an encore they sang "To Sir with Love." Poitier laughed, buried his face in his hands, crouched down, and proclaimed, "This will happen to you!"[51]

In the film, the "sneakers" are not footwear but security consultants from society's fringe. The former 1960s radical Martin Bishop (Redford) leads a paranoid computer genius (Aykroyd), a teenage computer genius (Phoenix), and a blind computer genius (David Straithairn). Poitier plays a retired CIA agent, Crease, who brings dignity to the ragtag crew. Bishop's team gets blackmailed into stealing a computer chip that could collapse the world economy. In the process they topple a sinister radical-gone-awry (Kingsley).

Filled with cool gadgets and light repartee, *Sneakers* offered a comic-book charm. It won a considerable audience. No one gave a sterling performance, but they all embraced the frivolous spirit, even when the story devolved into nonsense. "I rarely have seen anything that I understood less or enjoyed more," wrote Rex Reed upon its September 1992 release.[52]

Poitier occupied a familiar niche. *Sneakers* maintained the boundaries on black actors: the white hero, Redford, had the romance. It also lacked the import of *Separate but Equal*: rather than recite Thurgood Marshall, he says, "Motherfuckers mess with me and I'll split your head!" *Sneakers* nevertheless allowed him both strength and fun. After forty years in the business, Poitier could finally indulge in those simple pleasures.

❖

Yet simple pleasures were not enough. In the last half-century, Poitier had trained himself in reading and diction, honed his acting, branched into directing and producing, and agonized over his personal and professional responsibilities. "I want roles that require me to dig a little deeper," he said in 1992. "I know I'm asking a lot, and that's why I don't work much anymore." This compulsion for self-improvement had driven his success, even as it compensated for his sticky anxieties. The old ghosts still haunted him.[53]

Watching a one-woman show by Anna DeVere Smith at a Los Angeles theater, Poitier was stirred to action. He remembered learning pantomime in the early 1950s. He had perfected those silent skills, and he had once considered forming them into a nightclub routine. Forty years later, the ambition reawakened. He wanted to do a solo stage show about his life. "First, I needed to settle obligations owed to self," he recalled. "Second, in the process I wanted to spin enough magic to close out what had been for me a genuinely magical career."[54]

That awareness of mortality drove the show. His old friend Charles Blackwell co-wrote the script. Recently diagnosed with prostate cancer, Blackwell wore an ostomy bag under his clothing. Then doctors diagnosed Poitier with the same disease. After four biopsies, Poitier underwent prostate surgery in June 1993. He was playing golf three weeks after leaving the hospital, and they soon finished the script. Alas, a Broadway producer nixed it. They considered rewriting the show, but Blackwell's cancer returned, and he died in June 1995.[55]

Poitier never again acted on stage, and he never again assumed such an artistic risk. Nor did his demons ever disappear. But they faded into the background. Now Poitier sought projects that reinforced his legacy, that imparted his values of tolerance and self-reliance, that connected him to the dreams and lessons of his past.

He returned to acting for *Children of the Dust*, a CBS miniseries that aired over two nights in February 1995. The Western recalls *Buck and the Preacher*. His character, Gypsy Smith, is a half-black, half-Cherokee bounty hunter. He protects black settlers during the land rush to the Oklahoma Territory in the 1880s, and he becomes marshal of Freedom, an all-black settlement. Yet he refuses to homestead himself, since he sympathizes with the deposed Cheyennes. In the final scene he fends off a Ku Klux Klan attack.[56]

Gypsy Smith, Poitier explained, "has a code of conduct that appealed to me." The cowboy helps both blacks and Indians, and he possesses the courage to challenge white bounty hunters. He also has tender exchanges with a schoolteacher, played by Regina Taylor. Motion pictures offered few roles for old-fashioned, senior-citizen heroes. But television's older audiences appreciated Poitier in *Children of the Dust* (repackaged for commercial release as *A Good Day to Die*). Poitier, for his part, embraced the revisionist update on the virtuous cowboy that he worshiped as a boy.[57]

Poitier's next project was even more personal, even more linked to his past. He reprised Mark Thackeray for an April 1996 television sequel, *To Sir, with Love II*. "It was my idea," he explained. "I felt that this character, had he stayed at the game, would have matured into quite an impressive individual." Directed by Peter Bogdanovich, the film begins with the teacher's retirement from his East End School. Some of the original actors make cameos. A middle-aged Lulu belts the title song again. Then Thackeray moves to Chicago, where he teaches a remedial class at a South Side school.[58]

If the original's classroom transformation is hard to swallow, then the sequel's is completely implausible. In an inner-city school plagued by guns, prostitution, and gang warfare, Thackeray offers dictums on self-esteem and manners. "When we address someone with respect, we are more likely to get respect," he lectures. "Please, thank you, excuse me — magical words, magical words." Of course, he salvages the teenagers' lives. Poitier followed the pattern set by *Blackboard Jungle*, *To Sir, with Love*, and *A Piece of the Action*; again he imparted his cherished values of pride and courtesy, learned on Cat Island.[59]

In line with his inclination to represent moral integrity, Poitier sought to play Nelson Mandela. As early as 1986, Poitier expressed interest in a Mandela miniseries produced by Harry Belafonte. ABC approved the project in June 1995, and Belafonte announced a cast with Danny Glover and Susan Sarandon. Then Poitier withdrew, citing script problems. "Harry knows and accepts that there have not been and never will be any artistic favors done between us," said Poitier. But Belafonte stewed. "Even if I'm a guest in his house," he said, "there are some things he just will not invite me to — situations where he feels it will just make it uncomfortable for the people he's going to be with." As both neared seventy, their relationship possessed the same masked tensions, petty jealousies, grudging respect, and brotherly love of their early Harlem days.[60]

Instead of Belafonte's project, Poitier starred in *Mandela and de Klerk*, an original production for Showtime. Richard Wesley, Poitier's collaborator on two First Artists pictures, wrote a screenplay that captured the dissolution of apartheid through the personal, emotional experiences of the two statesmen. Michael Caine, Poitier's co-star in *The Wilby Conspiracy*, again played his foil — this time as President F. W. de Klerk, the reluctant convert to racial democracy.[61]

Mandela and de Klerk crowned Poitier's experience with South Africa. In 1950 he was a lonely young man indentured to his white director. In 1996 he brought his family to a nation that had dismantled the racial state and elected Mandela to the presidency. During filming, Mandela invited Poitier to his Cape Town office, even though Mandela was planning a competing project based on his memoir *Long Walk to Freedom* and Mandela's literary agent was threatening a lawsuit. In addition, the national actors' union protested that foreigners were playing South Africans. Nevertheless, the statesman received Poitier with humility, vigor, and an aura of nobility. Poitier was overwhelmed. He composed himself enough to study Mandela's speech patterns and limping gait.[62]

In the movie, which aired in February 1997, Poitier captures his subject's dignity and warmth. The picture dramatizes Mandela's twenty-seven years in prison, his clandestine negotiations with de Klerk, his release to freedom, and his ascension to the presidency. It also portrays the crude ethnic nationalism of the white Conservative Party, the frightening militarism of the black Inkatha faction, and the political and personal failings of Winnie Mandela. De Klerk emerges morally ambivalent, though he deserves a harsher portrayal (the South African government sanctioned thousands of black deaths under him). Nelson Mandela is a hero — a characterization familiar to Poitier and appropriate to history.[63]

Poitier seemed settled into television projects that taught lessons of history and decency. Then in November 1997 he reappeared on the big screen in *The Jackal*, a high-budget remake of the 1973 film *The Day of the Jackal*. He again played an FBI agent. The film stars Bruce Willis as the Jackal, an international assassin, and Richard Gere as Declan Mulqueen, an imprisoned Irish terrorist. The Jackal plans a high-profile murder. Mulqueen knows the mysterious killer, and Poitier's Carter Preston enlists the Irishman's help. Mulqueen and Preston eventually thwart the assassination of the First Lady.

The story sprawls from Moscow to Helsinki to Washington, and the script's plausibility erodes as the government manhunt becomes a personal struggle between the Jackal and Mulqueen. The remake falls short of the original. Still, there are copious thrills. Poitier acts with remarkable gusto. He looks at least ten years younger than his actual age. *The Jackal* might not have won any Oscars or taught any lessons, but it proved that Poitier could survive and thrive into his eighth decade.[64]

Oprah Winfrey, Poitier's successor as the titan of black entertainment, supplied his next role. Poitier joined a television remake of *David and Lisa*, a low-budget black-and-white from 1962. "This is about something!" Poitier remembered thinking upon reading the script. "How imperfect we are, our frailties." For an introspective man guided by years of therapy, the story resonated. He played Jack Miller, the gentle psychiatrist who counsels David, a genius averse to touching, and Lisa, a schizophrenic who speaks in rhyme. The patients come to share a human connection. *Oprah Winfrey Presents: David and Lisa* aired on ABC in November 1999. Poitier remained the kind, intelligent professional that the public admired.[65]

Three months later, Sidney Poitier appeared in the Showtime original movie *Free of Eden* with a surprising co-star: Sydney Poitier. Like their half-sisters Pamela and Sherri, both Sydney and Anika had pursued acting careers. Before *Free of Eden*, however, Sydney was working as an assistant at a record company. Poitier the elder, as executive producer, proposed her for a minor part. Realizing the marketing opportunity, her acting capabilities, and her stunning looks (she was one of *People*'s "Fifty Most Beautiful People" in 2001), Showtime instead cast her for the lead.[66]

Sydney plays Nicole Turner, a young woman stuck in a Brooklyn housing project. Will Cleamons, Sidney's teacher-turned-businessman, advises her. Both undergo life-changing experiences. Nicole learns self-empowerment, like the teenagers of *Blackboard Jungle* and *To Sir, with Love*. Cleamons explores his painful past, which began in the ghetto. *Free of Eden* launched Sydney's career, and it followed Sidney's tendency to cast himself as a mentor.[67]

Poitier's last two projects — both CBS television movies — continued in this vein. In *The Simple Life of Noah Dearborn*, which aired in May 1999, he plays a ninety-one-year-old carpenter who still powers his scroll saw with a foot pedal. When realtors offer to buy his land, he resists, even fending off an investigation into his mental health. In *The Last Brick-maker in America*, broadcast in April 2001, he plays a craftsman who misses his dead wife. Modern technology has supplanted his brickmaking skill. He mentors a troubled boy, and each copes through hard work. Both movies are impossibly corny, but Poitier carries them with warmth and pride. He bore strong connections to these characters. Each had shades of his father—a proud man, wearied by a new economic order, reliant on traditional values. Poitier honored his father's legacy: the dignity of labor, the merit of responsibility.[68]

But while Poitier saluted his father, the nation celebrated Poitier. The Museum of the Moving Image honored him in 1989. "He was the only strong black figure I saw in the movies when I was growing up," said Spike Lee. "I'm able to do what I can today because of the hell that Sidney Poitier went through." In 1992, the American Film Institute gave Poitier its Life Achievement Award. For the occasion, they renamed the Louis B. Mayer Building on the old MGM lot after Poitier. The audience included Hollywood stars, Rosa Parks, and all six of Poitier's daughters. Denzel Washington, Danny Glover, and John Singleton paid homage. The praise approached the hagiographic. "I bow before your spirit," said Rod Steiger. "I emulate you," said Quincy Jones. Dan Aykroyd called him a "saint."[69]

The next year Poitier and Harry Belafonte shared the first-ever Thurgood Marshall Lifetime Achievement Award. Again the stars turned out: Quincy Jones, Berry Gordy, Gregory Peck, even Diahann Carroll. The two honorees reflected upon their tumultuous rapport. "Harry is an example of what a friend can be," said Poitier. "He's terrific." While Poitier lauded Thurgood Marshall, Belafonte delivered zingers. "When they told me that Sidney would be sharing it," he said, "there was no question that I deserved it."[70]

The accolades flowed: a 1992 film festival in Virginia, a 1994 honorary degree from Sarah Lawrence College, a 1995 Career Achievement Award from the National Board of Review, a 1995 commendation at the Kennedy Center Honors, a 1998 salute by the Motion Picture Academy of Arts and Sciences, a 1998 Lifetime Achievement Award from the Anti-Defamation League, a 2000 Lifetime Achievement Award from the Screen Actors Guild, a 2001 Directors Guild of America honor, and a 2001 Hall of Fame induction at the NAACP Image Awards. In some acceptance speeches, Poitier explained his career as the product of Evelyn and Reginald Poitier. At the Kennedy Center Honors, after Paul Newman extolled his "pilgrimage of startling grace," President Bill Clinton and First Lady Hillary Clinton cheered him from two adjacent seats, while applause washed over him. He cast his arms wide, thanking his admirers. He looked to the heavens. "My mother," he mouthed. "My father."[71]

The awards helped shape Poitier's legacy as a pioneer, as an icon of grace. He symbolized an era. A&E and PBS produced documentaries about his life and career. He participated in filmed tributes to others, including William Wellman, Michael Caine, and Ralph Bunche. The television series *In the Heat of the Night* inspired memories of his groundbreaking film. He even appeared as a cartoon giant in an episode of *South Park*.[72]

He also occupied positions of authority: the Walt Disney Company elected him to the Board of Directors, and the Bahamas named Poitier their ambassador to Japan. In 1997, he presented his credentials before Emperor Hirohito. Seventy years after his birth—an uncertain, premature birth that provoked his mother's desperation—Poitier fulfilled the predictions of a Miami soothsayer. He walked with kings.[73]

❖

By the turn of the century, Poitier showed some effects from seventy-three years, two wives, six children, four grandchildren, forty-six feature films, ten television movies, four Broadway plays, and one exceptional life. His hair had receded, and it assumed a touch of gray. Now he moved with slight deliberation. Grandfatherly poise replaced sizzling verve.

Yet he still possessed ample energy. He ran Verdon-Cedric Productions, searched for acting vehicles, and maintained a public presence. In 1994 he and Joanna moved to New York City, buying a two-story, thirteen-room, $2.5 million co-op on Fifth Avenue. Seven years later, they sold the apartment (for double the price) and moved back to Beverly Hills, where they bought an opulent Mediterranean-style home. Wherever their primary residence, the Poitiers bounced between the two coasts, visited the Bahamas, and traveled the world. Even in these luxurious golden years, however, Poitier maintained his self-discipline. He eschewed alcohol, red meat, milk, even sugar. He ate vegetables at breakfast. Age had mellowed his temper, but he still regulated his "demons." "I know that my biggest job is to keep them controlled," he told Brent Staples. "They are—what's the word?—seismic."[74]

In 2000 Poitier published a second memoir. *The Measure of a Man: A Spiritual Autobiography* explored questions of identity, spirituality, and responsibility. As he wrote, "I wanted to find out, as I looked back at a long and complicated life, with many twists and turns, how well I've done at measuring up to the values I espouse, the standards I myself have set." The struggles of his parents inform this quest. His father's adage — "The measure of a man is how well he provides for his children" — lends the title. In early chapters on the Bahamas, his migrations, and Harlem, Poitier commends his parents for instilling him with a work ethic and independent spirit.[75]

Poitier renounces straight narrative in *The Measure of a Man*, instead analyzing American values through his Bahamian past. When considering his survival during the blacklist era, he remembers his mother's advice: "Charm them, son, into neutral." When recalling the struggle over *A Raisin in the Sun*, he interprets Walter Lee Younger through his father. He lauds such pictures as *The Defiant Ones* and *A Patch of Blue* as extensions of his principles. He discusses his intellectual growth, his parenting philosophies, his spiritual ethos.[76]

And he defends himself. Coolly, matter-of-factly, he recounts the backlash against *To Sir, with Love, In the Heat of the Night*, and *Guess Who's Coming to Dinner*. The frustration simmers beneath, a cool boil. "In essence," he wrote, "I was being taken to task for playing exemplary human beings." He believes that he made necessary and important choices. Though he acknowledges his imperfections (there is only an oblique reference to Diahann Carroll), he implicitly suggests that his life has affirmed his ideals.[77]

Poitier deserves that credit, even if he smooths over some shortcomings. For a generation he shouldered a burden, created sympathy for black equality, delivered liberal films within a conservative system. He became the screen symbol of a morally righteous political movement. As the texture of black politics changed, he experienced both soaring popularity and withering criticism. The struggle tested him, and he emerged a better man. *The Measure of a Man* became a *New York Times* bestseller, and Poitier's recorded reading won a Grammy for best spoken-word album. Whether in print, on tape, or on screen, the public still appreciated the man and his image.[78]

His legacy informs modern black Hollywood. Poitier proved that large audiences would attend pictures featuring a black person as something other than an asinine servant or happy-go-lucky entertainer. His success paved the way for contemporary black actors and filmmakers.[79]

But the old barriers persevere, even if the lines have grown fuzzy. Morgan Freeman, Louis Gossett Jr., and Danny Glover often replicate the patterns from Poitier movies: their characters exist to enlighten white co-stars. Handsome stars such as Will Smith and Laurence Fishburne receive few romantic roles. Black actresses from Whoopi Goldberg to Angela Bassett rarely find roles worthy of their talents. Hollywood may no longer relegate blacks to particular stereotypes, but it still pigeonholes them into familiar categories.[80]

Denzel Washington best illustrates these barriers. He long admired Poitier. Once, during Washington's early career, Poitier saw him on a studio lot. "I pulled him aside and told him something that I know he already knew, but I needed to say it anyway," recalled Poitier. "I told him he had an amazing gift and with that gift came responsibility. Never lose sight of that."[81]

Indeed, Washington seemed to mold his public persona after Poitier, even as he resisted direct comparisons to his mentor. Like Poitier, he presented a figure of broad appeal. He played proud, upstanding, intelligent characters. He urged the media not to confine their discussions to racial topics. And in such pictures as *The Pelican Brief* and *The Mighty Quinn*, Washington insisted on cutting out kissing scenes between him and white women. Poitier's old dilemma — capturing a broad audience while satisfying a core contingent of African Americans — now applied to Washington.[82]

Thanks to his monumental talent, Washington became a top-rung movie star — and a reluctant standard-bearer for black Hollywood, in the Poitier mold. Yet like Poitier, he never received consideration for most major roles. "There is a ceiling for black actors, no doubt about that," he said. "But I try to keep thinking of it as a glass ceiling, one that can be broken at some point." Because blacks found so few opportunities to play three-dimensional characters, they rarely achieved recognition. Gossett, Washington, Goldberg, and Cuba Gooding Jr. won Academy Awards for supporting roles, but no black actor since Poitier had won for a leading role. The Academy of Motion Picture Arts and Sciences spurned Washington despite his astonishing performances in both *Malcolm X* (1992) and *The Hurricane* (1999). No black woman ever won Best Actress. Then, for the 2002 Academy Awards, a trio of African Americans won leading role nominations: Halle Berry for *Monster's Ball*, Will Smith for *Ali*, and Denzel Washington for *Training Day*.[83]

Sidney Poitier reigned over the Oscar ceremony, both literally and figuratively. He watched the proceedings with his family from a box next to the stage at the Kodak Theatre. The Academy gave him an honorary

Oscar. Washington, along with Walter Mirisch, introduced a short film that featured almost every modern black actor of significance. Gooding, recalling Poitier's first Oscar, said that "it rose us all up as Americans. We all became better because of it." Ving Rhames said that when Poitier slapped the white aristocrat in *In the Heat of the Night*, "it made a statement to me about what it is to be a man." Berry called him "a national treasure."

Poitier emerged to accept his Oscar. He stood before a long standing ovation by thousands of respectful admirers, and he gave a formal, restrained speech. "I arrived in Hollywood at the age of twenty-two in a time different than today's," he began, "a time in which the odds of my standing here tonight fifty-three years later would not have fallen in my favor." But instead of recounting his own experiences, he commended the filmmakers who made his career possible: Joe Mankiewicz, Darryl Zanuck, Richard Brooks, Ralph Nelson, Walter Mirisch, Guy Green, Norman Jewison, Stanley Kramer. He acknowledged his predecessors, accepting the award "in memory of all the African American actors and actresses who went before me in the difficult years, on whose shoulders I was privileged to stand to see where I might go." Last, he thanked Martin Baum and his family. The speech completed his enshrinement as a humble exponent of black dignity.[84]

That evening, Poitier was a living, breathing reminder of the history of black Hollywood. The television cameras often panned to him, especially during references to the historic trio of nominations. About an hour after Poitier's speech, Halle Berry won Best Actress. Through shaking tears, she began: "This moment is so much bigger than me." She recognized Dorothy Dandridge, Lena Horne, Diahann Carroll. She called herself a "vessel" for other women of color.

During the Best Actor presentation, Poitier grew larger than life. "I kissed Sidney Poitier tonight," giggled Julia Roberts before announcing the nominees. She opened the envelope and revealed the winner: Denzel Washington. Thirty-eight years after Poitier's triumph, another black actor won the highest honor accorded a movie actor. (In an ironic and revealing twist, Washington won by departing from his noble hero character; he played an engaging "bad cop" in *Training Day*.)

"Forty years I've been chasing Sidney," said Washington, laughing that even on the night of his triumph, Poitier overshadowed him. "I'll always be chasing you, Sidney. I'll always be following in your footsteps. There's nothing I would rather do, Sir. God bless you." Poitier saluted Washington with his own Oscar. As the audience roared, the two men shared a moment—capping off a triumphant evening, acknowledging the milestone, symbolizing an awareness of their shared burden.

❖

As with Poitier's Oscar in 1964, the triple black triumph on Oscar Night 2002 generated speculation about its import. "As a country, we are better because of moments like this," said filmmaker Kasi Lemmons. "Something groundbreaking, historical happened." Black entertainers reacted with joy, and some believed that a new era had dawned. Perhaps for the first time, many producers and directors paid attention to the black image on film.[85]

But were the Oscars mere tokens? "Only time will tell whether the symbol becomes the substance," said NAACP chairman Julian Bond. Awards did not mean equality. Bond called for black actors, directors, screenwriters, and craft personnel in numbers representative of their percentage of the population. Cultural critic Stanley Crouch added that the Academy Awards gained attention only because of the film industry's long history of exclusion. But the ghosts of the past—the wild-eyed bucks of *Birth of a Nation*, the loyal slaves of *Gone With the Wind*, Stepin Fetchit— still hover over Hollywood, so the Oscars represent a milestone.[86]

Poitier is a ghost of black Hollywood, too. He has become consecrated as a heroic pioneer, but he was also a stereotype. His image served a worthy purpose. At a time when racial integration depended on white public opinion, Poitier expressed everything that blacks could be: noble, intelligent, proud. He also expressed everything that blacks could *not* be: resentful of racism, sexually charged, justified of eye-for-an-eye violence. In a nation of Rodney King and O. J. Simpson, where race still molds social perceptions, where political life still gets sifted through popular culture, Poitier's legacy continues to resonate.[87]

So the past debates over his image must influence the present understanding of the man. To uncritically admire Poitier does not just recognize his characters' virtues or his career's milestones. It also indulges the corrosive fantasy that racial equality depends on black people with the goodness and grace associated with Sidney Poitier.

APPENDIX : PERFORMANCES BY SIDNEY POITIER

No Way Out
(Twentieth Century-Fox, 1950)
Producer: Darryl Zanuck
Director: Joseph Mankiewicz
Screenplay: Joseph Mankiewicz, Lesser
Samuels
Photography: Milton Krasner
Music: Alfred Newman
Editor: Barbara McLean
Art Direction: Lyle Wheeler, George
Davis
Cast: Richard Widmark (Ray Biddle),
Linda Darnell (Edie Johnson), Stephen
McNally (Dr. Daniel Wharton), Sidney
Poitier (Dr. Luther Brooks), Mildred
Joanne Smith (Cora Brooks), Harry
Belaver (George Biddle), Don Hicks
(Johnny Biddle), Stanley Ridges (Dr.
Moreland), Dots Johnson (Lefty), Ruby
Dee (Connie), Ossie Davis (John)

Cry, the Beloved Country
(London Films, 1952)
Producer: Zoltan Korda
Director: Zoltan Korda
Screenplay: Alan Paton, from his novel
Photography: Robert Krasker
Editor: David Easy
Art Direction: Wilfrid Shingleton
Cast: Canada Lee (Stephen Kumalo),
James Jarvis (Charles Carson), Sidney
Poitier (Reverend Msimangu), Joyce
Carey (Margaret Jarvis), Geoffrey Keen
(Father Vincent), Michael Goodliffe
(Martens), Edric Connor (John
Kumalo), Charles McCrae (Kumalo's
Friend), Lionel Ngakane (Absalom),
Vivien Clinton (Mary), Albertina
Temba (Mrs. Kumalo), Bruce Anderson
(Farmer Smith), Bruce Meredith Smith

(Captain Jaarsveldt), Berdine
Brunewald (Mary Jarvis), Ribbon
Dhlamini (Gertrude Kumalo), Stanley
Van Beers (Judge)

Red Ball Express
(Universal-International, 1952)
Producer: Aaron Rosenberg
Director: Budd Boetticher
Screenplay: John Michael Hayes, from
the Marcel Klauber and Billy Grady Jr.
story
Photography: Maury Gertsman
Editor: Edward Curtiss
Art Direction: Bernard Herzbrun,
Richard Riedel
Cast: Jeff Chandler (Lt. Chick
Campbell), Alex Nicol (Sgt. Ernest
Kallek), Charles Drake (Partridge),
Hugh O'Brian (Wilson), Frank Chase
(Higgins), Jack Kelly (Heyman), Judith
Braun (Joyce McClellan), Cindy Garner
(Kitty Walsh), Jacqueline Duval
(Antoinette DuBois), Howard Petrie
(Gen. Gordon), Sidney Poitier (Corp.
Andrew Robertson), Bubber Johnson
(Taffy Smith), Robert Davis (Dave
McCord), John Hudson (Sgt. Max),
Palmer Lee (Tank Lt.), Jack Warden
(Major)

Go, Man, Go!
(Sirod Productions, released by United
Artists, 1954)
Producer: Anton M. Leader (Alfred
Palca)
Director: James Wong Howe
Screenplay: Arnold Becker (Alfred
Palca)
Photography: Bill Steiner
Editor: Faith Elliott
Music: Alex North

Art Direction: Howard Bay
Technical Director: Harry Hannin
Cast: Dane Clark (Abe Saperstein),
Sylvia Saperstein (Pat Breslin), Sidney
Poitier (Inman Jackson), Edmon Ryan
(Zack Leader), Bram Nossen (James
Willoughby), Anatol Winogradoff
(Papa Saperstein), Celia Boodkin
(Mama Saperstein), Carol Sinclair (Fay
Saperstein), Ellsworth Wright (Sam),
Slim Galliard (Slim), Frieda Altman
(Ticket Seller), Mort Marshall (MC),
Jean Shore (Secretary), Ruby Dee (Irma
Jackson), Marty Glickman (Announcer
No. 1), Bill Stern (Announcer No. 2),
Lew Hearn (Appraiser), Harlem
Globetrotters (themselves)

Blackboard Jungle
(Metro-Goldwyn-Mayer, 1955)
Producer: Pandro S. Berman
Director: Richard Brooks
Screenplay: Richard Brooks, from the
Evan Hunter novel *The Blackboard
Jungle*
Photography: Russell Harlan
Music: Bill Haley and the Comets
Editor: Ferris Webster
Art Direction: Cedric Gibbons, Randall
Duell
Cast: Glenn Ford (Richard Dadier),
Anne Francis (Anne Dadier), Louis
Calhern (Jim Murdock), Margaret
Hayes (Lois Hammond), John Hoyt
(Mr. Warneke), Richard Kiley (Joshua
Edwards), Emile Meyer (Mr. Halloran),
Warner Anderson (Dr. Bradley), Basil
Ruysdael (Prof. A. R. Kraal), Sidney
Poitier (Gregory Miller), Vic Morrow
(Artie West), Dan Terranova (Belazi),
Rafael Campos (Pete Morales), Paul
Mazursky (Emmanuel Stoker), Horace
McMahon (Detective), Jameel Farah
(Santini), Danny Dennis (De Lica)

Goodbye, My Lady
(Warner Brothers, 1956)
Producer: Batjac Productions
Director: William A. Wellman

Screenplay: Sid Fleishman, from the
James Street novel
Photography: William H. Clothier
Music: Laurindo Almeida, George Field
Editor: Fred MacDowell
Production Manager: Nate H. Edwards,
Gordon B. Forbes
Cast: Walter Brennan (Uncle Jesse), Phil
Harris (Cash), Brandon de Wilde
(Skeeter), Sidney Poitier (Gates),
William Hopper (Grover), Louise
Beavers (Bonnie Dew), Vivian Vance
(Wife), William Frawley (Husband)

Edge of the City
(Metro-Goldwyn-Mayer, 1957)
Producer: David Susskind
Director: Martin Ritt
Screenplay: Robert Alan Aurthur, from
his teleplay *A Man is Ten Feet Tall*
Photography: Joseph Brun
Music: Leonard Rosenman
Editor: Sidney Meyers
Art Direction: Richard Sylbert
Cast: John Cassavetes (Axel North),
Sidney Poitier (Tommy Tyler), Jack
Warden (Charles Malik), Kathleen
Maguire (Ellen Wilson), Ruby Dee
(Lucy Tyler), Robert Simon (Mr.
Nordmann), Ruth White (Mrs.
Nordmann), William A. Lee (Davis),
Val Avery (Brother), John Kellogg
(Detective), David Clarke (Wallace),
Estelle Helmsley (Lucy's Mother),
Charles Jordan (Old Stevodore), Ralph
Bell (Nightboss)

Something of Value
(Metro-Goldwyn-Mayer, 1957)
Producer: Pandro S. Berman
Director: Richard Brooks
Screenplay: Richard Brooks, from the
Robert Ruark novel
Photography: Russell Harlan
Music: Miklos Rosza
Editor: Ferris Webster
Art Direction: William A. Horning,
Edward Carfagno
Cast: Rock Hudson (Peter McKenzie),

Dana Wynter (Holly Keith), Wendy Hiller (Elizabeth Newton), Sidney Poitier (Kimani), Juano Hernandez (Njogu), William Marshall (Leader), Robert Beatty (Jeff Newton), Walter Ftizgerald (Henry McKenzie), Michael Pate (Joe Matson), Ivan Dixon (Lathela), Ken Renard (Karanja), Samadu Jackson (Witch Doctor), Frederick O'Neal (Adam Marenga), John J. Akar (Waithaka)

Band of Angels
(Warner Brothers, 1957)
Director: Raoul Walsh
Screenplay: John Twist, Ivan Goff, Ben Roberts, from the Robert Penn Warren novel
Photography: Lucien Ballard
Music: Max Steiner
Editor: Folmar Blangsted
Art Direction: Franz Blachelin
Cast: Clark Gable (Hamish Bond), Yvonne DeCarlo (Amantha Starr), Sidney Poitier (Rau-Ru), Efrem Zimbalist Jr. (Ethan Sears), Patric Knowles (Charles de Marigny), Rex Reason (Seth Parton), Torin Thatcher (Capt. Canavan), Andrea King (Miss Idell), Ray Teal (Mr. Calloway), Russ Evans (Jimmee), Carolle Drake (Michele), Raymond Bailey (Stuart), Tommie Moore (Dollie), William Forrest (Aaron Starr), Noreen Corcoran (Young Manty)

Mark of the Hawk
(Universal-International, 1958)
Producer: Lloyd Young, W. Burston Marton
Director: Michael Audley
Screenplay: H. Kenn Carmichael and Lloyd Young, from the Young original story
Photography: Erwin Hillier, Toge Fujihara
Music: Matyas Seiber
Editor: Edward Jarvis
Art Direction: Terence Verity

African Location Unit Director: Gilbert Gunn
Cast: Eartha Kitt (Renee), Sidney Poitier (Obam), Juano Hernandez (Amugu), John McIntire (Craig), Helen Horton (Barbara), Marne Maitland (Sundar Lal), Gerard Heinz (Governor General), Patrick Allen (Gregory), Earl Cameron (Prosecutor), Clifton Macklin (Kanda), Ewen Solon (Inspector), Lionel Ngakane (African Doctor), Andy Ho (Chinese Doctor), John A. Tinn (Chinese Soldier)

The Defiant Ones
(Stanley Kramer, released by United Artists, 1958)
Director: Stanley Kramer
Screenplay: Nathan E. Douglas (Nedrick Young) and Harold Jacob Smith
Photography: Sam Leavitt
Music: Ernest Gold
Editor: Frederic Knudtson
Art Direction: Fernando Carrere
Costume: Joe King
Special Effects: Walter Elliott
Cast: Tony Curtis (John "Joker" Jackson), Sidney Poitier (Noah Cullen), Theodore Bikel (Sheriff Max Muller), Charles McGraw (Capt. Frank Gibbons), Cara Williams (The Woman), Lon Chaney (Big Sam), King Donovan (Solly), Claude Akins (Mac), Lawrence Dobkin (Editor), Whit Bissell (Lou Gans), Carl Switzer (Angus), Kevin Coughlin (The Kid)

Virgin Island
(Countryman Films, released by Films-Around-the-World, 1958)
Producer: Leon Close, Grahame Thorpe
Director: Pat Jackson
Screenplay: Philip Rush (Ring Lardner Jr.) and Pat Jackson, from the Robb White novel *Our Virgin Island*
Photography: Freddie Francis
Music: Clifton Parker
Editor: Gordon Pilkington

Cast: John Cassavetes (Even), Virginia Maskell (Tina), Sidney Poitier (Marcus), Isabel Dean (Mrs. Lomax), Colin Gordon (Commissioner), Howard Marion Crawford (Prescott), Edric Connor (Captain Jason), Ruby Dee (Ruth), Gladys Boot (Mrs. Carruthers), Julian Mayfield (Band Leader), Reginald Hearne (Doctor), Arnold Bell (Heath), Alonzo Bozon (Grant)

Porgy and Bess
(Samuel Goldwyn, released by Columbia Pictures, 1959)
Director: Otto Preminger
Screenplay: Richard Nash, from the George Gershwin operetta *Porgy and Bess*, from the Dorothy and Dubose Heyward play *Porgy*, from the Dubose Heyward novel *Porgy*
Photography: Leon Shamroy
Music: George Gershwin, Andre Previn
Editor: Daniel Mandell
Choreography: Hermes Pan
Cast: Sidney Poitier (Porgy), Dorothy Dandridge (Bess), Sammy Davis Jr. (Sportin' Life), Pearl Bailey (Maria), Brock Peters (Crown), Diahann Carroll (Clara), Leslie Scott (Jake), Ruth Attaway (Serena), Clarence Muse (Peter), Ivan Dixon (Jim), Everdinne Wilson (Annie), Joel Fluellen (Robbins), Earl Jackson (Mingo), Roy Glenn (Lawyer Frazier), Claude Akins (Detective), Maurica Manson (Coroner)

All the Young Men
(Hall Bartlett, released by Columbia Pictures, 1960)
Director: Hall Bartlett
Screenplay: Hall Bartlett
Photography: Daniel Fapp
Music: George Dunning
Editor: Al Clark
Art Direction: George Dunning
Cast: Alan Ladd (Kincaid), Sidney Poitier (Towler), James Darren (Cotton), Glenn Corbett (Wade), Mort Sahl (Crane), Anna St. Clair (Maya),

Paul Richards (Bracken), Dick Davalos (Casey), Lee Kinsolving (Dean), Joe Gallison (Jackson), Paul Baxley (Lazitech), Charles Quinlivan (Lieutenant), Michael Davis (Cho), Mario Alcalde (Hunter), Maria Tsien (Korean Woman), Ingemar Johansson (Torgil)

A Raisin in the Sun
(David Susskind and Philip Rose, released by Columbia Pictures, 1961)
Director: Daniel Petrie
Screenplay: Lorraine Hansberry, from her play
Photography: Charles Lawton
Music: Laurence Rosenthal
Editor: William A. Lyon, Paul Weatherwax
Art Direction: Carl Anderson
Cast: Sidney Poitier (Walter Lee Younger), Claudia McNeil (Lena Younger), Ruby Dee (Ruth), Diana Sands (Beneatha), Ivan Dixon (Asagai), John Fiedler (Mark Lindner). Louis Gossett (George Murchison), Stephen Perry (Travis), Joel Fluellen (Bobo), Roy Glenn (Willie Harris), Ray Stubbs (Bartender), Rudolph Monroe (Taxi Driver), George De Normand (Employer)

Paris Blues
(Sam Shaw, released by United Artists, 1961)
Producer: George Glass and Walter Seitzer
Director: Martin Ritt
Screenplay: Jack Sher, Irene Kamp, and Walter Bernstein, from the Lulla Adler adaptation of the Harold Flender novel
Photography: Christian Matras
Music: Duke Ellington
Editor: Roger Dwyre
Art Direction: Alexander Trauner
Cast: Paul Newman (Ram Bowen), Joanne Woodward (Lillian Corning), Sidney Poitier (Eddie Cook), Louis Armstrong (Wild Man Moore), Diahann Carroll (Connie Lampson),

Serge Reggiani (Michel Dugivne), Barbara Laage (Marie Seoul), Andre Luguet (Rene Bernard), Marie Versini (Nicole), Moustache (Drummer), Aaron Bridgers (Pianist), Roger Blin (Gypsy Guitarist), Niko (Ricardo)

Pressure Point
(Stanley Kramer, released by United Artists, 1962)
Director: Hubert Cornfield
Screenplay: Hubert Cornfield and S. Lee Pogostin, from a chapter of the Robert Lindner book *The Fifty Minute Hour*
Photography: Ernest Haller
Music: Ernest Gold
Editor: Fred Knudtson
Art Direction: Rudy Sternad
Cast: Sidney Poitier (Doctor), Bobby Darin (Patient), Peter Falk (Psychiatrist), Carl Benton Reid (Chief Medical Officer), Mary Munday (Bar Hostess), Barry Gordon (Boy), Howard Caine (Tavern Owner), Anne Barton (Mother), James Anderson (Father), Yvette Vickers (Drunken Woman)

Lilies of the Field
(Ralph Nelson, released by United Artists, 1963)
Director: Ralph Nelson
Screenplay: James Poe, from the William Barrett novella *The Lilies of the Field*
Photography: Ernest Haller
Music: Jerry Goldsmith
Editor: John McCafferty
Cast: Sidney Poitier (Homer Smith), Lilia Skala (Mother Maria), Lisa Mann (Sister Gertrude), Isa Crino (Sister Agnes), Francesca Jarvis (Sister Albertine), Pamela Branch (Sister Elizabeth), Stanley Adams (Juan), Dan Frazer (Father Murphy), Ralph Nelson (Harold Ashton)

The Long Ships
(Warwick Avala Productions, released by Columbia Pictures, 1964)

Producer: Irving Allen
Director: Jack Cardiff
Screenplay: Berkeley Mather and Beverly Cross, from the Franz Bengtsson novel
Photography: Christopher Challis
Music: Dusan Radles
Editor: Geoff Foot
Cast: Richard Widmark (Rolfe), Sidney Poitier (Ali Mansuh), Russ Tamblyn (Orm), Rosanna Schiaffino (Aminah), Bebe Loncar (Gerda), Oscar Holmolka (Krok), Edward Judd (Sven), Clifford Evans (King Harald), Jeanne Moody (Ylva), Colin Blakely (Rhykka), Gordon Jackson (Vahlin), David Lodge (Olla), Paul Stassino (Raschild), Lionel Jeffries (Ariz)

The Greatest Story Ever Told
(George Stevens, released by United Artists, 1965)
Executive Producer: Frank I. Davis
Associate Producer: George Stevens Jr., Antonion Vellani
Director: George Stevens
Screenplay: George Stevens, James Lee Barrett from the books of the Old and New Testament, other ancient writings, the Fulton Oursler book, and other writings by Henry Dreker, with the creative consultation of Carl Sandburg
Photography: Loyal Griggs, William C. Mellor
Music: Alfred Newman
Editor: Harold F. Kress, Argyle Nelson Jr., Frank O'Neill
Art Direction: Richard Day, William Creber
Costumes: Vittorio Nino Novarese, Marjorie Best
Set Design: David Hall
Special Effects: J. McMillan Johnson, Clarence Silfer, A. Arnold Gillespie, Robert A. Hoag
Cast: Max Von Sydow (Jesus), Dorothy McGuire (Mary), Robert Loggia (Joseph), Calude Rains (Herod the Great), Jose Ferrer (Herod Antipas),

Marian Seldes (Herodias), John Abbott (Aben), Rodolfo Acosta (Captain of Lancers), Charlton Heston (John the Baptist), Michael Anderson (Little James), Robert Blake (Simon the Zealot), Burt Brinkerhoff (Andrew), John Considine (John), Jamie Farr (Thaddeus), David Hedison (Philip), Peter Mann (Nathaniel), David McCallum (Judas), Roddy McDowall (Matthew), Gary Raymond (Peter), Tom Reese (Thomas), David Sheiner (James the Elder), Pat Boone (Young Man at Tomb), Victor Buono (Sorak), Richard Conte (Barabbas), Philip Coolidge (Chuza), John Crawford (Alexander), Joanna Dunham (Mary Magdalene), Angela Lansbury (Claudia), Frank Silvera (Caspar), Ed Wynn (Old Aram), Martin Landau (Caiaphas), John Wayne (Roman Captain), Sidney Poitier (Simon of Cyrene), Kim Hamilton (Simon of Cyrene's Wife), Frank DeKova (Tormentor), Van Heflin (Bar Amand), Martin Landau (Caiaphas), Vic Lundin (Pilate's Aid), Janet Margolin (Mary of Bethany), Sal Mineo (Uriah), Gil Perkins (Jacob), Nehemiah Persoff (Shemiah), Donald Pleasance (Dark Hermit), Telly Savales (Pilate), Joseph Schildkraut (Nicodemus), Joe Sirola (Dumah), Abraham Solger (Joesph of Arimathea), Paul Stewart (Quester), Harold Stone (General Varus), John Wayne (Centurion), Shelley Winters (Woman of No Name)

The Bedford Incident
(Bedford Productions, released by Columbia Pictures, 1965)
Producer: James B. Harris and Richard Widmark
Associate Producer: Dennis O'Dell
Director: James B. Harris
Screenplay: James Poe, from the James Rascovich novel
Photography: Gilbert Taylor
Music: Gerard Schurmann

Editor: John Jympson
Art Direction: Arthur Lawson
Cast: Richard Widmark (Capt. Eric Finlander), Sidney Poitier (Ben Munceford), James MacArthur (Ensign Ralston), Martin Balsam (Dr. Chester Potter), Wally Cox (Seaman Merlin Queffle), Eric Portman (Commodore Schrepke), Michael Kane (Commandant Allison), Gary Cockrell (Lt. Bascombe), Phil Brown (Chief Hospitalman McKinley), Brian Davies (Lt. Beckman), Edward Bishop (Lt. Hacker), George Roubichek (Lt. Berger), Michael Graham (Lt. Krindlemeyer), Bill Evans (Lt. Hazelwood), Donald Sutherland (Hospital Man), Warren Stanhope (Hospital Man), Colin Maitland (Seaman), Paul Tamarin (Seaman), Frank Lieberman (Seaman)

A Patch of Blue
(Metro-Goldwyn-Mayer, 1965)
Producer: Pandro S. Berman
Director: Guy Green
Screenplay: Guy Green, from the Elizabeth Kata novel *Be Ready with Bells and Drums*
Photography: Robert Burks
Music: Jerry Goldsmith
Editor: Rita Roland
Art Direction: George W. Davis, Urie McCleary
Cast: Sidney Poitier (Gordon Ralfe), Shelley Winters (Rose-Ann D'Arcey), Elizabeth Hartman (Selina D'Arcey), Wallace Ford (Ole Pa), Ivan Dixon (Mark Ralfe), Elisabeth Fraser (Sadie), John Qualen (Mr. Faber), Kelly Flynn (Yanek Faber), Debi Storm (Selina, Age 5), Renata Vanni (Mrs. Favolaro), Saverio LoMedico (Mr. Favolaro)

The Slender Thread
(Paramount, 1966)
Producer: Stephen Alexander
Director: Sydney Pollack
Screenplay: Stirling Siliphant, from the

Shana Alexander article "Decision to Die"
Photography: Loyal Griggs
Music: Quincy Jones
Editor: Thomas Stanford
Art Direction: Hal Pereira and Jack Poplin
Cast: Sidney Poitier (Alan Newell), Anne Bancroft (Inga Dyson), Telly Savalas (Dr. Coburn), Steven Hill (Mark Dyson), Edward Asner (Det. Judd Ridley), Indus Arthur (Marion), Paul Newlan (Sgt. Harry Ward), Dabney Coleman (Charlie), H. M. Wynant (Doctor), Robert Hoy (Patrolman Steve Peters), Greg Jarvis (Chris Dyson), Jason Wingreen (Medical Technician), Marjorie Nelson (Mrs. Thomas), Steven Marlo (Arthur Foss), Thomas Hill (Liquor Salesman), Lane Bradford (Al McArdle), Janet Dudley (Edna), John Napier (Dr. Alden Van)

Duel at Diablo
(Fred Engel and Ralph Nelson, released by United Artists, 1966)
Director: Ralph Nelson
Screenplay: Marvin Alpert and Michael Grilikhes, from the Alpert novel *Apache Rising*
Photography: Charles F. Wheeler
Music: Neal Hefti
Editor: Fredric Steinkamp
Assistant Directors: Emmett Emerson, Philip N. Cook
Cast: James Garner (Jess Remsberg), Sidney Poitier (Toller), Bibi Andersson (Ellen Grange), Dennis Weaver (Willard Grange), Bill Travers (Lt. Scotty McAllister), William Redfield (Sgt. Ferguson), John Hoyt (Chata), John Crawford (Clay Dean), John Hubbard (Major Novak), Kevin Coughlin (Norton), Jay Ripley (Tech), Jeff Cooper (Casey), Ralph Bahnsen (Nyles), Bobby Crawford (Swenson), Richard Lapp (Forbes), Armand Alzamora (Ramirez), Alf Elson (Col. Foster), Dawn Little Sky (Chata's Wife), Eddie Little Sky (Alchise), Al Wyatt (First Miner), Bill Hart (Corporal Harrington), J. R. Randall (Crowley), John Daheim (Stableman), Phil Schumacher (Burly Soldier), Richard Farnsworth (First Wagon Driver), Joe Finnegan (Second Wagon Driver)

To Sir, with Love
(James Clavell, released by Columbia Pictures, 1967)
Executive Producer: John R. Sloan
Director: James Clavell
Screenplay: James Clavell, from the E. R. Braithwaite memoir
Photography: Paul Beeson
Music: Ron Grainer
Editor: Peter Thornton
Cast: Sidney Poitier (Mark Thackeray), Christian Roberts (Denham), Judy Geeson (Pamela Dare), Suzy Kendall (Gillian), Faith Brook (Mrs. Evans), Christopher Chittell (Potter), Geoffrey Bayldon (Weston), Patricia Routledge (Clinty), Adrienne Posta (Moira Jackson), Edward Burnham (Florian), Rita Webb (Mrs. Joseph), Fiona Duncan (Miss Phillips), Lulu [Marie Lawrie] (Barbara Pegg)

In the Heat of the Night
(Walter Mirisch, released by United Artists, 1967)
Director: Norman Jewison
Screenplay: Stirling Siliphant, from the John Ball novel
Photography: Haskell Wexler
Music: Quincy Jones
Editor: Hal Ashby
Art Direction: Paul Groesse
Cast: Sidney Poitier (Virgil Tibbs), Rod Steiger (Bill Gillespie), Warren Oates (Sam Wood), Lee Grant (Leslie Colbert), James Patterson (Purdy), Quentin Dean (Dolores Purdy), Larry Gates (Eric Endicott), Scott Wilson (Harvey Oberst), Jack Teter (Philip Colbert), Matt Clark (Packy Harrison),

Anthony James (Ralph Henshaw), Karmit Murdock (H. E. Henderson), Khalil Bezaleel (Jess), Peter Whitney (George Courtney), William Watson (Harold Courtney), Timothy Scott (Shagbag Martin), Fred Stewart (Dr. Martin), Arthur Malet (Ted Ulam), David Stinehart (Baggage Master), Buzz Barton (Conductor)

Guess Who's Coming to Dinner
(Stanley Kramer, released by Columbia Pictures, 1967)
Director: Stanley Kramer
Screenplay: William Rose
Associate Producer: George Glass
Photography: Sam Leavitt
Music: Frank De Vol
Editor: Robert C. Jones
Production Design: Robert Clatworthy
Cast: Spencer Tracy (Matt Drayton), Sidney Poitier (John Prentice), Katharine Hepburn (Christina Drayton), Katharine Houghton (Joey Drayton), Cecil Kellaway (Monsignor Ryan), Beah Richards (Mrs. Prentice), Roy Glenn (Mr. Prentice), Isabel Sanford (Tillie), Virginia Christie (Hilary St. George), Alexandra Hay (Carhop), Barbara Randolph (Dorothy), D'Urville Martin (Frankie), Tom Heaton (Peter), Grace Gaynor (Judith), Skip Martin (Delivery Boy), John Hopkins (Cab Driver)

For Love of Ivy
(Palomar Pictures, released by Cinerama, 1968)
Producer: Edgar J. Scherick, Jay Weston
Director: Daniel Mann
Screenplay: Robert Alan Aurthur, from Sidney Poitier's original story
Photography: Joseph Coffey
Music: Quincy Jones
Editor: Patricia Jaffe
Production Design: Peter Dohanos
Cast: Sidney Poitier (Jack Parks), Abbey Lincoln (Ivy Moore), Beau Bridges (Tim Austin), Nan Martin (Doris Austin),

Lauri Peters (Gena Austin), Carroll O'Connor (Frank Austin), Leon Bibb (Billy Talbot), Hugh Hird (Jerry), Lon Satton (Harry), Stanley Greene (Eddie)

The Lost Man
(Universal Pictures, 1969)
Producer: Edward Muhl, Melville Tucker
Director: Robert Alan Aurthur
Screenplay: Robert Alan Aurthur, from Frederick Green's screenplay *Odd Man Out*
Photography: Jerry Finnerman
Music: Quincy Jones
Editor: Edward Mann
Art Direction: Alexander Golitzen, George C. Webb
Cast: Sidney Poitier (Jason Higgs), Joanna Shimkus (Cathy Ellis), Al Freeman Jr. (Dennis), Michael Tolan (Hamilton), Leon Bibb (Eddie), Richard Dysart (Barnes), David Steinberg (Photographer), Beverly Todd (Sally), Paul Winfield (Orville), Bernie Hamilton (Reggie), Richard Anthony Williams (Ronald), Virginia Capers (Theresa), Vonette McGee (Diane), Frank Marth (Warren), Maxine Stuart (Miss Harrison), George Tyle (Plainsclothesman), Pauline Mayers (Grandma), Lee Weaver (Willie), Morris Erby (Miller), Doug Johnson (Teddy), Lincoln Kilpatrick (Minister)

They Call Me Mister Tibbs!
(Walter Mirisch, released by United Artists, 1970)
Producer: Herbert Hirschman
Director: Gordon Douglas
Screenplay: Alan R. Trustman and James R. Webb, from the Trustman story, based on the John Ball characters
Photography: Gerald Finnerman
Music: Quincy Jones
Editor: Bud Molin
Art Direction: Addison F. Hehr
Cast: Sidney Poitier (Virgil Tibbs), Martin Landau (Rev. Logan Sharpe),

Barbara McNair (Valeri Tibbs), Anthony Zerbe (Rice Weedon), Jeff Corey (Capt. Marden), David Sheiner (Herbert Kenner), Juano Hernandez (Mealie), Norma Crane (Marge Garfield), Edward Asner (Woody Garfield), Ted Gehring (Sgt. Deutsch), Beverly Todd (Puff), Linda Towne (Joy Sturges), George Spell (Andrew Tibbs), Wanda Spell (Ginny Tibbs)

Brother John
(E&R Productions, released by Columbia Pictures, 1971)
Producer: Joel Glickman
Director: James Goldstone
Screenplay: Ernest Kinoy
Photography: Gerald Perry Finnerman
Music: Quincy Jones
Sound: William Randall
Editor: Edward A. Biery
Art Direction: Al Brenner
Set Decoration: Audrey Blasdel
Assistant Director: Tom Schmidt
Cast: Sidney Poitier (John Kane), Will Geer (Doc Thomas), Bradford Dillman (Lloyd Thomas), Beverly Todd (Louisa MacGill), Ramon Bieri (Orly Bail), Warren J. Kemmerling (George), Lincoln Kirkpatrick (Charles Gray), P. Jay Sidney (Rev. MacGill), Richard Ward (Frank), Paul Winfield (Henry Birkhardt), Zara Cutty (Miss Nettie)

The Organization
(Walter Mirisch, released by United Artists, 1971)
Director: Don Medford
Screenplay: James R. Webb, based on the John Ball characters
Photography: Joseph Biroc
Music: Gil Melle
Editor: Ferris Webster
Art Direction: George Chan
Cast: Sidney Poitier (Virgil Tibbs), Barbara McNair (Valeri Tibbs), Gerald O'Loughlin (Jack Pecora), Sheree North (Mrs. Morgan), Fred Bier (Bob Alford), Allen Garfield (Benjy), Ron O'Neal (Joe

Peralez), Lani Miyazaki (Annie Sekido), George Spell (Andrew Tibbs), Wanda Spell (Ginny Tibbs)

Buck and the Preacher
(E&R Productions and Belafonte Enterprises, released by Columbia Pictures, 1972)
Executive Producer: Sidney Poitier, Harry Belafonte
Producer: Joel Glickman
Director: Sidney Poitier
Screenplay: Ernest Kinoy, from the Kinoy and Drake Walker story
Photography: Alex Phillips Jr.
Music: Benny Carter, featuring Sonny Terry and Brownie McGhee
Editor: Pembroke J. Herring
Production Designer: Sydney Z. Litwack
Costume Designer: Guy Verhille
Cast: Sidney Poitier (Buck), Harry Belafonte (Preacher), Ruby Dee (Ruth), Cameron Mitchell (Deshay), Denny Miller (Floyd), Nita Talbot (Madame Esther), John Kelly (Sheriff), Tony Brubaker (Headman), James McEachin (Kingston), Clarence Muse (Cudjo), Lynn Hamilton (Sarah), Doug Johnson (Sam), Errol John (Joshua), Ken Menard (Little Henry), Pamela Jones (Delilah), Drake Walker (Elder), Dennis Hines (Little Toby), Fred Waugh (Mizoo), Bill Shannon (Tom), Phil Adams (Frank), Walter Scot (Earl), John Howard (George), Enrique Lucero (Indian Chief), Julie Robinson (Sinsie), Jose Carlo Ruiz (Brave), Jerry Gatlin (Deputy), Ivan Scott (Express Agent), John Kennedy (Bank Teller)

A Warm December
(First Artists, released by National General Pictures, 1973)
Producer: Melville Tucker
Director: Sidney Poitier
Screenplay: Lawrence Roman
Photography: Paul Beeson
Music: Coleridge-Taylor Perkinson

Editor: Pembroke J. Herring, Peter Pitt
Art Direction: Elliot Scott
Assistant Director: David Tomblin
Cast: Sidney Poitier (Matt Younger), Esther Anderson (Catherine), Yvette Curtis (Stephanie), George Baker (Henry Barlow), Johnny Sekka (Myomo), Earl Cameron (George Oswandu), Hilary Crane (Marsha Barlow), John Beardmore (Burberry), Milos Kurek (Gen. Kuznouski), Ann Smith (Carol Barlow), Stephanie Smith (Janie Burlow), Letta Mbula (Singer)

Uptown Saturday Night
(First Artists, released by Warner Brothers, 1974)
Producer: Melville Tucker
Director: Sidney Poitier
Screenplay: Richard Wesley
Photography: Fred J. Koenekamp
Music: Tom Scott
Editor: Pembroke J. Herring
Production Design: Alfred Sweeney
Cast: Sidney Poitier (Steve Jackson), Bill Cosby (Wardell Franklin), Flip Wilson (The Reverend), Richard Pryor (Sharp Eye Washington), Rosalind Cash (Sarah Jackson), Roscoe Lee Browne (Congressman Lincoln), Paula Kelly (Leggy Peggy), Lee Camberlin (Madame Zenobia), Johnny Sekka (Geechie's Henchman), Lincoln Kilpatrick (Slim's Henchman), Harold Nicholas (Little Seymour), Calvin Lockhart (Silky Slim), Ketty Lester (Irma Franklin), Harry Belafonte (Geechie Dan Buford)

The Wilby Conspiracy
(Martin Baum, released by United Artists, 1975)
Director: Ralph Nelson
Screenplay: Rod Amateau and Harold Nebenzal, from the Peter Driscoll novel
Photography: John Coquillon
Music: Stanley Myers
Editor: Ernest Walter
Cast: Sidney Poitier (Shack Twala), Michael Caine (Jim Keogh), Nicol Williamson (Major Horn), Prunella Gee (Rina), Persis Khambatta (Persis Ray), Saeed Jaffrey (Mukerjee), Ryk de Gooyer (Van Heerden), Rutger Hauer (Baline Nierkirk), Joseph De Graf (Wilby), Brian Empson (Judge), Abdullah Sunado (Headman), Archie Duncan (Gordon), Helmut Dantine (Counsel)

Let's Do It Again
(First Artists, released by Warner Brothers, 1975)
Producer: Melville Tucker
Director: Sidney Poitier
Screenplay: Richard Wesley
Photography: Donald M. Morgan
Music: Curtis Mayfield
Editor: Pembroke J. Herring
Production Design: Alfred J. Sweeney
Cast: Sidney Poitier (Clyde Williams), Bill Cosby (Billy Foster), Jimmie Walker (Bootney Farnsworth), Calvin Lockhart (Biggie Smalls), John Amos (Kansas City Mack), Denise Nicholas (Beth Foster), Lee Chamberlin (Dee Dee Williams), Mel Stewart (Ellison), Ossie Davis (Elder Johnson), Billy Eckstine (Zack), Julius Harris (Bubbletop Woodson), Paul E. Harris (Jody Tipps), Val Avery (Lt. Bottomley)

A Piece of the Action
(First Artists, released by Warner Brothers, 1977)
Producer: Melville Tucker
Director: Sidney Poitier
Screenplay: Charles Blackwell
Photography: Donald M. Morgan
Music: Curtis Mayfield
Editor: Pembroke J. Herring
Production Design: Alfred Sweeney
Cast: Sidney Poitier (Manny Durrell), Bill Cosby (Dave Anderson), James Earl Jones (Joshua Burke), Denise Nicholas (Lila French), Hope Clarke (Sarah Thomas), Tracy Reed (Nikki McLean), Frances Foster (Bea Quitman), Titos Vandis (Bruno), Janet Dubois (Nellie

Bond), Marc Lawrence (Lovie), Cyril
Poitier (Mr. Theodore), Sherri Poitier
(Cookie), Edward Love (Willie
Maunger), Sheryl Lee Ralph (Barbara
Hanley)

Stir Crazy
(Columbia Pictures, 1980)
Producer: Hannah Weinstein
Director: Sidney Poitier
Screenplay: Bruce Jay Friedman
Photography: Fred Schuler
Music: Tom Scott
Editor: Harry Keller
Cast: Gene Wilder (Skip Donahue),
Richard Pryor (Harry Monroe), Georg
Standford Brown (Rory Schultebrand),
Jo Beth Williams (Meredith), Miguel
Angel Suarez (Jesus Ramirez), Craig T.
Nelson (Deputy Ward Wilson), Barry
Corbin (Warden Walter Beatty), Charles
Weldon (Blade), Nicolas Coster
(Warden Henry Sampson), Joel Brooks
(Len Garber), Jonathan Banks (Jack
Graham), Erland Van Lidth De Jeude
(Grossberger), Lewis Van Bergen
(Guard No. 1), Lee Purcell (Susan)

Hanky Panky
(Columbia Pictures, 1982)
Producer: Martin Ransohoff
Director: Sidney Poitier
Screenplay: Henry Rosenbaum and
David Taylor
Photography: Arthur Ornitz
Music: Tom Scott
Editor: Harry Keller
Cast: Gene Wilder (Michael Jordan),
Gilda Radner (Kate Hellman), Kathleen
Quinlan (Janet Dunn), Richard Widmark
(Ransom), Robert Prosky (Hiram
Calder), Josef Sommer (Adrian Pruitt),
Johnny Sekka (Lacey), Jay O. Sanders
(Katz), Sam Gray (Dr. John Wolff), Larry
Bryggman (Stacy), Pat Corley (Pilot),
Johnny Brown (Bus Driver)

Fast Forward
(Columbia Pictures, 1985)

Producer: John Patrick Veitch
Director: Sidney Poitier
Screenplay: Richard Wesley, from the
Timothy March story
Photography: Matthew F. Leonetti
Music: Tom Scott and Jack Hayes
Editor: Harry Keller
Cast: John Scott Clough (Matt
Sherman), Don Franklin (Michael
Stafford), Tamara Mark (June Wolsky),
Tracy Silver (Francine Hackett),
Gretchen F. Palmer (Valerie
Thompson), Monique Cintron (Rita
Diaz), Debra Varnado (Debbie
Hughes), Noel Conlon (Mr. Stanton)

Shoot to Kill
(Touchstone Pictures, released by Buena
Vista, 1988)
Executive Producer: Philip Rogers
Producer: Ron Silverman, Daniel Petrie
Jr.
Director: Roger Spottiswoode
Screenplay: Harv Zimmel, Michael
Burton, Daniel Petrie Jr., from the
Zimmel story
Photography: Michael Chapman
Music: John Scott
Editor: Garth Craven, George Bowers
Production Design: Richard Sylbert
Cast: Sidney Poitier (Warren Stantin),
Tom Berenger (Jonathan Knox), Kirstie
Alley (Sarah), Clancy Brown (Steve),
Richard Masur (Norman), Andrew
Robinson (Harvey), Kevin Scannell
(Ben), Frederick Coffin (Ralph),
Michael McRae (Fournier), Robert
Lesser (Minelli)

Little Nikita
(Columbia Pictures, 1988)
Producer: Harry Gittes
Director: Richard Benjamin
Screenplay: John Hill and Bo Goldman,
from the Tom Musca and Terry
Schwartz story
Photography: Laszlo Kovacs
Music: Marvin Hamlisch
Editor: Jacqueline Cambas

Production Design: Gene Callahan
Cast: Sidney Poitier (Roy Parmenter),
River Phoenix (Jeff Grant), Richard
Jenkins (Richard Grant), Caroline Kava
(Elizabeth Grant), Richard Bradford
(Konstantin Karpov), Richard Lynch
(Scuba), Loretta Devine (Verna
McLaughlin), Lucy Deakins (Barbara
Kerry)

Ghost Dad
(Universal Pictures, 1990)
Producer: Terry Nelson
Director: Sidney Poitier
Screenplay: Chris Reese, Brent
Maddock, S. S. Wilson, from the
Maddock and Wilson story
Photography: Andrew Laszlo
Music: Henry Mancini
Editor: Pembroke Herring
Production Design: Henry Bumstead
Cast: Bill Cosby (Elliot), Kimberly
Russell (Diane), Denise Nicholas
(Joan), Ian Bannen (Sir Edith Moser),
Salim Grant (Danny), Brooke Fontaine
(Amanda), Dana Ashbrook (Tony
Ricker), Omar Gooding (Stuart),
Christine Ebersole (Carol)

Sneakers
(Universal Pictures, 1992)
Producer: Walter F. Parkes, Lawrence
Lasker
Director: Phil Alden Robinson
Screenplay: Lawrence Lasker, Walter F.
Parkes, and Phil Alden Robinson
Photography: John Lindley
Music: James Horner
Editor: Tom Rolf
Production Designer: Patrizia von
Brandenstein
Cast: Robert Redford (Bishop), Sidney
Poitier (Crease), Gery Hershberger
(Young Bishop), David Straithairn
(Whistler), Dan Aykroyd (Mother), River
Phoenix (Carl), George Hearn (Gregor),
Timothy Busfield (Dick Gordon), Mary
McDonnell (Liz), Ben Kingsley (Cosmo),
Jojo Marr (Young Cosmo)

The Jackal
(Universal Pictures, 1997)
Executive Producer: Terence Clegg, Hal
Lieberman, Gary Levinsohn, Mark
Gordon
Producer: James Jacks, Sean Daniel,
Michael Caton-Jones, Kevin Jarre
Director: Michael Caton-Jones
Screenplay: Chuck Pfarrer, from the
Kenneth Ross screenplay *The Day of
the Jackal*
Photography: Karl Walter Lindenlaub
Editor: Jim Clark
Music: Carter Burwell
Production Design: Michael White
Cast: Bruce Willis (The Jackal), Richard
Gere (Declan Mulqueen), Sidney Poitier
(Carter Preston), Diane Venora
(Valentina Koslova), Tess Harper (First
Lady), J. K. Simmons (Witherspoon),
Mathilda May (Isabella), Stephen
Spinella (Douglas), Richard Lineback
(McMurphy), Jack Black (Lamont),
John Cunningham (Donald Brown),
David Hayman (Terek Murad), Steve
Bassett (George Decker), Ravil Isyanov
(Ghazzi Murad), Serge Houde
(Beaufres)

DOCUMENTARY FILMS

*King: A Filmed Record . . . Montgomery
to Memphis* (1970)
Producer: Ely Landau, Commonwealth
United Productions
Director: Joseph Mankiewicz, Sidney
Lumet
Narrators: Sidney Poitier, Paul
Newman, Joanne Woodward, Ruby
Dee, Ben Gazzara, Charlton Heston,
James Earl Jones, Clarence Williams
3rd, Harry Belafonte, Burt Lancaster

Paul Robeson: Tribute to an Artist
(1979)
Producer: Janus Films
Director: Saul Turell
Writer: Saul Turell
Narrator: Sidney Poitier

Bopha! (1987)
  Producer: Oasis Media
  Director: Daniel Rosenfeld
  Writer: Percy Mtwa
  Narrator: Sidney Poitier

Ralph Bunche: An American Odyssey
(2000)
  Producer: William Greaves, Louise
  Archimbault
  Director: William Greaves
  Writer: William Greaves and Leslie Lee,
  from Brian Urquhard's biography
  Narrator: Sidney Poitier

TELEVISION DRAMAS AND SPECIALS

Parole Chief
  (NBC, Philco Television Playhouse,
  16 November 1952)
  Producer: Fred Coe
  Director: Delbert Mann
  Based on: David Dressler's
  autobiography Parole Chief
  Cast: Harry Townes (David Dressler),
  Donald Foster (Pat Byron), Sidney
  Poitier (Ernest Adams), Allen Nourse
  (Townsend), Perry Wilson (Belle
  Dressler), Mario Gallo (Louie Dabit),
  Terry Becker (Larry), Leo Penn (Roy)

The Fascinating Stranger
  (ABC, ABC Pond Theater, 23 June
  1955)
  Based on: Booth Tarkington's story
  "The Fascinating Stranger"
  Cast: Larry Gates (Alfred Tuttle),
  Sidney Poitier (Clifford Hill)

A Man Is Ten Feet Tall
  (NBC, Philco Television Playhouse,
  2 October 1955)
  Producer: Fred Coe
  Director: Robert Mulligan
  Writer: Robert Alan Aurthur
  Cast: Tommy Tyler (Sidney Poitier),
  Axel North (Don Murray), Charlie
  Malik (Martin Balsam), Hilda Simms
  (Lucy Tyler)

The Strollin' Twenties
  (CBS, 21 February 1966)
  Producer: Harry Belafonte
  Writer: Harry Belafonte and Langston
  Hughes, from Hughes's novel The Big
  Sea
  Cast: Sidney Poitier, Sammy Davis Jr.,
  Duke Ellington, Diahann Carroll, Paula
  Kelly, Joe Williams, Nipsey Russell,
  Gloria Lynne, George Kirby

A Time for Laughter: A Look at Negro
Humor in America
  (ABC, Stage 67, 6 April 1967)
  Producer: Harry Belafonte
  Cast: Sidney Poitier, Harry Belafonte,
  Godfrey Cambridge, Diahann Carroll,
  Redd Foxx, Dick Gregory, George
  Kirby, Jackie "Moms" Mabley, Pigmeat
  Markham, Richard Pryor, Diana Sands,
  Nipsey Russell

Separate but Equal
  (ABC, 7 April 1991–8 April 1991)
  Producer: George Stevens Jr. and Stan
  Margulies
  Director: George Stevens Jr.
  Writer: George Stevens Jr.
  Cast: Sidney Poitier (Thurgood
  Marshall), Burt Lancaster (John W.
  Davis), Earl Warren (Richard Kiley),
  Cleavon Little (Robert Carter), Gloria
  Foster (Buster Marshall), John
  McMartin (Gov. James F. Byrnes),
  Graham Beckel (Josiah B. Tulley), Ed
  Hall (Rev. J. A. DeLaine), Lynne
  Thigpen (Alice Stovall)

Children of the Dust
  (CBS, 26 February 1995 and
  28 February 1995)
  Executive Producer: Frank Konigsberg,
  Joyce Eliason
  Producer: Harold Tichenor
  Director: David Greene
  Writer: Joyce Eliason, from Clancy
  Carlile's novel
  Cast: Sidney Poitier (Gypsy Smith),
  Michael Moriarty (John Maxwell),

Joanna Going (Rachel Maxwell), Hart
Bochner (Shelby Hornbeck), Billy
Worth (White Wolf/Corby), Farrah
Fawcett (Nora Maxwell)

To Sir, with Love II
(NBC, 7 April 1996)
Director: Peter Bogdanovich
Cast: Sidney Poitier (Mark Thackeray),
Daniel J. Travanti (Horace Weaver),
Judy Geeson (Pamela Dare), Lulu
(Barbara Pegg)

Mandela and de Klerk
(Showtime, 16 February 1997)
Director: Joseph Sargent
Cast: Sidney Poitier (Nelson Mandela),
Michael Caine (F. W. de Klerk), Tina
Lefford (Winnie Mandela), Gerry
Maritz (P. W. Botha), Ian Roberts
(Kobie Coetsee), Jerry Mofokeng
(Walter Sisulu), Kwesi Kobus (Chris
Hani)

Oprah Winfrey Presents: David and Lisa
(ABC, 1 November 1998)
Producer: Oprah Winfrey
Director: Lloyd Kramer
Writer: Lloyd Kramer, Eleanor Perry, and
Theodore Isaac Rubin, from Rubin's case
history and Perry's original script
Cast: Sidney Poitier (Dr. Jack Miller),
Lukas Haas (David), Brittany Murphy
(Lisa)

Free of Eden
(Showtime, 21 February 1999)
Producer: Cedric Scott
Director: Leon Ichaso
Writer: Delle Chatman and Yule Caise,
from Chatman's story
Cast: Sidney Poitier (Will Cleamons),
Sydney Tamiia Poitier (Nicole Turner),
Desiree Cleamons (Phylicia Rashad),
Robert Hooks (Joe Sherman)

The Simple Life of Noah Dearborn
(CBS, 9 May 1999)
Producer: Mark Amin

Director: Gregg Champion
Writer: Sterling Anderson
Cast: Sidney Poitier (Noah Dearborn),
Dianne Wiest (Sarah McClellan), Mary-
Louise Parker (Dr. Valerie Crane), Greg
Newbern (Christian Nelson), Roxzane
T. Mims (Noah's mother), Afemo
Omilami (Noah's father), Bernie Casey
(Silas), James Thomas Lee Knight
(eight-year-old Noah), Christopher
Ryan Dunn (ten-year-old Noah)

The Last Brickmaker in America
(CBS, 15 April 2001)
Director: Gregg Champion
Cast: Sidney Poitier (Henry Cobb),
Cody Newton (Danny Potter), Piper
Laurie (Mrs. Potter), Jay O. Sanders
(Mike), Wendy Crewson (Karen), Mert
Hatfield (Charlie Reddin), Christopher
Simmons (Forklift Operator)

BROADWAY PLAYS

Lysistrata
(Belasco Theatre, opened 17 October
1946, 4 performances)
Producer: James Light, Max J. Jelin
Director: James Light
Writer: Gilbert Seldes, from
Aristophanes's play
Choreography: Felicia Sorel
Music: Harry Bryant
Cast: Pearl Gaines (Leader of Old
Women's Chorus), Etta Moten
(Lysistrata), Fredi Washington
(Kalonika), Mildred Smith (Myrrhina),
Mercedes Gilbert (Lampito), Leigh
Whipper (Leader of Old Men's Chorus),
Rex Ingram (President of the Senate),
Maurice Ellis (Spartan Envoy), Emmett
Babe Wallace (Kineslas), John de Battle
(Trygeus), Larry Williams (Nikias),
Sidney Poitier (Polydorus), Emory S.
Richardson (Lykon)

Anna Lucasta
(National Theatre, opened 22
September 1947, 32 performances)

Producer: John Wildberg
Director: Harry Wagstaff Gribble
Writer: Philip Yordan
Cast: Wesleen Foster (Katie), Rosette Le Noire (Stella), Laura Bowman (Theresa), Roy Allen (Stanley), Warren Coleman (Frank), Frank Wilson (Joe), Ralf Coleman (Eddie), Slim Thompson (Noah), Claire Jay (Blanche), Merritt Smith (Officer), Isabelle Cooley (Anna), Lance Taylor (Danny), Sidney Poitier (Lester), Duke Williams (Rudolf)

A Raisin in the Sun
(Ethel Barrymore Theatre, opened 11 March 1959, 198 performances with Poitier)
Producer: Philip Rose, David J. Cogan
Director: Lloyd Richards
Writer: Lorraine Hansberry
Cast: Ruby Dee (Ruth Younger), Glynn Turman (Travis Younger), Sidney Poitier (Walter Lee Younger), Diana Sands (Beneatha Younger), Claudia McNeil (Lena Younger), Ivan Dixon (Joseph Asagai), Louis Gossett (George Murchison), Lonnie Elder 3rd (Bobo), John Fiedler (Karl Lindner), Ed Hall (Moving Man), Douglas Turner (Moving Man)

Carry Me Back to Morningside Heights
(John Golden Theatre, opened 27 February 1968, 7 performances)
Producer: Saint Subber, Harold Loeb
Director: Sidney Poitier
Writer: Robert Alan Aurthur
Cast: Louis Gossett (Willie Nurse), David Steinberg (Seymour Levin), Johnny Brown (Henry Hardy), Cicely Tyson (Myrna Jessup), Diane Ladd (Alma Sue Bates)

SPOKEN-WORD ALBUMS

Poetry of the Negro
(Glory Records, 1955), 33⅓ rpm
Poitier Meets Plato
(Warner Brothers, 1964), 33⅓ rpm
Journeys inside the Mind: The Dialogues
(Warner Brothers, 1968) 33⅓ rpm
The Measure of a Man: A Spiritual Autobiography
(Harper Audio, 2000)

NOTES

Abbreviations

CBFSC
   Celeste Bartos Film Study Center, Museum of Modern Art, New York, New York
CTL
   Cinema and Television Library, University of Southern California, Los Angeles, California
ELL
   Eli Lilly Library, Indiana University, Bloomington, Indiana
HTC
   Harvard Theatre Collection, Cambridge, Massachusetts
MHL
   Margaret Herrick Library, Motion Picture Academy of Arts and Sciences, Los Angeles, California
MPSVB
   Motion Picture, Sound, and Video Branch, National Archives, College Park, Maryland
MTR
   Museum of Television and Radio, New York, New York
NYPLPA
   New York Public Library for the Performing Arts, New York, New York
SCRBC
   Schomburg Center for Research in Black Culture, New York Public Library, New York, New York
UCLA
   Special Collections, University of California–Los Angeles, Los Angeles, California
UCLA Arts
   Arts Special Collections, University of California–Los Angeles, Los Angeles, California

WBC
   Warner Brothers Collection, University of Southern California, Los Angeles, California
WSHS
   Wisconsin State Historical Society, Madison, Wisconsin

Introduction

1. "Sidney Poitier: The Defiant One"; *Variety*, 23 August 1967.

2. *Report of the United States National Advisory Commission on Civil Disorders*; Weisbrot, *Freedom Bound*, 264–65; *Variety*, 12 July 1967; *Pittsburgh Courier*, 26 July 1967.

3. *Atlanta Journal*, 15 August 1967; *Pittsburgh Courier*, 26 August 1967; *New York Times*, 15 August 1967, 19 August 1967.

4. Lerone Bennett Jr., "Hollywood's First Negro Movie Star," *Ebony*, May 1959, 100. On Poitier's career, see Keyser and Ruszkowski, *Cinema of Sidney Poitier*; Marill, *Films of Sidney Poitier*; Kelley, "Evolution of Character Portrayals"; Cripps, *Making Movies Black*, 250–94.

5. On Poitier's life, see Poitier, *This Life*; Poitier, *Measure of a Man*; Ewers, *Long Journey*; Hoffman, *Sidney*; Bergman, *Sidney Poitier*.

6. On black film, see Cripps, *Slow Fade to Black*; Bogle, *Toms, Coons, Mulattoes, Mammies, and Bucks*; Leab, *From Sambo to Superspade*; Reid, *Redefining Black Film*; Diawara, *Black American Cinema*; Guerrero, *Framing Blackness*; Mapp, *Blacks in American Films*; Nesteby, *Black Images in American Films*; Null, *Black Hollywood*.

7. On race and popular culture, see Boskin, *Sambo*; Bogle, *Dorothy Dandridge*; Duberman, *Paul Robeson*; Ely, *Adventures of Amos 'n' Andy*; Epstein, *Nat King Cole*; Levine, *Black Culture and Black Consciousness*; Rampersad, *Jackie Robinson*; Remnick, *King of the World*; Rogin, *Blackface, White Noise*; Tygiel, *Baseball's Great Experiment*; Watkins, *On the Real Side*.

8. On the civil rights movement, see Branch, *Parting the Waters*; Branch, *Pillar of Fire*; Dittmer, *Local People*; Garrow, *Bearing the Cross*; Morris, *Origins of the Civil Rights Movement*; Sitkoff, *Struggle for Black Equality*; Weisbrot, *Freedom Bound*. On obfuscation of barriers between entertainment and politics, see Boorstin, *Image*; Schickel, *Intimate Strangers*; Gabler, *Life the Movie*. This book adopts a broad definition of political action, one inclusive of what Ben Keppel calls "the cultural politics of race," or how black personalities use language and symbols to shape and understand shifting racial realities. See Keppel, *Work of Democracy*; Smith, *Dancing in the Street*.

9. *Variety*, 26 July 1967; *New York Times*, 10 September 1967.

10. Du Bois, *Souls of Black Folk*, 1–5.

Chapter One

1. Poitier, *This Life*, 1–2.

2. Poitier, *Measure of a Man*, 16–17.

3. Craton and Saunders, *Islanders in the Stream*, 1:48–114.

4. Ibid., 179–95.

5. Beckles, "The Self-Liberation Ethos of Enslaved Blacks," in *Caribbean Slavery in the Atlantic World*, ed. Shepherd and Beckles, 869–78; Lyn Tornabene, "Walking with Sidney Poitier," *McCall's*, July 1969, 122.

6. Craton and Saunders, *Islanders in the Stream*, 2:2–236. See also Johnson, *Race Relations in the Bahamas*.

7. Craton and Saunders, *Islanders in the Stream*, 2:240–41.

8. Hughes, *Race and Politics in the Bahamas*, 14–15.

9. Craton and Saunders, *Islanders in the Stream*, 2:152, 282.

10. Poitier, *This Life*, 5.

11. Craton and Saunders, *Islanders in the Stream*, 2:152–54; Poitier, *This Life*, 5.

12. Normand Poirier, "Sidney Poitier's Long Journey," *Saturday Evening Post*, 20 June 1964, 26–27.

13. Ibid., 26.

14. *Los Angeles Times*, 30 October 1977; Poitier, *This Life*, 7; Poirier, "Sidney Poitier's Long Journey," 26.

15. Jenkins, *Bahamian Memories*, 83, 259–60; Poitier, *Measure of a Man*, 28; Craton and Saunders, *Islanders in the Stream*, 2:161–65.

16. Milburn Smith, "The Night Sidney Poitier Cried for His Mother," *Photoplay*, August 1968, 76; Tom Seligson, "I No Longer Feel I Have to Prove Anything," *Parade*, 28 February 1988, 4; Poitier, *Measure of a Man*, 4–12; Tornabene, "Walking with Sidney Poitier," 122; Poirier, "Sidney Poitier's Long Journey," 26.

17. *Nassau Guardian*, 1 May 1964.

18. Poitier, *This Life*, 7–8; Poitier, *Measure of a Man*, 4; Tom Prideaux, "Poitier's Search for the Right Corner," *Life*, 27 April 1959, 142.

19. Poitier, "Sidney Poitier's Long Journey," 29; *New York Post*, 10 February 1968.

20. Poitier, *This Life*, 11–14.

21. Poitier, *Measure of a Man*, 7.

22. American Film Institute Seminar with Sidney Poitier, 7; Prideaux, "Poitier's Search for the Right Corner," 141.

23. Craton and Saunders, *Islanders in the Stream*, 2:282; Hughes, *Race and Politics in the Bahamas*, 24–25; Sidney Poitier, interview by Tom Brokaw, NBC television broadcast, 23 June 1980, Michigan State University Voice Library.

24. Hughes, *Race and Politics in the*

Bahamas, 11; Craton and Saunders, *Islanders in the Stream*, 2:283; Poitier, *This Life*, 13.

25. Poitier, *Measure of a Man*, 25; Craton and Saunders, *Islanders in the Stream*, 2:263–64. See also Jenkins, *Bahamian Memories*, 33–34.

26. Frederick Simpich, "Bahama Holiday," *National Geographic*, February 1936, 245.

27. Poirier, "Sidney Poitier's Long Journey," 27.

28. *New York Post*, 10 February 1968.

29. Johnson, *Bahamas in Slavery and Freedom*, 153; Craton, *History of the Bahamas*, 285; Poitier, *Measure of a Man*, 38. See also *Pittsburgh Courier*, 27 January 1968.

30. Craton, *History of the Bahamas*, 138; Hughes, *Race and Politics in the Bahamas*, 24–29; Williams, *Negro in the Caribbean*, 57–69.

31. Poitier, *Measure of a Man*, 34–36.

32. Poitier, *This Life*, 17; Hughes, *Race and Politics in the Bahamas*, 15.

33. Craton and Saunders, *Islanders in the Stream*, 2:264; Bryan Darnton, "Sunny Isles of Leisure," *New York Times Magazine*, 21 July 1940, 11.

34. Craton and Saunders, *Islanders in the Stream*, 2:248–51, 267–72; Hughes, *Race and Politics in the Bahamas*, 41–42.

35. Poitier, *This Life*, 30, 17; Poitier, *Measure of a Man*, 213–14.

36. Poitier, *Measure of a Man*, 38–39.

37. Poitier, *This Life*, 17–19.

38. Ibid., 19–21; Poirier, "Sidney Poitier's Long Journey," 29.

39. Poitier, *This Life*, 32–34.

40. Ibid., 29.

41. *New York Post*, 31 March 1959; Poitier, *This Life*, 24–25.

42. Poitier, *This Life*, 25; Craton and Saunders, *Islanders in the Stream*, 2:276.

43. Craton, *History of the Bahamas*, 274–75.

44. Craton and Saunders, *Islanders in the Stream*, 2:286–88.

45. Poitier, *This Life*, 27; *New York Post*, 31 March 1959.

46. *Pittsburgh Courier*, 4 January 1969; Poitier, *This Life*, 26–27; *New York Post*, 31 March 1959.

47. Poitier, "Sidney Poitier's Long Journey," 30.

48. "Sidney Poitier: One Bright Light."

49. Slotkin, *Gunfighter Nation*, 271–77.

50. Poitier, *This Life*, 31; "Sidney Poitier: One Bright Light."

51. Gabler, *An Empire of Their Own*; Sklar, *Movie-Made America*, 3–246; Ray, *Certain Tendency of the Hollywood Cinema*, 25–88; May, *Screening Out the Past*; Bergman, *We're in the Money*; Tompkins, *West of Everything*, 3–67; Mellen, *Big Bad Wolves*, 3–5, 132–33.

52. Keyser and Ruszkowski, *Cinema of Sidney Poitier*, 12.

53. Cripps, *Slow Fade to Black*, 273–74.

54. See Williams, *Playing the Race Card*, 96–135.

55. *Crisis* 10 (May 1915): 33; *Crisis* 11 (December 1915): 76.

56. Guerrero, *Framing Blackness*, 11–18; John Hope Franklin, "*Birth of a Nation* — Propaganda as History," in Mintz and Roberts, *Hollywood's America*, 42–52.

57. Mintz and Roberts, *Hollywood's America*, 142–52; Cripps, *Slow Fade to Black*; Donald Bogle, *Toms, Coons, Mulattoes, Mammies, and Bucks*, 1–116; Leab, *From Sambo to Superspade*, 1–143; Ely, *Adventures of Amos 'n' Andy*; Rogin, *Blackface, White Noise*, 3–208.

58. Bogle, *Toms, Coons, Mulattoes, Mammies and Bucks*, 39–43; Cripps, *Slow Fade to Black*, 284–86; Leab, *From Sambo to Superspade*, 89–90.

59. Cripps, *Slow Fade to Black*, 363–64; Williams, *Playing the Race Card*, 187–219.

60. Snead, *White Screens, Black Images*, 121–49.

61. Poirier, "Sidney Poitier's Long Jour-

ney," 30; Sidney Poitier, "Dialogue on Film," September 1976, 35.

62. Poitier, *This Life*, 30–31.

63. Craton and Saunders, *Islanders in the Stream*, 2:250–51; Poirier, "Sidney Poitier's Long Journey," 30.

64. Poitier, *This Life*, 27–28.

65. *Los Angeles Mirror-News*, 17 March 1958; Poitier, *This Life*, 29–30.

66. Poitier, *Measure of a Man*, 14–15.

Chapter Two

1. Poitier, *This Life*, 38–39.

2. Poitier, *Measure of a Man*, 189.

3. Ibid., 40–41.

4. Frederic Morton, "The Audacity of Sidney Poitier," *Holiday*, June 1962, 105.

5. Johnson, "Bahamian Labor Migration," 90, 95; Mohl, "Black Immigrants," 271–72, 286.

6. Craton and Saunders, *Islanders in the Stream*, 2:173–74; Anthony P. Maingot, "Immigration from the Caribbean Basin," in *Miami Now!*, ed. Grenier and Stepick, 28–29; Poitier, *Measure of a Man*, 14.

7. Craton and Saunders, *Islanders in the Stream*, 221–22; Johnson, "Bahamian Labor Migration."

8. Reid, *Negro Immigrant*, 189; Craton and Saunders, *Islanders in the Stream*, 2:296; "Sidney Poitier: One Bright Light."

9. Poitier, *This Life*, 41–43; Morton, "Audacity of Sidney Poitier," 103.

10. Dunn, *Black Miami in the Twentieth Century*, 158–60; Mormino, "GI Joe Meets Jim Crow"; Poitier, *This Life*, 43–44; Morton, "Audacity of Sidney Poitier," 106; *New York Post*, 31 March 1959.

11. *New York Post*, 31 March 1959.

12. Hernton, *Sex and Racism in America*, 1–2; Lemann, *Promised Land*, 24–37.

13. Tebeau, *History of Florida*, 243–45, 289–90.

14. George, "Colored Town"; Mohl, "Black Immigrants," 340; Dunn, *Black Miami in the Twentieth Century*, 171.

15. Raymond A. Mohl, "The Pattern of Race Relations in Miami since the 1920s," in *African American Heritage of Florida*, ed. Colburn and Landers, 338; Dunn, *Black Miami in the Twentieth Century*, 164–67; *Guide to Miami and Dade County*, 5.

16. George, "Colored Town," 436–37; Mohl, "Making the Second Ghetto," 397–99.

17. George, "Colored Town," 438–40; Dunn, *Black Miami in the Twentieth Century*, 143–55; Reed, "Funky Nights in Overtown."

18. Poitier, *This Life*, 43.

19. *New York Post*, 31 March 1959; Hoffman, *Sidney*, 34.

20. Poitier, *This Life*, 45–46.

21. Poitier, *Measure of a Man*, 129–31.

22. Morton, "Audacity of Sidney Poitier," 105.

23. Dunn, *Black Miami in the Twentieth Century*, 131–37; George, "Colored Town," 443–46.

24. Mohl, "Pattern of Race Relations," 346–47; Mohl, "Making the Second Ghetto," 408–9.

25. Poitier, *This Life*, 46–47.

26. Ibid., 48–50; *New York Post*, 31 March 1959.

27. Poitier, *This Life*, 48–52.

28. Poitier, *Measure of a Man*, 44–46; Johnson, *Black Manhattan*, 3.

29. Arna Bontemps and Jack Conroy, "The Exodus Train," in *Up South*, ed. Malaika Adero, 208–9; Stewart E. Tolnay and E. M. Beck, "Rethinking the Role of Racial Violence," in *Black Exodus*, ed. Alferdteen Harrison, 22; Mandle, *Not Slave, Not Free*, 78–89.

30. Brandt, *Harlem at War*, 39; Osofsky, *Harlem*, 92–141.

31. Lewis, *When Harlem Was in Vogue*.

32. McKay, *Harlem*, 118.

33. Johnson, *Black Manhattan*, 162–69; Ottley, *New World A-Coming*, 82–88; McKay, *Harlem*, 33–49; Anderson, *This Was Harlem*, 291–94, 319–23.

34. Ottley, *New World A-Coming*, 41–

47; Reid, *Negro Immigrant*, 54–60, 107–12; Anderson, *This Was Harlem*, 299–303. See also Sowell, *Essays and Data on American Ethnic Groups*, 43–48; Bryce-Laporte, "Black Immigrants"; Holder, "Causes and Composition."

35. Poitier, *Measure of a Man*, 43.

36. Smith, "Politics of Income and Education Differences"; Foner, "West Indians in New York City and London."

37. Poitier, *This Life*, 54–56.

38. Malcolm X with Alex Haley, *Autobiography of Malcolm X*, 82–97; Poitier, *This Life*, 56–57.

39. Poitier, *This Life*, 57–58.

40. *New York Amsterdam News*, 29 May 1943, 24 July 1943, 31 July 1943, 7 August 1943; Bogle, *Toms, Coons, Mulattoes, Mammies and Bucks*, 128–32.

41. Bogle, *Toms, Coons, Mulattoes, Mammies and Bucks*, 139–41; Null, *Black Hollywood*, 119–21; Cripps, *Slow Fade to Black*, 370–73; Nesteby, *Black Images in American Film*, 233; Koppes and Black, "Blacks, Loyalty, and Motion Picture Propaganda," 398.

42. Poitier, *This Life*, 58–59.

43. Ibid., 59–60.

44. *New York Post*, 12 June 1974, 10 October 1975.

45. *Los Angeles Mirror-News*, 17 March 1959; Sidney Poitier, "Why I Became an Actor," *Negro Digest*, December 1961, 81; Sidney Poitier, interview by Hedda Hopper, Sidney Poitier file, Hedda Hopper Collection, MHL.

46. Sitkoff, "Racial Militancy and Interracial Violence," 665.

47. *New York Amsterdam News*, 15 May 1943, 22 May 1943, 5 June 1943; Greenberg, "Politics of Disorder," 422–24; Walter White, "Behind the Harlem Riot of 1943," in *Urban Racial Violence in the Twentieth Century*, ed. Joseph Boskin, 58; Anderson, *This Was Harlem*, 99.

48. Brandt, *Harlem at War*, 183–86; Baldwin, *Notes of a Native Son*, 99.

49. *People's Voice*, 7 August 1943,

14 August 1943; Brandt, *Harlem at War*, 186–88; White, "Behind the Harlem Riot of 1943," 59.

50. Poitier, *This Life*, 60–61.

51. Ibid., 61–62.

52. *People's Voice*, 14 August 1943; Poitier, *This Life*, 62.

53. Brandt, *Harlem at War*, 194–227; Baldwin, *Notes of a Native Son*, 99.

54. Lerone Bennett Jr., "Hollywood's First Negro Movie Star," *Ebony*, May 1959, 102–3.

55. Poitier, *This Life*, 63–65.

56. Ibid., 66; Fleming and Burkel, *Who's Who in Colored America*, 420.

57. *New York Post*, 31 March 1959.

58. Poitier, *This Life*, 66–69.

59. Brandt, *Harlem at War*, 102–12.

60. *People's Voice*, 10 June 1944, 17 June 1944; Poitier, *This Life*, 66–69.

61. Poitier, *Measure of a Man*, 52–55.

62. Poitier, *This Life*, 71–72.

63. Ibid., 72–76. See also Vickerman, *Crosscurrents*, 2–6, 139; Waters, *Black Identities*, 44–93.

64. Ibid., 77–78.

65. *New York Post*, 31 March 1959.

66. Poitier, *This Life*, 79–82.

67. *Los Angeles Mirror-News*, 17 March 1959; *Sidney Poitier: The Defiant One*.

Chapter Three

1. Undated "Harlem Portraits" in *Pittsburgh Courier*, Box 2, Frederick O'Neal Papers, SCRBC; *Chicago Defender*, 12 May 1945; *New York Times*, 28 April 1945. See also Simmons, *Frederick Douglass O'Neal*.

2. Poitier, *This Life*, 82–83.

3. "Sidney Poitier: One Bright Light"; Poitier, "Dialogue on Film," *American Film*, September 1976, 35.

4. Poitier, *This Life*, 82–85; *New York Post*, 1 April 1959.

5. Marill, *Films of Sidney Poitier*, 17; Sidney Poitier file, Jack Hirshberg Collec-

tion, MHS; *Los Angeles Mirror-News*, 18 March 1959.

6. Sidney Poitier, "Why I Became an Actor," *Negro Digest*, December 1961, 83; Sidney Poitier, *This Life*, 85–87; Sidney Poitier file, Hedda Hopper Collection, MHL.

7. Keyssar, *Curtain and the Veil*; Krasner, *Resistance*; Curtis, *First Black Actors*.

8. *New York Amsterdam News*, 5 January 1946; Pitts, "American Negro Theatre," 17–27.

9. *Rhythm*, March 1947.

10. Pitts, "American Negro Theatre," 33–42; Mitchell, *Voices of the Black Theatre*, 117–26; *New York Times*, 24 September 1944.

11. Pitts, "American Negro Theatre," 27, 57; Box 1, Folder 27, and Box 1, Folder 10, ANT Records, SCRBC; *Smith College Spectator*, February 1945.

12. *New York Morning-Telegraph*, 19 June 1944; Yordan, *Anna Lucasta*; *New York Times*, 10 September 1944.

13. *New York Times*, 17 June 1944; *PM*, 25 June 1944; *New York World Telegram*, 19 June 1944; *Variety*, 5 July 1944; *New York Post*, 19 June 1944; *Brooklyn Eagle*, 17 June 1944; *New York Journal-American*, 17 June 1944; *People's Voice*, 24 June 1944.

14. *New York Morning-Telegraph*, 1 September 1944; *New York Times*, 31 August 1944; *New York Daily News*, 31 August 1944; *New York Daily Mirror*, 31 August 1944; *Women's Wear Daily*, 31 August 1944; *New York World Telegram*, 31 August 1944; *New York Sun*, 31 August 1944; *New York Journal-American*, 31 August 1944; *Variety*, 6 September 1944; *Newark Evening News*, 31 August 1944; *Brooklyn Citizen*, 31 August 1944; *New Leader*, 24 February 1945; *Brooklyn Daily Eagle*, 31 August 1944; Mantle, *Best Plays of 1946–47*, 500.

15. *New York Post*, 31 August 1944; *New York Times*, 10 September 1944;

P.M., 31 August 1944; *New York Herald-Tribune*, 31 August 1944; *Brooklyn Daily Eagle*, 18 September 1944; *New York Amsterdam News*, 9 September 1944.

16. *New York Times*, 24 September 1944.

17. Box 1, Folder 9, ANT Records; Pitts, "American Negro Theatre," 46–47; *Daily Worker*, 2 February 1948.

18. Poitier, *This Life*, 87–89; Cosgrove, "Zoot Suit and Style Warfare"; Tom Prideaux, "Poitier's Search for the Right Corner," *Life*, 27 April 1959, 141.

19. Poitier, *This Life*, 89–90; Poitier, "Dialogue on Film," September 1976, 37.

20. Poitier, *This Life*, 90–92; Pitts, "American Negro Theatre," 102–9.

21. George Goodman, "Durango: Poitier Meets Belafonte," *Look*, 24 August 1971, 58; *New York Post*, 1 April 1959; Sidney Poitier, telephone interview with the author, 9 May 2001.

22. Poitier, *This Life*, 91–92; Poitier, "Dialogue on Film," September 1976, 37.

23. *New York Post*, 1 April 1959; Mitchell, *Voices of the Black Theatre*, 122.

24. Poitier, *Measure of a Man*, 76–79.

25. *New York Amsterdam News*, 1 June 1946; *Pittsburgh Courier*, 8 June 1946; Poitier, *This Life*, 97–98.

26. Shaw, *Belafonte*, 19–27.

27. Ibid., 1–41.

28. Poitier, *This Life*, 99–100.

29. Ibid., 100–101.

30. Moss Hart and George S. Kaufman, "You Can't Take It with You," in *Three Comedies of American Family Life*, ed. Joseph E. Mersand, 225–314; *Daily Worker*, 25 August 1946.

31. Aristophanes, *Lysistrata*, revised by Gilbert Seldes (New York: Heritage Press, 1934).

32. Jefferson, "Negro on Broadway, 1945–1946"; *New York Amsterdam News*, 29 June 1946.

33. *Negro Digest*, December 1947; Loften Mitchell, "The Negro Theatre and the Harlem Community," in *Harlem*

U.S.A., ed. John Henrik Clarke, 113; Lovell, "Roundup"; *Norfolk (Va.) Journal and Guide*, 16 February 1946.

34. Lysistrata playbill, SCRBC.

35. Poitier, "Dialogue on Film," September 1976, 37.

36. Poitier, *This Life*, 105; "Sidney Poitier: One Bright Light."

37. Jefferson, "Negro on Broadway, 1946–1947," 154; *New York Sun*, 18 October 1946; *New York World Telegram*, 18 October 1946; *New York Herald-Tribune*, 18 October 1946; *New York Post*, 18 October 1946; *New York Journal-American*, 18 October 1946; *New York Times*, 18 October 1946; *PM*, 20 October 1946; *New York Daily News*, 18 October 1946.

38. *New York Amsterdam News*, 12 October 1946; Mantle, *Best Plays of 1946–47*, 500; *Hartford Times*, 3 October 1946; *Northampton Hampshire-Gazette*, 10 October 1946; *Schenectady Union-Star*, 11 October 1946; Poitier, *This Life*, 105–6.

39. Davis and Dee, *With Ossie and Ruby*, 266–67; *Washington Post*, 3 December 1995.

40. Davis and Dee, *With Ossie and Ruby*, 266–67.

41. Poitier, *This Life*, 92–96, 106–8, 115–16.

42. Ibid., 116–18.

43. Marill, *Films of Sidney Poitier*, 19; *New York Herald-Tribune*, 10 August 1947. For reviews of the original version of *John and Mary*, see *New York Times*, 5 February 1947; *New York Daily News*, 5 February 1947; *New York Post*, 5 February 1947.

44. *Anna Lucasta* playbill, 29 September 1947, New York Public Library for the Performing Arts, New York City; *Variety*, 24 September 1947.

45. *Women's Wear Daily*, 23 September 1947; *New York Morning-Telegraph*, 24 September 1947; Cruse, *Crisis of the Negro Intellectual*, 528.

46. Pitts, "American Negro Theatre," 79.

47. Ibid., 80.

48. *Variety*, 22 August 1945; Jefferson, "Negro on Broadway, 1946–1947," 56; Box 1, Folder 14, ANT Records.

49. *New York World Telegram*, 21 December 1945; *PM*, 28 March 1946; Pitts, "American Negro Theatre," 83–85; Ethel Pitts, "The American Negro Theatre," in *Theater of Black Americans: A Collection of Critical Essays*, ed. Errol Hill, 60–61.

50. Undated letter in *Daily Worker*, in American Negro Theatre Scrapbook, 1945–1947, SCRBC; Box 1, Folder 11, and Box 1, Folder 13, ANT Records.

51. Box 1, Folder 11, and Box 1, Folder 12, ANT Records; Pitts, "American Negro Theatre," 123.

52. Box 1, Folder 14, and Box 1, Folder 18, ANT Records; *New York Amsterdam News*, 28 February 1948.

53. Kenneth White, "Freight," in *Best One-Act Plays 1946–1947*, ed. Margaret Mayorga, 17–50.

54. Jefferson, "Negro on Broadway, 1948–1949," 107; *New York Times*, 4 February 1949.

55. Archer, *Black Images in the American Theatre*, 90; Anderson, *This Was Harlem*, 349.

56. Frederic Morton, "The Audacity of Sidney Poitier," *Holiday*, June 1962, 109; *New York Post*, 1 April 1959.

57. *New York Post*, 1 April 1959.

58. Sidney Poitier, telephone interview with the author, 16 August 2000; Marill, *Films of Sidney Poitier*, 219; Raines, *Getting the Message Through*, 269–71; *Daily Worker*, 23 December 1945; Poitier, *This Life*, 122.

59. Henry Louis Gates Jr., "Belafonte's Balancing Act," *New Yorker*, 26 August and 2 September 1996, 135; Article draft by Frank London, Box 262, Stanley Kramer Papers, Special Collections, UCLA; Jones, *Q*, 102, 252; Edmiston and Cirino, *Literary New York*, 302; Cruse, *Crisis of the Negro Intellectual*, 217–19; Poitier, *This Life*, 119–20.

60. Poitier, *This Life*, 121–23.

61. Sidney Poitier, interview by Hedda Hopper, in Sidney Poitier file, Hedda Hopper Collection, MHL.

62. Poitier, *This Life*, 125–26; *Los Angeles Mirror-News*, 18 March 1959; *Chicago Defender*, 29 July 1950.

63. Poitier, *This Life*, 126–28.

Chapter Four

1. John Ford Papers, ELL. See also Cripps, *Making Movies Black*, 35–63.

2. Robinson, *I Never Had It Made*, 26–37; Tygiel, *Baseball's Great Experiment*, 64–70; Rampersad, *Jackie Robinson*, 124–31.

3. Knight, "Negro in Films Today."

4. Ceplair and Englund, *Inquisition in Hollywood*, 254–98.

5. Whitfield, *Culture of the Cold War*, 1–26; Dudziak, *Cold War Civil Rights*, 3–46. See also May, *Big Tomorrow*.

6. Gomery, *Shared Pleasures*, 83–102; Balio, *American Film Industry*, 315–31.

7. Cripps, *Making Movies Black*, 217–18; Leab, *From Sambo to Superspade*, 137; *New York Age*, 9 March 1946; *Los Angeles Sentinel*, 9 May 1946.

8. Cripps, *Making Movies Black*, 215–49; Rogin, *Blackface, White Noise*, 228–42; *New Republic*, 16 May 1949.

9. *Variety*, 20 October 1949; Cripps, *Making Movies Black*, 220; Buchanan, "Study of the Attitudes," 172; Bloom, "Social Psychological Study," 98–101, 255; Smith, *Not Just Race, Not Just Gender*, 35–60; Ellison, *Shadow and Act*, 273–81.

10. "No Way Out" File, Box 322, Twentieth Century-Fox Legal Files, UCLA Arts; *Variety*, 13 April 1949; *New York Times*, 9 January 1949, 30 July 1950.

11. Folder 1, "No Way Out" File, Twentieth Century-Fox Collection, CTL.

12. Folders 1–2, "No Way Out" File, Twentieth Century-Fox Collection, CTL.

13. Folder 1, "No Way Out" File, Twentieth Century-Fox Collection, CTL; PCA

files for "No Way Out," MHL. See also Dick, *Joseph L. Mankiewicz*, 81–85; Custen, *Twentieth Century's Fox*, 333–36.

14. *Los Angeles Daily News*, 17 October 1949; Cripps, *Slow Fade to Black*, 90–92; de Graaf, "Negro Migration to Los Angeles," 199–204; Wheeler, *Black California*, 225–44; Davis and Dee, *With Ossie and Ruby*, 193; Poitier, *This Life*, 128.

15. Box 322, "No Way Out" Legal Files, UCLA Arts; *People's World*, 18 August 1949.

16. "No Way Out" Production Notes, MHL; *Los Angeles Times*, 6 August 1950.

17. Poitier, *This Life*, 129–30; Davis and Dee, *With Ossie and Ruby*, 196–97.

18. Davis and Dee, *With Ossie and Ruby*, 198; Geist, *Pictures Will Talk*, 156; Folder 3, "No Way Out" File, Twentieth Century-Fox Collection, CTL.

19. Geist, *Pictures Will Talk*, 157.

20. Ibid., 155; *Negro Digest*, December 1950.

21. On the emergence of the Poitier icon, see Kelley, "Evolution of Character Portrayals," 95–100; Stam and Shohat, *Unthinking Eurocentrism*, 198–204; Leab, *From Sambo to Superspade*, 163–64; Bogle, *Toms, Coons, Mulattoes, Mammies and Bucks*, 175–79. On *No Way Out* see also Burke, "Presentation of the American Negro in Hollywood Films," 204–15.

22. Kracauer, "National Types as Hollywood Presents Them," 70.

23. Frazier, *Black Bourgeoisie*, 24–26; Hare, *Black Anglo-Saxons*, 37–45.

24. *Variety*, 8 August 1950; *Motion Picture Herald*, 2 September 1950; *Time*, 21 August 1950; *Look*, 12 September 1950; *New York Times*, 17 August 1950; *New York Herald-Tribune*, 17 August 1950; *Newsweek*, 21 August 1950; *New Yorker*, 26 August 1950.

25. *Pittsburgh Courier*, 5 August 1950 and 12 August 1950; "No Way Out" Production Notes, Herrick Library; *New*

York *Amsterdam News,* 22 June 1950; *Chicago Defender,* 12 August 1950.

26. *New Republic,* 4 September 1950; *Saturday Review,* 2 September 1950. See also *Nation,* 28 October 1950; Stam and Shohat, *Unthinking Eurocentrism,* 203–4; Sayre, *Running Time,* 36–48.

27. *Saturday Review,* 14 October 1950.

28. Wolfenstein and Leites, "Two Social Scientists View 'No Way Out.'"

29. *Motion Picture Herald,* 5 August 1950; *Hollywood Reporter,* 2 August 1950; *Film Daily,* 2 August 1950; *Variety,* 29 July 1950, 2 August 1950, 30 August 1950; *Independent Film Journal,* 12 August 1950; Gerald Weales, "Pro-Negro Films in Atlanta," 300; "No Way Out" file, PCA Files, MHL.

30. *Variety,* 23 August 1950; "No Way Out" file, PCA Files, MHL.

31. *Variety,* 23 August 1950; *Los Angeles Citizen-News,* 24 August 1950; *New York Herald-Tribune,* 25 August 1950; *Variety,* 30 August 1950; *Hollywood Reporter,* 31 August 1950; *Motion Picture Herald,* 2 September 1950.

32. "No Way Out" file, PCA Files, MHL.

33. *New York Post,* 1 April 1959.

34. *New York Post,* 15 August 1950.

35. Poitier, *This Life,* 130–31; Kulik, *Alexander Korda,* 211; *New York Times,* 22 April 1951.

36. Poitier, *This Life,* 137–38; *Nassau Guardian,* 1 May 1964.

37. Poitier, *This Life,* 138–41.

38. *Nassau Guardian,* 1 May 1964; Poitier, *This Life,* 141–43; *The Record,* 26 June 1974 (in Sidney Poitier file, 1970–1979, NYPLPA).

39. Craton and Saunders, *Islanders in the Stream,* 2:302–10.

40. Ibid., 308–10; Poitier, *This Life,* 157–58.

41. Poitier, *This Life,* 131–35.

42. *New York Post,* 22 May 1950; *Variety,* 24 May 1950.

43. Poitier, *This Life,* 143–44.

44. *Detroit Free Press,* 6 August 1967.

45. Poitier, *This Life,* 144–45, 150–51.

46. Korda, *Charmed Lives,* 41; Kulik, *Alexander Korda,* 135–37, 210–11.

47. Kulik, *Alexander Korda,* 310–14; Edward Callan, "Introduction" to Paton, *Cry, the Beloved Country,* 20–29; Alexander, *Alan Paton: A Biography,* 244, 260; Carr, *Left Side of Paradise,* 88–89; *Pacific Film Archive,* 17 October 1996.

48. Paton, *Journey Continued,* 43; Poitier, *This Life,* 145–46; *Variety,* 16 August 1950; *New York Amsterdam News,* 26 August 1950.

49. Thompson, *History of South Africa,* 110–86.

50. Ibid., 187–91.

51. Poitier, *This Life,* 145–47; *New York Herald-Tribune,* 11 May 1952.

52. *New York Post,* 27 January 1952; Poitier, *This Life,* 145–47.

53. *New York Times,* 22 April 1951.

54. *New York Times,* 22 April 1951; Poitier, *This Life,* 148–49; "Scandalize My Name: Stories from the Blacklist."

55. *New York Times,* 16 December 1951; "Cry, the Beloved Country" Production Notes, MHL.

56. Paton, *Journey Continued,* 43.

57. *Variety,* 20 March 1951; *New York Times,* 22 April 1951; Alexander, *Alan Paton,* 263–64; Paton, *Journey Continued,* 48–53.

58. Alexander, *Alan Paton,* 277; Paton, *Journey Continued,* 53–54. See also Davis, *In Darkest Hollywood,* 38–45.

59. *New York Times,* 16 December 1951. See also Nixon, "Cry White Season."

60. *Variety,* 23 January 1952; *Hollywood Reporter,* 18 September 1952; *Los Angeles Times,* 18 September 1952; *Hollywood Reporter,* 30 April 1952 and 27 June 1952; *Variety,* 2 June 1952.

61. See *Saturday Review,* 2 February 1952; *New York Herald-Tribune,* 27 January 1952.

62. *Time,* 18 February 1952; *Newsweek,* 28 January 1952; *New Yorker,* 2 February 1952; *New Republic,* 11 Feb-

ruary 1952; *New York Times*, 27 January 1952; *Hollywood Reporter*, 27 August 1952; *Saturday Review*, 29 August 1953.

63. Stam and Shohat, *Unthinking Eurocentrism*, 101–22, 137–51; Davis, *In Darkest Hollywood*, 1–9; Ukadike, "Western Film Images of Africa."

64. *Pittsburgh Courier*, 2 February 1952.

65. *New York Post*, 2 April 1959; Poitier, *This Life*, 151–52.

66. Poitier, *This Life*, 152–55.

67. Noble, "Entertainment, Politics, and the Movie Business," 22.

Chapter Five

1. Duberman, *Paul Robeson*, 1–335.

2. Ibid., 336–42.

3. Rampersad, *Jackie Robinson*, 210–16.

4. Duberman, *Paul Robeson*, 359–62.

5. Poitier, *This Life*, 156–57.

6. *New York Amsterdam News*, 16 August 1958; Interview Draft from 23 May 1958, Sidney Poitier File, Hedda Hopper Collection, MHL.

7. *New York Amsterdam News*, 16 August 1958.

8. Poitier, *This Life*, 158.

9. *New York Times*, 22 April 1951; Simmons, *Frederick Douglass O'Neal*, 114–15.

10. Ceplair and Englund, *Inquisition in Hollywood*, 361–66; Brownstein, *Power and the Glitter*, 114–15; J. B. Matthews, "Did the Movies Really Clean House?," *American Legion Magazine*, December 1951, 49–56; *Los Angeles Examiner*, 11 March 1952.

11. Ceplair and Englund, *Inquisition in Hollywood*, 371–86; *Los Angeles Examiner*, 23 March 1951; *Hollywood Reporter*, 6 June 1951; *Variety*, 13 October 1950, 2 April 1951.

12. Ceplair and Englund, *Inquisition in Hollywood*, 387–93; Kanfer, *Journal of the Plague Years*, 93.

13. Killens, "Broadway in Black and White," 75; *Red Channels*; McGilligan and Buhle, *Tender Comrades*, 149; Navasky, *Naming Names*, 189–92.

14. *Daily Worker*, 13 May 1952; *New York Herald-Tribune*, 11 May 1952; Kanfer, *Journal of the Plague Years*, 179–82; "Scandalize My Name." See also Gill, "Canada Lee," and Gill, "Careerist and Casualty."

15. *Counterattack*, 9 February 1951; Duberman, *Paul Robeson*, 381–88; Navasky, *Naming Names*, 187–94; Dudziak, *Cold War Civil Rights*, 61–63.

16. Cripps, *Making Movies Black*, 182–83; Duberman, *Paul Robeson*, 390–91.

17. Poitier, *This Life*, 120; Henry Louis Gates Jr., "Belafonte's Balancing Act," *New Yorker*, 26 August and 2 September 1996, 135.

18. Noble, "Entertainment, Politics, and the Movie Business," 21; Duberman, *Paul Robeson*, 390–91; Poitier, *Measure of a Man*, 88.

19. Cruse, *Crisis of the Negro Intellectual*, 18, 224; Poitier, *This Life*, 167–68.

20. Horne, *Race Woman*, 114; Cole, *Hollywood Red*, 343–44; *Counterattack*, 8 August 1952.

21. *Counterattack*, 9 February 1951, 9 May 1952, 26 September 1952, 25 September 1953, 8 January 1954. See also Box 2, Folder 2, and Box 5, Folder 16, Ossie Davis and Ruby Dee Papers, SCRBC.

22. *Counterattack*, 29 March 1957.

23. FBI Bureau File 100-138754, *Communist Activity in the Entertainment Industry* 26:13–14; Cruse, *Crisis of the Negro Intellectual*, 207–20.

24. *New York Amsterdam News*, 4 August 1951; Noble, "Entertainment, Politics, and the Movie Business," 21; Poitier, *Measure of a Man*, 86–87.

25. *New York Times*, 27 December 1950; *Variety*, 11 October 1950; *Daily Compass*, 22 September 1950; *New York Amsterdam News*, 7 April 1951; *New York Post*, 6 April 1951; Sidney Poitier,

telephone interview with the author, 22 December 2000.

26. Poitier, *This Life*, 158–60.

27. *New York Daily News*, 4 August 1951; *Variety*, 8 August 1951.

28. *New York Amsterdam News*, 11 August 1951; Loften Mitchell, "The Negro Theatre and the Harlem Community," in *Harlem U.S.A.*, ed. Clarke, 114–15; Cruse, *Crisis of the Negro Intellectual*, 17.

29. Poitier, *This Life*, 161–62.

30. Ibid., 162–63.

31. Keyser and Ruszkowski, *Cinema of Sidney Poitier*, 22; Bogle, *Toms, Coons, Mulattoes, Mammies, and Bucks*, 44, 93; Ely, *Adventures of Amos 'n' Andy*, 194–244; *New York Amsterdam News*, 4 August 1951; *Chicago Defender*, 16 January 1954, 23 January 1954.

32. See Bogle, *Toms, Coons, Mulattoes, Mammies and Bucks*, 146–47; *Counterattack*, 17 August 1951.

33. Folders #08138 and #09556, Production #1688, Universal Collection, CTL; Poitier, *This Life*, 163–64.

34. Colley, *Road to Victory*, 67–72, 177–82.

35. *New York Times*, 19 May 1951.

36. See Franklin and Moss, *From Slavery to Freedom*, 507.

37. *New York Times*, 30 May 1952; *New York Herald-Tribune*, 30 May 1952. See also *Los Angeles Examiner*, 26 May 1952; *Hollywood Citizen-News*, 28 May 1952; *Los Angeles Times*, 26 May 1952; *Time*, 16 June 1952.

38. *Chicago Defender*, 12 April 1952; *Ebony*, June 1952, 51–53.

39. Gerald Weales, "Pro-Negro Films in Atlanta," 301.

40. *Hollywood Reporter*, 30 April 1952; *Motion Picture Daily*, 30 April 1952; *New York Times*, 30 May 1952.

41. *Hollywood Citizen-News*, 13 June 1952; Vaughn, "Ronald Reagan and the Struggle for Black Dignity," 9–10.

42. Sidney Poitier, telephone interview with the author, 22 December 2000; Parish and Terrace, *Complete Actors' Television Credits*, 1:390; Dressler, *Parole Chief*; Marill, *Films of Sidney Poitier*, 223; Sidney Poitier, telephone interview with the author, 9 May 2001.

43. MacDonald, *One Nation under Television*, 97–99; Kindem, *Live Television Generation of Hollywood Film Directors*, 150–52; *Counterattack*, 20 March 1953, 8 May 1953, 26 February 1953.

44. Poitier, *This Life*, 164–65; Poitier, *Measure of a Man*, 181.

45. *New York Mirror*, 28 March 1955; Sidney Poitier, interview by Tom Brokaw, NBC television broadcast, 23 June 1980, Michigan State University Voice Library; Cooper, *Amateur Night at the Apollo*, 216; *New York Post*, 2 April 1959.

46. *New York Post*, 3 April 1959; Moore, *Archie Moore Story*, 132–36; Douroux, *Archie Moore*, 140–53.

47. Stan Helleur, "Paul Mann's Actor's Workshop," *Mayfair*, September 1957, 37, 77. See also Stanislavsky, *An Actor Prepares*.

48. Helleur, "Paul Mann's Actor's Workshop," 38, 77; Biography sheet in Paul Mann file, NYPLPA; *Show Business*, 29 October 1951, 19 January 1953, 2 September 1953; *New York Times*, 23 September 1953.

49. Manso, *Brando*, 243, 262–63; *Counterattack*, 27 October 1950, 4 January 1952.

50. *New York Times*, 20 August 1997; *Variety*, 19 August 1953; Higham, *Hollywood Cameramen*, 93.

51. *New York Times*, 20 August 1997.

52. *New York Times*, 20 August 1997, 22 August 1997; *Variety*, 5 September 1953, 11 December 1953; *Hollywood Reporter*, 1 October 1997.

53. *Time*, 8 February 1954.

54. Roberts and Olson, *Winning Is the Only Thing*, 30–31.

55. See Dworkin, "New Negro on Screen," February 1961, 39.

56. *Newsweek*, 25 January 1954; *Vari-*

ety, 20 January 1954. See also *New York Times*, 10 March 1954; *Hollywood Reporter*, 13 January 1954; *Motion Picture Daily*, 18 January 1954; *Hollywood Citizen-News*, 21 January 1954; *New York Herald-Tribune*, 10 March 1954; *Los Angeles Times*, 20 March 1954; *Los Angeles Examiner*, 21 January 1954.

57. *Variety*, 2 September 1953; *Hollywood Reporter*, 16 December 1953; *Variety*, 12 August 1953, 27 January 1954, 7 April 1954.

58. Poitier, *This Life*, 164–66.

59. *Counterattack*, 8 January 1954, 12 February 1954.

60. Navasky, *Naming Names*, 193.

61. Poitier, *Measure of a Man*, 86; *Counterattack*, 7 August 1953, 16 October 1953, 27 November 1953; Box 2, Folder 2, Ossie Davis and Ruby Dee Papers, SCRBC; Kanfer, *Journal of the Plague Years*, 224–25.

62. Pandro S. Berman Oral History, MHL, 116–17; Folder 1, "Blackboard Jungle" File, Metro-Goldwyn-Mayer Collection, CTL; Hunter, *Blackboard Jungle*; *Hollywood Reporter*, 13 April 1954; *Variety*, 18 November 1954.

63. Pandro S. Berman Oral History, MHL, 118; Gabler, *An Empire of Their Own*, 209–18, 411–17.

64. Pandro S. Berman Oral History, MHL, 118; Pandro S. Berman Oral History, Ronald L. Davis Oral History Collection, MHL, 44; Schary, *Heyday*, 285–86.

65. "Blackboard Jungle" file, PCA Files, MHL. See also Richard Brooks, "Dialogue on Film," *American Film*, October 1977, 47–48, and *American Film*, February 1978.

66. *New York Times*, 6 March 1955; "Blackboard Jungle" Pressbook, MHL; *Los Angeles Herald-Examiner*, 13 January 1983.

67. Poitier, *This Life*, 169; *Variety*, 30 May 1954.

68. Poitier, *This Life*, 169–71.

69. Poitier, *Measure of a Man*, 87–90;

"Blackboard Jungle" Production Notes, MHL.

Chapter Six

1. Brustein, "America's New Culture Hero"; Manso, *Brando*, 219–381.

2. See Wilkinson, *From Brown to Bakke*, 11–57; Patterson, *Brown v. Board of Education*, 1–117; Lemann, *Promised Land*, 59–107.

3. Warren Susman with Edward Griffin, "Did Success Spoil the United States? Dual Representations in Postwar America," in *Recasting America*, ed. May, 19–37.

4. Gilbert, *Cycle of Outrage*, 63–66.

5. *Variety*, 26 January 1955; *Los Angeles Times*, 6 March 1955; "Blackboard Jungle" Pressbook, MHL.

6. Bertrand, *Race, Rock, and Elvis*, 41–92; George Lipsitz, "Land of a Thousand Dances: Youth, Minorities, and the Rise of Rock and Roll," in *Recasting America*, ed. May, 267–84; Aquila, *That Old Time Rock & Roll*, 3–8; Steussy, *Rock and Roll*, 31–34; Szatmary, *Time to Rock*, 22–25.

7. Kantor, Blacker, and Kramer, *Directors at Work*, 35–36. See also Biskind, *Seeing Is Believing*, 202–17.

8. *Hollywood Reporter*, 28 February 1955; *Variety*, 28 February 1955; *Saturday Review*, 2 April 1955; *Time*, 21 March 1955; *New York Post*, 21 March 1955; *New York World Telegram*, 21 March 1955.

9. Cripps, *Making Movies Black*, 287; *Los Angeles Times*, 9 April 1955; *Catholic Tidings*, 9 September 1955; *Variety*, 31 September 1955; *Kinematograph Weekly*, 22 September 1955.

10. Gilbert, *Cycle of Outrage*, 175.

11. *Variety*, 22 June 1955; Steussy, *Rock and Roll*, 33–34; *Los Angeles Herald-Examiner*, 13 January 1983; *New York Times*, 21 May 1955.

12. *New York Times*, 27 March 1955, 3 April 1955.

13. *Independent Film Journal*, 16 April 1955; *Variety*, 23 March 1955, 29 March 1955; *New York Daily News*, 28 March 1955; *Nation*, 2 April 1955; *New Republic*, 11 April 1955. See also *New Yorker*, 26 March 1955; *Los Angeles Examiner*, 12 May 1955; *New York Daily Mirror*, 21 March 1955; *Los Angeles Times*, 12 May 1955; *Christian Science Monitor*, 1 March 1956.

14. *Los Angeles Times*, 9 March 1956; *Life*, 28 March 1955.

15. *Los Angeles Citizen-News*, 14 June 1955; *Los Angeles Times*, 6 March 1955; *Catholic Tidings*, 9 September 1955.

16. *Variety*, 30 March 1955, 13 April 1955; *Boxoffice*, 2 April 1955; *Motion Picture Daily*, 13 April 1955, 17 May 1955.

17. *New York Times*, 13 April 1955, 4 June 1955; *Variety*, 8 June 1955, 29 June 1955, 13 July 1955; *Showmen's Trade Review*, 9 July 1955; *Hollywood Citizen-News*, 6 July 1955.

18. *Variety*, 18 May 1955, 19 May 1955, 20 May 1955, 25 May 1955, 1 June 1955, 1 September 1955.

19. "Blackboard Jungle" PCA Files, MHL; *Variety*, 18 March 1955, 20 April 1955, 21 April 1955, 13 July 1955; *Hollywood Reporter*, 21 March 1955.

20. Gorman, *Kefauver*, 196–98.

21. United States Senate Committee on the Judiciary, *Motion Pictures and Juvenile Delinquency, 1955*, 2–4, 8–19, 46–47, 52–54, 61–71.

22. *New York Times*, 27 August 1955; *Variety*, 26 August 1955, 29 August 1955, 31 August 1955, 1 September 1955; *Hollywood Reporter*, 26 August 1955, 30 August 1955; *Hollywood Citizen-News*, 27 August 1955, 1 September 1955.

23. *Variety*, 20 April 1955, 31 August 1955; *New York Times*, 4 September 1955, 11 September 1955.

24. *Los Angeles Mirror-News*, 2 September 1955; *Los Angeles Examiner*, 4 September 1955; *Motion Picture Her-* ald, 10 September 1955; *Motion Picture Daily*, 22 September 1955, 30 September 1955; *Variety*, 30 September 1955, 5 October 1955; *Independent Film Journal*, 16 April 1955; *Variety*, 21 March 1955, 1 September 1955.

25. Robert M. W. Vogel Oral History, MHL; *Hollywood Reporter*, 23 November 1955, 22 January 1956; *Variety*, 9 September 1955, 1 November 1955, 9 November 1955, 23 November 1955, 30 November 1955, 2 December 1955.

26. *Hollywood Reporter*, 20 October 1955; *Variety*, 10 November 1955; *Hollywood Citizen-News*, 8 September 1955, 9 September 1955; *Motion Picture Daily*, 18 January 1956.

27. *Hollywood Reporter*, 31 May 1957; Poitier, *This Life*, 171–72; *New York Mirror*, 28 March 1955.

28. Rose, *You Can't Do That on Broadway!*, 45–55; *Poetry of the Negro* (Glory Records, 1955), 33 1/ rpm; undated article from *Cashbox*, Box 17, David Susskind Papers, WSHS.

29. *Newsweek*, 13 May 1957.

30. Poitier, *Measure of a Man*, 94; Brownstein, *Power and the Glitter*, 182–83.

31. Poitier, *This Life*, 172–73; *New York Post*, 2 April 1959; *Variety*, 20 July 1955.

32. Allison Samuels, "Will It Be Denzel's Day?," *Newsweek*, 25 February 2002, 57.

33. Poitier, *This Life*, 173.

34. Parrish and Terrace, *Complete Actors' Television Credits*, 1:390; Tarkington, *Fascinating Stranger*, 1–56; Sidney Poitier, telephone interview with the author, 22 December 2000; Marill, *Films of Sidney Poitier*, 223.

35. Street, *Good-bye, My Lady*; Poitier, *This Life*, 173–174; Folders #174A and #2442B, WBC.

36. *Variety*, 17 June 1955; Wellman, *Short Time for Insanity*, 97; Folders #174A and #2951, WBC.

37. *Hollywood Reporter*, 4 April 1956; *Variety*, 4 April 1956; Folders #2951 and

#174A, WBC; *Catholic World*, May 1956; *Commonweal*, 25 May 1956; Wellman, *Short Time for Insanity*, 97.

38. See Dworkin, "New Negro on Screen," October 1960, 41.

39. Poitier, *This Life*, 174; Sidney Poitier, telephone interview with the author, 22 December 2000.

40. Poitier, *This Life*, 174–75.

41. Robert Alan Aurthur, "All Original, All Live," *TV Guide*, 17 March 1973, 6.

42. Museum of Television and Radio Seminar Series, "The Dynamics of Live Television: A Conversation with Three Prominent Directors," MTR; Barnouw, *Tube of Plenty*, 163–65.

43. Aurthur, "All Original, All Live," 7; *New York Post*, 2 April 1959.

44. Barnouw, *Tube of Plenty*, 154–67.

45. Kisseloff, *Box*, 230; *Los Angeles Times*, 13 July 1956.

46. "Dynamics of Live Television," MTR.

47. Aurthur, "All Original, All Live," 8–10; Poitier, *This Life*, 176–78.

48. Kindem, *Live Television Generation of Hollywood Film Directors*, 54–56, 133; Poitier, *This Life*, 178.

49. Live television recording of "A Man Is Ten Feet Tall," MTR. For script, see Folder 1, "Edge of the City" File, MGM Collection, CTL.

50. "Dynamics of Live Television," MTR; Aurthur, "All Original, All Live," 10; Box 17, Susskind Papers, WSHS; MGM Press Release, 30 November 1955, "A Man Is Ten Feet Tall" file, NYPLPA.

51. Aurthur, "All Original, All Live," 10; *New York Herald-Tribune*, 30 October 1962; *Jet*, 24 November 1955.

52. *Hollywood Reporter*, 12 October 1955; Barnouw, *Tube of Plenty*, 166; Kisseloff, *Box*, 230; Gianakos, *Television Drama Series Programming*.

53. Box 17, Susskind Papers; *Variety*, 7 December 1955; *Urbana (Ill.) Courier*, 19 April 1956.

54. *Counterattack*, 26 September 1952, 19 May 1953; Jackson, *Picking Up the Tab*, 26–37; McGilligan and Buhle, *Tender Comrades*, 561–62.

55. *New York Times*, 15 April 1956; Box 17, Susskind Papers, WSHS.

56. *New York Times*, 15 April 1956.

57. Box 17, Susskind Papers, WSHS; *Columbus (Ind.) Republican*, 10 March 1956.

58. *Urbana (Ill.) Courier*, 19 April 1956; Folder 1, "Edge of the City" File, MGM Collection, CTL; Gow, *Hollywood in the Fifties*, 97.

59. Miller, *Films of Martin Ritt*, 22; Boxes 17 and 27, Susskind Papers, WSHS; *Variety*, 2 January 1957.

60. *Time*, 14 January 1957; *Variety*, 2 January 1957. See also *New York Times*, 20 January 1957, 30 January 1957, 3 February 1957; *New York Post*, 30 January 1957; *Cue*, 2 February 1957.

61. *New Yorker*, 9 February 1957; *Variety*, 2 January 1957; *New York Herald-Tribune*, 30 January 1957; *New York Times*, 3 February 1957; Box 17, Susskind Papers, WSHS.

62. *New York Herald-Tribune*, 30 January 1957; *New Yorker*, 9 February 1957; *Newsweek*, 7 January 1957; *Saturday Review*, 12 January 1957; Wood, *America in the Movies*, 133; "Edge of the City" PCA Files, MHS.

63. See Johnson, "Beige, Brown, or Black," 39; Godfrey, "Tall When They're Small," 43; Dworkin, "New Negro on Screen," October 1960, 39; Burke, "Presentation of the American Negro in Hollywood Films," 250–58.

64. Branch, *Parting the Waters*, 120–30; Marisa Chappell, Jenny Hutchinson, and Brian Ward, " 'Dress modestly, neatly . . . as if you were going to church': Respectability, Class and Gender in the Montgomery Bus Boycott and the Early Civil Rights Movement," in *Gender in the Civil Rights Movement*, ed. Ling and Monteith, 69–100.

65. Branch, *Parting the Waters*, 136–68.

66. Ibid., 167–205. See also Morris,

Origins of the Civil Rights Movement, 1–173.

67. Box 17, Susskind Papers, WSHS. See also Williams, *Playing the Race Card*, 10–44, 218.

68. *Pittsburgh Courier*, quoted in Buchanan, "Study of the Writers of the Negro Press," 113. See also a review of *Edge of the City* by a young black woman in *Daily Worker*, 14 February 1957.

69. *Chicago Defender*, 16 March 1957; Gow, *Hollywood in the Fifties*, 97.

70. *Chicago Defender*, 15 September 1956; *Pittsburgh Courier*, 20 October 1956; "Edge of the City" Pressbook, Box 6, Black Films Collection, SCRBC.

71. *New York Daily News*, 30 January 1957, 6 February 1957.

72. *New York Daily News*, 6 February 1957.

Chapter Seven

1. *Variety*, 9 May 1956. See also *Ebony*, December 1955.

2. *New York Times*, 2 April 1961.

3. *Variety*, 5 January 1955; Royce, *Rock Hudson*, 12; *Richmond Times-Dispatch*, 2 December 1956; *Hollywood Reporter*, 28 September 1955; "Inter-Office Memos" Folder and Folders 1–4, "Something of Value" File, MGM Collection, CTL; "Something of Value" Pressbook, NYPLPA.

4. Ruark, *Something of Value*; *New Yorker*, 18 May 1957; *Good Housekeeping*, June 1957.

5. Kershaw, *Mau Mau from Below*, 212–15; Clough, *Mau Mau Memoirs*, 26–28.

6. Kershaw, *Mau Mau from Below*, 215–63.

7. Clough, *Mau Mau Memoirs*, 2–4, 34–42.

8. "Something of Value" Pressbook, NYPLPA; "Something of Value" PCA files, MHL.

9. "Inter-Office Memos" Folder, "Some-thing of Value" File, MGM Collection, CTL; Gates and Thomas, *My Husband, Rock Hudson*, 144; *New York Post*, 1 April 1959.

10. Gates and Thomas, *My Husband, Rock Hudson*, 137–44; Hudson and Davidson, *Rock Hudson*, 56–57, 96–102; Clark with Kleiner, *Rock Hudson: Friend of Mine*, 72.

11. Gates and Thomas, *My Husband, Rock Hudson*, 144; Oppenheimer and Vitek, *Idol*, 62.

12. Oppenheimer and Vitek, *Idol: Rock Hudson*, 61–62.

13. Poitier, *This Life*, 181–84.

14. "Something of Value" Pressbook, NYPLPA.

15. Rock Hudson Oral History, Ronald L. Davis Oral History Collection, MHL, 29–32; McGilligan, *Backstory 2*, 54–55; Sidney Poitier, telephone interview with the author, 9 May 2001.

16. Shooting Schedule, "Something of Value" File, MHL; *Los Angeles Examiner*, 30 September 1956; *New York Post*, 2 April 1959; Interview Draft, 23 May 1958, Sidney Poitier File, Hedda Hopper Collection, MHL.

17. *New Yorker*, 18 May 1957; *Saturday Review*, 18 May 1957; *Newsweek*, 13 May 1957. See also *Hollywood Reporter*, 29 April 1957; *Showmen's Trade Review*, 29 April 1957; *Cue*, 11 May 1957; *Montreal Star*, 6 July 1957; Martin S. Dworkin, "New Negro on Screen," November 1960, 35.

18. *Variety*, 1 May 1957.

19. Ibid.; *Motion Picture Daily*, 29 April 1957; *New York Times*, 11 May 1957; *Time*, 20 May 1957; *Hollywood Citizen-News*, 8 June 1957.

20. *Variety*, 15 May 1957; *Pittsburgh Courier*, 22 May 1957.

21. *New York Amsterdam News*, 11 May 1957; *Ebony*, April 1957; *Hollywood Reporter*, 25 April 1957; *New York Times*, 10 February 1958, 28 August 1957, 9 September 1957, 15 September 1957.

22. *Newsweek*, 13 May 1957.

23. Ibid.

24. Poitier, *This Life*, 186; Sidney Poitier, "Why I Became an Actor," *Negro Digest*, December 1961, 92.

25. *Look*, 28 October 1958; Davis and Dee, *With Ossie and Ruby*, 267.

26. Poitier, *This Life*, 193–94; Poitier, "Why I Became an Actor," 96–97.

27. Poitier, *This Life*, 194–95; *New York Post*, 3 April 1959; Article Draft, 13 July 1965, Folder 84, Sidney Skolsky Collection, MHL.

28. Poitier, *This Life*, 185–86; Davis and Dee, *With Ossie and Ruby*, 268.

29. "Mark of the Hawk" Production Notes, NYPLPA; *Pittsburgh Courier*, 5 January 1957; *New York Post*, 6 March 1958; Poitier, *This Life*, 186–88.

30. "Mark of the Hawk" Pressbook, Box 7, Black Films Collection, SCRBC; Kitt, *Confessions of a Sex Kitten*, 157–58; Poitier, *This Life*, 188–90.

31. Kitt, *Confessions of a Sex Kitten*, 158–62.

32. For scripts, see "Mark of the Hawk" Folder, Box 60, and "Mark of the Hawk" Folder, Box 21, in the Universal Collection, CTL.

33. *Los Angeles Examiner*, 28 November 1958; *Los Angeles Times*, 7 August 1958; *Cue*, 8 March 1958. See also *Christian Science Monitor*, 4 March 1958; *Film Daily*, 26 February 1958; *New York Times*, 6 March 1958, 9 March 1958; *New York Post*, 6 March 1958; uncited reviews in "Mark of the Hawk" file, CBFSC.

34. Folder 12668B, "Mark of the Hawk" file, Universal Collection, CTL; *Variety*, 12 March 1958; *Motion Picture Herald*, 15 February 1958.

35. Folder 12283, "Mark of the Hawk" File, Universal Collection, CTL; *New York Amsterdam News*, 23 September 1957.

36. "Mark of the Hawk" Pressbook, Box 7, Black Films Collection, SCRBC; *Variety*, 26 November 1958.

37. *New York Journal*, 1 February 1957; *New York Daily News*, 6 February 1957; *New York Times*, 17 February 1957, 15 February 1957.

38. *Time*, 25 March 1957; Doherty, *Teenagers and Teenpics*, 99–101.

39. Henry Louis Gates Jr., "Belafonte's Balancing Act," *New Yorker*, 26 August and 2 September 1996, 138; "Lead Man Holler," *Time*, 2 March 1959, 40–43; *Cue*, 9 March 1957; *Down Beat*, 6 March 1957; *New York Post*, 19 August 1956, 18 November 1958.

40. Shaw, *Belafonte*, 115–18, 194–221, 298–99; Harry Belafonte, "Why I Married Julie," *Ebony*, July 1957, 90–95.

41. *Daily Worker*, 6 May 1957; *New York Times*, 11 May 1957, 4 August 1957, 14 August 1957, 17 August 1957, 18 August 1957, 22 October 1957; *Ebony*, July 1957; *Time*, 2 March 1959.

42. Mailer, "White Negro." See also Levine, "Body's Politics," 57–89.

43. Gates, "Belafonte's Balancing Act," 139; Shaw, *Belafonte*, 192. See also Michelle A. Stephens, "The 'First Negro Matinee Idol': Harry Belafonte and American Culture in the 1950s," unpublished manuscript in the author's possession.

44. Tom Prideaux, "Poitier's Search for the Right Corner," *Life*, 27 April 1959, 142; *New York Amsterdam News*, 2 February 1957, 9 February 1957.

45. Warren, *Band of Angels*; Blotner, *Robert Penn Warren*, 290–91, 298–302; Watkins, Hiers, and Weaks, *Talking with Robert Penn Warren*, 262.

46. Bogle, *Toms, Coons, Mulattoes, Mammies, and Bucks*, 57–60, 150–54, 166–75; Graham, *Framing the South*, 68.

47. See Van Deburg, *Slavery and Race in American Popular Culture*, 109–26.

48. Wayne, *Clark Gable*, 264–73; Samuels, *King*, 291–315.

49. Tornabene, *Long Live the King*, 353–54; Poitier, *This Life*, 200–201.

50. Folders 646B, 1442A, 1442B, 3105B, "Band of Angels" file, WBC; DeCarlo with Warren, *Yvonne*, 200.

51. Uncited articles on Reel 1, George L. Johnson Collection, UCLA; Folder 1442B, "Band of Angels" file, WBC.

52. *Ebony*, September 1957; *New York Amsterdam News*, 16 February 1957; *Counterattack*, 29 March 1957.

53. Campbell, *Celluloid South*, 167; Folder 714, "Band of Angels" File, WBC. See also hooks, *Reel to Real*, 83–90.

54. Popkin, "Hollywood Tackles the Race Issue."

55. *Newsweek*, 29 July 1957; *New Yorker*, 20 July 1957; *Los Angeles Mirror-News*, 10 August 1957. See also *Variety*, 10 July 1957; *Hollywood Reporter*, 10 July 1957; *New York Herald-Tribune*, 10 July 1957; *New York Post*, 11 July 1957; *New York Journal-American*, 11 July 1957; *New York Mirror*, 11 July 1957; *New York Daily News*, 11 July 1957; *Los Angeles Times*, 8 August 1957; *Time*, 5 August 1957.

56. *Chicago Defender*, 3 August 1957.

57. Folder 1499B, "Band of Angels" File, WBC.

58. *Chicago Defender*, 3 August 1957, 20 July 1957; *Pittsburgh Courier*, 3 August 1957, 6 July 1957, 20 July 1957. See also *Ebony*, September 1957.

59. *Chicago Defender*, 3 August 1957; John Oliver Killens, "Hollywood in Black and White," in *State of the Union*, ed. Boroff, 102–3.

60. Killens, "Hollywood in Black and White," 103.

61. Ibid., 103–4.

62. *Variety*, 8 May 1957.

63. *Hollywood Reporter*, 28 October 1957; *New York Times*, 29 October 1957, 10 November 1957; *Pittsburgh Courier*, 9 November 1957.

64. See Wood, *America in the Movies*, 16–20, 129–36; Thomas Cripps, "African Americans and Jews in Hollywood," in *Struggles in the Promised Land*, ed. Salzman and West, 257–74.

65. *Pittsburgh Courier*, 16 February 1957. See also *Pittsburgh Courier*, 11 May 1957; *Daily Worker*, 2 May 1957.

66. *New York Amsterdam News*, 2 March 1957, 10 August 1957, 24 August 1957; *Pittsburgh Courier*, 2 November 1957.

67. Brownstein, *Power and the Glitter*, 168; *New York Amsterdam News*, 25 May 1957; *Pittsburgh Courier*, 25 May 1957; Branch, *Parting the Waters*, 216–18.

68. Carby, *Race Men*, 4–5; Brownstein, *Power and the Glitter*, 168.

69. *New York Post*, 11 September 1957.

70. Ibid.

Chapter Eight

1. *New York Amsterdam News*, 31 August 1957, 14 September 1957; Davis and Dee, *With Ossie and Ruby*, 275. See also White, *Our Virgin Island*.

2. See *Motion Picture Herald*, 2 March 1960; *New York Times*, 24 March 1960; *Cue*, 26 March 1960.

3. *Variety*, 5 November 1958.

4. *New York Morning-Telegraph*, 21 January 1959.

5. *Pittsburgh Courier*, 15 March 1958; *New York Times*, 23 March 1960; Poitier, *This Life*, 202–3.

6. *New York Amsterdam News*, 16 November 1957; *New York Times*, 5 November 1957.

7. Berg, *Goldwyn*, 427–29.

8. See Gabler, *An Empire of Their Own*.

9. Berg, *Goldwyn*, 1–349; Loudon Wainwright, "One-Man Gang Is in Action Again," *Life*, 16 February 1959, 103–16.

10. Balio, *American Film Industry*, 315–31; Leff and Simmons, *Dame in the Kimono*, 224–25.

11. Berg, *Goldwyn*, 460–61.

12. *Los Angeles Times Magazine*, 5 April 1959; Heyward, *Porgy*.

13. Dorothy and DuBose Heyward, *Porgy: A Play in Four Acts*.

14. *New York Times*, 14 September

1943, 21 June 1959; *Variety*, 12 September 1944.

15. *Hollywood Reporter*, 10 March 1953, 14 August 1954; Jefferson, "Negro on Broadway, 1952–1953," 270–72; "Porgy and Bess" Compilation of Stage Productions, "Porgy and Bess" File, CBFSC; *Los Angeles Times Magazine*, 5 April 1959.

16. Buchanan, "Study of the Attitudes of the Writers of the Negro Press," 213–18; Langston Hughes, "Negro and American Entertainment," in *American Negro Reference Book*, ed. Davis, 842–46; *New York Amsterdam News*, 6 September 1958; *Variety*, 13 October 1954.

17. "Porgy and Bess" PCA Files, MHL; *Hollywood Reporter*, 11 October 1935; *New York Times*, 9 May 1957; Berg, *Goldwyn*, 478–79.

18. *Pittsburgh Courier*, 22 June 1957; Bogle, *Dorothy Dandridge*, 395–99; *The Jewish Advocate*, 24 October 1957, and *The Call*, 1 November 1957, have notes about distribution to newspaper syndicates in Folder 4, Box 34, Richard N. Nash Papers, WSHS.

19. *New York Times*, 5 November 1957.

20. *New York Amsterdam News*, 16 November 1957.

21. *New York Times*, 11 November 1957, 20 November 1957; *Daily Defender*, 14 November 1957; *New York Post*, 14 November 1957, 21 November 1957.

22. Poitier, *This Life*, 204–5.

23. Wainwright, "One-Man Gang Is in Action Again," 110; *New York Times*, 11 December 1957; *Variety*, 12 December 1957; *New York Herald-American*, 3 January 1958; *Los Angeles Mirror-News*, 4 January 1958; *Jet*, 23 January 1958.

24. Poitier, *This Life*, 206–7.

25. Kramer, *Mad, Mad, Mad, Mad World*, 1–146; *New York Herald-Tribune*, 4 August 1958.

26. Poitier, *This Life*, 207–8.

27. Ibid., 208–10; Box 18, Stanley

Kramer Papers, UCLA; uncited article, Reel 10, George L. Johnson Collection, UCLA; *New York Times*, 14 December 1957.

28. Berg, *Goldwyn*, 479–82; Davis and Jane and Burt Boyar, *Why Me?*, 66–67; Davis, *Hollywood in a Suitcase*, 53.

29. Hughes, "Negro and American Entertainment," 845; Poitier, *This Life*, 208–11.

30. Box 18, Stanley Kramer Papers, UCLA; Kramer, *Mad, Mad, Mad, Mad World*, 146–50; Manso, *Brando*, 347–48, 522–23; *New York Post*, 5 September 1958.

31. Curtis and Parks, *Tony Curtis*, 132–42.

32. Kramer, *Mad, Mad, Mad Mad World*, 150–52; Curtis and Parks, *Tony Curtis*, 142; Box 18, Stanley Kramer Papers, UCLA. See also Theodore Bikel Oral History, Ronald L. Davis Oral History Collection, MHL; Bikel, *Theo*, 197–99.

33. "Defiant Ones" Production Notes, MHL; "Defiant Ones" Pressbook, Box 6, Black Films Collection, SCRBC; *Chicago Defender*, 9 August 1958; *New York Times*, 6 July 1958.

34. *Limelight*, May 1996; Robb, "Naming the Right Names," 25; *Variety*, 12 May 1958.

35. Folder 5, Box 9, Nedrick Young Papers, WSHS; *New York Times*, 9 March 1958; Hutchens, "Defiance in 'The Defiant Ones.'" See also Box 18, Stanley Kramer Papers, UCLA; PCA Files for "Defiant Ones," MHL.

36. See Rogin, *Blackface, White Noise*, 239; Carby, *Race Men*, 181–84; Stam and Shohat, *Unthinking Eurocentrism*, 236–37. See also Frank, "Unchained: Perspectives on Change."

37. *Variety*, 22 July 1958; "Defiant Ones" Pressbook, Box 6, Black Films Collection, SCRBC; *New York Times*, 10 June 1958, 30 June 1958, 9 July 1958, 13 July 1958.

38. *New York Times*, 9 July 1958,

20 August 1958; uncited article dated 11 July 1958, Reel 10, Johnson Collection, UCLA.

39. *Pittsburgh Courier*, 26 July 1958; *New York Amsterdam News*, 26 July 1958, 27 September 1958; "Defiant Ones" Pressbook, Box 6, Black Films Collection, SCRBC.

40. "Defiant Ones" Pressbook, Box 6, Black Films Collection, SCRBC; Baldwin, *Devil Finds Work*, 66.

41. Uncited article entitled " 'Defiant Ones' Is Launched" from "Defiant Ones" file, CBFSC; *Film Daily*, 4 September 1958; *Chicago American*, 14 August 1958; *Chicago Daily Tribune*, 14 August 1958; *Chicago Sun-Times*, 14 August 1958; *Chicago Defender*, 6 September 1958. See also *Saturday Review*, 26 July 1958; *Life*, 11 August 1958.

42. *New York Times*, 25 September 1958, 5 October 1958; *Boston Globe*, 5 October 1958; *Hollywood Reporter*, 5 August 1958; *Film Daily*, 5 August 1958; *Variety*, 6 August 1958; *New York Journal-American*, 25 September 1958; *Los Angeles Examiner*, 2 October 1958; *Los Angeles Times*, 2 October 1958, 17 October 1958. See also *Hollywood Reporter*, 31 July 1958; *Newark Evening News*, 2 October 1958.

43. *Newsweek*, 25 August 1958; *Ebony*, October 1958; *Pittsburgh Courier*, 9 August 1958, 16 August 1958; *Chicago Defender*, 9 August 1958, 16 August 1958; *New York Amsterdam News*, 16 August 1958, 27 September 1958, 17 January 1959. See also Dworkin, "New Negro on Screen," January 1961, 36–37.

44. Box 17, Stanley Kramer Papers, UCLA; *New York Times*, 20 October 1958, 31 December 1958; *Variety*, 4 September 1958; *Chicago Defender*, 20 September 1958; *New York Daily Mirror*, 4 April 1959; *New York Times*, 24 February 1959; *People's World*, 7 March 1959; *Los Angeles Mirror-News*, 19 March 1959.

45. *New York Amsterdam News*, 28 February 1959; Cripps, *Making Movies Black*, 190–93; *New York Times*, 1 March 1959, 7 April 1959, 8 April 1959. See also Dick Williams column in *Los Angeles Mirror-News*, Reel 1, Johnson Collection, UCLA.

46. *New York Times*, 1 January 1959, 14 January 1959, 17 January 1959, 8 February 1960, 9 February 1960, 3 May 1960, 11 September 1960, 4 June 1961; *Variety*, 21 January 1959; *Boxoffice*, 9 February 1959; Box 8, Nedrick Young Papers, WSHS. See also Ceplair and Englund, *Inquisition in Hollywood*, 418–19.

47. *Variety*, 2 July 1961; *Hollywood Reporter*, 7 February 1961; Box 18, Stanley Kramer Papers, UCLA. See also undated articles in Nedrick Young Papers, WSHS.

48. *Variety*, 25 March 1959; *New York Times*, 10 April 1959, 2 April 1961; undated article in *New York Post*, in Sidney Poitier file, NYPLPA.

49. *New Republic*, 1 September 1958.

50. *New York Times*, 8 February 1959. See also *New York Times*, 1 February 1959, 15 March 1959, and uncited essay by Chestyn Everett on Reel 4, Johnson Collection, UCLA.

51. Terkel, *Spectator*, 287–88; Baldwin, *Devil Finds Work*, 66, 62.

52. Gow, *Hollywood in the Fifties*, 98.

53. *New York Post*, 26 August 1958; *New York Mirror*, 17 August 1958; undated article from *New York Daily News*, in Nedrick Young Papers, WSHS.

54. *Look*, 27 October 1958; *New York Amsterdam News*, 16 August 1958; Sidney Poitier file, Hedda Hopper Collection, MHL. Versions of the Hopper interview appear in her syndicated feature. See *Chicago Sunday Tribune Magazine*, 31 August 1958; *Los Angeles Times Magazine*, 31 August 1958.

55. *New York Times*, 22 May 1958.

56. "Porgy and Bess" PCA File, MHL; Folder 5, Box 34, Richard Nash Papers, WSHS; *Variety*, 30 April 1958.

57. *Life*, 15 June 1959; *Los Angeles Times*, 3 July 1958; *New York Times*, 3 July 1958.

58. Wainwright, "One-Man Gang Is in Action Again," 107; *Chicago Defender*, 30 August 1958; Poitier, *This Life*, 212–13. On Carroll, see *Time*, 7 December 1959.

59. Carroll, *Diahann*, 75–76; *Ebony*, September 1965.

60. Rampersad, *Jackie Robinson*, 332–34; Poitier, *This Life*, 213–17; Poitier, *Measure of a Man*, 163–68.

61. Rouben Mamoulian Oral History, Ronald L. Davis Oral History Collection, MHL, 39–41; Michael Freedland, *Goldwyn Touch*, 242–44.

62. Mamoulian Oral History, 41–43; *Variety*, 28 July 1958, 30 July 1958; *New York Times*, 28 July 1958.

63. *New York Times*, 31 July 1958, 3 August 1958, 4 August 1958; *Variety*, 6 August 1958, 10 September 1958; Preminger, *Preminger*, 136; *Chicago Defender*, 30 August 1958; Berg, *Goldwyn*, 485–86; *Hollywood Reporter*, 5 August 1958.

64. *New York Post*, 5 August 1958; *Hollywood Reporter*, 7 August 1958; *New York Times*, 7 August 1958.

65. *New York Times*, 8 August 1958; *Variety*, 13 August 1958; *New York Amsterdam News*, 16 August 1958; *Chicago Defender*, 23 August 1958.

66. *Los Angeles Tribune*, 15 August 1958; *Hollywood Reporter*, 25 August 1958.

67. *Chicago Defender*, 17 August 1958; *New York Mirror*, 17 August 1958; Sidney Poitier, "They Call Me a Do-It-Yourself Man," *Films and Filming*, September 1959, 7.

68. *New York Times*, 9 August 1958, 17 August 1958, 11 February 1959; *Variety*, 11 February 1959.

69. Preminger, *Preminger*, 136–37; Bogdanovich, *Who the Devil Made It*, 623, 630; Berg, *Goldwyn*, 485–86.

70. Folder 7, Box 34, Richard Nash Papers, WSHS; Frederic Morton, "Audacity of Sidney Poitier," *Holiday*, June 1962, 109.

71. Morton, "Audacity of Sidney Poitier," 109; *Chicago Defender*, 13 September 1958.

72. Preminger, *Preminger*, 137–38; Davis, *Hollywood in a Suitcase*, 58–60, 77.

73. Bogle, *Dorothy Dandridge*, 400–416; Bailey, *Between You and Me*, 184–87.

74. Preminger, *Preminger*, 138; Bogle, *Dorothy Dandridge*, 416–20.

75. Davis, *Hollywood in a Suitcase*, 59; *New York Amsterdam News*, 25 October 1958; Poitier, *This Life*, 220–21.

76. Poitier, *This Life*, 221–22.

77. Carroll, *Diahann*, 56–73.

78. Ibid., 76; Poitier, *This Life*, 223–25.

79. Carroll, *Diahann*, 79–82; Poitier, *This Life*, 225–26.

80. "Porgy and Bess" Production Notes, NYPLPA; *New York Times*, 8 December 1958; *Los Angeles Mirror-News*, 10 December 1958; *Baltimore Sun*, 15 December 1958; *Newark News*, 19 December 1958.

81. Carroll, *Diahann*, 84.

82. *Chicago Defender*, 20 June 1959, 27 June 1959; *Pittsburgh Courier*, 11 July 1959; Bogle, *Dorothy Dandridge*, 449–50.

83. *Film Daily*, 25 June 1959; *Motion Picture Herald*, 27 June 1959; *Cue*, 4 July 1959; *Hollywood Reporter*, 25 June 1959; "Porgy and Bess" Press Packet, CBFSC; *New York Times*, 25 June 1959, 28 June 1959, 2 August 1959.

84. *Saturday Review*, 4 July 1959; *New Yorker*, 4 July 1959; *Time*, 6 July 1959.

85. *Variety*, 15 March 1961, 22 March 1961, 27 March 1963; *New York Amsterdam News*, 9 August 1959, 17 October 1959; Berg, *Goldwyn*, 487; *New York Times*, 11 April 1959; *Los Angeles Examiner*, 11 April 1959.

86. *Variety*, 13 January 1960, 3 February 1960, 1 March 1961.

87. *Variety*, 1 March 1961. See also *New York Amsterdam News*, 8 April 1961.

88. *Christian Science Monitor*, 30 June 1959; *Time*, 6 July 1959; *Los Angeles Mirror-News*, 16 August 1959.

89. *Chicago Defender*, 7 March 1959, 25 August 1959; *New York Amsterdam News*, 13 June 1959, 4 July 1959.

90. *Variety*, 27 May 1959; Baldwin, "On Catfish Row," 246–48. See also Cruse, *Crisis of the Negro Intellectual*, 100–107.

91. Baldwin, "On Catfish Row," 248. See also Dworkin, "New Negro on Screen," February 1961, 40.

92. *New York Times*, 6 August 1967.

Chapter Nine

1. Poitier, *This Life*, 227.

2. Ibid., 227–30; Poitier, *Measure of a Man*, 181–82.

3. Keppel, *Work of Democracy*, 23–26, 187–90.

4. *New York Times*, 8 March 1959, 9 April 1959.

5. Hansberry, *Raisin in the Sun*.

6. Hansberry, *To Be Young, Gifted, and Black*, 210. See also Brown-Guillory, *Their Place on Stage*, 34–36, 93–94, 117–19; Carter, *Hansberry's Drama*, 26–32; Cheney, *Lorraine Hansberry*, 55–71.

7. Rose, *You Can't Do That on Broadway!*, 56–69.

8. Ibid., 70–74, 98–99.

9. Carroll, *Diahann*, 87.

10. Ibid.

11. Ibid., 88–94.

12. *Chicago Defender*, 21 February 1959; *Patriot Ledger* (Mass.), 1 September 1988; Mitchell, *Black Drama*, 180–82.

13. Rose, *You Can't Do That on Broadway!*, 20–22.

14. Sidney Poitier, "Dialogue on Film," September/October 1991, 21; Ward, "Lorraine Hansberry and the Passion of

Walter Lee"; Turner, "Visions of Love and Manliness in a Blackening World." See also Marriott, *On Black Men*, viii–x; Manning Marable, "The Black Male: Searching beyond Stereotypes," in *American Black Male*, ed. Majors and Gordon, 69–77.

15. Lorraine Hansberry, "An Author's Reflections: Willy Loman, Walter Younger, and He Who Must Live," *Village Voice*, 12 August 1959; Rose, *You Can't Do That on Broadway!*, 22–24.

16. Rose, *You Can't Do That on Broadway!*, 22.

17. *Hartford Times*, 22 January 1959; Davis and Dee, *With Ossie and Ruby*, 282–83; Poitier, *This Life*, 232.

18. Rose, *You Can't Do That on Broadway!*, 25, 106; *Philadelphia Daily News*, 29 January 1959.

19. James Baldwin, "Sweet Lorraine," introduction to Hansberry, *Young, Gifted, and Black*, xii; Keppel, *Work of Democracy*, 177–82. See also *New York Amsterdam News*, 7 February 1959.

20. Rose, *You Can't Do That on Broadway!*, 27–33; *Chicago Tribune*, 11 February 1959; *New York Herald-Tribune*, 1 March 1959; *New York Amsterdam News*, 14 February 1959.

21. Rose, *You Can't Do That on Broadway!*, 31, 106–7.

22. Poitier, *This Life*, 232–34.

23. Sidney Poitier, "Why I Became an Actor," *Negro Digest*, December 1961, 84–85; *New York Post*, 30 March 1959; undated article from *Christian Science Monitor* entitled "Star of 'Raisin in the Sun' Explains His Need for 'Prohuman' Scripts," "Raisin in the Sun" file, NYPLPA. Poitier, *Measure of a Man*, 148–58. See also McDonough, *Staging Masculinity*, 140–43.

24. Poitier, *This Life*, 234; Sidney Poitier, telephone interview with the author, 9 May 2001.

25. Langston Hughes, "The Negro and American Entertainment," in *American Negro Reference Book*, ed. Davis, 834–

35; *New York Amsterdam News*, 13 September 1958; *New York Daily News*, 24 May 1960.

26. Winters, *Shelley II*, 204–5. See also *New York Times*, 16 May 1958.

27. *New York Journal-American*, 12 March 1959; Rose, *You Can't Do That on Broadway!*, 9–11.

28. "Sidney Poitier: One Bright Light"; Rose, *You Can't Do That on Broadway!*, 12; *New York Amsterdam News*, 21 March 1959.

29. *New York Post*, 12 March 1959; *New York Daily News*, 12 March 1959; *New York Journal-American*, 12 March 1959; *New York Times*, 12 March 1959; *New York Daily Mirror*, 12 March 1959; *New York World Telegram*, 12 March 1959; *New York Herald-Tribune*, 12 March 1959.

30. Hansberry, *Young, Gifted, and Black*, 128; *New York Times*, 13 March 1959; *New Yorker*, 9 May 1957; Roosevelt, *My Day*, 207; *Pittsburgh Courier*, 10 January 1959; *New York Amsterdam News*, 21 March 1959, 14 April 1959, 16 May 1959, 23 May 1959, 1 August 1959, 29 August 1959, 4 June 1960; *Chicago Defender*, 14 February 1959, 21 February 1959.

31. Lerone Bennett Jr., "Hollywood's First Negro Movie Star," *Ebony*, May 1959, 107–8.

32. *Coronet*, July 1959; *Louisville Courier-Journal*, 5 April 1959; Rose, *You Can't Do That on Broadway!*, 133–36; Poitier, *Measure of a Man*, 155.

33. *Los Angeles Mirror-News*, 18 March 1959; *New York Times*, 8 April 1959; *New York Herald-Tribune*, 8 April 1959; Weales, "Thoughts on 'A Raisin in the Sun,'" 527; *New Republic*, 13 April 1959.

34. *Village Voice*, 25 March 1959, 22 April 1959.

35. *New York Times*, 8 March 1959, 12 March 1959, 29 March 1959, 9 April 1959, 11 October 1964; *New York Post*, 12 March 1959; *New York Daily News*,

12 March 1959; *New York Journal-American*, 12 March 1959; *New York Daily Mirror*, 12 March 1959; *New York World Telegram*, 12 March 1959; *New York Herald-Tribune*, 12 March 1959.

36. See Keyssar, *Curtain and the Veil*, 113–44.

37. Hansberry, "An Author's Reflections," 195–96; Terkel, *Spectator*, 282–83; Keppel, *Work of Democracy*, 197–202; Anderson, *Mammies No More*, 32–35; Davis, "Significance of Lorraine Hansberry."

38. Woodie King Jr., "Lorraine Hansberry's Children"; Davis and Dee, *With Ossie and Ruby*, 290; Keppel, *Work of Democracy*, 21–27; Cruse, *Crisis of the Negro Intellectual*, 277–83; Rahman, "To Be Black, Female, and a Playwright."

39. *New York Daily Mirror*, 4 April 1959; *New York Times*, 24 February 1959; *People's World*, 7 March 1959; Box 17, Stanley Kramer Papers, UCLA.

40. *New York Times Magazine*, 25 January 1959; *New York Morning-Telegram*, 21 January 1959; *New York Journal*, 29 June 1959; *New York Herald-Tribune*, 4 October 1959; *Newark Sunday News*, 13 September 1959; *Current Biography*, May 1959, 364–66; *Chicago Defender*, 24 January 1959; 31 January 1959, 3 May 1959; Tom Prideaux, "Poitier's Search for the Right Corner," *Life*, 27 April 1959, 140–43; Bennett, "Hollywood's First Negro Movie Star," 100–108; *Los Angeles Mirror-News*, 16 March 1959–19 March 1959; *New York Post*, 30 March 1959–3 April 1959; Noble, "Entertainment, Politics, and the Movie Business," 21; Carroll, *Diahann*, 79.

41. Boorstin, *Image*, 37, 57; Sidney Poitier, telephone interview with the author, 9 May 2001. See also Schickel, *Intimate Strangers*; Gabler, *Life the Movie*.

42. *New York Amsterdam News*, 21 March 1959; Prideaux, "Poitier's Search for the Right Corner," 140; Bennett, "Hollywood's First Negro Movie

Star," 107; *New York Post*, 28 August 1960; *Los Angeles Mirror-News*, 19 March 1959.

43. Poitier, "They Call Me a Do-It-Yourself Man"; *Los Angeles Mirror-News*, 16 March 1959; *New York Post*, 8 April 1959.

44. *New York Post*, 1 April 1959; *New York Morning Telegram*, 21 January 1959; *Los Angeles Mirror-News*, 16 March 1959, 19 March 1959.

45. *New York Journal*, 29 June 1959; *New York Post*, 3 April 1959; *New York Morning-Telegraph*, 21 January 1959.

46. *New York Post*, 30 March 1959, 3 April 1959, 28 August 1960.

47. *Newsweek*, 19 September 1960.

48. Prideaux, "Poitier's Search for the Right Corner," 143; *New York Daily News*, 16 April 1961, 28 October 1962.

49. *New York Post*, 30 March 1959; "Sidney Poitier: One Bright Light." See also Marwick, *Sixties*, 412–17.

50. *New York Post*, 30 March 1959; *New York Herald-Tribune*, 4 October 1959.

51. Brown, *Actors Talk*, 167; *New York Herald-Tribune*, 4 October 1959; Reel 5, George L. Johnson Collection, UCLA; *Los Angeles Times*, 29 November 1959.

52. Box 29, David Susskind Papers, WSHS; Rose, *You Can't Do That on Broadway!*, 72; *Variety*, 21 January 1959; *New York Amsterdam News*, 24 January 1959.

53. *New York Times Magazine*, 22 February 1959; *New York Times*, 26 May 1959; *Chicago Defender*, 24 January 1959; *Pittsburgh Courier*, 2 May 1959; *New York Amsterdam News*, 30 April 1960; *Ebony*, July 1959, September 1960; Levine, *Black Culture and Black Consciousness*, 433–40.

54. "Belafonte Becomes 'Big Business,'" *Ebony*, June 1958, 17–24; Emily Coleman, "Organization Man Named Belafonte," *New York Times Magazine*, 13 December 1959, 35–42; Eleanor Harris, "The Stormy Success of Harry Belafonte," *Redbook*, May 1958, 44–47, 101–5; *New York Post*, 5 April 1959; *Pittsburgh Courier*, 19 July 1958; *New York Times*, 15 March 1959; *Cue*, 25 April 1959; *Redbook* quoted from *Pittsburgh Courier*, 26 April 1958.

55. Leab, *From Sambo to Superspade*, 219–21; Cripps, *Making Movies Black*, 265–73.

56. *Newsweek*, 19 September 1960; *New York Times*, 28 July 1959.

57. Hall Bartlett Oral History, Ronald L. Davis Oral History Collection, MHL, 21; "All the Young Men" Production Notes, CBFSC; Dworkin, "New Negro on Screen," December 1960, 35–36; *Saturday Review*, 20 August 1960.

58. Bartlett Oral History, 21; *Hollywood Reporter*, 4 March 1959; *New York Amsterdam News*, 27 August 1960; *New York Times*, 2 September 1959. See also "All the Young Men" PCA files, MHL.

59. *Variety*, 1 June 1960.

60. *New York Times*, 7 October 1959; *Hollywood Reporter*, 29 September 1959, 13 October 1959; *Screen Stories*, September 1960.

61. *Screen Stories*, September 1960; *Los Angeles Examiner*, 8 November 1959.

62. Sidney Poitier, *Measure of a Man*, 84–85.

63. Poitier, *This Life*, 236–37; *New York Amsterdam News*, 12 December 1959.

64. Linet, *Ladd*, 237; *Hollywood Citizen-News*, 8 September 1960; Bartlett Oral History, 24–25.

65. *Newsweek*, 5 September 1960; *Time*, 29 August 1960; *New Yorker*, 10 September 1960; *New York Times*, 27 August 1960; *New York Herald-Tribune*, 27 August 1960; *Cue*, 27 August 1960; *Los Angeles Times*, 8 September 1960; *Playboy*, November 1960.

66. *Variety*, 4 August 1960; *Motion Picture Daily*, 3 August 1960; *Film Daily*, 4 August 1960; *Hollywood Reporter*, 3 August 1960; *Motion Picture Herald*, 6 August 1960; *New York Times*, 11 Sep-

tember 1960; *Ebony*, August 1960; *New York Amsterdam News*, 6 August 1960; *Motion Picture Herald*, 17 September 1960.

67. *Motion Picture Herald*, 17 September 1960; *Variety*, 27 December 1967.

68. Weisbrot, *Freedom Bound*, 1–3, 19–44.

69. Undated article from *Christian Science Monitor* entitled "Star of 'Raisin in the Sun' Explains His Need for 'Prohuman' Scripts," "Raisin in the Sun" file, NYPLPA.

70. *New York Post*, 22 March 1959; Box 34, Susskind Papers, WSHS; *New York Herald-Tribune*, 26 March 1961.

71. *Time*, 12 September 1960; *New York Herald-Tribune*, 26 March 1961; *Variety*, 1 April 1961; *New York Times*, 17 July 1960; Box 34, Susskind Papers, WSHS.

72. *Los Angeles Examiner*, 21 August 1960; Box 34, Susskind Papers, WSHS.

73. Hansberry, *Raisin in the Sun: The Original Unfilmed Screenplay*.

74. Box 34, Susskind Papers, WSHS. On transition of *A Raisin in the Sun* from play to film, see also Keppel, *Work of Democracy*, 210–11; Carter, *Hansberry's Drama*, 70–78; Cheney, *Lorraine Hansberry*, 26–28; Reid, *Redefining Black Film*, 57–60. See also "Raisin in the Sun" PCA files, MHL.

75. *New York Amsterdam News*, 23 July 1960; *New York Times*, 17 July 1960.

76. *New York Amsterdam News*, 28 May 1960; *Variety*, 3 March 2000.

77. Box 34, Susskind Papers, WSHS; *Screen Stories*, May 1961; "Raisin in the Sun" Production Notes, CBFSC.

78. *New York Times*, 19 August 1960.

79. *Los Angeles Examiner*, 21 August 1960; *New York Times*, 17 July 1960; *New York Herald-Tribune*, 8 September 1960.

80. Frederic Morton, "Audacity of Sidney Poitier," *Holiday*, June 1962, 103–5.

81. *Films and Filming*, July 1961; *Time*, 31 March 1961. See also *Life*, 21 April 1961; *New York Times*, 30 March 1961; *New York Herald-Tribune*, 30 March 1961; *Variety*, 29 March 1959.

82. *New York Amsterdam News*, 11 March 1961, 22 April 1961, 24 June 1961; *New York Times*, 26 April 1961.

83. *New York Herald-Tribune*, 2 April 1961; *Motion Picture Daily*, 28 March 1961; *Hollywood Reporter*, 28 March 1961. See also *Village Voice*, 6 April 1961, 13 April 1961, 20 April 1961; *Time*, 31 March 1961, 21 April 1961; *Esquire*, September 1961; *New Republic*, 20 March 1961.

84. *Newsweek*, 10 April 1961. See also *New Yorker*, 8 April 1961; *Films and Filming*, July 1961; *Film Daily*, 24 March 1961; Baldwin, *Devil Finds Work*, 60–61.

85. *Hollywood Reporter*, 29 March 1961; *Limelight*, 30 March 1961; *Motion Picture Herald*, 1 April 1961; Morton, "Audacity of Sidney Poitier," 109–10; *New York Times*, 19 May 1961; *Hollywood Citizen-News*, 19 May 1961.

86. Box 34, Susskind Papers, WSHS; *Variety*, 10 January 1962; Reid, *Redefining Black Film*, 60–61.

87. *Christian Science Monitor*, 5 April 1961.

88. "Conversation with Actor Sidney Poitier," Audio Tape in CBS News Audio Resource Library, Vital History Cassette Series, June 1980.

89. *New York Amsterdam News*, 8 October 1960; *Screen Stories*, May 1961.

Chapter Ten

1. Carroll, *Diahann*, 94–95; *New York Amsterdam News*, 12 December 1959, 24 September 1960.

2. Carroll, *Diahann*, 95.

3. Quirk, *Paul Newman*, 1–109; Landry, *Paul Newman*, 61–62.

4. Carroll, *Diahann*, 96–97.

5. Flender, *Paris Blues*; Stovall, *Paris*

Noir; Baldwin, *Notes of a Native Son*; Heath, *Deep Are the Roots*.

6. *New York Times*, 5 November 1961; *Hollywood Reporter*, 1 September 1960.

7. Miller, *Films of Martin Ritt*, 39–43; Quirk, *Paul Newman*, 109; *Newsweek*, 2 October 1961.

8. *Newsweek*, 2 October 1961; Nicholson, *Reminiscing in Tempo*, 324–26.

9. *New York Amsterdam News*, 8 October 1960; "Paris Blues" Production Notes, NYPLPA; *Ebony*, August 1961; *Newsweek*, 2 October 1961. See also Godfrey, "Tall When They're Small," 44.

10. "Paris Blues" Pressbook, Box 7, Black Films Collection, SCRBC; Erenberg, *Swingin' the Dream*, 211–53.

11. "Paris Blues" Pressbook, Box 7, Black Films Collection, SCRBC; Lisa E. Davenport, "Jazz and the Cold War: Black Culture as an Instrument of American Foreign Policy," in *Crossing Boundaries*, ed. Hine and McLeod, 286–88, 305.

12. Gabbard, *Jammin' at the Margins*, 193–203, 228–30.

13. See Rogin, *Blackface, White Noise*, 226; Stovall, *Paris Noir*, 242–49.

14. See Thompson, "Paris Blues, Visited."

15. "Paris Blues" Pressbook, Box 7, Black Films Collection, SCRBC.

16. *Time*, 13 October 1961; *Variety*, 27 September 1961; *Limelight*, 28 September 1961; *Motion Picture Herald*, 11 October 1961; *New Yorker*, 11 November 1961; *Cue*, 11 November 1961; *New York Times*, 8 November 1961; *Saturday Review*, 28 October 1961; *New Republic*, 9 October 1961; Johnson, "Negro in American Films," 6.

17. Folder 6, Box 1, Pandro Berman Papers, WSHS.

18. Poitier, *This Life*, 237–38; Carroll, *Diahann*, 98.

19. Poitier, *This Life*, 238.

20. Carroll, *Diahann*, 99–100.

21. Brownstein, *Power and the Glitter*, 145–53; Box 1, Folder 1, Otto Preminger Papers, WSHS.

22. *New York Times*, 21 January 1961; *Ebony*, March 1961; *New York Amsterdam News*, 14 January 1961; Levy, *Rat Pack Confidential*, 160–78.

23. *New York Times*, 29 March 1960, 21 February 1961; Branch, *Parting the Waters*, 295–96, 370–71, 579–80, 771–72.

24. *New York Times*, 18 May 1960; Anderson, *Bayard Rustin*, 228; *New York Amsterdam News*, 16 April 1960, 7 May 1960.

25. *New York Amsterdam News*, 21 January 1961, 4 February 1961.

26. *New York Post*, 3 April 1959; Branch, *Parting the Waters*, 275.

27. *New York Times*, 29 November 1961, 3 December 1961; *New York Amsterdam News*, 9 December 1961, 23 December 1961; Brownstein, *Power and the Glitter*, 171–72.

28. Martin S. Dworkin, "New Negro on Screen," October 1960–February 1961; *New York Amsterdam News*, 11 February 1961. See also *Variety*, 27 April 1960; Manchel, "Man Who Made the Stars Shine Brighter," 41.

29. *New York Times*, 26 March 1961; *New York Amsterdam News*, 1 April 1961.

30. Funke and Booth, *Actors Talk about Acting*, 371–94. The interview was reprinted as Sidney Poitier, "Why I Became an Actor," *Negro Digest*, December 1961, 80–97, and excerpted in *New York Times Magazine*, 1 October 1961.

31. *New York Morning-Telegraph*, 6 July 1959; *Chicago Defender*, 11 August 1959; Poitier, "Thinking of Corruption"; *New York Amsterdam News*, 23 January 1960, 27 May 1961; Hall, "Pride without Prejudice," January 1972, 41; *New York Times*, 21 May 1961; Folder 274, William Gordon Collection, MHL.

32. *New York Amsterdam News*, 18 March 1961; Poitier, "Why I Became an Actor," 94; *Newsweek*, 19 September 1960. See also Hill, *Shakespeare in Sable*, 8–9, 40–41.

33. Carney, *American Dreaming*, 77; *Los Angeles Times*, 9 February 1961; *New York Times*, 26 March 1961; *New York Amsterdam News*, 1 April 1961, 3 June 1961; Poitier, "Thinking of Corruption," 7; Cole, *Hollywood Red*, 363–64.

34. *Newsweek*, 19 September 1960; *New York Times*, 26 March 1961; Poitier, "Thinking of Corruption," 7; uncited article on Reel 1, George L. Johnson Collection, UCLA.

35. *New York Times*, 21 May 1961; Marshall, *Brown Girl, Brownstones*; Keyser and Ruszkowski, *Cinema of Sidney Poitier*, 64–65.

36. Poitier, "Why I Became an Actor," 95; *New York Amsterdam News*, 2 September 1961, 21 April 1962, 16 June 1962; *New York Times*, 11 June 1962.

37. James Baldwin, "Sidney Poitier," *Look*, 23 July 1968, 58; *New York Amsterdam News*, 15 June 1962, 24 November 1962; Baldwin, *Blues for Mister Charlie*; Sidney Poitier, telephone interview with the author, 15 February 2002. See also Leeming, *James Baldwin*, 238–39.

38. *New York Amsterdam News*, 31 August 1963; *New York Journal-American*, 29 March 1964; Ray Rogers, "The Negro Actor," in *Anthology of the American Negro in the Theatre*, ed. Patterson, 137–39; *New York Times*, 7 March 1962, 23 September 1964; *New York Herald-Tribune*, 9 April 1962, 31 May 1962.

39. *New York World Telegram and Sun*, 25 October 1961.

40. Jones and Niven, *James Earl Jones*, 129–30; Poitier, "Why I Became an Actor," 94–95.

41. "Sidney Poitier Talks about His Early Poverty in New York City," Interview with Tom Brokaw, Audio Tape of NBC-TV Broadcast, 23 June 1980; "Conversation with Actor Sidney Poitier," Audio Tape from CBS News Audio Resource Library, Vital History Cassette Series, June 1980; *New York Daily News*, 23 October 1963; Poitier, "Why I Became an Actor," 95.

42. *New York Herald-Tribune*, 23 May 1961; *New York Daily News*, 28 October 1963.

43. Normand Poirier, "Sidney Poitier's Long Journey," *Saturday Evening Post*, 20 June 1964, 31; Frederic Morton, "Audacity of Sidney Poitier," *Holiday*, June 1962, 109; Hoffman, *Sidney*, 99–104.

44. *New York Times*, 21 July 1961; Morton, "Audacity of Sidney Poitier," 109; Poitier, *This Life*, 239.

45. Poitier, *This Life*, 247–48; Carroll, *Diahann*, 100–102.

46. Carroll, *Diahann*, 103.

47. Poitier, *This Life*, 30, 254–55.

48. Ibid., 241–45.

49. *New York Amsterdam News*, 9 December 1961; Poirier, "Sidney Poitier's Long Journey," 29; *Ebony*, June 1965.

50. Poitier, *This Life*, 259–62; Tom Seligson, "I No Longer Feel I Have to Prove Anything," *Parade*, 28 February 1988, 6.

51. Poitier, *This Life*, 263–66; Morton, "Audacity of Sidney Poitier," 108.

52. Lindner, *Fifty-Minute Hour*; *Variety*, 27 October 1961; *Hollywood Reporter*, 27 October 1961, 29 November 1961; Box 48, Stanley Kramer Papers, UCLA.

53. *New York Herald-Tribune*, 7 January 1962; *Variety*, 28 November 1961; *New York Amsterdam News*, 9 December 1961. See also "Pressure Point" Pressbook, Box 7, Black Films Collection, SCRBC.

54. Bosley Crowther, "Hollywood's Producer of Controversy," *New York Times Magazine*, 10 December 1961, 76–85; DiOrio, *Borrowed Time*, 118–21; Bobby Darin, "Why I Played a Film Bigot," *Ebony*, November 1962, 45–50; *New York Amsterdam News*, 25 November 1961; *New York Daily News*, 28 October 1962; Reel 10, Johnson Collection,

UCLA; Box 48, Stanley Kramer Papers, UCLA.

55. Spoto, *Stanley Kramer*, 237–41; *New York Times*, 11 October 1962; *Hollywood Citizen-News*, 20 September 1962.

56. See Cripps, "Death of Rastus," 273.

57. Johnson, "Negro in American Films," 19.

58. Box 48, Stanley Kramer Papers, UCLA.

59. Lincoln, *Black Muslims in America*, 3–32, 107–8.

60. Hampton and Fayer, *Voices of Freedom*, 250–51.

61. *Variety*, 4 September 1962; *Hollywood Reporter*, 7 September 1962; *Film Daily*, 12 September 1962; *Saturday Review*, 15 September 1962; *Los Angeles Times*, 20 September 1962; *New York Herald-Tribune*, 11 October 1962; *Cue*, 13 October 1962; Box 48, Stanley Kramer Papers, UCLA; *Films and Filming*, November 1963; *New Republic*, 20 October 1962.

62. Carroll, *Diahann*, 117–18.

63. Poitier, *Measure of a Man*, 182–86.

64. *New York Times*, 23 May 1962, 24 May 1962; Dudziak, *Cold War Civil Rights*, 152–55; *New York Post*, 26 April 1964.

65. *Los Angeles Times*, 15 November 1962; *New York Post*, 28 October 1962, 2 November 1962, 13 November 1962; *New York Times*, 30 October 1962; *New York Herald-Tribune*, 30 October 1962.

66. Mapp, *Blacks in American Films*, 62–63; Barrett, *Lilies of the Field*; *Newsday*, 6 June 1982; Henry Louis Gates Jr., "Belafonte's Balancing Act," *New Yorker*, 26 August–2 September 1996, 139.

67. Article Draft in Sidney Poitier file, Jack Hirshberg Collection, MHL; *New York Times*, 9 February 1964.

68. *New York Times*, 29 September 1963; Keyser and Ruszkowski, *Cinema of Sidney Poitier*, 72.

69. *New York Times*, 29 September 1963, 9 February 1964.

70. *Hollywood Reporter*, 27 November 1962; "Lilies of the Field" Production Notes, MHL; *Los Angeles Times*, 5 December 1962; *New York Times*, 9 February 1964.

71. Article Draft in Sidney Poitier file, Jack Hirshberg Collection, MHL; *New York Times*, 9 February 1964; *Los Angeles Times*, 28 July 1963.

72. "Lilies of the Field" Shooting Script, Box 3, Stanley Scheuer Collection, CTL.

73. Keyser and Ruszkowski, *Cinema of Sidney Poitier*, 77.

Chapter Eleven

1. *New York Times*, 26 March 1963; *New York Amsterdam News*, 13 April 1963; Bengtsson, *Long Ships*; Michael Buckley, "Richard Widmark (Part Three)," *Films in Review*, June/July 1986, 327; "The Long Ships" Production Notes, MHL; *Motion Picture Herald*, 30 October 1963; Poitier, *This Life*, 256–57; *Cinema*, April 1965; *Los Angeles Times*, 9 May 1963.

2. George Stevens Collection, Folder #1154, MHL; Oursler, *Greatest Story Ever Told*; *Los Angeles Times*, 3 May 1954; *Variety*, 10 June 1960, 1 July 1960; *Hollywood Reporter*, 10 June 1960, 1 July 1960, 14 September 1960, 7 October 1960; *New York Times*, 30 October 1960.

3. Balio, *United Artists*, 133–36; "Greatest Story Ever Told" Production Notes, MHL; *Variety*, 1 September 1961; *Hollywood Reporter*, 6 September 1961, 7 November 1961; *Los Angeles Times*, 6 September 1961, 13 September 1961; *New York Times*, 10 September 1961, 11 November 1961; *B'nai Brith Messenger*, 13 July 1962; *New York Times* (Western Edition), 9 February 1963.

4. McWhorter, *Carry Me Home*, 303–454; Weisbrot, *Freedom Bound*, 68–75.

5. McWhorter, *Carry Me Home*, 455–65; Weisbrot, *Freedom Bound*, 75–76.

6. *New York Times*, 13 June 1963, 26 June 1963, 27 June 1963, 30 June 1963, 19 July 1963, 20 July 1963, 28 July 1963, 31 July 1963, 2 August 1963, 22 August 1963, 29 December 1963.

7. *New York Times*, 28 July 1963, 3 August 1963; *Washington Post*, 21 June 1964; *Hollywood Citizen-News*, 16 October 1963. See also Dudziak, *Cold War Civil Rights*, 152–202.

8. Brownstein, *Power and the Glitter*, 169–70; Buford, *Burt Lancaster*, 233–34.

9. Heston, *Actor's Life*, 178–79; Heston, *In the Arena*, 316; *New York Times*, 25 August 1963.

10. *New York Times*, 25 August 1963; *Pittsburgh Courier*, 7 September 1963; Branch, *Parting the Waters*, 872–77. See also Lewis, *W. E. B. Du Bois*, 1–3.

11. Branch, *Parting the Waters*, 876–83.

12. *New York Times*, 29 August 1963; Manso, *Brando*, 655; Davis and Jane and Burt Boyar, *Why Me?*, 147; *New York Daily News*, 28 October 1963.

13. See Matusow, *Unraveling of America*, 60–92.

14. See Kelley, "Evolution of Character Portrayals," 126–29, 134–36.

15. Johnson, "Negro in American Films," 18. See also *Films and Filming*, May 1964.

16. *Variety*, 2 October 1963; Sidney Poitier file, Hedda Hopper Collection, MHL.

17. *Variety*, 26 June 1963, 28 June 1963, 17 July 1963; *Los Angeles Times*, 5 July 1963; *Film Daily*, 7 August 1963; *Motion Picture Exhibitor*, 7 August 1963; *Hollywood Reporter*, 23 July 1963; *Motion Picture Herald*, 21 August 1963; *Cinema*, August/September 1963; Sidney Poitier File, Hedda Hopper Collection, MHL; "Lilies of the Field" Pressbook, Box 6, Black Films Collection, SCRBC.

18. *Hollywood Reporter*, 26 September 1963; *Boxoffice*, 18 November 1963; *New York Amsterdam News*, 28 September 1963.

19. *Cue*, 5 October 1963; *New York Morning-Telegraph*, 2 October 1963; *New York*, October 1963; *Ebony*, October 1963.

20. *New York Daily News*, 28 October 1963; Sidney Poitier File, Hedda Hopper Collection, MHL; *Los Angeles Times*, 12 October 1963; *Film Daily*, 8 January 1964, 6 March 1964; *Hollywood Reporter*, 31 January 1964, 6 March 1964; *Motion Picture Exhibitor*, 18 March 1964; Sidney Poitier File, Jack Hirshberg Collection, MHL.

21. *Saturday Review*, 7 September 1963; *New York Times*, 2 October 1963, 6 October 1963.

22. *Newsweek*, 14 October 1963; *Film Quarterly*, Spring 1964.

23. *AFI Report*, May 1973.

24. *Los Angeles Times*, 17 July 1963, 6 October 1963; *Chicago Defender*, 6 October 1963.

25. *Variety*, 2 October 1963.

26. *Ebony*, October 1963; *New York Times*, 11 February 1964; Brownstein, *Power and the Glitter*, 172–73.

27. *Newsday*, 7 October 1963; *Los Angeles Times*, 6 October 1963; *New York Amsterdam News*, 21 July 1962; *New York Times*, 31 May 1964.

28. *Hollywood Citizen-News*, 29 March 1964.

29. *New York Times*, 27 January 1964, 2 February 1964, 9 February 1964, 31 May 1964.

30. *Pittsburgh Courier*, 26 October 1963; *New York Post*, 26 April 1964.

31. *Time*, 24 April 1964; *New York Times*, 12 April 1964.

32. Poitier, *This Life*, 248; *New York Times*, 19 April 1964.

33. "News of the Day," 19 April 1964, Black and White Newsreel, Vol. 35, No. 271, MPSVB; *Time*, 24 April 1964; *New York Post*, 26 April 1964; *Memories*, April/May 1989.

34. *New York Post*, 26 April 1964; "News of the Day," 19 April 1964, MPSVB; *New York Times*, 15 April 1964; *Sepia*, June 1964; Poitier, *This Life*, 251.

35. *New York Journal-American*, 14 April 1964; *New York Times*, 15 April 1964; *New York Post*, 26 April 1964; "Sidney Poitier: One Bright Light."

36. *New York Times*, 14 April 1964, 19 April 1964; *New York Morning-Telegraph*, 15 April 1964; *New York World Telegram and Sun*, 18 April 1964.

37. *Washington Post*, 16 April 1964; *Moncton (N.J.) Transcript*, 23 April 1964.

38. *Chicago Defender*, 25 April 1964–1 May 1964; *Pittsburgh Courier*, 25 April 1964; *Hollywood Citizen-News*, 2 May 1964.

39. *Variety*, 22 April 1964; *New York Herald-Tribune*, 19 April 1964; *Hollywood Citizen-News*, 2 May 1964; *Time*, 24 April 1964; *New York Times*, 26 April 1964.

40. *New York Times*, 21 April 1964; *New York Post*, 22 April 1964; *Variety*, 22 April 1964.

41. Poirier, "Sidney Poitier's Long Journey," 26–27; *Nassau Guardian*, 2 May 1964, 3 May 1964.

42. Craton and Saunders, *Islanders in the Stream*, 2:310–16, 337–38; *Nassau Guardian*, 2 May 1964, 3 May 1964; Poirier, "Sidney Poitier's Long Journey," 30.

43. Poirier, "Sidney Poitier's Long Journey," 30.

44. *Nassau Guardian*, 5 May 1964; *Pittsburgh Courier*, 23 May 1964; Poirier, "Sidney Poitier's Long Journey," 30.

45. *Hollywood Reporter*, 8 June 1964, 18 June 1964, 19 June 1964, 22 June 1964; *New York Times*, 5 April 1966; *Variety*, 22 April 1964, 19 August 1964.

46. *Los Angeles Herald-Examiner*, 25 November 1964; "Patch of Blue" Pressbook, MHL.

47. *New York Herald-Tribune*, 25 June 1964. See also *Time*, 12 June 1964; *New York Times*, 25 June 1964.

48. *Los Angeles Times*, 17 July 1963; *Pittsburgh Courier*, 20 July 1963; *Ebony*, March 1964; "Long Ships" Pressbook, Box 6, Black Films Collection, SCRBC; *Hollywood Reporter*, 29 May 1964; *New York Daily News*, 25 June 1964; *Films and Filming*, April 1964; *Variety*, 6 March 1964.

49. "Long Ships" PCA Files, MHL; *Variety*, 17 June 1964; *New York Post*, 10 February 1968.

50. Wilson, *In Search of Democracy*, 334–35; Sidney Poitier file, Hedda Hopper Collection, MHL. See also *Los Angeles Times*, 24 May 1964; uncited article in Sidney Poitier file, HTC.

51. Uncited article by Myra McPherson entitled "Senate Rights Apathy Disturbing to Poitier," in Sidney Poitier File, NYPLPA; Branch, *Pillar of Fire*, 336–37.

52. Davis and Dee, *With Ossie and Ruby*, 307–8; Hampton and Fayer, *Voices of Freedom*, 260.

53. *Village Voice*, 25 June 1964, 9 July 1964, 23 July 1964.

54. *Washington Post*, 21 June 1964; Cruse, *Crisis of the Negro Intellectual*, 193–205.

55. *Washington Post*, 21 June 1964; Feinstein, "Three in Search of Cinema," 23; *New York Times*, 27 June 1964.

56. Sidney Poitier, interview with the author, 9 May 2001; Henry Louis Gates Jr., "Belafonte's Balancing Act," *New Yorker*, 26 August and 2 September 1996, 140; Branch, *Parting the Waters*, 185, 810–11; King, *Why We Can't Wait*, 51–52, 74.

57. Gates, "Belafonte's Balancing Act," 139; Manso, *Brando*, 655.

58. *Hollywood Citizen-News*, 11 August 1964; Poitier, *This Life*, 276–77; Branch, *Pillar of Fire*, 450.

59. Branch, *Pillar of Fire*, 450; Noble, "Entertainment, Politics, and the Movie Business," 22.

60. Sutherland, *Letters from Mississippi*, 183–84.

61. Poitier, *This Life*, 279–80; Branch, *Pillar of Fire*, 451.

62. Forman, *Making of Black Revolutionaries*, 385.

63. Carroll, *Diahann*, 123; Poitier, *This Life*, 270–71.

64. Undated cite from *Jet*, Reel 10, George L. Johnson Collection, UCLA; *Sepia*, June 1965. On *Synanon* casting, see *Hollywood Reporter*, 5 May 1964; Folder 274, William Gordon Collection, MHL.

65. Carroll, *Diahann*, 123–24.

66. Ibid., 124–26.

67. *Los Angeles Times*, 13 October 1964; *Hollywood Reporter*, 6 October 1964.

68. *Boston Traveler*, 15 October 1964; *Variety*, 21 October 1964.

69. Sidney Poitier File, Hedda Hopper Collection, MHL; *Los Angeles Herald-Examiner*, 25 November 1964; *Poitier Meets Plato* (Warner Brothers, 1964), 33⅓ rpm.

70. *Variety*, 4 November 1964.

Chapter Twelve

1. *Hollywood Reporter*, 28 August 1964; *Variety*, 28 August 1964, 23 September 1964, 23 October 1964, 28 October 1964, 18 November 1964, 8 January 1965, 9 March 1965; *Los Angeles Times*, 25 February 1965.

2. Reviews from *Hollywood Citizen-News*, *Los Angeles Herald-Examiner*, and *Miami Herald* quoted from Pressbook, "The Greatest Story Ever Told" file, MHL; *Variety*, 15 February 1965, 24 February 1965, 9 March 1965, 17 March 1965, 15 August 1965; *Boxoffice*, 8 March 1965.

3. *New Yorker*, 28 February 1965; *Newsweek*, 22 February 1965; *Saturday Review*, 27 February 1965; *Commonweal*, 12 March 1965; *New York Herald-Tribune*, 16 February 1965; *New York Times*, 16 February 1965; *Time*, 26 February 1965; *Variety*, 10 March 1965.

4. *New York Times*, 31 January 1963, 14 February 1965, 16 February 1965; *Time*, 26 February 1965; *Variety*, 15 February 1965; *Los Angeles Times*, 19 April 1965.

5. Boykin Sanders, "In Search of a Face for Simon the Cyrene," in *Recovery of Black Presence*, ed. Bailey and Grant, 51–63. See also Cullen, *On These I Stand*, 8.

6. Garrow, *Bearing the Cross*, 357–430; Weisbrot, *Freedom Bound*, 158–61; Matusow, *Unraveling of America*, 180–216, 345–62.

7. Garrow, *Bearing the Cross*, 418–20. See also Silberman, *Crisis in Black and White*, 10.

8. Cohen, *Essential Lenny Bruce*, 28–31.

9. Hernton, *White Papers for White Americans*, 53–70.

10. *New York Times*, 30 April 1965, 9 July 1965; *Pittsburgh Courier*, 20 November 1965, 18 December 1965; *Variety*, 19 May 1965, 13 October 1965; John Oliver Killens, "Hollywood in Black and White," in *State of the Nation*, ed. Boroff, 100–107.

11. *New York Times*, 29 August 1965.

12. Bogle, *Toms, Coons, Mulattoes, Mammies, and Bucks*, 200–204; Leab, *From Sambo to Superspade*, 198–200.

13. *New York World Telegram and Sun*, 9 August 1965.

14. Folder 84, Sidney Skolsky Collection, MHL; *Variety*, 15 July 1965, 22 July 1965; *Los Angeles Times*, 26 August 1965.

15. Leeming, *James Baldwin*, 248, 257; *New York Word Telegram and Sun*, 3 April 1965.

16. *Variety*, 12 March 1965, 17 March 1965.

17. *New York Times*, 13 June 1965; Sidney Poitier, telephone interview with the author, 15 February 2002.

18. Henry Louis Gates Jr., "Belafonte's Balancing Act," *New Yorker*, 26 August and 2 September 1996, 139.

19. Rascovich, *Bedford Incident*, 7; *Los Angeles Times*, 28 February 1964; *Los Angeles Herald-Examiner*, 11 November 1965.

20. *Hollywood Reporter*, 30 May 1964; Folder 274, William Gordon Collection, MHL; "Bedford Incident" Production

Notes, MHL; *New York Times*, 20 August 1964, 8 August 1965; *Los Angeles Times*, 22 November 1965; Slide, *Actors on Red Alert*, 34–35; *Variety*, 3 August 1964; *Hollywood Citizen-News*, 18 December 1964.

21. Henrikson, *Dr. Strangelove's America*, 304–44; Boyer, *By the Bomb's Early Light*, 352–56.

22. *Variety*, 3 November 1965, 17 November 1965, 8 December 1965; *Life*, 5 November 1965; *Newsweek*, 22 November 1965; *Saturday Review*, 13 November 1965, 4 December 1965; *Time*, 29 October 1965; *America*, 13 November 1965; *New Yorker*, 16 November 1965; *Films and Filming*, March 1966; *New York Times*, 3 November 1965.

23. *Cue*, 6 November 1965; *New Yorker*, 6 November 1965. See also *New York Herald-Tribune*, 3 November 1965; *Christian Science Monitor*, 13 November 1965.

24. *Hollywood Reporter*, 11 October 1965; *Variety*, 13 January 1965; *Film Daily*, 4 November 1965.

25. *Saturday Review*, 8 January 1966.

26. Shana Alexander, "Decision to Die," *Life*, 29 May 1964, 75–89; "Slender Thread" Production Notes, Celeste Bartos Film Center; "Slender Thread" PCA Files, MHL; Box 62, Folder 2, Stirling Siliphant Papers, UCLA.

27. *Los Angeles Times*, 24 July 1965, 27 June 1965. See also "Slender Thread" Pressbook, Box 7, Black Films Collection, SCRBC.

28. *Hollywood Reporter*, 14 June 1965, 5 November 1965; "Slender Thread" Production Notes, CBFSC.

29. See *New Yorker*, 15 January 1966; Meyer, *Sydney Pollack*, 30–35.

30. *Commonweal*, 21 January 1966; *Christian Science Monitor*, 24 March 1966; *Films and Filming*, May 1966; *New York Morning-Telegraph*, 24 December 1965; *Saturday Review*, 8 January 1966. See also Taylor, *Sydney Pollack*, 23–24, 33–36.

31. *Newsweek*, 10 January 1966; *Time*, 4 January 1966; *New York Times*, 24 December 1965; *New York Herald-Tribune*, 24 December 1965.

32. *Hollywood Reporter*, 10 December 1965.

33. See *America*, 22 January 1966; *Catholic Film Newsletter*, 24 February 1966.

34. Kata, *Be Ready with Bells and Drums*; Box 1, Folder 6, Pandro Berman Papers, WSHS.

35. Pandro S. Berman Oral History, Ronald L. Davis Oral History Collection, MHL, 62–63; Box 1, Folder 6, Pandro Berman Papers, WSHS.

36. Box 1, Folder 6, Pandro Berman Papers, WSHS.

37. *Variety*, 23 October 1964; Box 1, Folder 6, and Box 2, Folder 3, Pandro Berman Papers, WSHS; Pandro Berman Oral History, 54–55.

38. "Patch of Blue" PCA Files, MHL; Box 1, Folders 6–7, and Box 2, Folder 2, Pandro Berman Papers, WSHS; *Variety*, 4 May 1965.

39. Box 1, Folder 7, Pandro Berman Papers, WSHS.

40. See Barnes, "Portraits of Interracial Romance and Sexuality in Hollywood Cinema," 1–74.

41. *New York Times*, 6 August 1967.

42. *New Yorker*, 25 December 1965; *Newsweek*, 27 December 1965; *Los Angeles Times*, 10 December 1965; *Vogue*, 15 January 1966.

43. *Newsweek*, 27 December 1965; *New York Times*, 16 December 1965; *Film Quarterly*, Summer 1966; *Village Voice*, 19 May 1966; *America*, 22 January 1966; *New Yorker*, 25 December 1965; *Vogue*, 15 January 1966; *New York Morning-Telegraph*, 16 December 1966.

44. *Time*, 17 December 1965; *Variety*, 8 December 1965; *Hollywood Reporter*, 7 December 1965; *Commonweal*, 24 December 1965; *Cue*, 18 December 1965; *Films and Filming*, September 1966; *Sat-*

urday Review, 8 January 1966; New York
Herald-Tribune, 19 December 1965.

45. Box 1, Folders 7–8, Pandro Berman
Papers, WSHS.

46. Hollywood Reporter, 19 November 1965, 23 February 1966; Variety,
9 March 1966, 30 March 1966, 3 January
1968.

47. Hollywood Reporter, 14 April
1966; Film Daily, 5 June 1966; Boxoffice,
24 May 1966; Box 1, Folder 8, Pandro
Berman Papers, WSHS.

48. Variety, 5 April 1966; Box 29,
Folder 3, Pandro Berman Papers, WSHS;
Hollywood Reporter, 25 February 1966.

49. Box 1, Folder 8, Pandro Berman
Papers, WSHS; Variety, 5 April 1966.

50. Motion Picture Exhibitor, 13 April
1966; Variety, 11 May 1966, 3 August
1966.

51. Hollywood Reporter, 22 December
1965; Variety, 10 December 1965,
30 March 1966; New York Amsterdam
News, 18 December 1965, 25 December
1965; New York World Telegram and
Sun, 8 January 1966.

52. New York Times, 19 December
1965; Hollywood Reporter, 21 December
1965.

53. Fleischer, Just Tell Me When to Cry,
235–43.

54. Ibid., 243–57.

55. Ibid., 257–59.

56. Life, 4 February 1966; New York
Daily News, 20 February 1966; Pittsburgh Courier, 26 February 1966,
5 March 1966.

57. Epstein, Nat King Cole, 269–91;
Gates, "Belafonte's Balancing Act," 140.

58. Louisville Courier-Journal, 20 October 1963; "Pressure Point" Pressbook,
Box 7, Black Films Collection, SCRBC;
Article Draft from 13 July 1965, Folder
84, Sidney Skolsky Collection, MHL;
MacDonald, Blacks and White TV, 81–
82. See also New York Times, 18 August
1963.

59. Pittsburgh Courier, 26 February
1966, 5 March 1966; Pageant, October

1965; Time, 17 June 1963; Newsweek,
31 January 1966; New York Post, 23 February 1964, 22 July 1967; New York
Times, 10 September 1965, 17 October
1965, 8 January 1966; Saturday Review,
5 February 1966, 26 March 1966. See
also Bogle, Prime Time Blues, 115–25.

60. Pittsburgh Courier, 5 March 1966.
Recording of Strollin' Twenties, MTR.

61. New York Post, 21 February 1965;
New York Times, 13 June 1965.

62. Undated Jet article, Reel 10, George
L. Johnson Collection, UCLA; Sepia, June
1965.

63. Sepia, June 1965; Modern Screen,
February 1968; Jet, 27 April 1967;
undated Jet article, Reel 10, George L.
Johnson Collection, UCLA; Ebony, Sep-
tember 1965; New York Journal-
American, 9 July 1965; Hollywood
Citizen-News, 9 July 1965; New York
Times, 10 July 1965; Newsweek, 19 July
1965; New York World Telegram and
Sun, 9 August 1965.

64. Poitier, This Life, 272–73; Carroll,
Diahann, 126.

65. Killens, "Broadway in Black and
White," 74.

66. Film Daily, 8 September 1965; New
York Times, 13 June 1965.

67. Poitier, This Life, 272–73; People,
4 August 1980.

68. Carroll, Diahann, 126–27.

69. Poitier, This Life, 273; Carroll,
Diahann, 127.

70. Durham and Jones, Negro Cowboys; New York Times, 23 May 1965.

71. New York Times, 13 June 1965.

72. Catholic Standard and Times,
28 July 1967; Los Angeles Herald-
Examiner, 17 July 1966; Albert, Apache
Rising.

73. United Artists Press Release, "Duel
at Diablo" File, CBFSC; Variety, 2 September 1964, 2 December 1964; Strait,
James Garner, 153–65, 240.

74. Variety, 21 April 1965; Film Daily,
8 September 1965; Hollywood Reporter,
28 September 1965; Hollywood Citizen-

News, 7 October 1965; *Los Angeles Times Calendar*, 17 July 1966; "Duel at Diablo" Pressbook, Box 6, Black Films Collection, SCRBC; *Variety*, 27 September 1965.

75. *Variety*, 16 May 1966; *Hollywood Reporter*, 16 May 1966; undated article from *Film Daily*, "Duel at Diablo" File, CBFSC. On Apache resistance, see William T. Hagan, "How the West Was Lost," in *Indians in American History*, ed. Hoxie and Iverson, 162–65.

76. Slotkin, *Gunfighter Nation*, 534–61; *New York Times*, 16 June 1966. See also *Films and Filming*, September 1966.

77. *Time*, 1 July 1966; undated review from *Commonweal*, "Duel at Diablo" File, CBFSC; *Los Angeles Times*, 22 June 1966; Keyser and Ruszkowski, *Cinema of Sidney Poitier*, 93; Slotkin, *Gunfighter Nation*, 560–61, 631.

78. *New York Post*, 16 June 1966; Andy Wood, "Why Negroes Love Sidney Poitier — but Not Sammy Davis," *Photoplay*, 84; *Playboy*, September 1966.

79. *Film Daily*, 4 August 1966.

80. Sitkoff, *Struggle for Black Equality*, 209.

81. Ibid., 209–14; Matusow, *Unraveling of America*, 351–60.

82. *New York Times*, 21 June 1966, 26 June 1966; Davis and Jane and Burt Boyar, *Why Me?*, 187–90.

83. *Variety*, 15 July 1965; *New York Times*, 15 April 1966, 13 December 1966.

84. *New York World Telegram and Sun*, 17 February 1966, 22 March 1966; *New York Journal-American*, 22 March 1966.

85. *New York Times*, 8 July 1966, 12 July 1966, 17 July 1966.

86. *New York World Telegram and Sun*, 9 August 1965; Wallace, *The Man*; *Detroit Free Press*, 6 August 1967.

87. *Variety*, 8 June 1966; *St. Louis Post-Dispatch*, 2 October 1966; Sidney Poitier, telephone interview with the author, 15 February 2002; Jones and Niven, *James Earl Jones*, 298.

88. *New York Times*, 6 August 1967,

18 December 1966; *Hollywood Citizen-News*, 28 October 1966.

Chapter Thirteen

1. Carroll, *Diahann*, 128–30.

2. Ibid., 130; Milburn Smith, "Diahann: A Doll Who Has Been Known to Cry," *Photoplay*, November 1968, 93.

3. *Photoplay*, August 1968; Josh Greenfield, "What's the Secret of Sidney Poitier's Zooming Appeal?," *Good Housekeeping*, May 1968, 164.

4. *Los Angeles Times*, 19 February 1967.

5. *Los Angeles Times*, 5 March 1967.

6. Craton and Saunders, *Islanders in the Stream*, 2:338–43; Hughes, *Race and Politics in the Bahamas*, 107–17; Poitier, *This Life*, 314–15.

7. Craton and Saunders, *Islanders in the Stream*, 2:344; *Nassau Guardian*, 9 January 1967, 10 January 1967. See also Fitzroy A. Baptiste, "United States–Caribbean Relations from World War II to the Present: The Social Nexus," in *U.S.-Caribbean Relations*, ed. Palmer, 7–52.

8. Poitier, *This Life*, 315–16.

9. *Nassau Guardian*, 9 February 1967, 10 February 1967; Hughes, *Race and Politics in the Bahamas*, 124–26; Poitier, *This Life*, 316–17.

10. *Village Voice*, 26 January 1967; *Jet*, 6 April 1967, 27 April 1967.

11. *Time*, 5 February 1965, 6 April 1970; *Coronet*, August 1966; *Los Angeles Examiner*, 31 March 1968; Watkins, *On the Real Side*, 479–525; Boskin, *Sambo*, 198–224.

12. Watkins, *On the Real Side*, 328; *Los Angeles Herald-Examiner*, 6 April 1967; *Saturday Review*, 29 April 1967.

13. *New York Times*, 16 April 1967; *Pittsburgh Courier*, 17 June 1967. See also *Variety*, 19 April 1967; *Saturday Review*, 29 April 1967.

14. *Report of the National Commission on Civil Disorders*, 1; Sitkoff, *Struggle*

for *Black Equality*, 202–4; *Newsweek*, 7 August 1967.

15. Sitkoff, *Struggle for Black Equality*, 204; *Report of the National Commission on Civil Disorders*, 2; Boskin, *Urban Racial Violence in the Twentieth Century*, 151–52.

16. *Variety*, 26 July 1967, 2 August 1967, 9 August 1967, 16 August 1967, 6 September 1967, 3 January 1968, 24 January 1968.

17. Matusow, *Unraveling of America*, 275–394; *Variety*, 9 August 1967; Brown, *Die Nigger Die!*, 144.

18. Carmichael and Hamilton, *Black Power*; Cleaver, *Soul on Ice*, 88–89.

19. *New York Amsterdam News*, 11 November 1967.

20. Hacker, *Two Nations*, 19; *Report of the National Commission on Civil Disorders*, 7.

21. Poitier, *This Life*, 281; Braithwaite, *To Sir, with Love*; *Senior Scholastic*, 7 April 1967; *New York Amsterdam News*, 16 September 1967.

22. *Hollywood Citizen-News*, 22 September 1967; *Hollywood Reporter*, 31 July 1967; Poitier, *Measure of a Man*, 187–89.

23. *Hollywood Citizen-News*, 22 September 1967; *Hollywood Reporter*, 31 July 1967; *Variety*, 15 May 1966, 20 September 1967.

24. *Senior Scholastic*, 7 April 1967; *McCall's*, July 1967; *Hollywood Citizen-News*, 22 September 1967; Article draft, Box 262, Stanley Kramer Papers, UCLA. See also Folder 291, William Gordon Collection, MHL.

25. *Los Angeles Times*, 14 August 1966.

26. George, *Blackface*, 21.

27. Braithwaite, *To Sir, with Love*, 186–88. See also Marwick, *Sixties*, 77, 560.

28. Braithwaite, *To Sir, with Love*, 93–97, 145–50; First and Second Scripts, *To Sir, with Love*, Screenplay Collection, MHL.

29. Release Script, *To Sir, with Love*, Screenplay Collection, MHL.

30. See Levine, "Body's Politics," 134–38, 148–51; Barnes, "Portraits of Interracial Romance and Sexuality," 65–68; Jacquie Jones, "Construction of Black Sexuality," in *Black American Cinema*, ed. Diawara, 247–56.

31. *Cosmopolitan*, April 1967; *Playboy*, April 1967; *Variety*, 14 June 1967; *Hollywood Reporter*, 13 June 1967.

32. "To Sir, with Love" Pressbook, Box 7, Black Films Collection, SCRBC; Keyser and Ruszkowski, *Cinema of Sidney Poitier*, 100; *Variety*, 19 July 1967.

33. *Cue*, 17 June 1967; *Hollywood Citizen-News*, 25 September 1967; *Motion Picture Herald*, 21 June 1967; *Boxoffice*, 21 June 1967; *Film Daily*, 15 June 1967; *Films and Filming*, November 1967.

34. *Greater Amusement*, July 1967; *Motion Picture Herald*, 21 June 1967; *Boxoffice*, 21 June 1967; *New York Times*, 15 June 1967.

35. *New York Amsterdam News*, 17 June 1967; *Ebony*, April 1967.

36. *Village Voice*, 7 December 1967; *Film Quarterly* 22 (Winter 1968): 57. See also *Saturday Review*, 8 July 1967.

37. *New Yorker*, 17 June 1967.

38. *Film Quarterly* 22 (Winter 1968): 57; *New Republic*, 15 July 1967.

39. Ball, *In the Heat of the Night*; "In the Heat of the Night" Production Notes, MHL; Box 26, Walter Mirisch Papers, WSHS; Walter Mirisch Oral History, Ronald L. Davis Oral History Collection, MHL, 26; Box 10, Norman Jewison Papers, WSHS; *New York Times*, 19 June 1965; *New York World Telegram and Sun*, 9 August 1965.

40. "In the Heat of the Night" Production Notes, MHL; *Los Angeles Herald-Examiner*, 15 July 1967; *Variety*, 18 August 1966.

41. *Sparta News-Plaindealer*, 6 October 1966; *Southern Illinoisian*, 9 October

1966; *St. Louis Post-Dispatch*, 2 October 1966; *Jet*, 15 December 1966.

42. *St. Louis Post-Dispatch*, 2 October 1966; *Jet*, 17 November 1966; Poitier, *This Life*, 286–87.

43. Poitier, *Measure of a Man*, 135–37.

44. Box 40, Folder 5, Stirling Siliphant Papers, UCLA; Box 10, Norman Jewison Papers, WSHS.

45. Meeker, "Novel to Script to Film," 1–63; Box 10, Norman Jewison Papers, WSHS.

46. Poitier, *This Life*, 287; *Variety*, 7 February 1968; Hutchinson, *Rod Steiger*, 23–127.

47. *New York Times*, 7 January 1968; *St. Louis Post-Dispatch*, 2 October 1966; "In the Heat of the Night" Production Notes, MHL.

48. Kantor, Blacker, and Kramer, *Directors at Work*, 135.

49. Poitier, *Measure of a Man*, 137, 142–44.

50. "In the Heat of the Night" Production Notes, MHL; Meyer, "South and Black Cinema," 39–40; *Hollywood Reporter*, 23 February 2001; *Variety*, 8 November 1966, 14 November 1966.

51. See Box 11, Norman Jewison Papers, WSHS; *New York Amsterdam News*, 29 July 1967.

52. *New York Amsterdam News*, 22 July 1967; *Cue*, 5 August 1967; *Hollywood Citizen-News*, 24 June 1967; *New York Times*, 3 August 1967; *Saturday Review*, 8 July 1967; *Women's Wear Daily*, 4 August 1967; *Listener*, 31 August 1967; *New York Post*, 3 August 1967; *New York Daily News*, 3 August 1967; *Saturday Review*, 19 August 1967; *Time*, 11 August 1967; *Life*, 28 July 1967. See Box 10 and Box 11, Norman Jewison Papers, WSHS.

53. Graham, *Framing the South*, 125, 168–72, 179–82; Levine, "Body's Politics," 171–72; *Readers and Writers*, November–January 1968.

54. Wiegman, *American Anatomies*, 138–40; Levine, "Sidney Poitier's Civil

Rights," 377–81; *The Thunderbolt: The White Man's Viewpoint*, October 1967.

55. *Newsweek*, 14 August 1967; *Kansas City Star*, 13 August 1967; *New York Times*, 3 March 1968; *Chicago Sun-Times*, 17 August 1967.

56. See Bogle, *Toms, Coons, Mulattoes, Mammies, and Bucks*, 140–41; Reid, *Redefining Black Film*, 78; Clyde Taylor, "Ironies of Palace-Subaltern Discourse," in *Black American Cinema*, ed. Diawara, 196–97.

57. *New Yorker*, 5 August 1967; *Esquire*, September 1967; *Los Angeles Free Press*, 1 September 1967; *Toronto Globe and Mail*, 5 August 1967; *London Daily Telegraph*, 25 August 1967; *Village Voice*, 17 August 1967.

58. *Christian Century*, 6 December 1967; *Show*, September 1972. See also *New York Amsterdam News*, 5 August 1967.

59. Baldwin, *Devil Finds Work*, 50–57.

60. *Variety*, 12 July 1967, 9 August 1967; *Hollywood Reporter*, 7 August 1967.

61. *Variety*, 9 August 1967, 16 August 1967, 23 August 1967, 30 August 1967.

62. *Variety*, 13 September 1967, 20 September 1967, 4 October 1967, 11 October 1967, 22 November 1967, 3 January 1968, 16 February 1968, 18 March 1968; *Pittsburgh Courier*, 11 November 1967; Meyer, "South and Black Cinema," 40–43; *New York Times*, 29 December 1967, 29 January 1968; *New York Amsterdam News*, 11 November 1967, 23 December 1967; Box 11, Norman Jewison Papers, WSHS; *Hollywood Reporter*, 31 July 1967.

63. *Variety*, 31 May 1967, 26 July 1967, 25 October 1967, 14 February 1968; *Jet*, 13 April 1967, 20 April 1967, 7 July 1967; *Pittsburgh Courier*, 5 August 1967, 10 February 1968; *Chicago Defender*, 30 September–6 October 1967, 28 October–3 November 1967, 6 January–12 January 1968.

64. *New York Times*, 18 November

1967. See also *Pittsburgh Courier*, 13 January 1968; *New York Amsterdam News*, 27 April 1968.

65. *New York Times*, 18 November 1967; *Variety*, 21 June 1967, 9 August 1967; *Hollywood Reporter*, 21 June 1967; *Newsweek*, 3 July 1967; *Los Angeles Times*, 23 August 1967.

66. *Hollywood Reporter*, 22 October 1967, 21 November 1967; *Variety*, 1 November 1967; Box 4, Folder 9, Ossie Davis and Ruby Dee Papers, SCRBC.

67. *Variety*, 26 July 1967, 16 August 1967; *New York Amsterdam News*, 17 June 1967, 2 December 1967; *New York Times*, 23 July 1967.

68. *Atlanta Journal*, 15 August 1967; *Variety*, 23 August 1967; *New York Post*, 20 September 1967; "Sidney Poitier: One Bright Light."

69. *New York Times*, 6 August 1967.

70. *Variety*, 26 July 1967.

71. Ibid.

72. *San Francisco Examiner*, 26 November 1967.

73. *Variety*, 29 November 1967, 27 December 1967, 17 January 1967. See also *New York Amsterdam News*, 23 December 1967.

74. *Village Voice*, 17 August 1967.

75. *Saturday Review*, 8 July 1967; *San Francisco Examiner*, 22 August 1967; *Boston*, September 1967.

76. Cripps, "Death of Rastus," 275; Sugy, "Black Men or Good Niggers," 20.

77. Cruse, *Crisis of the Negro Intellectual*, 111, 455; *Variety*, 20 December 1967.

78. *New York Times*, 2 April 1967; *Detroit Free Press*, 6 August 1967; *New York Daily News*, 27 August 1967; *Newsweek*, 11 December 1967; *San Francisco Examiner*, 26 November 1967; *Los Angeles Herald-Examiner*, 26 November 1967; *Catholic Standard and Times*, 28 July 1967.

79. Article draft by Frank London, Box 262, Kramer Papers, UCLA.

80. *Camden Courier-Post*, 5 August 1967; *Boston Record-American*, 4 July 1967.

81. *Variety*, 4 October 1967; *Chicago Sun-Times*, 16 July 1967; *Chicago Tribune*, 20 August 1967; *Los Angeles Herald-Examiner*, 20 August 1967; *Syracuse Herald Journal*, 3 July 1967.

82. *New York Times*, 6 August 1967.

83. Ibid.

84. *New York Times*, 10 September 1967.

85. Ibid.

86. *New York Times*, 1 October 1967.

87. Ibid.

88. Poitier, *This Life*, 333–37; *Newsweek*, 11 December 1967.

89. *The Record*, 26 July 1974 (Sidney Poitier File, 1970–1979, NYPLPA); Poitier, *This Life*, 333.

Chapter Fourteen

1. *New York Times*, 11 June 1967; *Variety*, 14 June 1967; "Last Visit with Two Undimmed Stars," *Look*, 11 June 1967, 26–35.

2. Leaming, *Katharine Hepburn*, 306–13, 383–425.

3. Ibid., 426–90.

4. Kael, *Kiss Kiss Bang Bang*, 203–14.

5. Boxes 290 and 291, Stanley Kramer Papers, UCLA.

6. Kramer, *Mad, Mad, Mad, Mad World*, 220–21; Mike Frankovich Oral History, Ronald L. Davis Oral History Collection, MHL, 18–19.

7. Boxes 262 and 356, Stanley Kramer Papers, UCLA; Newquist, *Special Kind of Magic*, 39–41.

8. Box 292, Stanley Kramer Papers, UCLA.

9. Box 291, Stanley Kramer Papers, UCLA; Folder 117, William Gordon Collection, MHL.

10. Leaming, *Katharine Hepburn*, 490–92; Andersen, *An Affair to Remember*, 294; Kramer, *Mad, Mad, Mad, Mad World*, 221–22.

11. Poitier, *Measure of a Man*, 121–24; Newquist, *Special Kind of Magic*, 92–93.

12. Kramer, *Mad, Mad, Mad, Mad World*, 222, 226; Andersen, *An Affair to Remember*, 295; Poitier, *This Life*, 284.

13. "Guess Who's Coming to Dinner" Pressbook, Box 6, Black Films Collection, SCRBC; *New York Post*, 10 February 1968.

14. *Life*, 5 January 1968; Edwards, *Remarkable Woman*, 338–39.

15. *Life*, 5 January 1968; Leaming, *Katharine Hepburn*, 492–93.

16. Stanley Kramer, "He Could Wither You with a Glance," *Life*, 30 June 1967, 74; Andersen, *An Affair to Remember*, 298; Leaming, *Katharine Hepburn*, 493–94.

17. *Hollywood Reporter*, 8 December 1967; "Last Visit with Two Undimmed Stars," *Look*, 11 June 1967, 26–35; *New York Times*, 18 June 1967; Kramer, "He Could Wither You with a Glance," *Life*, 30 June 1967, 69–74; Roy Newquist, "Katharine Hepburn," *McCall's*, July 1967; Newquist, *Special Kind of Magic*; "Aunt Kat," *Life*, 5 January 1968; Kennedy, *Interracial Intimacies*, 104–8, 272–78; *Jet*, 5 October 1967; *Ebony*, December 1967.

18. See Kelley, "Evolution of Character Portrayals," 160, 171.

19. Box 111, Stanley Kramer Papers, UCLA.

20. Levine, "Sidney Poitier's Civil Rights," 374–75.

21. Levine, "Body's Politics," 155–60; *New York Times*, 6 October 1974.

22. *Variety*, 10 January 1968, 14 February 1968, 21 February 1968, 13 March 1968, 21 March 1968, 3 April 1968, 8 May 1968.

23. Box 81, Stanley Kramer Papers, UCLA. See also *Ebony*, July 1968.

24. *New York Daily News*, 12 December 1967; *New York Post*, 12 December 1967; *New York Morning-Telegraph*, 12 December 1967; *New York Times*, 12 December 1967, 17 December 1967;

Variety, 6 December 1967, 3 January 1968.

25. *Newsweek*, 25 December 1967; *New Republic*, 16 December 1967; *Christian Advocate*, 13 June 1968; *New Yorker*, 16 December 1967; *Saturday Review*, 16 December 1967.

26. *New Yorker*, 16 December 1967; *Saturday Review*, 16 December 1967; *Esquire*, February 1968; *Harper's*, January 1968; *New Republic*, 16 December 1967; Crist, *Private Eye*, 254; *Newsweek*, 25 December 1967.

27. *Variety*, 10 January 1968; Omatsu, "Guess Who Came to Lunch?," 20–21; *Action*, March–April 1968; *New York Times*, 26 May 1968, 19 June 1968; Marill, *Films of Sidney Poitier*, 156.

28. *Los Angeles Sentinel*, 23 November 1967; *Ebony*, January 1968; *Chicago Defender*, 4 November 1967, 6 January 1968, 27 January 1968; Box 81, Stanley Kramer Papers, UCLA; *New York Amsterdam News*, 9 December 1967, 16 December 1967.

29. *New York Amsterdam News*, 16 December 1967; Charles L. Sanders, "Sidney Poitier: The Man behind the Superstar," *Ebony*, April 1968, 179.

30. Poussaint, "Education and Black Self-Image," 337; *New York Times*, 16 June 1968; Elliston, "Two Sidney Poitier Films," 28.

31. *Punch*, 19 June 1968; *New York Times*, 23 July 1968, 24 July 1968.

32. Undated article from *Wall Street Journal*, Blacks in Films, 1966–1969 File, MHL; "Guess Who's Coming to Dinner" Production File, MHL; Box 85, Stanley Kramer Papers, UCLA.

33. *The Thunderbolt: The White Man's Viewpoint*, December 1967, quoted in Elliston, "Two Sidney Poitier Films," 32; Box 82, Stanley Kramer Papers, UCLA.

34. "Guess Who's Coming to Dinner" Production File, MHL; *Variety*, 20 March 1968, 16 October 1968.

35. *New York Times*, 7 March 1968; *Variety*, 13 March 1968.

36. *New York Times*, 3 March 1968. See also uncited Adler article in Reel 10, George L. Johnson Collection, UCLA.

37. James Baldwin, "Sidney Poitier," *Look*, 23 July 1968, 50–58; Baldwin, *Devil Finds Work*, 68–76.

38. Baldwin, "Sidney Poitier," 58.

39. Josh Greenfield, "What's the Secret of Sidney Poitier's Zooming Appeal?," *Good Housekeeping*, May 1968, 92–93, 164–70; Andy Wood, "Why Negroes Love Sidney Poitier — but Not Sammy Davis," *Photoplay*, September 1968, 44–45, 84–85; "Why White Women Dig Sidney Poitier," *Modern Screen*, August 1968, 46–48, 81–82; *Variety*, 4 December 1968; *New York Times*, 17 March 1968; *Pittsburgh Courier*, 1 May 1968; *Washington Post*, 21 April 1968; Sanders, "Sidney Poitier: The Man behind the Superstar"; *Ebony*, July 1968; *Look*, 3 September 1968. See also *Pittsburgh Courier*, 13 April 1968.

40. *Newsweek*, 11 December 1967; Newquist, *Special Kind of Magic*, 123–26; *Seventeen*, February 1968.

41. Greenfield, "What's the Secret of Sidney Poitier's Zooming Appeal?," 166–68; *San Francisco Examiner*, 3 November 1967; *Los Angeles Herald-Examiner*, 24 February 1968; *Variety*, 12 June 1968.

42. *Pittsburgh Courier*, 9 March 1968; *Los Angeles Herald-Examiner*, 24 February 1968; *New York Times*, 6 February 1968; *New York Post*, 10 February 1968.

43. Woodie King Jr., "Problems Facing Negro Actors," in *Anthology of the American Negro in the Theatre*, ed. Patterson, 141–44.

44. *Liberator*, April 1965, June 1965; *New York Post*, 17 March 1966, 19 December 1967; *New York Times*, 18 March 1966; Cruse, *Crisis of the Negro Intellectual*, 520, 536–38.

45. *Women's Wear Daily*, 28 February 1968; *Los Angeles Times*, 1 March 1968; *Variety*, 6 March 1968. See also Reel 2, George L. Johnson Collection, UCLA.

46. *New York Amsterdam News*,

2 March 1968; *New York Times*, 28 March 1968; *New York Post*, 28 February 1968; *New York Daily News*, 28 February 1968; *New York Morning-Telegraph*, 29 February 1968; *Village Voice*, 7 March 1968; *Wall Street Journal*, 29 February 1968; Poitier, *This Life*, 292–93.

47. Garrow, *Bearing the Cross*, 620–24; Weisbrot, *Freedom Bound*, 269–71; *New York Amsterdam News*, 20 April 1968.

48. Memos dated 7 April 1968 and 8 April 1968, FBI Files on Sanitation Workers Strike at Memphis, Tennessee, 1968; Poitier, *This Life*, 321–33; George Goodman, "Durango: Poitier Meets Belafonte," *Look*, 24 August 1971, 59.

49. Manso, *Brando*, 668–69; *Pittsburgh Courier*, 20 April 1968; *Variety*, 1 May 1968; *New York Amsterdam News*, 27 April 1968; *New York Times*, 6 April 1968, 7 April 1968.

50. *Variety*, 3 April 1968, 10 April 1968, 17 April 1968, 24 April 1968, 1 May 1968.

51. *Pittsburgh Courier*, 13 April 1968.

52. *Variety*, 20 February 1968; *Los Angeles Herald-Examiner*, 1 March 1968; *Los Angeles Times*, 9 April 1968.

53. *Time*, 19 April 1968; *Film and Television Daily*, 19 April 1968; *New York Post*, 11 April 1968; *New York Times*, 11 April 1968.

54. *New York Times*, 11 April 1968; *Variety*, 17 April 1968; *New York Post*, 11 April 1968.

55. Box 11, Norman Jewison Papers, WSHS; Walter Mirisch Oral History, Ronald L. Davis Oral History Collection, MHL, 26; *Variety*, 14 August 1968; *Film Daily*, 6 November 1968; *Hollywood Citizen-News*, 31 December 1968; *Journeys inside the Mind: The Dialogues* (Warner Brothers: Seven Arts Records, 1968), 33⅓ rpm; undated article from 1968 in *Hartford Times*, Sidney Poitier File, 1960–1969, NYPLPA.

56. *Boxoffice*, 17 February 1969; Box 12, Norman Jewison Papers, WSHS; *Vari-*

ety, 13 March 1969; *S.A. Film Weekly*, 15 February 1968, 9 May 1968; *Los Angeles Times*, 19 June 1972; *New York Times*, 6 February 1969.

57. Abernathy, *And the Walls Came Tumbling Down*, 510–14; *Screen and TV Album*, January 1969; *New York Times*, 8 June 1968, 22 June 1968. See also Matusow, *Unraveling of America*, 395–439.

58. *Hollywood Reporter*, 24 January 1969; undated article by Charles Champlin in *Los Angeles Times*, Reel 10, George L. Johnson Collection, UCLA; *Film-TV Daily*, 28 January 1969.

59. Greenfield, "What's the Secret of Sidney Poitier's Zooming Appeal?," 166; *New York Post*, 10 February 1968; *Screen Stars*, December 1969; Milburn Smith, "The Night Sidney Poitier Cried for His Mother," *Photoplay*, August 1968, 76.

60. *New York Post*, 10 February 1968.

61. *New York Post*, 10 February 1968, 22 July 1968; Poitier, *Measure of a Man*, 182–87.

62. Poitier, *This Life*, 295–98; *New York Post*, 10 February 1968.

63. Greenfield, "What's the Secret of Sidney Poitier's Zooming Appeal?," 166; Smith, "The Night Sidney Poitier Cried for His Mother," 76; *New York Post*, 10 February 1968.

64. *Modern Screen*, July 1967; *Screen and TV Album*, January 1969; *Screenland*, February 1969; *Ebony*, April 1968; Poitier, *This Life*, 293–95.

65. *Urban West*, February 1970; Greenfield, "What's the Secret of Sidney Poitier's Zooming Appeal?," 166; *Screen Stars*, December 1969; *Screenland*, February 1969; undated *Los Angeles Sentinel* column, Reel 10, Johnson Collection, UCLA; *Movie Life Yearbook*, July 1969.

66. Holly, *One Life*, 99–100.

67. *Movie Screen*, December 1969.

68. *Variety*, 10 April 1968, 17 April 1968; *Newsweek*, 15 July 1968; *Time*, 24 May 1968; *New York Times*, 30 June

1968, 3 July 1968; *Pittsburgh Courier*, 20 July 1968; *Hollywood Reporter*, 3 July 1968.

69. *Hollywood Reporter*, 4 June 1968.

70. *Variety*, 13 December 1967, 24 January 1968, 12 June 1968, 24 July 1968; *Hollywood Reporter*, 6 September 1968; *New York Times*, 2 April 1968; *New York Amsterdam News*, 13 April 1968.

71. Bogle, *Toms, Coons, Mulattoes, Mammies, and Bucks*, 225–26; *Variety*, 21 February 1968, 28 February 1968; Leeming, *James Baldwin*, 284–302.

72. Styron, *Confessions of Nat Turner*; Clarke, *William Styron's Nat Turner*; *New York Amsterdam News*, 25 November 1967, 9 December 1967, 30 December 1967, 27 April 1968; *Pittsburgh Courier*, 18 November 1967, 9 March 1968, 11 November 1968; *Variety*, 3 April 1968, 12 June 1968; *New York Times*, 10 November 1968.

73. *New York Times*, 10 November 1968.

Chapter Fifteen

1. *New York Times*, 14 May 1967. See also Anderson, *Mammies No More*; Edward Mapp, "Black Women in Films: A Mixed Bag of Tricks," in *Black Films and Film-makers*, ed. Patterson, 196–205; Carby, *Race Men*; Haskell, *From Reverence to Rape*; Gill, " 'Her Voice Was Ever Soft, Gentle, and Low.' "

2. *New York Times*, 18 August 1968; Bogle, *Prime Time Blues*, 140–56; *Saturday Review*, 20 April 1968; *Newsweek*, 30 September 1968; undated *Wall Street Journal* article, Blacks and Film — 1968 File, MHL.

3. *New York Times*, 6 August 1967; *Variety*, 8 January 1969.

4. *After Dark*, June 1968; *Variety*, 4 October 1967, 12 June 1968, 8 January 1969.

5. *New York Amsterdam News*, 14 October 1967; *Ebony*, October 1968; *New*

York Times, 14 January 1968; *Variety*, 8 January 1969.

6. *Hollywood Reporter*, 2 October 1967; *Variety*, 11 October 1967; *Village Voice*, 12 October 1967; *New York Times*, 12 October 1967.

7. "For Love of Ivy" Pressbook, Box 6, Black Films Collection, SCRBC; *Ebony*, October 1968; *Film Daily*, 29 September 1967, 8 March 1968; *After Dark*, June 1968.

8. *Films and Filming*, October 1968.

9. *New Yorker*, 27 July 1968; *Playboy*, September 1968; *New Republic*, 10 August 1968; *London Observer*, 21 July 1968; *New York*, 20 July 1968; *Cue*, 20 July 1968.

10. *Variety*, 10 July 1968; *Hollywood Reporter*, 1 July 1968; *New York Post*, 18 July 1968; *New York Daily News*, 18 July 1968; *New Republic*, 10 August 1968; *McCall's*, September 1968; *Saturday Review*, 3 August 1968; *Time*, 2 August 1968; *Newsweek*, 29 July 1968.

11. *Pittsburgh Courier*, 20 July 1968.

12. See Ray, *Certain Tendency of the Hollywood Cinema*, 296–325; Mordden, *Medium Cool*, 149–52, 180–91; Frank, *Conquest of Cool*, 1–33; Roberts and Olson, *John Wayne*, 535–81; Schickel, *Clint Eastwood*, 135–256; Brantley, *Conversations with Pauline Kael*, 37–38.

13. *New Republic*, 10 August 1968; *Soul Illustrated*, Fall 1968.

14. *New York Times*, 25 August 1968, 1 September 1968; Elliston, "Two Sidney Poitier Movies," 30.

15. *Ebony*, October 1968; *New York Post*, 27 July 1968; *Newsweek*, 12 August 1968.

16. Naipaul, *Guerrillas*, 30–31.

17. *New York Times*, 18 August 1968.

18. *Variety*, 2 November 1967; *Hollywood Reporter*, 2 November 1967; *New York Times*, 17 December 1967, 10 November 1968.

19. Poitier, *This Life*, 300–301.

20. *New York Times*, 10 November 1968, 19 June 1970; *New York Post*, 23 June 1970; *New York Daily News*, 2 August 1970; *Photoplay*, January 1971.

21. Poitier, *This Life*, 301–3.

22. Ibid., 303–7.

23. "Lost Man" Production Notes, CBFSC; Rhines, *Black Film/White Money*, 148.

24. *Soul Illustrated*, April 1969; "Lost Man" Pressbook, Box 6, Black Films Collection, SCRBC.

25. *Soul Illustrated*, April 1969; *Cinemeditor*, Fall 1969.

26. *Cinemeditor*, Fall 1969; *Soul Illustrated*, April 1969.

27. Brown, *Actors Talk*, 208–9.

28. Box 115, Stanley Kramer Papers, UCLA.

29. Marill, *Films of Sidney Poitier*, 223; *Pittsburgh Courier*, 14 December 1968, 21 December 1968; *Los Angeles Times*, 2 February 1969; undated *Chicago Defender* article, Reel 10, George L. Johnson Collection, UCLA.

30. *Variety*, 14 May 1969; *Hollywood Reporter*, 14 May 1969; *Boxoffice*, 26 May 1969; *Motion Picture Exhibitor*, 28 May 1969.

31. *Esquire*, August 1969; *Saturday Review*, 28 June 1969; *Playboy*, August 1969. See also Kelley, "Evolution of Character Portrayals," 183–84, 211–16.

32. *Los Angeles Herald-Examiner*, 29 June 1969; *New Republic*, 28 June 1969; *Film Quarterly*, Fall 1969; *Time*, 18 July 1969.

33. *Esquire*, August 1969, September 1969; *New York Times*, 26 June 1969.

34. *Soul Illustrated*, August 1969; *Nommo*, 26 August 1969; *New York Times*, 3 August 1969.

35. *New York Post*, 4 February 1969; Poitier, *This Life*, 307–8.

36. Poitier, *This Life*, 308–9.

37. *Screen and TV Album*, January 1969; *Los Angeles Times*, 15 January 1969; Poitier, *This Life*, 309.

38. *New York Post*, 4 February 1969; Poitier, *This Life*, 309–10.

39. *New York Times*, 6 August 1967;

Photo Screen, September 1969. See also Fanon, *Black Skin, White Masks*, 63.

40. *Hollywood Reporter*, 8 January 1969; uncited articles from Reel 10, George L. Johnson Collection, UCLA; *Screenland*, February 1969; *Los Angeles Sentinel*, 23 January 1969; *Los Angeles Times*, 15 January 1969.

41. Poitier, *This Life*, 310.

42. *New York Post*, 4 February 1969; *Photo Screen*, September 1969.

43. *Screen Stars*, December 1969; *Movie Mirror*, April 1969; Poitier, *This Life*, 311–12, 351–57; *Photo Screen*, September 1969; *Modern Screen*, May 1969, September 1969.

44. *Modern Screen*, May 1969; Louie Robinson, "The Expanding World of Sidney Poitier," *Ebony*, November 1971, 111.

45. Lyn Tornabene, "Walking with Sidney Poitier," *McCall's*, July 1969, 122; Poitier, *This Life*, 357–59.

46. *New York Times*, 2 February 1969; *TV Guide*, 14 March 1970; Carroll, *Diahann*, 140–64.

47. *Newsweek*, 23 June 1969; *New York Times*, 23 December 1979; "Harold Lloyd Master Seminar," available on-line from ⟨http://www.afionline.org/haroldlloyd/poitier/script.9.html⟩, 14 February 2000.

48. *New York Times*, 12 June 1969; *Los Angeles Herald-Examiner*, 5 May 1969; Box 4, Folder 9, Ossie Davis and Ruby Dee Papers, SCRBC.

49. *Look*, 12 January 1969; *Hollywood Citizen-News*, 22 April 1969; *Ebony*, October 1969; *Movie/TV Marketing*, March 1970; Guerrero, *Framing Blackness*, 70–71, 79; Leab, *From Sambo to Superspade*, 234–46.

50. Poitier, *This Life*, 338.

51. Quinn, *One Man Tango*, 351–55.

52. Poitier, *This Life*, 314; Tornabene, "Walking with Sidney Poitier," 122; Craton and Saunders, *Islanders in the Stream*, 2:346–58; *New York Times*, 23 August 1970; *Urban West*, February

1970; uncited article from Reel 10, Johnson Collection, UCLA.

53. *People*, 14 August 1980; *Los Angeles Herald-Examiner*, 24 November 1969.

54. Poitier, *This Life*, 337–38; *Los Angeles Herald-Examiner*, 26 September 1969.

55. *Los Angeles Herald-Examiner*, 24 November 1969; *Variety*, 30 September 1969; "They Call Me Mister Tibbs!" Pressbook, Box 7, Black Films Collection, SCRBC.

56. James W. Merrick Vertical File, MHL.

57. See *New York Times*, 25 March 1971.

58. *Variety*, 8 July 1970; *Hollywood Reporter*, 8 July 1970; *Motion Picture Daily*, 8 July 1970; *New York Post*, 9 July 1970; *Cue*, 18 July 1970; *Village Voice*, 23 July 1970; *Motion Picture Herald*, 29 July 1970; *Boston After Dark*, 4 August 1970; *Los Angeles Herald-Examiner*, 14 August 1970; *Playboy*, October 1970; *Films and Filming*, April 1971.

59. *New York Daily News*, 5 July 1970; *Los Angeles Times*, 13 August 1970; *New York Times*, 18 September 1970; *New Yorker*, 18 July 1970; *Newsweek*, 20 July 1970.

60. *New York Times*, 9 July 1970, 19 July 1970.

61. *Los Angeles Times*, 27 June 1971.

62. *Hollywood Reporter*, 20 October 1971; *Los Angeles Herald-Examiner*, 20 October 1971; *Variety*, 21 October 1971; *New York Times*, 21 October 1971; *New York Daily News*, 21 October 1971; *New York Post*, 21 October 1971; *Cue*, 30 October 1971; *Saturday Review*, 6 November 1971; *Playboy*, January 1972.

63. *Boxoffice*, 15 June 1970; Poitier, *This Life*, 311, 325.

64. "Brother John" Production Notes, CBFSC; *Variety*, 23 April 1970, 4 June 1970; undated *Los Angeles Sentinel* article, Reel 10, George L. Johnson Collection, UCLA.

65. *Life*, 30 April 1971; *New York*, 29 March 1971; *Variety*, 24 March 1971; *Hollywood Reporter*, 24 March 1971; *New York Post*, 25 March 1971; *New York Daily News*, 25 March 1971; *Cue*, 27 March 1971; *Los Angeles Herald-Examiner*, 7 April 1971; *Playboy*, May 1971.

66. *New York Times*, 25 March 1971.

67. Bogle, *Toms, Coons, Mulattoes, Mammies, and Bucks*, 234–39; Leab, *From Sambo to Superspade*, 248–52.

68. Charles Michener, "Black Movies," *Newsweek*, 23 October 1972, 74; *New York Times*, 17 December 1972.

69. Lerone Bennett Jr., "The Emancipation Orgasm: Sweetback in Wonderland," *Ebony*, September 1971, 118.

70. Guerrero, *Framing Blackness*, 82–85; Cripps, *Hollywood's High Noon*, 227–30; *Variety*, 8 September 1971, 23 February 1972, 14 September 1972; Box 6, Black Films Collection, SCRBC.

71. Poitier, *This Life*, 338–40; Robinson, "Expanding World of Sidney Poitier," 112. See also Hughes, *Race and Politics in the Bahamas*, 181–82.

72. *New York Times*, 6 September 1970; *Variety*, 16 September 1970; Poitier, *This Life*, 298–99.

73. *New York Amsterdam News*, 15 December 1973.

74. *Films in Review*, February 1970; *New York Times*, 28 September 1969, 1 October 1969; *New York Daily News*, 7 July 1974.

75. *Variety*, 18 November 1970; *New York Times*, 28 March 1969, 1 October 1969, 3 September 1971; *Negro History Bulletin*, November 1970; Fishgall, *Against Type*, 261; *Ebony*, September 1971.

76. Hauser, *Muhammad Ali*, 209–11. See also Remnick, *King of the World*.

77. Plimpton, *Shadow Box*, 162–63.

78. Wolfe, *Radical Chic & Mau-Mauing the Flak Catchers*, 1–113.

79. Lorraine Gauguin, "Black Machismo," *Photoplay*, January 1975, 67; *Players*, November 1973.

80. *Hollywood Citizen-News*, 27 June 1969; *Los Angeles Times*, 2 February 1969, 27 June 1969; *Urban West*, February 1970; uncited articles from Reel 10, George L. Johnson Collection, UCLA.

81. *Los Angeles Herald-Examiner*, 11 July 1971; Robinson, "Expanding World of Sidney Poitier," 112.

82. Box 4, Folder 9, Ossie Davis and Ruby Dee Papers, SCRBC.

83. Ibid.

Chapter Sixteen

1. Poitier, *This Life*, 322–23.

2. *Hollywood Reporter*, 9 December 1970; *Variety*, 9 December 1970; *New York Morning-Telegraph*, 6 July 1959; Rhines, *Black Film/White Money*, 149–50; *Washington Post*, 6 May 1972.

3. Poitier, *This Life*, 323–26; George Goodman, "Durango: Poitier Meets Belafonte," *Look*, 24 August 1971, 59–60.

4. *Variety*, 24 February 1971, 9 March 1971; undated article from *Look* entitled "Behind the Scenes," "Buck and the Preacher" File, MHL.

5. *Variety*, 17 February 1971, 19 February 1971, 9 March 1971; Goodman, "Durango: Poitier Meets Belafonte," 62; Poitier, *This Life*, 326–27.

6. *Variety*, 9 March 1971; *Los Angeles Herald-Examiner*, 11 July 1971; "Buck and the Preacher" Production Notes, MHL.

7. "They Call Me Mister Tibbs!" Production Notes, CBFSC; Poitier, "Dialogue on Film," *American Film*, September 1976, 34.

8. Poitier, *This Life*, 328–29; Goodman, "Durango: Poitier Meets Belafonte," 62; *Washington Post*, 15 March 1972.

9. *Los Angeles Times*, 27 June 1971; Davis and Dee, *With Ossie and Ruby*, 354–55; "Buck and the Preacher" Production Notes, MHL.

10. *New York Daily News*, 26 March 1972; *Boxoffice*, 15 May 1972; Goodman, "Durango: Poitier Meets Belafonte," 60; Keyser and Ruszkowski, *Cinema of Sidney Poitier*, 150; *Washington Post*, 15 March 1972.

11. *Hollywood Citizen-News*, 30 July 1970; *New York Times*, 2 July 1972; *Los Angeles Herald-Examiner*, 28 May 1972.

12. *Variety*, 28 April 1971; Louie Robinson, "The Expanding World of Sidney Poitier," *Ebony*, November 1971, 106.

13. See Painter, *Exodusters*.

14. See Ray, *Certain Tendency of the Hollywood Cinema*.

15. Slotkin, *Gunfighter Nation*, 628–33.

16. *Boxoffice*, 15 May 1972; *Commonweal*, 26 May 1972; *New York Times*, 10 September 1972; *Chicago Tribune*, 27 April 1972; *Essence*, August 1972. See also Yearwood, *Black Film as a Signifying Practice*, 87–88.

17. *New York*, 1 May 1972; *Los Angeles Herald-Examiner*, 4 May 1972; *New York Times*, 7 May 1972; *Newsweek*, 15 May 1972; *Playboy*, June 1972; *Films and Filming*, June 1972.

18. *New York Times*, 13 August 1972; "Proceedings of a Symposium on Black Images in Films," 56–57.

19. *Variety*, 19 April 1972; *Washington Post*, 5 May 1972; *Saturday Review*, 3 June 1972; *Hollywood Reporter*, 20 April 1972; *Boston Globe*, 15 May 1972; Poitier, *This Life*, 329–30.

20. *New York Times*, 29 April 1972; *Time*, 29 May 1972; *Life*, 9 June 1972; Noble, "Entertainment, Politics, and the Movie Business," 18.

21. Woodard, *Nation within a Nation*, 202–3; Charles Musser and Adam Knee, "William Greaves, Documentary Filmmaking, and the African-American Experience," in *Cinemas of the Black Diaspora*, ed. Martin, 400–401.

22. Sidney Poitier, telephone interview with the author, 15 February 2002;
Poitier, *This Life*, 331; Keyser and Ruszkowski, *Cinema of Sidney Poitier*, 157.

23. Robinson, "Expanding World of Sidney Poitier," 106; *New York Daily News*, 26 March 1972; "Warm December" Production Notes, CBFSC.

24. *Variety*, 19 July 1972; Box 7, Black Films Collection, SCRBC; Press Release from National General Pictures titled "The Style-Setting Look of 'A Warm December,' " CBFSC; "Warm December" Production Notes, CBFSC.

25. *Chicago Tribune*, 28 May 1973.

26. *New York Daily News*, 8 June 1973; *Films and Filming*, July 1973; *New York Times*, 24 May 1973; *Real Paper*, 30 May 1973; *Los Angeles Times*, 23 May 1973; *Washington Post*, 26 May 1973; *Cue*, 26 May 1973; *Women's Wear Daily*, 24 May 1973; *Playboy*, June 1973; *Time*, 4 June 1973; *Variety*, 18 April 1973; *Christian Science Monitor*, 25 May 1973.

27. *Jet*, 3 May 1973; *Hollywood Reporter*, 16 April 1973; *Chicago Tribune*, 26 May 1973; *World*, 10 April 1973; *New York*, 28 May 1973. See also Wailoo, *Dying in the City of Blues*, 182; *New York Times*, 6 October 1974.

28. *New York Times*, 17 December 1972; B. J. Mason, "The New Films: Culture or Con Game?," *Ebony*, December 1972, 60–68; Charles Michener, "Black Movies: Renaissance or Ripoff?," *Newsweek*, 23 October 1972, 72–81.

29. *New York Times*, 17 December 1972; *Jet*, 14 September 1972. See also *New Yorker*, 2 December 1972.

30. *New York Times*, 18 July 1972, 17 December 1972; Alvin Poussaint, "Cheap Thrills That Degrade Blacks," *Psychology Today*, February 1974, 22–32, 98; Michener, "Black Movies," 77; Mason, "New Films," 64. See also Leab, *From Sambo to Superspade*, 258; Stephens, "Black Women in Film," 168.

31. Michael Mattox, "The Day Black Movie Stars Got Militant," in *Black Films and Film-makers*, ed. Patterson, 190–95;

Hollywood Reporter, 18 September 1972;
Mason, "New Films," 62.

32. Michener, "Black Movies," 77–78;
Jet, 12 October 1972; *New York Times*,
17 December 1972; *Hollywood Reporter*,
6 June 1972.

33. *Jet*, 17 January 1974; Guerrero,
Framing Blackness, 69–111.

34. Poitier, *This Life*, 343–44; *Variety*,
10 September 1972.

35. Poitier, "Dialogue on Film," 47;
Variety, 5 December 1973; Box 7, Black
Films Collection, SCRBC; *Jet*, 25 July
1974; *New York Amsterdam News*,
22 December 1973; *Chicago Tribune*,
30 June 1974; *New York Daily News*,
7 July 1974.

36. "Uptown Saturday Night" Production Notes, CBFSC; *New York Amsterdam News*, 11 May 1974.

37. Poitier, "Dialogue on Film," 42–43;
George, *Blackface*, 40; *Variety*,
21 December 1973.

38. *New Yorker*, 17 June 1974; *New
York Post*, 17 June 1974; *Players*, January
1975.

39. *New York Daily News*, 17 June
1974; *Los Angeles Times*, 21 June 1974;
Chicago Tribune, 24 June 1974; *Village
Voice*, 27 June 1974.

40. *Time*, 1 July 1974.

41. *Variety*, 12 June 1974; *Hollywood
Reporter*, 12 June 1974; *Cue*, 17 June
1974; *New York*, 24 June 1974; *Films and
Filming*, August 1975.

42. *New York Amsterdam News*,
25 May 1974, 22 June 1974, 13 July
1974.

43. *New York Amsterdam News*,
22 June 1974, 13 July 1974; *New York
Times*, 11 July 1974, 16 July 1974.

44. *Jet*, 25 July 1974; *Variety*, 16 July
1974, 17 July 1974, 30 July 1974; *Holly-
wood Reporter*, 16 July 1974; *Boxoffice*,
22 July 1974; *Warner Brothers Rambling
Reporter*, August 1974; *Los Angeles
Herald-Examiner*, 4 August 1974; Noble,
"Entertainment, Politics, and the Movie
Business," 18.

45. *New York Times*, 13 March 1973,
21 May 1975. See also *New York Times*,
5 January 1968, 24 December 1968,
16 November 1969, 23 November 1969,
30 November 1969, 16 December 1969;
Baraka, *Autobiography of Leroi Jones*.

46. Baraka, *Sidnee Poet Heroical*.

47. Ibid.

48. *New York Times*, 21 May 1975;
Watts, *Amiri Baraka*, 286–89.

49. Reilly, *Conversations with Amiri
Baraka*, 215; Brown, *Actors Talk*, 209.

50. *Boston Globe*, 4 August 1974; *Variety*, 28 August 1968, 29 August 1973,
5 December 1973; *Boxoffice*, 10 September 1973; Driscoll, *Wilby Conspiracy*;
"Wilby Conspiracy" Production Notes,
NYPLPA.

51. *Variety*, 13 March 1974; Nelson,
Kenya, 54–60; Caine, *What's It All
About?*, 315–16.

52. Caine, *What's It All About?*, 318–
19.

53. *Films and Filming*, April 1975; *Variety*, 25 June 1975; *Hollywood Reporter*,
24 June 1975; *Los Angeles Times*, 30 July
1975; *New York Times*, 4 September
1975; *New York Post*, 4 September 1975;
New York Daily News, 4 September
1975; *Cue*, 13 September 1975; *Time*,
6 October 1975; *Essence*, November
1975; *Chicago Tribune*, 23 June 1975.

54. "Wilby Conspiracy" Production
Notes, NYPLPA; Davis, *In Darkest Hollywood*, 75–79.

55. *Wall Street Journal*, 4 August 1975;
New Yorker, 15 September 1975; *New
Republic*, 20 September 1975. See also
Fredrickson, *Black Liberation*, 238–52,
265–76, 298–313.

56. Davis, *In Darkest Hollywood*, 76–
80; Massie, *Loosing the Bonds*, 262–332.

57. *New York Daily News*, 6 April 1975.

58. *New York Amsterdam News*, 9 December 1972; *Hollywood Reporter*,
21 December 1972; *Sepia*, March 1973;
New York Times, 21 September 1972.

59. *New York Amsterdam News*,
15 December 1973.

60. Craton and Saunders, *Islanders in the Stream*, 2:349–62; Hughes, *Race and Politics in the Bahamas*, 179–206; Poitier, *This Life*, 317–19; Sidney Poitier, telephone interview with the author, 16 August 2000.

61. *New York Daily News*, 7 July 1974, 23 February 1975; *New York Daily Mail*, 3 July 1974; Poitier, *This Life*, 351, 360–61; Marill, *Films of Sidney Poitier*, 38; *Los Angeles Herald-Examiner*, 23 January 1976; *Los Angeles Times*, 24 January 1976.

62. *Black Stars*, September 1978; *New York Daily News*, 21 September 1976, 27 March 1977; *Los Angeles Times*, 28 August 1978.

63. *Los Angeles Times*, 24 June 1974, 3 March 1975, 16 December 1976; Rose, *You Can't Do That on Broadway!*, 225–26.

64. *Los Angeles Times*, 20 September 1975; *Boxoffice*, 22 September 1975; Louie Robinson, "Have Blacks Really Made It in Hollywood?," *Ebony*, June 1975, 33–42.

65. "Let's Do It Again" Production Notes, CBFSC; *New York Amsterdam News*, 14 May 1975; *Variety*, 9 April 1975, 7 May 1975; *Boxoffice*, 26 May 1975; *New York Daily News*, 1 June 1975.

66. Smith, *Cosby*, 142; *Boston Globe*, 1 November 1975.

67. *Hollywood Reporter*, 6 October 1975; *Variety*, 8 October 1975; *New York Times*, 13 October 1975; *New York Post*, 13 October 1975; *Cue*, 18 October 1975; *Time*, 27 October 1975; *Films and Filming*, September 1976; Noble, "Entertainment, Politics, and the Movie Business," 18.

68. *New Yorker*, 3 November 1975.

69. *Washington Post*, 29 February 1976; *White Plains Reporter Dispatch*, 27 October 1977.

70. *New York Times*, 23 February 1978, 29 October 1979, 23 December 1979; "Harold Lloyd Master Seminar,"

available on-line from ⟨http://www.afionline.org/haroldlloyd/poitier/script.9.html⟩, 14 February 2000.

71. "Piece of the Action" Pressbook, Box 7, Black Films Collection, SCRBC; *New York Daily News*, 7 October 1977; *New York Post*, 8 October 1977; *Christian Science Monitor*, 10 November 1977; "Piece of the Action" Production Notes, CBFSC; *Time*, 21 March 1977; *Boxoffice*, 26 June 1976, 25 April 1977, 23 May 1977; *Chicago Tribune*, 11 May 1977.

72. *Variety*, 5 October 1977; *Hollywood Reporter*, 7 October 1977; *Los Angeles Times*, 7 October 1977; *New York Times*, 8 October 1977; *New York Post*, 8 October 1977; *Washington Post*, 14 October 1977; *Village Voice*, 17 October 1977; *Newsweek*, 31 October 1977; *Time*, 14 November 1977; *After Dark*, December 1977; *Playboy*, January 1978.

73. *Los Angeles Times*, 2 February 2000.

74. *Los Angeles Times*, 14 June 1975.

75. *New York Post*, 12 June 1974, 10 October 1975; *Daily Breeze*, 11 August 1980; "Sidney Poitier Talks about His Early Poverty in New York City," interview with Tom Brokaw, audio tape of NBC-TV broadcast, 23 June 1980, Michigan State University Voice Library.

76. *Washington Post*, 16 April 1973, 29 February 1976; Poitier, "Dialogue on Film"; Noble, "Entertainment, Politics, and the Movie Business"; Louie Robinson, "Sidney Poitier Tells How to Stay on Top in Hollywood," *Ebony*, November 1977, 53–54.

77. *Los Angeles Times*, 30 October 1977; *Boston Globe*, 4 January 1978; *People*, 4 August 1980.

78. *Los Angeles Times*, 30 October 1977; Michael J. Bandler, "Poitier: His Thoughts Fly Back," *American Way*, July 1980, 54–58; *Washington Post*, 6 July 1980.

79. Quotation from Poitier, *This Life*, 11.

80. See *Los Angeles Times*, 28 August

1980; Carroll, *Diahann*; *New York Post*, 8 May 1986.

81. *New Republic*, 10 May 1980; *Washington Post*, 25 May 1980, 6 July 1980; *Los Angeles Times*, 1 June 1980, 8 February 1981; *New York Times*, 2 June 1980; *New Yorker*, 2 June 1980; *Ebony*, June 1980; *Los Angeles Herald-Examiner*, 6 July 1980; *Chicago Tribune*, 27 July 1980; *New York Times Book Review*, 17 August 1980. A portion of *This Life* is excerpted in *American Film*, April 1980.

Chapter Seventeen

1. *New York Post*, 11 December 1978, 23 May 1979; *Hollywood Reporter*, 7 December 1978, 1 March 1979; *Variety*, 13 December 1978, 11 May 1979, 29 August 1979, 17 March 1980, 10 November 1980; *Boxoffice*, 18 December 1978; *Chicago Defender*, 16 December 1978; *New York Times*, 27 November 1979; *Los Angeles Times*, 16 January 1979.

2. *Cue*, 26 November 1977; *New York Times*, 27 November 1979, 13 June 1980.

3. *Hollywood Reporter*, 11 March 1980, 18 April 1980; *Los Angeles Times*, 18 May 1980; "Stir Crazy" Production Notes, CBFSC.

4. *Los Angeles Times*, 18 May 1980; *Variety*, 17 March 1980; *New York Post*, 9 January 1981.

5. Pryor, *Pryor Convictions and Other Life Sentences*, 181–82; *Variety*, 1 May 1980, 2 May 1980, 7 May 1980, 11 June 1980; *Hollywood Reporter*, 7 May 1980, 28 May 1980; *On Cable*, April 1982.

6. *New York*, 15 December 1980; *Variety*, 1 December 1980; *Hollywood Reporter*, 2 December 1980; *New York Times*, 12 December 1980; *Village Voice*, 10–16 December 1980; *New York Daily News*, 12 December 1980; *Los Angeles Herald-Examiner*, 12 December 1980; *Newsweek*, 15 December 1980; *Los Angeles Reporter*, 17 December 1980;

New Republic, 27 December 1980; *Motion Picture Product Digest*, 31 December 1980; *Boxoffice*, January 1981; *Time*, 12 January 1981; *Los Angeles Times*, 11 February 1981.

7. *New York Times*, 13 December 1980, 5 May 1981; *Hollywood Reporter*, 23 December 1980, 5 May 1981; *New York Post*, 15 August 1985.

8. *Boston Globe*, 18 April 1982.

9. *Los Angeles Times*, 8 February 1981; *Los Angeles Herald-Examiner*, 20 February 1981; *Variety*, 28 October 1981; *Essence*, November 1981; *Hollywood Reporter*, 2 June 1983; *Boston Globe*, 7 November 1987.

10. *Patriot Ledger* (Mass.), 28 August 1981; *Boston Globe*, 30 August 1981, 2 September 1981; *Variety*, 24 July 1981; *US*, 30 March 1982.

11. *Film Journal*, 24 May 1982; *Variety*, 2 June 1982; *Hollywood Reporter*, 2 June 1982; *New York Times*, 4 June 1982; *New York Daily News*, 4 June 1982; *Los Angeles Herald-Examiner*, 5 June 1982; *Philadelphia Inquirer*, 8 June 1982; *Motion Picture Product Digest*, 16 June 1982; *Newsweek*, 21 June 1982; *Time*, 7 June 1982; *Inquiry*, June 1982.

12. "Fast Forward" Production Notes, MHL; *USA Today*, 5 March 1985; *Variety*, 7 December 1983, 25 June 1984, 5 September 1984.

13. *Variety*, 13 February 1985; *Hollywood Reporter*, 14 February 1985; *Boxoffice*, April 1985; *Pittsburgh Post-Gazette*, 16 February 1985; *Philadelphia Inquirer*, 18 February 1985; *New York Times*, 19 February 1985; *Village Voice*, 26 February 1985; *Boston Phoenix*, 26 February 1985; *Boston Globe*, 15 February 1985; *Los Angeles Weekly*, 15 February 1985; *Los Angeles Herald-Examiner*, 16 February 1985; *Washington Post*, 15 February 1985, 20 February 1985.

14. *Boston Globe*, 15 February 1985.

15. Herbert Nipson, "Sidney Poitier Is Back," *Ebony*, May 1988, 34–35; *New York Post*, 8 February 1988.

16. *Jet*, 14 March 1988; *New York Daily News*, 6 March 1989; *New York Times*, 4 May 1987; *Cable Guide*, April 1989; *Newsweek*, 22 February 1988.

17. *Los Angeles Times*, 20 September 1983; *Time*, 5 December 1983.

18. *New York Post*, 8 February 1988; *Newsweek*, 22 February 1988; *Chicago Tribune*, 25 May 1980; Michael Bandler, "Poitier: His Thoughts Fly Back," *American Way*, July 1980, 54–58; *Essence*, November 1981.

19. Tom Seligson, "I No Longer Feel I Have to Prove Anything," *Parade*, 28 February 1988, 6; *New York Amsterdam News*, 14 April 1990; *Women's Wear Daily*, 24 June 1980; *Jet*, 23 September 1985; *Cable Guide*, April 1989.

20. *Los Angeles Times*, 5 March 1987; *Boston Phoenix*, 12 February 1988; *New York Times*, 28 February 1989; *Newsweek*, 22 February 1988.

21. Sidney Poitier, "Dialogue on Film," *American Film*, September–October 1991, 49; *New York Times*, 28 February 1989; *Newsweek*, 22 February 1988; *Los Angeles Times*, 28 February 1989.

22. Yule, *Fast Fade*, 256–57; *New York Times*, 20 February 1987, 4 May 1987; *Jet*, 23 March 1987; *Los Angeles Times*, 5 March 1987; "Little Nikita" Production Notes, MHL.

23. *New York Daily News*, 7 March 1986; *Jet*, 14 March 1988; "Shoot to Kill" Production Notes, CBFSC; Nipson, "Sidney Poitier Is Back," 31.

24. *Los Angeles Times*, 19 February 1988; *Boston Globe*, 12 February 1988; *Village Voice*, 23 February 1988; *Los Angeles Herald-Examiner*, 12 February 1988; *Wall Street Journal*, 18 February 1988.

25. *Variety*, 8 February 1988; *Hollywood Reporter*, 8 February 1988; *New York Times*, 12 February 1988; *Village Voice*, 14 March 1988; *Boxoffice*, April 1988; *Time*, 29 February 1988. See also *Los Angeles Times*, 20 September 1987.

26. *New York Times*, 18 March 1988; *Boston Globe*, 18 March 1988; *Philadelphia Inquirer*, 19 March 1988; *People*, 18 April 1988; *Chicago Tribune*, 18 March 1988; Yule, *Fast Fade*, 267, 349.

27. See Bogle, *Toms, Coons, Mulattoes, Mammies, and Bucks*, 267–303; *Jet*, 28 November 1988.

28. Willis, *High Contrast*, 27–59. See also Sharkey, "Knocking on Hollywood's Door"; Quart, "Jews and Blacks in Hollywood"; Bourne, "African American Image in Cinema."

29. See Wilson, *Declining Significance of Race*; Pinkney, *Myth of Black Progress*.

30. *New York Times*, 19 October 1983, 31 July 1990; Jeannie Kasindorf, "Six Degrees of Impersonation," *New York*, 25 March 1991, 42.

31. *New York Times*, 21 June 1990, 31 July 1990; Kasindorf, "Six Degrees of Impersonation," 42–43.

32. *New York Post*, 18 October 1983; *New York Times*, 18 October 1983.

33. *New York Times*, 21 June 1990. See also *Los Angeles Reader*, 24 December 1993.

34. *New York Times*, 19 October 1983, 20 November 1983, 10 January 1984, 21 June 1990.

35. Kasindorf, "Six Degrees of Impersonation," 45; *New York Times*, 10 June 1990.

36. *New York Times*, 10 June 1990, 15 June 1990, 1 July 1990, 9 November 1990; *New York Daily News*, 9 November 1990; *Newsday*, 9 November 1990; *Newsweek*, 26 November 1990; *Diversion*, June 1991; *New Yorker*, 31 May 1993.

37. *New York Times*, 31 July 1990, 26 March 1991, 7 May 1991, 7 November 1991; Kasindorf, "Six Degrees of Impersonation," 39, 46; *Variety*, 4 May 1992; *Hollywood Reporter*, 25 September 1992.

38. *Variety*, 13 December 1993; *Los Angeles Times*, 10 December 1993; *New York*, 13 December 1993; *New York Post*,

8 December 1993; *Newsday*, 8 December 1993; *Newsweek*, 20 December 1993; *Village Voice*, 14 December 1993; *Boston Globe*, 22 December 1993; *New York Times*, 21 June 1990, 16 May 1993; *USA Today*, 25 May 1993.

39. Guare, *Six Degrees of Separation*.

40. Richard Zoglin, "Cosby, Inc.," *Time*, 28 September 1987; *Village Voice*, 23 October 1984.

41. *Essence*, June 1990; *Los Angeles Times*, 27 May 1990; *Hollywood Reporter*, 9 May 1989; *Jet*, 2 July 1990.

42. *Essence*, June 1990; *Los Angeles Times*, 27 May 1990; *Variety*, 21 June 1989; *Boston Phoenix*, 29 June 1990; "Ghost Dad" Production Notes, CBFSC.

43. *Variety*, 25 June 1990; *Wall Street Journal*, 28 June 1990; *New York Times*, 29 June 1990; *Boston Herald*, 29 June 1990; *Boston Phoenix*, 29 June 1990; *Philadelphia Inquirer*, 29 June 1990; *Village Voice*, 10 July 1990; *Time*, 16 July 1990.

44. *Hollywood Reporter*, 25 June 1990; *Los Angeles Times*, 29 June 1990.

45. *Los Angeles Herald-Examiner*, 15 January 1988; *Variety*, 21 June 1989, 10 October 1989, 30 October 1989; *Newark Star-Ledger*, 24 March 1991; *New York Post*, 8 November 1989.

46. *New York Times*, 29 June 1990, 7 April 1990; *Los Angeles Times*, 7 April 1991; *Newark Star-Ledger*, 24 March 1991; *Jet*, 22 April 1991.

47. Buford, *Burt Lancaster*, 333–35; Fishgall, *Against Type*, 391–92.

48. "Separate but Equal" Viewer Guide, Sidney Poitier File, CBFSC; *New York Times*, 5 April 1991, 8 April 1991; *New York*, 8 April 1991; *Time*, 8 April 1991.

49. *New York Times*, 6 April 1991.

50. *New York Times*, 19 April 1991. See also Carlton Moss Oral History, MHL, 398.

51. "Sneakers" Production Notes, MHL; *Premiere*, October 1992.

52. *New York Observer*, 14 September 1992; *New York Times*, 9 September 1992; *Los Angeles Times*, 9 September 1992; *Philadelphia Inquirer*, 11 September 1992; *Village View*, 11 September 1992; *Variety*, 14 September 1992; *Time*, 14 September 1992; *New Yorker*, 21 September 1992; *Newsweek*, 21 September 1992; *Boston Globe*, 22 September 1992.

53. *Orange County Register*, 11 September 1992.

54. Poitier, *Measure of a Man*, 231–37. On Smith, see *Current Biography Yearbook 1994*, 544–47.

55. Poitier, *Measure of a Man*, 237–41; *Variety*, 29 June 1993.

56. *Variety*, 20 February 1995; *New York*, 27 February 1995.

57. *Jet*, 13 February 1995; *TV Guide*, 25 February 1995; *Los Angeles Times*, 26 February 1995.

58. *Washington Post*, 3 December 1995; *Variety*, 1 April 1996; *Los Angeles Times*, 7 April 1996.

59. *New York Times*, 6 April 1996; *Variety*, 1 April 1996; *Boston Globe*, 5 April 1996.

60. *Jet*, 24 November 1986; *Los Angeles Daily News*, 12 June 1995; Henry Louis Gates Jr., "Belafonte's Balancing Act," *New Yorker*, 26 August and 2 September 1996, 141–42.

61. *Los Angeles Times*, 13 February 1997.

62. *New York Times*, 30 May 1996; Mandela, *Long Walk to Freedom*; *Parade*, 1 November 1998; *Washington Post*, 13 February 1997; *Los Angeles Times*, 13 February 1997.

63. *New York*, 17 February 1997; *Jet*, 17 February 1997; Goodman, *Fault Lines*, 14.

64. *Variety*, 10 November 1997; *New York Times*, 14 November 1997; *Los Angeles Times*, 14 November 1997; *New York Post*, 14 November 1997; *Newsday*, 14 November 1997; *Newsweek*, 24 November 1997; *Village Voice*, 25 November 1997.

65. Farber and Green, *Hollywood on the Couch*, 161–63; *Parade*, 1 November 1998. See also Rubin, *Jordi/Lisa and David*; Reach, *David and Lisa*.

66. *Vogue*, January 1999; *Time*, 22 September 1997; *People*, 14 May 2001; *Jet*, 22 February 1999; *Los Angeles Times*, 13 June 1998.

67. *Jet*, 22 February 1999; *People*, 16 April 2001.

68. *Variety*, 2 May 1997.

69. *New York Times*, 1 March 1989, 3 April 1992; *Jet*, 20 March 1989; *People*, 30 March 1992; *Variety*, 11 March 1992, 12 March 1992; *Hollywood Reporter*, 16 March 1992.

70. *New York Times*, 17 November 1993; *Jet*, 13 December 1993.

71. *Jet*, 23 November 1992, 27 March 2000, 19 March 2001; *New York Times*, 21 May 1994, 18 November 1994, 4 December 1995; *Los Angeles Times*, 13 June 1998, 5 January 1999; *Washington Post*, 4 December 1995; *Hollywood Reporter*, 22 February 2001; *Variety*, 26 February 2001; "Sidney Poitier: One Bright Light."

72. *Los Angeles Times*, 4 March 1988, 2 February 2000; *Variety*, 18 December 1996, 1 April 1996; *Jet*, 24 January 2000; "Sidney Poitier: The Defiant One"; "Sidney Poitier: One Bright Light."

73. *Jet*, 12 December 1994, 5 May 1997; *Variety*, 2 May 1997.

74. *Los Angeles Times*, 8 March 1992, 26 June 1994, 28 October 2001; *New York*, 26 March 2001; *New York Times*, 16 April 2000.

75. Poitier, *Measure of a Man*, xii.

76. *New York Times*, 28 May 2000.

77. Poitier, *Measure of a Man*, 118.

78. *Publishers Weekly*, 5 March 2001.

79. See Guerrero, *Framing Blackness*, 157–208.

80. See *Boston Globe*, 7 December 1999; Carby, *Race Men*, 169–91.

81. Allison Samuels, "Will It Be Denzel's Day?," *Newsweek*, 25 February 2002, 59–60.

82. See Brode, *Denzel Washington*.

83. Samuels, "Will It Be Denzel's Day?," 57; Levy, *Oscar Fever*, 117–18; *Jet*, 16 April 1990, 4 March 2002.

84. Speech available on-line at ⟨http://www.oscars.com/oscarnight/winners/winner—poitier.html⟩, 30 March 2002; *New York Post*, 26 March 2002; *Wall Street Journal*, 27 March 2002.

85. *USA Today*, 25 March 2002; *Washington Post*, 26 March 2002.

86. *Boston Globe*, 26 March 2002.

87. See Shipler, *Country of Strangers*; Terkel, *Race*; Linda Williams, *Playing the Race Card*, 252–310.

BIBLIOGRAPHY

Archival Collections

Bloomington, Indiana
  Black Films Center/Archive, Indiana
  University
    Films not yet commercially released
  Eli Lilly Library, Indiana University
    John Ford Papers
Cambridge, Massachusetts
  Harvard Theatre Collection
    Clippings files by play and
    personality
College Park, Maryland
  Motion Picture, Sound, and Video
  Branch, National Archives
    Newsreels
Los Angeles, California
  Arts Special Collections, University of
  California–Los Angeles
    Stirling Siliphant Papers
    Twentieth Century-Fox Legal Files
  Cinema and Television Library,
  University of Southern California
    Constance McCormack Collection
    Metro-Goldwyn Mayer Collection
    Stanley Scheuer Collection
    Twentieth Century-Fox Collection
    Universal Collection
  Margaret Herrick Library, Academy of
  Motion Picture Arts and Sciences
    Charles Champlin Collection
    Clippings files by film, personality,
    and subject
    Jack Hirshberg Collection
    Oral History Collection
    Production Code Administration of
    America Files
    Ronald L. Davis Oral History
    Collection
    Screenplay Collection
    Sidney Skolsky Collection
    William Gordon Collection

Special Collections, University of
  California–Los Angeles
    George L. Johnson Collection
    Stanley Kramer Papers
Warner Brothers Collection, University of
  Southern California
    Files on Warner Brothers films
Madison, Wisconsin
  Wisconsin State Historical Society
    David Susskind Papers
    Norman Jewison Papers
    Otto Preminger Papers
    Pandro Berman Papers
    Richard Nash Papers
    Walter Mirisch Papers
New York, New York
  Celeste Bartos Film Study Center,
  Museum of Modern Art
    Clippings files by film and personality
  Museum of Television and Radio
    Recordings of television programs
  New York Public Library for the
  Performing Arts
    Clippings files by film, play, and
    personality
    Pressbook collections
  Schomburg Center for Research in
  Black Culture, New York Public
  Library
    American Negro Theatre Records
    American Negro Theatre Scrapbook
    Black Films Collection
    Frederick O'Neal Papers
    Ossie Davis and Ruby Dee Papers
Washington, D.C.
  Motion Picture and Television Reading
  Room, Library of Congress
    Films not yet commercially released

Newspapers and Periodicals

AFI Report
After Dark

America
American Film
American Legion Magazine
American Way
Atlanta Journal
Black Stars
B'nai Brith Messenger
Boston
Boston After Dark
Boston Globe
Boston Phoenix
Boston Record-American
Boston Traveler
Boxoffice
Brooklyn Citizen
Brooklyn Daily Eagle
Cable Guide
The Call
Camden Courier-Post
Catholic Film Newsletter
Catholic Standard and Times
Catholic Tidings
Catholic World
Chicago American
Chicago Defender
Chicago Sun-Times
Chicago Tribune
Christian Advocate
Christian Century
Christian Science Monitor
Cinema
Cinemeditor
Columbus (Ind.) Republican
Commonweal
Coronet
Cosmopolitan
Counterattack
Crisis
Cue
Current Biography
Daily Compass
Daily Worker
Detroit Free Press
Diversion
Ebony
Esquire
Essence
Film Culture
Film Daily

Film Journal
Film Quarterly
Films and Filming
Film-TV Daily
Good Housekeeping
Greater Amusement
Harper's
Hartford Times
Holiday
Hollywood Citizen-News
Hollywood Reporter
Independent Film Journal
Inquiry
Jet
Jewish Advocate
Liberator
Life
Limelight
Listener
London Daily Telegraph
London Observer
Look
Los Angeles Citizen-News
Los Angeles Examiner
Los Angeles Free Press
Los Angeles Herald-Examiner
Los Angeles Mirror-News
Los Angeles Reader
Los Angeles Reporter
Los Angeles Sentinel
Los Angeles Times
Los Angeles Weekly
Louisville Courier-Journal
Mayfair
Memories
McCall's
Modern Screen
Moncton (N.J.) Transcript
Montreal Star
Motion Picture Daily
Motion Picture Exhibitor
Motion Picture Herald
Motion Picture Product Digest
Movie Life Yearbook
Movie Mirror
Movie Screen
Movie/TV Marketing
Nassau Guardian
Nation

National Geographic
Negro Digest
Negro History Bulletin
Newark Evening News
New Leader
New Republic
Newsweek
New York
New York Amsterdam News
New York Daily Mirror
New York Daily News
New Yorker
New York Herald-Tribune
New York Journal-American
New York Morning-Telegraph
New York Post
New York Sun
New York Times
New York World Telegram and Sun
Nommo
Norfolk (Va.) Journal and Guide
Northampton (Mass.) Hampshire-Gazette
On Cable
Orange County Register
Parade
Patriot Ledger (Mass.)
People
People's Voice
People's World
Philadelphia Inquirer
Photoplay
Photo Screen
Phylon
Pittsburgh Courier
Pittsburgh Post-Gazette
Playboy
Players
PM
Psychology Today
Publishers Weekly
Punch
Readers and Writers
Real Paper
Rhythm
Richmond Times-Dispatch
S.A. Film Weekly
San Francisco Examiner
Saturday Evening Post
Saturday Review

Schenectady (N.Y.) Union-Star
Screen and TV Album
Screenland
Screen Stars
Screen Stories
Senior Scholastic
Sepia
Seventeen
Showmen's Trade Review
Smith College Spectator
Soul Illustrated
Southern Illinoisian
Sparta News-Plaindealer
St. Louis Post-Dispatch
Syracuse Herald Journal
The Thunderbolt: The White Man's
    Viewpoint
Time
Toronto Globe and Mail
TV Guide
Urbana (Ill.) Courier
Urban West
USA Today
Variety
Village Voice
Vogue
Wall Street Journal
Warner Brothers Rambling Reporter
Washington Post
White Plains Reporter Dispatch
Women's Wear Daily
World

Books

Abernathy, Ralph David. *And the Walls Came Tumbling Down.* New York: Harper and Row, 1989.

Adero, Malaika, ed. *Up South: Stories, Studies, and Letters of This Century's Black Migrations.* New York: New Press, 1993.

Albert, Marvin H. *Apache Rising.* Greenwich, Conn.: Fawcett Gold Medal, 1957.

Alexander, Peter F. *Alan Paton: A Biography.* New York: Oxford University, 1994.

Andersen, Christopher. *An Affair to Remember: The Remarkable Love*

Story of Katharine Hepburn and Spencer Tracy. New York: William Morrow, 1997.

Anderson, Jervis. *Bayard Rustin: Troubles I've Seen*. New York: HarperCollins, 1997.

———. *This Was Harlem: A Cultural Portrait, 1900–1950*. New York: Farrar, Straus and Giroux, 1983.

Anderson, Lisa M. *Mammies No More: The Changing Image of Black Women on Stage and Screen*. Lanham, Md.: Rowman and Littlefield, 1997.

Aquila, Richard. *That Old Time Rock & Roll: A Chronicle of an Era, 1954–1963*. New York: Schirmer Books, 1989.

Archer, Leonard C. *Black Images in the American Theatre*. Brooklyn, N.Y.: Pageant-Poseidon, 1973.

Aristophanes. *Lysistrata*. Revised by Gilbert Seldes. New York: Heritage Press, 1934.

Bailey, Pearl. *Between You and Me: A Heartfelt Memoir on Learning, Loving, and Living*. New York: Doubleday, 1989.

Bailey, Randall C., and Jacquelyn Grant, eds. *The Recovery of Black Presence: An Interdisciplinary Exploration*. Nashville, Tenn.: Abingdon Press, 1995.

Baldwin, James. *Blues for Mister Charlie*. 1964. Reprint, New York: Vintage Books, 1992.

———. *The Devil Finds Work*. New York: Dial Press, 1976.

———. *Notes of a Native Son*. 1955. Reprint, New York: Dial Press, 1963.

Balio, Tino. *The American Film Industry*. Madison: University of Wisconsin Press, 1985.

———. *United Artists: The Company That Changed the Film Industry*. Madison: University of Wisconsin Press.

Ball, John. *In the Heat of the Night*. New York: Harper and Row, 1965.

Baraka, Amiri. *The Autobiography of Leroi Jones*. Chicago: Lawrence Hill Books, 1997.

———. *The Sidnee Poet Heroical in 29 Scenes*. New York: Ishmael Reed Books, 1979.

Barnouw, Erik. *Tube of Plenty: The Evolution of American Television*. Rev. ed. New York: Oxford University Press, 1982.

Barrett, William. *The Lilies of the Field*. Garden City, N.Y.: Doubleday, 1962.

Bengtsson, Frans G. *The Long Ships: A Saga of the Viking Age*. Translated by Michael Meyer. London: Collins, 1954.

Berg, A. Scott. *Goldwyn: A Biography*. New York: Alfred A. Knopf, 1989.

Bergman, Andrew. *We're in the Money: Depression America and Its Films*. New York: New York University Press, 1971.

Bergman, Carol. *Sidney Poitier*. Los Angeles: Melrose Square Publishing, 1990.

Bertrand, Michael T. *Race, Rock, and Elvis*. Urbana: University of Illinois Press, 2000.

Bikel, Theodore. *Theo*. New York: HarperCollins, 1994.

Biskind, Peter. *Seeing Is Believing: How Hollywood Taught Us to Stop Worrying and Love the Fifties*. New York: Pantheon, 1983.

Blotner, Joseph. *Robert Penn Warren: A Biography*. New York: Random House, 1997.

Bogdanovich, Peter. *Who the Devil Made It*. New York: Alfred A. Knopf, 1997.

Bogle, Donald. *Dorothy Dandridge: A Biography*. New York: Amistad, 1997.

———. *Prime Time Blues: African Americans on Network Television*. New York: Farrar, Straus and Giroux, 2001.

———. *Toms, Coons, Mulattoes, Mammies and Bucks: An Interpretive History of Blacks in American Films*. Rev. expanded ed. New York: Continuum, 1993.

Boorstin, Daniel J. *The Image: A Guide to Pseudo Events in America*. New York: Harper-Colophon Books, 1961.

Boroff, David, ed. *The State of the Union*.

Englewood Cliffs, N.J.: Prentice-Hall, 1965.

Boskin, Joseph. *Sambo: The Rise and Demise of an American Jester*. New York: Oxford University Press, 1986.

———. *Urban Racial Violence in the Twentieth Century*. Beverly Hills, Calif.: Glencoe Press, 1969.

Boyer, Paul. *By the Bomb's Early Light: American Thought and Culture at the Dawn of the Atomic Age*. 1984. Reprint, Chapel Hill: University of North Carolina Press, 1994.

Braithwaite, E. R. *To Sir, with Love*. New York: Jove Books, 1959.

Branch, Taylor. *Parting the Waters: America in the King Years, 1954–1963*. New York: Simon and Schuster, 1988.

———. *Pillar of Fire: America in the King Years, 1963–65*. New York: Simon and Schuster, 1998.

Brandt, Nat. *Harlem at War: The Black Experience in WWII*. Syracuse, N.Y.: Syracuse University Press, 1996.

Brantley, Will, ed. *Conversations with Pauline Kael*. Jackson: University Press of Mississippi, 1996.

Brode, Douglas. *Denzel Washington: His Films and Career*. Secaucus, N.J.: Birch Lane Press, 1997.

Brown, Dennis. *Actors Talk: Profiles and Stories from the Acting Trade*. New York: Limelight Editions, 1999.

Brown, H. Rap. *Die Nigger Die!* New York: Dial Press, 1969.

Brown-Guillory, Elizabeth. *Their Place on Stage: Black Women Playwrights on Stage*. New York: Greenwood Press, 1988.

Brownstein, Ronald. *The Power and the Glitter: The Hollywood-Washington Connection*. New York: Pantheon Books, 1990.

Buford, Kate. *Burt Lancaster: An American Life*. New York: Alfred A. Knopf, 2000.

Caine, Michael. *What's It All About?* London: Century, 1992.

Campbell, Edward D. C., Jr. *The Celluloid South: Hollywood and the Southern Myth*. Knoxville: University of Tennessee Press, 1981.

Carby, Hazel V. *Race Men*. Cambridge, Mass.: Harvard University Press, 1998.

Carmichael, Stokely, and Charles V. Hamilton. *Black Power: The Politics of Liberation in America*. New York: Random House, 1967.

Carney, Raymond. *American Dreaming: The Films of John Cassavetes and the American Experience*. Berkeley: University of California Press, 1985.

Carr, Gary. *The Left Side of Paradise: The Screenwriting of John Howard Lawson*. Ann Arbor, Mich.: UMI Research Press, 1984.

Carroll, Diahann, with Ross Firestone. *Diahann: An Autobiography*. Boston: Little, Brown, 1986.

Carson, Clayborne. *Malcolm X: The FBI File*. New York: Carroll and Graf, 1991.

Carter, Steven F. *Hansberry's Drama: Commitment and Complexity*. Urbana: University of Illinois Press, 1991.

Ceplair, Larry, and Steven Englund. *The Inquisition in Hollywood: Politics in the Film Community*. Garden City, N.Y.: Anchor Press/Doubleday, 1980.

Cheney, Anne. *Lorraine Hansberry*. Boston: Twayne Publishers, 1984.

Clark, Tom, with Dick Kleiner. *Rock Hudson: Friend of Mine*. New York: Pharos Books, 1989.

Clarke, John Henrik, ed. *Harlem U.S.A.* New York: Collier Books, 1971.

———. *William Styron's Nat Turner: Ten Black Writers Respond*. Westport, Conn.: Greenwood Press, 1968.

Cleaver, Eldridge. *Soul on Ice*. New York: McGraw-Hill, 1968.

Clough, Marshall S. *Mau Mau Memoirs: History, Memory, Politics*. Boulder, Colo.: Lynne Rienner Publishers, 1998.

Cohen, John, ed. *The Essential Lenny Bruce*. New York: Ballantine Books, 1967.

Colburn, David R., and Jane L. Landers,

eds. *The African American Heritage of Florida*. Gainesville: University Press of Florida, 1995.

Cole, Lester. *Hollywood Red: The Autobiography of Lester Cole*. Palo Alto, Calif.: Ramparts Press, 1981.

Colley, David. *The Road to Victory: The Untold Story of World War II's Red Ball Express*. Washington, D.C.: Brassey's, 2000.

Cooper, Ralph, with Steve Dougherty. *Amateur Night at the Apollo*. New York: HarperCollins, 1990.

Craton, Michael. *A History of the Bahamas*. 2nd ed. London: Collins, 1968.

Craton, Michael, and Gail Saunders. *Islanders in the Stream: A History of the Bahamian People*. Athens: University of Georgia Press, 1998.

Cripps, Thomas. *Black Film as Genre*. Bloomington: Indiana University Press, 1979.

——. *Hollywood's High Noon: Moviemaking and Society before Television*. Baltimore: Johns Hopkins University Press, 1997.

——. *Making Movies Black: The Hollywood Message Movie from World War II to the Civil Rights Era*. New York: Oxford University Press, 1993.

——. *Slow Fade to Black: The Negro in American Film, 1900–1942*. New York: Oxford University Press, 1977.

Crist, Judith. *The Private Eye, the Cowboy, and the Very Naked Girl: Movies from Cleo to Clyde*. Chicago: Holt, Rinehart and Winston, 1968.

Cruse, Harold. *The Crisis of the Negro Intellectual: A Historical Analysis of the Failure of Black Leadership*. 1967. Reprint, New York: Quill, 1984.

Cullen, Countee. *On These I Stand*. 1927. Reprint, New York: Harper and Row, 1947.

Curtis, Susan. *The First Black Actors on the Great White Way*. Columbia: University of Missouri Press, 1998.

Curtis, Tony, and Barry Parks. *Tony Curtis: The Autobiography*. New York: William Morrow, 1993.

Custen, George F. *Twentieth Century's Fox: Darryl F. Zanuck and the Culture of Hollywood*. New York: BasicBooks, 1997.

Davis, John P., ed. *The American Negro Reference Book*. Englewood Cliffs, N.J.: Prentice-Hall, 1966.

Davis, Ossie, and Ruby Dee. *With Ossie and Ruby: In This Life Together*. New York: William Morrow, 1998.

Davis, Peter. *In Darkest Hollywood: Exploring the Jungles of Cinema's South Africa*. Athens: Ohio University Press, 1996.

Davis, Sammy, Jr. *Hollywood in a Suitcase*. New York: William Morrow, 1980.

Davis, Sammy, Jr., and Jane and Burt Boyar. *Why Me? The Sammy Davis, Jr. Story*. New York: Farrar, Straus and Giroux, 1989.

DeCarlo, Yvonne, with Doug Warren. *Yvonne: An Autobiography*. New York: St. Martin's Press, 1971.

Diawara, Manthia, ed. *Black American Cinema*. New York: Routledge, 1993.

Dick, Bernard F. *Joseph L. Mankiewicz*. Boston: Twayne Publishers, 1983.

DiOrio, Al. *Borrowed Time: The 37 Years of Bobby Darin*. Philadelphia: Running Press, 1981.

Dittmer, John. *Local People*. Urbana: University of Illinois Press, 1994.

Doherty, Thomas. *Teenagers and Teenpics: The Juvenalization of American Movies in the 1950s*. Boston: Unwin Hyman, 1988.

Douroux, Marilyn. *Archie Moore: The Old Mongoose*. Boston: Brandon Publishing, 1991.

Dressler, David. *Parole Chief*. New York: Viking, 1951.

Driscoll, Peter. *The Wilby Conspiracy*. Philadelphia: Lippincott, 1972.

Duberman, Martin Bauml. *Paul Robeson*. New York: Alfred A. Knopf, 1988.

Du Bois, W. E. Burghardt. *The Souls of*

Black Folk: Essays and Sketches.
Chicago: A. C. McClurg, 1903.

Dudziak, Mary L. *Cold War Civil Rights: Race and the Image of American Democracy.* Princeton, N.J.: Princeton University Press, 2000.

Dunn, Marvin. *Black Miami in the Twentieth Century.* Gainesville: University Press of Florida, 1997.

Durham, Philip, and Everett L. Jones. *The Negro Cowboys.* New York: Dodd, Mead and Co., 1965.

Edmiston, Susan, and Linda D. Cirino. *Literary New York: A History and Guide.* Boston: Houghton Mifflin, 1976.

Edwards, Anne. *A Remarkable Woman: A Biography of Katharine Hepburn.* New York: William Morrow, 1985.

Ellison, Ralph. *Shadow and Act.* New York: Random House, 1953.

Ely, Melvin Patrick. *The Adventures of Amos 'n' Andy: A Social History of an American Phenomenon.* New York: Free Press, 1991.

Epstein, Daniel Mark. *Nat King Cole.* New York: Farrar, Straus and Giroux, 1999.

Erenberg, Lewis A. *Swingin' the Dream: Big Band Jazz and the Rebirth of American Culture.* Chicago: University of Chicago Press, 1998.

Ewers, Carolyn. *Sidney Poitier: The Long Journey.* New York: New American Library, 1969.

Fanon, Frantz. *Black Skin, White Masks.* 1952. Reprint, New York: Grove Press, 1967.

Farber, Stephen, and Marc Green. *Hollywood on the Couch: A Candid Look at the Overheated Love Affair between Psychiatrists and Moviemakers.* New York: William Morrow, 1993.

Fishgall, Gary. *Against Type: The Biography of Burt Lancaster.* New York: Scribner, 1995.

Fleischer, Richard. *Just Tell Me When to Cry: A Memoir.* New York: Carroll and Graf, 1993.

Fleming, G. James, and Christian E. Burkel, eds. *Who's Who in Colored America.* 7th ed. Yonkers-on-Hudson, N.Y.: Christian E. Bruckel and Associates, 1950.

Flender, Harold. *Paris Blues.* New York: Ballantine Books, 1957.

Forman, James. *The Making of Black Revolutionaries.* New York: Macmillan, 1972.

Frank, Thomas. *The Conquest of Cool: Business Culture, Counterculture, and the Rise of Consumerism.* Chicago: University of Chicago Press, 1997.

Franklin, John Hope, and Alfred A. Moss Jr. *From Slavery to Freedom: A History of African Americans.* 1947. 8th ed., Boston: McGraw-Hill, 2000.

Frazier, E. Franklin. *Black Bourgeoisie: The Rise of a New Middle Class.* New York: Free Press, 1957.

Fredrickson, George M. *Black Liberation: A Comparative History of Black Ideologies in the United States and South Africa.* New York: Oxford University Press, 1995.

Freedland, Michael. *The Goldwyn Touch: A Biography of Sam Goldwyn.* London: Harrap, 1986.

Funke, Lewis, and Paul E. Booth. *Actors Talk about Acting.* New York: Random House, 1961.

Gabbard, Krin. *Jammin' at the Margins: Jazz and the American Cinema.* Chicago: University of Chicago Press, 1994.

Gabler, Neal. *An Empire of Their Own: How the Jews Invented Hollywood.* New York: Crown Publishers, 1988.

———. *Life the Movie.* New York: Alfred A. Knopf, 1998.

Garrow, David J. *Bearing the Cross: Martin Luther King, Jr. and the Southern Christian Leadership Conference.* 1986. Reprint, New York: Vintage, 1993.

Gates, Phyllis, and Bob Thomas. *My Husband, Rock Hudson.* Garden City, N.Y.: Doubleday, 1987.

Geist, Kenneth L. *Pictures Will Talk: The Life and Films of Joseph L. Mankiewicz.* New York: Charles Scribner's Sons, 1978.

George, Nelson. *Blackface: Reflections on African-Americans and the Movies.* New York: HarperCollins, 1994.

Gianakos, Larry James. *Television Drama Series Programming: A Comprehensive Chronicle, 1947–1959.* Metuchen, N.J.: Scarecrow Press, 1980.

Gilbert, James. *A Cycle of Outrage: America's Reaction to the Juvenile Delinquent in the 1950s.* New York: Oxford University Press, 1986.

Gomery, Douglas. *Shared Pleasures: A History of Movie Presentation in the United States.* Madison: University of Wisconsin Press, 1992.

Goodman, David. *Fault Lines: Journeys into the New South Africa.* Berkeley: University of California Press, 1999.

Gorman, Joseph Bruce. *Kefauver: A Political Biography.* New York: Oxford University Press, 1971.

Gow, Gordon. *Hollywood in the Fifties.* New York: A. S. Barnes, 1971.

Graham, Allison. *Framing the South: Hollywood, Television, and Race during the Civil Rights Struggle.* Baltimore: Johns Hopkins University Press, 2001.

Grenier, Guillermo J., and Alex Stepick III, eds. *Miami Now! Immigration, Ethnicity, and Social Change.* Gainesville: University Press of Florida, 1992.

Guare, John. *Six Degrees of Separation.* New York: Random House, 1990.

Guerrero, Ed. *Framing Blackness: The African American Image in Film.* Philadelphia: Temple University Press, 1993.

A Guide to Miami and Dade County: Including Miami Beach and Coral Gables. Writers' Program of the Works Progress Administration in the State of Florida. Northport, N.Y.: Bacon, Percy, and Daggett, 1941.

Hacker, Andrew. *Two Nations: Black and White, Separate, Hostile, Unequal.* New York: Charles Scribner's Sons, 1992.

Hampton, Henry, and Steve Fayer, eds. *Voices of Freedom: An Oral History of the Civil Rights Movement from the 1950s to the 1980s.* New York: Bantam Books, 1990.

Hansberry, Lorraine. *A Raisin in the Sun.* 1958. Reprint, New York: Vintage Books, 1988.

———. *A Raisin in the Sun: The Original Unfilmed Screenplay.* Edited by Robert Nemiroff. New York: Plume, 1992.

———. *To Be Young, Gifted, and Black.* Adapted by Robert Nemiroff. New York: Signet, 1970.

Hare, Nathan. *The Black Anglo-Saxons.* New York: Marziani and Munsell, 1965.

Harrison, Alferdteen, ed. *Black Exodus: The Great Migration from the American South.* Jackson: University Press of Mississippi, 1991.

Haskell, Molly. *From Reverence to Rape: The Treatment of Women in the Movies.* New York: Rinehart and Winston, 1973.

Hauser, Thomas. *Muhammad Ali: His Life and Times.* New York: Touchstone, 1991.

Hay, Samuel A. *African American Theatre: A Historical and Cultural Analysis.* New York: Cambridge University Press, 1994.

Heath, Gordon. *Deep Are the Roots: Memoirs of a Black Expatriate.* Amherst: University of Massachusetts Press, 1992.

Heldenfels, R. D. *Television's Greatest Year: 1954.* New York: Continuum, 1994.

Henrikson, Margot A. *Dr. Strangelove's America: Society and Culture in the Atomic Age.* Berkeley: University of California Press, 1997.

Hernton, Calvin C. *Sex and Racism in America.* 1965. Reprint, New York: Anchor Books, 1988.

———. *White Papers for White Americans*. Garden City, N.Y.: Doubleday, 1966.

Heston, Charlton. *The Actor's Life: Journals 1956–1976*. Edited by Hollis Alpert. New York: E. P. Dutton, 1978.

———. *In the Arena: An Autobiography*. New York: Simon and Schuster, 1995.

Heyward, DuBose. *Porgy*. New York: George H. Doran, 1925.

Heyward, Dorothy and DuBose. *Porgy: A Play in Four Acts*. Garden City, N.Y.: Doubleday, Doran, 1928.

Higham, Charles. *Hollywood Cameramen: Sources of Light*. London: Thames and Hudson in association with the British Film Institute, 1970.

Hill, Errol. *Shakespeare in Sable: A History of Black Shakespearean Actors*. Amherst: University of Massachusetts Press, 1984.

———, ed. *The Theater of Black Americans: A Collection of Critical Essays*. New York: Applause, 1987.

Hine, Darlene Clark, and Jacqeline McLeod, eds. *Crossing Boundaries: Comparative History of Black People in Diaspora*. Bloomington: Indiana University Press, 1999.

Hoffman, William. *Sidney*. New York: Lyle Stuart, 1971.

Holly, Ellen. *One Life: The Autobiography of an African American Actress*. New York: Kodesha International, 1996.

hooks, bell. *Reel to Real: Race, Sex, and Class at the Movies*. New York: Routledge, 1996.

Horne, Gerald. *Race Woman: The Lives of Shirley Graham DuBois*. New York: New York University Press, 2000.

Hoxie, Frederick E., and Peter Iverson, eds. *Indians in American History: An Introduction*. 2nd ed. Wheeling, Ill.: Harlan Davidson, 1998.

Hudson, Rock, and Sara Davidson. *Rock Hudson: His Story*. New York: William Morrow, 1986.

Hughes, Colin A. *Race and Politics in the Bahamas*. New York: St. Martin's Press, 1981.

Hunter, Evan. *The Blackboard Jungle*. New York: Simon and Schuster, 1954.

Hutchinson, Tom. *Rod Steiger: Memoirs of a Friendship*. New York: Fromm International, 2000.

Hyatt, Marshall, ed. *The Afro-American Cinematic Experience: An Annotated Bibliography and Filmography*. Wilmington, Del.: Scholarly Resources, 1983.

Jackson, Carlton. *Picking Up the Tab: The Life and Movies of Martin Ritt*. Bowling Green, Ohio: Bowling Green State University/Popular Press, 1994.

Jenkins, Olga Culmer. *Bahamian Memories: Island Voices of the Twentieth Century*. Gainesville: University Press of Florida, 2000.

Johnson, Howard. *The Bahamas in Slavery and Freedom*. Kingston, Jamaica: Ian Randle Publishers, 1991.

Johnson, James Weldon. *Black Manhattan*. 1930. Reprint, New York: Arno Press, 1968.

Johnson, Whittington B. *Race Relations in the Bahamas, 1784–1834: The Nonviolent Transformation from a Slave to a Free Society*. Fayetteville: University of Arkansas Press, 2000.

Jones, James Earl, and Penelope Niven. *James Earl Jones: Voices and Silences*. New York: Charles Scribner's Sons, 1993.

Jones, Quincy. *Q: The Autobiography of Quincy Jones*. New York: Doubleday, 2001.

Kael, Pauline. *Kiss Kiss Bang Bang*. Boston: Little, Brown, 1965.

Kanfer, Stefan. *A Journal of the Plague Years*. New York: Atheneum, 1973.

Kantor, Bernard R., Irwin R. Blacker, and Anne Kramer. *Directors at Work: Interviews with American Film-Makers*. New York: Funk and Wagnalls, 1970.

Kata, Elizabeth. *Be Ready with Bells and Drums*. New York: St. Martin's Press, 1961.

Kennedy, Randall. *Interracial Intimacies: Sex, Marriage, Identity, and Adoption.* New York: Pantheon, 2003.

Keppel, Ben. *The Work of Democracy: Ralph Bunche, Kenneth B. Clarke, Lorraine Hansberry, and the Cultural Politics of Race.* Cambridge, Mass.: Harvard University Press, 1995.

Kershaw, Greet. *Mau Mau from Below.* Oxford: James Currey, 1997.

Keyser, Lester J., and Andre H. Ruszkowski. *The Cinema of Sidney Poitier: The Black Man's Changing Role on the American Screen.* San Diego, Calif.: A. S. Barnes, 1980.

Keyssar, Helen. *The Curtain and the Veil: Strategies in Black Drama.* New York: Burt Franklin, 1981.

Killens, John Oliver. *Black Man's Burden.* New York: Trident Press, 1965.

Kindem, Gorham. *The Live Television Generation of Hollywood Film Directors: Interviews with Seven Directors.* Jefferson, N.C.: McFarland, 1994.

King, Martin Luther, Jr. *Why We Can't Wait.* New York: Harper and Row, 1963.

Kisseloff, Jeff. *The Box: An Oral History of Live Television, 1920–1961.* New York: Viking, 1995.

Kitt, Eartha. *Confessions of a Sex Kitten.* London: Barricade Books, 1989.

Klotman, Phyllis Rauch. *Frame by Frame: A Black Filmography.* Bloomington: Indiana University Press, 1979.

———. *Frame by Frame II: A Filmography of the African American Image, 1978–1994.* Bloomington: Indiana University Press, 1997.

Korda, Michael. *Charmed Lives.* New York: Random House, 1979.

Kramer, Stanley, with Thomas M. Coffey. *A Mad, Mad, Mad, Mad World: A Life in Hollywood.* New York: Harcourt Brace, 1997.

Krasner, David. *Resistance, Parody, and Double Consciousness in African American Theatre, 1895–1910.* New York: St. Martin's Press, 1997.

Kulik, Karol. *Alexander Korda: The Man Who Could Work Miracles.* London: W. H. Allen, 1975.

Landry, J. C. *Paul Newman.* New York: McGraw-Hill, 1983.

Leab, Daniel. *From Sambo to Superspade: The Black Experience in American Films.* Boston: Houghton Mifflin, 1985.

Leaming, Barbara. *Katharine Hepburn.* New York: Crown Publishing, 1995.

Leeming, David. *James Baldwin: A Biography.* New York: Alfred A. Knopf, 1994.

Leff, Leonard J., and Jerold L. Simmons. *The Dame in the Kimono: Hollywood, Censorship, and the Production Code Adminstration from the 1920s to the 1960s.* New York: Grace Weidenfeld, 1990.

Lemann, Nicholas. *The Promised Land: The Great Black Migration and How It Changed America.* New York: Alfred A. Knopf, 1991.

Levine, Lawrence. *Black Culture and Black Consciousness.* New York: Oxford University Press, 1977.

Levy, Emanuel. *Oscar Fever: The History and Politics of the Academy Awards.* New York: Continuum, 2001.

Levy, Shawn. *Rat Pack Confidential.* New York: Doubleday, 1998.

Lewis, David Levering. *W. E. B. Du Bois: Biography of a Race, 1868–1919.* New York: Henry Holt, 1993.

———. *When Harlem Was in Vogue.* New York: Alfred A. Knopf, 1981.

Lincoln, C. Eric. *The Black Muslims in America.* Boston: Beacon Press, 1961.

Lindner, Robert. *The Fifty-Minute Hour: A Collection of True Psychoanalytic Tales.* New York: Rinehart, 1954.

Linet, Beverly. *Ladd: The Life, the Legend, the Legacy of Alan Ladd.* New York: Arbor House, 1979.

Ling, Peter J., and Sharon Monteith, eds. *Gender in the Civil Rights Movement.* New York: Garland Publishing, 1999.

MacDonald, J. Fred. *Blacks and White TV: African Americans in Television since 1948*. Chicago: Nelson-Hall, 1992.

——. *One Nation under Television: The Rise and Decline of Network TV*. New York: Pantheon Books, 1990.

Majors, Richard G., and Jacob U. Gordon, eds. *The American Black Male: His Present Status and His Future*. Chicago: Nelson-Hall, 1994.

Malcolm X, with Alex Haley. *The Autobiography of Malcolm X*. 1964. Reprint, New York: Ballantine Books, 1992.

Mandela, Nelson. *Long Walk to Freedom*. Boston: Little, Brown, 1994.

Mandle, Jay. *Not Slave, Not Free: The African American Economic Experience since the Civil War*. Durham, N.C.: Duke University Press, 1992.

Manso, Peter. *Brando: The Biography*. New York: Hyperion, 1994.

Mantle, Burns, ed. *The Best Plays of 1946–47*. New York: Dodd Mead, 1947.

Mapp, Edward. *Blacks in American Films*. Metuchen, N.J.: Scarecrow Press, 1972.

Marill, Alvin. *The Films of Sidney Poitier*. Secaucus, N.J.: Citadel Press, 1978.

Marriott, David. *On Black Men*. New York: Columbia University Press, 2000.

Marshall, Paule. *Brown Girl, Brownstones*. New York: Random House, 1959.

Martin, Michael T., ed. *Cinemas of the Black Diaspora: Diversity, Dependence, and Oppositionality*. Detroit: Wayne State University Press, 1995.

Marwick, Arthur. *The Sixties: Cultural Revolution in Britain, France, Italy, and the United States, c. 1958–c. 1974*. New York: Oxford University Press, 1998.

Massie, Raymond Kinloch. *Loosing the Bonds: The United States and South Africa in the Apartheid Years*. New York: Nan A. Talese/Doubleday, 1997.

Matusow, Allen J. *The Unraveling of America: A History of Liberalism in the 1960s*. New York: Harper Torchbooks, 1984.

May, Lary. *The Big Tomorrow: Hollywood and the Politics of the American Way*. Chicago: University of Chicago Press, 2000.

——. *Screening Out the Past: The Birth of Mass Culture and the Motion Picture Industry*. New York: Oxford University Press, 1980.

——, ed. *Recasting America: Culture and Politics in the Age of the Cold War*. Chicago: University of Chicago Press, 1989.

Mayorga, Margaret, ed. *The Best One-Act Plays 1946–1947*. New York: Dodd Mead, 1947.

McDonough, Carla J. *Staging Masculinity: Male Identity in Contemporary American Drama*. Jefferson, N.C.: McFarland, 1997.

McGilligan, Pat, ed. *Backstory 2: Interviews with Screenwriters of the 1940s and 1950s*. Berkeley: University of California Press, 1991.

McGilligan, Patrick, and Paul Buhle. *Tender Comrades: A Backstory of the Hollywood Blacklist*. New York: St. Martin's Press, 1997.

McKay, Claude. *Harlem: Negro Metropolis*. New York: E. P. Dutton, 1940.

McWhorter, Diane. *Carry Me Home: Birmingham, Alabama: The Climactic Battle of the Civil Rights Revolution*. New York: Simon and Schuster, 2001.

Mellen, Joan. *Big Bad Wolves: Masculinity in the American Film*. New York: Pantheon Books, 1977.

Mersand, Joseph E., ed. *Three Comedies of American Family Life*. New York: Washington Square Press, 1961.

Meyer, Janet L. *Sydney Pollack: A Critical Filmography*. Jefferson, N.C.: McFarland, 1991.

Miller, Gabriel. *The Films of Martin Ritt: Fanfare for the Common Man*. Jackson: University Press of Mississippi, 2000.

Mintz, Steven, and Randy Roberts. *Hollywood's America: United States History through Its Films*. St. James, N.Y.: Brandywine Press, 1993.

Mitchell, Loften. *Black Drama*. New York: Hawthorn Books, 1967.

———. *Voices of the Black Theatre*. Clifton, N.J.: J. T. White, 1975.

Moore, Archie. *The Archie Moore Story*. London: Nicholas Kaye, 1960.

Mordden, Ethan. *Medium Cool: The Movies of the 1960s*. New York: Alfred A. Knopf, 1990.

Morris, Aldon. *The Origins of the Civil Rights Movement: Black Communities Organizing for Change*. New York: Free Press, 1984.

Murray, James P. *To Find an Image*. New York: Bobbs-Merrill, 1973.

Naipaul, V. S. *Guerrillas*. 1975. Reprint, New York: Vintage Books, 1990.

Navasky, Victor S. *Naming Names*. New York: Viking Press, 1980.

Nelson, Harold D. *Kenya: A Country Study*. Washington, D.C.: United States Government as represented by the Secretary of the Army, 1984.

Nesteby, James R. *Black Images in American Films, 1896–1954: The Interplay between Civil Rights and Film Culture*. Washington, D.C.: University Press of America, 1982.

Newquist, Roy. *A Special Kind of Magic*. New York: Rand McNally, 1967.

Nicholson, Stuart. *Reminiscing in Tempo: A Portrait of Duke Ellington*. Boston: Northeastern University Press, 1999.

Null, Gary. *Black Hollywood*. New York: Citadel Press, 1970.

———. *Black Hollywood: From 1970 to Today*. New York: Citadel Press, 1993.

Oppenheimer, Jerry, and Jack Vitek. *Idol: Rock Hudson*. New York: Villard, 1986.

Osofsky, Gilbert. *Harlem: The Making of a Ghetto*. New York: Harper and Row, 1966.

Ottley, Roi. *New World A-Coming*. 1943. Reprint, New York: Arno Press, 1968.

Oursler, Fulton. *The Greatest Story Ever Told*. Garden City, N.Y.: Doubleday, 1949.

Painter, Nell Irvin. *Exodusters: Black Migration to Kansas after Reconstruction*. New York: Alfred A. Knopf, 1977.

Palmer, Ransford W. *Pilgrims from the Sun: West Indian Migration to America*. New York: Twayne Publishers, 1995.

———. *U.S.-Caribbean Relations: Their Impact on Peoples and Culture*. Westport, Conn.: Praeger, 1998.

Parrish, James Robert, and Vincent Terrace. *The Complete Actors' Television Credits, 1948–1988*. 2nd ed. Metuchen, N.J.: Scarecrow Press, 1989.

Paton, Alan. *Cry, the Beloved Country*. 1948. Reprint, New York: Simon and Schuster, 1987.

———. *Journey Continued: An Autobiography*. New York: Charles Scribner's Sons, 1988.

Patterson, James T. *Brown v. Board of Education: A Civil Rights Milestone and Its Troubled Legacy*. New York: Oxford University Press, 2001.

Patterson, Lindsay. *Black Films and Film-makers*. New York: Dodd, Mead, 1975.

———, ed. *Anthology of the American Negro in the Theatre: A Critical Approach*. New York: Publishers Company, 1969.

Pinkney, Alphonso. *The Myth of Black Progress*. New York: Cambridge University Press, 1984.

Plimpton, George. *Shadow Box*. New York: G. P. Putnam's Sons, 1977.

Poitier, Sidney. *The Measure of a Man*. San Francisco: Harper San Francisco, 2000.

———. *This Life*. New York: Alfred A. Knopf, 1980.

Preminger, Otto. *Preminger: An Autobiography*. Garden City, N.Y.: Doubleday, 1977.

Pryor, Richard, with Todd Gold. *Pryor Convictions and Other Life Sentences*. New York: Pantheon Books, 1995.

Quinn, Anthony, with Daniel Paisner. *One Man Tango*. New York: HarperCollins, 1995.

Quirk, Lawrence J. *Paul Newman*. Dallas: Taylor Publishing, 1996.

Raines, Rebecca Robbins. *Getting the Message Through: A Branch History of the U.S. Army Signal Corps*. Washington, D.C.: Center of Military History, United States Army, 1996.

Rampersad, Arnold. *Jackie Robinson*. New York: Alfred A. Knopf, 1997.

Rascovich, Mark. *The Bedford Incident*. New York: Atheneum, 1963.

Ray, Robert B. *A Certain Tendency of the Hollywood Cinema, 1930–1980*. Princeton, N.J.: Princeton University Press, 1985.

Reach, James. *David and Lisa: A Play in Two Acts*. New York: Samuel French, 1967.

Red Channels: The Report of Communist Influence in Radio and Television. New York: American Business Consultants, 1950.

Reid, Ira De A. *The Negro Immigrant: His Background, Characteristics and Social Adjustment, 1899–1937*. New York: Columbia University Press, 1939.

Reid, Mark A. *Redefining Black Film*. Berkeley: University of California Press, 1993.

Reilly, Charlie, ed. *Conversations with Amiri Baraka*. Jackson: University Press of Mississippi, 1994.

Remnick, David. *King of the World*. New York: Random House, 1998.

Report of the National Advisory Commission on Civil Disorders. New York: E. P. Dutton, 1968.

Rhines, Jesse Algeron. *Black Film/White Money*. New Brunswick, N.J.: Rutgers University Press, 1996.

Roberts, Randy, and James S. Olson. *John Wayne: American*. New York: Free Press, 1995.

———. *Winning Is the Only Thing: Sports in America since 1945*. Baltimore: Johns Hopkins University Press, 1989.

Robinson, Jackie. *I Never Had It Made: An Autobiography*. 1972. Reprint, Hopewell, N.J.: Ecco Press, 1995.

Rogin, Michael. *Blackface, White Noise: Jewish Immigrants in the Hollywood Melting Pot*. Berkeley: University of California Press, 1996.

Roosevelt, Eleanor. *My Day*. Vol. 3, *First Lady of the World*. Edited by David Elmblidge. New York: Pharos Books, 1991.

Rose, Philip. *You Can't Do That on Broadway! A Raisin in the Sun and Other Theatrical Improbabilities*. New York: Limelight Editions, 2001.

Royce, Brenda Scott. *Rock Hudson: A Bio-Bibliography*. Westport, Conn.: Greenwood Press, 1995.

Ruark, Robert. *Something of Value*. Garden City, N.Y.: Doubleday, 1955.

Rubin, Theodore Isaac. *Jordi/Lisa and David*. New York: Ballantine Books, 1962.

Salzman, Jack, and David West, eds. *Struggles in the Promised Land: Toward a History of Black-Jewish Relations*. New York: Oxford University Press, 1997.

Samuels, Charles. *The King: A Biography of Clark Gable*. New York: Coward-McCann, 1962.

Sayre, Nora. *Running Time: Films of the Cold War*. New York: Dial Press, 1982.

Schary, Dore. *Heyday: An Autobiography*. Boston: Little, Brown, 1979.

Schickel, Richard. *Clint Eastwood: A Biography*. New York: Vintage, 1996.

———. *Intimate Strangers: The Culture of Celebrity*. Garden City, N.Y.: Doubleday, 1985.

Shaw, Arnold. *Belafonte: An Unauthorized Biography*. Philadelphia: Chilton, 1960.

Shepherd, Verene A., and Hillary McD. Beckles. *Caribbean Slavery in the Atlantic World*. Kingston, Jamaica: Ian Randle Publishers, 2000.

Shipler, David K. *A Country of Strangers:*

Blacks and Whites in America. New York: Alfred A. Knopf, 1997.

Silberman, Charles. *Crisis in Black and White.* New York: Random House, 1964.

Simmons, Renee A. *Frederick Douglass O'Neal: Pioneer of the Actor's Equity Association.* New York: Garland Publishing, 1996.

Sitkoff, Harvard. *The Struggle for Black Equality, 1954–1980.* New York: Hill and Wang, 1981.

Sklar, Robert. *Movie-Made America: A Cultural History of American Movies.* New York: Random House, 1975.

Slide, Anthony. *Actors on Red Alert: Career Interviews with Five Actors and Actresses Affected by the Blacklist.* Lanham, Md.: Scarecrow Press, 1999.

Slotkin, Richard. *Gunfighter Nation: The Myth of the Frontier in Twentieth-Century America.* New York: Atheneum, 1992.

Smith, Ronald L. *Cosby.* New York: St. Martin's Press, 1986.

Smith, Suzanne. *Dancing in the Street: Motown and the Cultural Politics of Detroit.* Cambridge, Mass.: Harvard University Press, 1999.

Smith, Valerie. *Not Just Race, Not Just Gender: Black Feminist Readings.* New York: Routledge, 1998.

Snead, James. *White Screens, Black Images: Hollywood from the Dark Side.* New York: Routledge, 1994.

Sowell, Thomas. *Essays and Data on American Ethnic Groups.* Washington, D.C.: Urban Institute, 1978.

Spoto, Donald. *Stanley Kramer: Film Maker.* New York: G. P. Putnam's Sons, 1978.

Stam, Robert, and Ellen Shohat. *Unthinking Eurocentrism: Multiculturalism and the Media.* New York: Routledge, 1994.

Stanislavsky, Constantin. *An Actor Prepares.* Translated by Elizabeth Reynolds Hapgood. New York: Theatre Arts Books, 1936.

Steussy, Joe. *Rock and Roll: Its History and Stylistic Development.* 2nd ed. Englewood Cliffs, N.J.: Prentice Hall, 1994.

Stovall, Tyler. *Paris Noir: African Americans in the City of Light.* Boston: Houghton Mifflin, 1996.

Strait, Raymond. *James Garner: A Biography.* New York: St. Martin's Press, 1985.

Street, James. *Good-bye, My Lady.* Philadelphia: Lippincott, 1954.

Styron, William. *The Confessions of Nat Turner.* New York: Random House, 1967.

Sutherland, Elizabeth, ed. *Letters from Mississippi.* New York: McGraw-Hill, 1965.

Szatmary, David. *A Time to Rock: A Social History of Rock 'n' Roll.* New York: Schirmer Books, 1996.

Tarkington, Booth. *The Fascinating Stranger and Other Stories.* Garden City, N.Y.: Doubleday, Page, 1923.

Taylor, William. *Sydney Pollack.* Boston: Twayne Publishers, 1981.

Tebeau, Charlton W. *A History of Florida.* Coral Gables, Fla.: University of Miami Press, 1971.

Terkel, Studs. *Race: How Blacks and Whites Think and Feel about the American Obsession.* New York: New Press, 1992.

———. *The Spectator: Talk about Movies and Plays with the People Who Make Them.* New York: New Press, 1999.

Thompson, Leonard. *A History of South Africa.* New Haven, Conn.: Yale University Press, 1995.

Tompkins, Jane. *West of Everything: The Inner Life of Westerns.* New York: Oxford University Press, 1992.

Tornabene, Lynn. *Long Live the King: A Biography of Clark Gable.* New York: G. P. Putnam's Sons, 1976.

Tygiel, Jules. *Baseball's Great Experiment.* New York: Oxford University Press, 1983.

United States Senate Committee on the

Judiciary. *Motion Pictures and Juvenile Delinquency, 1955*. Washington, D.C.: Government Printing Office, 1956.

Van Deburg, William L. *Slavery and Race in American Popular Culture*. Madison: University of Wisconsin Press, 1984.

Vickerman, Milton. *Crosscurrents: West Indian Immigrants and Race*. New York: Oxford University Press, 1999.

Wailoo, Keith. *Dying in the City of Blues: Sickle Cell Anemia and the Politics of Race and Health*. Chapel Hill: University of North Carolina Press, 2001.

Wallace, Irving. *The Man*. New York: Simon and Schuster, 1964.

Warren, Robert Penn. *Band of Angels*. New York: Random House, 1955.

Waters, Mary C. *Black Identities: West Indian Immigrant Dreams and American Realities*. New York: Russell Sage Foundation, 1999.

Watkins, Floyd C., John T. Hiers, and Mary Louise Weaks, eds. *Talking with Robert Penn Warren*. Athens: University of Georgia Press, 1990.

Watkins, Mel. *On the Real Side: Laughing, Lying, and Signifying — The Underground Tradition of African-American Humor That Transformed American Culture, from Slavery to Richard Pryor*. New York: Simon and Schuster, 1994.

Watts, Jerry Gafio. *Amiri Baraka: The Politics and Art of a Black Intellectual*. New York: New York University Press, 2001.

Wayne, Jane Ellen. *Clark Gable: Portrait of a Misfit*. London: Robson Books, 1993.

Weisbrot, Robert. *Freedom Bound: A History of America's Civil Rights Movement*. New York: Norton, 1990.

Wellman, William. *A Short Time for Insanity: An Autobiography*. New York: Hawthorn Books, 1974.

Wheeler, B. Gordon. *Black California: The History of African Americans in the Golden State*. New York: Hippocrene Books, 1993.

White, Robb. *Our Virgin Island*. Garden City, N.Y.: Doubleday, 1953.

Whitfield, Stephen J. *The Culture of the Cold War*. Baltimore: Johns Hopkins University Press, 1996.

Wiegman, Robyn. *American Anatomies: Theorizing Race and Gender*. Durham, N.C.: Duke University Press, 1995.

Wilkinson, J. Harvie. *From Brown to Bakke: The Supreme Court and School Integration*. New York: Oxford University Press, 1979.

Williams, Eric. *The Negro in the Caribbean*. New York: Negro Universities Press, 1942.

Williams, Linda. *Playing the Race Card: Melodramas of Black and White from Uncle Tom to O. J. Simpson*. Princeton, N.J.: Princeton University Press, 2001.

Willis, Sharon. *High Contrast: Race and Gender in Contemporary Hollywood Film*. Durham, N.C.: Duke University Press, 1997.

Wilson, Sondra Kathryn. *In Search of Democracy: The NAACP Writings of James Weldon Johnson, Walter White, and Roy Wilkins*. New York: Oxford University Press, 1999.

Wilson, William Julius. *The Declining Significance of Race*. Chicago: University of Chicago Press, 1978.

Winters, Shelley. *Shelley II: The Middle of My Century*. New York: Simon and Schuster, 1989.

Wolfe, Tom. *Radical Chic & Mau-Mauing the Flak Catchers*. New York: Bantam Books, 1970.

Woll, Allen L., and Randall M. Miller. *Ethnic and Racial Images in American Film and Television: Historical Essays and Bibliography*. New York: Garland, 1987.

Wood, Michael. *America in the Movies; or "Santa Maria, It Had Stripped My Mind."* New York: Basic Books, 1975.

Woodard, Komozi. *A Nation within a Nation: Amiri Baraka (Leroi Jones) and*

Black Power Politics. Chapel Hill: University of North Carolina Press, 1999.

Yearwood, Gladstone L. *Black Film as a Signifying Practice: Cinema, Narration and the African American Aesthetic Tradition.* Trenton, N.J.: Africa World Press, 2000.

Yordan, Philip. *Anna Lucasta.* New York: Random House, 1945.

Yule, Andrew. *Fast Fade: David Puttnam, Columbia Pictures, and the Battle for Hollywood.* New York: Delacorte Press, 1989.

Articles, Dissertations, and Symposia

American Film Institute Seminar with Sidney Poitier, 28 January 1976. Beverly Hills, Calif.: American Film Institute, 1978.

Baldwin, James. "On Catfish Row: 'Porgy and Bess' in the Movies." *Commentary* (September 1959): 246–48.

Barnes, Dawn Cooper. "Portraits of Interracial Romance and Sexuality in Hollywood Cinema: 1965–1975." Ph.D. diss., University of Maryland, 1992.

Bloom, Samuel. "A Social Psychological Study of Motion Picture Audience Behavior: A Case Study of the Negro Image in Mass Communication." Ph.D. diss., University of Wisconsin, 1956.

Bourne, St. Clair. "The African American Image in Cinema." *Black Scholar* 21 (March–May 1990): 12–19.

Brustein, Robert. "America's New Culture Hero." *Commentary* (February 1958): 123–29.

Bryce-Laporte, Roy Simon. "Black Immigrants: The Experience of Invisibility and Inequality." *Journal of Black Studies* 3 (1) (1972): 29–56.

Buchanan, Singer Alfred. "A Study of the Attitudes of the Writers of the Negro Press toward the Depiction of the Negro in Plays and Films." Ph.D. diss., University of Michigan, 1968.

Burke, William Lee. "The Presentation of the American Negro in Hollywood Films, 1946–1961: Analysis of a Selected Sample of Feature Films." Ph.D. diss., Northwestern University, 1965.

Cosgrove, Stuart. "The Zoot-Suit and Style Warfare." *Radical America* 18 (6) (1984): 39–50.

Cripps, Thomas. "The Death of Rastus: Negroes in American Films since 1945." *Phylon* 28 (Fall 1967): 267–76.

Davis, Ossie. "The Significance of Lorraine Hansberry." *Freedomways* 5 (3) (1965): 397–402.

de Graaf, Lawrence Brooks. "Negro Migration to Los Angeles, 1930 to 1950." Ph.D. diss., University of California–Los Angeles, 1962.

Dworkin, Martin S. "The New Negro on Screen." *The Progressive* (October 1960): 39–41.

———. "The New Negro on Screen." *The Progressive* (November 1960): 33–36.

———. "The New Negro on Screen." *The Progressive* (December 1960): 34–36.

———. "The New Negro on Screen." *The Progressive* (January 1961): 36–38.

———. "The New Negro on Screen." *The Progressive* (February 1961): 38–41.

Elliston, Maxine Hall. "Two Sidney Poitier Films." *Film Comment* 5 (Winter 1969): 29–31.

Feinstein, Herbert. "Three in Search of Cinema." *Columbia University Forum* (Summer 1965): 22–24.

Foner, Nancy. "West Indians in New York City and London: A Comparative Analysis." *International Migration Review* 13 (2) (1979): 284–97.

Frank, Michelle Klagsbrun. "Unchained: Perspectives on Change." *Journal of Popular Film and Television* 18 (3) (Autumn 1990): 123–29.

George, Paul S. "Colored Town: Miami's Black Community, 1896–1930." *Florida Historical Quarterly* 56 (4) (1978): 432–47.

Gill, Glenda. "Canada Lee: Black Actor in

Non-Traditional Roles." *Journal of Popular Culture* 25 (3) (1981): 79–89.

———. "Careerist and Casualty: The Rise and Fall of Canada Lee." *Freedomways* 21 (1) (1981): 15–27.

———. " 'Her Voice Was Ever Soft, Gentle, and Low, an Excellent Thing' in Ruby Dee." *Journal of Popular Culture* 28 (Summer 1994): 61–71.

Godfrey, Lionel. "Tall When They're Small: The Films of Martin Ritt." *Films and Filming* (August 1968): 43–48.

Greenberg, Cheryl. "The Politics of Disorder: Reexamining Harlem's Riots of 1935 and 1943." *Journal of Urban History* 18 (4) (1992): 395–441.

Hall, Dennis John. "Pride without Prejudice." *Films and Filming* 20 (December 1971): 40–44.

———. "Pride without Prejudice." *Films and Filming* 20 (January 1972): 41–44.

Holder, Calvin B. "The Causes and Composition of West Indian Immigration to New York City, 1900–1952." *Afro-Americans in New York Life and History* 1 (January 1987): 7–27.

Hutchens, Gordon. "The Defiance in *The Defiant Ones*." *Film Culture* 50–51 (Fall and Winter 1970): 63–65.

Jackson, Joyce. "African American and West Indian Folklife in South Florida." *South Florida History Magazine* 3 (1970): 11–18.

Jefferson, Miles M. "The Negro on Broadway, 1945–1946." *Phylon* 7 (2) (1946): 185–91.

———. "The Negro on Broadway, 1948–1949." *Phylon* 10 (2) (1949): 103–11.

———. "The Negro on Broadway, 1952–1953: Still Cloudy, Fair Weather Ahead." *Phylon* 14 (3) (1953): 268–79.

Johnson, Albert. "Beige, Brown, or Black." *Film Quarterly* 13 (Fall 1959): 39–42.

———. "The Negro in American Films: Some Recent Works." *Film Quarterly* 18 (4) (Summer 1965): 14–30.

Johnson, Howard. "Bahamian Labor Migration to Florida in the Late Nineteenth and Early Twentieth Centuries." *International Migration Review* 22 (1) (1988): 84–103.

Kelley, Samuel L. "The Evolution of Character Portrayals in the Films of Sidney Poitier, 1950–1978." Ph.D. diss., University of Michigan, 1980.

Killens, John Oliver. "Broadway in Black and White." *African Forum* 1 (Winter 1966): 66–76.

King, Woodie, Jr. "Lorraine Hansberry's Children: Black Artists and *A Raisin in the Sun*." *Freedomways* 19 (4) (1979): 219–21.

Knight, Arthur. "The Negro in Films Today: Hollywood's New Cycle." *Films in Review* 1 (1950): 14–19.

Koppes, Clayton R., and Gregory D. Black. "Blacks, Loyalty, and Motion-Picture Propaganda in World War II." *Journal of American History* 73 (September 1986): 383–406.

Kracauer, Siegfried. "National Types as Hollywood Presents Them." *Public Opinion Quarterly* 13 (Spring 1949): 53–72.

Levine, Andrea Beth. "The Body's Politics: Race and Gender in the 'Authentic' Sixties." Ph.D. diss., University of Virginia, 1997.

———. "Sidney Poitier's Civil Rights: Rewriting the Mystique of White Womanhood in *Guess Who's Coming to Dinner* and *In the Heat of the Night*." *American Literature* 73 (June 2001): 365–86.

Lovell, John, Jr. "Roundup: The Negro in American Theatre." *Crisis* 54 (July 1947): 212–17.

Mailer, Norman. "The White Negro (Superficial Reflections on the Hipster)." *Dissent* 4 (3) (1957): 276–93.

Manchel, Frank. "The Man Who Made the Stars Shine Brighter: An Interview with Woody Strode." *Black Scholar* 25 (Spring 1995): 37–46.

Meeker, Darcy Sue. "Novel to Script to

Film: The Case of *In the Heat of the Night*." M.A. thesis, University of Florida, 1981.

Meyer, Stephen G. "The South and Black Cinema: An Exploration." *Southern Historian* 13 (1992): 36–47.

Mohl, Raymond A. "Black Immigrants in Early Twentieth-Century Miami." *Florida Historical Quarterly* 65 (3) (1987): 271–97.

———. "Making the Second Ghetto in Metropolitan Miami, 1940–1960." *Journal of Urban History* 21 (3) (1995): 395–427.

Mormino, Gary R. "GI Joe Meets Jim Crow: Racial Violence and Reform in World War II Florida." *Florida Historical Quarterly* 73 (1) (1994): 23–42.

Nixon, Rob. "Cry White Season: Apartheid, Liberalism, and the American Screen." *South Atlantic Quarterly* 90 (3) (1991): 499–529.

Noble, Gil. "Entertainment, Politics, and the Movie Business: An Interview with Sidney Poitier." *Cineaste* (Winter 1977–78): 16–28.

Omatsu, Mary. "Guess Who Came to Lunch?" *Take One* 1 (January–February 1968): 20–21.

Pitts, Ethel Louise. "The American Negro Theatre: 1940–1949." Ph.D. diss, University of Missouri, 1975.

Poitier, Sidney. "Dialogue on Film." *American Film* (September 1976): 33–48.

———. "Dialogue on Film." *American Film* (September–October 1991): 18–21.

———. "Entertainment, Politics, and the Movie Business." *Cineaste* 8 (3) (Winter 1977–78): 16–23.

———. "They Call Me a Do-It-Yourself Man." *Films and Filming* (September 1959): 7.

———. "Thinking of Corruption." *Films and Filming* (August 1961): 7.

Popkin, Henry. "Hollywood Tackles the Race Issue." *Commentary* (October 1957): 354–57.

Poussaint, Alvin F. "Education and Black Self-Image." *Freedomways: A Quarterly Review of the Freedom Movement* 8 (Fall 1968): 337.

"Proceedings of a Symposium on Black Images in Films, Stereotyping, and Self-Perception as Viewed by Black Actresses." Boston University, 13 and 14 April 1973. Boston: Boston University Afro-American Studies Program, 1974.

Quart, Leonard. "Jews and Blacks in Hollywood." *Dissent* 39 (Fall 1992): 528–31.

Rahman, Aishah. "To Be Black, Female, and a Playwright." *Freedomways* 19 (4) (1979): 256–60.

Reed, Eve. "Funky Nights in Overtown." *South Florida History Magazine* 21 (2–3) (1993): 8–14.

Robb, David. "Naming the Right Names: Amending the Hollywood Blacklist." *Cineaste* 22 (2) (1996): 25.

Sharkey, Betsy. "Knocking on Hollywood's Door." *American Film* (July–August 1989): 22–27.

Simpson, Donald. "Black Images in Film—The 1940s to the Early 1960s." *Black Scholar* 21 (March–May 1990): 20–29.

Sitkoff, Harvard. "Racial Militancy and Interracial Violence in the Second World War." *Journal of American History* 58 (3) (1971): 661–81.

Smith, J. Owens. "The Politics of Income and Education Differences between Blacks and West Indians." *Journal of Ethnic Studies* 13 (3) (1985): 17–30.

Stephens, Lenora Clodfelter. "Black Women in Film." *Southern Quarterly* 19 (September–December 1981): 164–70.

Sugy, Catherine. "Black Men or Good Niggers: Race in the New Movies." *Take One* 1 (November–December 1967): 18–21.

Thompson, Cliff. "Paris Blues, Visited." *Iowa Review* 26 (1) (1996):167–71.

Turner, Darwin T. "Visions of Love and

Manliness in a Blackening World: Dramas of Black Life since 1953." *Black Scholar* 25 (Spring 1995): 2–12.

Ukadike, N. Frank. "Western Film Images of Africa: Genealogy of an Ideological Formulation." *Black Scholar* 21 (2) (1990): 30–48.

Vaughn, Stephen. "Ronald Reagan and the Struggle for Black Dignity in Cinema, 1937–1953." *Journal of Negro History* 77 (Winter 1992): 1–16.

Ward, Douglas Turner. "Lorraine Hansberry and the Passion of Walter Lee." *Freedomways* 19 (4) (1979): 223–25.

Weales, Gerald. "Pro-Negro Films in Atlanta." *Phylon* 13 (Winter 1952): 300–301.

———. "Thoughts on 'A Raisin in the Sun.'" *Commentary* (June 1959): 527–30.

Wolfenstein, Martha, and Nathan Leites. "Two Social Scientists View 'No Way Out': The Unconscious vs. the 'Message' in an Anti-Bias Film." *Commentary* (October 1950): 388–91.

Documentaries

"Scandalize My Name: Stories from the Blacklist." BET Movies. 60 mins., 1999, videocassette.

"Sidney Poitier: One Bright Light." PBS *American Masters*. 60 mins., 2000, videocassette.

"Sidney Poitier: The Defiant One." A&E Television Networks. 50 mins., 1996, videocassette.

INDEX

Darnell, Linda, 72
Darren, James, 181–82
David and Lisa, 374
Davis, Bette, 194
Davis, Blevins, 148
Davis, Miles, 191
Davis, Ossie, 53, 58, 67–68, 88–89, 97,
129, 149, 180, 204, 210, 222, 289, 291,
296, 326, 339. *See also* Dee, Ruby; *No
Way Out*
Davis, Robert, 93
Davis, Sammy, Jr., 199, 216–17, 244–
45, 288, 324, 326–27, 365; political
activity, 141, 194–95, 210–11, 221,
250–51, 291; *Porgy and Bess*, 151, 160,
162, 164
Day, Doris, 317
Days of Our Youth, 49–50
Dean, Isabel, 145
Dean, James, 104
Dean, Quentin, 267
DeCarlo, Yvonne, 137–38
Dee, Ruby, 129, 315, 333, 335; on stage,
53, 68; political activity, 88–89, 141,
169–70, 172–73, 204, 222, 291; on
film, 97, 117, 145, 185–86, 339, 341.
See also *Buck and the Preacher*; *Go,
Man, Go!*; *No Way Out*; *A Raisin in the
Sun* (film and play); *Virgin Island*
Deep Are the Roots, 51, 190
The Defiant Ones, 150–58, 171, 183–84,
196, 209, 211, 217, 233, 245, 270, 350,
360, 363–64, 377
De Klerk, F. W., 373
DeMille, Cecil B., 147, 231
Dennis, Sandy, 255
Desk Set, 277
Detective Story, 91
The Devil at Four O'Clock, 197
Devine, Loretta, 364
DeWilde, Brandon, 113
Die Hard, 364
Dietrich, Marlene, 164
Dillman, Bradford, 330
Dixon, Ivan, 149, 240
Dixon, Thomas, 21
Doctor Doolittle, 244
Dr. Strangelove, 235–36
Doctor Zhivago, 265

Domino, Fats, 105
Douglas, Kirk, 152, 279
The Drum, 77
Du Bois, W. E. B., 4, 21, 45, 47
Duel at Diablo, 247–50, 270, 275,
349
Duff, Gordon, 114
Dulles, John Foster, 132
Dunbar, Paul Laurence, 111
Durante, Jimmy, 194
Dylan, Bob, 210

E&R Productions, 270–71, 321, 326,
330, 337, 342
Earl, Fred, 206
Eastwood, Clint, 317
Eckstine, Billy, 353
Edge of the City, 117–23, 157
Edwards, James, 92, 190
Eisenhower, Dwight, 105, 132
Elliott, Inger, 366
Elliott, Osborn, 366
Ellington, Duke, 33, 191–92, 216, 244
The Emperor Jones, 84, 139
Evers, Medgar, 209
Exodus, 156
The Exorcist, 344

Fagan, Myron C., 92
Fail-Safe, 235–36
Falk, Peter, 204
Fargas, Antonio, 326
The Fascinating Stranger, 112–13
Fast Forward, 361
Feldman, Phil, 354
Ferrer, Mel, 66
Fetchit, Stepin (Lincoln Perry), 22, 63–64,
69, 92, 140–41, 241, 249, 255, 273,
287, 295, 380
Fine, Arthur, 225
Finney, Albert, 216
First Artists Production Company, 326,
342, 344–45, 348–49, 354
Fishburne, Laurence, 378
Fitzgerald, Ella, 33, 58
Fleischer, Richard, 244
Flender, Harold, 190
Fluellen, Joel, 164
Fonda, Henry, 194